# 2012
# Deskbook Encyclopedia of
# American School Law

**Students with Disabilities**

**Threats and Bullying**

**Freedom of Speech**

**School Athletics**

**Student Search and Seizure**

**Discipline**

**Electronic Communications**

*Center for*
*Education & Employment Law*

CEEL

Center for Education & Employment Law
P.O. Box 3008
Malvern, Pennsylvania 19355

> "This publication is designed to provide accurate and authoritative information in regard to
> the subject matter covered. It is sold with the understanding that the publisher is not engaged
> in rendering legal, accounting or other professional service. If legal advice or other expert
> assistance is required, the services of a competent professional person should be sought." —
> *from a Declaration of Principles jointly adopted by a Committee of the American Bar
> Association and a Committee of Publishers and Associations.*

ISBN 978-1-933043-54-8
ISSN 1058-4919

**The Library of Congress has cataloged this serial title as follows:**
Deskbook Encyclopedia of American School Law.— 1980/81 — Rosemount, Minn.:
Informational Research Systems, 1981-

v.; 23 cm.

Annual.
Published 2011                          by: Center for Education & Employment Law
Prepared by the editors of: Legal Notes for Education,
1980/81-
1. Educational law and legislation—United States—Digests. 2. Educational law and legislation—
United States—Periodicals. I. Informational Research Systems (Washington, D.C.) II. Oakstone Legal
& Business Publishing III. Center for Education & Employment Law IV. Legal Notes for Education.
V. Title: Encyclopedia of American School Law.
KF4114.D46                                   92-054912
                                    344.73'07'02638 — dc19
                                       [347.304702638]
                                                    AACR 2#M#MARC-S

Library of Congress        [8704r86]rev

Cover Design by Patricia Jacoby

Other Titles Published By
Center for Education & Employment Law:

*Deskbook Encyclopedia of Employment Law*
*Deskbook Encyclopedia of Public Employment Law*
*Higher Education Law in America*
*Keeping Your School Safe & Secure: A Practical Guide*
*Legal Update for Teachers: The Complete Principal's Guide*
*Private School Law in America*
*Students with Disabilities and Special Education*

# TABLE OF CONTENTS

## CHAPTER ONE
## Student Rights

## CHAPTER TWO
## Student Discipline

## CHAPTER THREE
## Freedom of Speech and Association

## CHAPTER FOUR
## Religion and the Public Schools

## CHAPTER FIVE
## Academic Practices

## CHAPTER SIX
## Students with Disabilities

## CHAPTER SEVEN
## Employment Practices

## CHAPTER EIGHT
## Employment Discrimination

## CHAPTER NINE
## Employment Termination, Resignation and Retirement

## CHAPTER TEN
### Tenure and Due Process

## CHAPTER ELEVEN
### Labor Relations

TABLE OF CONTENTS

# CHAPTER TWELVE
## School Liability and Safety

## CHAPTER THIRTEEN
### Interscholastic Athletics

## CHAPTER FOURTEEN
### School Operations

## CHAPTER FIFTEEN
## Private Schools

## TABLE OF CONTENTS

### REFERENCE SECTION

# INTRODUCTION

The *2012 Deskbook Encyclopedia of American School Law* is a completely updated encyclopedic compilation of state and federal appellate court decisions that affect education. These decisions have been selected and edited by the editorial staff of Center for Education & Employment Law, publishers of *Legal Notes for Education*. Topical classifications have been revised and edited to reflect rapid changes in education law, and many cases reported in previous editions have been re-edited or reclassified.

This edition contains a brief introductory note on the American judicial system and an updated appendix of recent U.S. Supreme Court cases. Also included are portions of the U.S. Constitution that are most frequently cited in education cases. This publication is intended to provide educators and lawyers with access to the most current available cases in education. We believe that you will find this edition even more readable and easier to use than previous editions.

# ABOUT THE EDITORS

**James A. Roth** is the editor of *Legal Notes for Education* and *Special Education Law Update*. He is a co-author of *Students with Disabilities and Special Education Law* and an adjunct program assistant professor at St. Mary's University in Minnesota. Mr. Roth is a graduate of the University of Minnesota and William Mitchell College of Law. He is admitted to the Minnesota Bar.

**Thomas D'Agostino** is a managing editor at the Center for Education & Employment Law and is the editor of *Higher Education Legal Alert*. He graduated from the Duquesne University School of Law and received his undergraduate degree from Ramapo College of New Jersey. He is a past member of the American Bar Association's Section of Individual Rights and Responsibilities as well as the Pennsylvania Bar Association's Legal Services to Persons with Disabilities Committee. Mr. D'Agostino is admitted to the Pennsylvania bar.

**Curt J. Brown** is the Group Publisher of the Center for Education & Employment Law. Prior to assuming his present position, he gained extensive experience in business-to-business publishing, including management of well-known publications such as *What's Working in Human Resources, What's New in Benefits & Compensation, Keep Up to Date with Payroll, Supervisors Legal Update,* and *Facility Manager's Alert.* Mr. Brown graduated from Villanova School of Law and graduated magna cum laude from Bloomsburg University with a B.S. in Business Administration. He is admitted to the Pennsylvania Bar.

# HOW TO USE YOUR DESKBOOK

We have designed the *2012 Deskbook Encyclopedia of American School Law* in an accessible format for both attorneys and non-attorneys to use as a research and reference tool toward prevention of legal problems.

## Research Tool

As a research tool, our deskbook allows you to conduct your research on two different levels – by topics or cases.

*Topic Research*

♦ If you have a general interest in a particular **topic** area, our **table of contents** provides descriptive chapter headings containing detailed subheadings from each chapter.

➢ For your convenience, we also include the chapter table of contents at the beginning of each chapter.

**Example:**
For more information on alternative placements, the table of contents indicates that a discussion of this topic begins in Chapter Two on page 45:

### CHAPTER TWO
### Student Discipline

♦ If you have a specific interest in a particular **issue**, our comprehensive **index** collects all of the relevant page references to particular issues.

---

**Example:**
  For more information on misconduct by coaches, the index provides references to all of the cases dealing with coaches instead of only those cases dealing with misconduct:

Coaching-related issues, 506-516
  defamation, 510-512
  employment, 506-510
  liability, 512-515
➤  misconduct, 516

---

## Case Research

♦ If you know the **name** of a particular case, our **table of cases** will allow you to quickly reference the location of the case.

---

**Example:**
  If someone mentioned a case named *Zelman v. Simmons-Harris,* looking in the table of cases, which has been arranged alphabetically, the case would be located under the "Z" section.


**Z**

 Zager v. Chester Community Charter School, 181
➤ Zelman v. Simmons-Harris, 169, 170, 172
 Zepeda v. Boerne Independent School Dist., 23
 Zobrest v. Catalina Foothills School Dist., 249, 590
 Zorach v. Clauson, 152, 154, 596

---

✓ Each of the cases summarized in the deskbook also contains the case citation, which will allow you to access the full text of the case if you would like to learn more about it. *See How to Read a Case Citation, p. 623.*

◆ If your interest lies in cases from a **particular state**, our **table of cases by state** will identify the cases from your state and direct you to their page numbers.

---

**Example:**

If cases from Texas were of interest, the table of cases by state, arranged alphabetically, would list all of the case summaries contained in the deskbook from Texas.

**➡ TEXAS**

A.M. v. Cash, 101
Abbott v. North East Independent School Dist., 282
Academy of Skills & Knowledge v. Charter Schools, 188
Adams v. Groesbeck Independent School Dist., 311
Alvin Independent School Dist. v. Patricia F., 230

---

✓ Remember, the judicial system has two court systems – state and federal court – which generally function independently from each other. *See The Judicial System, p. 619.* We have included the federal court cases in the table of cases by state according to the state in which the court resides. However, federal court decisions often impact other federal courts within that particular circuit. Therefore, it may be helpful to review cases from all of the states contained in a particular circuit.

## *Reference Tool*

As a reference tool, we have highlighted important resources that provide the framework for many legal issues.

◆ If you would like to see specific wording of the **U.S. Constitution**, refer to **Appendix A**, which includes relevant provisions of the U.S. Constitution such as the First Amendment (freedom of speech and religion).

◆ If you would like to review **U.S. Supreme Court decisions** in a particular subject matter area, our topical list of U.S. Supreme Court case citations located in **Appendix B** will be helpful.

We hope you benefit from the use of the *2012 Deskbook Encyclopedia of American School Law*. If you have any questions about how to use the deskbook, please contact Jim Roth at jroth@pbp.com.

# TABLE OF CASES

# TABLE OF CASES

# TABLE OF CASES

# TABLE OF CASES

# TABLE OF CASES

# TABLE OF CASES

# TABLE OF CASES

# TABLE OF CASES

# TABLE OF CASES

# TABLE OF CASES

# TABLE OF CASES

# TABLE OF CASES

# TABLE OF CASES

xxvi

# TABLE OF CASES BY STATE

# TABLE OF CASES BY STATE

## INDIANA

## IOWA

TABLE OF CASES BY STATE

# TABLE OF CASES BY STATE

# TABLE OF CASES BY STATE

# TABLE OF CASES BY STATE

# TABLE OF CASES BY STATE

# TABLE OF CASES BY STATE

# CHAPTER ONE

## Student Rights

## I.   SEXUAL HARASSMENT

*Title IX of the Education Amendments of 1972 prohibits sex discrimination by all recipients of federal funding. In* Davis v. Monroe County Board of Educ., *this chapter, the Supreme Court held school districts may be held liable under Title IX for student-on-student harassment. To establish liability under* Davis, *students must show (1) sexual harassment by peers; (2) deliberate indifference by school officials with actual knowledge of harassment; and (3) harassment so severe, pervasive and objectively offensive it deprived the student of access to educational opportunities. A teacher's knowledge of peer harassment is sufficient to create "actual knowledge" that may trigger liability for a district.*

*In* Fitzgerald v. Barnstable School Committee, *the U.S. Supreme Court held Title IX does not bar Equal Protection claims under 42 U.S.C. § 1983. Section 1983 is a federal statute that creates no rights itself, but enforces rights created by federal laws and the Constitution. Section 1983 imposes liability on a school district that has a policy or custom of violating constitutional rights.*

1

## A. Texting, Sexting and Electronic Harassment

*Facebook, texting and other electronic communication forms have created new concerns about inappropriate contacts among students, and between school employees and students. The relatively high liability standards under both Title IX and Section 1983 have been criticized as not preventing the sexual abuse of students. One response by school attorneys has been to urge school districts to enforce strict boundaries between students and school employees.*

◆ Parents began complaining about text messages from an Arkansas coach to female students. He agreed to stop the texting, but he also told one student that "her mother could stay with him" when the team had an out-of-town game. Another student told the superintendent that her ninth-grade cousin "might have a crush" on the coach. She said the ninth-grader often left classes to visit him in the gym. The student went to the ninth-grader's house to inform her mother of her suspicions. The coach denied anything was going on. The mother later approached the principal during a school board meeting to discuss rumors about a relationship between the coach and her daughter. The cousin tearfully volunteered more information and allegedly identified staff members who knew of inappropriate conduct. According to the ninth-grader's parent, the principal said she would investigate further, but she failed to do so before going on maternity leave. While she was on leave, the coach was accused of texting a student "OMG you look good today." After the principal returned from her leave, she received two new reports of misconduct by the coach. Based on these and other concerns, the district made preparations to nonrenew his contract.

When students reported details of sexual contact between the coach and ninth-grader, the coach was arrested. He was eventually prosecuted and sentenced to 10 years in prison. The ninth-grader's parents filed a Title IX case against the school district, principal and other school officials. They added constitutional claims under 42 U.S.C. § 1983. A federal district court dismissed the claims against the school district and most of the claims against the officials, but the principal was denied immunity. On appeal, the U.S. Court of Appeals, Eighth Circuit, found the principal could be held liable for constitutional violations if she was deliberately indifferent to a pattern of unconstitutional acts by the coach. This required proof that she knew of his conduct but failed to take remedial action in a manner that caused the ninth-grader's injury. **The court held the coach's text messages did not provide the principal "actual notice of sexual abuse." Inappropriate comments alone did not alert her to a possible sexual relationship.** Even the most suggestive text message – "OMG you look good today" – did not indicate sexual conduct or abuse. The principal and superintendent investigated each report they received, and during the relevant time there was no evidence of improper contact. The court held "a student's familiar behavior with a teacher or even an 'excessive amount of time' spent with a teacher, without more, does not automatically give rise to a reasonable inference of sexual abuse." As a result, the lower court's denial of qualified immunity to the principal was reversed. Nor was the school district liable under Title IX. *Doe v. Flaherty*, 623 F.3d 577 (8th Cir. 2010).

◆   A New York student received three emails from a male classmate's school email account. One was profane and disparaged her appearance, and the others sought sexual relations. Although the student promptly reported the emails to the school administration, the classmate denied sending them and claimed other students had his email password. The classmate's account was later disabled, but the sender of the emails was never conclusively identified. Believing that the school district's investigation was inadequate, the student sued the school district in a federal district court for violating Title IX and other federal laws. The court held that no reasonable jury could find the student met the liability standard under Title IX for peer sexual harassment established in *Davis v. Monroe County School Board*, this chapter. The student appealed to the U.S. Court of Appeals, Second Circuit, which explained the *Davis* standard.

**To prevail on a Title IX claim, the student had to show the school district acted with deliberate indifference that was so severe, pervasive, and objectively offensive that it barred her access to an educational opportunity or benefit.** As the district court held, the student did not meet these requirements. While the emails were offensive, they fell well short of the kind of conduct necessary to create liability under Title IX. Since three offensive emails in a 10-day time period did not demonstrate "severe and pervasive harassment," the Title IX claim had been properly resolved in favor of the school district. The student's equal protection claim based on the district's allegedly more aggressive investigation and pursuit of a prior incident of race-based misconduct did not persuade the court, and the judgment was affirmed. *R.S. v. Board of Educ. of the Hastings-on-Hudson Union Free School Dist.*, 371 Fed.Appx. 231 (2d Cir. 2010).

◆   A Michigan high school soccer coach addressed players with obscenities, engaged them in "flirtatious conversations," and made suggestive remarks. He called players and sent them emails at unusual hours. He told one student on the team that he had "a special interest" in a particular teammate. The student said that when she discouraged the coach from pursuing the teammate, he threatened the entire team with consequences. The assistant principal, principal and athletic director met with him to address complaints by parents about his late-evening communications. The administrators composed a memo prohibiting him from late calls and from emailing players unless he copied the assistant principal. The coach was prohibited from counseling players about personal matters, conducting activities off-campus without parents present, and from inappropriate relationships. The teammate later informed the student she had broken off her relationship with the coach. According to the student, the coach blamed her for this and threatened to "break her nose and take out her knees so she would never play soccer again." The coach then threatened suicide. Police arrived at his residence, recovered a pistol, and took him to a hospital.

The coach resigned and was prohibited from entering school property. The student transferred to a different school and sued the district, coach and school officials. The case reached the U.S. Court of Appeals, Sixth Circuit, which held that **the coach's threats to harm the student did not involve any sexual communication.** While the threats were an abuse of authority, they did not pertain to sex. Verbal or physical conduct or communications that are not sexual in nature cannot be considered sexual harassment. The court noted that liability can be imposed for creating hostile environment harassment only if there is reasonable notice and failure to take action by officials. Here, the extent of the coach's misconduct did not become known until he resigned. *Henderson v. Walled Lake Consolidated Schools*, 469 F.3d 479 (6th Cir. 2006).

### B. Sexual Harassment by Students

◆    An Illinois student told her mother that a Junior Reserve Officer Training Corps (JROTC) instructor had improperly touched her at school and at JROTC stations. After the instructor admitted wrongdoing, he was charged criminally and resigned from his position. According to the student's stepfather, the JROTC supervisor told him "this incident has happened before, and it just in time goes away." After the charges against the instructor were published, two other female students came forward and reported that he abused them as well.

In a federal district court sexual harassment action, the student included an equal protection claim under 42 U.S.C. § 1983 against the district and the JROTC supervisor. She also brought a claim under Title IX against the district. The court found the Title IX claim precluded any Section 1983 claim based on supervisory liability. Judgment was entered for the school district, and the student appealed. The U.S. Court of Appeals, Seventh Circuit, found the dismissal of the Section 1983 claim for equal protection violations was based on a theory of supervisory liability. It noted the U.S. Supreme Court held Title IX did not bar Section 1983 claims against school officials in *Fitzgerald v. Barnstable School Committee*, below. But as the Section 1983 claim was based on supervisory liability, the court held **the lack of any knowledge of the instructor's misconduct by either the school district or the JROTC supervisor was fatal to the claim**. No school official knew of any sexual abuse of the student until the day she reported it. The court found remarks attributed to the JROTC supervisor were insufficient to pursue the Section 1983 claims. As a result, they had been properly dismissed. In urging Title IX liability, the student said that after she reported the abuse by the JROTC instructor, other students taunted her, put gum in her hair and threatened her. But the court refused to consider this as a form of "student-on-student harassment" that might create Title IX liability for the school district. As there was no legal support for the student's Title IX theory, the judgment for the district and supervisor was affirmed. *Trentadue v. Redmon*, 619 F.3d 648 (7th Cir. 2010).

◆    A Massachusetts kindergarten student told her parents that a third-grader on her school bus bullied her into lifting her skirt. The parents reported this to the principal, but the third-grader repeatedly denied the report, and the school could not corroborate the student's account. After she said the boy made her pull down her underpants and spread her legs, the school called the police, who found insufficient evidence for criminal charges. Finding insufficient evidence for school discipline, the principal suggested transferring the kindergartner to a different bus or leaving rows of empty seats between students of different ages.

The parents suggested moving the third-grader instead, or placing a monitor on the bus. The superintendent denied the requests. After the parents reported that the student had experienced more encounters with the third-grader at school, she began staying home. The family sued the school committee under 42 U.S.C. § 1983, claiming a violation of Title IX. A federal court and the First Circuit held that Title IX's private remedy precluded using 42 U.S.C. § 1983 to advance Title IX claims. The U.S. Supreme Court reversed the judgment. It held that Title IX was not meant to be the exclusive mechanism for addressing gender discrimination in the schools. Nor was it meant to be a substitute for parallel Section 1983 lawsuits as a means of enforcing constitutional rights. According to the Supreme Court, **Section 1983 was available as a remedy to enforce Equal Protection claims for gender discrimination in schools**. *Fitzgerald v. Barnstable School Committee*, 129 S.Ct. 788 (U.S. 2009).

◆ A Texas cheerleader claimed an African-American player on her high school's basketball team sexually assaulted her at a party. She stated that the player and another African-American were arrested for the assault, but that due to racial division in the grand jury, there was no indictment against them. At a school basketball game, the cheerleader cheered for the team but refused to cheer for the African-American player. School officials required her to either cheer when others cheered or go home. After the cheerleader left, she was removed from the squad for the school year. In a federal district court action against the school district and several officials, she asserted constitutional rights violations.

The court dismissed the case, and appeal went to the U.S. Court of Appeals, Fifth Circuit. It reviewed the cheerleader's claim that school officials deprived her of a due process right to be free from bodily injury and stigmatization. There was no allegation of a violation of bodily integrity. The court found that psychological injury alone was not a violation of a due process right to bodily integrity. As the Supreme Court of Texas has held, "students do not possess a constitutionally protected interest in their participation in extracurricular activities." The lower court correctly dismissed the case under the terms of the cheerleading contract, since failure to cheer was a valid ground for removal. **There was no basis for an equal protection claim, as the cheerleader did not show she was treated differently from others or show that gender had motivated any actions by officials.** There was no merit to her claims for First Amendment violations based on her refusal to cheer. Since the lower court judgment was not reached in error, the court affirmed it. *Doe v. Silsbee Independent School Dist.*, No. 09-41075, 2010 WL 3736233 (5th Cir. 9/16/10).

◆ An Ohio school bus monitor reported that a 12-year-old student performed oral sex on a 17-year-old high school student in the back of their school bus. Police and child protection authorities were called, and both students were suspended from school for 10 days. When the student returned from her suspension, she was required to sit at the front of the bus. The high school student was assigned to another bus. The student claimed others on the bus called her a "whore" and a "slut." After her stepfather called the school to complain, the taunting stopped. Although the student's mother said she reported the taunting and spoke to the principal three times, he later denied this. A few days after the student returned to school from her suspension, she was suspended again for 10 days for stealing an iPod and for lying. An expulsion was proposed based on theft, lying and earlier rules violations. After a board hearing, the student was expelled for theft, disruption and lying. Her mother sued the school district in a federal district court for failure to respond to sexual harassment in violation of Title IX.

According to the court, **federal funding recipients may be held liable for student-on-student harassment if the recipient is deliberately indifferent to harassment that is so severe, pervasive and objectively offensive that it deprives a victim of access to educational opportunities**. The board was not liable for the assault, as no prior incidents gave it reason to suspect the high school student would force the student to engage in oral sex on the bus. After the incident, the high school student was immediately disciplined and assigned to another bus. Damages are unavailable for insults, banter, teasing, shoving and pushing, even if it is gender-specific. As the verbal harassment did not deny the student equal access to educational opportunities, the board and principal were entitled to pretrial judgment on the harassment claims. But the court found enough evidence to allow the student's retaliation claims to proceed. The proximity in time between the complaints of harassment and the referral for expulsion created an inference that the family's complaints may have motivated the discipline. The Title IX retaliation claim and a related First Amendment claim were not dismissed. *Marcum v. Board of Educ. of Bloom-Carroll Local School Dist.*, 727 F.Supp.2d 657 (S.D. Ohio 2010).

◆    A Georgia fifth-grader complained to her teacher of sexual harassment by a male student. The teacher did not immediately notify the principal about it. Although the harasser was eventually charged with sexual battery, school officials took no action against him. The fifth-grader sued the school board for Title IX violations. A federal district court dismissed the case, and the U.S. Court of Appeals, Eleventh Circuit, affirmed. The U.S. Supreme Court reversed the judgment, holding that **school districts may be held liable under Title IX for deliberate indifference to known acts of peer sexual harassment, where the school's response is clearly unreasonable under the circumstances**.

A recipient of federal funds may be liable for student-on-student sexual harassment, where the recipient is deliberately indifferent to known sexual harassment and the harasser is under the recipient's disciplinary authority. To create Title IX liability, the harassment must be so severe, pervasive and objectively offensive that it deprives the victim of access to educational opportunities or benefits. The Court held the harassment alleged by the student in this case was sufficiently severe enough to avoid pretrial dismissal. The judgment was reversed and the case was returned to the lower courts. *Davis v. Monroe County Board of Educ.*, 526 U.S. 629 (1999).

◆    An Illinois kindergartner reported that a male classmate jumped on her back during a recess period near the start of the school year. He continued to exhibit inappropriate behavior, including repeatedly unzipping his pants. He also jumped on and kissed other female students. The principal suspended the classmate for two days and reassigned him to a new classroom, lunch and recess period. However, the classmate and kindergartner were later returned to the same lunch and recess periods, and the classmate's behavior apparently continued. A counselor diagnosed the kindergartner as having acute stress disorder and separation anxiety, and she received therapy. The school district granted the parents' request to transfer her to a different school for first grade, and they sued the district for sexual harassment.

The case reached the U.S. Court of Appeals, Seventh Circuit, which held that kindergartners could not engage in sexual harassment. Young students are still learning how to act appropriately, and they "regularly interact in a manner that would be unacceptable among adults." For this reason, **"simple acts of teasing and name calling among children" do not create Title IX liability**. The kindergartner was unable to report conduct other than "vague and unspecific" allegations that the classmate "bothered her by doing nasty stuff." This did not provide the court with necessary details to evaluate its severity and pervasiveness. The kindergartner was not denied access to an education, as neither her grades nor her attendance suffered. As the district's response to the harassment was not clearly unreasonable and did not amount to deliberate indifference, the court held for the district. *Gabrielle M. v. Park Forest-Chicago Heights School Dist. 163*, 315 F.3d 817 (7th Cir. 2003).

◆   Two female second-graders claimed a boy repeatedly chased, touched and grabbed them and often made sexual remarks and gestures, but they did not communicate the sexual nature of his actions, and no adult saw him engage in overtly sexual behavior. Near the end of the school year, a third girl began attending the school and promptly complained to her teacher that the boy had told her to "suck his dick." The third girl's mother contacted the principal and teacher and was told that the school was working with the boy's parents to resolve his problems. After meeting with the third girl's mother, the principal suspended the boy. The principal instructed the teacher to keep him away from the third girl. When the girls' attorney notified the principal that the boy's misconduct was continuing, the school suspended him for the rest of the school year. The families sued the school board under Title IX.

The case reached the Eleventh Circuit, which stated that **damages are not available for "simple acts of teasing and mere name-calling"** among children even when comments target differences in gender. Although the conduct alleged by the first two girls persisted for months and was sexually explicit and vulgar, it was not so severe, pervasive or offensive that it denied them access to their education. They suffered no physical exclusion from school facilities. While the third girl's complaints were more explicit, the school responded to them and it was not deliberately indifferent. The court ruled for the school board. *Hawkins v. Sarasota County School Board*, 322 F.3d 1279 (11th Cir. 2003).

### C.  Sexual Harassment by Staff

◆   In 1998, the U.S. Supreme Court examined the liability of school districts for sexual harassment of students by teachers and other staff under Title IX. The case involved a Texas student who had a sexual relationship with a teacher. The Court rejected the liability standard advocated by the student and by the U.S. government, which resembled *respondeat superior* (vicarious) liability under Title VII. Title IX contains an administrative enforcement mechanism that assumes actual notice has been provided to officials prior to the imposition of enforcement remedies. **An award of damages would be inappropriate in a Title IX case unless an official with the authority to address the discrimination failed to act despite actual knowledge of it, in a manner amounting to deliberate indifference** to discrimination. Here, there was insufficient evidence that a school official should have known about the relationship to impose Title IX liability. Accordingly, the district could not be held liable for the teacher's misconduct. *Gebser v. Lago Vista Independent School Dist.*, 524 U.S. 274, 118 S.Ct. 1989, 141 L.Ed.2d 277 (1998).

◆ An Alabama personnel director investigated a teacher's misconduct three times, and each time the teacher denied the charge. After the third incident, the school board transferred him from a high school to an elementary school. There, a female student complained that he made an inappropriate comment. The principal told him that additional reports would result in discharge. Later in the same school year, female students complained about the way the teacher told them to do push-ups. The principal "ordered him not to place himself in such a questionable situation." An 11-year-old disabled student sought to transfer from his class, stating that classmates teased her about her disabilities. Over a year later, she told a school counselor that the teacher had raped her. The counselor promptly notified the student's parents and school officials.

The personnel director immediately placed the teacher on administrative leave and began investigating. The teacher retired, and the parents sued the school board and personnel director, asserting that the district was deliberately indifferent to the risk of harm to their child. The case reached the Supreme Court of Alabama, which held that the board was not an arm of the state for purposes of Eleventh Amendment immunity. However, the director was entitled to qualified immunity. **His failure to recommend the teacher's termination did not amount to deliberate indifference to the student's constitutional rights.** *Madison County Board of Educ. v. Reaves*, 1 So.3d 980 (Ala. 2008).

◆ An Idaho teacher had sexual relations with an 18-year-old student. When this was revealed, the teacher resigned. The student sued the teacher, school district and school officials, including claims for negligent supervision and violation of Title IX. She presented evidence of post-traumatic stress disorder (PTSD), but offered no medical records or damage estimates. The school district offered testimony from a psychologist who stated that her emotional problems were triggered by the lawsuit itself, not the sexual relationship. The jury found the district liable for negligent supervision. However, it found that the student did not prove any damages, and it awarded her none. On appeal, the Supreme Court of Idaho held a reasonable jury could have found the student proved no damages. **Her own experts disagreed as to her condition, with one finding she did not have PTSD.** The district's expert had found the student had no significant psychological difficulties until after the lawsuit was filed. The court upheld the jury's findings. *Hei v. Holzer*, 181 P.3d 489 (Idaho 2008).

◆ A Virginia gym teacher was accused of improperly touching two girls. The school principal responded to the complaints, investigated them and reported her findings to her supervisor. Her investigation set into motion police and child protection investigations, which found both complaints unfounded. A school investigator found that the teacher's actions were unintentional. Four years after the incidents, the teacher was fired for unprofessional conduct and insubordination. An adult former student learned of his misconduct and claimed he had improperly touched her when she was an elementary school student. She sued the school district and principal for sexual harassment, but a federal district court found no deliberate indifference by the principal.

The former student appealed to the U.S. Court of Appeals, Fourth Circuit, which noted that the standard of "deliberate indifference" is a high one. **Supervisory officials may be held liable for a subordinate's constitutional violations, but only if they have knowledge of the misconduct.** It must be demonstrated that the supervisor's response was so inadequate as to show deliberate indifference or "tacit authorization of the alleged offensive practices," and a link to the injury. To show "deliberate indifference" by the principal, the adult former student would have to show "continued inaction in the face of documented widespread abuses." The principal had responded reasonably to the risk that the gym teacher was sexually abusing students. As there was no evidence that closer supervision would have made any difference in this case, the lower court had properly held for the principal. *Sanders v. Brown*, 257 Fed.Appx. 666 (4th Cir. 2007).

◆ An assistant school superintendent in Georgia received an anonymous email during the school year, accusing a teacher of having inappropriate relationships with a list of students who had graduated or dropped out of school. She learned of a similar complaint against the teacher three years earlier, but the student involved in that incident vehemently denied anything inappropriate. The teacher denied both the report and the email accusation. The assistant superintendent warned her, both orally and in writing, to avoid any appearance of impropriety with students and situations where she would be alone with male students. Vehicles owned by the teacher and the troubled student were later seen parked together in some woods. The superintendent promptly notified the school board and the police, and asked the state Professional Standards Commission (PSC) to investigate the incident. She told the principal to monitor the two, prevent unnecessary contact between them and to report suspicious behavior to her. The teacher resigned and surrendered her teaching certificate after a substitute teacher discovered a note written by the student that threatened to expose their relationship if she did not comply with certain demands. The parents sued the district for Title IX and civil rights violations under 42 U.S.C. § 1983. The court held for the school district, and the parents appealed.

The U.S. Court of Appeals, Eleventh Circuit, held that the parents failed to show that school officials acted with deliberate indifference. They responded to each report of misconduct by investigating the charges and interviewing relevant persons. The officials consistently monitored the teacher and warned her about her interaction with students. They requested a PSC investigation after they received the first report specifically linking the teacher and student, monitored her and confronted her when the explicit note was discovered. In light of the many corrective measures taken by district officials, they were not deliberately indifferent. **A district is not deliberately indifferent because the**

**measures it takes are ultimately ineffective in stopping the harassment.** The court affirmed the judgment for the district. *Sauls v. Pierce County School Dist.*, 399 F.3d 1279 (11th Cir. 2005).

## D. Sexual Orientation

*In the following case, the Court of Appeal of California observed that school administrators are better situated to address peer sexual harassment than are courts. Administrators can take affirmative steps to combat racism, sexism and other forms of bias which the courts cannot. And administrative actions are typically resolved far more quickly than private lawsuits.*

◆ Two California students claimed they were subjected to so much severe verbal and physical anti-gay harassment that they had to leave school. They kept logs of anti-gay peer harassment and gave them to school administrators. After getting little response, the students completed their high school careers in home study programs. They sued the school district, principal, assistant principal and district superintendent. A jury found that the district violated the Education Code and that the principal and assistant principal violated the male student's rights under the Equal Protection Clause. According to the jury, the principal violated the female student's equal protection rights. The verdict awarded the male student $175,000 in damages and the female student $125,000. They also received attorneys' fees of over $427,000. The Court of Appeal of California found the students had made out a successful claim for "deliberate indifference" to known anti-gay harassment. This satisfied the stringent Title IX standard.

In finding for the students on their equal protection claims, the jury had found that **administrators had actual notice of harassment but were deliberately indifferent to it**. As the principal was an appropriate person to act on behalf of the school district to address peer sexual orientation harassment, and there was evidence that the administrators took no meaningful action to stop the harassment, the judgment was upheld. *Donovan v. Poway Unified School Dist.*, 167 Cal.App.4th 567, 84 Cal.Rptr.3d 285 (Cal. Ct. App. 2008).

◆ A New Jersey student claimed he was repeatedly and severely taunted by classmates who directed homosexual epithets at him beginning in grade four. He endured slurs in the halls and was struck while in the school cafeteria, when 10 to 15 students surrounded and taunted him. The assistant principal did not punish or reprimand the students. During the student's eighth-grade year, his mother claimed a school guidance counselor simply urged her son to "toughen up and turn the other cheek." The principal later agreed to let the student leave classes to report problems directly to him, and the school began to discipline perpetrators. Verbal abuse persisted, but to a lesser degree. When the student entered high school, the harassment resurfaced. To avoid derision on school buses, he decided to walk home from school. He reported being followed by others as he walked home. Other students punched him and knocked him down, and he had to miss school. The students were suspended for 10 days and one pled guilty to assault charges. The student never returned to the high school, and his mother filed a harassment complaint with the state Division on Civil Rights. The student won $50,000 in emotional distress damages, and his mother won $10,000 for emotional distress. The district was fined $10,000 and ordered to pay attorneys' fees. A state appellate division court affirmed the $50,000 award for the student, but it reversed the award for his mother. On appeal, the Supreme Court of New Jersey **recognized a cause of action against school districts for student-on-student harassment based on perceived sexual orientation**. Liability would be imposed for peer harassment only if a district failed to reasonably address harassment and the district knew or should have known about it. The case was returned to the lower courts. *L.W. v. Toms River Regional Schools Board of Educ.*, 189 N.J. 381, 915 A.2d 535 (N.J. 2007).

◆   An Iowa student claimed that he endured years of severe harassment at school due to a perception that he was homosexual. He stated that school administrators failed to provide a safe environment after dozens of incidents of vandalization and physical assault. The school resource officer advised him to either ignore a harassing classmate or confront him. When the student confronted the classmate, the two got into a fight. The school suspended both students, and they were arrested for disorderly conduct. The student sued the district and several school and police officials for civil rights violations. A court upheld the school's anti-fighting policy as content and viewpoint neutral. The school had a strong interest in maintaining order to promote its learning environment, and the anti-fighting policy helped promote this interest. **The district could not be held liable for "negligent" failure to stop harassment.** The student showed a likelihood of success on his Title IX claim by alleging repeated harassment resulting in a hostile environment that forced him to leave school. He also claimed administrators knew of the harassment but were deliberately indifferent to it. Despite the student's strong showing on his Title IX claim, he was not entitled to a preliminary order preventing his suspension. *Doe v. Perry Community School Dist.*, 316 F.Supp.2d 809 (S.D. Iowa 2004).

◆   A group of California students who were (or were perceived by peers to be) gay, lesbian or bisexual claimed harassment by classmates over a seven-year period. The students stated that school officials took little or no action to protect them, and they sued the school district, its board and several school administrators. A federal district court held that the students presented evidence of official failure to remedy peer harassment and that this failure was based on sexual orientation. As the students' right to be free from sexual orientation discrimination was clearly established, the officials were not entitled to immunity. The officials appealed to the Ninth Circuit, which found evidence of years of harassment during which school administrators failed to enforce policies to protect the students. **There was evidence that school administrators were motivated by intentional discrimination or acted with deliberate indifference, despite many complaints.** This included failure to respond or inadequate response to at least two assault incidents, as well as repeated verbal harassment and pornography given to the students or placed in lockers. The district court had properly denied immunity to the administrators. *Flores v. Morgan Hill Unified School Dist.*, 324 F.3d 1130 (9th Cir. 2003).

◆ A lesbian student was allowed to proceed with discrimination claims against California school administrators who barred her from taking a physical education class based on her sexual orientation. She sued the school district and officials for violations of the Equal Protection Clause through 42 U.S.C. § 1983, also asserting state law claims. A court denied the school officials' motion for pretrial judgment based on Eleventh Amendment immunity. **Sexual orientation discrimination gives rise to an equal protection claim.** *Massey v. Banning Unified School Dist.*, 256 F.Supp.2d 1090 (C.D. Cal. 2003).

## E.  Students with Disabilities

◆ A Philadelphia special education student had difficulty speaking and asking for help, and she had significantly below-average communications skills. When she was 16 and in tenth grade, another special education student approached her sexually. As a result, her parent sought one-on-one supervision for her. Some time later, the student was led away from the school cafeteria by a male student to an auditorium balcony. Students were not permitted there, but they could and did manipulate the doors to gain entry without permission. In the balcony area, five male students sexually assaulted the student. In a lawsuit against the school district, school officials, the student perpetrators and their parents, the student's parent claimed school officials knew that the balcony created a hazard.

A federal district court considered evidence that the high school had been identified as a "persistently dangerous school" under the No Child Left Behind Act. A school safety advocate stated that the school district had under-reported violent incidents in prior years and that the district had a policy of not expelling students, even if they committed serious offenses involving assault or weapons. The court held that to establish municipal liability, a party must show that a constitutional violation occurred as the result of a custom or policy. It had to be shown that a school decisionmaker was deliberately indifferent to a risk of a constitutional violation, despite notice of harm. According to the court, **the Due Process Clause is a limitation on state power and not "a guarantee of certain minimal levels of safety and security."** There was no state obligation to prevent harm by a private person. Assurances of protection could not form the basis of a due process violation claim. Alleged failure by the school to keep the balcony area sealed and failure to report and properly discipline students could not be construed as "affirmative acts." An argument based on allowing violent students to persist in unlawful behavior due to failure to discipline them did not support a claim for a "state-created danger." *Brown v. School Dist. of Philadelphia*, Civil Action No. 08-2787, 2010 WL 2991741 (E.D. Pa. 7/28/10).

◆ A Michigan student endured harassment and bullying by classmates for years. When he reported harassment, an administrator allegedly said "kids will be kids, it's middle school." The harassment escalated during seventh grade, and a teacher even teased him in front of a full class, after which he became withdrawn and said he wanted to quit school. His grades fell, and he hid during lunch to avoid taunting. When he entered grade eight, he was found eligible for special education. An individualized education program (IEP) placed him in a resource room where the teacher helped him cope with peers. After a good eighth-grade experience, the student advanced to grade nine, where the high school principal refused to let him use the old resource room, even though it was in the same building. When the student was a junior, a baseball team member sexually assaulted him in the locker room as another student prevented his escape. While the assaulting student was expelled for eight days, the other student was only verbally reprimanded. The student refused to return to the high school, and his family sued the school district for violating Title IX.

A court found no deliberate indifference by the district under Title IX. On appeal, the U.S. Court of Appeals, Sixth Circuit, noted that each time the family reported an incident and the school knew who the perpetrators were, the district responded. This was not "deliberate indifference." However, **refusing to let the student use the old resource room might be deliberate indifference, opening the door for Title IX liability**. The court returned the case to the lower court. *Patterson v. Hudson Area Schools*, 551 F.3d 438 (9th Cir. 2008).

When the case returned to the district court, the school district sought to dismiss it for failure to first request a due process hearing under the Individuals with Disabilities Education Act (IDEA). The district also sought to exclude from evidence any testimony of a non-sexual nature. The court held that even though the student had an IEP, the case arose under Title IX of the Education Amendments of 1972, not the IDEA or other laws protecting disabled persons. The court found Title IX intends to protect students from sex discrimination, not general bullying. While damages are available in a Title IX action for harassment that is so severe, pervasive and objectively offensive that it denied equal access to education, they are not available for simple acts of teasing and name-calling. Some evidence that the school district sought to exclude had sexual overtones and might be more than just teasing or bullying. But the court held materials relating to any time after the student stopped going to school could be excluded. *Patterson v. Hudson Area Schools*, No. 05-74439, 2010 WL 455410 (E.D. Mich. 2/3/10).

◆ A 16-year-old Texas special education student with mental retardation and a speech impairment functioned at the approximate level of a second-grader. According to her family, she was sexually assaulted at her middle school by a male special needs student with a previous disciplinary record of violence and displaying pornographic material. Despite this history, the students were left unattended in a classroom for 15-20 minutes. The student reported to an aide that the male student exposed himself to her, grabbed her, kissed her and raised up her dress. Although the aide separated the two immediately, she did not report the incident until the next day. The principal called the school district police, and police officers questioned the male student and a teacher. No police action was taken against the male student, but the school separated the students and assigned an escort to the female student between all her classes. After he shouted intimidating profanities at her, he was sent to another school.

The student's family sued the school district for sexual harassment under Title IX. A federal district court dismissed the case, and the U.S. Court of Appeals, Fifth Circuit, affirmed the judgment. It held that to establish school liability under Title IX, there must be sexual harassment so severe, pervasive and objectively offensive that it deprives the victim of access to educational opportunities or benefits. In addition, **a school district must have actual knowledge of harassment, yet act with deliberate indifference to it**. According to the court, the student did not prove the requirements for Title IX liability. The actions in this case were not "so severe, pervasive and objectively offensive" as to deprive the student of access to education. And the school district took several remedial actions designed to prevent future incidents. *Watkins v. La Marque Indep. School Dist.*, 308 Fed.Appx. 781 (5th Cir. 2009).

## II.  RACE AND NATIONAL ORIGIN DISCRIMINATION

*Title VI of the Civil Rights Act of 1964 prohibits race discrimination in any program that receives federal funds. Title VI is based on equal protection principles, and many discrimination complaints allege violations of Title VI, the Equal Protection Clause, and analogous state law provisions.* **Courts require proof of intentional discrimination in Title VI cases.** *School officials may be held liable under Title VI if they are deliberately indifferent to clearly established student rights. This occurs where a pattern or practice of civil rights violations is shown that is attributable to policy-making employees.*

◆   A Minnesota special school district opened an alternative school to serve immigrant students with limited English skills and little or no formal education. Thirteen students claimed that the placement provided little educational benefit and effectively guaranteed that they would not graduate. They claimed that the school warehoused them and had no coherent curriculum. Several failed to pass a state test required for high school graduation. A report by the state education department found that the school improperly refused to test students at the school for special education eligibility until they had at least three years of English Language Learner instruction. Although some of the students had graduated, they filed a federal district court action against the school and the district for violating the Equal Educational Opportunities Act (EEOA), Title VI of the Civil Rights Act of 1964, and the Minnesota Human Rights Act (MHRA).

After the court ruled for the school district, the students appealed. The U.S. Court of Appeals, Eighth Circuit, held **Title VI prohibits only intentional discrimination**. There was no strong evidence of discrimination in this case based on the statements by school personal. Significantly, **the students did not identify students who were treated more favorably by the school district to whom they could be compared**. Eleven of the students presented no evidence of injury from the policy of not testing ELL students for special education needs until they took three years of ELL classes. As for the remaining two, the district stated it did not believe they could be reliably assessed for special services until they had been in the country long enough to learn English. The court found this was a legitimate, nondiscriminatory reason. No school or district policy singled out foreign-born students. The testing policy applied to ELL students, not those born outside the U.S. According to the court, "language and national origin are not interchangeable." A policy treating ELL students differently than others in the district was not one that discriminated on the basis of national origin. Review of the legislative history of the EEOA revealed that the act did not offer monetary damage awards. The MHRA was interpreted similarly to the EEOA, and as all the claims failed, the court affirmed the judgment. *Mumid v. Abraham Lincoln High School*, 618 F.3d 789 (8th Cir. 2010).

◆  Nine North Carolina students sued the Durham Public School System, asserting a "wholesale challenge" to its disciplinary process. They claimed that they were disciplined more severely than white students for less serious offenses. In addition, the students claimed that the board's anti-gang policy was unconstitutionally vague. A state trial court dismissed the action, and the students appealed. The Court of Appeals of North Carolina held that most of the claims had been properly dismissed, as each individual student failed to allege a claim for relief against each individual official. But the lower court would have to reconsider a due process claim brought on behalf of a now-deceased student who had been suspended for 13 days. His mother claimed that the superintendent of schools misled her and backdated correspondence to make a long-term suspension appear to be a short-term suspension. The trial court was also to reconsider a challenge to the school board's anti-gang policy. On appeal, the Supreme Court of North Carolina held the student had an adequate remedy under state law. So he could not sue the board for due process violations. Here, **two North Carolina statutes allowed any student who was suspended in excess of 10 school days to appeal to the education board, and then to a state court**. The court did not consider the gang policy issue, which was to return to the trial court. *Copper v. Denlinger*, 688 S.E.2d 426 (N.C. 2010).

◆  New Jersey school officials called the police after discovering an African-American student had a knife at school. He petitioned the state department of education to reverse his 10-day suspension. According to the student and his father, white students were only suspended three to five days for similar conduct. After the suspension was upheld, the student's father, who served as the student's attorney, filed a state court action against the school district for civil rights violations. He also filed a series of requests for public records and court actions seeking statistics about violent incidents in the district to support his discrimination claim. These requests were made under the state Open Public Records Act (OPRA). When the district provided copies of disciplinary records, the father made an OPRA request for additional records that he believed were in the district's possession. When this request did not yield the information being sought, he filed another state court action. This time, he sought the names of the police departments and officers who responded to 47 weapons-related incidents in district schools from 2001 to 2007. The school district disputed that there were 47 weapons incidents and provided records for a lower number.

A state trial court eventually resolved the three OPRA actions in favor of the district. It held there had been a sufficient response under the OPRA, and it found that 249 Violence, Vandalism and Substance Abuse Incident reports sought by the father did not exist. The district was not required to research, analyze records and report "incident details" as the father sought. In the civil rights case, the court held for the district and denied a request for extension of the pretrial discovery period. Appeal went before a New Jersey Appellate Division Court, which consolidated the three OPRA cases with the civil rights action. It held there was no denial of access to records under the OPRA or common law. The court found the father had received all the records he was due. The OPRA and common law claims for access to documents "kept the parties in a continuous, multi-faceted battle" and complicated the litigation. As for the civil rights claim, **the court found the student did not show any discrimination in his discipline or the report to the police. A 10-day suspension was not significantly different from the suspensions imposed on white students.** Since there was no statistically or legally significant basis to support a finding of discrimination based on the suspension or the call to police, the court affirmed the judgment. *O.R. v. Kniewel*, Nos. L-2293, L-2380-07, L-2686-06, L-2316-06, 2010 WL 1191088 (N.J. Super. Ct. App. Div. 3/17/10).

◆   Georgia school administrators received a report that an African-American student stole an MP3 player from another student's locker and tried to sell it. A white male stated that he and the African-American student stole the player together after going locker to locker. He accused the African-American student of selling the MP3 player for $40. The assistant principal interviewed the African-American student, who denied the allegations. She then searched his locker and found a dead cell phone that was later determined to be stolen from a middle school in the district. Investigators questioned the African-American student a second time about the stolen MP3 player. He admitted trying to sell it to a friend but claimed he did not steal it and was not aware that it had been stolen. After school officials suspended him for eight days, he sued them.

A federal district court held that the search and seizure claims did not state a Fourth Amendment or due process violation. As for the equal protection claims, they failed because the student did not show that he was "similarly situated" to his white classmate. On appeal, the U.S. Court of Appeals, Eleventh Circuit, affirmed, noting that in cases involving short-term suspensions of 10 days or less, **"once school administrators tell a student what they heard or saw, ask why they heard or saw it, and allow a brief response, a student has received all the process that the Fourteenth Amendment demands."** *Roy v. Fulton County School Dist.*, 288 Fed.Appx. 686 (11th Cir. 2008).

◆   A Kansas student claimed that the principal and teachers at his alternative school repeatedly forbade students of Hispanic origin from speaking Spanish. According to the student, the principal suspended him after telling him "he was not in Mexico" and that "he should speak only English on school premises." The student's father brought the suspension notice to the superintendent, who overturned the suspension. The family sued the superintendent, principal, teachers, school board and district, and members of the school board. The complaint alleged race and national origin discrimination in violation of Title VI and the Equal Protection Clause.

The court noted that the EEOC has stated that rigid English-only workplace rules may violate Title VII of the Civil Rights Act. **By claiming that school officials singled out students of Hispanic origin and targeted them for attributes based upon race or national origin, the student made out a valid equal protection claim.** But the principal and teacher were entitled to qualified immunity from liability because no case had established a right to speak a foreign language at a public school. However, the school district could still be held liable for the principal's acts, because she had authority to take corrective action to end the discrimination. *Rubio v. Turner Unified School Dist.*, 453 F.Supp.2d 1295 (D. Kan. 2006).

◆ An Oklahoma school district maintained a "fight policy" subjecting second-time offenders to expulsion for a semester. After the district expelled two African-American students for violating the fight policy, they alleged that white students were not expelled despite similar conduct. They claimed that the principal tolerated racial slurs and epithets by white students and allowed swastikas and the letters "KKK" to be inscribed in desks and placed in the lockers or notebooks of African-American students. The students sued the district for violating Title VI. A court awarded pretrial judgment to the district, and the students appealed to the Tenth Circuit.

The court noted that since the students could not disprove the school's legitimate reasons for discipline, pretrial judgment was appropriate on the intentional discrimination claim. However, the students were entitled to an opportunity to prove their assertions of the principal's inaction in the face of a racist environment. **School administrators could be liable under Title VI for remaining "deliberately indifferent" to known acts of "student-on-student harassment."** The hostile race environment claim was remanded to the district court, with instructions to apply the standard of liability for peer sexual harassment claims from *Davis v. Monroe County Board of Educ.*, this chapter. The hostile race environment claim was returned to the district court so it could determine if the harassment was so severe, pervasive and objectively offensive that it deprived the victims of access to educational benefits or opportunities. *Bryant v. Independent School Dist. No. I-38, Garvin County, Oklahoma*, 334 F.3d 928 (10th Cir. 2003).

## III.  RELIGIOUS DISCRIMINATION

*Cases involving religion and public schools typically arise under the Establishment and Free Exercise Clauses of the First Amendment. Those cases are summarized in Chapter Four of this volume. The following cases involve claims of discrimination under the Equal Protection Clause or state law.*

◆ A Delaware fourth-grade student from a Muslim family said her teacher isolated her by reading Christmas books and telling a candy cane story that was supposed to symbolize Christian beliefs. She said her teacher's classroom discussions deviated from a textbook and framed the events of 9/11 "as a war of Christians versus Muslims." But the student was afraid to complain about the teacher. She said that her classmates teased her. When the student finally complained to her mother that she was upset by the Christian books and Christmas discussions in her classroom, the mother asked school officials for an apology and a statement to the class that she had done nothing wrong. The mother's suggestions were rejected, but after the ACLU became involved, the teacher agreed to let the student make a presentation to the class. A transfer of the student then followed, but her friends shunned and taunted her.

In a federal district court action, the student filed claims under Article I, Section One of the Delaware Constitution, which the court found analogous to the Establishment and Free Exercise Clauses of the First Amendment. As the Supreme Court has held, **the government cannot promote or affiliate itself with any religious doctrine or organization, nor is it permitted to discriminate on grounds of religious belief or practice**. Although school officials claimed the student was not coerced in violation of her Free Exercise rights, the court allowed the claim to proceed. There were fact issues about whether the teacher violated the student's rights under the state constitution's Preference Clause. A reasonable jury might find that phrases from the teacher's candy cane story, such as "Jesus is the pure Lamb of God," and "Jesus is the Christ," lacked any secular purpose and endorsed Christianity. As a result, pretrial judgment was denied regarding discussions about Christian readings and the candy cane story. But the court found the 9/11 textbook portrayed historic events evenhandedly and served a secular educational purpose that neither enhanced nor inhibited religion. A claim alleging retaliation for protected speech required further consideration. The court found a reasonable jury might agree with the student that her transfer to another classroom was an adverse action. An equal protection claim also required further consideration, since the court found the teacher read Christmas books to the class every day for about one month but did not recognize other religious holidays. *Doe v. Cape Henlopen School Dist.*, Civ. No. 05-424-SLR, 2011 WL 64073 (D. Del. 1/7/11).

◆    A New York parent claimed a charter school principal forced her child to eat during a fast. Without the help of an attorney, the parent sued the charter school and principal in a federal district court for religious discrimination. She claimed the principal defied her instructions, isolated the child in the cafeteria and presented her with food. The complaint asserted only that this "violated her freedom of religion." The court found the complaint legally deficient. There was no direct claim that the school or the principal were "acting under color of state law," which was necessary to find a constitutional rights violation under 42 U.S.C. § 1983. It was unclear whether charter schools were "state actors" subject to liability under 42 U.S.C. § 1983. Even if the charter school was a state actor, the parent did not allege misconduct that resulted from an official policy or custom, which is a prerequisite for Section 1983 liability.

While the Free Exercise Clause is "an unflinching pledge to allow our citizenry to explore religious beliefs in accordance with the dictates of their conscience," the court held "not every belief put forward as 'religious' is elevated to constitutional status." **To survive dismissal, the court found there had to be a reasonable possibility that the parent had sincerely held convictions with theological, rather than secular grounds.** She also had to show the school put a substantial burden upon her and interfered with a central religious doctrine. In this case, the parent did not assert religious beliefs that were genuine and sincerely held. She stated no facts concerning her religious beliefs or their importance. Even if the parent's view was believed, the court found a general reference to "familial religious practice," without explanation of the importance of fasting, was insufficient to allege a sincerely held religious belief. As a result, the religious free exercise challenge failed. Regarding the Equal Protection Clause claim, the court held the parent had to show intentional discrimination based on a protected classification, such as religious belief. But she did not allege that the school and principal knew what her religion was or even offer any facts concerning the family's religion. As filed, the complaint was deficient. However, the court offered the parent a second chance to file a complaint so she could include facts supporting her claims. *Meadows v. Lesh*, No. 10-CV-00223(M), 2010 WL 3730105 (W.D.N.Y. 9/17/10).

## IV.   ADMISSIONS AND ATTENDANCE

*The Equal Protection Clause of the Fourteenth Amendment requires government agencies to apply the law equally to all persons. Due the history of official segregation prior to* Brown v. Board of Educ., *347 U.S. 483 (1954), all government classifications based on race are subject to strict judicial scrutiny.*

### A.  Race, Admission and School Assignment

◆   Seattle never operated a dual system of racially segregated schools, but it used race as a tiebreaker in allocating ninth-grade slots for oversubscribed high schools. Jefferson County, Kentucky formerly operated a dual school system, but a federal court declared the system unitary in 2000 and freed it from federal court supervision. Both school districts voluntarily adopted student assignment plans that relied in part upon race. Jefferson County considered race when making some elementary school assignments and in ruling on transfer requests. It tried to assure that a school's racial balance was within a range reflecting the district's racial composition. Parents of students who were denied the school assignment of their choice sued the school systems. Federal circuit courts later upheld the student assignment plans used in both of the school systems.

Appeal reached the U.S. Supreme Court, which noted that the plans did not allow meaningful individual review of applicants but instead relied on racial classifications in a "non-individualized, mechanical way." The classifications would only shift a small number of students. By contrast, consideration of race was critical in tripling minority representation at Michigan Law School in *Grutter v. Bollinger*, below. The diversity interest approved by the Court in *Grutter* "was not focused on race alone but encompassed 'all factors that may contribute to student body diversity.'" The plans in this case "employ only a limited notion of diversity, viewing race exclusively in white/nonwhite terms in Seattle and black/'other' terms in Jefferson County." The Court found that enrolling students without regard to race would yield "a substantially diverse student body without any definition of diversity." **Allowing racial balancing was unconstitutional, and using it as a compelling end in itself would assure that race would always be relevant.** This could justify permanent racial classifications, promote notions of racial inferiority and lead to racial hostility. The Court reversed the judgments. *Parents Involved in Community Schools v. Seattle School Dist. No. 1*, 551 U.S. 701, 127 S.Ct. 2738 (2007).

◆    Parents of students attending school in Berkeley Unified School District (BUSD) had to rank the school program they preferred for their children. While BUSD attempted to assign students on the basis of parental preference, it made assignments in priority categories. BUSD used neighborhood demographics when assigning students to elementary schools and high school programs. Instead of considering individual student race, BUSD used neighborhood data based on 445 "planning areas" of four-to-eight city blocks. Students in these areas were assigned a score based on their area's demographics. Areas were evaluated by average neighborhood household income, average education level of adults residing in the neighborhood, and neighborhood racial composition.

Each student within an area was treated the same in assignments, regardless of his or her own race. A parent group charged BUSD with violating Proposition 209, which prohibits state and local government units (including school districts) from discriminating against, or granting preferential treatment to, any individual or group based on race, sex, color, ethnicity or national origin in public employment, education or contracting. The Court of Appeal of California held that the plan did not violate the state constitution, as it did "not show partiality, prejudice, or preference to any student on the basis of that student's race." **All students in an area were treated equally, regardless of individual race or personal characteristics.** To the extent that any preference was given, it was on the basis of the collective composition of a student's neighborhood. *American Civil Rights Foundation v. Berkeley Unified School Dist.*, 172 Cal.App.4th 207, 90 Cal.Rptr.3d 789 (Cal. Ct. App. 2009).

◆    Massachusetts state officials pressured the Lynn School Committee to stop approving transfers that had a segregative effect on its schools. Lynn officials amended the district school attendance plan to guarantee student attendance in neighborhood schools by **only allowing transfers that "improved the racial balance in either the neighborhood school or the destination school."** Objecting parents sued, raising Equal Protection Clause and related claims. After an 11-day trial, the court held that "since the implementation of the Plan the Lynn schools have become a success story." The court upheld the plan. The U.S. Court of Appeals, First Circuit, affirmed, and the U.S. Supreme Court denied review, apparently ending the case. However, when the U.S. Supreme Court struck down student assignment policies in *Parents Involved in Community Schools v. Seattle School Dist. No. 1*, this chapter, the Lynn parents took note of the similarities among the assignment policies in Seattle, Louisville and Lynn. They filed a complaint to overcome the 2005 First Circuit judgment. A federal court dismissed the case, and the First Circuit refused to reopen it. *Comfort v. Lynn School Committee*, 560 F.3d 22 (1st Cir. 2009).

◆    Los Angeles Unified School District (LAUSD) operated magnet programs under a desegregation order which ended 18 years of state court litigation. A state court entered a final order in 1981 that approved an integration plan relying in part on magnet schools and a Permit With Transportation (PWT) program. Both programs took student race or ethnicity into account in school applications and admissions. The case ended when the U.S. Supreme Court let stand LAUSD's magnet and PWT programs in *Crawford v. Board of Educ*, 458

U.S. 527 (1982). In 1996, California voters approved Proposition 209 to amend the state constitution to prohibit public education programs from discriminating against, or giving preferential treatment to any individual or group on the basis of race, ethnicity or national origin. LAUSD continued to assign students to magnet schools on a priority point system that relied in part on student racial and ethnic designations. In 2005, an organization sued LAUSD, claiming that it relied on racial classifications in violation of Proposition 209.

The case reached the California Court of Appeal, which agreed with LAUSD and its expert that desegregation orders do not terminate simply because court supervision of plan implementation has ended. Desegregation efforts were still under way in LAUSD schools in 1996. The 1981 court order had never been reversed, overruled, vacated, revoked, modified or withdrawn. **The Supreme Court has held that school districts may rely on the ongoing validity of a desegregation order.** The court mandate for LAUSD was to take reasonably feasible steps to desegregate its schools, and LAUSD remained subject to this constitutional duty. As the 1981 *Crawford* order was in existence when Proposition 209 took effect in 1996, the magnet and PWT programs were upheld. *American Civil Rights Foundation v. Los Angeles Unified School Dist.*, 169 Cal.App.4th 436, 86 Cal.Rptr.3d 754 (Cal. Ct. App. 2008).

◆  In two cases involving the University of Michigan, the Supreme Court considered the use of race in higher education admissions.

In the first case, the U.S. Court of Appeals, Sixth Circuit, upheld the University of Michigan Law School's admissions policy. The appeals court found that the law school had a compelling interest in achieving a diverse student body. The Supreme Court noted that any governmental distinction based on race must be examined under the strict scrutiny standard. Under this standard, the classification must be "narrowly tailored to further compelling governmental interests." The Court concluded, based on *Regents of the Univ. of California v. Bakke*, 438 U.S. 265 (1978), that the goal of having a diverse student body is a compelling governmental interest. **The law school admissions policy utilized a narrowly tailored method of achieving that interest through its consideration of race as a "plus" factor.** The Court held the policy was flexible, and it did not create an impermissible quota system. One of the most important factors supporting the decision was the individualized review of applicants that considered several race-neutral factors. *Grutter v. Bollinger,* 539 U.S. 306, 123 S.Ct. 2325, 156 L.E.2d 304 (2003).

The second Michigan case involved the undergraduate admissions policy for the university's College of Literature, Science and the Arts. During the course of the litigation, the policy was changed several times. The policy being considered by the Supreme Court awarded applicants from underrepresented minority groups 20 points. Applicants were awarded points for a variety of factors, and they needed at least 100 points for admission. The Court applied the strict scrutiny analysis to the policy and held that it was not narrowly tailored to achieve the compelling state interest in diversity declared by the university.

**The policy impermissibly gave underrepresented minority students an advantage or preference** by automatically awarding them 20 points. The policy was also deficient because it failed to require an individualized review of each applicant, which is essential when race is a consideration. *Gratz v. Bollinger,* 539 U.S. 244, 123 S.Ct. 2411, 156 L.Ed.2d 257 (2003).

◆    A Wisconsin school district had no formal policy or practice for elementary school class assignments, but a principal issued a memo to staff, urging the balancing of classes according to student gender, ethnicity, academic ability, special needs and parental input. The parents of an African-American student requested their daughter learn from a teacher with high expectations. They also expressed concerns about some negative incidents she had experienced with special education students. After the start of the school year, the student's teacher divided her class into five small groups and put two African-American students in each group, so that they sat together in pairs. She justified this because she believed "African-American students need a buddy, and sometimes it works well if they have someone else working with them because they view things in a global manner." She also seated Hispanic students in pairs.

   The student's family sued the school district and school officials, alleging that the assignment and seating policies violated the Equal Protection Clause. The court awarded pretrial judgment to the district and officials, finding the decision to place the student was the result of race-neutral factors. It found no evidence that the teacher's seating policy resulted in different treatment of the student. The U.S. Court of Appeals, Seventh Circuit, affirmed the decision concerning the school assignment policy. The student's assignment took into consideration her parents' race-neutral concerns. But the lower court should not have awarded pretrial judgment to the teacher on the Equal Protection claim. **Even if the teacher believed she was acting in the best interests of minority students by seating them in pairs, her action was based purely on race.** Because the law in this area was well established, the teacher was not entitled to qualified immunity on the equal protection claim arising from the seating policy. The court reversed in part and remanded the case. *Billings v. Madison Metropolitan School Dist.,* 259 F.3d 807 (7th Cir. 2001).

## B.  Age and Residency Requirements

   *Federal law requires schools to provide homeless students with access to the same free, appropriate public education as other children receive. This includes transportation, special education, English learner, gifted and talented programs and school lunch programs for which students meet eligibility requirements. Under the McKinney-Vento Homeless Assistance Act, homeless children cannot be stigmatized or segregated from a "mainstream school environment on the basis of their being homeless." The No Child Left Behind (NCLB) Act reauthorized the McKinney-Vento Act.*

   *If a homeless student's school enrollment is disputed, the Act requires school districts to immediately admit a student to the school in which enrollment is sought, pending resolution of the dispute.*

   *Schools must notify the parents of homeless children about the NCLB Act's school choice provisions. Schools must continue the education of a homeless student in the student's "school of origin," or enroll the student in a public school that non-homeless students in the same attendance area are eligible to attend. NCLB section 722(g), codified at 42 U.S.C. § 11432, defines "school of origin" as the school a child attended when permanently housed or "the school in which the child or youth was last enrolled."*

◆   A five-year-old Texas student went to live with his aunt. His birth mother lived outside the school district. The aunt sought to pre-enroll the student in a kindergarten class, but the school registrar informed her that she could not enroll him without proof that she had the legal right to act as his guardian or parent. Later in the day, the registrar rejected a power of attorney document signed by the student's mother. The aunt obtained a legal aid attorney, who asserted that a power of attorney was sufficient to establish residency under a section of the Texas Education Code. The section requires non-resident persons under 18 years of age to establish that their presence in a school district is not for the primary purpose of participation in extracurricular activities. The school district maintained that the section did not create a basis for school enrollment. Instead of pursuing the board's grievance procedure, the aunt filed a lawsuit.

The district superintendent then decided to admit the student on the basis of the power of attorney. When the aunt tried to continue the lawsuit anyway, claiming that the district might again exclude the student, a federal district **court dismissed the case, finding the district had never denied the student admission.** The U.S. Court of Appeals, Fifth Circuit, affirmed. Had the aunt awaited a decision by the superintendent or filed a proper grievance, she would have forced the district's initial decision-maker to take a definitive position. *Zepeda v. Boerne Independent School Dist.*, 294 Fed.Appx. 834 (5th Cir. 2008).

◆   Six New York families claimed that homeless children in Suffolk County missed significant amounts of school time due to a systematic failure to provide them with access to education and transportation. The families sued state education officials, who sought to dismiss the case. A federal court explained that the McKinney-Vento Act required states to assure that homeless children had access to a free and appropriate public education. The Act directed local education agencies to immediately enroll homeless students, even if they were unable to produce the records normally required for enrollment. **Enrolling schools must immediately contact the school last attended by a homeless student to obtain necessary records, and they must help parents of homeless students obtain necessary immunizations or medical records.** The court held that Congress intended to create a private right of action to enforce the McKinney-Vento Act. Thus, the families were appropriate representatives of homeless students in Suffolk County, and the court certified the case as a class action. *National Law Center on Homelessness and Poverty, R.I. v. State of New York*, 224 F.R.D. 314 (E.D.N.Y. 2004).

*The New York Court of Appeals applied state law consistently with the No Child Left Behind Act in the following case, in which a homeless student's last permanent residence counted, not his brief stay in a homeless shelter.*

◆   A New York family rented a house in Springs School District for parts of two school years. The family was evicted, and the children moved to temporary homes, including stays in motels and with relatives. The mother was jailed for part of this time, and the family moved into a homeless shelter in the Longwood School District. The county Department of Social Services (DSS) placed the children in foster care, and they then began attending Longwood schools. DSS forms indicated Springs as the "district of origin" for the children. Longwood filed a claim against Springs for tuition reimbursement for the children. When Springs refused, Longwood sued Springs. A state trial court held for Longwood, ruling the mother's last permanent home was in the Springs School District.

The New York Supreme Court, Appellate Division, reversed the judgment, holding that the mother's temporary stay in the homeless shelter obligated Longwood to pay for the children's education. The New York Court of Appeals noted that the school district in which a child resided at the time of a social services placement had to bear the child's instructional costs. The court agreed with Longwood that the family's last permanent residence was what counted, not a brief stay in a shelter. **Residence was established by physical presence as an inhabitant within the district, combined with an intent to remain.** Districts were required to provide tuition-free education only to students whose parents or guardians resided in the district. The "temporary stayovers" following the eviction, including time in the homeless shelter, did not change the family residence. As a result, the court reversed the judgment. *Longwood Cent. School Dist. v. Springs Union Free School Dist.*, 1 N.Y.3d 385, 774 N.Y.S.2d 857, 806 N.E.2d 970 (N.Y. 2004).

◆    A disabled Colorado student and her family moved out of her school district when she was in second grade. The district permitted her to stay in her school for the rest of the year. It readmitted her to the school for third and fourth grade under the state's school choice law. However, the district denied her application to re-enroll for grade five, stating that its special education program had exceeded its capacity. A special education due process hearing officer held for the district, and an administrative law judge affirmed. The parents moved back into the school district and re-enrolled their daughter in the school she had formerly attended. They sued the district for violating the state school choice law, among others. The court awarded pretrial judgment to the district.

On appeal, the state court of appeals held that the school choice law allowed elementary students who became district "nonresidents" during a school year or between school years to remain in their schools. This right extended only to the next school year and did not entitle a nonresident student to return for subsequent school years, as the parents argued. The district's special education programs exceeded nonresident enrollment limits. **The school choice statute authorized the district to deny re-enrollment based on nonresident status.** The district had a "potentially limitless" obligation to provide special education to disabled resident students, but this was distinct from any obligation to accept nonresidents under the school choice law. The court affirmed the judgment. *Bradshaw v. Cherry Creek School Dist. No. 5*, 98 P.3d 886 (Colo. Ct. App. 2003).

◆    A parent who lived in Chicago sent her daughter to North Carolina after the girl was threatened with assault. The student's uncle attempted to enroll her in a local school, but the district superintendent denied admission because she was not domiciled in a county school administrative unit. The family filed a state court action that reached the North Carolina Court of Appeals.

The court observed that **a child who is not domiciled in a local administrative unit may attend its schools without paying tuition if the child resides with an adult in the unit as the result of a parent or guardian's death, serious illness, incapacity or incarceration**. A non-domiciliary student may also enroll in school in another administrative unit in cases of abandonment, child abuse or natural disaster. In these cases, the student must present an affidavit including a statement that the claim to residency is not primarily related to attendance at a particular school and that an adult with whom the child resides accepts responsibility for the child's educational decisions. The court rejected the family's argument that the law violated due process and equal protection rights. In *Martinez v. Bynum* (this chapter), the U.S. Supreme Court upheld a Texas law conditioning public school enrollment on residency within a school district or proof that enrollment was not being sought for the sole purpose of attending school within the district. The North Carolina statute, like the Texas law, was a reasonable standard for determining the residential status of public school students. *Graham v. Mock*, 545 S.E.2d 263 (N.C. Ct. App. 2001).

◆ The Texas Education Code permitted school districts to deny free admission to minors who lived apart from a "parent, guardian, or the person having lawful control of him" if the minor's primary purpose in being in the district was to attend local public schools. A minor left his parent's home in Mexico to live with his sister in a Texas town for the purpose of attending school there. When the school district denied his application for tuition-free admission, his sister sued, alleging that the law was unconstitutional. A federal court held for the state, and the Fifth Circuit Court of Appeals affirmed.

The U.S. Supreme Court upheld the residency requirement. **A bona fide residence requirement, appropriately defined and uniformly applied, furthered a substantial state interest** in assuring that services provided for residents were enjoyed only by residents. Such a requirement with respect to attendance in public free schools did not violate the Equal Protection Clause. Residence generally requires both physical presence and intention to remain. As long as the child was not living in the district for the sole purpose of attending school, he satisfied the statutory test. The Court held that this was a bona fide residency requirement and that the Constitution permits a state to restrict eligibility for tuition-free education to its bona fide residents. *Martinez v. Bynum*, 461 U.S. 321, 103 S.Ct. 1838, 75 L.Ed.2d 879 (1983).

◆ In May 1975, the Texas legislature revised its education laws to withhold from school districts any state funds for the education of children who were not legally admitted into the U.S. It authorized school districts to deny enrollment to these children. A group filed a class action on behalf of school-age children of Mexican origin who could not establish they had been legally admitted into the U.S. The action complained of the exclusion of the children from public school. A federal court prevented the school district from denying a free education to the children, and the U.S. Court of Appeals, Fifth Circuit, upheld the decision. The legislation was also challenged by numerous other plaintiffs. The court held that the law violated the Equal Protection Clause, and the Fifth Circuit affirmed. The Supreme Court granted review. The state claimed that undocumented aliens were not "persons" within the jurisdiction of Texas, and so were not entitled to equal protection of its laws. The Court rejected this argument, stating that **whatever an alien's status under the immigration laws, an alien is a "person" in any sense of the term**.

The term "within its jurisdiction" was meant as a term of geographic location, and the Equal Protection Clause extended its protection to all persons within a state, whether citizen or stranger. The statute could not be upheld because it did not advance any substantial state interest. The Texas statute imposed a lifetime hardship on a discrete class of children not accountable for their disabling status. There was no evidence to show the exclusion of the children would improve the overall quality of education in the state. *Plyler v. Doe*, 457 U.S. 202, 102 S.Ct. 2382, 72 L.Ed.2d 786 (1982).

## V.   COMPULSORY ATTENDANCE

*States have a compelling interest in providing public education and may establish and enforce reasonable school attendance laws.*

### A.   Compulsory Attendance and Truancy

◆   A Maryland school attendance worker recorded a student as absent from school 74 days during the 2006-07 school year. State prosecutors filed an adult truancy petition against the student's parent for violating the state compulsory attendance act. The parent and student claimed that the student usually arrived at school on a regular basis. But the student admitted that once at school, she often cut her classes and was "hanging out" in school hallways. The parent asserted that after her child was at school, she was in the care and custody of school officials. The trial judge expressed disbelief at the parent for failing to ask her child about missing classes and found her "involved in" the child's truancy. After the court upheld the petition and placed the parent on probation, she appealed to the Court of Appeals of Maryland.

The lower court had found the parent's testimony both "incomprehensible" and incredible. As it was error for the trial court judge to make an inference that the opposite of her testimony must be true, the parent was entitled to a new trial. Once the daughter entered the school building, her custody shifted to the school. No language in the compulsory attendance law made it clear to a parent that criminal liability would be imposed on a parent whose child cut classes. **While children were being educated during the school day, their parents transferred to school officials the power to act as their guardians.** Evidence that the student was not in her homeroom when attendance was taken would be sufficient to establish that she did not attend school on that day. In order to find that the parent violated the compulsory attendance law at a new trial, there had to be "proof beyond a reasonable doubt" that her child did not attend school. *In re Gloria H.*, 410 Md. 562, 979 A.2d 710 (Md. 2009).

◆ A Kentucky middle school student accumulated 21 unexcused absences in a two-month period, and a family court complaint was filed against him. He argued that his school district should have determined if his truancy was a manifestation of a disability prior to filing the action. A school attendance coordinator testified that she made a home visit, mailed numerous letters and made many phone calls to gain compliance. Her intervention did not help and the student only complained that "he did not like school." After a hearing, the court found the student habitually truant. While he could remain at home, he was required to attend counseling and school, and cooperate with a state family services agency. On appeal, the Court of Appeals of Kentucky found that **prior to filing a truancy complaint, a school director of pupil personnel must determine the causes of a student's truancy, assess home conditions and conduct home visits**. All these requirements were met and ample evidence supported the finding of habitual truancy. And nothing in the Individuals with Disabilities Education Act (IDEA) required a manifestation determination to see if his truancy related to a disability. The court affirmed the judgment. *R.B.J. v. Comwlth. of Kentucky*, No. 2008-CA-001349-ME, 2009 WL 1349219 (Ky. Ct. App. 5/15/09).

◆ A New Mexico student of African-American and Hispanic heritage received special education for a specific learning disability. In eighth grade, she stopped coming to school, due in part to family problems. The student was charged with aggravated battery and assault of her mother and brother with a deadly weapon. After serving time in juvenile facilities, she was placed in a residential treatment center. Upon returning to school, the student used drugs and alcohol at school and received numerous disciplinary referrals for truancy. She skipped school to provoke her mother's boyfriend into leaving their home.

The student became pregnant and was sent to a day shelter. She was then suspended for fighting at school. Her mother claimed the school district denied her access to a Wilson Reading System program and filed an unsuccessful special education due process action. The student transferred to another school district, where she enrolled in a Wilson class. She earned a 4.0 grade average for grade nine, then dropped out due to more family turmoil and drug use. The parent sued the residence school district for equal protection and Title VI violations. A court found no merit to the student's claim that she did not benefit from her education. On appeal, the U.S. Court of Appeals, Tenth Circuit, denied her claim under the Individuals with Disabilities Education Act. **She was seeking the very services she would have received by simply returning to school.** For more details about the special education claims, see Chapter Six, Section II.C. of this volume. *Garcia v. Board of Educ. of Albuquerque Public Schools*, 520 F.3d 1116 (10th Cir. 2008).

◆ A St. Louis city ordinance made parents responsible for truancy by their minor children. Parents who knowingly allowed their children to miss school without excuse could be fined $25 for each day of school missed. A city municipal court judge directed a minor student who had an infant child to participate in therapy, attend school every day and refrain from using force against her own parents. The family was ordered to cooperate with the court or face contempt charges. The minor student's mother claimed the student assaulted her. The judge held the minor student in contempt of court and encouraged the mother to file criminal charges against her. She filed charges but dropped them within a few days. The judge later ordered the mother to be incarcerated for several days until her next appearance. The mother claimed that while she was incarcerated, state social workers took custody of her grandson.

The grandson, who was the truant minor student's son, was then adopted by a foster family. The mother sued the judge and city for civil rights violations. A court awarded judgment to the city and found the judge was entitled to immunity. The U.S. Court of Appeals, Eighth Circuit, found **a municipality is liable for federal civil rights violations only where an official with final policymaking responsibility makes a deliberate choice to violate constitutional rights**. The judge's order was a judicial decision for which the city could not be held responsible. As the order incarcerating the mother was not a final policy decision of the type creating municipal liability, the court affirmed the judgment. *Granda v. City of St. Louis*, 472 F.3d 565 (8th Cir. 2007).

◆    **Wisconsin's compulsory school attendance statute requires any person having control of a school-age child to "cause the child to attend school regularly. …"** The statute cross-references other Wisconsin statutes detailing state procedures for truancy, including a statute that requires each school board to establish written attendance policies. The parent of a student who was absent without excuse eight times during a three-month period failed to respond to repeated notices from the school to meet with officials. The district attorney's office brought charges against the student's parent, resulting in a misdemeanor conviction. On appeal to the Court of Appeals of Wisconsin, the parent argued that the compulsory attendance statute was unconstitutionally vague because it did not define "regularly." The court found the statute sufficiently definite and understandable to a person of average intelligence. It sufficiently cross-referenced other statutes so that the full statutory scheme of mandatory attendance was clear. The court rejected the parent's defense that the student was uncontrollable, because evidence indicated she had a consistent pattern of unexcused absences dating from kindergarten. The court upheld the statute and affirmed the conviction. *State v. White*, 509 N.W.2d 434 (Wis. Ct. App. 1993).

◆    An 18-year-old West Virginia student missed five days of school without an excuse. He was warned that continued absences could result in criminal prosecution. After continuing unexcused absences, the county prosecutor's office filed a criminal complaint against the student. After he was convicted of violating a state compulsory attendance statute, he petitioned the Supreme Court of Appeals of West Virginia for review. The court observed that the compulsory attendance statute mandated school attendance for children between the ages of six and 16 and provided enforcement sanctions against parents, guardians or custodians, but not against individual students. **There was no possibility of liability under the statute for a non-attending student, regardless of age.** The court ruled for the student. *State ex rel. Estes v. Egnor*, 443 S.E.2d 193 (W. Va. 1994).

## B.  Home Study Programs

◆   Pennsylvania law permitted home education programs. School districts reviewed home education programs for compliance with minimum hours of instruction, course requirements and student progress. Parents of children being homeschooled had to file affidavits every year indicating their compliance with compulsory attendance law requirements, and had to get annual written evaluations of each child's work. School superintendents were charged with ensuring that home-schooled children received an appropriate education. If a superintendent determined appropriate education was not taking place, there could be a request for more information and the possibility of a hearing. A hearing officer who found that an appropriate education was not taking place could order the student into a remedial program, or a public or private school.

A group of parents who homeschooled their children sought exemptions from the Religious Freedom Protection Act. The districts denied their requests. After truancy prosecutions were begun, the parents filed separate suits against the districts that were eventually consolidated before a federal district court. The cases reached the U.S. Court of Appeals, Third Circuit. It found that **in practice, school districts exercised a "limited level of oversight" over home education programs**. The court held the Free Exercise Clause does not relieve persons from a valid and neutral law of general applicability. A law was "neutral" if it did not target religiously motivated conduct. In this case, the act was a neutral law of general applicability. It did not target religious practices or selectively burden religiously motivated conduct. Nothing suggested school officials discriminated against religiously based home education programs. The act was rationally related to legitimate government objectives. As the right of parents to control the education of their children was "neither absolute nor unqualified," the court held for the school districts. *Combs v. Homer-Center School Dist.*, 540 F.3d 231 (3d Cir. 2008).

◆   A California family had a 20-year history of intervention by children and family services. The parents were subject to a dependency court proceeding for charges of physical abuse, neglect and failure to prevent sexual abuse. They were uncooperative with authorities, and the mother once attempted to hide the children from them. After two children were declared dependent due to the abuse and neglect of their siblings, their attorney sought an order requiring that they be sent to a public or private school, rather than educated at home. The request was made to allow the children to be in regular contact with mandatory reporters. A state superior court refused the request, finding "parents have an absolute constitutional right to home school their children."

On appeal, the state court of appeal found that state law does not expressly permit homeschooling. But recent provisions of law indicated that the legislature recognized homeschooling is taking place. The court explained that homeschooling arose as an issue in the case because one child, who had been homeschooled by the mother, wanted to attend public school. The children and families agency claimed the child was dependent on the additional basis that her parents' refusal to send her to public school placed her at risk of serious emotional damage. The superior court had incorrectly found there was an absolute parental right to homeschool children. Instead, **the constitutional liberty interest of parents to direct the education of their children had to yield to the state interest in child protection and safety**. The court noted this was a dependency case in which the children had been found dependent due to abuse and neglect of a sibling. "The parents in dependency have been judicially determined not to be fit," wrote the court. Without contact with mandated reporters at school, the court found child safety might not be guaranteed. By allowing the children to attend school, they could remain in their home, while educators would provide "an extra layer of protection." The court returned the case to the superior court for reconsideration. *Jonathan L. v. Superior Court*, 165 Cal.App.4th 1074, 81 Cal.Rptr.3d 517 (Cal. Ct. App. 2008).

◆   The Court of Appeals of Michigan upheld an order by a family court to exercise jurisdiction over a student with disabilities whose mother claimed she was homeschooling him. Evidence indicated that she was not even at home during most of the school day. The family court found that the student had missed 111 out of the 134 days of the current school year. The court noted the mother's reluctance to use negative consequences for improper conduct by the student. The court found that it was not in the student's best interests to be homeschooled, especially where this required him to be unsupervised for most of the day. **The court found the mother's home-schooling plan "painfully neglectful" of his educational needs.** Although this was not a severe case of educational neglect, it was proper for the trial court to assume jurisdiction over the student. *Manchester Public Schools v. Flint*, No. 240251, 2003 WL 22244692 (Mich. Ct. App. 2003).

◆   Two Massachusetts children were not enrolled in school and lacked approved home-schooling plans. The parents contended that school committee approval of their home-schooling activities would conflict with their learner-led approach to education, and that the Constitution prohibited infringement on their privacy and family rights. The school committee initiated a state district court proceeding for the care and protection of the children. The court found the parents had failed over a two-year period to show the children's educational needs were being met, effectively preventing any evaluation of their educational level and instructional methods. The parents did not comply with a court order to file educational plans, resulting in adjudication of the children as in need of care and protection. The court transferred legal custody of the children to the social services department, although they remained in their parents' physical custody. The parents appealed to the Appellate Court of Massachusetts.

The court noted that the trial court order had required the parents to submit a detailed home-schooling plan to the school committee to allow assessment of the program and the children's progress. **This was a legitimate educational condition that a school committee could impose on a home-school proposal without infringing on the constitutional rights of a family.** The U.S. Supreme Court has recognized a degree of parental autonomy to direct the education of children, but state laws effectively incorporated this requirement by allowing for flexibility in the evaluation of private instruction. The parents rejected accommodations proposed by the school committee, and the custody order was entered only after they had received a final opportunity to comply with the committee's requests. The court affirmed the order for temporary care and protection. *In re Ivan*, 717 N.E.2d 1020 (Mass. App. Ct. 1999).

## C. Attendance Policies

◆ The Court of Appeal of Louisiana denied relief to a student who was expelled in her eighth-grade year and sought to return the next year as a ninth-grader. She based her claim on her progress as a home-schooled student and her passing score on the state's LEAP test with mastery achievement levels. The parents had sought to have the school board evaluate the student since August 2006, but a state trial court denied their request and the case became mired in appeal procedures. The court of appeal chastised the school board and trial court for allowing the student to go without an evaluation until February 2007. Both the court of appeal and state supreme court had ordered such an evaluation. **The school board's decision to return the student to grade eight appeared to be arbitrary.** However, only 65 days remained in the school year, and it was now too late for her to meet the relevant attendance and lesson requirements. *B.W.S., Jr. v. Livingston Parish School Board*, 960 So.2d 997 (La. Ct. App. 2007).

◆ An Alabama high school handbook required the referral of tardy students first into parent conferences, then for discipline or alternative programs. After a student's third unexcused absence in a semester, the handbook provided for referral to an "early warning program" conducted by the county juvenile court system. After a student's tenth tardy in one semester, the school principal reported her to the school truant officer. The principal did not refer her to the early warning program or contact her parents, as specified in the school handbook. The truant officer filed a child in need of supervision petition in the juvenile court. After a trial, the court adjudicated the student a child in need of supervision and placed her on probation for the rest of the school year.

On appeal, the student asserted that the principal violated the Compulsory School Attendance Law and school policy by failing to investigate the causes of her tardiness before referring her to the truant officer. **The Alabama Court of Civil Appeals found nothing in state law requiring the principal to investigate the causes of a student's tardiness.** The principal did not violate the student's due process rights by failing to follow the student handbook's progressive discipline policies before submitting her name to the truant officer. The handbook placed a duty on students to provide a timely excuse for their absences. The student was unable to show that the school selectively enforced the prosecution of truancy cases. The court affirmed the judgment. *S.H. v. State of Alabama*, 868 So.2d 1110 (Ala. Civ. App. 2003).

◆ An Ohio school policy required the school to provide parents with written notification of state compulsory education laws upon a student's third unexcused absence. After the fifth absence, the school was required to hold an informal conference with the parents, student and a probation officer, and upon the tenth absence, a formal hearing was mandated. A student was absent without excuse approximately 20 days during a four-month period. On some occasions the parents explained there was a medical problem. The school accepted these explanations until the parents applied to the county educational service center for permission to home-school the student. But the school did not send them any notices concerning truancy proceedings. The service center advised the principal that the student's home school application was being denied, and the principal filed a complaint against the parents in an Ohio county court on charges of contributing to the delinquency of a minor.

The court conducted a jury trial and sentenced the parents to seven days in jail and fines of $250. They appealed to a state appeals court, which reversed the judgment. The state failed to meet its burden of proof to show that under local standards, the student was habitually truant. **Because truancy involved more than absenteeism, the court held the state was required to show a lack of excuse or permission as established by school policy.** In this case, the state failed to prove that it had sent the parents written notices that their daughter was absent without an excuse for three or more days. Without this proof, the state could not satisfy the essential element of habitual truancy. *State v. Smrekar*, No. 99 CO 35, 2000 Ohio App. Lexis 5381, 2000 WL 1726518 (Ohio Ct. App. 2000).

## VI. CORPORAL PUNISHMENT

*The U.S. Supreme Court held in* Ingraham v. Wright, *below, that the infliction of corporal punishment implicates student liberty interests under the Due Process Clause of the Fourteenth Amendment. However, as corporal punishment was authorized by common law, the Court refused to create any procedural safeguards for students beyond those offered by state law. Corporal punishment is distinguishable from "reasonable physical force" to restrain unruly students, maintain order and prevent injury, as permitted by state law.*

*In 2009, Florida legislators amended state law to limit the use of zero-tolerance policies and require school boards that permit corporal punishment as a form of discipline to review such policies every three years.*

◆  The U.S. Supreme Court held that the use of corporal punishment is a matter of state law. Two Florida students were paddled by school administrators. One was beaten so severely he missed 11 days of school. The other suffered a hematoma and lost the use of his arm for a week. The parents sued school authorities, alleging cruel and unusual punishment and due process violations. **The Supreme Court held that the Eighth Amendment prohibition against cruel and unusual punishment did not apply to corporal punishment in schools.** The Court's reasoning for this decision lay in the relative openness of the school system and its surveillance by the community. The Eighth Amendment was intended to protect the rights of incarcerated persons, not students. State civil and criminal penalties restrained school employees from issuing unreasonable punishment. While corporal punishment implicated the Due Process Clause, state law vested the decision to issue it with school officials. The Court found corporal punishment served important educational interests. There was no requirement for notice and a hearing prior to imposing corporal punishment as the practice was authorized and limited by state law. *Ingraham v. Wright*, 430 U.S. 651, 97 S.Ct. 1401, 51 L.Ed.2d 711 (1977).

## A. Student Due Process Rights

◆  A Florida student with autism became aggressive and had trouble obeying rules and completing schoolwork. He pushed and bit others, growled, cursed, scratched himself and threatened to blow up his school. According to the student, the teacher used profanity daily and called him names. The teacher was placed on leave after two aides reported she had held down another child in the student's class until his eyes swelled and his lips turned blue. Reports were made to the state child abuse hotline, and the teacher was suspended and barred from school grounds. She was eventually convicted of one out of four counts of child abuse. A federal district court action was filed against the teacher on behalf of the student. In pretrial activity, two teaching aides stated that the teacher, who weighed almost 300 pounds, had straddled the student or pinned him against an object and pulled his arms behind his back. One aide testified that the teacher had used restraints in a way that could cause asphyxiation.

The court dismissed claims under the Due Process Clause of the Fourteenth Amendment and Section 504 of the Rehabilitation Act. On appeal, the Eleventh Circuit affirmed the judgment. It held only the most egregious official conduct violates the Constitution. **Corporal punishment has been held actionable by courts only when it is arbitrary, egregious and shocks the conscience.** A tripping incident was not corporal punishment. As for the other incidents, it appeared to the court that the teacher was attempting to restore order, maintain discipline or protect the student from harming himself. In each case, the student refused to go to his "cool down room," called the teacher names or threatened her. The court found no evidence that the teacher provoked the student into misbehaving. Evidence established that the teacher used restraints only until the student calmed down or agreed to comply with her instructions. Each incident lasted only a few minutes. There was also no evidence that the punishment of the student was based on his disability, defeating any discrimination claim. *T.W. v. School Board of Seminole County, Florida*, 610 F.3d 588 (11th Cir. 2010).

◆  A Tennessee student claimed two basketball coaches routinely paddled him for missing basketball practice, being late or other misconduct. He claimed one of the coaches punched him in the chest and paddled him for missing a car wash. The student said coaches sometimes paddled him for getting poor grades or misconduct. The student transferred schools in his eleventh-grade year and sued the coaches, school principal, the Memphis City Schools and its superintendent in a federal district court. After dismissing some of the claims, the court held a jury trial. A jury returned a verdict for the school system and officials on the remaining claims, and the student appealed.

On appeal, the U.S. Court of Appeals, Sixth Circuit, reviewed evidence that neither the student nor his parent ever complained about the paddlings to the principal or other officials. He never sought medical treatment and admitted he was not seriously harmed. One of the coaches stated that he might have paddled the student two or three times in all. The other coach stated he had paddled the student about 10 times over a three-year period. The Sixth Circuit noted that **Section 49-6-4103 of the Tennessee Code permits teachers and principals to use corporal punishment** "in a reasonable manner against any pupil for good cause in order to maintain discipline and order within the public schools." A school policy also permitted paddling. A 1944 state supreme court decision held that **"if corporal punishment is moderate and is inflicted with a proper instrument the teacher is as a rule, not liable civilly for assault and battery."** As only excessive punishment will subject a teacher to civil liability, the state law assault and battery claims failed. As for the constitutional claims, the court explained that there is a due process liberty interest in freedom from bodily injury. But the standard for a violation is high, and to prevail, the student had to show force so severe and so disproportionate to the need and "so inspired by malice or sadism" as to literally be "shocking to the conscience." He admitted he was not seriously injured, and the judgment was affirmed. *Nolan v. Memphis City Schools*, 589 F.3d 257 (6th Cir. 2009).

◆    A Georgia eighth-grade student was assigned to a remedial reading class. He arrived late to class, then talked to a classmate. The teacher told the classmate to leave the room, and the student tried to leave with him, refusing to return to his seat when she instructed him to do so. The teacher yelled and shook her finger at him. As the student moved to the door, she blocked it, and he initiated some physical contact with her. The teacher then grabbed the student by the neck. He claimed she squeezed his neck until he could not breathe. The teacher said she was afraid the student was preparing to hit her and put her hands on him to protect herself. The district placed her on administrative leave, and she soon resigned. The student sued the teacher, principal, district superintendent and school district. A federal court awarded pretrial judgment to the school officials, and the student appealed.

The U.S. Court of Appeals, Eleventh Circuit, held that regardless of whether the teacher acted in self-defense or imposed corporal punishment, there was no constitutional violation. **School officials violate substantive due process rights under the Fourteenth Amendment only when their conduct is considered arbitrary or "shocking to the conscience."** Neither party disputed that the teacher was acting within the scope of her discretionary authority. The force she used was not "obviously excessive," and she acted only after he repeatedly disobeyed her. She was entitled to official immunity. *Peterson v. Baker*, 504 F.3d 1331(11th Cir. 2007).

◆    An 18-year-old Texas student attended a public charter school during the 2003-04 school year. The principal disciplined her for leaving campus during a school day. He attempted to administer corporal punishment with a wooden paddle. The student resisted and received temporary, minor injuries to her hand by trying to block the paddle. She sued the school and principal. The case reached the U.S. Court of Appeals, Fifth Circuit, which held that **corporal punishment of public school students deprives them of substantive due process rights only when "arbitrary, capricious or wholly unrelated to the legitimate state goal of maintaining an atmosphere conducive to learning."**

Corporal punishment is not arbitrary so long as the state affords local remedies. Texas law afforded adequate remedies for excessive corporal punishment claims. For this reason, the student's due process claims failed. There was no merit to her claim that adult status increased her rights. While the student did not have to attend school past the age of 18, she had voluntarily chosen to do so. Having agreed to attend school, she was not free to disregard school rules. *Serafin v. School of Excellence in Educ.*, 252 Fed.Appx. 684 (5th Cir. 2007).

◆    The U.S. Court of Appeals, Eleventh Circuit, upheld a federal court order denying qualified immunity to an Alabama principal accused of beating a student. The student claimed the principal called him into his office for disciplinary reasons and hit him in the head, ribs and back with a metal cane. His mother sued the district and principal for violating his federal civil rights. The principal sought pretrial judgment, asserting qualified immunity. He alleged that the student had previously been disciplined for bringing a weapon to school, justifying his use of force. The court denied the request for immunity, and the principal appealed to the Eleventh Circuit. The court held that repeatedly striking a 13-year-old with a metal cane was an obvious constitutional violation. It rejected the principal's assertion that any prior incident involving weapons possession allowed him to beat the student. *Ingraham v. Wright* held that the deliberate infliction of physical pain by school authorities as punishment implicated student due process rights. The Alabama Supreme Court has held that **corporal punishment deprives students of their substantive due process rights when it is arbitrary, capricious or unrelated to the legitimate goal of maintaining an atmosphere conducive to learning**. The principal was not entitled to qualified immunity. The case required a trial. *Kirkland v. Greene County Board of Educ.*, 347 F.3d 903 (11th Cir. 2003).

◆    A Hawaii elementary school teacher sent a student to the office for fighting. Once there, the student refused to stand still against a wall for time-out punishment. The vice principal warned the student that he would take him outside and tape him to a tree if he did not stand still. He then made good on his threat by taping the student to the tree with masking tape. After about five minutes, a fifth-grade student told the vice principal that "she did not think he should be doing that." The vice principal allowed her to remove the tape from the student. The student's family sued the state education department and vice principal for constitutional rights violations. A court denied the vice principal's motion for pretrial judgment. He appealed to the Ninth Circuit, which held that school seizures violated the Fourth Amendment if they were objectively unreasonable under the circumstances. There was no suggestion in this case that the student was a danger to others. **Taping an eight-year-old to a tree was objectively unreasonable conduct.** The court affirmed the judgment. *Doe v. State of Hawaii*, 334 F.3d 906 (9th Cir. 2003).

◆    When a teacher observed an Arkansas ninth-grader violently kicking a vending machine, she attempted to stop him. The student initially ignored the teacher, but stopped kicking the machine when she began to shake him by the arms. The principal of the adjacent high school grabbed the student's neck and shirt collar, led him from the school and "threw" him on a bench, where he landed on his shoulder. The principal instructed the school's resource officer to handcuff the student, and he was taken to the county jail. The student's mother then took him to an emergency room, where he was diagnosed with a strained neck and treated. The student's mother sued the principal, and a federal court awarded pretrial judgment to the principal. On appeal, the Eighth Circuit stated that the principal's conduct could not be considered shocking to the conscience unless it was malicious and sadistic. There was no evidence that he disliked the student or had even met him before. **School administrators are entitled to substantial deference in their efforts to maintain order and discipline.** The principal responded quickly and decisively to an incident of serious student misbehavior, and the court affirmed the judgment in his favor. *Golden ex rel. Balch v. Anders*, 324 F.3d 650 (8th Cir. 2003).

## B.  Teacher Liability Protection

*Subpart Five of the No Child Left Behind (NCLB) Act (20 U.S.C. §§ 6731-38) is the Paul D. Coverdell Teacher Protection Act. This NCLB Act provision protects school staff from liability if they act on behalf of the school, within the scope of their employment, in conformity with law and "in furtherance of efforts to control, discipline, expel, or suspend a student or maintain order or control in the classroom or school.;" ... and there is no willful or criminal misconduct, gross negligence or reckless misconduct or flagrant disregard for rights. The Coverdell Act provision parallels state law provisions protecting school employees from liability when they restrain students in order to preserve order in the school or to prevent injury. For example, Oklahoma law prohibits any liability from the use of necessary and reasonable force to control and discipline a student, or from taking good faith actions to suspend a student.*

*The NCLB provision also prohibits punitive damage awards against teachers unless there is "clear and convincing evidence that the harm was proximately caused by an act or omission of such teacher that constitutes willful or criminal misconduct" or flagrant indifference to rights.*

◆    A Nevada teacher was accused of grabbing and choking a student who was trying to push open a door where entry was not allowed. Although the teacher denied choking the student, he admitted touching his chest and admonishing him. After the incident, the student visited a doctor and an uncertified counselor for "emotional and psychological treatments." In an arbitration proceeding, the student won past medical expenses for his family practitioner and a physical therapist. However, the arbitrator did not award costs for the counselor due to his inadequate credentials. The student then sued the teacher and school district in a state court for negligence. On the first day of trial, the teacher and district moved for immunity. They cited the Paul D. Coverdell Teacher Protection Act, described in the paragraphs above. The court found the teacher's conduct was unreasonable and outside the act's protections.

The court awarded general damages and expenses of $27,270, an amount that was slightly lower than the arbitration award. This included the $5,700 charged by the counselor that had not been allowed in arbitration. Appeal reached the Supreme Court of Nevada, where the student claimed a Coverdell Act defense could not be raised at the beginning of a trial. Instead, he argued the act created an "affirmative defense" that had to be raised at the time of the initial response to a complaint. The court agreed that **the Coverdell Act defense was an affirmative defense which had to be asserted in the response to the complaint**. It then found the counselor's fees were excessive and unreasonable. When the state legislature enacted laws regulating psychologists, it intended to prevent laypersons from practicing the profession. As a result, the award of $5,700 for the counselor's services was found "illegal and not recoverable." *Webb v. Clark County School Dist.*, 145 Nev. 47, 218 P.3d 1239 (Nev. 2009).

◆ An Ohio student's mother claimed that a teacher grabbed, choked and shoved her son in front of the rest of his first-grade class, causing serious physical injury. She sued the school system, its board, and the teacher for negligence and intentional conduct. A court awarded pretrial judgment to the school board but denied it to the teacher. The Court of Appeals of Ohio explained that the trial court had properly awarded judgment to the school system. It then considered the teacher's claim to state law immunity and noted that **the family's assertion that she willfully, wantonly and recklessly grabbed, choked and shoved the student was sufficient to deny immunity**. The case against her would proceed. *Rogers v. Akron City School System*, No. CV 2006-05-2869, 2008 WL 2439674 (Ohio Ct. App. 6/18/08).

◆ An Ohio school district banned corporal punishment in its schools in 1987. Substitute teachers had to undergo training on the subject before becoming eligible for hire. During orientation, they were informed of the district policy prohibiting corporal punishment and told how to handle student misconduct. Substitutes had to seek assistance from the principal or assistant principal if a student disciplinary situation occurred. One substitute worked for the school district for four years when a third grader claimed that the substitute "slammed her into a chalkboard, threw her on the ground, and choked her" for a minute because she did not have a pencil with her. Her parent sued the school district.

    The case reached the U.S. Court of Appeals, Sixth Circuit, which rejected the parent's claim that the state Tort Liability Act violated the Ohio Constitution. To show corporal punishment violates the Constitution, a student must show the force applied caused injury so severe, was so disproportionate to the need presented, and was so inspired by malice or sadism that it amounted to a brutal and inhumane abuse of official power that was shocking to the conscience. In this case, **the student did not show that the district was deliberately indifferent to student abuse by substitute teachers**. There had been only two incidents in a two-year period in a school district with 127 schools serving over 69,000 students. This did not create "notice" of constitutional problems. The court affirmed the judgment for the school district. *Ellis v. Cleveland Municipal School Dist.*, 455 F.3d 690 (6th Cir. 2006).

◆ In a case involving a student with attention deficit hyperactivity disorder, the Louisiana Court of Appeal ruled that a school properly applied corporal punishment, which was expressly allowed in Louisiana. The rules governing its use allowed corporal punishment only after other methods had failed. The court found the rules protected student due process rights, required a staff witness, and specified the paddle and the number of strokes to be used. An assistant principal testified that he paddled the student because of the severity of the misconduct and only after other methods failed. He complied with board rules and felt the student needed immediate negative reinforcement. The student had a pattern of misbehavior, including fighting, kicking, cursing, biting and taking things. His parents complained of other methods and refused counseling. **The law did not require advance parental consent.** *Setliff v. Rapides Parish School Board*, 888 So.2d 1156 (La. Ct. App. 2004).

◆    **A Colorado school custodian broke up a fight between two students in a school hallway. He "head-butted" the student he perceived to be the aggressor** and told him "there's always someone bigger than you. Now get out of here." The district investigated the incident and proposed discharging the custodian for inappropriate contact with a student. After a hearing before the superintendent under the collective bargaining agreement, discharge for deliberate or inappropriate conduct was recommended, and the school board approved this. In a state court action, the court held the discharge was unlawful, and it ordered the district to reinstate the custodian to his job with back wages. In doing so, the court conducted a new hearing, described by courts as "*de novo* review." But the Supreme Court of Colorado held the trial court should not have conducted a separate review. Instead, it should have relied on the school board hearing. The district provided the custodian a hearing as required by the collective bargaining agreement. School boards, not courts, retained discretion over employees and the enforcement of their own conduct and discipline codes. *Widder v. Durango School Dist. No. 9-R*, 85 P.3d 518 (Colo. 2004).

◆    A Florida teacher called school security to escort a student from class for disruptive behavior. A security officer brought the student to a detention room. The two "got into a disagreement," and the student claimed the officer began to beat him. Two more security officers then arrived at the room and allegedly kicked and punched the student. The student and his family sued the school board and officers for constitutional rights violations and battery. The Florida District Court of Appeal noted that **in general, state subdivisions were not liable for the acts or omissions of employees who acted outside the scope of their employment**. However, the security officers here acted within the scope of their authority when escorting the student from class and restraining him. Thus, a trial court would have to consider whether their actions were within the scope of a state statute on immunity. The court remanded the case to determine whether the board had immunity under that statute. *Carestio v. School Board of Broward County*, 866 So.2d 754 (Fla. Dist. Ct. App. 2004).

# CHAPTER TWO

## Student Discipline

## I. EXPULSIONS AND SUSPENSIONS

### A. Due Process

*The Due Process Clause of the Fourteenth Amendment prohibits the states from depriving any person of life, liberty or property without due process of law. "Due process" requires school districts to provide students all the notices and procedural protections to which they are entitled under state law or school policies when they are faced with school discipline.*

*The U.S. Supreme Court first recognized due process rights in a student disciplinary case in* Goss v. Lopez, *below. Students facing short-term suspensions and other minor school discipline have minimal due process rights. An informal discussion between the student and administrator typically satisfies due process for suspensions of up to 10 days. The student must be advised of the charges supporting the suspension and receive an opportunity to tell his or her side of the story. When a suspension is for a longer term, greater procedural protections apply, which may include a formal hearing.*

*The Supreme Court's decision in* Mathews v. Eldridge, *424 U.S. 319 (1976), indicated that* Goss *is merely a starting point for a due process analysis in longer term suspension and expulsion cases.* Mathews *explained that "due process is flexible, and calls for such procedural protections as the particular situation demands." State laws typically explain the specific procedures that are required, and afford greater protections for long-term discipline.*

◆    In *Goss v. Lopez*, the U.S. Supreme Court recognized a due process right to receive notice and a hearing in student disciplinary actions. In *Goss*, Ohio students had been suspended from school for up to 10 days for participating in demonstrations and other school disturbances. Their suspensions were handed down without a hearing either before or after the school board's ruling. The Supreme Court held that students facing temporary suspensions from a public school have property and liberty interests in their education that are protected by the Due Process Clause of the Fourteenth Amendment. **Students faced with suspension or expulsion must be given oral or written notice of the charges against them along with some opportunity to present their version of what happened.** Recognizing that situations often do not allow time to follow adequate procedures prior to the suspensions, such as in cases where there is a danger to students or property, the Court stated that, at the very least, **proper notice and a hearing should be given as soon after the suspension as is practicable.** The Court also stated that if a student is threatened with a suspension longer than 10 days, more elaborate procedural safeguards may be necessary. *Goss v. Lopez*, 419 U.S. 565, 95 S.Ct. 729, 42 L.Ed.2d 725 (1975).

### 1.  Notice and Procedural Protections

◆    A Minnesota student hit another student over the head with a hard plastic tray, disrupting the school cafeteria. The student believed she would be expelled for violating a disciplinary policy against assault and fighting, and she waived her right to a hearing before the school board. The board then expelled her for a full calendar year. Her case reached the Court of Appeals of Minnesota, which found the board did not explain its decision as required by the state Pupil Fair Dismissal Act. When the case returned to the board, it made a new resolution explaining its decision and finding the student committed two offenses: "assault with the lunch tray (used as a weapon)," and attempting to break away when being escorted from the cafeteria in order to harm the other student. In its initial notices to the student and her family, the board did not specify that it considered the lunch tray a "weapon." As other students had been expelled for a full calendar year for assault incidents, the board felt it had to do so in this case.

On appeal, the state commissioner of education found the board violated the student's due process rights. The case came before the court of appeals a second time. It noted the board did not refer to the weapons policy until after the student had waived her right to a hearing. While the board had removed references to the weapons policy after the commissioner's decision, the court found this did not absolve it from its previous reliance upon an improper consideration. The board failed to explain in sufficient detail why the student's conduct warranted a full calendar year expulsion. At no time prior to the hearing did the school board indicate that it viewed the use of a lunch tray as a weapons policy violation. **Education is a fundamental right under the state constitution and is protected by the Due Process Clause of the Fourteenth Amendment, and the board could not deny a student's due process rights.** As the board reached its decision in violation of the student's due process rights, the court affirmed the commissioner's decision in her favor. *Matter of Expulsion of N.Y.B.*, No. A09-670, 2010 WL 1541260 (Minn. Ct. App. 4/20/10).

◆   A Washington student who was accused of off-campus marijuana smoking received a new chance to avoid a 55-day suspension. Reversing a lower court decision, the U.S. Court of Appeals, Ninth Circuit, noted the suspension was based on hearsay statements by people having no affiliation with the school. In issuing the suspension, **the school district did not question or produce the witnesses and did not reveal the substance of their statements**. The case was sent back to a federal district court to determine if the student had a due process interest in state regulations permitting students to question and confront witnesses in certain cases. It also had to be determined whether the student had asked for a chance to question the witnesses. *T.T. v. Bellevue School Dist.*, 376 Fed.Appx. 769 (9th Cir. 2010).

◆   South Carolina brothers were approached by other students as they walked through the school parking lot to a football practice. After a heated exchange, a coach intervened, but was unable to stop a fight. One student inadvertently hit the coach. As a result, the students were immediately suspended from school. The brothers pursued hearings and appeared before a school panel. But the panel voted to expel them, and the decision was upheld by the school board. Instead of appealing to a state court, the brothers sued the board for negligence, due process violations and other constitutional claims. The district sought dismissal of all claims. The case reached the Court of Appeals of South Carolina, where the brothers argued a direct appeal from the expulsion order would have been futile because the school year in question would have ended by the time of a court hearing. State law permitted a civil action for damages in lieu of a direct appeal from a school board expulsion, relieving them of any administrative exhaustion requirement. **Since a direct appeal from the board order would not have provided immediate relief, the court refused to dismiss the due process issue** and let the case proceed. *Stinney v. Sumter School Dist. 17*, 382 S.C. 352, 675 S.E.2d 760 (S.C. Ct. App. 2009).

◆   A Nevada student took a knife on a school-sponsored choir trip. He was suspended for 10 days pending expulsion. The next school day, a vice principal drafted a letter explaining the district's weapons policy and detailing the violation. A school disciplinary panel held a hearing at which the charges against the student were read, and a police liaison officer testified. The student claimed he had brought the knife to school accidentally, and his parents verified this. After the hearing, the panel recommended expulsion for the remaining weeks of the school year. The school board met with the assistant superintendent in a closed session, and accepted his expulsion recommendation. The family was excluded from the session, and a federal district court action followed. The court noted that **some form of hearing is required before a student can be deprived of a property interest in public school attendance**.

In long-term disciplinary cases, the Ninth Circuit has required procedural protections such as representation by counsel, the opportunity to present witnesses and the ability to cross-examine adverse witnesses. In this case, the disciplinary panel hearing met the heightened requirements for expulsions. The student was provided with the relevant regulations before a hearing where he could present evidence, call and cross-examine witnesses and have counsel. There was nothing improper about the assistant superintendent's presence at the board meeting. A school administrator involved with initiating disciplinary charges may participate in the deliberations. The court held for the district. *Hardie v. Churchill County School Dist.*, No. 3:07-CV-310-RAM, 2009 WL 875486 (D. Nev. 3/30/09).

◆    North Carolina students accused school officials of disciplining them in a discriminatory manner and sued them for due process and equal protection violations. They also alleged that the school board's anti-gang policy was unconstitutional. A state court dismissed the case, and the Court of Appeals of North Carolina, held that most of the due process claims were legally insufficient as they failed to allege a claim for relief on behalf of each individual student against each individual official. An exception was a due process claim asserting that the superintendent wrote a misleading letter to a student's mother that was "designed to cut off" his appeal rights. Punitive damages would be available if the claim was successful. The right to a notice and opportunity to be heard was clearly established by the Supreme Court. For that reason, the superintendent could not claim immunity. The trial court would have to reconsider a challenge to the school board policy on gangs and gang-related activity. *Copper v. Denlinger*, 667 S.E.2d 470 (N.C. Ct. App. 2008).

On appeal, the Supreme Court of North Carolina explained that to bring a direct state constitutional claim against an education board, it must be alleged that no adequate state law remedy existed. Two North Carolina statutes allowed any student who was suspended in excess of 10 school days to appeal to the education board, and then to a state court. **As there was a statutory right to appeal, an adequate state law remedy existed, and any constitutional claim was barred.** For similar reasons, federal due process claims against the superintendent failed. The gang policy issue was returned to the trial court for further proceedings. *Copper v. Denlinger*, 688 S.E.2d 426 (N.C. 2010).

◆    An Illinois security guard wrote up a student for "posturing" with a group of students who were flashing gang signs in the school cafeteria. A police officer became involved, and the school suspended the student for 10 days pending an expulsion hearing. A school hearing officer wrote the student a letter that expulsion for "subversive organizations" was being recommended. At the hearing, the hearing officer charged the student with another offense for

"Fighting/Mob Action." The student admitted lending support to Latin Kings gang members. The security guard and police officer did not attend the hearing, at which the student's father made several remarks in English. After the hearing, the school board voted to expel the student. He sued the school district and officials in a federal district court for due process violations, including the district's failure to provide his parents with a Spanish-language interpreter.

After the court held for the school district, the U.S. Court of Appeals, Seventh Circuit, affirmed the judgment. It noted that the student had admitted wrongdoing, and he received notice and a meaningful opportunity to be heard. **Due process does not require schools to offer the trial-type safeguards of a delinquency proceeding.** Under *Goss v. Lopez*, this chapter, no delay is necessary between the time notice is given and the time of the discussion with the student. While a two-semester expulsion was a harsh punishment, the due process claim could not succeed. *Coronado v. Valleyview Public School Dist. 365-U*, 537 F.3d 791 (7th Cir. 2008).

◆   Parents of an Iowa student who was arrested and detained in a juvenile detention center could not claim any monetary damages in a civil action against her school district. The state court of appeals affirmed a trial court ruling that the district had no duty to notify the parents that their daughter had been arrested. **There was no deprivation of any parental rights, and the parents had no standing to assert a claim based on their child's due process rights.** School officials made many attempts to contact them after the student was detained. *Simmons v. Sioux City Community School Dist.*, 743 N.W.2d 872 (Table) (Iowa Ct. App. 2007).

◆   A California student was suspended for placing liquid white board cleaner in a teacher's water bottle. After investigating, the principal sent the student a "notice of extension of suspension," stating that his presence at school would threaten the instructional process. The student was charged with participating in the placement of the cleaner in the water bottle, and puncturing the cleaner's container with a knife he brought to school. The student's parents submitted written apologies on his behalf and sought his return to school. They rejected alternative placement offers. After weeks of negotiations, a school district placement counselor notified the parents of an "administrative placement" of their son at a different middle school. An appeal panel upheld the transfer.

The case reached the Court of Appeal of California, which noted that the state **Education Code allowed an initial student suspension of five days**. The principal was only authorized to extend the suspension until the school board made a decision. Here, the student had been suspended for over 60 days, and his involuntary transfer was part of an expulsion process. The district had filed documents indicating that he committed an expellable offense. However, it never provided a school board hearing, and placed the student in a regular middle school. The district did not provide the student with an expulsion hearing, and the administrative appeal did not comply with the Education Code. *Gliane v. Long Beach Unified School Dist.*, No. B193345, 2007 WL 2111045 (Cal. Ct. App. 7/24/07).

◆   **A Mississippi school board did not deprive a student of due process by failing to provide him with a list of witnesses in advance of his expulsion hearing** for selling drugs at school. The state court of appeals rejected his claim that he was not informed of the charges against him because a key witness had changed his story. The witness had only changed the date of one alleged drug purchase. As the charges were based on continuous incidents, this change was insignificant. *T.B. v. Board of Trustees of Vicksburg Warren School Dist.*, 931 So.2d 634 (Miss. Ct. App. 2006).

◆   A Louisiana school board expelled a student for 12 months during her eighth-grade year. Near the end of the school year, her parents petitioned a trial court for an order requiring the board to evaluate her for placement in ninth grade. The court denied the request, as the 12-month expulsion period was not yet complete. The court of appeal directed the board to answer seven questions, then granted the family's request. The Louisiana Supreme Court vacated the court of appeal's decision. It held that **appellate courts are prohibited from receiving new evidence**. The case was returned to the trial court for an expedited hearing to consider whether the board was obligated to provide the student with any alternative education. *B.W.S. v. Livingston Parish School Board*, 936 So.2d 181 (La. 2006).

◆   The Wyoming Supreme Court held that a school board's appeal from a lower court decision reversing a student suspension was moot, as the student had already graduated. The board had expelled the student for violating a state law prohibiting the possession, use, transfer, carrying or selling of a deadly weapon on school property or grounds. The expulsion was modified to a 10-day in-school suspension and the student was required to abide by a behavior contract. **The student appealed to a state court, which held that the board violated the notice and hearing requirements of Wyoming law.** The court also found insufficient evidence to support the discipline. The appeal to the supreme court was moot, as the student had already served his suspension and graduated. *Board of Trustees of Fremont County School Dist. #25 v. BM*, 129 P.3d 317 (Wyo. 2006).

◆   The Supreme Court of Colorado affirmed a lower court decision vacating a student expulsion order, because **the student's school board refused to allow her to call witnesses to provide evidence of her good character at her expulsion hearing**. The district expelled the student for fighting, but it denied her request to present statements from her teachers at her hearing. The supreme court agreed with the trial court that the school district violated her due process rights and made it "as difficult as possible" to present evidence in her favor. *Nichols v. DeStefano*, 84 P.3d 496 (Colo. 2004).

◆   Several South Carolina seniors vandalized a high school they did not attend. After they were suspended, a state trial court granted their request for a temporary injunction, but the South Carolina Court of Appeals held that the trial court had no jurisdiction to hear any case involving a short-term student suspension. The students appealed to the state supreme court, which noted that state law did not permit judicial review of student suspensions of 10 days or less. Otherwise, students and parents might burden the court system and strain school resources with a flood of appeals from short-term suspensions. The students received notice, an explanation and an opportunity to respond, which was all the process they were due under *Goss v. Lopez*. The court affirmed the appellate court's decision. *Floyd v. Horry County School Dist.*, 569 S.E.2d 343 (S.C. 2002).

## 2.  Alternative Placements

◆   A North Carolina student was suspended for the second semester of her sophomore year for fighting. She was not offered alternative education. After a hearing, a school panel upheld the superintendent's decision to suspend her without services. In a state court lawsuit, the student asserted violation of her right to a sound basic education under the North Carolina constitution. A state trial court dismissed the case, and appeal reached the Supreme Court of North Carolina. It held state law vested school administrators with authority to issue long-term suspensions to students who willfully violated school conduct policies. But the law required education boards to establish alternative learning programs and to adopt guidelines for assigning students to long-term discipline.

According to the court, state law provided a comprehensive scheme that granted students a right to an alternative education "when feasible and appropriate" during long-term suspensions. **There was no constitutional right to an alternative education, but there was a constitutional right for a suspended student to know the reason for exclusion from school.** In reaching this conclusion, the court accepted the student's claim that prior rulings on state educational funding applied to her case. The funding cases established that "equal access to participation in our public school system is a fundamental right, guaranteed by our state constitution and protected by considerations of procedural due process." While students had a right to a sound basic education under the state constitution, the court held school administrators had to articulate an important or significant reason for denying a student access to an alternative education. In this case, administrators did not articulate a reason for denying the student access to alternative education. Since she had a right to education guaranteed by the North Carolina Constitution, the court reversed the judgment and returned the case to the lower courts so the education board could have an opportunity to explain why alternative education had been denied. *King v. Beaufort County Board of Educ.*, 364 S.E.2d 368 (N.C. 2010).

◆   A Texas student was assigned to an alternative school for being involved in a brawl in his high school hallway. A school assistant principal allegedly reported that the student was arrested after striking an officer. Part of the fight was videotaped, and the assistant principal observed the student's behavior. At an informal hearing among the assistant principal, student and parents, the family was notified of a three-day suspension followed by a 45-day assignment to an alternative education program. A district administrator heard an appeal by the family but upheld the decision. In response, the student sued the school district and several officials in a federal district court for civil rights violations. **The**

**court held placement in alternative education programs did not implicate due process rights.** Instead, they were considered transfers from one school program to another "with stricter discipline." Since the student had an opportunity to explain his version of the facts in the meeting with the assistant principal, due process was satisfied. Many courts, including the Supreme Court in *Goss v. Lopez*, this chapter, have recognized that **sometimes a school disciplinarian may be a witness to the conduct forming the basis for discipline.** Nothing indicated the assistant principal or a police officer in this case had any preexisting bias toward the student. Finding no due process violation, the court held for the school district. *Salas v. United Independent School Dist.*, Civ. No. L-08-22, 2009 WL 1035068 (S.D. Tex. 4/17/09).

◆    A Texas school security officer opened a purse found on school property to help determine who owned it. A cheerleader's school athletic pass and what was later identified as a hydrocodone pill were found inside the purse. The school district held a hearing to consider expelling the cheerleader for violating its zero-tolerance anti-drug policy. A school hearing officer determined that the pill most likely belonged to the parent of another student and not the cheerleader. The district placed the cheerleader in an alternative education program for 36 days and excluded her from the cheerleading squad for the 2005-06 school year, as specified by the school's "cheerleader constitution." The school board upheld the decision, and the cheerleader completed the alternative assignment. She later obtained a court order reinstating her to the cheerleading squad, and the school district appealed. The Court of Appeals of Texas held that **a board's decision regarding an alternative education program was final and unappealable.** The court upheld the placement and the district's decision to keep incident records. *Flour Bluff Independent School Dist. v. R.S.*, No. 13-05-623-CV, 2006 WL 949968 (Tex. Ct. App. 2006).

◆    A Michigan student dropped out of high school but was admitted to an alternative education program called "Skills Quest." Enrollment in the program was discretionary with the district superintendent and required students to comply with its attendance policy and the district's student code of conduct. The student was charged with murder and jailed in an adult correctional facility. A state court ordered the county sheriff to segregate him from adult prisoners as required by state law. The student expressed suicidal thoughts and was placed on "suicide watch." He was later released from jail after a preliminary hearing, based on lack of admissible evidence. The superintendent rejected his request to reenter Skills Quest, but reversed himself after another individual confessed to the murder. The student reenrolled in Skills Quest but dropped out after only a month. He then sued state, county and school officials in a federal district court for civil rights violations. The district court granted pretrial judgment to the sheriff and district but denied it to the superintendent. The parties appealed.

The U.S. Court of Appeals, Sixth Circuit, noted that the student chose to forgo his right to a free public education when he dropped out of school. **Neither the Michigan Constitution nor state law mandated alternative education programs.** The student could not show a legitimate claim to participate in Skills Quest, since participation was "entirely at the discretion of the superintendent and continues only so long as the participant abides by the program's rules and policies." As the student had no right to an alternative education, he could not show a due process violation. The court ruled for the sheriff, school district and superintendent. *Daniels v. Woodside*, 396 F.3d 730 (6th Cir. 2005).

◆   A Wyoming school district expelled three students for marijuana violations. One was enrolled in special education programs and continued receiving the educational services described in his individualized education program. The others were adjudicated delinquent in juvenile court proceedings. The court held that the Wyoming Constitution imposed a duty on the school district to provide the students a free appropriate education during their expulsion periods.

The Supreme Court of Wyoming held that while education is a fundamental right under the Wyoming Constitution, the state interest in student safety and welfare was compelling enough to temporarily interfere with this right. It noted with approval *Fowler v. Williamson*, 39 N.C. App. 715, 251 S.E.2d 889 (N.C. Ct. App. 1979), a North Carolina case recognizing that educational services are contingent upon appropriate conduct. The school district had offered students an education system that conformed to its constitutional obligation to provide an equal opportunity for a quality education. **Reasonable suspension rules did not deny the right to an education; they only denied students an opportunity to misbehave.** Students could be temporarily denied educational services if their conduct threatened the safety and welfare of others. School districts were in the best position to judge student actions, and the district was not required to provide lawfully expelled students with an alternate education under the circumstances of this case. The court rejected the claim that the expulsions violated the non-disabled students' equal protection rights. Special education students must receive services under federal law, even after discipline is imposed. *In re R.M.*, 102 P.3d 868 (Wyo. 2004).

### 3.  Zero-Tolerance Policies

◆   Texas school officials found a small amount of alcohol in a vehicle parked on school property. Under the school district's zero-tolerance policy, the student who had driven the vehicle to school had to be placed in an alternative school. After several hearings, an alternative school assignment was upheld. According to the district superintendent, the student would have been allowed to avoid the placement had he presented evidence to support his claim that he did not know there was any alcohol in his vehicle. The student sued the school district and officials in the state court system for due process violations. The court held for the district, and he appealed to the Court of Appeals of Texas, arguing the district's disciplinary procedures did not meet minimal due process standards.

According to the student, the school district's policy subjected students to punishment even if they did not knowingly or consciously possess alcohol. The court held he did not show the zero-tolerance policy was unconstitutional as it was applied to him. It noted that zero-tolerance policies "have promoted consistency over rationality." **Strict adherence to a zero-tolerance policy, without consideration of a student's state of mind, "would appear to run afoul of substantive due process notions."** But there was no due process violation in this case, because the superintendent offered the student a chance to show he did not know about the alcohol. As the district provided him "an escape mechanism in lieu of strict application of the zero-tolerance policy," his due process challenge failed. *Hinterlong v. Arlington Independent School Dist.*, No. 2-09-050-CV, 2010 WL 522641 (Tex. Ct. App. 2/11/10).

◆    The Fifth Circuit affirmed the assignment of a Mississippi honor student to an alternative school after a cup of beer was found in a car she had parked in a school lot. Her parent had left the beer in the car, and she said she did not know about it. She appealed the transfer decision to the school board and a federal court, without success. She withdrew from school and obtained a GED. The Fifth Circuit held that however misguided the school district might have been for applying its zero-tolerance policy, the case had to be dismissed. The Supreme Court has observed that public education relies upon the discretion and judgment of school administrators and board members. **An alternative school assignment implicated no constitutional rights.** *Langley v. Monroe County School Dist.*, 264 Fed.Appx. 366 (5th Cir. 2008).

◆    A Florida student who was suspended for violating a school's zero-tolerance policy against weapons possession had no right to appeal the school board decision to the state court system. The Court of Appeal of Florida held the case was properly dismissed because **the Florida Administrative Procedure Act does not permit court review of a suspension order**. The court rejected the student's assertion that he could appeal his suspension because he faced a possible expulsion. Instead, only a hearing that results in an actual expulsion is available for court review. *D.K. v. Dist. School Board of Indian River County*, 981 So.2d 667 (Fla. Dist. Ct. App. 2008).

◆    A drug dog alerted on an honor student's truck during a routine check of a Texas school parking lot. The student consented to a search by the police, who found brass knuckles in the glove box. The brass knuckles belonged to a friend, and the student didn't know they were there. But school board policy held students responsible for the contents of their vehicles. A hearing officer ruled that the Texas Education Code required expulsion. The board voted to expel the student for one day and to assign him to an alternative school for the rest of the school year. After a state court granted the student's request for a preliminary order halting the expulsion, the school board appealed. The Court of Appeals of Texas found the Texas Education Code required school districts to specify whether they considered intent or lack of intent as a factor in student expulsions. **School districts could choose between adopting zero-tolerance policies, or allowing alternatives for involuntary possession of prohibited weapons.** In this case, the district policy allowed it to consider intent, and it could decline to expel the student if possession of a weapon was involuntary. The hearing officer incorrectly interpreted the Education Code as requiring expulsion, even if possession of a prohibited weapon was unknowing. The trial court did not abuse its discretion in issuing a temporary injunction to halt the expulsion. *Tarkington Independent School Dist. v. Ellis*, 200 S.W.3d 794 (Tex. Ct. App. 2006).

◆ A California school district regulation required an immediate suspension with a recommended expulsion for three or more fighting incidents in a year. A 12-year-old student was involved in three fights in one school year. A hearing panel upheld the principal's recommendation for expulsion, and the student was placed in an alternative program. The student was suspended there for physically confronting a staff member. The school district placed her in a community school, where she claimed older male students sexually harassed and physically assaulted her. She sued the district in a state court, which dismissed her personal injury claim. But the court held the district's policy requiring the principal to recommend expulsion violated state law and the Due Process Clause. On appeal, the Court of Appeal of California noted that state law permitted an impartial hearing panel to hold expulsion hearings. **The court found the district's zero-tolerance provision consistent with the education code.** The policy did not require expulsion for specified offenses. It only put these cases before an impartial hearing panel. The elimination of a principal's discretion to refrain from referring a case to a hearing did not deprive students of due process. The court reversed the judgment. *T.H. v. San Diego Unified School Dist.*, 122 Cal.App.4th 1267, 19 Cal.Rptr.3d 532 (Cal. Ct. App. 2004).

## B. Misconduct

### 1. Sexual Harassment

◆ South Carolina school officials charged a 14-year-old girl with a "sexual offense" for entering a boys' lavatory. A video camera recorded her following a male student into the lavatory, where she remained for about a minute. The student claimed she went into the lavatory to retrieve a comb that the male had taken from her. But the school suspended her for 10 days and recommended an expulsion for the rest of the year, based on a sexual offense. Earlier in the school year, she had been suspended for two days for a verbal altercation with a classmate. Prior to an expulsion hearing, a school administrator and a hearing officer watched the videotape of the student entering the lavatory. But the tape was recorded over before the student was allowed to view it. The hearing officer found the student committed a sexual offense and expelled her for the rest of the school year. A state court reversed the decision, finding no substantial evidence of a sexual offense. It also found a violation of due process rights.

On appeal, the Court of Appeals of South Carolina noted that the school district did not present any additional evidence to support the charge of sexual offense beyond the videotape. Any prior acts of disruption by the student had no bearing on the case. The school district had chosen not to expel her for her prior conduct. **The only evidence of a sexual offense was the student's voluntary entry into the boys' lavatory for about one minute in pursuit of another student.** Since there was no evidence of sexual activity by the student or the male, and no male student indicated that anything sexual had occurred, there was no substantial evidence in support of the expulsion. The judgment for the student was affirmed. *Doe v. Richland County School Dist. Two*, 382 S.C. 656, 677 S.E.2d 610 (S.C. Ct. App. 2009).

◆    A Michigan school counselor made a presentation to a language arts class. She saw a student place his fingers in his mouth and believed he was making a sexual gesture about her. The school suspended the student and he appealed to the district superintendent, who interviewed the counselor, student and a classmate who saw the gesture. The students asserted that the gesture simply indicated boredom. The superintendent found the counselor more reliable and upheld the suspension for "indecency," as defined in the high school's student handbook. A trial court affirmed the discipline, and the student appealed.

The Court of Appeals of Michigan held that courts are bound by school administrators' findings when there is any evidence in the record to support them. **A student must be guilty of some willful or malicious act of detriment to a school before being suspended or expelled.** This is "something more than a petty or trivial offense" against school rules. The court found the student's gesture qualified as "gross misbehavior and misconduct," as it was both willful and malicious. The school complied with due process requirements for a short-term suspension by giving him oral notice of the general nature of the charges and a chance to be heard. Allowing him to go unpunished for embarrassing a school employee would welcome more disrespect. *Kloberdanz v. Swan Valley School Dist.*, No. 256208, 2006 WL 234880 (Mich. Ct. App. 2006).

◆    A California student was accused of sexually related misconduct, including grabbing a girl by the buttocks, groping other boys, making inappropriate comments or gestures, and simulating masturbation or sex. He denied most of the allegations, explaining that he had accidentally touched the girl. The student's father, an attorney, attended a meeting to consider discipline. The school principal said that he had interviewed several credible witnesses and issued a five-day suspension. The student served his suspension, then graduated. He sued the school district under 42 U.S.C. § 1983. A court held that the district violated his due process rights and awarded him general damages of $45,000, punitive damages of $50,000 and attorneys' fees of $72,268.

The school district appealed to the California Court of Appeal, which found **the principal had complied with the "notice and opportunity to respond" requirements of *Goss v. Lopez*** (this chapter). He had adequately explained the reasons for the suspension and was not required to give the student any further procedural protections to comply with *Goss*. The student was not entitled to learn the identities of his accusers, and had the principal done so, the school district might be exposed to further lawsuits. The district had issued a proper suspension, and the court reversed the judgment. *Granowitz v. Redlands Unified School Dist.*, 129 Cal.Rptr.2d 410 (Cal. Ct. App. 2003).

◆    A Massachusetts high school student sodomized a six-year-old and was charged with various felonies. His principal obtained a police report in which the student described the incident as "a joke." The principal suspended the student, finding he posed a threat to the safety, security and welfare of students at the high school. After a hearing, the superintendent upheld the suspension, but a court later reversed the suspension, finding the superintendent's action was an abuse of discretion. On appeal, the Massachusetts Supreme Judicial Court observed that a felony charge against a student, by itself, is an insufficient basis for suspension.

There must be a finding that the student's continued presence in school would have a substantial detrimental effect on the general welfare of the school.

A suspension may be overturned only if it is so arbitrary and capricious that it constitutes an abuse of discretion and lacks any rational explanation. **Here, the superintendent's decision was within his discretion because it was fully supported by the evidence.** The principal was permitted to draw inferences from the nature of the crime and the student's lack of remorse. Given the seriousness of the charges, the principal reasonably concluded there was a danger the student would attempt similar behavior at school. The court reversed and remanded the case. *Doe v. Superintendent of Schools of Stoughton*, 437 Mass. 1, 767 N.E.2d 1054 (Mass. 2002).

## 2. Drugs, Alcohol and Weapons Possession

*In a case involving off-campus alcohol consumption by an Arkansas student, the U.S. Supreme Court limited the role of federal courts to construe school regulations differently than a school board. An Arkansas school board had a rule requiring the mandatory suspension of students who were "under the influence of" or in possession of narcotics, hallucinogenics, drugs or controlled substances. The Supreme Court held the board had authority to expel a student for drinking alcohol off campus and returning to school.* Board of Educ. v. McCluskey, 458 U.S. 966, 102 S.Ct. 3469, 73 L.Ed.2d 1273 (1982). *But in the following case, an Alabama school board improperly disciplined a student for being under the influence of alcohol at a school prom under a rule that only addressed the "use" of alcohol while on school property or at a school function.*

◆    Alabama high school staff members noticed a student smelled of alcohol at a school prom. A Breathalyzer test showed his blood-alcohol level was between .001 and .006. A disciplinary committee held a hearing and found no evidence of alcohol possession at the prom. The student was also not "under the influence of alcohol to the extent that he would have been guilty of ... criminal offenses." Based on findings that he drank alcohol on the day of the prom, the board suspended him and sent him to an alternative school. The reason stated was being under the influence of alcohol at the prom in violation of a school handbook provision. In a juvenile court hearing, the court found the term "use" from the school policy meant "to ingest alcohol while on school property or at any other school function." As there was no evidence that the student had "used" alcohol on school property or at a school function, the court held he did not violate the policy. In addition to reinstating the student, the court found the school's alcohol policy did not address punishment and the discipline imposed was unreasonable. Appeal reached the Court of Civil Appeals of Alabama.

The court noted a 1985 decision by the state supreme court held that "a board of education must comply with the policies it adopts." Rules and regulations governing student conduct had to be sufficiently definite to provide them reasonable notice that they must conform their conduct to the expected requirements. In this case, the school had applied a student handbook provision to students who used alcohol shortly before going to the prom. **A policy that did not notify the student of possible consequences for arriving at the prom**

**after drinking alcohol deprived him of due process.** The court affirmed the juvenile court's decision reinstating him to school. *Monroe County Board of Educ. v. K.B.*, No. 2090746, 2010 WL 3611918 (Ala. Civ. Ct. App. 9/17/10).

◆   After a Mississippi student reportedly sold drugs on campus, the school principal searched his backpack and found an item described as either a nail file or a knife. A school district appeals committee voted to expel the student after a hearing, and the school board met to review the case. At his hearing, the student was permitted to argue that the item was a nail file. But since the item was unavailable for inspection, the board assigned to the superintendent the decision of determining whether it was a prohibited item. He decided it was a knife. The board upheld the expulsion, and the student was placed in an alternative school. Within weeks, he was accused of possessing marijuana.

Another appeals committee hearing was scheduled to review a new expulsion recommendation. A notice to the student described his offense and the charges. In addition, the notice offered the student a right to have counsel present and to cross-examine witnesses. After the student spoke at the hearing, the committee accepted the expulsion recommendation. The student appealed, and the Supreme Court of Mississippi found **a reasonable basis for the board to find that the item was a knife and not a nail file.** The Mississippi Code did not require the school board to physically examine the weapon. As the student was permitted to speak on his own behalf before the appeals committee, due process was satisfied. The court reinstated the board's decision. *Hinds County School Dist. Board of Trustees v. D.L.B.*, 10 So.3d 387 (Miss. 2008).

◆   A Wisconsin high school student admitted writing a note that a bomb was in a school locker, resulting in the school being evacuated and students being moved off-campus. The school lost over four hours of instructional time. A state court placed the student on probation after he pled no contest to making a bomb scare under a state criminal statute. In addition to ordering him to perform 100 hours of community service, the court ordered him to pay the school district restitution of over $18,000. The student appealed the order to pay restitution. The Court of Appeals of Wisconsin noted that most of the amount represented salaries and benefits of teachers and staff who had been working but had to evacuate the school due to his note. According to the student, the district did not suffer a true financial loss. But the court held that a determination of restitution is within a court's discretion. **Pay for teachers and staff who had to vacate the building amounted to "special damages" that could form the basis of an order for restitution.** As deprivation of employee productivity was a "loss in itself," restitution was reasonable. *State of Wisconsin v. Vanbeek*, 316 Wis.2d 527, 765 N.W.2d 834, 2009 WI App 37 (Wis. Ct. App. 2009).

◆   A Pennsylvania student said another student told him he had vodka in a bottle of iced tea he brought to lunch. He admitted taking a drink from the bottle, "because he didn't believe him." The student said he knew a third student had also taken a drink prior to lunch. School administrators suspended the student and brought expulsion proceedings against him. The school board expelled him for 18 days, based on his admission and the results of Breathalyzer testing administered in school. The student appealed to a state court. Meanwhile, he completed his expulsion period and performed community service that was imposed as a prerequisite for his return to school. The court affirmed the school board's order, and the student appealed.

The Commonwealth Court of Pennsylvania observed that school administrators had not required the student to give a statement. Instead, they merely provided him with an opportunity to voluntarily do so. The board drew a reasonable inference that there was alcohol in the bottle of iced tea based on the student's statement and Breathalyzer testing. The student argued that a school district policy (based on a federal law) had been violated. The policy (and the law) prohibited surveys, analysis or evaluations revealing illegal, antisocial, self-incriminating and demeaning behavior by minors, without prior consent by parents. The court rejected this argument, noting that the provision did not apply to interviews conducted by school administrators for student disciplinary purposes. School officials "have a substantial interest in maintaining a safe and educational environment on school grounds." The court affirmed the judgment. *Haas v. West Shore School Dist.*, 915 A.2d 1254 (Pa. Commw. Ct. 2007).

◆ A Missouri high school student brought toy guns to school twice. The toys shot small pieces of plastic. On the first occasion, the student shot at another student who was standing outside their school. On the second, two toy guns were found locked in his car on school property. The school superintendent issued an immediate 10-day suspension for the incidents, finding the student in possession of a "weapon" which he had used on school property. The school board voted in a closed session to exclude the student from school for one year. The student was provided a hearing where he was represented by an attorney, allowed to present evidence and to call and cross-examine witnesses.

The board voted to uphold the 180-day suspension. The student appealed, arguing that the school handbook definition of "weapon" did not include toys and other look-alike items. The Court of Appeals of Missouri **found that superintendents may modify expulsion requirements on a case-by-case basis to comply with requirements of federal laws,** including the Individuals with Disabilities Education Act. The school board had adopted a weapons guide separate from the student handbook several years earlier. The guide's definition of "weapon" included any object designed to look like or imitate a dangerous weapon. While the guidelines were not personally handed to each student or parent, they were accessible through a school district website and upon request. The guidelines were properly applied to the student. The toy guns were "dangerous instruments" because they could cause an eye injury. The court upheld the suspension. *Moore v. Appleton City R-II School Dist.*, 232 S.W.3d 642 (Mo. Ct. App. 2007).

◆ A New York student talked with other students about a gun while they were in the school cafeteria. Police decided to lockdown the school, and guns were found off school grounds. The student was suspended for the rest of the school year. The state education commissioner affirmed the suspension, but a New York court held the hearing officer denied the student a fair hearing and vacated the discipline. The student sued the board and hearing officer for civil rights violations. A state court dismissed the student's due process claim, since he had already received notice and a hearing to consider his suspension. This was all the process to which he was entitled. The state court had vacated the discipline, curing any procedural defects. The court held that talking with students about handguns was a material and substantial disruption of the educational process. The suspension did not violate the student's substantive due process rights.

**The court agreed with the board that public school students may be disciplined for conduct off school grounds, if there is a connection between the behavior and the school.** Misconduct occurring off campus may adversely affect the educational process or endanger students. However, the court refused to dismiss the student's speech rights claim. He raised a valid equal protection claim by asserting that the other students implicated in the conversation were only suspended for three weeks, while he was suspended for the rest of the school year. The court refused to dismiss the equal protection claims against the board and hearing officer, and held they were not entitled to qualified immunity. *Cohn v. New Paltz Cent. School Dist.*, 363 F.Supp.2d 421 (N.D. N.Y. 2005). The Second Circuit affirmed the decision in a brief memorandum. *Cohn v. New Paltz Cent. School Dist.*, 171 Fed.Appx. 877 (2d Cir. 2006).

◆   A Kentucky high school received a bomb threat. A private company under contract with the district to provide canine detection services found no explosives, but a dog alerted to a car parked in the school parking lot. The principal called the student from his class but did not accompany him to the parking lot, despite a board policy requiring principals or their designees to be present when any student search was conducted. A dog handler went with the student to the car and found marijuana inside it. The student was suspended pending an expulsion hearing, then expelled by the board.

When the student sued, the Court of Appeals of Kentucky held that **the board's policy mandated that the school principal or designee be present during any student search.** Because the evidence for the expulsion was obtained in violation of the board's own policy, the decision to expel the student was arbitrarily based on incompetent evidence. The board had to comply with its own policy. Since the only evidence used against the student was inadmissible, the expulsion was in error. *M.K.J. v. Bourbon County Board of Educ.*, No.2003-CA-0003520MN, 2004 WL 1948461 (Ky. Ct. App. 2004).

◆   A Pennsylvania court held that **a school district had no power to expel an honor student for using drugs on a school playground after school hours, when no school activity was taking place.** A trial court properly found that the student was not under school supervision at the time of the incident and had exceeded its statutory powers by expelling him. The school board had voluntarily reinstated the student to school prior to the trial court decision, and the court's order required it to expunge the expulsion from his record. *D.O.F. v. Lewisburg Area School Dist.*, 868 A.2d 28 (Pa. Commw. Ct. 2004).

◆   A New Mexico school security guard noticed a car parked in a faculty lot without a required permit. He contacted a law enforcement agency to check its registration and then observed a knife in plain view between the passenger seat and console. The guard called the student who had driven the car from his class and had him open the car. He found a sheathed hunting knife, handgun, ammunition and drug paraphernalia. The student claimed he did not know the items were in the car, which belonged to his brother. He was then suspended pending a hearing. A hearing officer held that the student should be suspended for a year. The school board upheld the decision, and the student sued for civil rights violations. A court found that the board could not suspend a student who unknowingly brought drugs or weapons to school. It granted the student a preliminary injunction that allowed him to return to school and graduate.

Appeal reached the U.S. Court of Appeals, Tenth Circuit, which held that a school suspension decision is to be upheld unless it is arbitrary, lacking a rational basis or shocking to the conscience. Here, the board did not suspend the student for "unknowingly" bringing a knife to school. Instead, it found that he should have known he was in possession of a knife, since it was in plain view to persons standing outside the car. He also should have known that he was responsible for the vehicle and its contents. **The possession of weapons on school property threatened the board's interest in school safety, and there was a rational basis for the one-year suspension.** The suspension did not violate the student's civil rights. *Butler v. Rio Rancho Public Schools Board of Educ.*, 341 F.3d 1197 (10th Cir. 2003).

◆ An Indiana middle school student gave caffeine pills to eight classmates. One classmate was taken to the emergency room for a rapid heartbeat and other symptoms. An assistant principal confiscated the pills from the student's locker. The school suspended the student for five days, pending expulsion. At the expulsion hearing, the assistant principal read into the record statements by six students who took pills. The hearing officer upheld the expulsion and ordered the student to complete a substance abuse assessment, enroll in counseling and perform 15 hours of community service. Students who accepted pills were barred from extracurricular activities and field trips for the semester. The student sued the school system in a federal district court, which found she admitted distributing the pills. **A reasonably intelligent 13-year-old would understand that the distribution of caffeine pills at school was improper.**

The presentation of student testimony through the assistant principal did not violate the student's due process rights. She had no constitutional right to cross-examine these students. The district was relieved of more formal procedures because the need to protect student witnesses greatly outweighed the slight value of providing the student their names. Also, the student's equal protection claims failed, despite her claim that the expulsion was "grossly unfair" in comparison with the discipline imposed on other students. The court awarded judgment to the district and officials. *Wagner v. Fort Wayne Community Schools*, 255 F.Supp.2d 915 (N.D. Ind. 2003).

◆ An Idaho student left a pellet gun in a car parked on school grounds. Another student took the gun and superficially wounded a third student with it. The first two students admitted possessing the gun, and the principal suspended them. The superintendent and principal met with the students and their parents to discuss the suspensions and inform them of a hearing. Letters from the principal and superintendent confirmed the hearing. The board suspended both students for 13 days after their hearing, then voted to expel them for over three months. The students were notified of their expulsions for violating Idaho law.

At a second hearing, the board again voted for expulsion. A state trial court found that the board had acted arbitrarily and abused its discretion, but the Idaho Supreme Court reversed this decision. It stated that while procedural errors during a suspension may justify judicial relief, there were none in this case. By the time the students had requested a court order, their suspensions had been over for two months. **State procedures for student discipline are not as strict as criminal or juvenile protections.** In school disciplinary cases, notice of the incidents giving rise to discipline is generally sufficient. The board reasonably found their presence detrimental to others at the school. *Rogers v. Gooding Public Joint School Dist. No. 231*, 20 P.3d 16 (Idaho 2001).

### 3.  Extracurricular and Co-Curricular Events

◆    A group of Ohio students attended a school-sponsored student exchange program in Germany. Before the trip, a teacher explained to students that they would stay with a "host family" for two weeks. While in Germany, a number of students consumed alcoholic beverages at biergartens with their "host parents." They were of legal drinking age in Germany and believed they were permitted to drink without supervision. Upon returning home, the school suspended the students for three to five days for violating student code prohibitions on consuming or possessing alcohol while in the school's control and custody.

The students asked for a hearing before the school board, arguing that the teacher had "verbally created an exception to the school's code of conduct regarding the consumption of alcohol." The board overturned the suspensions but required the students to perform community service. An Ohio trial court vacated the discipline, and the Court of Appeals of Ohio affirmed. **Here, the teacher had "engrafted an exception on the disciplinary code's provisions concerning alcohol consumption."** The students and their parents had all stated that their understanding of the policy allowed parents and host parents to determine the circumstances for alcohol consumption by students. *Brosch v. Mariemont City School Dist. Board of Educ.*, No. C-050283, 2006 WL 250947, 2006-Ohio-453 (Ohio Ct. App. 2006).

◆    Missouri cheerleading squad members reported that two cheerleaders were drinking alcohol before a school football jamboree. An investigation by the squad's faculty advisor was inconclusive. The principal later began a new investigation, but the parents of the cheerleaders did not cooperate, and one of them removed her daughter from school. The parents then sued the school district and school officials. The principal continued his investigation and obtained statements from several students who said they had seen the two cheerleaders drinking alcohol. The principal suspended both cheerleaders for 10 days for being under the influence of alcohol at a school event. He advised the parents of the decision, and the district sent them written confirmations of the suspensions, informing them of the reason for the action and their right to school board review. The parents did not respond. The court held for the district and officials, and the parents appealed.

The U.S. Court of Appeals, Eighth Circuit, noted evidence that the cheerleaders knew drinking alcohol before a school event violated the school disciplinary code. The court rejected the parents' claim that the district "patently failed to train" its employees. The district provided coaches with triennial training sessions for responding to student misconduct. **To establish school liability for failing to train staff, the parents would have to prove that the district showed deliberate indifference to student rights.** The court found no deliberate indifference by the district in this case. The cheerleaders received proper notice that they were being charged with a violation of the school code. Although the parents complained that the district had deprived their daughters of due process, they themselves had terminated contact with the principal. The students had the opportunity to present their side of the story, satisfying due process requirements. As the suspensions were based on violations of a longstanding, published policy, the judgment was affirmed. *Jennings v. Wentzville R-IV School Dist.*, 397 F.3d 1118 (8th Cir. 2005).

◆ An Indiana wrestling coach confiscated some negatives from a student who was a member of the school wrestling team. A school administrator instructed the coach to develop the negatives, which revealed the student and three other wrestlers naked in the boys' shower room. The school principal recommended expelling the student for "possessing or distributing pornographic material." The student's attorney argued at an expulsion hearing that the district code did not specify this offense. The hearing officer upheld the recommendation for expulsion, but the decision was reversed after a school administrative review.

The student returned to school after six weeks and made up his work. A federal district court reviewed his complaint and held that the principal and hearing officer were entitled to qualified immunity in the case. The student appealed to the U.S. Court of Appeals, Seventh Circuit, which held that the conduct of the principal and hearing officer did not meet the high threshold for proving a substantive due process violation. **School officials are entitled to qualified immunity for federal civil rights violations, unless the unlawfulness of their conduct is apparent in light of preexisting law.** While the school administrators had "exercised questionable judgment," they were entitled to qualified immunity. *Tun v. Whitticker*, 398 F.3d 899 (7th Cir. 2005).

### 4. Fighting and Violence

*Michigan's highest court held a group of teachers and their employee association could pursue an action against their school board to enforce a state law requiring the expulsion of students who assaulted employees.*

◆ Section 380.1311a(1) of Michigan Compiled Laws requires the permanent expulsion of a student in grade six or above for a physical assault at school against a school employee, volunteer or contractor. If an assault is reported to the school, the school board is required by law to "expel the pupil from the school district permanently." Four teachers claimed that pupils in grade six or higher physically assaulted them in their classrooms and that the assaults were reported to a school administrator. Instead of expelling the students, the school district only suspended them. The teachers and their association filed an action in the state court system against the school board under Section 380.1311a(1).

The court held it had no authority to supervise a school district's exercise of discretion, and the state court of appeals affirmed the decision. Appeal reached the Supreme Court of Michigan, which first held the teachers had legal standing to pursue the case. They were likely to suffer an injury that other members of the public did not face. The lower court decisions denying standing to the teachers would "slam the courthouse door" on numerous controversies, and the court reversed the judgment. **The legislative history of Section 380.1311 revealed an intent to create a safe school environment and a more effective workplace for teachers.** As a result, the lower court decisions for the board were reversed. The court of appeals would have to rule on the remaining issues that had not been considered. *Lansing Schools Educ. Ass'n MEA/NEA v. Lansing Board of Educ.*, 487 Mich. 387, 792 N.W.2d 686 (Mich. 2010).

◆  North Carolina school staff members tried to break up a fight between two students in the cafeteria. One of the students admitted hitting a teacher about 20 seconds after being separated from the other student. An assistant principal interviewed the students, staff members and witnesses. Police also conducted an investigation. The student was charged as a juvenile with assault on a school employee and disorderly conduct, and the other student was charged as an adult with a misdemeanor. The school board suspended the student for 10 days for violating four school board policies, including one providing for a long-term suspension for assaulting a school employee. After the suspension was imposed under North Carolina law, the student received a hearing where he was represented by an attorney and had the opportunity to present evidence, call witnesses and make arguments. A hearing panel voted to affirm a recommendation to place him in an alternative setting. The panel decision was affirmed by a discipline review committee, and the superintendent approved it.

Another hearing was held before the school board, where the student was again represented by counsel. Again, the long-term suspension was upheld. A state superior court affirmed the decision, and appeal reached the Court of Appeals of North Carolina. It appeared to the court that the student had an opportunity to learn the nature of his offense and respond to the charges. He received two hearings, which included an "exhaustive fact-finding inquiry" by the school board. **While the student asserted self-defense, he had admitted a delay of 20 seconds from the end of the fight to the time he hit the teacher.** No witnesses supported his claim of self-defense. **State law required imposing a long-term suspension for violating the policy against assaulting school employees.** Protecting school employees is a goal of school discipline, so the court upheld a long-term suspension. There was no showing that an alternative placement was inadequate to provide a sound, basic education. Federal privacy laws prevented the student from obtaining the educational records of his fight opponent. The court affirmed the judgment. *Watson-Green v. Wake County Board of Educ.*, 700 S.E.2d 249 (N.C. Ct. App. 2010).

◆ A Washington student threatened his older sisters at home with scissors and a knife. The girls barricaded themselves in a room and called their father. He called 911, and police took the student into custody, then informed school administrators of the incident. The principal told the student's mother that the student could not remain at school, and the district superintendent expelled the student on an emergency basis, advising the parents that he would have to undergo a violence risk assessment by a district-approved mental health professional as a condition for re-entering school. After he missed 10 days of school, a therapist found he was not a danger to himself or others. The student returned to school and later sued the district and superintendent. A court held that the district did not violate his due process rights, and that where a student poses a continuing danger, the school need not provide prior notice of discipline.

The student appealed to the U.S. Court of Appeals, Ninth Circuit, which held that the student and his mother had met with a district representative, who gave them oral notice of the exclusion pending a meeting with the superintendent. The superintendent later met with them for several hours to discuss the incident and his pending expulsion. Accordingly, the student received adequate notice of the charge and a hearing under *Goss*. **The expulsion did not violate the student's due process rights.** *Doe v. Mercer Island School Dist. No. 400*, 288 Fed.Appx. 426 (9th Cir. 2008).

◆ Two North Carolina students transferred into a new school system, where they were bullied by other students. In their first semester there, one of them became involved in a fight with another student at a school basketball game. Both children were removed from the attendance roll for the next semester, based on the family's out-of-district residency and one student's violation of the student code. Before the education board issued a final decision, the parent sued it for breach of contract, violation of board policy and constitutional violations. The court dismissed the case, and the Court of Appeals of North Carolina affirmed. State law provided for appeal to a local education board following a final administrative decision for the discipline of a student, violations of law, school board rules and policies, and policies regarding grade retention of students. **The parent was first required to obtain a final decision of the board before proceeding to court.** Here, the board had not issued a final decision at the time she filed her state court action. *Hentz v. Asheville City Board of Educ.*, 658 S.E.2d 520 (N.C. Ct. App. 2008).

◆ An Arkansas student shouted at a classmate near their school cafeteria and approached her until a teacher intervened. The principal received a handwritten note from the student in which she threatened the classmate's life and described her plan to initiate a fight. The principal suspended the student pending a recommended expulsion, and the school board expelled her. She obtained a court order allowing her to return to school a few days later, and the district appealed. The Arkansas Court of Appeals agreed with the district that the county court had ignored its proper role by substituting its judgment for that of the school board. **The Arkansas Code requires school boards to hold students strictly accountable for disorderly conduct in school**, and there is a general policy against court intervention in matters that are properly before school authorities. The county court had no power to substitute its judgment for that of the school board, and the appeals court reversed its judgment. *Cross County School Dist. v. Spencer*, 58 S.W.3d 406 (Ark. Ct. App. 2001).

### 5. Cell Phones and Electronic Devices

*Off-campus student electronic communications often have a negative impact on school grounds, forcing educators to consider discipline for events that take place off-campus. In such cases, schools may seek the involvement of law enforcement officials and look to criminal laws to justify school discipline.*

◆    An Arkansas teacher confiscated a student's cell phone as he was using it in violation of a school rule. Although his parents demanded the return of the phone, it remained in the school office for two weeks, as required by a district policy. It was then returned, but the family sued the teacher and principal in a state court for trespass and taking property without due process of law. The court held for the district, and appeal reached the Supreme Court of Arkansas.

On appeal, the parents claimed Section 6-18-502 of the Arkansas Code did not authorize the confiscation. They argued that Americans have Fourth Amendment rights to be secure in their persons and property and to be free from unreasonable searches and seizures without due process. The court explained that Section 6-18-502 pertained only to the suspension or dismissal of students from public schools. It was insufficient to simply claim that no law authorized the confiscation. In prior decisions, the court made clear that a party's argument will not be considered unless it is convincing or supported by authority. **Section 6-18-502 declared that school policies were to "prescribe minimum and maximum penalties, including students' suspension or dismissal from school."** Arkansas school boards have broad discretion to direct school operations, and "courts have no power to interfere with such boards in the exercise of that discretion unless there is a clear abuse of it." The court refused to interfere with the board's decision about the best way to enforce its policy. The family did not cite any authority defining a property right to have a cell phone at school. As a result, the judgment for school officials was affirmed. *Koch v. Adams*, No. 09-829, 2010 WL 986775 (Ark. 3/18/10).

◆    An investigation of "sexting" among high school students was begun when Tunkhannock, Pennsylvania school officials found photos of nude and semi-nude female students on cell phones. Officials learned that male students traded the images over their cell phones. The district attorney investigated and made a public statement to the media that possession of inappropriate images of minors could justify criminal prosecution for possession or distribution of child pornography. The district attorney presented teens suspected of sexting with a choice of either attending an education program or facing child pornography charges. As part of the education program, female students would have to write a report detailing "why you are here," "what you did," and "why it was wrong."

Three parents brought a federal court action to halt the proceeding, arguing the threatened prosecution came in retaliation for refusal to attend the education program. The court granted them preliminary relief. An appeal was made to the

U.S. Court of Appeals, Third Circuit. While the appeal was pending, the district attorney dropped charges against two students. The other student and her parent pursued the appeal. The court stated that parents have a Fourteenth Amendment Due Process right to raise their children without undue state interference. The court found the parent objected to the lessons in morality, and held **the government cannot coerce parents to accept official ideas of morality and gender roles**. While the district attorney could offer a voluntary education program, he could not coerce attendance by threatening prosecution. The parent showed a reasonable likelihood of prevailing on both her claim that the district attorney violated her right to parental autonomy and her daughter's right to be free from compelled speech. Government action requiring an individual to state a particular message is coercive and violates the First Amendment. As it appeared the district attorney made a retaliatory threat of prosecution, the court upheld the preliminary order. *Miller v. Mitchell*, 598 F.3d 139 (3d Cir. 2010).

◆ A Mississippi school faculty member confiscated a student's cell phone in his class. Pictures on the phone showed the student dancing at home and a classmate holding a BB gun at the student's house. Deeming the items "gang pictures," the principal suspended the student under a school discipline rule prohibiting students from wearing or displaying clothing, accessories, drawings or messages associated with gangs or crime. At a school disciplinary hearing, a municipal police sergeant said he recognized gang signs in the pictures, and the principal said the student "was a threat to school safety." The hearing officer recommended expelling the student for the rest of the school year, and the board of education affirmed the order. **A federal district court held the search of the cell phone did not violate the Fourth Amendment. The city was entitled to dismissal of the claim, and city and school officials had immunity.** A crucial factor was that the student was using his phone in violation of a school rule.

The court said that once the staff member saw the student improperly using the phone, it was reasonable for him to find out why he was using it. The student might have been using the phone to cheat or talk to another student. But the court found no explanation for finding the student was a threat to the school. The sergeant did not state a basis for believing the pictures had gang signs. The court was "troubled" that the student "somehow found himself expelled for an entire school year when the only offense he committed was the minor offense of bringing a phone on school grounds." It was clear to the court that he did not violate the anti-gang policy. The pictures were taken at the student's home, and it appeared that the district misapplied its anti-gang policy. As the most likely reason for expulsion was the principal's testimony that the student was "a threat to school safety," the court found it possible that the expulsion was based on subjective beliefs and not conduct. In a footnote, the court advised the district to consider a settlement. *J.W. v. Desoto County School Dist.*, Civil Action No. 2:09-cv-00155-MPM-DAS, 2010 WL 4394059 (N.D. Miss. 11/1/10).

◆ At a school event called Class Day, an Arkansas student played an audio clip from his cell phone of a female student saying "oh my gosh, I'm horny!" A school official confiscated the phone, suspended him for three days and barred him from graduation ceremonies. The family sued the school district and officials in a state court for violating the state Civil Rights Act and the student's speech and due process rights. It was asserted that the discipline was retaliatory because the female in the clip was the stepdaughter of a school board member who happened to be in attendance at the assembly. A state circuit court held for the district, since the student was immediately advised of his improper conduct and his parents received written notification of the discipline and an opportunity to meet with the superintendent. As the district provided the due process required by *Goss v. Lopez*, 419 U.S. 565 (1975), the court found no violation.

Regarding the speech rights claim, the court cited *Bethel School Dist. No. 403 v. Fraser*, 478 U.S. 675 (1986) for the proposition that schools may determine what constitutes lewd, indecent or offensive speech. Since the court found no speech rights violation and no violation of the Arkansas Civil Rights Act, it held for the school district. On appeal, the Supreme Court of Arkansas found the student had to assert a deprivation of a right, privilege or immunity secured by the Arkansas Constitution to prevail. **Since the family did not show why federal decisions should be applied to find a violation of the state Civil Rights Act, the court refused to develop an argument on his behalf.** Instead, it held the circuit court judgment for the district and officials should be affirmed. *Walters v. Dobbins,* No. 09-1004, 2010 WL 2131869 (Ark. 5/27/10).

◆   New York City school rules forbade students from bringing cell phones into public schools without authorization from principals. A state court held that any enforcement system focusing on the use, rather than possession, of cell phones would require teachers to observe and enforce the ban. Teachers would become involved in confronting students and punishment decisions. For that reason, the board had a rational basis for a complete ban. The involvement of teachers in enforcing the cell phone ban would take time from their teaching mission and increase the perception of teachers as adversaries to students. Each principal could address specific situations by allowing students to carry cell phones when there was a special need for it. The court refused to recognize a "constitutional right to bear cell phones," and it rejected claims by parents who asserted a right to be able to communicate with their children at school.

On appeal, the New York Supreme Court, Appellate Division, upheld the cell phone policy, finding it beyond court review. It was not unreasonable for the school system to ban cell phones, which by their nature could be used surreptitiously and in violation of school rules. Significantly, the court held that "the department has a rational interest in having its teachers and staff devote their time to educating students and not waging a 'war' against cell phones." **The use of cell phones for cheating, sexual harassment, prank calls and intimidation was a threat to order in the schools.** The judgment was affirmed. *Price v. New York City Board of Educ.,* 51 A.D.3d 277, 855 N.Y.S.2d 530 (N.Y. App. Div. 2008).

◆   A student with a record of computer-related misconduct admitted helping another student hack into a Pennsylvania school district computer system. He admitted supplying the other student user names and passwords to allow him to install software and manipulate the district's database. The student was suspended pending an expulsion hearing for violating the school's computer use policy. The policy allowed discipline for violating local, state or federal law. After a school board hearing, the board found the student had violated the computer use policy as well as the state school code and felony provisions of the state crimes code. The board expelled him for the rest of the school year. The student's attorney noted that the school computer use policy did not specify that a violation of the policy could lead to expulsion, but a state common pleas court affirmed the board's decision. On appeal, the Commonwealth Court of Pennsylvania, held **"[g]iven his history, a 10-day suspension was not likely to get his attention because he did not learn from his prior suspension for computer misconduct."** Since the student's conduct would be a felony under the state crimes code, "an expulsion was entirely appropriate." The board had properly exercised its discretion to expel him, and the judgment was affirmed. *M.T. v. Cent. York School Dist.*, 937 A.2d 538 (Pa. Commw. Ct. 2007).

◆    A Tennessee eighth-grade teacher seized a student's cell phone when it began to ring in a classroom. A student code provision prohibited cell phones and other devices on school property during school hours. Violations were to be reported to the principal, and the phone or device was to be confiscated for 30 days. The code of conduct imposed a one-day, in-school suspension for first offenses and required minimal due process. The student's parent went to the school to retrieve the phone, but the principal refused to return it. The vice principal then assigned the student a day of in-school suspension. The parents sued the school board, principal and vice principal in a federal district court for constitutional rights violations. The court dismissed the father's due process claim for retention of the phone, but not the student's due process claim.

The school board appealed to the U.S. Court of Appeals, Sixth Circuit. The court reviewed *Goss v. Lopez*, this chapter, and held an in-school suspension could deprive a student of educational opportunities in the same way an out-of-school suspension would. However, the in-school suspension in this case did not resemble the suspensions issued in *Goss*. The student was allowed to do her school work. Her attendance was recorded in the same manner as if she had attended regular classes by state law. The court found other courts have held **in-school suspensions do not implicate a student's property interest in public education**. In *Wise v. Pea Ridge School Dist.*, 855 F.2d 560 (8th Cir. 1988), a special education student was suspended for three days in a special classroom due to tardiness. The *Wise* court refused to apply *Goss* to a temporary, in-school suspension. The court agreed with *Wise*, as **"in-school suspension does not exclude the student from school and consequently a student's property interest in public education is not implicated."** A one-day in-school suspension, during which the student was recorded as in attendance and was allowed to do her schoolwork did not deprive her of any due process rights, and the court reversed the judgment. *Laney v. Farley*, 501 F.3d 577 (6th Cir. 2007).

◆    A Delaware student used his cell phone at a school assembly, in violation of the school code of conduct. He refused to surrender his phone to a staff member, and the principal asked him four times to hand it over. The principal told the student he would have to come with him to the office. The student still refused to move, and the principal tried to escort him from the assembly by the elbow. The student struggled, pushed the principal and stepped on his foot. After being removed from the assembly, he continued to use his cell phone. The student remained disruptive in the school office and told the principal "you can't touch me," and "just wait till I call my mom. She'll sue you." He also threatened other students and teachers. The police arrived at the school and took the student into custody. The school board expelled the student for the rest of the school year and assigned him to an alternative school. The state board of education affirmed the action, and the student appealed to a state superior court.

The court held the state board could overturn a local board decision only if it was contrary to state law or state regulations, was not supported by substantial evidence, or was arbitrary and capricious. The court found sufficient evidence that the student had pushed the principal and stepped on his foot. **The student had intentionally and offensively touched the principal in violation of the school code.** Expulsion with referral to an alternative program was not disproportionate to the misconduct. *Jordan v. Smyrna School Dist. Board of Educ.*, No. 05A-02-004, 2006 WL 1149149 (Del. Super. Ct. 2006).

## C.  Academic Expulsions or Suspensions

◆   An Ohio student and his parents were Chinese citizens in the U.S. on visas. In addition to earning straight As, the student was a master violinist. After being questioned about a recent high grade on a biology test, the student admitted obtaining a biology test bank via the Internet by guessing the teacher's password and accessing a school computer. The assistant principal completed a notice of removal and/or intended suspension form that indicated a five-day suspension. It also stated that expulsion was possible. The assistant principal notified the family he was recommending expulsion for violating Ohio laws against computer break-ins. Due to the student's visa status and pending criminal charges, he faced possible deportation. A board hearing officer limited the hearing's duration to one hour because "it was a busy day." After the hearing, the hearing officer notified the family that the suspension should be upheld. However, no conclusions of fact were sent to the family as required by Ohio statute. A state court affirmed the suspension. On appeal, the Court of Appeals of Ohio agreed with the family that there should have been a hearing in the trial court under the statute to supplement the deficient administrative record.

As the hearing transcript did not record all the statements, and the hearing officer did not file any conclusions of law, the parents were entitled to submit additional evidence at another hearing. In the absence of a record, the court was unable to tell what rules the student may have violated, or the evidence upon which the board relied. **While the student's behavior was not to be condoned, he deserved an opportunity to present additional evidence under the circumstances.** *Huang v. Kent City School Dist. Board of Educ.*, No. 2008-P-0038, 2008 WL 4901779 (Ohio Ct. App. 11/14/08).

◆   An Oregon student had Attention Deficit Hyperactivity Disorder. With the help of the school football team's quarterback, he created counterfeit money. Both students were caught passing counterfeit bills at the student store. The student was charged with forgery and suspended for ongoing disciplinary issues, including a minor-in-possession charge, two harassment and misconduct complaints, and at least one athletic code violation. The school informed the student that since he intended to finish his course load outside of the classroom, the district was recommending expulsion for the rest of the year. The actual proceedings would be stayed if certain conditions were met. The quarterback received an in-school suspension for four days, and a three-week suspension from athletic activity and community service/grounds work at the high school.

In a federal district court action, the student asserted the greater punishment assigned to him was based on his learning disabilities. The court noted that **as long as there was a rational basis for the difference in the way the students were treated, the district was entitled to judgment**. This was because disabled students are not a "protected class" under the Equal Protection Clause. The court noted the student's prior disciplinary record and the fact that the quarterback had no disciplinary history. This distinction permitted disciplining the learning disabled student differently. *Schneider v. Corvallis School Dist. 509J*, No. CIV 05-6375-TC, 2006 WL 3827457 (D. Or. 2006).

◆  A student enrolled in the University of Michigan's "Inteflex" program – a special six-year course of study leading to both an undergraduate and medical degree. He struggled with the curriculum and failed the NBME Part I, receiving the lowest score in the brief history of the Inteflex program. The university's medical school executive board reviewed the student's academic career and decided to drop him from registration in the program. It denied his request to retake the NBME Part I. The student sued the university in a federal court, claiming due process violations. The evidence showed that the university had a practice of allowing students who had failed the NBME Part I to retake the test up to four times. The student was the only person ever refused permission to retake the test. Nonetheless, the court held that his dismissal did not violate the Due Process Clause. The U.S. Supreme Court agreed. The **Due Process Clause was not offended because "the University's liberal retesting custom gave rise to no state law entitlement to retake NBME Part I."** *Regents of Univ. of Michigan v. Ewing*, 474 U.S. 214, 106 S.Ct. 507, 88 L.Ed.2d 523 (1985).

## II.  STUDENT SEARCH AND SEIZURE

*In* New Jersey v. T.L.O., *below, the Supreme Court held the warrant and probable cause requirement of the Fourth Amendment does not apply to school officials who search students suspected of violating a law or school rules. Instead, the legality of a student search depends upon the reasonableness of the search in light of all the circumstances. A search performed by school officials must be "reasonable at its inception" and "not overly intrusive under all the circumstances." A student's age and sex are relevant considerations when evaluating the intrusiveness of a search. The Supreme Court revisited* T.L.O. *in* Safford Unified School Dist. #1 v. Redding, *Subsection II.A.3, below. The Supreme Court clarified that "justified at its inception" means reasonable grounds for suspecting that a search will turn up evidence of a rules violation.*

## A. Fourth Amendment "Reasonable Suspicion"

### 1. Searches Based on Individualized Suspicion

◆    A teacher at a New Jersey high school found two girls smoking in a school lavatory in violation of school rules. She brought them to the assistant vice principal's office, where one of the girls admitted to smoking in the lavatory. However, the other girl denied even being a smoker. The assistant vice principal then asked the latter girl to come to his private office, where he opened her purse and found a pack of cigarettes. As he reached for them, he noticed rolling papers and decided to thoroughly search the entire purse. He found marijuana, a pipe, empty plastic bags, a substantial number of one dollar bills and a list of "people who owe me money." The matter was then turned over to the police. A juvenile court hearing was held, and the girl was adjudicated delinquent. She appealed the juvenile court's determination, contending that her constitutional rights had been violated by the search of her purse. She argued that the evidence against her should have been excluded from the juvenile court proceeding.

The U.S. Supreme Court held the search did not violate the Fourth Amendment. It said: "The legality of a search of a student should depend simply on the reasonableness, under all the circumstances, of the search." Two considerations are relevant in determining the reasonableness of a search. First, **the search must be justified initially by reasonable suspicion of a violation**. Second, **the scope and conduct of the search must be reasonably related to the circumstances which gave rise to the search, and school officials must take into account the student's age, sex and the nature of the offense**. The Court upheld the search of the student in this case because the initial search for cigarettes was supported by reasonable suspicion. The discovery of rolling papers then justified the further searching of the purse, since such papers are commonly used to roll marijuana cigarettes. The Court affirmed the delinquency adjudication, ruling the "reasonableness" standard was met by school officials in these circumstances and the evidence was properly obtained. *New Jersey v. T.L.O.*, 469 U.S. 325, 105 S.Ct. 733, 83 L.Ed.2d 720 (1985).

◆    A New York middle school teacher reported that her classroom was being disturbed by a musical noise from a cell phone. The dean of the school arrived to investigate and enforce the school's rule prohibiting cell phone use in class. After a student realized the dean intended to search each student in the room for the source of the noise, he removed a hunting knife with a six-inch blade from his pocket and handed it over to the dean. As he was 15 years old, he was charged in a state family court with the delinquent act of weapons possession. The student moved to suppress evidence of his knife possession, claiming it was unlawfully obtained in violation of the state and federal constitutions. The court denied the motion and adjudicated him delinquent. On appeal, the New York Supreme Court, Appellate Division, held **the dean did not perform a "search" of the student, because he was holding the knife and it was in plain view**.

**Even if there was a search, the dean's actions were justified.** Asking students to empty their pockets was a non-intrusive, practical means of finding an unauthorized cell phone. The dean had a reasonable basis to believe a student in the class was violating school rules, and that the sound was disruptive. The family court had properly found the dean was trying to restore order, "which is not a law enforcement interest." Accordingly, he required neither probable cause nor reasonable suspicion to justify asking the students to empty their pockets. The appellate court upheld the family court's finding of delinquency. *In re Elvin G.*, 47 A.D.3d 527, 851 N.Y.S.2d 129 (N.Y. App. Div. 2008).

◆     A California elementary school prohibited personal articles and clothing suggesting tobacco, drug or alcohol use, sexual promiscuity, profanity, vulgarity and other inappropriate subjects. A seventh grader wore a shirt with pro-life messages and images of fetuses to school. She claimed the images were "similar to images of unborn infants regularly contained in health and science textbooks." She claimed that a school clerk stopped her from eating her breakfast, subjected her to ridicule, and led her to the school office. There she was ordered to remove the shirt, which was confiscated for the school day.

According to the student, other students were allowed to wear clothes to school with personal messages. She brought multiple claims against the school district and officials, including one that school officials had confiscated her shirt without legal justification. **The court held that seizures of a student or personal items are subject to a reasonableness standard.** Since the student raised issues of possible arbitrary, capricious or unreasonable conduct, the court denied the district's motion for dismissal of the Fourth Amendment claim. *T.A. v. McSwain Union Elementary School Dist.*, No. CV-F-08-1986, 2009 WL 1748793 (E.D. Cal. 6/18/09).

◆     A student informant identified an 18-year-old adult student as one of several students who might be involved in drug dealing at an Ohio high school. The assistant principal summoned the adult student to the office, where he agreed to a pat-down search. Several hundred dollars were found in his wallet, which he claimed was pay from his job. Administrators asked to search his car, and he told them they would only find cigarettes. A search confirmed that the student possessed cigarettes and lighters, and he was suspended for three days.

The school board rejected the student's appeal, and an Ohio common pleas court upheld the suspension. On appeal to the Court of Appeals of Ohio, the student argued the informant's report was an insufficient reason for a search or questioning. Moreover, he admitted having the cigarettes, making a search unnecessary. **The court found a student search is justified at its inception when there are reasonable grounds for suspecting it will turn up evidence of a violation of school rules or a law.** The assistant principal believed the informant was trustworthy, making the search justified at its inception. The search was reasonable in scope because the student admitted contraband would be found in his car. A school policy called for only a warning to adult school district employees who possessed tobacco, while students were subject to suspension. Since students were distinguishable from district employees and could be treated differently, the court found no equal protection violation and upheld the discipline. *Mayeux v. Board of Educ. of Painesville Township School Dist.*, No. 2007-L-099, 2008 WL 754979 (Ohio Ct. App. 3/21/08).

◆    A Florida student felt dizzy at school and lost consciousness in a lavatory. He then told a school monitor he did not feel well. The monitor escorted the student to a school office. The assistant principal later said that the student was quiet, subdued and a little pale. She ordered the student to empty out his pockets and bookbag. After noticing a plastic baggie that appeared to contain marijuana, she called the police. The contents of the bag tested positive for marijuana. The student was arrested and charged with marijuana possession. A Florida court denied his motion to suppress the evidence and adjudicated him delinquent. The student appealed to a Florida District Court of Appeal. The court explained that school officials must have reasonable grounds to suspect that a search will result in evidence that the student has violated the law or school rules. Here, the search was premised upon the student's lavatory incident and his appearance. **The student's pale or quiet appearance alone was "entirely consistent with non-criminal behavior such as illness."** The court reversed the adjudication of delinquency. *C.G. v. State of Florida*, 941 So.2d 503 (Fla. Dist. Ct. App. 2007).

◆    A California school security employee saw three teenagers sitting on the front lawn of a high school during school hours. Because the employee did not recognize any of them as students, he called a police officer. The officer approached the intruders and asked them for identification. One of them produced identification from another school. The officer decided to escort the three intruders to the office to verify their identities. For his own safety, he decided to pat them down. The officer discovered a knife with a locking blade on one intruder and confiscated it. The intruder was charged with unlawful possession of the knife on school property. A state superior court denied his motion to exclude the knife as evidence, and he appealed.

The Court of Appeal of California held that the special need for schools to maintain a safe and orderly learning environment required different search and seizure rules than those for the general public. **Searches of students are justified if there is reasonable suspicion of a violation of a law, school rule or regulation.** Students may be detained without any particularized suspicion, so long as the detention is not arbitrary, capricious or for the purpose of harassment. Here, the intruder did not attend the school. He had a lesser right of privacy than students who were properly on school grounds. The officer had ample cause to believe the intruder did not belong on campus. The state's interest in preventing violence on a high school campus outweighed the minimal invasion to the intruder's privacy rights. As the pat-down search was proper, the court affirmed the judgment. *In re Jose Y.*, 141 Cal.App.4th 748, 46 Cal.Rptr.3d 268 (Cal. Ct. App. 2006).

◆    A Pennsylvania student had his cell phone on, in violation of a school policy. When a teacher confiscated the phone, a text message appeared on its screen from another student requesting marijuana. The teacher and an assistant principal then called nine students listed in the cell phone's directory to see if their phones were turned on in violation of school policy. They accessed the student's text messages and voice mail and used the phone's instant messaging feature. The student stated the district superintendent later told the press that the student was a drug user or peddler, and the family sued the teacher, assistant principal, superintendent and school district in a federal district court. It held the superintendent could not assert absolute immunity for his statements to the press. The teacher and assistant principal also had no immunity for the invasion of privacy claims. **The court agreed with the family that accessing the phone directory, voice mail and text messages, and use of the phone to call persons listed in the directory amounted to a "search or seizure" under the Fourth Amendment.** The court found no basis for the "search," as it was not done to find evidence of wrongdoing by the student, but instead to obtain evidence of possible misconduct by others. The Fourth Amendment claims would proceed. *Klump v. Nazareth Area School Dist.*, 425 F.Supp.2d 622 (E.D. Pa. 2006).

◆   An Atlanta high school resource officer was instructed by another officer to stop a car with some possible truant students in it. When the officer stopped the car, the front seat passenger tried to jump out. He removed marijuana from his pocket when the officer approached. The officer handcuffed all four of the car's occupants. An assistant principal arrived and instructed the officer to search the others for marijuana. A search of one student revealed car keys and $500. The officer and assistant principal searched this student's car and found a handgun in it. A K-9 unit arrived and found 15 bags of marijuana in the car. A county superior court held the search "bore no relation to the stated reason for the stop." It was based on the discovery of a key, some money, rumors and suspicion. Such actions were "whimsical, tyrannical and unreasonable" under *State v. Young*, 234 Ga. 488, 216 S.E.2d 586 (Ga. 1975).

On appeal, the Court of Appeals of Georgia noted that **searches by school officials are "subject only to the most minimal restraints necessary to insure that students are not whimsically stripped of personal privacy and subjected to petty tyranny."** The state supreme court gave great leeway to school officials in *Young*, but distinguished between searches conducted by school officials and those involving police. *Young* was inapplicable if a school official directed a search by the police. The court held a police resource officer should be considered a law enforcement officer and not a school official. The student's first contact with the police came when the car was stopped. *Young* did not apply, and the search was governed by the Fourth Amendment. The court rejected the state's assertion that the stop was valid on the basis of suspected truancy. As the stop was not justified, and the student's consent to search was obtained illegally, the court upheld his motion to suppress evidence seized from his car. *State v. Scott*, 279 Ga.App. 52, 630 S.E.2d 563 (Ga. Ct. App. 2006).

◆   A Pennsylvania assistant principal detained a student for nearly four hours while investigating a classmate's claim that the student touched her in a sexual manner without her consent. The student denied unwanted touching. The assistant principal told him to remain in a conference room while he interviewed witnesses. The student remained there and did school work for several hours. The principal later suspended him for four days for inappropriate conduct. The student sued the school district, board and administrators in a federal district court for constitutional rights violations. The court held for the district, and he appealed. On appeal, the U.S. Court of Appeals, Third Circuit, held confinement in a conference room for nearly four hours was a "seizure."

Public school searches are governed by the "reasonableness standard" of *New Jersey v. T.L.O.*, above. **What is reasonable depends on the context of the search. In school cases, the courts balance the need for a search against the personal invasion which the search entails.** The court noted the detention was to investigate the incident, and to determine appropriate punishment. **In light of the serious nature of the charge, it was reasonable for the school to detain the student.** The court rejected his due process claim, as the assistant principal allowed him to present his side of the story before discipline was administered. *Shuman v. Penn Manor School Dist.*, 422 F.3d 141 (3d Cir. 2005).

◆ A Massachusetts school administrator saw three students in a parking lot when they should have been in class. A search of one student yielded a small bag of marijuana. A juvenile court denied his motion to suppress the marijuana evidence and found him delinquent. On appeal, the Supreme Judicial Court of Massachusetts explained that **reasonable suspicion is not a hunch or "unparticularized suspicion," but instead requires common-sense conclusions about human behavior.** In this case, the student had recently been truant and failed to bring his mother to a meeting to discuss it. School officials had no evidence he possessed contraband or had violated a law or school rule. The court rejected the argument that the search was appropriate based on the student's truancy. A violation of school rules, standing alone, would not provide reasonable grounds for a search unless the specific facts of the violation created a reasonable suspicion of a violation. As there was no information of an individualized nature that the student might have contraband, any search was unreasonable at its inception and the court vacated the juvenile court order. *Comwlth. of Massachusetts v. Damian D.*, 752 N.E. 2d 679 (Mass. 2001).

◆ A California high school security officer observed a student in an area that was off limits to students. When she approached him, she noticed he became "very paranoid and nervous." After the student entered a classroom, the officer and a colleague summoned him to the hallway and performed a pat-down search that yielded a knife. The state filed charges against the student and placed him on probation. On appeal, the Supreme Court of California explained that schools may enact disciplinary rules and regulations and enforce them through police or security officers. The school environment calls for immediate, effective action, and school officials are allowed to exercise the same degree of physical control over students as parents are privileged to exercise.

**Students are deprived of liberty while at school, and detention by a school official for questioning does not increase the limitations already in effect by being in school.** Student may be stopped, told to remain in or leave a classroom, sent to the office and held after school. Individualized suspicion is usually needed to perform a search or seizure, but special needs exist at schools that relax this requirement. Detentions on school grounds did not violate the Constitution, so long as they were not arbitrary, capricious or for the purposes of harassment. Since the student did not allege the officer acted arbitrarily, capriciously or in a harassing manner, the court affirmed the judgment. *In re Randy G.*, 26 Cal. 4th 556, 110 Cal. Rptr. 2d 516, 28 P. 3d 239 (Cal. 2001).

◆  A Maryland student attended a school for students with emotional, learning and behavioral difficulties. The school system's search and seizure policy allowed administrators to search students or their lockers if there was probable cause to believe that a student had items whose possession would constitute a Maryland criminal offense, including weapons, drugs and drug paraphernalia, alcohol or pagers. The principal pursued an anonymous tip that there were drugs or weapons at the middle school and authorized a search of all middle school lockers. A school security officer opened the student's locker in the student's absence and found a book bag containing a folding knife and pager.

In juvenile court proceedings, the student admitted possessing the items but moved to suppress them as evidence, claiming the school policy created a reasonable expectation of privacy in his locker. The juvenile court disagreed, and appeal reached the state's highest court. The Court of Appeals of Maryland held state law, not school policy, defined and controlled the authority of school officials to conduct locker searches. The only evidence indicating the student had a privacy expectation in his locker was the school policy. **Maryland Education Article Section 7-308 permitted reasonable searches of students based on a reasonable belief that a student possessed an item whose possession would create a criminal offense.** School lockers are designated school property and subject to search by school officials. Accordingly, the school policy was invalid and could not serve as the basis for a reasonable privacy expectation. *In re Patrick Y.*, 358 Md. 50, 746 A.2d 405 (Md. 2000).

## 2. Off-Campus Searches

◆  Minnesota students attending an auto shop class were bused to a body shop for class instruction. En route, the teacher observed a student holding a knife that was passed to him from a classmate. When the bus arrived at the body shop, the teacher called a school coordinator to report the knife. The coordinator and principal decided each student should be searched, and the principal called a school liaison officer. Before the search began, the classmate voluntarily handed over the knife. The liaison officer found a collapsible baton in the student's pocket, and he was charged with violating a state law prohibiting possession of a dangerous weapon on school property. The district brought an expulsion proceeding against the student for violating its ban on weapons and look-alikes.

The student pursued civil rights claims against the liaison officer and his municipality. The case reached the Eighth Circuit, which noted that while law officers are normally required to have probable cause of wrongdoing to support a search or seizure of persons or property, the more lenient standard of "reasonable suspicion" applies to searches and seizures in the context of public schools. School officials may conduct a search that is "justified at its inception" and reasonable in scope. The court held that **the *New Jersey v. T.L.O.* standard applies to law enforcement officers who conduct student searches away from traditional school grounds.** School administrators initiated the search, and one of them played a substantial role in it. The fact that the search took place off school grounds did not call for imposing the stricter probable cause standard. The liaison officer's conduct was reasonable, as he did not know whether other students might also have weapons. As the search was justified and reasonable in scope, the officer was entitled to immunity. *Shade v. City of Farmington, Minnesota*, 309 F.3d 1054 (8th Cir. 2002).

◆ Before leaving for a school-sponsored trip, New York students were informed that drugs and alcohol were banned and that participants would be subject to room searches. Each student signed a pledge to avoid alcohol and drugs. The pledge recited that a violation would result in disqualification from senior activities and graduation ceremonies. During the trip, the school principal smelled marijuana where many of the students had congregated in the hallway of their motel. He then obtained a hotel security pass key and searched most of their rooms. The principal found marijuana in the safe of one room. He sent two students home early and suspended them from school for three days.

The students sued the principal and school district. A court held that students under supervision in school activities, including field trips, are subject to the reasonable suspicion standard for student searches first announced by the U.S. Supreme Court in *New Jersey v. T.L.O.*, not the more stringent Fourth Amendment probable cause standard. **The students had no legitimate reason to expect complete privacy in their hotel rooms, and it was reasonable for the principal to search the rooms** based on his detection of marijuana smoke and the gathering of students. This was true even though he was without individualized suspicion that any one student possessed drugs. The court upheld the search. *Rhodes v. Guarricino*, 54 F.Supp.2d 186 (S.D.N.Y. 1999).

### 3. Strip Searches

*In* Safford Unified School Dist. #1 v. Redding, *below, the Supreme Court discussed the distinction between the "probable cause" standard for police searches and the "reasonable suspicion" standard for school searches. It held "probable cause" requires evidence that raises "a fair probability" or a "substantial chance of discovering evidence of criminal activity."* **By contrast, the Court held "the standard for school searches could as readily be described as a moderate chance of finding evidence of wrongdoing."**

◆ An Arizona assistant middle school principal questioned a 13-year-old student about knives, lighters and a cigarette found in her planner. When the student denied owning any of the contraband, the assistant principal questioned her about prescription-strength ibuprofen pills and an over-the-counter painkiller. After the student denied knowing about the pills, the assistant principal told her he had received a report from a male student that she was giving pills to others at school. She denied this and allowed the assistant principal to search her belongings. He found no contraband there but told female staff members to further search the student in the nurse's office. An administrative assistant and school nurse asked the student to remove her jacket, socks, shoes, pants and t-shirt. They then instructed her to pull her bra to the side and shake it. Finally, the two staff members told the student to pull out the elastic of her underpants.

No pills were found in the search. The student's mother filed a federal district court action against the school district and school officials for Fourth Amendment violations. The case reached the U.S. Supreme Court, which noted that *New Jersey v. T.L.O.*, this chapter, used "a standard of reasonableness that stops short of probable cause." In this case, the male student's report created suspicion enough to justify the search of the student's backpack and outer clothing. But asking her to pull away her underwear and expose her breasts and pelvic area made the search **"categorically distinct, requiring distinct elements of justification on the part of school authorities for going beyond a search of outer clothing and belongings."** The Court cited a psychology journal study that found a strip search can cause serious emotional damage. Some schools find strip searches are never reasonable. While the indignity of a search did not necessarily outlaw it, the Court found "the suspicion failed to match the degree of intrusion." The assistant principal had no reason to suspect the student was hiding drugs or painkillers in her underwear. The Court stated "the *T.L.O.* concern to limit a school search to reasonable scope requires the support of reasonable suspicion of danger or of resort to underwear for hiding evidence of wrongdoing before a search can reasonably make the quantum leap from outer clothes and backpacks to exposure of intimate parts." Despite the constitutional violation, the law regarding student searches was not so well established as to deprive school officials of qualified immunity from liability. The case was returned to the district court for further consideration. *Safford Unified School Dist. #1 v. Redding*, 129 S.Ct. 2633 (U.S. 2009).

◆   Two students in an Ohio high school nursing class reported missing cash, a credit card and gift cards. The other 15 or 16 students in the class were taken to the first aid room, where their purses, books, shoes, socks and pockets were searched. After a search of each student's locker, staff members received a report that an unidentified student was hiding the missing items in her bra. The school director then instructed a female instructor to search the students in the lavatory. Eleven students sued the school district, instructors and other school officials in a federal district court for violating their Fourth Amendment rights. The court denied the officials' request for qualified immunity. On appeal, the U.S. Court of Appeals, Sixth Circuit, affirmed the judgment, and the officials appealed to the U.S. Supreme Court. It returned the case to the Sixth Circuit in view of its decision in *Safford Unified School Dist. #1 v. Redding*, above.

The Sixth Circuit held there must be "reasonable grounds for suspecting that the search will turn up evidence that the student has violated or is violating either the law or the rules of the school." **A student handbook policy did not create mutual consent to conduct the strip searches, as the district argued.** There was no waiver of privacy expectations, as some students did not even know about the policy. Repeating its finding in *Beard v. Whitmore Lake School Dist.*, this chapter, the court held "students have a significant privacy interest in their unclothed bodies." The severity of the school's need in this case was held "slight." A search for money served a much less important interest than a search for drugs or weapons. Any interest in searching for the missing items was "diluted considerably" when the entire class was searched. The court found the search was unlikely to uncover any evidence and violated the students' rights. As a result, the court again denied the officials' claim to immunity. *Knisley v. Pike County Joint Vocational School Dist.*, 604 F.3d 977 (6th Cir. 2010).

◆   A federal district court held Illinois charter school officials were immune to claims filed by a student who was strip-searched by a security guard and police officer. Prior to a trial, the school principal and dean sought to dismiss the federal law claims on the basis of qualified immunity. In *Safford Unified School Dist. v. Redding*, this chapter, the Supreme Court held that a school official searching a student may claim qualified immunity where no clearly established law reveals a constitutional violation. In this case, the student could not show the law regarding school strip searches was "clearly established" at the time of the search. Although the *Redding* case found Arizona school officials violated a middle school student's rights by conducting an overly intrusive search, the decision was not released until after the search in this case. As for the other claims, the court rejected the student's argument that school and municipal officials placed her in a position of danger by allowing the search to go forward.

There was no allegation of an official policy or practice of civil rights violations, requiring dismissal of the claims against the school and its board. The court found the student did not allege any other incident of failure to train employees. **A single, isolated incident of wrongdoing by a non-policymaker was insufficient to establish municipal liability.** Rejecting other state law claims such as intentional infliction of emotional distress and false arrest, the court disposed of many of the student's claims prior to any trial. *S.J. v. Perspectives Charter School*, 685 F.Supp.2d 847 (N.D. Ill. 2010).

◆   A Georgia high school student violated a ban on electronic communication devices by bringing an iPod and cell phone to class. After confiscating the iPod and putting it in a drawer, the teacher left the room, and a classmate took it from the drawer. When the teacher returned, he found the iPod missing and asked who had taken it. After no student admitted having the iPod, all of them were told to open their book bags, turn out their pockets and untuck their shirts. A classmate later confided the identity of the iPod taker to the assistant principal. He avoided confronting the iPod taker to protect the identity of the informer, and told the school discipline secretary to take each of the girls to a closet where they were to shake out their blouses and roll down their waistbands.

Although the identity of the iPod taker was already known, the secretary told a student to remove her pants and underwear. The student sued the teacher, district and others in a federal district court. It held student searches must be "justified at its inception." **This meant reasonable grounds for suspecting that the search will turn up evidence of a violation of rules must be present.** In *Thomas v. Roberts*, 261 F.3d 1160 (11th Cir. 2001), the Eleventh Circuit considered a strip search of Georgia fifth-graders for $26 in missing cash. *Roberts* put schools on notice that a strip search for non-dangerous contraband violates the Fourth Amendment. Officials lacked individualized suspicion that the student had the iPod, and the assistant principal acknowledged the search was to protect the informant. As the search was not based on individualized suspicion that the student had an iPod, a jury could find a Fourth Amendment violation if she was searched as she claimed. But as the assistant principal was not a "final policymaker" for the district, there could be no district liability on the federal claims. *Foster v. Raspberry*, 652 F.Supp.2d 1342 (M.D. Ga. 2009).

◆   An Alabama seventh-grade teacher reported her $450 makeup bag and $12 in cash were missing. The principal, an assistant principal and a counselor told students to empty their book bags and purses and take off their shoes and socks. Students were told to pull out their pants pockets, and the assistant principal and counselor patted down a few of them. The assistant principal stuck her hand into a student's pockets. The counselor reached into the pockets of male students and ran her hand down one student's thigh. The principal took some boys into the hallway for questioning. He then found the makeup bag in a trash can. The $12 was not in the bag, but the teacher said she was no longer concerned about it. Despite this response, the principal took the boys to the boys' lavatory, where he told them to drop their pants and raise their shirts. The counselor took the girls to the lavatory and asked most of them to do the same. A few were also told to pull up their bras. Parents of the students sued the school board, principal, assistant principal, and counselor for Fourth Amendment violations.

A federal district court noted the school handbook warned school officials to avoid group searches where individualized suspicion was lacking. School officials were to call the police and parents if a more intrusive search was required. The policy forbade strip searching. The court found that the officials did not have any individualized suspicion that any student took the makeup bag. The classroom searches which did not involve the touching of students were justified, but **a strip search for the possible theft of $12 was unreasonable. The strip searches were intrusive and violated the district's own policy.** As the search was beyond the school officials' authority, they were not entitled to qualified immunity from the Fourth Amendment violation claims. *H.Y. v. Russell County Board of Educ.*, 490 F.Supp.2d 1174 (M.D. Ala. 2007).

◆   Connecticut school officials held a security search prior to the boarding of buses to a senior class picnic. A student was found with a pack of cigarettes, but no action was taken against her. A classmate then reported to a teacher that the student said she planned to hide marijuana in her pants after the security check. The principal instructed the nurse to search the student's underpants. The nurse expressed apprehension, and the student's mother was called. While waiting for her, the principal searched the student's purse and found cigarettes and a lighter inside it. The mother arrived and agreed to help with the search after being told the police would be called otherwise. The nurse and mother then performed the search behind a curtain. The student was required to raise her shirt, pull down her bra and skirt, and pull her underpants away from her body. The search revealed no marijuana, and she was allowed to attend the picnic. She later sued the principal and other officials for constitutional violations. A federal district court upheld the search under *New Jersey v. T.L.O.*, (this chapter).

The U.S. Court of Appeals, Second Circuit, considered the case and reviewed *Cornfield v. Consolidated High School Dist.*, 991 F.2d 1316 (7th Cir. 1993), an Illinois case that found an intrusive strip search required such a high level of suspicion that it approached probable cause. Here, the factors relied on by the school officials were insufficient to create reasonable suspicion for a strip search. While the teacher may have been entitled to rely on the classmate as a reliable informant, the principal was not. After receiving the tip, the principal did not investigate or try to corroborate the classmate's account. **A student's** history of drug use could be a factor justifying a school search. However, the student in this case was not previously disciplined for any drug offense. The "discovery" of cigarettes and a lighter had only a tenuous connection to the report of marijuana possession. School officials had already seen this contraband during the security check and did not confiscate any items or express concern. *Phaneuf v. Fraikin*, 448 F.3d 591 (2d Cir. 2006).

◆ A Michigan student told her gym teacher that money had been stolen from her during class. A teacher who was acting principal called the police. The gym teacher searched backpacks of male students in the class, without success. A male teacher searched the boys in their locker room, instructing them to lower their pants and underwear and remove their shirts. A police officer arrived and told the teacher to continue searching, and said the girls should be checked in the same way as the boys "to prevent any claims of gender discrimination." The acting principal and a female teacher then searched the girls in their locker room, requiring them to pull up their shirts and pull down their pants. About 25 students were searched, but the stolen money was not discovered. The students sued the school district, teachers and police officer in a federal district court.

The case reached the U.S. Court of Appeals, Sixth Circuit, which stated that a **search for missing money served a less important governmental interest than a search for drugs or weapons**. This interest was further diluted when a school searched over 20 students with no reason to suspect any one in particular. The search was unlikely to succeed and was unlawful. But as *New Jersey v. T.L.O.* and relevant Sixth Circuit cases did not discuss strip searches, the law was sufficiently unclear that the teachers and officer were entitled to qualified immunity. *Beard v. Whitmore Lake School Dist.*, 402 F.3d 598 (6th Cir. 2005).

After the district court dismissed other claims, the students brought a second appeal to the Sixth Circuit. The court held that to hold the school district liable for not sufficiently training its teachers and maintaining a custom or policy of tolerating unconstitutional searches the students had to show "deliberate indifference" by the district. But the district had a two-page policy governing student searches and seizures, plus five pages of guidelines. The teachers had disregarded these policies when performing the search. It was unclear that the search was unconstitutional at the time it was performed, and the need for further training was not so obvious that the school district could be found "deliberately indifferent" to student constitutional rights. The court rejected the students' additional arguments and affirmed the judgment. *Beard v. Whitmore Lake School Dist.*, 244 Fed.Appx. 607 (6th Cir. 2007).

### 4.   State Constitutional Cases

*In* In re P.E.A., *754 P.2d 382 (Col. 1988), the Colorado Supreme Court held the search of a student's car for contraband was justified at its inception. The Supreme Court of New Jersey looked to the Colorado decision in* State v. Best, *below, to support the application of a reasonableness standard to the search of vehicles parked on school property. Officials took action that was reasonably related to the objectives of the search and not excessively intrusive.*

◆   A New Jersey assistant principal (AP) received a report that a high school student was under the influence of drugs. After being taken to the AP's office and interviewed, the student denied any wrongdoing. A search of the student's pockets yielded three white capsules. The AP then searched the student's car and denied his request to call his father. The car search yielded contraband, including a bag containing what appeared to be illegal drugs. A school resource officer arrested the student, who waived his right to remain silent and admitted that the contraband belonged to him. In juvenile proceedings, the student moved to suppress evidence seized from his car as a violation of his right to be free from unreasonable searches and seizures. Based on a finding that the AP's search of the car was reasonably related to a suspicion that the student had drugs and posed a danger to the school, the trial court denied the student's motion.

A state appellate division court affirmed the judgment, and the student appealed to the Supreme Court of New Jersey. On appeal, the court explained that under *New Jersey v. T.L.O.*, this chapter, the school setting required some easing of police search standards in view of the need to maintain school discipline and safety. **The court found no reason to avoid the *T.L.O.* standard in vehicle cases, as "the school setting calls for protections geared toward the safety of students."** The court was not convinced by the student's claim to a greater expectation of privacy in his car than he might have in a locker or purse. A reasonable grounds standard applied to the search of a student's car on school property by school authorities. Based on a classmate's statements and his apparent drug use, and the student's statements and possession of pills, it was reasonable for the AP to extend the search to the student's car. The court affirmed the judgment. *State v. Best*, 201 N.J. 100, 987 A.2d 605 (N.J. 2010).

*Oregon's highest court held a "reasonable suspicion" standard from federal law could apply to student searches in cases decided under the state constitution. But the court limited the standard to serious threats of harm.*

◆   An Oregon assistant high school principal learned a student had been seen trying to sell marijuana near the school. The student was called to the office and told that an anonymous witness saw him trying to sell drugs. After speaking to his mother, the student agreed to turn his pockets inside out. Marijuana, plastic bags and a pipe were found, and he admitted he had tried to sell marijuana. In juvenile court proceedings, the student claimed any evidence seized by school officials should be excluded from trial because there was no probable cause for a search. Finding probable cause was unnecessary, the juvenile court utilized the "reasonable suspicion" standard used by federal courts in deciding public school students' Fourth Amendment claims. Applying this standard, the court held the search was lawful. It also concluded that the student was delinquent.

Appeal reached the Supreme Court of Oregon. It discussed Article I, Section 9, of the Oregon Constitution, which prohibits unreasonable searches or seizures. The court held school searches are different from law enforcement searches. **But only searches involving safety concerns justify a departure from the warrant and probable cause requirements.** When school officials perceive an immediate threat to safety, they need the ability to take prompt, reasonable steps. School officials have wide latitude to take safety precautions. This latitude applies when officials have reasonable suspicion based on specific and articulable facts that an individual poses a threat to safety or possesses an item posing such a threat. Reasonable suspicion applies to searches for drugs on school property. Important limits apply to searches under the new rule. School officials cannot rely on generalizations about suspected drug use or use information that is not specific or current. Since officials reasonably suspected that the student had illegal drugs at the time of the search and that he intended to sell them at school, the judgment was affirmed. *State ex rel. Juvenile Dep't of Clackamas County v. M.A.D.*, 348 Or. 381, 233 P.3d 437 (Or. 2010).

◆   Several people told a Florida middle school principal that a student had been drinking alcohol with her friend at home the day before. Upon interviewing the student, the principal learned that the two girls drank alcohol before school. A sibling of the student then took them to school. A child study committee met and found the student was under the influence of alcohol at school. A school board hearing was held to consider expulsion for attending school after drinking alcohol and disrupting the orderly conduct of the school.

A final school board order expelled the student for substantially disrupting the orderly conduct of the school and for gross misconduct in violation of a school policy against drinking alcohol. On appeal, a Florida District Court of Appeal found **Section 1006.07 of Florida Statutes and the own school's policy limited the board's power to punish students to conduct occurring on school grounds or during school-provided transportation**. In this case, the consumption of alcohol occurred at the student's residence about 45 minutes before school began. As she argued, the board could not punish her for drinking alcohol at home. There was no evidence that the student was under the influence of alcohol at school or that she behaved in an impaired manner. Since the court found no evidence that the student disrupted the learning environment despite her ingestion of alcohol, she could not be expelled under the school policy. As a result, the court vacated the school board's decision. *A.B.E. v. School Board of Brevard County*, 33 So.3d 795 (Fla. Dist. Ct. App. 2010).

## B.  Random Search Policies

*The U.S. Supreme Court has upheld random testing programs for students seeking to participate in extracurricular activities and use school parking facilities. According to the Court, students participating in extracurricular programs have a reduced expectation of privacy when compared to the general student population, justifying random testing. See Chapter Thirteen for more cases concerning random searches of students in interscholastic athletics.*

◆   An Oregon school district responded to increased student drug use by instituting a random drug-testing policy for all students wishing to participate in varsity athletics. A student who wanted to play football refused to sign the drug-testing consent form and was suspended from sports for the season. His parents sued the district in a federal district court. The court upheld the policy, but the Ninth Circuit held it violated the U.S. and Oregon Constitutions. On appeal, the Supreme Court noted **students have a lesser expectation of**

**privacy than the general populace, and that student-athletes had an even lower expectation of privacy in the locker room.** The Supreme Court held the invasion of privacy in this case was no worse than what was typically encountered in public restrooms. Positive test results were disclosed to only a limited number of school employees. **The insignificant invasion of student privacy was outweighed by the district's important interest in addressing drug use by students who risked physical harm while playing sports.** The Court vacated the judgment and remanded the case. *Vernonia School Dist. 47J v. Acton*, 515 U.S. 646, 115 S.Ct. 2386, 132 L.Ed.2d 564 (1995).

◆ An Oklahoma school district adopted a policy requiring all students who sought to participate in extracurricular activities to submit to random drug testing. A student challenged the policy in a federal district court, which awarded summary judgment to the board. On appeal, the Tenth Circuit held student drug use in the Oklahoma district was far from epidemic or an immediate crisis and reversed the judgment. The board appealed to the U.S. Supreme Court, which noted the testing policy was adopted to protect students.

   **The Court found no reason to limit drug testing to student-athletes, extending *Vernonia* to cover all extracurricular activities participants.** Participants in these activities had limited privacy rights, as they voluntarily subjected themselves to certain intrusions on their privacy. They also agreed to abide by extracurricular club rules and requirements that did not apply to the student body at large. The policy's intrusion on student privacy was minimal. Test results could have no impact on student discipline or academics, but could only lead to the limitation of extracurricular activities participation. By contrast, the district and board had an important interest in preventing student drug use. The Court found sufficient evidence of drug use by students to justify the policy. **It deemed the policy a reasonably effective means of addressing legitimate concerns in preventing, deterring and detecting student drug use.** *Board of Educ. of Independent School Dist. 92, Pottawatomie County v. Earls*, 536 U.S. 822, 122 S.Ct. 2559, 153 L.Ed.2d 735 (2002).

◆ A federal district court held that daily searches of disabled students at segregated facilities operated by a public school special education cooperative violated the Fourth Amendment prohibition on unreasonable searches and seizures. **The court found the cooperative's programs were educational and not punitive in nature.** This distinguished the case from *C.N.H. v. Florida*, 927 So.2d 1 (Fla. Dist. Ct. App. 2006), where a court approved of daily pat-down searches at an alternative school where students attended by court order and in lieu of confinement. In this case, the students did not attend school in lieu of detention. **A policy of daily, suspicionless searches was unconstitutional.** A jury would have to decide whether daily searches over a course of years was "highly offensive" under state law principles. *Hough v. Shakopee Public Schools*, 608 F.Supp.2d 1087 (D. Minn. 2009).

◆ An Arkansas district handbook permitted random searches of book bags, backpacks, purses and other containers at all times on school property. A staff member found some marijuana in a student's purse after all the students in her classroom were ordered to wait in the hall during a search. The student sued the district for constitutional rights violations. A court awarded pretrial judgment to the district, and the student appealed. The Eighth Circuit held that students have a legitimate, though limited, privacy expectation in their personal belongings while in school. Subjecting them to full-scale searches without any suspicion of wrongdoing virtually eliminated their privacy interests. There was no evidence of any special circumstances that would justify the intrusiveness of the district policy. **Searches involving "people rummaging through personal belongings" were much more intrusive than searches involving metal detectors or police dogs.** As the policy was highly intrusive and not justified by any significant school interest, the court held that it violated the Fourth Amendment. *Doe v. Little Rock School Dist.*, 380 F.3d 349 (8th Cir. 2004).

◆    A Pennsylvania school district required students who sought to participate in extracurricular activities or obtain a school parking permit to agree to random urinalysis testing. The policy was intended to deter drug use, prevent physical harm and require students to serve as role models for their peers. Two students sued the district for violating Article I, Section 8 of the Pennsylvania Constitution, which prohibits unreasonable searches and seizures. The court held for the district, but the Commonwealth Court of Pennsylvania reversed.

On appeal, the Supreme Court of Pennsylvania said Article I, Section 8 recognized stronger privacy interests than those recognized by the Fourth Amendment. And here, the policy was not a trivial incursion on student privacy. Students had a reasonable expectation that their excretory functions would only be modestly diminished at school. The district suggested no specialized need to test students for drugs and alcohol based on an existing problem, and there was no showing the group targeted for testing presented a drug problem. The policy unconstitutionally authorized a direct invasion on student privacy, with no suspicion that targeted students used drugs or alcohol in greater numbers than those who were exempt. The court held that **random testing of all students in extracurricular activities was unreasonable**, and it affirmed the judgment. *Theodore v. Delaware Valley School Dist.*, 575 Pa. 321, 836 A.2d 76 (Pa. 2003).

◆    A New Jersey school district implemented a series of policies to deter students from using drugs and alcohol, and to refer those with abuse problems into counseling. The school board implemented a random drug-and alcohol-testing program for all interscholastic sports participants. It later accepted a task force recommendation to expand the testing to all extracurricular participants and those who held school parking permits. Test results were confidential and those who tested positive for drug or alcohol use did not face other school penalties or criminal prosecution. Parents sued the board and superintendent for violating Article I, Paragraph 7 of the New Jersey Constitution.

The case reached the Supreme Court of New Jersey, which commented that Article I, Paragraph 7 was nearly identical to the Fourth Amendment. The court employed the *Vernonia* factors for evaluating the constitutionality of testing programs for interscholastic sports participants. It embraced U.S. Supreme Court language approving of the use of minimally obtrusive drug testing to address the nationwide drug epidemic. The testing program was justified by the special need to maintain school order and safety. **Extracurricular activities participants and those seeking parking privileges subjected themselves to additional regulation that did not apply to all students.** The collection process afforded privacy and protected personal dignity. The court rejected the parents' invitation to interpret the state constitution as providing greater protection of individual rights than the Fourth Amendment. It affirmed the decision, cautioning other districts not to interpret its holding as "an automatic green light" to replicate the district's program. *Joye v. Hunterdon Cent. Regional High School Board of Educ.*, 176 N.J. 568, 826 A.2d 624 (N.J. 2003).

◆ An Indiana district adopted a random drug-testing policy for students in grades 7-12 who participated in school athletics, extracurricular and co-curricular activities, and those who wished to park vehicles on campus. Positive tests did not result in academic penalties, were not documented and were not disclosed to legal authorities. Those who submitted negative retests had their privileges reinstated, but those who submitted positive retests could be retested and barred from returning to activities for up to a year. Two students who participated in extracurricular activities sued the district for violations of the Indiana Constitution. A state court held for the district, and the case reached the Supreme Court of Indiana. It rejected the students' claim that the policy should be analyzed under the "individualized suspicion standard" applicable to police. **School searches were substantively different from law enforcement searches because the relationship between school officials and students was not adversarial.** School officials did not offer test results to law enforcement agencies or use them for school discipline, undercutting the rationale for use of an individualized suspicion standard. Students enjoy less privacy at school than do adults in comparable situations. The voluntary decision to submit to drug testing further decreased student privacy expectations. The policy only deprived students of participation in the extracurricular part of an activity and was upheld. *Linke v. Northwestern School Corp.*, 763 N.E.2d 972 (Ind. 2002).

## C. Police Involvement

*School officials are not agents of the police, as they act to ensure student safety and maintain school order, not combat crime. For this reason, the courts have held school officials do not need to advise students of their Fifth Amendment rights or have probable cause to conduct student searches. However, the presence of municipal police during a school search may complicate the correct constitutional standard to apply.*

### 1. *Miranda* Warnings

*When persons are taken into police custody, they must be advised of their Fifth and Sixth Amendment rights. Otherwise, any statement may not be used in juvenile or criminal proceedings. The advisory includes the right to remain silent, to know that any statement can be used against the person in court, and the right to have assistance of counsel. This is known as a "Miranda warning," based on* Miranda v. Arizona, *384 U.S. 436 (1966).*

*Courts in Texas, Rhode Island, New Jersey, Massachusetts, Florida and California have held school liaison officers need not issue* Miranda *warnings when questioning students about school rules violations, but the Supreme Court of Pennsylvania has held they must. The Oregon Court of Appeals refused to apply the* Miranda *requirement in a civil action to reverse a school expulsion.*

◆   An anonymous informant told Wisconsin school officials that a student had drugs at school. He consented to the search of his person, book bag and locker by a school liaison officer and a municipal police officer. When no drugs were found, an assistant principal searched the student's car and found marijuana, a pipe, Oxycontin and cash. She turned over these items to the police, who arrested the student and took him to the police station, where he received his criminal rights warnings, known as "*Miranda* rights." Prior to trial, the student sought to exclude evidence seized from his car and any statements he made during the investigation. He claimed he was "in custody" of the police at the time he was questioned in the parking lot. If this was the case, it was necessary to read him his *Miranda* rights at that time. The court denied the student's motions to suppress his statements and the evidence seized from his car.

On appeal, the Court of Appeals of Wisconsin found ***Miranda* warnings are only required when a person is in police "custody."** Whether a person is in custody depends upon the circumstances. Formal arrest, restraint on freedom of movement, or interrogation that is likely to elicit an incriminating response are examples of "custody" for *Miranda* purposes. Here, while the student was "escorted" to his car by police, an assistant principal was still in control of the investigation, up to and including the search of the car. Moreover, the student was not cuffed, and he was not detained for more than 15 minutes. Finding that a reasonable person would not have considered himself to be in "custody" at the time, the student was not entitled to have his *Miranda* rights read to him in the parking lot. The court also found the search reasonable under the circumstances. *State of Wisconsin v. Schloegel*, 769 N.W.2d 130 (Wis. Ct. App. 2009).

◆   A Tennessee student told a school resource officer that marijuana found in his truck belonged to him. As they returned to the school building, the student also admitted he had left school to smoke marijuana with a friend that morning. The resource officer took the student to juvenile court and charged him. The student later moved to suppress his statements on grounds that she did not inform him of his *Miranda* rights prior to questioning. The juvenile court denied the student's motion, finding the student was not in police custody at the time.

On appeal, the Supreme Court of Tennessee held that **the student was not confined for questioning, and he was not in police "custody."** Thus, his incriminating statements had been properly admitted into evidence. However, since *T.L.O.* was decided, there has been an increased presence of law enforcement officers in public schools. Municipalities have "blended" the traditional duties of school officials and law officers to protect the safety of students and teachers. Based on the resource officer's duties, a new trial would be held to find whether the search required probable cause or reasonable suspicion. *R.D.S. v. State of Tennessee*, 245 S.W.3d 356 (Tenn. 2008).

◆   A Boston middle school student showed a clear plastic bag containing over 50 bullets to other students. The school resource officer confiscated the bullets, and later conducted a pat-down search that yielded no further evidence. The officer then read the student his *Miranda* warnings and asked him to disclose the location of his gun. The student said he did not have a gun. His mother and grandmother arrived at school, and the officer continued questioning the student without informing the adults of the student's *Miranda* rights. After an expulsion hearing the same day, the student led the officer to the gun, which he had hidden in a yard in a residential area. In juvenile delinquency proceedings, the judge found the resource officer had unlawfully failed to provide the student *Miranda* warnings in the presence of an interested adult, as required by state law.

The case reached the Supreme Judicial Court of Massachusetts, which noted that the juvenile court judge refused to apply the "limited public safety exception" to *Miranda* established by the U.S. Supreme Court in *New York v. Quarles*, 467 U.S. 649 (1984). Here, the student was only 13 years old. **Juvenile suspects under 14 may not waive their *Miranda* rights in the absence of an interested adult, such as a parent.** But the resource officer here was faced with an emergency situation that required him to protect 890 middle school students as well as area residents. Under the circumstances, he reasonably concluded that there was an immediate need to question the student. The student's possession of 50 bullets was enough to support the inference that a gun was in close proximity. This was valid reason to invoke the public safety exception to *Miranda*. Accordingly, the court reversed the juvenile court order. *Comwlth. v. Dillon D.*, 448 Mass. 793, 863 N.E.2d 1287 (Mass. 2007).

◆   Several Virginia elementary school students reported to their teacher that a 10-year-old student brought a gun to school. An assistant principal questioned the student repeatedly in her office and searched her book bag and desk. After no weapon was found, the assistant principal allowed the student to leave. The following Monday, the assistant principal and principal interviewed some of the student witnesses. One of them said the student had thrown a handgun into the woods adjoining the school. School officials called police and brought the student to the office. They resumed the interrogation, despite her complaints of illness and requests to see her mother. The police continued interrogating the student, with school administrators present. The student repeatedly asked for her mother, but officials denied her requests. She claimed they detained her for over one hour and refused to let her go to the lavatory. The officers found no weapon and did not call the student's mother until after they left. The student and her mother sued school and police officials for due process and Fourth Amendment violations. But a federal district court dismissed the case.

The student appealed to the U.S. Court of Appeals, Fourth Circuit, which refused to adopt a general rule requiring school administrators to notify parents during school investigations, or to forbid student detentions of a particular length. Virginia law and school board rules required a principal to make reasonable efforts to contact parents or guardians before police interrogations. The Constitution imposed no parental notification duty while a student was detained. When school officials seize a student in a constitutional manner and tell police the basis for their suspicion, the detention is justified at its inception. **When a**

**student detention justifies police involvement, no Fourth Amendment violation occurs.** The officers detained the student only until they determined that no guns were on school grounds. The court found no fault with the efforts of the school officials to protect school safety, and it affirmed the judgment. *Wofford v. Evans*, 390 F.3d 318 (4th Cir. 2004).

◆    An Oregon student was suspended from school and subjected to a juvenile court adjudication. A vice principal called the student's mother several weeks later, and told her the student was again in the school office. The mother told the vice principal she was very uncomfortable with him talking to her son without his lawyer present. The next month, school officials questioned the student for two hours after a teacher smelled marijuana smoke coming from a restroom while the student and a classmate were there. The student first denied using marijuana, but later admitted it to the vice principal and other officials. As required by school policy, they reported this admission to municipal police.

After the school board voted for expulsion, the student appealed to an Oregon trial court, claiming he was entitled to *Miranda* warnings when he was questioned by school officials. The court dismissed the case because no police officers were involved and the matter was not a criminal prosecution. The student appealed to the Court of Appeals of Oregon, which **found no authority for suppressing evidence in a school disciplinary hearing on grounds of failure to administer *Miranda* warnings**. A school expulsion did not resemble the deprivation of liberty present in criminal cases. The differences between a school expulsion and a juvenile proceeding required affirming the judgment for the school officials. *T.M.M. v. Lake Oswego School Dist.*, 198 Or.App. 572, 108 P.3d 1211 (Or. Ct. App. 2005).

## 2.  Police-Assisted Searches

◆    A Texas school parking lot attendant told the principal that three students were smoking in a car parked in a school lot. The principal encountered the students and directed them to her office. She noted that one of them wore baggy shorts and believed he might have a concealed weapon. The student refused her request to empty his pockets and she obtained the assistance of a municipal police officer assigned to the high school. **The officer patted down the student and found him in possession of marijuana.** The state prosecuted the student in juvenile court for possession of marijuana in a drug-free zone. The court denied the student's pretrial motion to suppress the marijuana. He pleaded no contest to drug possession and was fined and placed under community supervision for one year. The student appealed to the Texas Court of Appeals.

On appeal, the student claimed the officer lacked reasonable suspicion to pat him down. The court held that **where school officials initiate a search, or police involvement is minimal, the "reasonable suspicion" test applies**, not the more exacting "probable cause" standard applicable to traditional law enforcement searches. Because the student was smoking in the parking lot, wore baggy shorts and refused to empty his pockets, reasonable grounds existed for suspecting a search would turn up evidence of a rules violation. The search was reasonably related to the objectives of the search and not excessively intrusive in view of the student's age and sex. So it did not violate the Fourth Amendment. *Russell v. State of Texas*, 74 S.W.3d 887 (Tex. Ct. App. 2002).

◆ A resource officer was assigned to work at a New Hampshire school by the municipal police department. Due to the many searches there, administrators agreed to investigate less serious matters, including drug possession, and refer those involving weapons or a threat to school safety to the officer. If the officer felt he lacked probable cause for an arrest, he would deem the case a "school issue" and let administrators handle it. A science teacher observed a student passing tinfoil to a classmate and reported it to the resource officer. The officer referred the student to an assistant principal. The assistant principal and another administrator questioned the student and asked if they could search him. He agreed and they discovered tinfoil that the student admitted "might be LSD." The administrators contacted the resource officer and returned the case to him.

A state court granted the student's motion to suppress evidence found by the administrators, finding they acted as agents of the police and had to provide him the safeguards afforded to criminal suspects. The state appealed to the New Hampshire Supreme Court, which noted that **school officials may take on the mantle of criminal investigators if they assume police duties. That is what occurred in this case**, as there was an understanding between the resource officer and school officials on how violations would be investigated. The court cautioned school administrators to "be vigilant not to assume responsibilities beyond the scope of their administrative duties" when establishing working relationships with police. Because an agency relationship existed between the police and school officials, the court affirmed the order for the student. *State of New Hampshire v. Heirtzler*, 789 A.2d 634 (N.H. 2001).

### 3. Drug-Sniffing Dogs

*In Burbank v. Canton Board of Educ., below, a Connecticut court applied a "public smell doctrine" to a search of school lockers and parking lots using police dogs. The court relied on a 1982 Texas case which reasoned that the **use of dogs to sniff for contraband in unattended lockers and cars is not a Fourth Amendment "search"** at all. Odors emanating from a person or property are "considered exposed to the public 'view' and, therefore, unprotected." Horton v. Goose Creek Independent School Dist., 690 F.2d 470 (5th Cir. 1982).*

◆ A Connecticut school board regulation authorized drug searches by dogs of school property to which students had access during the school day, including lockers, classrooms and parking areas. Dogs were not allowed to sniff persons and were not used in occupied classrooms. During the first period of a school day, the principals of a middle and high school announced a dog sweep search, and alerted students and faculty that they were to "stay put" in their classrooms, unless an emergency occurred. A dog alerted on one car in a school parking lot, and a student was arrested for a small amount of marijuana found there.

Students had to remain in their first period classes for about one hour and 50 minutes, and missed at least one full class period. Several parents asked a state court for a permanent order to either prohibit warrantless dog-sniff sweep searches, or require notice to parents at least 48 hours in advance of any search. The court stated that **dog-sniff searches of cars or unattended lockers were not even a "search" under the Fourth Amendment**. Requiring students to stay in their classrooms for over an hour was not a "seizure," as the families claimed. Here, the students would have normally been in class at the time of the search anyway. And the parents had no right to receive advance notice of dog-sniff searches, as they claimed. The court denied the parents' request for an order to halt the dog sweeps or to receive advance notice of future sweep searches. *Burbank v. Canton Board of Educ.*, No. CV 094043192S, 2009 WL 3366272 (Conn. Ct. Super. 9/14/09).

◆    An Alabama county sheriff's department conducted a drug-sweep search using drug-sniffing dogs at a school. A small package of drugs was found under a table where a student had been sitting. Law officers patted him down and asked him to empty his pockets. After a classmate said that the drugs belonged to the student, two male officers took him to a teachers' lounge, where a strip search yielded no further drugs. A second student was asked to empty his pockets onto a table in the cafeteria where all vocational students had been taken. The officers then led their dogs through the cafeteria and patted down students, even though no dogs alerted. A third student was called to the school parking lot when dogs alerted on his car. He then attempted to swallow a small package, and officers tried to make him spit it out. The third student admitted the package contained marijuana seeds, and the officers made him strip to his underwear while in the parking lot. The students sued the school board, school officials and law enforcement officers for violating their constitutional rights.

The court found the search of the first student was reasonable. Drugs were found at his table, and a classmate said he had placed them there. The police therefore had "individualized suspicion" of a violation. The second student did not show any constitutional violation occurred when he was required to empty his pockets. **A search may be conducted without individualized suspicion when student privacy interests are minimal and important governmental interests exist.** As the search was reasonably related to the objective of finding illegal drugs, it met the *T.L.O.* reasonableness standard. The search of the third student was supported by individualized suspicion, as sniffing dogs had alerted to his car. However, the search was excessively intrusive because the police officers required him to strip to his underwear while in a public parking lot. The school officials were entitled to judgment, however, as there was no evidence that they participated in any constitutional rights violation. *Rudolph v. Lowndes County Board of Educ.*, 242 F.Supp.2d 1107 (M.D. Ala. 2003).

### 4.  Liability Issues

*In* Chavez v. Martinez, *538 U.S. 760 (2003), the U.S. Supreme Court held courts cannot award damages against police investigators who wrongly induce suspects to provide incriminating information unless it is actually used in a criminal prosecution. Until compelled statements are used in a criminal case, there is no potential violation of the Fifth Amendment self-incrimination clause.*

◆ A Miami-area high school student was spotted walking away from the campus of a school he did not attend at 7:25 a.m. Police had warned him not to enter the school's safety zone on two prior occasions, and they arrested him. State prosecutors filed a delinquency petition against the student, and he was charged with trespass in a school safety zone and resisting arrest. The student moved to dismiss the petition, arguing that the law unconstitutionally restricted peaceful conduct and communication.

The case reached the Florida District Court of Appeal, Third District, which observed that a Florida statute makes it unlawful for any person to enter a "school safety zone" without legitimate business or other authorization at the school from one hour prior to the start of school until one hour after the end of school. The statute allowed those with proper authorization or legitimate business at a school to remain in a school zone. The student did not show that persons seeking to engage in constitutionally protected speech or assemblies could not receive "authorization" to do so. He did not show that persons who had received notices barring them from school safety zones have First Amendment rights to return to a school safety zone to express themselves. **The law was clearly intended to protect children, which is a compelling government interest.** The court affirmed the order declaring the student a juvenile delinquent. *J.L.S. v. State*, 947 So.2d 641 (Fla. Dist. Ct. App. 2007).

◆ An Idaho high school custodian discovered a stack of flyers in a school parking lot alleging sexual activities by a local judge's daughter. The principal investigated the incident and learned who made the documents. She also found that the documents were not produced at school. About two months later, the judge came to the school and sought to interview some students about a note he had received concerning his daughter's conduct. The principal allowed the judge and a staff member to interview three students without notice to their parents. This violated a school policy. The three students sued the principal and school district, asserting civil rights and tort claims. A federal district court held that there was no "search" under the Fourth Amendment. However, it was possible that the students were "seized" and underwent due process violations.

The students said they did not feel free to leave the office, and were aware of the judge's position. It appeared he had threatened at least one student with prosecution for failing to answer a question. Some of the questions had nothing to do with the note and might have been beyond the scope of the school's interest or authority. At the time of the interview, the principal already knew who had written the note. The court denied her request for qualified immunity, as she allowed the interviews without first contacting parents, in violation of district policies and due process guidelines. **There was no reasonable educational interest in asking students about their off-campus sexual activities or their interpersonal relationships.** A trial was required. *Howard v. Yakovac*, No. CV 04-202-S-ELJ, 2006 WL 1207615 (D. Idaho 2006).

◆ An Idaho student was developmentally disabled and had a form of autism. His school called a police officer to his class twice to observe his aggressive behavior with school staff. During one episode, the student hit the officer while she was trying to calm him. On another day, the student continuously tapped on his desk and was "verbally aggressive" toward teachers. School staff called the officer, who attempted to block the student from exiting, then took him to the floor, handcuffed him and hobbled his legs. After being restrained, the student was sent to hospital on "mental hold," while he struggled against confinement and remained verbally aggressive. The student later sued the school district and the police officer, claiming the district was negligent and the officer used excessive force in violation of the Fourth Amendment. A court held that the district and officer were immune. The student appealed to the U.S. Court of Appeals, Ninth Circuit, arguing that the district breached a duty to protect him by calling the police officer, creating an unreasonable risk of harm.

The court observed that the district did not employ the officer and had no real or apparent authority over her. **The district did not breach an asserted duty to intervene in her handling of the incident.** The student did not show that the district could have foreseen the officer would harm or endanger him. She knew of non-invasive techniques and had been able to calm him during past episodes. The type and amount of force the officer used was excessive. However, she was entitled to qualified immunity. There was no clearly established right to be free of the kind of force used in this case. *Hayenga v. Nampa School Dist. No. 131*, 123 Fed.Appx. 783 (9th Cir. 2005).

◆    A New York school employee told a middle school principal that two high school students regularly sold marijuana at their school. The principal accompanied the employee to the high school principal's office to report this. The employee learned from students that the high school students were planning to bring marijuana to school. She reported this to a state police officer, who came to the school and asked the principal to search the students. The principal agreed, and the students were searched separately by the principal, school dean and officer. They were asked to empty their pockets and book bags, to raise pants legs to expose their socks, and finally to drop their pants and turn around. Neither student was touched at any time, and no drugs were found.

One of the students alleged that other students saw him through the window of the principal's office in only his underwear. His father sued the district, principal and officer for civil rights violations. A court noted that *New Jersey v. T.L.O.* does not explain the legal standard to apply when police and school officials combine to conduct a school search. The court held for the district, principal and officer. A state appellate division court held that officials who perform discretionary functions are entitled to qualified immunity if their conduct does not violate clearly established rights of which a reasonable person would have known. The court acknowledged the ambiguous state of the law in mixed police/school searches. Given this ambiguity, **police officers of reasonable competence could have disagreed about whether probable cause was required for a search conducted by school officials.** The complaint against the officer had been correctly dismissed. *Doyle v. Rondout Valley Cent. School Dist.*, 770 N.Y.S.2d 480 (N.Y. App. Div. 2004).

# CHAPTER THREE

## Freedom of Speech and Association

## I. STUDENTS

*For over 40 years, courts have analyzed student speech cases under* Tinker v. Des Moines Independent Community School Dist., *393 U.S. 503 (1969).* Tinker *was the first U.S. Supreme Court case to recognize student speech rights in schools. In it, the Court held that in order to regulate student speech, school officials must show "the student's activities would materially and substantially disrupt the work and discipline of the school."* Tinker *remains the starting point for student speech rights cases, but as the U.S. Court of Appeals, Fifth Circuit, recently observed, "since* Tinker, *every Supreme Court decision looking at speech has expanded the kinds of speech schools can regulate."*

The Supreme Court declined to apply Tinker *in its most recent student speech rights case,* Morse v. Frederick, *551 U.S. 393 (2007), below, noting "the constitutional rights of students in public school are not automatically coextensive with the rights of adults in other settings."*

◆    A Mississippi student asked school administrators if she could attend her high school prom in a tuxedo with her same-sex partner. She was told that only boys were allowed to wear tuxedos to the prom and that girls would be required to wear dresses and could not slow dance together. After the student contacted the ACLU and threatened a lawsuit, the school board met and decided not to host a prom. In a federal district court action, the court found the board's claim that it only "withdrew its sponsorship" from the prom was "nothing more than semantics." The board had effectively cancelled the prom. The court found support for the student's First Amendment claim based on her identity and affiliation with a unique social group. **Government entities "cannot set-out homosexuals for special treatment."** In *Fricke v. Lynch*, 491 F.Supp. 381 (D.R.I. 1980), the court held a male student's desire to take a same-sex date to his prom "had significant expressive content which brought it within the ambit of the First Amendment." Additional support for the student's position came from a state circuit court in Alabama which held in 2008 that a school board could not legally cancel a prom to prevent a same-sex couple from attending.

**Based on clearly established case law, the court found the board violated the student's rights by denying her request to bring her girlfriend as her date to the prom.** Since she had been openly gay since eighth grade, the court held her wish to wear a tuxedo and attend the prom with a girl represented an intent to communicate a message that was protected by the First Amendment. While the student established a substantial likelihood of success on the merits of her First Amendment claim, she did not convince the court that the order she was requesting would be in the public interest. A parent-sponsored prom had been offered, and school officials represented that she would be welcome there. Relief was denied as against the public interest. *McMillen v. Itawamba County School Dist.*, 702 F.Supp.2d 699 (N.D. Miss. 2010).

◆    An 18-year-old Alaska high school student observed an Olympic Torch Relay that passed in front of his school. The school principal deemed the relay a school-approved social event or class trip. As torchbearers and camera crews passed, the student and his friends unfurled a 14-foot banner bearing the phrase "Bong Hits 4 Jesus." The principal instructed them to take down the banner, but the student refused to comply. She confiscated the banner and suspended him for 10 days. The district superintendent reduced the suspension to eight days. He found the principal had based the discipline on the banner's advocacy of illegal drug use, and not on any disagreement with the message. The school board also affirmed the suspension, and its decision was upheld by a federal district court.

Appeal reached the U.S. Supreme Court, which held the case involved "school speech." The relay was held during school hours and was sanctioned by the principal as "an approved social event or class trip." The board's rules were universally applied to school social events and class trips. The banner was directed to the school and was plainly visible to most students. **The principal reasonably determined that the banner would be interpreted by viewers as promoting illegal drug use.** While the message might be regarded as cryptic, offensive, amusing or nonsense, the Court agreed with the principal that it might advocate the use of illegal drugs. Supreme Court decisions on drug testing of student extracurricular programs have recognized that deterring drug use is an important and perhaps compelling interest. School officials in this case were dealing with a "far more serious and palpable" danger than that faced in *Tinker v. Des Moines Independent Community School Dist.*, below. The Court held that to allow the banner would have sent a powerful message to students that the school was not serious about its anti-drug message and the dangers of illegal drug use. *Morse v. Frederick*, 551 U.S. 393 (2007).

◆ In 1965, a group of Iowa adults and high school students publicized their objections to the hostilities in Vietnam by wearing black armbands during the holiday season. Three students and their parents had previously engaged in similar activities, and they decided to participate in this program. The principals of Des Moines schools became aware of the plan and adopted a policy that **any student wearing an armband to school would be asked to remove it or face suspension**. The three students wore their armbands and were all suspended until they agreed to come back without the armbands. The students did not return to their school until the planned protest period had ended.

The students sued the school district for First Amendment violations under 42 U.S.C. § 1983, seeking to prevent school officials from disciplining them, plus their nominal damages. A federal district court dismissed the complaint and the Eighth Circuit summarily affirmed the decision. On appeal, the Supreme Court stated neither students nor teachers shed their constitutional rights to freedom of speech or expression at the schoolhouse gate. **In order for school officials to justify prohibition of a particular expression of opinion, they must show something more than a mere desire to avoid the discomfort and unpleasantness associated with unpopular viewpoints.** Where there was no evidence that student expression would materially interfere with the requirements of appropriate discipline in the operation of the school, or collide with the rights of others, the prohibition was improper. The expressive act of wearing black armbands did not interrupt school activities or intrude in school affairs. The Court reversed the lower court decisions. *Tinker v. Des Moines Independent Community School Dist.*, 393 U.S. 503, 89 S.Ct. 733, 21 L.Ed.2d 733 (1969).

◆ A Washington high school student gave a speech nominating a classmate for a student election before an assembly of over 600 peers. All students were required to attend the assembly as part of the school's self-government program. **In his nominating speech, the student referred to his candidate in terms of an elaborate, explicit sexual metaphor, despite having been warned in advance by teachers not to do so.** Student reactions to the speech included laughter, graphic sexual gestures, hooting, bewilderment and embarrassment. When the student admitted he had deliberately used sexual innuendo in his speech, he was informed that he would be suspended for three days and that his name would be removed from the list of candidates for student speaker at graduation. The student sued the school district in a federal district court, claiming his First Amendment right to freedom of speech had been violated.

The court agreed and awarded him damages and attorneys' fees. It also ordered the school district to allow the student to speak at graduation. The decision was affirmed by the Ninth Circuit, under the authority of *Tinker*. On appeal, the Supreme Court reversed the decision, holding that **while public school students have the right to advocate unpopular and controversial views in school, that right must be balanced against the school interest in teaching socially appropriate behavior**. The Constitution does not protect obscene language, and a public school, as an instrument of the state, may legitimately establish standards of civil and mature conduct. *Bethel School Dist. No. 403 v. Fraser*, 478 U.S. 675, 106 S.Ct. 3159, 92 L.Ed.2d 549 (1986).

## A. Protected Speech

### 1. Disciplinary Cases

◆  A California student and three others walked out of their middle school with the intent of participating in protests against pending immigration reform measures. The middle school vice principal allegedly threatened them harshly with discipline upon their return, calling them "dumb, dumb and dumber" and warning them of the possible legal consequences of their truancy. He also allegedly threatened them with a $250 fine and juvenile sentencing, but this did not occur. After returning home on the day of the discipline, the student committed suicide, leaving a note that stated "I killed myself because I have too many problems. ... Tell my teachers they're the best and tell [the vice principal] he is a mother f#@(-)ker." The student's estate sued the school district, vice principal and others for constitutional and state law violations. The case reached the U.S. Court of Appeals, Ninth Circuit, which found that **no First Amendment retaliation claim could be based on threats of discipline if it was based on a lawful consequence that was never administered**.

The policy of disciplining truancy violated no First Amendment rights, even if the students sought to leave for expressive purposes. Further, the vice principal's words were not a form of corporal punishment, and nothing indicated that he had a retaliatory or discriminatory motive. Finally, since the suicide was not foreseeable, the estate failed to show negligence. The court affirmed the judgment. *Corales v. Bennett*, 567 F.3d 554 (9th Cir. 2009).

◆  Tennessee students claimed that their varsity football coach humiliated and degraded players, used inappropriate language and required them to participate in a year-round conditioning program that violated school rules. He also apparently hit a player in the helmet and threw away college recruiting letters sent to "disfavored players." One student typed a petition to remove the coach, which eighteen players signed. When the coach learned of this, he summoned players into his office one by one to interview them. Players who signed the petition were allowed to stay on the team if they apologized and said they wanted to play for him. Four players who did not apologize were taken off the team. These students sued the coach, school board and others for First Amendment violations. The case reached the U.S. Court of Appeals, Sixth Circuit, which noted that the players did not dispute their insubordinate actions during a team meeting. "Student athletes are subject to more restrictions than the student body at large." **The petition was a direct challenge to the coach's authority.** Therefore, it was not protected speech and there was no First Amendment violation. *Lowery v. Euverard*, 497 F.3d 584 (6th Cir. 2007).

◆    About 300 Hispanic students walked out of a Texas school to protest immigration reforms pending in Congress. Many wore T-shirts stating "We Are Not Criminals." The school principal, himself Hispanic, learned that some students planned to walk out of school the next day. Other faculty members believed some Caucasian and African-American students planned to wear T-shirts reading "Border Patrol" to antagonize them. The principal announced that any students who wore unauthorized shirts would be sent to the office, but about 130 students walked out of school. These students were suspended for three days. School administrators called most of their parents, but some students did not learn of the suspensions until they reported to school the next day. Many angry parents came to school, demanding to meet with the principal. After some parents refused to leave the building, school security asked them to leave.

Several families sued the district and superintendent in a federal district court for First Amendment violations. The court held **the principal acted to prevent disruption of the educational process**. Students were warned not to wear unauthorized T-shirts on the second day to prevent a possible race riot. "Where school administrators reasonably believe the students' uncontrolled exercise of expression would materially and substantially interfere with the work of the school or impinge upon the rights of other students, they may forbid such expression." The principal did not violate the First Amendment. *Doe v. Grove Public School Dist.*, 510 F.Supp.2d 425 (S.D. Tex. 2007).

◆    Most members of the boys varsity basketball team at an Oregon high school claimed that their head coach used abusive tactics, intimidated them, yelled incessantly and used profanity. After a game, the coach told them he would resign if they wanted it. The players drafted a petition requesting his resignation, and all but two players signed it. After the coach brought the petition to his principal, the school's athletic director and principal met with the team and told them they would have to board the team bus for a game that evening or forfeit their privilege to play in the game. Eight of them did not board the bus. The principal permanently suspended players who refused to board the bus from the team. They sued the coach, principal, and school district for speech rights violations. A federal court upheld the discipline, finding the students' speech and conduct were not constitutionally protected.

The students appealed to the Ninth Circuit, which found that the petition and grievances against the coach were "a form of pure speech." The students could not be disciplined unless there was a reasonable forecast of substantial disruption or material interference. The First Amendment protected the petition and the complaints to school administrators. However, the boycott of the game substantially disrupted and materially interfered with a school activity. **If**

**students decide not to participate in an extracurricular activity on the day it is scheduled to take place, "their conduct will inevitably disrupt or interfere with the activity."** This was true even if the event was not cancelled. The case was remanded for further proceedings. *Pinard v. Clatskanie School Dist. 6J*, 446 F.3d 964 (9th Cir. 2006).

## 2. Threats and Bullying

*In* Boim v. Fulton County School Board, *this chapter, the U.S. Court of Appeals, Eleventh Circuit, compared threatening speech to falsely yelling 'fire' in a crowded theater. The court cited* Schenck v. U.S., *249 U.S. 47 (1919), the Supreme Court decision in which Justice Oliver Wendell Holmes stated the famous "yelling fire in a movie house" rule.*

◆  Death threats and insults based on sexual orientation were posted to the website of a California private school student. After some classmates were implicated in the postings, the student's father called the police. Based on a recommendation by the police, the family moved. The private school newspaper reported the postings and revealed the family's new address. The student filed a state court action against the school for negligence, violation of state hate crime laws and related claims. The case was dismissed and arbitrated under an agreement in the private school contract. An arbitrator held the school was not liable for the student postings, even though some of them were made from school computers. Under the arbitration agreement, the prevailing party was entitled to its costs and legal fees. The state court of appeal reversed an award of fees and costs of more than $521,000 which the arbitrator had made to the school.

The student filed a separate action in a California court, asserting violation of state hate crimes laws, defamation and infliction of emotional distress. The classmate asserted his comments were of public interest and protected by the First Amendment. He also said he intended the message as "jocular humor." The court denied the classmate's motion to strike the claims under a state strategic lawsuit against public participation (anti-SLAPP) statute. The classmate appealed to the Court of Appeal of California, which held he did not show the student's complaint was subject to the anti-SLAPP statute. **The classmate did not show the message was protected speech.** Even if the message was a teenage joke, the court found it did not concern a public issue. *D.C. v. R.R.*, 182 Cal.App.4th 1190, 106 Cal.Rptr.3d 399 (Cal. Ct. App. 2010).

◆  A New York student was accused of making an insulting remark after a Hispanic student died in a motorcycle accident. The student said he was only repeating a remark he heard elsewhere, but Hispanic students confronted him at school and the police were called. He was escorted from school for his own protection. In the next few days, the principal denied requests by the student and his mother to read a letter declaring his innocence or to distribute copies of it. Meanwhile, the threats continued, and police were assigned to protect his house. At a hearing, the superintendent found the student should be expelled for the final weeks of the school year. But the state commissioner of education found insufficient evidence that the student made an offensive remark. As a result, the expulsion was annulled and his record was cleared. After more off-campus threats, the student was sent out of state for his own protection.

A federal district court suit was filed against the school district, board members and administrators for constitutional rights violations. After the court held for the district and officials, appeal reached the U.S. Court of Appeals, Second Circuit. It held the officials had qualified immunity from any liability. Even if the student had a right to return to school to address his classmates, the court found it was reasonable for the officials to believe they were acting within constitutional and statutory bounds. There was no question to the court that the student's "mere presence in the school, with or without his speech, would likely result in violence or the threat of violence." **The question was not whether there had been actual disruption, but whether it could be forecast.** It was reasonable for officials to forecast disruption if they readmitted the student. Since their conduct was objectively reasonable, the lower court correctly awarded them qualified immunity. The court affirmed the judgment. *DeFabio v. East Hampton Union Free School Dist.*, 623 F.3d 71 (2d Cir. 2010).

◆ A New York fifth-grade student turned in an assignment with the words "blow up the school with all the teachers in it." He was suspended from school for five days, with a day of in-school suspension. His parents sued the school district for First Amendment violations. A federal court dismissed the case, explaining that the student's writing created a foreseeable risk of substantial disruption. On appeal, the Second Circuit held that a reasonable jury might find a speech rights violation. **At the time of the incident, the student was in fifth grade. His "threat" was a crayon drawing in response to an assignment, and it was not shared with classmates.** No other discipline suggested the student was violent, and further proceedings were required to decide if there was a foreseeable risk of a material and substantial disruption. The case was returned to the lower court. *Cuff v. Valley Cent. School Dist.*, 341 Fed.Appx. 692 (2d Cir. 2009).

After further consideration, the district court found the student had a record of discipline for misbehavior on the school bus, during recess, in the hallway and in the cafeteria. School staff had found his assignment to be "disturbing." Before turning in the assignment, the student had drawn a person shooting bullets at a group of people and written a story about a squirrel who stalked other squirrels before killing them. There was evidence that the assignment had frightened a child and alarmed the teacher. The court found the student could have acted on his threat. **It held the district did not have to show a substantial disruption was inevitable. Officials only had to show a likelihood of substantial disruption.** Requiring schools to wait until actual disruption occurred before investigating would "cripple the officials' ability to maintain order" and would be "disastrous public policy." Whether the student had the capacity to blow up the school or not was not a deciding factor. Instead, the court held the objective reasonableness of the administration's response was relevant. Based on the facts, the school could have reasonably viewed the student's assignment as an indication of violent intentions. *Cuff v. Valley Cent. School Dist.*, 714 F.Supp.2d 462 (S.D.N.Y. 2010).

◆    A Minnesota student wrote an essay "detailing a fantasy murder-suicide inspired by the school shooting that took place at Columbine High School." He placed the essay in his folder, and his teacher read it a few weeks later. After the teacher reported the disturbing and graphic content of the essay, a child protection worker obtained an order to place the student in protective custody. The student was taken to a youth mental health facility, where he underwent a psychiatric evaluation. He was found not a threat to himself or others, and he was released after a total of 72 hours in custody. The family sued the school district, teacher, principal, and county law enforcement and child protection officials in a federal court for constitutional rights violations. Claims against the school district, teacher and principal were dismissed, but the family proceeded with speech and Fourth Amendment claims against law enforcement and child protection officials. The case reached the U.S. Court of Appeals, Eighth Circuit, which held **the student's essay was unprotected by the First Amendment, which does not protect a "true threat."** The essay was a serious threat, describing the student's "obsession with weapons and gore, a hatred for his English teacher," an attack at a high school, details of his teacher's murder and the narrator's suicide. *Riehm v. Engelking*, 538 F.3d 952 (8th Cir. 2008).

◆    A Texas student's notebook described a pseudo-Nazi group and a plan to commit a Columbine-style school shooting or a "coordinated shooting" at all schools in the district. The entries were reported to an assistant principal, who issued a three-day suspension for making terroristic threats. The student was then assigned to an alternative school. His parents sued the school district for First Amendment violations. The case reached the U.S. Court of Appeals, Fifth Circuit, which noted that the school environment made it possible for a single armed student to cause massive harm with little forewarning. Recent history demonstrated that threats against schools and students must be taken seriously. **Since school administrators could prohibit student speech that advocated illegal drug use, the same rule should apply to speech that threatens violence and massive death to a school population.** As student threats against a student body were not protected, the court found no constitutional violation. *Ponce v. Socorro Independent School Dist.*, 508 F.3d 765 (5th Cir. 2007).

◆    A Georgia high school student wrote a passage in her notebook labeled "Dream." It described, in first person, an account of a student's feelings while taking a gun to school, shooting her math teacher and being chased by the police. The student showed the notebook to a classmate. Her art teacher obtained the notebook and read the passage, then spoke with the school liaison officer and principal about it. The officer believed it was "planning in disguise as a dream," and the student was removed from class the next day.

At a meeting of school officials, the student and her parent, the student dismissed the narrative as creative fiction. The principal suspended the student for 10 days and recommended expelling her for threats of bodily harm, disregard of school rules and disrespectful conduct. The school board voted not to expel her, but it affirmed the suspension and retained a record of it. The student sued the school board for violation of her First Amendment rights. A federal district court held for the school board, and the student appealed to the

U.S. Court of Appeals, Eleventh Circuit. It held that writing the narrative and showing it to a classmate was reasonably likely to cause material and substantial disruption. In the climate of increasing school violence and government oversight, **the school had a compelling interest in acting quickly to prevent violence on school property**. The court found no First Amendment violation. *Boim v. Fulton County School Dist.*, 494 F.3d 978 (11th Cir. 2007).

◆   A South Carolina teacher claimed a student disrupted her classroom for over two hours and took a swing at her. Officials filed a juvenile delinquency petition against him for violating a state statute "by willingly, unlawfully, and unnecessarily interfering with and disturbing the students and teachers." The student argued the law was unconstitutionally vague and overbroad in violation of the First Amendment. A state court upheld the statute and committed the student to the juvenile justice department. The student appealed to the state supreme court, arguing the law was overly broad because it punished protected speech and was so vague that persons of common intelligence would have to guess at its meaning. The court held **the statute did not prohibit any speech that was protected by the First Amendment**. By its terms, it criminalized "conduct that 'disturbs' or 'interferes' with schools, or is 'obnoxious.'" The statute was not a substantial threat to free speech, and dealt with school disturbances, not public forums. The state had a legitimate interest in preserving discipline and could prohibit conduct interfering with the state's legitimate objectives. *In re Amir X.S.*, 371 S.C. 380, 639 S.E.2d 144 (S.C. 2006).

◆   The U.S. Court of Appeals, Third Circuit, held **"a school's authority to control student speech in an elementary school is undoubtedly greater than in a high school setting."** Accordingly, a New Jersey elementary student who was suspended for saying "I'm going to shoot you" during recess did not show any speech rights violation. Her principal was entitled to discretion in finding threats of violence and simulated firearms use unacceptable. Officials need not provide students the same latitude afforded to adults and need not tolerate speech that is inconsistent with a school's basic educational mission. *S.G., as Guardian of A.G. v. Sayreville Board of Educ.*, 333 F.3d 417 (3d Cir. 2003).

### 3. Internet Cases

*In* Doninger v. Niehoff, *527 F.3d 41 (2d Cir. 2008), below, the U.S. Court of Appeals, Second Circuit, found the courts are in "complete disarray" about student cyber-speech. It held school administrators were due immunity for disciplining a student who called them "douchebags," finding "it is certainly unreasonable to expect school administrators ... to predict where the line between on- and off-campus speech will be drawn in this new digital era."*

◆   A California student made a video off campus that showed some of her friends "ranting" about a classmate. The video was then posted on YouTube. An assistant principal viewed the video and told the student to take it off YouTube. Administrators suspended the student for two days, and she filed a federal district court action against the school district. In a 57-page order, the court found no Supreme Court case involving school regulation of off-campus student speech. **Several lower courts have held off-campus student speech that "makes its way onto campus" can be regulated, if the speech is reasonably likely to materially and substantially disrupt school.** The court found *Tinker v. Des Moines Independent Community School Dist.*, this chapter, relevant. It noted the U.S. Court of Appeals, Ninth Circuit, has applied *Tinker* "without regard to the location where the speech originated (off campus or on campus)."

Other courts have found "geographic boundaries generally carry little weight." Where a foreseeable risk of substantial disruption is established, "discipline for such speech is permissible." Applying *Tinker*, the court held school officials need more than undifferentiated fear or apprehension of a disturbance to overcome free expression. At most, the school had to address the concerns of an upset parent, and five students missed some class. *Tinker* did not support suspending the student based on the classmate's "hurt feelings," which "did not cause any type of school disruption." Finding no reasonable jury would believe the video disrupted the school, the court held for the student. Despite the speech rights violation, administrators had qualified immunity, as **the contours of student rights to make "a potentially defamatory and degrading video about a classmate" were not clearly established**. *J.C. v. Beverly Hills Unified School Dist.*, No. 2:08-cv-03824-SVW-CW (C.D. Cal. 11/16/09).

In a separate order, the court held school administrators also violated the student's due process rights. A school discipline manual and student handbook did not put her on notice that she could be punished for speech originating off campus. No language in the state Education Code placed students on notice that off-campus speech could lead to discipline. *J.C. v. Beverly Hills Unified School Dist.*, No. 2:08-cv-03824-SVW-CW (C.D. Cal. 12/8/09).

◆    A Pennsylvania middle school student used a home computer to make a fake profile of her school principal on MySpace.Com. The profile stated that the principal was a "married, bisexual man whose interests include 'fucking in his office' and 'hitting on' students and their parents." After investigating, the principal suspended the student for 10 days. She sued the school district for speech rights violations. Appeal reached the U.S. Court of Appeals, Third Circuit. It held **school authorities need not wait until a substantial disruption actually occurs in order to curb the offending speech**. Off-campus speech that caused (or reasonably threatened) substantial disruption of, or material interference with a school did not have to satisfy any "geographical technicality." The principal's concern was found valid. Insinuations about him on the profile struck at the heart of his fitness to serve in his position. As the profile was available to 22 middle school students with "friend" status on MySpace.com, the court found it was directly targeted at the school. *J.S. v. Blue Mountain School Dist.*, 593 F.3d 286 (3d Cir. 2010, *rehearing granted* 4/9/10).

◆    A Pennsylvania high school student made a MySpace.com parody of his principal at his grandmother's house, using her computer during non-school hours. He used a photo of the principal from the school website and created bogus answers to survey questions on the site which indicated that the principal was a drug user whose "interests" were "transgender, appreciators of alcoholic beverages." The student accessed his web page at school and showed it to others. Student use of computer labs was limited for a week due to the school's response to the web profile. After the principal identified the student as the parody's creator, he suspended him for 10 days, placed him in an alternative program, banned him from extracurricular programs and denied his participation in graduation ceremonies. The case reached the U.S. Court of Appeals, Third Circuit, which held **school officials did not establish a sufficient nexus between the student's communication and substantial disruption of the school environment**. While the school district attempted to characterize the web page as "on-campus speech" under various theories, the court was not persuaded. The court found the relationship between the student's conduct and the school "attenuated." Schools may punish off-campus speech in only limited circumstances, so the judgment was affirmed. *Layshock v. Hermitage School Dist.*, 593 F.3d 249 (3d Cir. 2010).

◆ A dispute arose between Connecticut high school administrators and some student council members over the postponement of a battle-of-the-bands event called "Jamfest." Council members sent a mass email from a school computer urging recipients to contact the district superintendent. A student officer later posted an Internet blog stating that "jamfest is cancelled due to douchebags in central office." She wrote that the email had "pissed off" the superintendent and caused her to cancel the event, and suggested others "write something or call her to piss her off more." Several students added blog comments, including one that referred to the superintendent as "a dirty whore." The superintendent and principal continued to receive calls and emails about Jamfest. The principal barred the student from class office and from giving a campaign speech.

The student's mother sued the school district for speech rights violations. Appeal reached the U.S. Court of Appeals, Second Circuit. It held that **off-campus conduct could create a foreseeable risk of substantial school disruption. The off-campus character of the speech did not insulate the student from discipline.** The posting was designed to reach the school, and it "foreseeably created a risk of substantial disruption within the school environment." As the student threatened to disrupt efforts to resolve the Jamfest dispute, and she frustrated student government operations, the court affirmed the judgment. *Doninger v. Niehoff*, 527 F.3d 41 (2d Cir. 2008).

After the student graduated, the district court considered her monetary damage claim. It held administrators could bar her from office based on vulgar, offensive off-campus speech that was likely to be heard at school. But the officials were not entitled to immunity for prohibiting students from wearing t-shirts to support her. *Doninger v. Niehoff*, 594 F.Supp.2d 211 (D. Conn. 2009).

◆ A Missouri high school student sent instant messages to another student, saying he was depressed and wanted to take guns to school, kill other students, then kill himself. The school principal learned of the electronic conversation and called police. Juvenile proceedings were brought against the student, and an assistant principal suspended him. The superintendent extended the suspension to cover the rest of the school year, and the school board affirmed this. When the student attained majority, he sued, seeking the expungement of discipline from his record. A court found that the case required a trial. The record did not show that the student substantially disrupted the school. But as he had received a hearing and opportunity to be heard, his due process rights were satisfied. All claims against the superintendent were dismissed. *Mardis v. Hannibal Public School Dist. #60*, No. 2:08CV63 JCH, 2009 WL 1140037 (E.D. Mo. 4/28/09).

The court later found that **the student's instant messages were "true threats" that were not due First Amendment protection**. He should have reasonably known his messages would reach other students. The student's state of mind and access to weapons made his threats believable. He expressed the wish to kill at least five classmates, and told the confidante that he had a .357 magnum pistol. Since a reasonable person would take these messages as "true threats," officials "acted entirely within their permissible authority in imposing sanctions." There was no merit to the student's claim that his speech did not disrupt the school. Complaints by parents who were scared to send their children to school indicated substantial disruption. *Mardis v. Hannibal Public School Dist. #60*, 684 F.Supp.2d 1114 (E.D. Mo. 2010).

◆   A New York student sent his friends instant messages with a small, crude icon depicting a pistol firing a bullet at a person's head, with dots representing blood. Beneath the drawing were the words "Kill [my English teacher]." The student used his parents' computer and did not send the instant message icon to the teacher or any other school official. However, a classmate told the English teacher about the icon, and the report was forwarded to school officials and the police. The student admitted making the icon, and the school suspended him for five days. A police investigator determined the icon was a joke and criminal proceedings were ended. But a school hearing officer found the icon threatened the health, safety and welfare of others and disrupted the school environment.

The student was suspended for a year, and his parents sued the school district for speech rights violations and retaliation. A federal court found the icon was a "true threat" that was unprotected by the First Amendment. The parents appealed to the U.S. Court of Appeals, Second Circuit, which found a reasonably foreseeable risk that the icon would come to the attention of school authorities, and that it would materially and substantially disrupt school work and discipline. Because of the risk of disruption caused by the icon, the student enjoyed no speech protection. The fact that he created it off school property did not insulate him from school discipline. **Off-campus conduct can create a foreseeable risk of substantial disruption in school.** *Wisniewski v. Board of Educ. of Weedsport Cent. School Dist.*, 494 F.3d 34 (2d Cir. 2007).

◆   An 14-year-old Indiana student posted profanity on a fake MySpace.com page about her principal. The state brought delinquency proceedings against the student, including the offense of harassment under the Indiana Criminal Code. A juvenile court found that the student committed an act of harassment which, if done by an adult, would have constituted a crime. It then adjudicated the student delinquent. Appeal reached the Supreme Court of Indiana. It noted that in juvenile delinquency cases, the state must prove every element of the offense "beyond a reasonable doubt." The postings were in a "private profile" site on MySpace.com, where they could not be seen by the general public. The court found no evidence that the student expected the principal would see or learn about the private profile. There was no evidence or reasonable inference to show that the student had a subjective expectation that her conduct would be likely to come to the principal's attention. **In order to commit the offense of harassment, a person must "have the intent to harass, annoy, or alarm another person but with no intent of legitimate communication."** The evidence did not prove beyond a reasonable doubt that the student had the requisite intent to harass, annoy or alarm the principal when she made the posting. *A.B. v. State of Indiana*, 885 N.E.2d 1223 (Ind. 2008).

### 4. Confederate Flags

*Recent federal appellate court decisions regarding Confederate flag displays at school have interpreted* Tinker v. Des Moines Independent Community School Dist. *as not requiring disruption to have actually occurred for officials to regulate student speech. Officials may bar Confederate flag displays based on a **forecast** of substantial disruption or material interference.*

◆ A Texas high school responded to race-related problems by prohibiting Confederate flag displays on school grounds. The number of reported race incidents decreased over the next three years, but racial graffiti remained common in a boys' lavatory. A home-made Confederate flag was raised on the school flagpole on Martin Luther King, Jr. day in 2006. When two students carried purses to school bearing large images of a Confederate flag, they were sent to the office. They were allowed to either go home or have a parent retrieve the purses. They chose to go home, but were not disciplined. They nevertheless sued the principal and school board for violating their constitutional rights.

A court awarded pretrial judgment to the school officials, and the girls appealed. Before the U.S. Court of Appeals, Fifth Circuit, the students argued they did not cause disruption, and that the flag symbolized their ancestry and Christian faith. They claimed that other ethnic groups were not prohibited from displaying Mexican flags, Malcolm X shirts and similar items. The court held that **school officials reasonably banned displays of the Confederate flag at school to prevent substantial and material disruption**. The decision was based on the history of racial hostility at the school, some of which involved Confederate flag displays. School officials reasonably anticipated that the flag would cause substantial disruption or material interference, based on evidence of racial hostility and tension. For this reason, the lower court had properly held for the school officials. *A.M. v. Cash*, 585 F.3d 214 (5th Cir. 2009).

◆ A Missouri high school community endured racially charged incidents and violence, leading to the withdrawal of three of the high school's 15-20 African-American students from school. A fight occurred at a high school basketball game after white players used racial slurs during the game. A Confederate flag was displayed near the locker rooms during the game. As a result of these and other incidents, the district superintendent banned students from displaying the Confederate flag on their clothing. Students who wore Confederate items to school were told to change their clothes. They later sued the school district, asserting First Amendment violations. A court found that no constitutional violation, as there was sufficient evidence of school disruption if the flag was allowed. The students appealed. The U.S. Court of Appeals, Eighth Circuit, held that the numerous racial events at the school made the school's actions constitutionally permissible. The court held *Tinker* **and cases interpreting it "allow a school to 'forecast' a disruption and take necessary precautions before racial tensions escalate out of hand."** As a result of the race-related incidents both in and out of school, the administration had reasonably banned in-school Confederate flag displays. The court affirmed the judgment for school officials. *B.W.A. v. Farmington R-7 School Dist.*, 554 F.3d 734 (8th Cir. 2009).

◆  A Tennessee school experienced racial fighting, and civil rights complaints and a lawsuit were filed against the school system. There were "multiple racially motivated threats and physical altercations," resulting in suspensions. Law enforcement officers maintained a presence at the school, and Confederate flag depictions were banned. Two students wore shirts depicting Confederate flags at school. After being told to either turn their shirts inside out or remove them, they filed a federal district court action. Appeal reached the U.S. Court of Appeals, Sixth Circuit, which held **school officials need not tolerate student speech that is inconsistent with their educational mission**. Schools may ban speech that would "materially and substantially interfere" with appropriate school discipline. But *Tinker v. Des Moines Independent Community School Dist.*, "does not require disruption to have actually occurred" for schools to regulate student speech. And *Tinker* did not require the expression itself to have been the source of past disruption. The graffiti was violent, and racial tensions had caused absenteeism, which the court found "the epitome of disruption in the educational process." As school officials had reasonably forecast disruption, they were entitled to judgment. *Barr v. LaFon*, 538 F.3d 554 (6th Cir. 2008).

## B.  Student Publications

*Student publications are not "public forums," so school administrators may exercise editorial control over them if a reasonable basis exists for the belief that a publication would materially disrupt class work, involve substantial disorder or violate the rights of others.*

◆  A Missouri high school principal objected to two articles prepared for publication in the school newspaper. Because the principal believed there was no time to edit the articles before the publication deadline, he deleted the two pages on which the articles appeared. Former students who were members of the newspaper staff sued, alleging that their First Amendment rights were violated when the pages were removed from the newspaper before publication.

A federal district court ruled in favor of the school district. The Eighth Circuit reversed, holding that the newspaper was a public forum "intended to be and operated as a conduit for student viewpoint." The U.S. Supreme Court agreed to hear the case and noted that school facilities, including school-sponsored newspapers, become public forums only if school authorities have intentionally opened those facilities for indiscriminate use by either the general public "or by some segment of the public, such as student organizations." The Court determined that since the district allowed a large amount of control by the journalism teacher and the principal, it had not intentionally opened the newspaper as a public forum for indiscriminate student speech. **School officials can exercise "editorial control over the style and content of student speech in school-sponsored expressive activities so long as their actions are reasonably related to legitimate pedagogical concerns."** Because the decision to delete two pages from the newspaper was reasonable, the Court found no violation of the First Amendment. *Hazelwood School Dist. v. Kuhlmeier*, 484 U.S. 260, 108 S.Ct. 562, 98 L.Ed.2d 592 (1988).

◆ A California high school student editor wrote an editorial for the school paper called "Immigration." He suggested all non-English speakers were illegal aliens. The principal allowed the publication of "Immigration," and Latino parents complained. After the superintendent instructed the principal to retract remaining copies of the paper, the principal apologized to students and parents for her "misinterpretation and misapplication of board policy in the publication of 'Immigration.'" Administrators wrote a letter to parents expressing regret over their decision to allow the publication. The student wrote another editorial entitled "Reverse Racism," which made provocative statements about race relations. The principal approved it for publication, but delayed publication until a counter-viewpoint editorial could be presented in the same issue.

The student sued in a state court for speech rights violations. The Court of Appeal of California held California Education Code Section 48907 protected student expression in school publications but prohibited "material which so incites students as to create a clear and present danger of the commission of unlawful acts on school premises or the violation of lawful school regulations." The editorial "Immigration" would not incite students to commit unlawful acts on school grounds, violate school rules, or pose a risk of substantially disrupting school operations. **Schools may only prohibit speech that incites disruption by specifically calling for a disturbance** or because the manner of expression "is so inflammatory that the speech itself provokes the disturbance." While the student was not disciplined, his rights were violated by the principal's statement that "Immigration" had been improperly published. *Smith v. Novato Unified School Dist.*, 150 Cal.App.4th 1439, 59 Cal.Rptr.3d 508 (Cal. Ct. App. 2007).

◆ The newly selected principal of a Washington high school threatened to sue her new school and the school newspaper's faculty advisor after the newspaper featured an article indicating that she was the student committee's "third choice" for principal. Student journalists claimed that after the new principal assumed her duties, she undertook many acts of retaliation based on the article. They claimed she objected to language for a new masthead for the newspaper declaring the paper was not subject to prior review. The current masthead stated that editorial decisions were student-made protected speech.

The students sued the school district in a federal court, which found that the newspaper was part of the curriculum, as students received grades and academic credit. A school policy provided for the review of all copy by the principal prior to publication. The court explained that "prior restraint" prohibited future speech, as opposed to punishing past speech. **The principal's "prior review" of the newspaper regulated only the time and manner of publication, and was not "prior restraint."** However, the court refused to dismiss their First Amendment challenge to the deletion of the proposed masthead. The newspaper was described as a school club in a student handbook and at freshman orientation. Students worked for long hours outside the school day to edit and produce each issue, and to sell advertising. The advisors had little control over the publication. The court also refused to dismiss the retaliation claims against the principal. *Lueneburg v. Everett School Dist. No. 2*, No. C05-2070RSM, 2007 WL 2069859 (W.D. Wash. 7/13/07).

◆   New Hampshire school yearbook editors considered publishing a picture of a student holding a shotgun and dressed in trap-shooting attire. The yearbook faculty advisor and the school principal encouraged the editors to make their own decision. The staff voted 8-2 not to publish the student's photograph in the senior portrait section of the yearbook. After the student's parents complained, the staff offered to publish the picture in the community sports section of the yearbook. The school board adopted a new publications policy banning the use of "props" in senior portraits. The student sued the board in a federal court for an order requiring the publication of the picture as his senior portrait. The court observed that the student editors were not coerced, unduly influenced or pressured by school officials to reject the student's picture. The editors believed that the display of a firearm would be inappropriate in a school publication, given school policies and recent tragedies such as Columbine. **The editorial judgment exercised by students was sufficiently independent from the school administration to avoid attribution to the school.** Thus, the student could not establish "state action." And while the revised board policy was state action, it was content neutral and viewpoint neutral. *Douglas v. Londonderry School Board*, 413 F.Supp.2d 1 (D.N.H. 2005).

## C. Non-School Publications

◆   A Michigan eighth-grader came to school with red tape over his mouth and wrists, a sweatshirt reading "Pray to End Abortion" and leaflets containing abortion statistics. After a teacher sent him to the office for causing a disruption, a guidance counselor told him to remove the tape and change his shirt or hide the message. The student returned to class but attempted to put his sweatshirt back on. The principal then repeated the directive not to wear it. As the student did not have approval to distribute the leaflets, the principal stated he could not hand them out. The principal had to pick up leaflets found in hallways. Although no discipline was imposed on the student, his parents sued the principal, school district and school officials in a federal district court. The parties agreed that the student could not come to school with tape on his mouth or wrists, but could wear the sweatshirt saying "Pray to End Abortion."

The court issued an order for the student, and the case reached the U.S. Court of Appeals, Sixth Circuit. It held **school hallways are "nonpublic forums" that do not possess the attributes of streets, parks and other places that are considered public forums**. School facilities may be deemed "public forums" only if authorities open them for indiscriminate use by the general public. Public forums are not created by government inaction. The school offered the student opportunities to post his leaflets on bulletin boards and to hand them out in the cafeteria during lunch. The court held regulation of his speech was "eminently reasonable." There was no indication of a desire to suppress his anti-abortion viewpoint. **It was reasonable for the school to require prior approval before permitting students to distribute literature at school.** The court reversed the judgment, holding the school policy on distribution of literature was not unconstitutional, as it was intended to prevent hallway clutter and congestion. *M.A.L. v. Kinsland*, 543 F.3d 841(6th Cir. 2008).

◆   Texas students and parents claimed an elementary school prevented speech about Christian religious beliefs and disallowed distributing religious items or literature at school. They filed a federal district court action against the school district, asserting First Amendment claims. The court held the "disruption" standard from *Tinker v. Des Moines Independent Community School Dist.*, this chapter, did not apply because the provisions being analyzed were content and viewpoint-neutral. **The policy was not targeted at nonschool materials based on their content or viewpoint.** The power of the principal to review materials was limited in time and scope and there was provision for an appeal.

The policy's numerical limit of 10 copies was not arbitrary, as the families urged. Instead, the court found a limit appropriately balanced the school's need to conserve resources with the interest in normal student interactions. The school district had a substantial interest in limiting time, place and manner restrictions to distributions of over 10 copies of an item. A provision delegating power to school principals to determine time, place and manner of distributions of over 10 documents had clear guidelines for principals and did not offer them excessive discretion. The court awarded pretrial judgment to the school district. *Pounds v. Katy Independent School Dist.*, 517 F.Supp.2d 901 (S.D. Tex. 2007).

## D.  Personal Appearance and Dress Codes

### 1.  Dress Codes

*Clothing with expressive content may be protected as "speech" under the First Amendment and is subject to the balancing of interests test from* Tinker v. Des Moines Independent Community School Dist., *(this chapter). But courts have rejected some claims that items such as T-shirts, jeans and body piercings are expressive at all. Officials may bar messages that materially disrupt school, involve substantial disorder or violate the rights of others. Dress codes implicate the Due Process Clause and must be specific enough to notify students of what speech is unacceptable, while not so broad as to prohibit protected expression.*

◆   A New Jersey school board adopted a uniform policy with significant input from the school community. Students could opt out of the policy for religious and medical reasons. A student tried to opt-out of the requirement based on "Constitutional Rights, Fundamental Freedom, Individual personal choice and Philosophical Beliefs." Upon being denied this request, he refused to comply, and after undergoing progressive discipline, he was suspended. When he entered high school, he again sought to opt out of the dress code, but was again denied his request. His family sued the board and several school officials. Appeal reached a New Jersey Appellate Division Court, where the parents claimed that a law authorizing education boards to adopt uniform dress codes violated the child's speech rights, as well as their own parental rights.

The court said parents have a fundamental right to decide whether to send their children to a public school, but do not have a fundamental right generally to direct how a public school teaches their children. The purpose of the law at issue was to assist in controlling the school environment and to keep the focus on learning. As these purposes were rationally related to the legitimate interest in quality education, the court found no constitutional violation. **Dressing as one chose was not expressive conduct that was due constitutional protection.** Here, the student "simply did not want to be told what to wear." The court also rejected the parents' claim based upon an asserted right to direct and control every aspect of their child's education, and the judgment was affirmed. *Dempsey v. Alston*, 405 N.J. Super. 499, 966 A.2d 1 (N.J. Super. Ct. App. Div. 2009).

◆   A Texas student wore a shirt to his school with "San Diego" printed on it. After an assistant principal told him this was a dress code violation, his parents brought him a "John Edwards for President '08" T-shirt to wear instead. But as the second shirt had a printed message, it also violated the dress code. Months later, the student sued the school district. By the time a hearing was held, a new dress code was in place. The court dismissed the case but asked to review the new dress code, which extended the ban on messages to polo shirts, and shirts with pro and university team logos or messages. Logos under two square inches, school spirit shirts, pins, buttons, wristbands, bumper stickers, and "principal-approved" messages of sponsored school clubs and teams were allowed. Each of the three shirts the student submitted to school administrators was disapproved. The court denied his request for an order to prevent enforcement of the dress code. He appealed to the U.S. Court of Appeals, Fifth Circuit.

The court rejected his argument that schools could only regulate specific kinds of speech. By allowing school logos and school-sponsored shirts, the school district did not suppress unpopular viewpoints. Instead, it provided students with more clothing options. As the code was content-neutral, it could be justified if it furthered an important government interest that was unrelated to expression. Among the reasons for adopting the dress code were improving student performance and attendance, instilling self-confidence, decreasing disciplinary referrals and lowering the drop-out rate. All these reasons furthered important government interests. Another valid goal was to promote professional and responsible dress for students preparing for the workforce. **"Federal courts should defer to school boards to decide what constitutes appropriate behavior and dress in public school."** The judgment was affirmed. *Palmer v. Waxahachie Independent School Dist.*, 579 F.3d 502 (5th Cir. 2009).

◆   A California school with a history of conflict over sexual orientation let a Gay-Straight Alliance group hold a "Day of Silence" to "teach tolerance." The 2003 event was accompanied by student fights. A group of students held an informal "Straight-Pride Day" and wore T-shirts with anti-gay slogans. Some students were asked to remove these shirts. Others were suspended for fighting. When the school allowed another "Day of Silence" in 2004, one student wore a T-shirt to school stating "I will not accept what God has condemned." The reverse of the shirt stated "homosexuality is shameful 'Romans 1:27.'" The student was detained in a school conference room for refusing to remove the shirt. Although he was not further disciplined, and no record of the incident was placed in his file, he sued the district and school officials for violating his speech and religious free exercise rights. The case reached the Ninth Circuit.

The court noted that *Tinker v. Des Moines Independent Community School Dist.* (this chapter) allows schools to **"prohibit speech that intrudes upon the rights of other students," or collides with the rights of others to be secure and to be let alone**. The T-shirt collided with other students' rights in the most fundamental way. Speech attacking minority students injured and intimidated them, damaged their sense of security and harmed their learning opportunities. Schools had a right to teach civic responsibility and tolerance, and did not have to permit hateful and injurious speech that ran counter to that message. *Harper v. Poway Unified School Dist.*, 445 F.3d 1166 (9th Cir. 2006).

After graduating, the students tried to pursue their claim for monetary damages. The case returned to the Ninth Circuit which held that the case was moot and that school officials had immunity from any damage claims. *Harper v. Poway Unified School Dist.*, 318 Fed.Appx. 540 (9th Cir. 2009).

◆   A Florida student had piercings and wore jewelry on her body, tongue, nasal septum, lip, navel and chest. She claimed her piercings were a way to express her "non-conformity and wild side" and expressed her individuality. An administrator told the student that her body jewelry violated the school dress code. The student refused to remove the jewelry and was assigned to lunch detention for four days for violating the dress code. She sued. A court ruled against her, and she appealed. The U.S. Court of Appeals, Eleventh Circuit, affirmed. It noted that students enjoy some speech rights at school, "but those constitutional rights are circumscribed by the special characteristics of the school environment." **While the First Amendment protects "symbolic speech," the Supreme Court has held that it does not apply unless "an intent to convey a particularized message was present."** The court questioned whether a jewelry ban implicated the First Amendment. Here, the student did not show that the First Amendment protected her right to express individuality at school by wearing body-piercing jewelry. Her conduct had insufficient communication to earn such protection. The board had enforced the dress code in a viewpoint-neutral manner and the rule was narrowly tailored to support the school interest in education. *Bar-Navon v. Brevard County School Board*, 290 Fed.Appx. 273 (11th Cir. 2008).

◆   Arkansas students wore black armbands to protest a mandatory uniform policy for grades seven through 12. After a few students wore armbands over their uniforms, the school disciplined them. One of the students handed out a flyer criticizing the uniform policy without first obtaining the principal's approval. This violated a district "literature review policy" requiring advance approval by the principal. The students sued the school district and school officials for constitutional violations. A court held that the uniform policy did not violate any constitutional provision, and that school board members were entitled to qualified immunity. On the other hand, the district superintendent and a junior high school principal were denied immunity in their individual capacities for imposing discipline to suppress a particular viewpoint. *Tinker v. Des Moines Independent Community School Dist.*, this chapter, established student rights to wear armbands in a non-disruptive way. After a jury found the students suffered no damages, the court awarded nominal damages. The district appealed to the U.S. Court of Appeals, Eighth Circuit, which found *Tinker* **was so similar in all relevant aspects that it required a judgment for the students**. *Lowry v. Watson Chapel School Dist.*, 540 F.3d 752 (8th Cir. 2008).

◆   An Illinois student who opposed a student "Day of Silence" wore a T-shirt stating: "Be Happy, Not Gay" and "My Day of Silence, Straight Alliance." A school official made him ink out the phrase "Not Gay," and to avoid discipline he did not wear the shirt. The student sued school officials, arguing that the First Amendment permitted his expression. A court refused to issue an order allowing him to wear the T-shirt, and he appealed. The U.S. Court of Appeals, Seventh Circuit, found the school banned "Be Happy, Not Gay" under a rule forbidding derogatory comments about race, ethnicity, religion, gender, sexual orientation or disability. But the slogan was a play on words that was not derogatory. The message was not targeted and "only tepidly negative." It was highly speculative that the T-shirt would provoke harassment of homosexuals. **While the student failed to qualify for an order suspending the school rule pending the outcome of his lawsuit, he could wear the shirt on a preliminary basis.** *Nuxoll v. Indian Prairie School Dist. #204*, 523 F.3d 668 (7th Cir. 2008).

◆   A Los Angeles middle school adopted a uniform policy for faculty and students after it was declared one of California's lowest-performing schools. The policy was expected to help students by reducing any distractions caused by clothing, allow easy identification of non-students, prevent students from leaving campus, and help prevent gang-related incidents. The school reported significant improvements in attendance and test scores, and a decrease in behavior problems after adopting the policy. The policy had a parental opt-out feature, but if students came to school out of uniform, their parents were called.

A student who opted out of the policy claimed that administrators, security guards and staff confronted her for appearing out of uniform. She said she was barred from a Valentine's Day dance and other activities. She sued, and a state court held for the district on most of her civil rights and speech claims. On appeal, the Court of Appeal of California explained that conduct "is protected by the First Amendment only if it 'is inherently expressive.'" **"Personal expression in clothing or hair style, without more, is not protected speech."** The student's "generalized desire to express her middle-school individuality" was an "unfocused message of personal expression" that was unprotected. The court affirmed the judgment. *Land v. Los Angeles Unified School Dist.*, No. B189287, 2007 WL 1413227 (Cal. Ct. App. 5/15/07, review denied, 8/15/07).

◆   Eighth-graders attended a gifted education program in a Chicago school. The school held annual contests to design a class T-shirt. The gifted students voted for a shirt depicting a boy with an enormous head, misshapen teeth, a dilated pupil and a missing hand. The reverse of the shirt had the word "Gifties," a reference to the gifted program. The "Gifties" shirt lost the school election, and the students were prevented from wearing the shirts at school. They said the shirts poked fun at themselves and had "irony." However, the principal stated that they mocked disabled people and threatened school safety. Many gifted students wore the shirts to school. Those who did so were confined to their homerooms. Although the school eventually permitted students to resume wearing the shirt, they sued the school board. A federal district court held that the T-shirt design did not contain a statement or symbolic message.

On appeal, the U.S. Court of Appeals, Seventh Circuit, held **the school did not violate the First Amendment by acting to exclude the shirts, because the images on them did not express an idea or opinion**. Schools may prohibit clothing with inappropriate words or slogans. As the principal acted reasonably and did not abuse his discretion, the court affirmed the judgment for the board. *Brandt v. Board of Educ. of City of Chicago*, 480 F.3d 460 (7th Cir. 2007).

◆   A New Jersey school district's mandatory uniform policy prompted two fifth-graders to wear buttons with the phrase "No School Uniforms," and a slashed red circle. The printing overlaid a photograph depicting hundreds of boys in uniform. While the photograph was identified as portraying Hitler Youth, no swastikas were visible. The school district sent letters to the students' parents stating that the background images on the buttons were "objectionable," and threatening the students with suspension if they wore the buttons to school again. The parents sued the school board for First Amendment violations. A court found it likely that some might find the button offensive, or in poor taste. On the other hand, the image was "a rather innocuous photograph – rows and rows of young men," with no visible swastikas. The image was not obscene, and "the young men might easily be mistaken for a historical photograph of the Boy Scouts." The court found that to prevent students from wearing the buttons, the board would have to show that they would "substantially interfere with the work of the school or impinge upon the rights of other students." **As the buttons did not cause disruption, and the board did not demonstrate a specific and significant fear of disruption, the censorship was unwarranted.** *DePinto v. Bayonne Board of Educ.*, 514 F.Supp.2d 633 (D.N.J. 2007).

◆   A Vermont high school student wore a T-shirt to school that read "George W. Bush, Chicken-Hawk-In-Chief." Surrounding a caricature of the president's face superimposed on a chicken's body were images of oil rigs, dollar symbols, cocaine, a razor blade and a martini glass. A parent complained about the shirt to a staff member, who decided that it violated a dress code provision barring images of drugs and alcohol. The student refused to turn the shirt inside-out or cover images of drugs and alcohol and the word "cocaine." He left school, but wore the shirt to school the next two days. He wrote the word "Censored" on duct tape and placed it on the shirt over the word "cocaine." The school disciplined the student and sent him home for wearing the shirt.

The student sued school officials, and a federal court found a speech rights violation. The parties appealed to the U.S. Court of Appeals, Second Circuit, which found that the student's T-shirt did not contain expression that was "vulgar, lewd, indecent or plainly offensive." *"Tinker* **established a protective standard"** **under which student speech cannot be suppressed based on its content, but only if it is substantially disruptive.** The "plainly offensive" standard of *Bethel School Dist. No. 403 v. Fraser*, this chapter, was not triggered whenever a school decided a student's message conflicted with its educational mission. The student was entitled to an order permitting him to wear the shirt and clearing his record. *Guiles v. Marineau*, 461 F.3d 320 (2d Cir. 2006).

◆   A Kentucky middle school adopted a policy generally requiring students to wear solid-colored clothing and restricting tight, baggy, revealing, form-fitting or "distressed" clothing, as well as clothing that was "too long" or not of appropriate size and fit. A parent sued the school district, stating that his daughter wanted to "be able to wear clothes that look nice on her, that she feels good in and that express her individuality." After the case was filed, the council modified the code to prohibit blue jeans. The court held for the school district, and the parent appealed. The U.S. Court of Appeals, Sixth Circuit, held that the school district could enforce a dress code regulating pants and tops where the student did not seek to convey any particular message through her clothing. The First Amendment does not apply unless there is a "particularized message." The student here had no message, wanting only to "wear clothes she feels good in." Her First Amendment claim failed, as she only stated "a generalized and vague desire to express her middle-school individuality." A person's choice of clothing "does not possess the communicative elements necessary to be considered speech-like conduct." The dress code also did not interfere with the parent's rights, as **parents have no fundamental right generally to direct how public schools teach their children.** The court affirmed the judgment. *Blau v. Fort Thomas Public School Dist.*, 401 F.3d 381 (6th Cir. 2005).

### 2.  Hair Length and Appearance

*In* Karr v. Schmidt, *460 F.2d 609 (5th Cir. 1972), the Fifth Circuit held that "there is no constitutional right to wear one's hair in a public high school in the length and style that suits the wearer." Karr created a* per se *rule that hair and grooming regulations are constitutional, so long as they are not arbitrary.*

◆   An African-American male student was told to remove braids from his hair, even though no policy prohibited them. The school board revised its dress code to require all students to "wear their hair in a standard, acceptable style." All students were required to wear uniforms. Any hairstyle detrimental to student performance or school activities was prohibited. Male students could not wear their hair in braids, spiked, or in a style distracting to other students. However, females could wear braids. The student claimed that the policy had a disparate impact on African-American males and violated his equal protection, free exercise and speech rights. He sued the school board. A federal district court rejected his claim that he had been denied a hairstyle favored by African-American males in violation of the First Amendment. There was also no violation of his equal protection rights. A school committee had revised the dress code in conjunction with a school safety policy. The court held the dress code should be upheld under *Karr v. Schmidt*, above. **According to the court, the board's policy advanced legitimate concerns for discipline, avoiding disruption and fostering respect for authority.** *Fenceroy v. Morehouse Parish School Board*, No. Civ.A. 05-0480, 2006 WL 39255 (W.D. La. 2006).

◆   A Texas school board adopted a student grooming policy prohibiting boys from wearing their hair below the shirt collar. An elementary school principal observed a third-grade boy with a ponytail and advised him and his mother that he was in violation of the grooming policy. The school board suspended the student for three days for refusing to comply, and it placed him on in-school suspension. The student's mother removed him from school and sued the board for violating the Texas Constitution and state law. A state court permanently enjoined the board from enforcing the policy. But the Supreme Court of Texas held **the grooming policy did not deprive males of equal educational opportunities or impose other improper barriers.** The regulation of hair length and other grooming or dress requirements was not discriminatory on the basis of sex, and the court reversed the judgment. *Board of Trustees of Bastrop Independent School Dist. v. Toungate*, 958 S.W.2d 365 (Tex. 1997).

◆   A fourth-grade Indiana boy wore an earring to school, even after the school board revised its handbook to bar the wearing of jewelry by male students. After a five-day suspension, a hearing examiner recommended transferring the student to another school that did not have similar policies. The board adopted the recommendations, but the student refused to transfer. The family sued the school district in the state court system for a declaration and order prohibiting enforcement of the policy. The Court of Appeals of Indiana rejected an argument that the policy violated equal protection of the law because girls were permitted to wear earrings. Enforcement of a strict dress code was a factor in improving student attitudes. **The policy served the valid educational purpose of instilling discipline and creating a positive educational environment.** *Hines v. Caston School Corp.*, 651 N.E.2d 330 (Ind. Ct. App. 1995).

### 3.  Gang Affiliation

*A federal district court held in* Brown v. Cabell County Board of Educ., *below, that schools may ban gang-related clothing if there is evidence of a potentially disruptive gang presence at school and gang-related disturbances. Borrowing language from recent Confederate flag cases, the court held the "test is not whether a student's statement has led to a disturbance or disruption, but whether it could reasonably be expected to lead to one."*

◆   Gang activities at a West Virginia high school escalated when a gang leader was arrested for shooting a police officer. Gang members verbally assaulted the faculty and staff at school, and fights and disturbances became prevalent. The principal advised staff members that the slogan "Free A-Train" was banned. A student wrote "Free A-Train" on his hands several times and was suspended for 10 days. He sued the school board in a federal district court for speech rights violations. The court held schools may ban gang-related clothing if evidence indicates a potentially disruptive gang presence and gang-related disturbances.

**Recent federal cases suggest schools may regulate expression if they can reasonably forecast material and substantial disruption at school.** This defeated the student's claim that speech must lead to an actual disruption before school administrators may suppress it. As students and parents had expressed fear over the use of the slogan, administrators could reasonably forecast that allowing the student to keep displaying it may have exacerbated the tensions and increased these fears. The court held the "distraction from classes or intimidation from passive displays of support may serve as the basis of a disruption," and found no speech rights violation. *Brown v. Cabell County Board of Educ.*, 714 F.Supp.2d 587 (S.D. W.Va. 2010).

◆   An Illinois school disciplinary code defined "gang activity" as "prohibited student conduct." Gang activity included any act in furtherance of a gang, and use or possession of gang symbols, such as drawings, hand signs and attire. The code stated that gangs and their activities substantially disrupted school by their very nature. A student was suspended three times for drawing gang-related symbols, including an inverted pitchfork and crowns with five points. Each time, the student was informed about the code prohibition on gang symbols and warned of its disciplinary implications. After the third incident, the superintendent notified the student's mother of a proposed expulsion, the date of a hearing and the right of the student to counsel.

A school resource officer testified at the hearing that the pitchfork and crowns were gang-related signs. She said drawing them could be dangerous if misconstrued as a sign of disrespect by another gang. The school board voted to expel the student for the second half of the school year, and his mother sued. **A federal district court held that the student code sufficiently defined the term "gang symbol," using specific examples of prohibited conduct.** The court rejected all of the student's First Amendment arguments. And his due process claim failed because the board gave him three chances to conform his behavior to the code. Both he and his mother had been warned that his conduct was a violation before he was expelled. The decision to expel the student after documented violations of the student code was not contrary to the evidence or in conflict with board policy, and judgment was awarded to the school board. *Kelly v. Board of Educ. of McHenry Community High School Dist. 156*, No. 06 C 1512, 2007 WL 114300 (N.D. Ill. 1/10/07).

◆   A Kentucky board of education devised a student dress code based on the need to address a school gang problem, promote safety, prevent violence and disputes over clothing, and enable the identification of non-students and intruders on campus. The dress code limited the clothing available to students as well as the way it could be worn. It prohibited logos, shorts, cargo pants, jeans, the wearing of certain jewelry outside clothes and other specified items. Some students who were disciplined for dress code violations sued the school board, and the case reached the U.S. Court of Appeals, Sixth Circuit. It held that **school officials had an important and substantial interest in creating an appropriate learning environment by preventing the gang presence and limiting fights**. The regulation of student expression furthered an important government interest without suppressing free speech. The board believed the dress code would help reduce gang activity, ease tension among students who fought over attire and otherwise enhance student safety. The dress code addressed those issues in a manner that was unrelated to the expressive nature of student dress. School officials may control student speech or expression that is inconsistent with a school's educational mission. *Long v. Board of Educ. of Jefferson County, Kentucky*, 21 Fed.Appx. 252 (6th Cir. 2001).

## II.  EMPLOYEES

### A.  Protected Speech

*In* Garcetti v. Ceballos, *547 U.S. 410 (2006) the Supreme Court held its public employee speech cases reflected "the common sense realization that government offices could not function if every employment decision became a constitutional matter." **A public employee's speech pursuant to official duties is not protected by the First Amendment.** Under* Garcetti, *courts must first determine if an employee's speech was made pursuant to official duties. If the speech was not made pursuant to official duties, the test from* Pickering v. Board of Educ., *391 U.S. 563 (1968), and* Connick v. Myers, *461 U.S. 138 (1983), applies. Under* Pickering *and* Connick, *employees have First Amendment protection (1) if they speak on matters of public concern and (2) their interest in public comment outweighs the government interest in efficient public service.*

◆   *Garcetti* involved a deputy district attorney in California who examined a search warrant affidavit presented by a defense attorney. He determined that it contained serious misrepresentations and recommended dismissing the case. At a subsequent meeting, a heated discussion ensued. The DA's office decided to proceed with the prosecution, and the deputy district attorney was reassigned, then transferred to another courthouse and denied a promotion. He sued county officials under 42 U.S.C. § 1983, claiming First Amendment violations. On appeal, **the U.S. Supreme Court held that "when public employees make statements pursuant to their official duties, the employees are not speaking as citizens for First Amendment purposes."** It was part of the deputy district attorney's job to advise his supervisors about the affidavit, and if his supervisors thought his speech was inflammatory or misguided, they had the authority to take corrective action against him. *Garcetti v. Ceballos*, 547 U.S. 410 (2006).

◆   A New York City teacher filed a grievance because school administrators failed to discipline a student who twice threw books at him. He understood that a student assault of a teacher violated a citywide policy. After the teacher told other teachers of his grievance, he claimed administrators retaliated against him by issuing bad performance reviews and a false report of sexually abusing a student. The board discharged the teacher, and he filed a federal district court case for speech rights violations. Applying *Garcetti v. Ceballos*, above, the court held the grievance was an aspect of the teacher's core duties of maintaining class discipline. But it held conversations with other teachers were not within the scope of his employment duties. The teacher appealed to the U.S. Court of Appeals, Second Circuit, regarding the grievance issue.

In addition to finding officials need wide latitude in managing government offices, *Garcetti* held that the First Amendment does not "constitutionalize the employee grievance." Statements made pursuant to official duties are not protected speech. According to the court, when the teacher filed a grievance to complain about his supervisor's failure to issue discipline to a student, he was "speaking pursuant to his official duties and thus not as a citizen." For this reason, the filing of the grievance was unprotected. In reaching this result, the court agreed with other federal circuits which have held that **under *Garcetti*, official duties need not be required by (or included in) an employee's job description**. Ability to maintain classroom discipline is "an indispensable prerequisite to effective teaching and classroom learning." As a grievance over the decision not to discipline the student was a means to fulfill a primary employment duty, the court held for the school board. *Weintraub v. Board of Educ. of City School Dist. of City of New York*, 593 F.3d 196 (2d Cir. 2010).

◆    A probationary California first-grade teacher complained about a student in her class who had severe behavior issues, and she told her principal she felt he should be evaluated for emotional disturbance. She had a poor relationship with the district's special education director, who eventually refused to speak to her without a witness. One of their encounters involved placement of the teacher's own disabled child. Other teachers complained that the teacher used her cell phone during classes and arrived late every day. Just prior to her discharge, the teacher left campus during lunch without permission. After the school board voted not to renew the teacher's contract, she sued the school district and several administrators in a state court under Section 44113 of the state Education Code.

The case reached the Court of Appeal of California, which explained that Section 44113 makes government employees liable for using official authority to interfere with a teacher's right to disclose improper governmental activities. The special education director and other non-supervisors of the teacher were exempt from Section 44113 liability. And the district was exempt from Section 44113 liability, since it was not an employee. But the principal, superintendent and a supervisory assistant superintendent were not exempt under the provision, as they had acted as "supervisory employees." Despite this finding, the court affirmed the decision for the school administrators, because the matters the teacher sought to disclose were not "improper governmental activities." **Her activities on behalf of special needs children were not considered a "protected disclosure" under Section 44113.** The teacher's complaints about unruly students and a failure to perform a timely special education assessment of her own child were unprotected, because they were made in a context of internal personnel or administrative matters. *Conn v. Western Placer Unified School Dist.*, 186 Cal.App.4th 1163, 113 Cal.Rptr.3d 116 (Cal. Ct. App. 2010).

◆   A Washington school employee made comments about her co-workers on an Internet blog. She was then transferred from a curriculum specialist position to a classroom teaching job. She claimed this was retaliation for her posting of blogs on the Internet that included "several highly personal and vituperative comments about her employers, union representatives and fellow teachers." In a federal district court action against the school district's human resources specialist, the employee claimed First Amendment protection for her postings.

The court held for the human resources specialist, and the employee appealed to the Ninth Circuit. The court found the employee's former position required her to enter into trusting mentor relationships with less experienced teachers, to whom she was to give honest, critical and private feedback. Her public blog resulted in complaints from co-workers, and one of them had refused to work with her, even though she had been assigned as her instructional coach. The transfer followed because **the blog fatally undermined her ability to enter into trusting relationships as an instructional coach**. The court found the blog had a harmful effect on the employee's working relationships, and common sense indicated that few teachers would expect to enter into a confidential and trusting relationship with her after reading her blog. Since the lower court properly found the employee's interest in speech did not outweigh the school district's interest in fulfilling its responsibilities, the court affirmed the judgment. *Richerson v. Beckon*, 337 Fed.Appx. 637 (9th Cir. 2009).

◆   A Nebraska school technical support coordinator claimed he was fired for telling staff members about pay irregularities, invalid contracts and funding discrepancies. He filed a federal district court action against the school district for speech rights violations. The case reached the U.S. Court of Appeals, Eighth Circuit, which found the coordinator admitted each instance of speech involved his job duties. **Since speech relating to a public employee's job duties is unprotected by the First Amendment, there was no constitutional violation.** *Anderson v. Douglas County School Dist.*, 342 Fed.Appx. 223 (8th Cir. 2009).

◆   An Idaho security employee advised a high school principal of student drug and weapons violations. He also expressed concern over school safety and emergency policies, which he felt were inadequate. Near this time, the principal took away some of the employee's job duties. The employee wrote a letter to district administrators complaining about the principal's handling of his reports. He criticized unresponsiveness to safety problems, inadequate staff training, concealment and insufficient documentation of safety violations, ineffective enforcement of truancy and sexual harassment policies, and inadequate fire safety planning. The employee substantiated his concerns with specific examples of students bringing weapons to school, harassing others and coming to school intoxicated. School officials later met with the employee at his home and outside school hours to discuss the concerns. At the end of the school year, his responsibilities were combined with those of three other positions in a new position. Another applicant was hired for this job and the employee sued the school district for retaliation in violation of state law and the First Amendment.

A federal court awarded pretrial judgment to the school district. On appeal, the Ninth Circuit explained that *Garcetti v. Ceballos*, this chapter, required it to determine whether the employee was speaking as a public employee or as a private citizen. However, the precise nature of the employee's duties was unclear. There was room for debate regarding whether he wrote the letter as part of his official duties. According to the Ninth Circuit, **the *Garcetti* inquiry was not a purely legal question over which a federal court could award pretrial judgment**. Speech rights present a mixed question of law and fact. There remained questions regarding the nature of the employee's duties, so the court reversed the judgment and returned the case to the lower court. *Posey v. Lake Pend Oreille School Dist. No. 84*, 546 F.3d 1121 (9th Cir. 2008).

◆   An Indiana teacher/coach had a history of addressing his opinions to the school board and other community members without first addressing them to his immediate supervisor, as required by a district "chain of command" policy. He allegedly provided an athletic club with information that encouraged a Title IX complaint against the school district, and also emailed the superintendent to ask how to file a Title IX suit. After the coach got into a fight with an assistant, 70 families presented the board with a petition requesting the coach's removal.

The school board voted to terminate the coach's contract, and he filed a federal court lawsuit for speech rights violations. The court held the chain of command policy was not an unconstitutional "prior restraint" on speech, and the U.S. Court of Appeals, Seventh Circuit, affirmed the judgment. Under *Garcetti v. Ceballos*, this chapter, the First Amendment does not protect employees while they make statements pursuant to their official duties. **The chain of command policy was not a "prior restraint" on speech.** It did not restrict any speech protected by the First Amendment, as it only implicated job responsibilities. The court found this did not limit speech rights, but only ensured that a speaker's views were not attributed to the board. There was no evidence that the board was motivated by retaliation when it voted to terminate the coach's contract. Instead, the record reflected that he lost his coaching job because of the troubled program he ran. *Samuelson v. LaPorte Community School Corp.*, 526 F.3d 1046 (7th Cir. 2008).

◆   A probationary Indiana teacher was in her first year of work for an elementary school. In response to a student's question, she stated that she had honked her car horn to show support for anti-war demonstrators who held a "Honk for Peace" sign denouncing military involvement in Iraq. Parents complained to the school principal, who told all teachers not to take sides in any political controversy. The teacher was not rehired, which she believed was based on her answer in the current events class. She sued the school system in a federal district court for violating the First Amendment. A court awarded pretrial judgment to the school system, and the teacher appealed to the Seventh Circuit. Although she admitted she made the comment while performing her official duties, she claimed she was still protected by academic freedom.

The court rejected her argument. Public school teachers "must hew to the approach prescribed by principals" and other school administrators. The court stated that "the school system does not 'regulate' teachers' speech as much as it hires that speech." **Teachers have to "stick to the prescribed curriculum" and have no constitutional right to interject their own views on curricular**

**subject matter.** Teachers could not use their classes as platforms to voice their own perspectives. Students in public schools are a captive audience and they "ought not be subject to teachers' idiosyncratic perspectives." The teacher had been told she could teach the controversy about policy toward Iraq, so long as she kept her opinions to herself. As teachers could not advocate viewpoints that departed from the curriculum, the court held for the school system. *Mayer v. Monroe County Community School Corp.*, 474 F.3d 477 (7th Cir. 2007).

◆   Colorado charter school teachers were hired by a K-8 charter school under contracts indicating that the school board welcomed "constructive criticism" to enhance the school's program. Each teacher received satisfactory evaluations, and their contracts were renewed. The next year, the teachers and a paraprofessional grew concerned about the school's operations, management and mission. They held off-campus meetings to discuss school matters. Parents and others also attended. The teachers expressed their concerns to the board, which invited grievances "without fear of retaliation." However, the teachers contended that their grievances were ignored, and that the principal gave them less favorable job evaluations. Each teacher submitted a resignation letter effective well before the end of the school year. The board discussed the letters during a meeting at which the principal also submitted her resignation. After the principal resigned, the teachers unsuccessfully tried to rescind their own resignations.

The teachers claimed that the board then "blacklisted them from future employment," and they sued the charter school and its chartering school district. A court issued an order for the school and the district. On appeal, the U.S. Court of Appeals, Tenth Circuit, held that **the vast majority of the speech at issue involved personal job duties, and not the public concern**. However, the statements regarding official impropriety, as well as political speech, were matters of public concern. And the teachers' comments about their freedom of speech and expression related to the public concern, so they were constitutionally protected. Their discussions about the future of the school and upcoming board elections were also protected. The case was returned to the lower court for it to determine if the teachers' discussions on these subjects outweighed the school's interest in avoiding disruption. *Brammer-Holter v. Twin Peaks Charter Academy*, 492 F.3d 1192 (10th Cir. 2007).

◆   A Texas high school employee was athletic director and head football coach of a Dallas high school. He repeatedly asked the school's office manager for information about athletic activity funds. The coach wrote memorandums to the office manager and school principal, protesting the lack of information and seeking immediate funding for a tournament entry fee for one of the school's teams. Four days after receiving the memo, the principal stripped the coach of his athletic director duties. The district then voted against renewing his coaching contract. The district placed the office manager and principal on administrative leave pending an investigation into school financial matters.

The coach sued the district and school officials in a federal district court, asserting that he was retaliated against for engaging in protected speech. Appeal reached the U.S. Court of Appeals, Fifth Circuit. **The Fifth Circuit held that public employee speech cases use a "balancing test" between the speaker's**

**expression and the employer's interests.** However, *Garcetti* "added a threshold layer" to the rules set by cases like *Pickering v. Board of Educ.* "Even if the speech is of great social importance, it is not protected by the First Amendment so long as it was made pursuant to the worker's official duties." The coach claimed that he wrote his memos as a taxpayer and a father, but the court disagreed, ruling that the memos focused on daily operations. The coach admitted he needed the information so he could operate the athletic department. As his speech was made in the course of performing his job, it was unprotected by the First Amendment. *Williams v. Dallas Independent School Dist.*, No. 05-11486, 2007 WL 504992 (5th Cir. 2/13/07).

◆   A Florida principal's school received a D grade on the Florida Comprehensive Assessment Test. The score improved to a C the next year, but the principal learned that the school would not receive additional staff or funding. He held a faculty vote to obtain teacher support for conversion to a charter school, as permitted by state law. The vote failed, but the principal continued his conversion efforts and advocacy. Although he had received a "high quality performance" rating four days earlier, the principal's contract was not renewed. He filed a complaint with the state education department, but an investigation found no direct correlation between non-renewal and his efforts to convert the school. The principal sued the district for First Amendment violations. A court held that the speech was unprotected, and the principal appealed to the Eleventh Circuit, which found that his efforts to convert the school were "part and parcel of his official duties."

In light of *Garcetti v. Ceballos*, this chapter, the principal's conduct was unprotected. Under *Garcetti*, **a public employee must speak both on a matter of public concern and as a citizen in order to gain First Amendment protection**. The Supreme Court held in *Garcetti* that public employee speech on official duties is not insulated from employer discipline. The principal sought to convert his school in his capacity as a public employee, and not as a citizen. As the lower court had properly entered judgment for the school board, the judgment was affirmed. *D'Angelo v. School Board of Polk County, Florida*, 497 F.3d 1203 (11th Cir. 2007).

◆   A New Mexico school district hired a new director for its noncompliant Head Start program. Within six months, the program substantially complied with federal requirements. The director then told the district superintendent that up to 50% of the families enrolled in Head Start had misstated their incomes or family sizes and were ineligible for the program. The superintendent repeatedly raised the Head Start issue to the school board and others, but was put off each time. She instructed the director to report to federal authorities. The U.S. government investigated, found improprieties and ordered the repayment of over $500,000 in federal aid. The superintendent filed a complaint with the state attorney general stating that the board had made decisions in executive session without proper notice. After the attorney general ordered corrective action, the board demoted the superintendent and decided not to renew her contract for the next school year. She sued the district, its new superintendent and school board members for retaliation. A federal court denied motions for pretrial judgment.

On appeal, the U.S. Court of Appeals, Tenth Circuit, **commented that** *Garcetti v. Ceballos* **"profoundly alters how courts review First Amendment retaliation claims."** The *Garcetti* standard defeated a First Amendment claim based on reporting Head Start program deficiencies, since the reports were part of the superintendent's official duties. But the reporting of open meetings act violations to the New Mexico attorney general was outside the scope of her official job duties. That part of the lawsuit required a trial. *Casey v. West Las Vegas Independent School Dist.*, 473 F.3d 1323 (10th Cir. 2007).

◆  A Pennsylvania special education teacher who was admonished for trying to arrange counseling sessions for a student with suicidal feelings enjoyed no First Amendment protection in a federal lawsuit against her school district. The student's individualized education program (IEP) did not include psychological services. However, the teacher arranged for sessions and transported the student to them. She claimed the district then retaliated against her for trying to help the student. The Third Circuit held **the scheduling of therapy sessions and other assistance was not "expression," and had no First Amendment protection.** *Montanye v. Wissahickon School Dist.*, 218 Fed.Appx. 126 (3d Cir. 2007).

## B. Personal Appearance and Dress Codes

*School officials have considerable authority to regulate employee speech that could be perceived by the public as representing an official school view.*

◆  New York City Board of Education (BOE) regulations required school employees to maintain neutrality regarding political candidates while on duty or with students and precluded the distribution, posting or display of materials supporting any political candidate or organizations in BOE buildings or staff mailboxes. BOE teachers claimed that the regulations violated employee speech rights. They sought an order from a federal district court to prohibit enforcement of them. The court held school officials may impose reasonable restrictions on the speech of teachers, unless an open forum has been intentionally opened for indiscriminate use by the general public. **Schools have more authority to regulate teacher speech when there is a risk that the public would view it as bearing the school's imprimatur than when regulating personal expression.** As the regulation was neutral and left teachers ample alternatives for expression, the court upheld a ban on political button-wearing by teachers at school. There was no risk of attribution of political views to the BOE when political materials were posted in areas not accessible to students, so the BOE was ordered to allow posting of political items on bulletin boards and teacher mailboxes. *Weingarten v. Board of Educ. of City School Dist. of City of New York*, 591 F.Supp.2d 511 (S.D.N.Y. 2008).

Months later, the court considered motions by both parties for a permanent order. Only the issue of political buttons remained in dispute. The court noted the Supreme Court has allowed schools to regulate teacher speech in classrooms for legitimate pedagogical reasons (see *Hazelwood School Dist. v. Kuhlmeier*, this chapter). **So long as the school acted in good faith and banned buttons for legitimate pedagogical concerns, the regulation was constitutional.** The board's findings relating to button-wearing by teachers was entitled to deference. Students were a captive audience in their classes, and the board found teacher displays of political partisanship were inconsistent with the school's mission. As the teachers could not undermine the deference due the board to exercise its judgment in good faith, the court held for the board. *Weingarten v. Board of Educ. of City School Dist. of City of New York*, 680 F.Supp.2d 595 (S.D.N.Y. 2010).

◆   A California school district and the association representing its teachers could not reach a new agreement as their contract neared expiration. The association called for teachers to wear buttons supporting its bargaining position. Most of the teachers taught in self-contained classrooms in which only teachers and students were present. The district superintendent advised teachers of a district policy preventing them from engaging in any political activity during work time. Teachers complied with the directive, but the association filed an unfair practice charge against the district. The state Public Employee Relations Board (PERB) found that the wearing of buttons was not political activity and held that the district had interfered with the teachers' rights. The district appealed to the state court of appeal, which held that **button-wearing was "political activity" that could be barred under the state Education Code**. It was reasonable to prohibit public school teachers from political advocacy during instructional activities. The wearing of union buttons during instructional time was "inherently political." The court held that keeping the labor relations dispute from spilling into the classroom was a proper restriction of political activity and reversed the PERB's decision. *Turlock Joint Elementary School Dist. v. PERB*, 5 Cal.Rptr.3d 308 (Cal. Ct. App. 2003).

◆   *Turlock Joint Elementary School Dist. v. PERB*, above, is limited to instructional time. **A ban on political advocacy could not be enforced in noninstructional settings.** Another California district prohibited employees from distributing partisan election materials on school grounds and from campaigning during work hours. The teachers association objected to the policy and demanded its rescission so that teachers could wear buttons expressing their opposition to a state education finance voter initiative. A state superior court held the policy violated the First Amendment speech rights of teachers.

The Court of Appeal of California held state law allows schools to restrict the political speech of teachers during work hours. Because public school teachers have considerable power and influence in classroom situations and their speech may be reasonably interpreted as reflecting the official view of their school districts, it was reasonable to prohibit them from wearing political buttons in classrooms. This restriction did not violate the First Amendment or the state constitution, as school authorities must have the power to disassociate themselves from political controversy and the appearance of approval of political messages. **But it was unreasonable for the school district to restrict political speech by teachers outside their classrooms.** The court modified the decision so that teachers were prohibited from wearing political buttons only in the classroom. *California Teachers Ass'n v. Governing Board of San Diego Unified School Dist.*, 53 Cal.Rptr.2d 474 (Cal. Ct. App. 1996).

## C.  Association Rights

*The following cases involve claims by or on behalf of individual rights to free association. For additional associational rights cases involving employee associations, collective bargaining, agency fees (fair sharing) and payroll deductions, please see Chapter Eleven, Section I of this volume.*

◆   A California teachers' association placed political endorsements for two school board candidates in school district employee mailboxes. While the association was authorized to communicate with its members though their mailboxes, an administrator advised the association that California Education Code Section 7054 prohibited the use of school mail facilities to distribute materials containing political endorsements. The association filed an unfair practice charge with the California Public Employee Relations Board (PERB).

The action was dismissed, but appeal later reached the Supreme Court of California. The court found Section 7054 prohibited school districts and community colleges from using funds, services, supplies or equipment to urge support for (or the defeat of) any ballot measure or candidate, including board candidates. **California law stated that "the government may not 'take sides' in election contests or bestow an unfair advantage on one of several competing factions."** The Legislature found the use of public funds in elections would be inappropriate. The court found Section 7054 was "designed to avoid the use of public resources to perpetuate an incumbent candidate or his or her chosen successor, or to promote self-serving ballot initiatives" that would compromise the integrity of elections. Since "equipment" was intended to include mailboxes such as those used by the school district, Section 7054 applied. Permitting the district to restrict political speech did not run afoul of Government Code Section 3543.1, which permits employee organizations to use school bulletin boards, mailboxes and other means "subject to reasonable regulation." The ban on political endorsements was upheld as reasonable. Under established First Amendment law, school mailboxes were considered nonpublic forums. This meant the district could impose viewpoint-neutral regulations on the content of items placed there. Since the district had an important government interest, it was entitled to judgment. *San Leandro Teachers Ass'n v. San Leandro Unified School Dist.*, 209 P.3d 73, 95 Cal.Rptr.3d 164 (Cal. 2009).

◆   The Colorado Education Association (CEA) and an affiliate recruited members for walks to support a state senate candidate. Two individuals claimed this violated Article XXVIII of the Colorado Constitution. They also asserted that payments for union staff salaries, office supplies and materials were unconstitutional "expenditures" or "contributions." The individuals challenged the union activity with the Colorado Secretary of State, seeking to impose a $170,000 civil penalty. An administrative law judge (ALJ) rejected the claim that the unions had "coordinated" activities with the candidate and found no evidence of any "expenditure." The ALJ found the unions did not communicate beyond their own membership, complying with a state constitutional exception that permits communications among union members. The case reached the Supreme Court of Colorado, which held that **unions were expressly permitted to** establish political committees and engage in other campaign activities among their members. The court found that campaign spending is a form of speech.

The First Amendment protects political association, and limitations on political expenditures place a substantial restraint on speech and association. The state constitution's broad membership communication exception protects employee free speech and association rights. There was no evidence that the unions made unlawful expenditures or campaign contributions. The union communicated with members, not voters or the general public. Any indirect benefit to the candidate was also permitted by the state constitution's membership communication exception. As the ALJ had properly found the unions acted for the benefit of their own members, the court upheld her judgment. *Colorado Educ. Ass'n v. Rutt*, 184 P.3d 65 (Colo. 2008).

◆   A newspaper incorrectly reported that a Tennessee school superintendent would speak at a convention sponsored by a congregation that was primarily gay and lesbian. He submitted statements to two newspapers, informing them that he had declined the speaking invitations, and declared "that he did not endorse, uphold or understand homosexuality, but that he would not refuse to associate with gay people or refuse the opportunity to share with them his beliefs." Several board members believed the article called his judgment into question, undermined public confidence in him, and impaired his functioning. The board did not hire the superintendent to become the director of schools.

When the superintendent sued, a federal court held for the board and board members. The U.S. Court of Appeals, Sixth Circuit, held that the superintendent's intended prayer or speech touched on the public concern. The speech concerned religion and perhaps homosexuality, and would occur on his own time. **The superintendent sought to share his religious beliefs with the congregation and the community. This conduct was protected.** "It would contravene the intent of the First Amendment to permit the Board effectively to terminate [the superintendent] for his speech and religious beliefs in this way." The court reversed the judgment for three school board members who had apparently changed their view of the superintendent on the basis of his intended speech. The superintendent also stated claims under the Equal Protection Clause. The board members were not entitled to qualified immunity, as he had a clearly established right to express his religious beliefs. The case was returned to the lower court for further proceedings. *Scarbrough v. Morgan County Board of Educ.*, 470 F.3d 250 (6th Cir. 2006).

## III.  ACADEMIC FREEDOM

*Schools have broad discretion in curricular matters and courts do not closely scrutinize reasonable school board decisions in this area. But once a decision has been made to place a particular book in a school library, the same level of discretion does not apply. In* ACLU of Florida v. Miami-Dade County School Board, *below, a federal appeals court held a Florida school board had the authority to determine what books were to appear on school library shelves.*

## A. Library Materials

*In* Board of Educ. v. Pico, *below, the Supreme Court held the removal of books from a school library would be unconstitutional if it was motivated by an intent to deny students access to ideas with which school officials disagreed.*

◆   A Miami parent was outraged to find a copy of "Vamos a Cuba" on the shelves of his daughter's public school library. As a former political prisoner from Cuba, he claimed the book was untruthful. After the book was removed from library shelves, the school board chairman said that the book offended the Cuban community. Another board member noted that the board was rejecting its school staff's recommendation due to political pressure. Still another board member suggested that if the board did not vote to remove the book from school libraries, they might find bombs under their cars. A different parent and two organizations sued the board for First Amendment and Due Process violations.

A federal district court prevented the board from removing the book, and the board appealed. On appeal, the U.S. Court of Appeals, Eleventh Circuit, noted the board found the book was inaccurate and had factual omissions. The board voted to replace the series with updated books. Here, the lower court improperly prevented the board from removing the book from school libraries. "Whatever else it prohibits, the First Amendment does not forbid a school board from removing a book because it contains factual inaccuracies, whether they be of commission or omission. **There is no constitutional right to have books containing mis-statements of objective facts shelved in a school library**." Rather than banning the book, the school board was "removing" it from its library shelves. As the board had the sole authority to determine what books were to appear on school library shelves, the court held in its favor. *ACLU of Florida v. Miami-Dade County School Board,* 557 F.3d 1177 (11th Cir. 2009).

◆   The U.S. Supreme Court held that the right to receive information and ideas is "an inherent corollary of the rights of free speech and press" embodied in the First Amendment. The case arose when a New York school board rejected the recommendations of a committee of parents and school staff it had appointed and ordered that certain books be removed from school libraries. The board characterized the books as "anti-American, anti-Christian, anti-Semitic, and just plain filthy." Students sued the board and its individual members, alleging the board's actions violated their rights under the First Amendment. The Supreme Court noted that while school boards have broad discretion in the management of curriculum, they do not have absolute discretion to censor libraries and are required to comply with the First Amendment. **A decision to remove books from a school library is unconstitutional if it is motivated by an intent to deny students access to ideas with which school officials disagree.** *Board of Educ. v. Pico,* 457 U.S. 853, 102 S.Ct. 2799, 73 L.Ed.2d 435 (1982).

◆   The Children's Internet Protection Act (CIPA) requires public schools and libraries receiving federal technology grants or e-rate discounts to install filtering systems on computers used by children 17 or younger. Local school boards or agencies can decide what software to install and what to block. Two complaints filed in federal courts alleged that the CIPA violated the First and Fifth Amendments and sought to permanently bar the Federal Communications Commission from implementing the law. A three-judge federal panel found the law unconstitutional because a library patron might wish to remain anonymous or might be too embarrassed to ask for the filters to be removed to view sensitive materials. On appeal, the U.S. Supreme Court held Internet access in public libraries is not a public forum. For this reason, **libraries have discretion to choose what parts of the Internet they will offer patrons, in the same way they choose which books to put on the shelves**. "A public library does not acquire Internet terminals in order to create a public forum for Web publishers to express themselves, any more than it collects books in order to provide a public forum for the authors of books to speak." The Court found any concerns about innocuous websites being wrongly blocked were addressed by CIPA provisions allowing librarians to disable filters when asked by adult patrons.

The Court rejected the contention that people seeking medical, sexual or other sensitive information would be reluctant to ask for unblocking. It concluded "the Constitution does not guarantee the right to acquire information at a public library without any risk of embarrassment." *U.S. v. American Library Ass'n Inc.*, 539 U.S. 194, 123 S.Ct. 2297, 156 L.E.2d 221 (2003).

◆   A gay and lesbian organization donated books with homosexual themes to a Kansas school district. One of the books was already on library shelves, but no one had ever checked it out. The media publicized the donation and opponents burned copies of the book on school property. The superintendent recommended removing copies from the libraries and rejecting the donation. The school board voted to remove the books and refuse the donation, and a teacher and some students sued. A federal district court found the book had no vulgarity or explicit language and had won many literary awards. The district had failed to abide by its own rules in rejecting the donation and removing copies from its shelves. Board members indicated that they disapproved of the book's subject matter and had voted to remove it because of their disagreement with it. The failure of the board to follow its own procedures for library procurement affirmed the court's belief that **board members had been motivated to remove the book based on their personal disagreement with ideas expressed in it**. Removal of the book violated the constitutional rights of students attending district schools. The court issued an order requiring school officials to return copies to district libraries. *Case v. Unified School Dist. No. 233*, 908 F.Supp. 864 (D. Kan. 1995).

### B.  Textbook Selection

*In* Chiras v. Miller, *below, the Fifth Circuit held students have no constitutional right to compel the selection of classroom materials.*

◆   A Texas student and the author of an environmental textbook had no constitutional right to compel the state board of education to select a particular textbook, according to the U.S. Court of Appeals, Fifth Circuit. Government can, without violating the constitution, selectively fund programs to encourage activities it believes are in the public interest, and may discriminate on the basis of viewpoint by choosing to fund one activity over another. Schools can thus promote policies and values of their own choosing, free from the forum analysis and the viewpoint-neutrality requirement. Devising the curriculum and selecting textbooks were core functions of the board, which needed to keep editorial judgment over the content of instructional materials for public school classrooms. The court agreed with the board that its selection of curricular materials was government speech. **Students have no constitutional right to compel the selection of classroom materials of their choosing.** *Chiras v. Miller*, 432 F.3d 606 (5th Cir. 2005).

◆   A group of parents whose children attended grade school in an Illinois school district sued for an order to prevent use of the Impressions Reading Series as the main supplemental reading program for grades kindergarten through five. The parents alleged that the series "foster[ed] a religious belief in the existence of superior beings exercising power over human beings" and focused on "supernatural beings" including "wizards, sorcerers, giants and unspecified creatures with supernatural powers." The court dismissed the lawsuit, and the parents appealed to the Seventh Circuit.

The court found the parents' argument (that use of the textbook series established a religion) speculative. Although the series contained some stories involving fantasy and make-believe, their presence in the series did not establish a coherent religion. The intent of the series was to stimulate imagination and improve reading skills by using the works of C.S. Lewis, A.A. Milne, Dr. Suess and other fiction writers. **The primary effect of using the series was not to endorse any religion, but to improve reading skills.** Use of the series did not impermissibly endorse religion under the Establishment Clause or the Free Exercise Clause. The court ruled for the school. *Fleischfresser v. Directors of School Dist. 200*, 15 F.3d 680 (7th Cir. 1994).

◆   A teacher in a Michigan public school taught a life science course using a textbook approved by the district's school board. He showed films to his class regarding human reproduction (*From Boy to Man* and *From Girl to Woman*) after obtaining approval from his principal. The films were shown to his seventh-grade classes with girls and boys in separate rooms, and only students with parental permission slips were allowed to attend. Both films had traditionally been shown to seventh-grade students in the school.

But after a board meeting where community residents demanded that the teacher be tarred and feathered for showing the films, the superintendent suspended the teacher with pay pending "administrative evaluation." The board approved this action. The teacher then sued the district for violating his First Amendment and other civil rights. A jury awarded the teacher $321,000 in compensatory and punitive damages. The U.S. Supreme Court reversed the decision and remanded the case. According to the Supreme Court, **an award of money damages may be made only to compensate a person for actual injuries caused by deprivation of a constitutional right**. Awards for abstract violations of the U.S. Constitution were not allowed. *Memphis Community School Dist. v. Stachura*, 477 U.S. 299, 106 S.Ct. 2537, 91 L.Ed.2d 249 (1986).

## C. School Productions

*In* Boring v. Buncombe County Board of Educ., *below, a federal appeals court held the selection of a school play was part of the curriculum, not a matter of public concern for which a teacher could claim constitutional protection.*

◆   A Nevada high school student selected a W.H. Auden poem containing the words "hell" and "damn" for recital at a statewide poetry reading competition. He practiced the poem twice a day for over two months. When the student recited the poem at a competition in the school, the dean of students emailed the English chair that it was objectionable due to inappropriate language. The student recited the poem again at a districtwide competition held off campus.

An administrator reprimanded English department members for allowing the recitation. The student learned he would have to choose a new poem for the state competition, as the Auden poem had profanity. He petitioned a federal district court for a temporary restraining order to prevent the school from interfering with his recitation. The court found the recitation of the Auden poem could not be considered vulgar, lewd, obscene or offensive. **Off-campus poetry recitation at a state competition sponsored by national organizations was not school-sponsored speech and was not a part of the curriculum or any regular classroom activity.** Where there was no showing that student speech would materially and substantially interfere with appropriate discipline, the court could not uphold speech restraint by school officials. A poem by a recognized poet, recited at an off-campus student competition authorized by the school, did not present even a remote risk of disruption. *Behymer-Smith v. Coral Academy of Science*, 427 F.Supp.2d 969 (D. Nev. 2006).

◆   A North Carolina high school English and drama instructor won numerous awards for directing and producing student plays. She selected a play for a state competition that depicted a divorced mother with a lesbian daughter and a daughter who was pregnant with an illegitimate child. Her advanced acting class won 17 of 21 possible awards at a regional competition for performing the play. But a parent objected to a scene from the play and the principal forbade students from performing it at the state finals. He later allowed the performance with the deletion of certain scenes. The school board approved a transfer of the teacher to a middle school for violating the district's controversial materials policy. She sued the board and school officials for retaliatory discharge.

After removal to a federal district court, the case was dismissed. A three-judge panel of the U.S. Court of Appeals, Fourth Circuit, rejected the board's argument that the First Amendment protects only original expression and not the selection of a play. The panel held that due to the important role that teachers play in society, the First Amendment extended to the selection of plays for high school drama classes. The full court reheard the case and vacated the panel decision, upholding the transfer. **The selection of a school play was part of a public school curriculum, and did not constitute a matter of public concern for which a teacher could claim constitutional protection.** *Boring v. Buncombe County Board of Educ.*, 136 F.3d 364 (4th Cir. 1998).

## IV.  PARENTAL SPEECH AND ASSOCIATION RIGHTS

*The Supreme Court has recognized a fundamental right of parents to direct and control the upbringing of their children. This does not include a parental right to direct and control public school curriculums or enter school campuses without restriction. Courts have approved state actions that intrude on parental liberty, such as sex and health education programs, community service and attendance requirements, uniform policies, and condom distribution programs.*

### A.  Access to School Campuses

◆  A New Jersey student said her varsity basketball coach routinely criticized her, singled her out due to her weight and went on "profanity-laced tirades" about her and some teammates. Her parent complained to school administrators and appeared at board meetings at least four times to urge action against the coach and to discuss the need to address civility in coaching. At one of the meetings, he spoke against reappointing the coach. Five others spoke in favor of the coaching staff, and the coach was reappointed. Months later, the parent was cut off about 30 seconds into an address to the board at a meeting to consider a policy against behavior diminishing individual dignity and safety. Other speakers were allowed to exceed a five-minute limit on remarks. The parent filed a state court action against the school board for retaliation and also raised other claims. A jury found the board and school officials liable for negligent supervision, but the court dismissed the daughter's claims.

The court refused to reverse a $100,000 verdict for the parent for emotional distress. Appeal reached the Supreme Court of New Jersey, which held there was enough evidence for a jury to find the board president had silenced the parent for his viewpoints. The public comment period of a school board meeting is a public forum that can be limited only if justified without reference to the content of speech. **Once the board opened the floor for discussion, it could not deny the forum to those wishing to express less-favored or controversial views.** The court held the jury was free to find the warning by the president revealed impatience and antagonism toward a view he did not want to hear. Since the president's motive was not content neutral, the court held the parent established a First Amendment violation. But the court found the evidence of emotional distress was limited to transient embarrassment and humiliation. The case was returned to the trial court to reduce the damage award or to hold a new trial on damages. *Besler v. Board of Educ. of West Windsor-Plainsboro Regional School Dist.*, 201 N.J. 544, 993 A.2d 805 (N.J. 2010).

◆  Four Tennessee high school football players were dismissed from the team after signing a petition stating they hated their head coach and did not want to play for him. They filed an unsuccessful lawsuit against the school board in a federal court (see *Lowery v. Euverard*, this chapter). Parents of the same students filed a new federal court action on their own behalf against the school board and two school officials. A jury held for the board and school officials, and the court ordered the parents to pay the board attorneys' fees and costs of over $87,000 as a sanction for bringing claims that were frivolous and intended to harass school officials. On appeal, the U.S. Court of Appeals, Sixth Circuit, found **a school board meeting was a "designated and limited public forum."**

The forum in this case was "limited," because people did not have to be allowed to engage in every type of speech there. **In a designated public forum, the government may regulate the time, place and manner of speech in a content-neutral fashion.** In this case, the board's content-neutral justifications for the policy had nothing to do with an individual's proposed speech. The court held the policy served a significant government interest in avoiding unstructured, chaotic school board meetings. There was no merit to the parents' claims that the policy was unconstitutionally vague and that the trial court had given the jury improper instructions. As the policy amounted to a content-neutral time, place and manner regulation, the court affirmed the judgment. But since the parents' claims were not frivolous, the court reversed the award of attorneys' fees for the board and school officials. *Lowery v. Jefferson County Board of Educ.*, 586 F.3d 427 (6th Cir. 2009).

◆   An Oklahoma parent agreed to check on another parent's daughter while volunteering at school. After obtaining approval to enter the classroom, the parent checked on the child, then spoke to a paraprofessional and other children for a few minutes. She then went to perform her volunteer duties and was again approached by the other parent to check on her daughter. The parent again looked in on the classroom. A school official sent her a letter banning her from school for five weeks for violating an Oklahoma law regarding "Interfering with Peaceful Conduct of Activities." After a hearing, the school reduced the time the parent was excluded from school, but she sued the district in federal district court for constitutional violations, including an interest in the care, custody and control of her children. The court held school officials were well within their bounds in limiting access, as "parents simply do not have a constitutional right to control each and every aspect of their children's education and oust the state's authority over that subject." **Public education is committed to the control of school authorities.** Federal courts in Kansas, Virginia, New Jersey, Texas and Michigan have held parents have no constitutional right to be on school grounds. *Mayberry v. Independent School Dist No. 1 of Tulsa County, Oklahoma*, No. 08-CV-416-GKF-PJC, 2008 WL 5070703 (N.D. Okla. 11/21/08).

◆   South Carolina legislators considered a bill to offer parents tax credits for private and home school expenses. A local school board believed the bill would undermine public school education, and it resolved to express opposition to the bill. The board instructed its director of community relations to communicate its position, and she did so on the district's website. The site was linked to other websites operated by bill opponents. The director emailed school employees and circulated fact sheets and opinions expressing the district's position. A parent sought to use the same channels to voice his support for the bill. The superintendent denied the request, and the parent sued the school district in a federal district court. The case reached the U.S. Court of Appeals, Fourth Circuit. It held government speech is exempt from First Amendment scrutiny.

**The Supreme Court has stated that "the government may advocate in support of its policies with speech that is not supported by all."** Generally, the government may support valid programs and policies and advocate particular positions. The district had approved a message of opposition to the bill and could deny access to its channels of communications. The district did not create a limited public forum, and the parent's speech rights were not implicated. *Page v. Lexington County School Dist. One*, 531 F.3d 275 (4th Cir. 2008).

◆    A Texas principal instructed students not to wear controversial T-shirts the day after about 300 Hispanic students walked out of school as part of nationwide demonstrations to protest pending immigration reform legislation in Congress. The principal issued about 130 suspensions for disobeying his order not to wear protest T-shirts the day after the nationwide demonstration. Many angry parents came to protest the suspension of their children. After some parents refused to leave the building, school security asked them to leave the campus. Several families sued, asserting First Amendment violations. A court upheld the principal's action, noting that he was responding to threats of violence at a school with a history of high racial tension. The court also rejected a claim by parents that they had been excluded from campus in violation of their rights. **A school can prevent parental access to the premises when necessary to maintain order and prevent disruptions to the education environment.** *Doe v. Grove Public School Dist.*, 510 F.Supp.2d 425 (S.D. Tex. 2007).

◆    An Illinois parent was convicted of a crime which defined him as a child sex offender. However, he was not required to register under the Illinois Sex Offender Registration Act. He brought his children to school activities, games and practices, and picked them up for medical appointments and emergencies. A 2005 law prohibited child sex offenders from being on or within 500 feet of school grounds when children were present, unless the offender was a parent or guardian of a student attending the school, and was there to meet or confer with school staff about the child's performance and adjustment in school. The law further required a child sex offender to notify the school principal of his or her presence at a school. School officials denied the parent's requests to come to school for his own children's activities. The parent sued the school district for an order to allow him to attend school events, concerts and games with his family. He also sought to proceed under the fictitious name "John Doe." The court found the parent's interests in privacy did not outweigh the public interest in the open nature of court proceedings, and it ordered him to proceed under his true name. **The court denied his motion for permission to attend school events during the litigation.** *Doe v. Paris Union School Dist. No. 95*, No. 05-2249, 2006 WL 44304 (C.D. Ill. 2006).

◆    An Illinois mother had sole custody of her two children, but her divorce decree specified that the children's father had joint, equal access rights to school records. The parents were required to cooperate to ensure authorities sent them dual notices of their children's school progress and activities. The father criticized a school principal at public meetings, complained that nothing was done when his son was bullied, and claimed the school did not provide him notices, records, correspondence and other documents sent to custodial parents. He wrote letters to the principal about these matters, then stated that the principal excluded him from the playground when he sought to observe his son during recess, and turned him down as a volunteer playground monitor.

The father sued the principal and school district for constitutional and state law violations. A federal court dismissed the case, and he appealed. The U.S. Court of Appeals, Seventh Circuit, noted the difficulty for schools to accommodate demands by divorced parents. The father's rights concerning his children's records were no greater than the school's interest in keeping as free as possible from divorce matters. **The only constitutional right concerning the education of one's child was the right to choose the child's school.** This was not a right to participate in the school's management. Schools also have a valid interest in limiting a parent's presence on campus. While most of the father's criticisms of administrators were "personal," he also was critical of them in public meetings and questioned their inadequate responses to bullying. The district and the principal prevailed on the father's due process claims, but the equal protection and speech rights claims were remanded to the lower court for further consideration. *Crowley v. McKinney*, 400 F.3d 965 (7th Cir. 2005).

## B.  Curriculum

*Courts have repeatedly rejected parental attempts to direct school curriculums through lawsuits. School boards have broad powers to direct and control curriculums. Parental rights to direct and control the education of children do not extend to the selection of the curriculum.*

◆   A New Hampshire taxpayer organization accused a school board of using public resources to engage in one-sided advocacy regarding election matters. The organization sued the board and town in state court, seeking an order to halt the board from sending any mailings on election issues. The court denied relief, finding "the government may use public funds to endorse its own measures." A final judgment for the board and town was affirmed by the state supreme court. The organization and its chairman then filed an action against the town and board in a federal district court, adding new claims and new taxpayers as parties. One claim alleged the town did not permit the organization to link its website to the town website while others were allowed to do so.

The court noted that most of the claims had (or could have) been raised in the state court case. It applied doctrines of *res judicata* and collateral estoppel, which bar claims between the same parties that have already been considered. On appeal, the U.S. Court of Appeals, First Circuit, held the addition of three new taxpayers did not change the outcome. Federal courts must give state court judgments the same effect they have under state law. **The court held the government may "speak for itself" and may use other parties to say its message.** For that reason, the town's decision to disallow the taxpayers from linking to their website was permissible. No similar group was allowed to link to the website. The town did not turn its website into a designated public forum by linking to a community event site. As the lower court had correctly held the remaining claims were barred, the judgment was affirmed. *Sutliffe v. Epping School Dist.*, 584 F.3d 314 (1st Cir. 2009).

◆   Pennsylvania parents who participated in elementary school curricular activities were subject to the same restriction on promotion of messages in class as their children. **So a parent could be barred from reading a religious text to kindergartners.** For more details about this case, see Chapter Four, Section I.A. *Busch v. Marple Newton School Dist.*, 567 F.3d 89 (3d Cir. 2008).

◆   An Anabaptist Mennonite parent protested Pledge of Allegiance recitations at his children's school by handing out flyers on a sidewalk near a district high school. The district rejected as inappropriate the parent's submission for an advertisement for "www.CivilReligionSucks.com" in the school yearbook purporting to offer "flag desecration products." His request to distribute flyers at an elementary school was also denied. After the district rejected the parent's request to place an advertisement in a school newspaper, he sued.

A federal court explained that while parents have a due process right to bring up their own children, states may condition that right. The parent's rights did not vest him with the authority to intervene and modify the school curriculum. The Pledge was being administered in a constitutional way. Students were allowed to remain quietly seated during recitations. Nothing required school officials to actively notify students of their rights to object. **The parent did not have the right to "dictate school curriculum to suit his own religious point of view."** And educators may exercise control over school publications, which are considered curricular. *Myers v. Loudoun County School Board*, 500 F.Supp.2d 539 (E.D. Va. 2007).

◆   A California volunteer mental health counselor developed a psychological assessment questionnaire as part of her master's degree program in psychology. The district agreed to survey first-, third- and fifth-graders and use the results for an intervention program to help children reduce barriers to learning created by anxiety, depression, aggression and verbal abuse. The counselor sought the consent of parents in a letter stating the nature and purpose of the questionnaire. She did not mention that 10 of the 79 questions involved sexual topics. After the survey was administered, parents learned of the survey questions about sex.

Students were asked if they felt they touched their private parts too much, could not stop thinking about sex, thought of touching others' private parts, had "sex feelings in my body," or washed themselves because of feeling "dirty on the inside." **Parents claimed they would not have consented to the survey had they known of these questions.** They sued the school district for constitutional privacy rights violations, and included a state law negligence claim. A federal district court dismissed the case, and the parents appealed. The U.S. Court of Appeals, Ninth Circuit, rejected the parents' claim to a fundamental right to control the upbringing of their children by "introducing them to matters of and relating to sex in accordance with their personal religious values and beliefs," and to exclusively determine when and how their children were exposed to sexually explicit subjects. Parents have a limited fundamental liberty interest to make decisions about the care, custody and control of their children. As they could not dictate the curriculum, the judgment was affirmed. *Fields v. Palmdale School Dist.*, 427 F.3d 1197 (9th Cir. 2005).

## V.  USE OF SCHOOL FACILITIES

*Schools may establish reasonable rules governing the time, place and manner of speech on school property, as discussed in Chapter Four, Section II. As in religious speech cases, the reasonableness of these rules depends upon the type of forum established by the school. A "limited public forum" exists on property that is generally open for use by the public. Time, manner and place regulations regarding a limited public forum must be content-neutral and narrowly tailored to serve a significant governmental interest. They must also provide for ample alternative channels of communication.*

### A.  Student Organizations and Demonstrations

*Student First Amendment rights are not coextensive with those of adults. School demonstrations may be enjoined if they are materially disruptive or invade the rights of others. Many student group access cases interpret the federal Equal Access Act (EAA), 20 U.S.C. §§ 4071-4074, which is more fully discussed in Chapter Four, Section II.C.*

*The U.S. Supreme Court relied on K-12 school law precedents in holding that a state-affiliated California law college could deny official recognition to a Christian student organization because the group only accepted members who shared the organization's beliefs about religion and sexual orientation.*

◆  Hastings College of Law allowed officially recognized Registered Student Organizations (RSOs) to use college communications channels, office space and email accounts. RSO events were subsidized by student fees. To gain RSO status, groups had to be non-commercial and comply with school policies, including a nondiscrimination policy. The Christian Legal Society (CLS) did not accept students whose religious convictions differed from its Statement of Faith, which affirmed belief in Christian tenets. The group also believed sexual activity should not take place outside marriage between a man and a woman. The CLS sought an exemption from the nondiscrimination policy, but Hastings found the group excluded students from membership based on their religion and sexual orientation. Hastings denied the request to recognize CLS as an RSO for noncompliance with its nondiscrimination policy. In a federal district court action against Hastings, the CLS asserted speech, religious free exercise and due process violations. The court upheld Hastings' policy. After the Ninth Circuit affirmed the judgment, the U.S. Supreme Court heard the case.

The Court held some restrictions on access to limited public forums are allowed. Regulations on speech are allowed only if they serve a compelling state interest. According to the Court, the CLS faced only indirect pressure to modify its policies. The group could still exclude any person for any reason if it decided to forego the benefits of RSO recognition. Hastings' policy applied to "all comers." **Among the Court's findings was that an all-comers policy ensured a student was not forced to fund any group that might exclude her.** An all-comers requirement helped Hastings "police" its policy without inquiring into the reasons for restricting RSO membership. The Court found Hastings reasonably believed its policy encouraged tolerance, cooperation and learning among its students. While the CLS could not take advantage of RSO benefits, electronic media and social networking sites reduced the importance of RSO channels. As for the CLS's argument that Hastings had no legitimate interest in regulating its membership, the Court held Hastings could "reasonably draw a line in the sand permitting all organizations to express what they wish but no group to discriminate in membership." The policy did not distinguish among groups based on viewpoint, and the Court held it was "textbook viewpoint neutral." *Christian Legal Society Chapter of the Univ. of California, Hastings College of Law v. Martinez*, 130 S.Ct. 2971 (U.S. 2010).

◆   A group of Florida students sought official recognition of a gay-straight alliance club. They claimed their purpose was to promote tolerance and equality among students, regardless of sexual orientation or gender identity. They sought to create a safe, respectful learning environment for all students and to work with the school administration and other clubs to end prejudice and harassment. The principal denied approval of official recognition as a school club with access to school facilities on the same basis as other student clubs. The club sued, asserting that the school board had violated the EAA. A court explained that the EAA prohibits schools from denying equal access and fair opportunities on the basis of religious, political, philosophical or other content of speech that may be expected at meetings of student groups in limited open forums. The school board claimed the club was "sex-based" and that its speech presented a threat to school order. The court held that **the board did not offer any evidence to refute the club's assertion that it did not discuss sex**, let alone promote sexual activity. The court also rejected the board's claim that the club would interfere with its abstinence-based sex education curriculum. The court ordered the board to recognize the club and grant the privileges given to other student clubs. *Gay-Straight Alliance of Okeechobee High School v. School Board of Okeechobee County*, 483 F.Supp.2d 1224 (S.D. Fla. 2007).

In later activity, the court held the club had a tolerance-based message that did not materially or substantially interfere with discipline in school operations. To justify its refusal to recognize the club as a school organization, the school board had to show more than mere discomfort and unpleasantness associated with an unpopular viewpoint. Despite prevailing, the club did not demonstrate compensable injury, and it was awarded only $1 in nominal damages. *Gonzalez v. School Board of Okeechobee County*, 571 F.Supp.2d 1257 (S.D. Fla. 2008).

◆   An 18-year-old Virginia student distributed small anti-abortion flyers at school in his sophomore and junior years as part of a "Pro-Life Day of Silent Solidarity." No disruption was reported. As a high school senior, the student again handed out anti-abortion literature in school hallways and the cafeteria during non-instructional times. The principal called the student to his office to tell him he could only distribute the flyers before or after school. The student contacted a lawyer, and within a month, the district devised a rule for students who were not associated with approved student organizations or curricular programs. It gave them no option for distributing non-school materials during the school day. The student sued the school district for an order to prohibit the enforcement of the ban on distribution of his materials.

The court found that the rule virtually banned the circulation of all written communication during the instructional day. It held the district had to show that the student's speech presented a reasonable fear of materially disrupting class work, creating substantial disorder, or invading the rights of others. **There was no evidence that the student's anti-abortion literature would cause disruption in the school.** The district had acted with a remote apprehension of disturbance rather than a specific and significant fear of disruption. The student had distributed similar literature the two previous school years without disruption. The rule was unreasonable. The court granted the student's request for a preliminary order preventing the board from enforcing the rule. *Raker v. Frederick County Public Schools*, 470 F.Supp.2d 634 (W.D. Va. 2007).

◆   A Texas school board adopted a policy allowing non-curriculum-related student clubs to meet and use school bulletin boards and public address systems. It also had an "abstinence-only policy" banning all speech about sexual activity. A gay/straight club sought permission to post notices about its meetings and to distribute flyers at school and use the school's PA system. Club members addressed the board and stated that their goals were to educate and help the community, improve relations between heterosexuals and homosexuals, and "educate willing youth about safe sex, AIDS, hatred, etc."

The board did not act on the club's request, and the club was not allowed to post advertisements in school. Administrators turned down further requests to use school facilities, and club members sued for First Amendment and Equal Access Act (EAA) violations. A federal district court held that **the district had a compelling interest in protecting student health and well-being and preventing recognition of groups based on sexual activity**. There was obscene material on the club's website. As club members failed to show that any other groups intended to discuss sexual content, they could not show discrimination against their viewpoint. The district was entitled to pretrial judgment on the First Amendment and EAA claims. The EAA does not limit a school's authority to maintain order and discipline on school grounds. The club's stated goals contradicted the district curriculum, and the superintendent was entitled to qualified immunity. *Caudillo v. Lubbock Independent School Dist.*, 311 F.Supp.2d 550 (N.D. Tex. 2004).

◆   A Kentucky high school's site-based decision-making council approved a proposal for a gay straight alliance (GSA) club. Students who opposed the GSA club protested, and many parents threatened to remove their children from the school system. The school board then voted to ban all non-curricular clubs. The principal let the GSA club use school facilities as an outside organization, but did not allow the club to meet in homerooms or before school in a classroom. Four other non-curriculum-related student organizations retained access to school facilities during this time. The GSA club and its members sued for an order requiring the board to afford it the same opportunity to use school facilities as other student clubs enjoyed. A federal district court rejected the board's argument that the other organizations were "curriculum related."

**A school opens up a "limited open forum" if it allows even one non-curriculum-related student group to use its facilities.** A club cannot be denied permission to meet at school during noninstructional time if others may do so. When a limited open forum has been created, a school may prohibit only meetings that materially and substantially interfere with school activities. Here, the school's treatment of the GSA club was a content-based restriction that was forbidden by the EAA. The board could not deny access to its facilities based on the uproar caused by recognition of the GSA club. *Boyd County High School Gay Straight Alliance v. Board of Educ. of Boyd County*, 258 F.Supp.2d 667 (E.D. Ky. 2003).

## B. Non-Student Groups

◆ Over time, Utah municipal officials accepted at least 11 monuments for display from private groups or individuals, including a wishing well, fire station, a September 11 monument, and a Ten Commandments monument. A Gnostic Christian organization called "Summum" sought to build a monument on public grounds containing its "Seven Aphorisms," or principles of creation. The organization stated that the Aphorisms had been handed down from God to Moses with the Ten Commandments, but withheld because the people were not ready to receive them. When the city declined Summum's request, the group sought a federal court order directing the city to permit its project.

The court denied the request, but the U.S. Court of Appeals, Tenth Circuit, held that the city had to allow the monument, as parks are traditionally considered public forums for speech. Appeal reached the U.S. Supreme Court, which held that **the First Amendment restricts government regulation of private speech, but does not regulate government speech**. The Court declared that government entities may "speak for themselves." Government entities may exercise the freedom to express their own views when receiving assistance from private sources when they deliver a "government-controlled message." Government speech must comply with constitutional provisions, such as the Establishment Clause, and the government was accountable to the electorate and the political process for its advocacy. When private speech was allowed in a public forum, the government could not place content-based restrictions upon private speech. In this case, the permanent monuments on display were "government speech" that the city could control. A "forum analysis" did not apply to the installation of permanent monuments on public property. The Court reversed the judgment. *Pleasant Grove City, Utah v. Summum*, 129 S.Ct. 1125 (U.S. 2009).

◆ Anti-abortion activists drove a truck around a California middle school, displaying enlarged, graphic images of early-term aborted fetuses. An assistant principal observed that some students became upset and felt that the pictures on the truck created a traffic hazard, so he contacted the sheriff's department. Two deputies arrived, detained the activists for about 75 minutes and searched their vehicles. Deputies talked with their supervisors about the legality of stopping the display. The assistant principal and a deputy instructed the activists to leave, after reading California Penal Code Section 626.8 to them. Section 626.8 prohibited a person from coming into school buildings or grounds where the person's "presence or acts interfere with the peaceful conduct of the activities of the school or disrupt the school or its pupils or school activities." The activists sued the deputies, the sheriff's department and assistant principal for violating their speech rights and for an unreasonable search and seizure.

A federal district court dismissed the case, and the activists appealed to the U.S. Court of Appeals, Ninth Circuit. The court agreed with the activists that the deputies and assistant principal applied section 626.8 unconstitutionally. **Peaceful public expressions of ideas cannot be prohibited because they may be offensive to others, or simply because bystanders may object.** Any disruption caused by the graphic display was a result of student reaction and discussion. Section 626.8 applied only to interference or disruption caused by the manner of a person's expressive conduct. The law could not be used to infringe upon the lawful exercise of protected speech. Thus, the judgment on the speech rights claim was reversed. While the deputies and assistant principal had violated the activists' speech rights, they were entitled to qualified immunity, since they made a reasonable mistake in believing that Section 626.8 applied. However, the deputies were denied immunity for the long detention of the activists. The investigation should not have taken more than the few minutes needed to check for outstanding warrants. *Center for Bio-Ethical Reform v. Los Angeles County Sheriff Dep't*, 533 F.3d 780 (9th Cir. 2008).

◆   A Montana speaker received $1,000 from a ministerial association to serve as the master of ceremonies at a religious rally held the evening after a school assembly. He claimed that the board reversed a decision to allow him to speak at the assembly in violation of the First Amendment. The U.S. Court of Appeals, Ninth Circuit, held that **the speaker had no protected interest in addressing a public school assembly**. He was not being paid by the board, and was thus not deprived of any valuable government benefit. The speaker later gave his speech off school grounds, and was paid by the ministerial association. No other federal circuit court had found that permission to speak at a school assembly was a valuable government benefit. *Carpenter v. Dillon Elementary School Dist. 10*, 149 Fed.Appx. 645 (9th Cir. 2005).

◆   The No Child Left Behind Act requires each local educational agency that receives assistance under the Act to provide military recruiters access to secondary student names, addresses and telephone numbers. The section, 20 U.S.C. § 7908, has a parental notice requirement. The Solomon Amendment, applicable to higher education institutions, has no such provision. In 2006, the Supreme Court held that law schools had to provide the military the same access granted to all other employment recruiters under the Solomon Act. It held that the broad and sweeping power of Congress to provide for defense included the authority to require campus access for military recruiters. **Congress was free to attach reasonable conditions to federal funding, and the Solomon Amendment regulated conduct, not speech.** *Rumsfeld v. Forum for Academic and Institutional Rights*, 547 U.S. 47 (2006).

# CHAPTER FOUR

## Religion and the Public Schools

## I.  RELIGIOUS ESTABLISHMENT

*The Establishment Clause of the First Amendment to the U.S. Constitution prohibits Congress from making any law respecting the establishment of a religion. Because public schools and administrators are subject to this mandate by operation of the Fourteenth Amendment, the courts have struck down practices that improperly entangle public schools with religion.*

*The U.S. Supreme Court has set forth various tests in Establishment Clause cases, but has held **"the touchstone for our Establishment Clause analysis is the principle that the First Amendment mandates government neutrality between religion and religion, and between religion and non-religion."***

### A.  Prayer and Religious Activity

◆ Illinois' "Silent Reflection and Student Prayer Act" allowed a voluntary moment of silence in public school classrooms. In 2007, an amendment to the act provided that "the teacher in charge **shall** observe a brief period of silence" at the start of every school day, "with the participation of all the pupils" in the classroom. It further provided that the period "shall not be conducted as a religious exercise but shall be an opportunity for silent prayer or for silent reflection on the anticipated activities of the day." A public high school student sued her school district and state officials in a federal district court, which held the amended act invalid.

On appeal, the U.S. Court of Appeals, Seventh Circuit, reviewed Supreme Court precedents including *Wallace v. Jaffree*, 472 U.S. 38 (1985), which involved an Alabama moment of silence act. **The court found the Illinois act served the secular purpose of helping calm students and prepare them for their school day.** No evidence indicated this purpose was a sham, as the student claimed. In *Wallace*, Alabama legislators openly admitted a legislative intent to "return prayer to the public schools." But review of the Illinois legislative debate confirmed a secular purpose and an intent to create uniformity across the state. Nothing indicated the act was motivated by a religious purpose. A review of moment of silence laws in other states revealed that federal courts had upheld similar laws in Georgia, Virginia and Texas. As the state argued, student prayer is permissible, and language in the act negated an impression that students could not pray silently during a moment of silence. A lack of specifics did not make the act so vague that guesswork was required. As a result, the court upheld the act. *Sherman v. Koch*, 623 F.3d 501 (7th Cir. 2010).

◆ A New Jersey head football coach led his teams in pregame prayers for many years. In 2005, parents began to complain, and administrators told him he could not lead, encourage or participate in student prayers. District guidelines emphasized student rights to pray on school property or at school events, so long as it did not interfere with school operations. However, the guidelines barred school representatives from participating in student-initiated prayers.

After temporarily resigning, the coach agreed to abide by the district's policy. He then sued the district and its superintendent. He emailed team co-captains and asked them if they would like to resume pre-game and pre-meal team prayers. After players voted to continue team prayers, the coach stood with them and bowed his head during pre-meal team prayers. He also knelt during pregame prayers. A federal district court found "nothing wrong with remaining silent and bowing one's head and taking a knee as a sign of respect for his players' actions and traditions." The school district appealed to the U.S. Court of Appeals, Third Circuit, which noted that the coach's silent expression of support and respect for the team was "not a matter of public concern." His conduct violated the Establishment Clause. In *Board of Educ. of Westside Community Schools v. Mergens*, 496 U.S. 226 (1990), this chapter, the U.S. Supreme Court held that faculty involvement in student religious groups was limited to a "nonparticipatory capacity." **The relevant question is whether a school official has improperly endorsed religion based on what a reasonable observer, familiar with the context and history of the display, would believe.** Here, the coach's prayer activities with his teams were well known. His conduct over 23 years signaled an unconstitutional endorsement of religion to any reasonable observer. The judgment was reversed. *Borden v. School Dist. of Township of East Brunswick*, 523 F.3d 153 (3d Cir. 2008).

◆   A Pennsylvania parent selected 10 Bible verses for her kindergartener to share with his class, including Psalms 118, Verse 14 which states "The Lord is my strength and my song, and is become my salvation." However, the principal informed the parent that reading the Bible to the class would be "against the law of separation of church and state." The parent sued for speech rights violations under the state and federal constitutions. A court held for the district, and the U.S. Court of Appeals, Third Circuit, affirmed. **A kindergarten class is a "unique forum" that is not a place for debate about issues of public importance.** Age and context are relevant, as "the age of the students bears an important inverse relationship to the degree and kind of control a school may exercise." The younger the student, the more control over speech a school could exercise. *Busch v. Marple Newton School Dist.*, 567 F.3d 89 (3d Cir. 2008).

◆   A New York school district with a Mohawk Indian majority permitted the saying of "Ohen: Ton Karihwatehkwen," also referred to as "the Thanksgiving Address," over the school's public address (PA) system. The address acknowledged people, Mother Earth, plants, fruits, grasses, water, fish, medicine, animals, trees, birds, Grandfather Thunders, Four Winds, Elder Brother Sun, Grandmother Moon, stars, Four Beings and a concept sometimes interpreted as "Creator." A parent who was not Mohawk complained that "the address could be a prayer." A district lawyer agreed, but stated that the school could allow student-initiated recitation of the address at a location chosen by students. The superintendent then let students go to the school auditorium for recitation of the address instead of having it said over the PA system. The saying of the address was also discontinued at pep rallies and at school lacrosse games. Mohawk students sued the school district, superintendent and other officials, asserting that discontinuing the address at school events violated their Equal Protection rights. A federal district court rejected their claim that they were treated differently than students who recited the Pledge of Allegiance.

Thanksgiving is not a religious holiday and is unrelated to a specific group or culture. The district did not broadcast Christmas carols or hymns over the PA system or at pep rallies or games. **Here, the district had attempted to promote diversity, pluralism and tolerance for culture, including Mohawk tradition.** The district continued to celebrate Mohawk culture in many ways. Students could still say the address in the auditorium, and their flag and traditional forms of dress were displayed on some occasions. The address' references to "the life forces of creation" resembled religious belief, as it described the relationship between Mohawks and the earth, using a word frequently translated as "creator." As the district acted reasonably by ending the recitation of the address at rallies, lacrosse games and over the PA system, the court ruled in its favor. On appeal, the U.S. Court of Appeals, Second Circuit, affirmed the judgment. *Jock v. Ransom*, No. 07-3162, 2009 WL 742193 (2d Cir. 3/20/09).

◆   A Louisiana parent claimed that his children's school permitted prayers to be said over the PA systems at sporting events and in school. Student-athletes prayed before and after games, and the school board opened its meetings with a prayer. The parent sued the school board in a federal court for Establishment Clause violations. The parties resolved challenges to most of the practices by consent judgment, but could not agree on the issue of prayers before board meetings. The court then held that these prayers violated the Establishment Clause under the traditional analysis of *Lemon v. Kurtzman*, 403 U.S. 602 (1971). The prayers fell outside a limited exception allowing prayers before legislative sessions found in *Marsh v. Chambers*, 463 U.S. 783 (1983).

The school board appealed to the Fifth Circuit. A three-judge panel of the court held that allowing Christian prayers was unconstitutional. The full court reheard the case and held that the parent did not have standing to bring the challenge. There was no evidence that the parent's own children were exposed to the prayers said at the school board meetings. **"Abstract knowledge" that the prayers were being said was not enough to grant standing to bring an Establishment Clause challenge.** As there was no proof that the parent or his children had ever attended school board meetings where prayers were said, the court vacated the judgment and instructed the lower court to dismiss the case. *Doe v. Tangipahoa Parish School Board*, 494 F.3d 494 (5th Cir. 2007).

◆   A New York school board directed a principal to have a prayer read aloud by each class in the presence of a teacher at the beginning of the school day. The procedure was adopted on the recommendation of the state board of regents. State officials had composed the prayer and published it as part of their "Statement on Moral and Spiritual Training in the Schools." The parents of 10 students sued the board, insisting that use of an official prayer in public schools violated the Establishment Clause of the First Amendment. The New York Court of Appeals upheld the practice as long as schools did not compel pupils to join in the prayer over the parents' objections. On appeal, the U.S. Supreme Court held that the practice was wholly inconsistent with the Establishment Clause. **There could be no doubt that the classroom invocation was a religious activity.** Neither the fact that the prayer was denominationally neutral nor that its observance was voluntary served to free it from the Establishment Clause. *Engel v. Vitale*, 370 U.S. 421, 82 S.Ct. 1261, 8 L.Ed.2d 601 (1962).

◆   Pennsylvania law required that "[a]t least ten verses from the Holy Bible shall be read, without comment, at the opening of each public school on each school day. Any child shall be excused from such Bible reading, or attending such Bible reading, upon written request of his parents or guardian." A family sued school officials to enjoin enforcement of the laws as violative of the First Amendment. The school commissioner of Baltimore had also adopted a rule that mandated the reading of a chapter of the Bible or the Lord's Prayer at the start of each school day without comment. That rule was also challenged. The U.S. Supreme Court consolidated the cases and held that both rules violated the Establishment Clause. The Court reiterated the premise of *Engel v. Vitale*, above, that **neither the state nor the federal government can constitutionally force a person to profess a belief or disbelief in any religion**. Nor can it pass laws that aid all religions as against nonbelievers. The primary purpose of the statutes and rule was religious. The compulsory nature of the ceremonies was not mitigated by the fact that students could excuse themselves. *Abington School Dist. v. Schempp*, 374 U.S. 203, 83 S.Ct. 1560, 10 L.Ed.2d 844 (1963).

◆   **The U.S. Supreme Court invalidated an Alabama statute allowing meditation or voluntary prayer in public school classrooms.** The case was initiated in 1982 by the father of three elementary students who challenged the validity of two Alabama statutes: a 1981 statute that allowed a period of silence for "meditation or voluntary prayer," and a 1982 statute authorizing teachers to lead "willing students" in a nonsectarian prayer composed by the state legislature. After a lower court found both statutes unconstitutional, the U.S. Supreme Court agreed to review only the portion of the lower court decision invalidating the 1981 statute that allowed "meditation or voluntary prayer." The Court concluded that the intent of the Alabama legislature was to affirmatively reestablish prayer in the public schools. Inclusion of the words "or voluntary prayer" in the statute indicated that it had been enacted to convey state approval of a religious activity and violated the First Amendment's Establishment Clause. *Wallace v. Jaffree*, 472 U.S. 38, 105 S.Ct. 2479, 96 L.Ed.2d 29 (1985).

◆   Two Texas students challenged a number of their school district's practices, including one allowing overtly Christian prayers at graduation ceremonies and football games. The district permitted nondenominational prayers at graduation ceremonies, read by students selected by vote of the graduating class. In response to the complaint, the district revised its policies for prayer at school functions by requiring them to be nonsectarian and non-proselytizing. Shortly thereafter, the district enacted new policies deleting the nonsectarian, non-proselytizing requirements for pre-game invocations and graduation prayers. A federal district court ordered the school district to enact a more restrictive policy, allowing only nonsectarian and non-proselytizing prayers.

The case reached the U.S. Supreme Court, which ruled that student-led, pre-game prayers violated the Establishment Clause. Although the district asserted that students determined the content of the pre-game message without review by school officials and with approval by the student body, school officials regulated the forum. **The majoritarian process for selecting speakers guaranteed that minority candidates would never prevail and that their views would be effectively silenced.** The degree of school involvement in the pre-game prayers created the perception and actual endorsement of religion by school officials. *Santa Fe Independent School Dist. v. Doe*, 530 U.S. 290, 120 S.Ct. 2266, 147 L.Ed.2d 295 (2000).

## B.  Instruction of Students

### 1.  Curriculum

◆   A California non-profit organization called Islamic Relief sponsored a charter school with two Minnesota campuses. For the 2008-09 school year, the academy expected $3.8 million in funds from the state of Minnesota. A vast majority of the academy's students were Somali Muslims. The ACLU claimed the academy violated the Establishment Clause by permitting prayer sessions during school hours in which parents, volunteers and teachers participated. The academy was accused of endorsing Islamic dress codes and dietary practices, and providing bus transportation only at the end of an after-school religious program. The ACLU sued academy officials, Islamic Relief and the Minnesota Department of Education in a federal district court, asserting that the academy preferred "Muslim" religious practices. The court found Islamic Relief was not a state actor, but had potential liability under the Establishment Clause due to its role in the traditionally exclusive function of public education.

Minnesota charter schools are a part of the public school system under state law, and the state Charter School Law required each school sponsor to assure compliance with nonsectarian requirements. The court rejected arguments for pretrial dismissal. Issues raised by the academy and Islamic Relief were factual in nature and should not be resolved at this stage of the litigation. For example, **religious entanglement created by the academy's dress code and the busing schedule required a factual inquiry**. The role played by Islamic Relief in the academy's operations also required further scrutiny. As a result, the case required a trial. *American Civil Liberties Union of Minnesota v. Tarek Ibn Ziyad Academy*, Civil No. 09-138 (DWF/JJG) (D. Minn. 7/21/09).

◆  A New York kindergartener made a poster for a class assignment with his mother's help. She wrote statements on the poster such as "prayer changes things" and "Jesus loves children." The student's teacher did not hang the poster, and the school principal later told her to have the student make a new one. After the mother helped her son make a new poster that also had religious themes, the teacher and principal folded it to obscure the religious content. The mother sued the school district and several officials for speech and religious rights violations in a federal district court. The court held for the district, and appeal reached the U.S. Court of Appeals, Second Circuit. In a 2005 decision, the court found the poster was a class assignment given under specific parameters which the school could regulate in a reasonable manner. **Schools may reasonably regulate speech and activities that are part of the school curriculum.** The Establishment Clause claim had been properly dismissed. *Peck v. Baldwinsville Cent. School Dist.*, 426 F.3d 617 (2d Cir. 2005).

The case was returned to the district court, which entered a judgment for the school district and officials. In 2009, the Second Circuit noted the case had been filed 10 years earlier. It held the student now lacked standing to pursue the case because he was seeking an injunction relying on a past, not a future injury. *Peck v. Baldwinsville Cent. School Dist.*, 351 Fed.Appx. 477 (2d Cir. 2009).

◆  A Michigan elementary school held a simulated marketplace event in the school gymnasium. Fifth-graders made products under assignment guidelines for sale at booths in the school gymnasium. Other students at the school visited the booths and purchased goods with faux school currency. A student accepted his mother's suggestion to sell Christmas candy cane-shaped tree ornaments made of pipe cleaners and beads. His father offered to make cards to attach to the canes, which bore a religious message. The student did not attach a sample card when he submitted his required prototype ornament, and he never told the school he intended to attach the cards. On the day of the marketplace event, the student's teacher learned about the card for the first time. She halted sales of the card, and the school principal informed the family that the student could not sell ornaments with the card. The principal stated that the marketplace event was considered instructional time and that the cards could not be attached due to their religious message. However, the student was permitted to sell cards in a school parking lot. Instead, the student sold the ornaments without the cards. He earned an A for the assignment and was not disciplined in any way.

The parents sued the school district and principal for speech rights violations. A court held for the school district, and the U.S. Court of Appeals, Sixth Circuit, affirmed. The marketplace event was part of the fifth-grade curriculum. **Educators do not offend the First Amendment by exercising editorial control over student speech in school-sponsored events.** The school's desire to avoid a curricular event that might offend parents and other children at the school qualified as a valid educational purpose, and the principal's decision to stop the sales of the religious card was based on her reasonable evaluation of legitimate pedagogical concerns. *Curry v. Hensiner,* 513 F.3d 570 (6th Cir. 2008).

◆   A Virginia high school Spanish teacher posted items with religious content on his classroom bulletin board. Following a complaint by a visitor, the principal took down five items, including a "National Day of Prayer" poster depicting George Washington kneeling in prayer, and four newspaper clippings discussing the Bible and religion. The school board had no written policy on teacher use of classroom bulletin boards and it relied on principals to decide which postings were appropriate. The principal's primary criterion for assessing postings was relevancy to the curriculum being taught by the particular teacher.

The teacher sued the board in a federal court, which held that the removed items were "curricular" in nature and that his speech was unprotected. On appeal, the U.S. Court of Appeals, Fourth Circuit, rejected his assertion that he could post any materials he wished in the classroom. His material was curricular in nature, and not a matter of public concern. **School boards have the right to regulate speech within a compulsory classroom setting.** The school had an interest in preventing in-class teacher speech that interfered with day-to-day operations. If speech is curricular in nature, it is not speech on a matter of public concern. Since the materials were likely to be attributed to the high school, the principal had the authority to remove them, and the court affirmed the judgment. *Lee v. York County School Division,* 484 F.3d 687 (4th Cir. 2007).

◆   Dover (Pennsylvania) area residents elected two Fundamentalist Christians to their school board. One became the board's president. He sought to include creationism and prayer in the district curriculum and recommended purchasing a textbook advocating "intelligent design." The board accepted 60 copies and forced teachers to use it as a reference text. The board then voted to change the district's ninth-grade biology curriculum so that "students will be made aware of gaps/problems in Darwin's theory and of other theories of evolution, including but not limited to intelligent design." Resident parents sued the board in a federal district court, asserting Establishment Clause violations.

The court held that **the intelligent design policy conveyed a message of religious endorsement**. None of the experts who testified at trial could explain how intelligent design "could be anything other than an inherently religious proposition." The disclaimer singled out evolution from everything else being taught in the district, suggesting evolution was a "highly questionable opinion or hunch." While evolution was "overwhelmingly accepted" by the scientific community, intelligent design had been refuted in peer-reviewed research papers. The conduct of the board members conveyed a strong message of religious endorsement. The court entered a permanent order preventing the district from maintaining the intelligent design policy and from requiring teachers to denigrate or disparage evolutionary theory. *Kitzmiller v. Dover Area School Dist.*, 400 F.Supp.2d 707 (M.D. Pa. 2005).

◆ **The U.S. Supreme Court let stand a decision by lower courts that a school district's Islam program did not violate the Establishment Clause of the First Amendment.** Prior to the Court's order denying review, the U.S. Court of Appeals, Ninth Circuit, held that the program activities were not "overt religious exercises that raise Establishment Clause concerns." The action was brought by two families who alleged that a middle school world history teacher asked them to choose Muslim names, learn prayers, simulate Muslim rituals and engage in other role-playing exercises. The Ninth Circuit held that the school district and individual school employees were entitled to qualified immunity "because they did not violate any constitutional right, let alone a clearly-established one." *Ecklund v. Byron Union School Dist.*, 549 U.S. 942 (U.S. cert. denied 10/2/06).

◆ In 1981, the Louisiana legislature enacted "Balanced Treatment for Creation Science and Evolution Science in Public School Instruction," an act providing that any school offering instruction in evolution must include equal time for instruction in "creation science." The act required that curriculum guides be developed and research services supplied for creation science but not for evolution. The stated purpose of the act was to protect academic freedom. A group of parents, teachers, and religious leaders challenged the law's constitutionality. A federal court and the Fifth Circuit both held that the act was an unconstitutional establishment of religion, and Louisiana state officials appealed to the U.S. Supreme Court. The Court addressed the issue of whether the Creationism Act was enacted for a clear secular purpose. It noted that **because the act provided for sanctions against teachers who chose not to teach creation science, it did not promote its avowed purpose of furthering academic freedom.** The Court ruled that "[b]ecause the primary purpose of the Creationism Act is to advance a particular religious belief, the Act endorses religion in violation of the First Amendment." The Creationism Act was therefore declared unconstitutional. *Edwards v. Aguillard*, 482 U.S. 578, 107 S.Ct. 2573, 96 L.Ed.2d 510 (1987).

## 2. Textbooks

◆ Massachusetts parents objected to their school district's presentation of books portraying diverse families to their children. This included depictions of families in which both parents were of the same gender. Massachusetts law required notification to parents and an opportunity to exempt their children from curriculums that primarily involved human sexuality. State law also mandated that academic standards include respect for cultural, ethnic and racial diversity, but did not mention or provide for notice to parents when a school curriculum included any discussion of homosexuality. Two families sued the school district, claiming that the exposure of their children to books describing diverse families violated a core belief of their religion that homosexual behavior and gay marriage are immoral and violate God's law. They claimed that two books were part of an effort by the public schools to systematically indoctrinate young children into the belief that homosexuality and homosexual marriage are moral and acceptable conduct. The court dismissed the case.

The U.S. Court of Appeals, First Circuit, found "Given that Massachusetts has recognized gay marriage under its state constitution, it is entirely rational for its schools to educate their students regarding that recognition." **Exposure to the books would not prevent the parents from raising their children in their religious beliefs.** Parental rights in the public school context are not absolute, and parents lack constitutional rights to control each and every aspect of their children's education. No federal case had recognized a due process right to allow parents an exemption from exposure to particular books used in the public schools. Requiring a student to read a particular book is not coercive, and public schools are not obligated to shield students from ideas that are potentially offensive. *Parker v. Hurley*, 514 F.3d 87 (1st Cir. 2008).

◆ A Georgia school district's textbook review committee recommended purchasing *Biology* by Miller and Levine as the best available text. School board members were concerned that their constituents wanted texts with "alternate theories of the origin of life." The board adopted a new policy and regulation providing that evolution would be taught in county science classes, and that religion would not be taught. A school attorney drafted a statement that was eventually written on stickers placed on each textbook. The stickers said: "This textbook contains material on evolution. Evolution is a theory, not a fact, regarding the origin of living things. This material should be approached with an open mind, studied carefully, and critically considered." Parents who believed the stickers endorsed religion sued the school board. A federal district court held that **an informed, reasonable observer would believe the stickers sent a message of approval to creationists**. As the board impermissibly entangled itself with religion, the court ordered it to remove the stickers.

The board appealed to the Eleventh Circuit. It found the lower court had improperly relied on a letter from a parent who objected to teaching evolution and a petition that she allegedly submitted to the board prior to its vote to place the stickers on the new textbooks. The lower court had relied on the timing of events in finding the stickers had the effect of endorsing religion. However, the record did not establish that the letter and petition were submitted to the board before the vote. The court recommended that the lower court issue new findings of fact and conclusions of law. Of particular importance would be what petition, if any, was submitted prior to the board's vote. The court vacated and remanded the decision. *Selman v. Cobb County School Dist.*, 449 F.3d 1320 (11th Cir. 2006). In late 2006, the board voluntarily agreed to refrain from placing any stickers or labels disclaiming evolutionary theory in textbooks.

### 3.   School Music Performances

*In* Nurre v. Whitehead, *below, a school district's tradition of letting seniors pick music for their graduation ceremonies was held to be a "limited public forum." But in* Stratechuk v. Board of Educ., South Orange-Maplewood School Dist., *below, a New Jersey holiday concert was not deemed a public forum. Schools are not public forums unless they are intentionally designated as such.*

◆   A Washington school district received complaints about religious music selections at a 2005 high school graduation ceremony. As the 2006 graduation approached, administrators rejected the school wind ensemble's selection of "Ave Maria," believing it created a risk of new complaints. They asked the ensemble to make another selection. A student member of the wind ensemble sued the school district and superintendent for constitutional violations. A federal district court held the district did not violate the student's rights. On appeal, the U.S. Court of Appeals, Ninth Circuit, held that **instrumental music was "speech" for First Amendment analysis**. Schools are not considered public forums for speech unless they are opened up by officials for indiscriminate use. A limited public forum for expression had been opened in this case because of the district's tradition of letting seniors select the music for their graduation ceremonies. In a limited public forum, restrictions can be based on subject matter, so long as any distinctions are reasonable in light of the purpose of the forum. Here, the school district acted reasonably to avoid repeating the prior year's controversy. The court affirmed the judgment for the district. *Nurre v. Whitehead,* 580 F.3d 1087 (9th Cir. 2009).

◆   A New Jersey school holiday activity policy stated that "special effort must be made to ensure the activity is not devotional and that pupils of all faiths and beliefs can join without feeling they are betraying their own faiths." After receiving complaints about religious music at a school concert, the policy was reexamined. A school fine arts director issued a memo clarifying that music selections representing religious holidays would be avoided. A parent complained this conveyed a message that Christianity was disfavored, and sued.

A federal court ruled for the school district, and the U.S. Court of Appeals, Third Circuit, affirmed the judgment. Applying the test from *Lemon v. Kurtzman,* 403 U.S. 602 (1971), the court found no Establishment Clause violation. As the lower court held, the district's intent was to avoid government endorsement of religious holidays and potential Establishment Clause violations. Although the parent maintained this was a "sham" purpose, the court held **the Constitution did not require schools to promote religion to the maximum extent allowed**. Failure to do so did not make the district "anti-religious," as he claimed. The policy did not preclude religious songs from classrooms or concerts, unless they were specific to a holiday. **School concerts are not public forums,** and as the lower court had correctly found the policy was reasonably related to legitimate pedagogical concerns, the judgment for the school district was affirmed. *Stratechuk v. Board of Educ., South Orange-Maplewood School Dist.,* 587 F.3d 597 (3d Cir. 2009).

## C. Commencement Ceremonies

*Important factual differences led two courts to reach opposite results in challenges to decisions to hold graduation ceremonies at churches. A Wisconsin school district had a new facility where future ceremonies would be held. But a Connecticut district did not use a cheaper alternate site, and the court found a reasonable observer would see religious endorsement when the board voted to hold ceremonies at school sites, then changed course under pressure.*

◆   After denying a motion for a preliminary order that would have halted a Wisconsin school district from holding 2009 graduation ceremonies at a church, a federal district court considered a permanent order. It reviewed evidence that the church was near both of the district's high schools, had air-conditioning, was accessible to disabled people, and had ample parking and a seating capacity of near 3,000. Observers would see many religious articles throughout the church. Some religious items could be covered or removed for graduation ceremonies, but the church was unwilling to remove or cover permanent structures. Alternate sites were suggested over the years, but senior classes had always voted to hold graduation ceremonies at the church. According to the court, **the purpose of the Establishment and Free Exercise Clauses "is to prevent, as far as possible, the intrusion of either the church or the state into the precincts of the other."** Total separation of church and state "is not possible in an absolute sense." The students and parents claimed that holding graduation ceremonies at the church had no secular purpose, but the history and context of the case showed otherwise. It appeared to the court that the ceremonies had been held at the church because it was convenient and cost-effective. This secular purpose was seen in the district's assertion that it would be holding future ceremonies in its new 3,500-seat field house. The objectors did not show rental of a church site created excessive religious entanglement. There was no attempt to "cleanse the Church of religious symbols and items" for ceremonies. The case was dismissed. *Does 1, 7, 8 and 9 v. Elmbrook Joint Common School Dist. No. 21*, No. 09-C-0409, 2010 WL 2854287 (E.D. Wis. 7/19/10).

◆   A Connecticut school district held its high school graduation ceremonies at a cathedral. Before the 2010 graduation ceremony, the school board voted to hold the ceremony on school grounds after learning of a threatened lawsuit. But the board later rescinded its vote after lobbying by a religious organization that promised free legal representation if the board agreed to hold the ceremonies at the cathedral. Alternative sites were rejected, including a symphony hall that would cost a total of $5,000 less than the cathedral. A federal district court case was filed to obtain an order prohibiting the board from holding 2010 graduation ceremonies at the cathedral. Among the court's findings was that many large crosses, banners and other religious items would be in view at the cathedral.

The court held **a reasonable observer would find selection of the cathedral for graduation ceremonies conveyed a message that the board embraced one religious view**. Observers would see religious objects, symbols and messages in the cathedral. Even with modifications, the cathedral remained a religious environment. By selecting the cathedral, the board sent a message that it was closely linked with a religious mission, and that it favored "the religious over the irreligious, and that it prefers Christians" over others. Any consideration of alternate sites did not appear to be open-minded. No precise criteria were stated, and the board rejected a cheaper site. And "the uneasy process of attempting to 'secularize' First Cathedral by covering some of its religious imagery" created excessive government entanglement with religion. Government coercion was found, since graduating seniors had no real choice to skip graduation. As the board failed the relevant Establishment Clause tests, the court issued a preliminary order for the students and parents. *Does 1, 2, 3, 4 and 5 v. Enfield Public Schools*, 716 F.Supp.2d 172 (D. Conn. 2010).

◆   A graduating Nevada high school senior was denied Supreme Court review of lower court decisions that rejected her claims against school officials who turned off her microphone when she deviated from her valedictory speech to talk about her faith in Christ. In a brief memorandum, **the U.S. Court of Appeals, Ninth Circuit, held school officials did not violate the student's rights under the Speech and Free Exercise Clauses of the first Amendment by "preventing her from making a proselytizing graduation speech."** It was also not an equal protection violation, as officials did not allow any other speakers to proselytize. *McComb v. Crehan*, 320 Fed.Appx. 507 (9th Cir. 2009). *McComb v. Crehan*, No. 08-1566, 130 S.Ct. 622 (U.S. cert. denied 11/16/09).

◆   A Colorado high school valedictorian submitted a speech for review by her school principal that did not mention religion. But at the ceremony, she encouraged attendees to learn about Jesus Christ and "the opportunity to live in eternity with Him." After the ceremony, the valedictorian learned she would not receive her diploma unless she publicly apologized. Instead of apologizing, she prepared a statement explaining that her speech reflected her beliefs and that it was made without the principal's prior approval. Although the valedictorian submitted the statement and received a diploma, she sued the school district in a federal district court. After the court held for the school district, she appealed to the U.S. Court of Appeals, Tenth Circuit. It applied *Hazelwood School Dist. v. Kuhlmeier*, 484 U.S. 260 (1988), which held **educators do not offend the First Amendment by exercising editorial control over student speech in school sponsored expressive activities**, "so long as their actions are reasonably related to legitimate pedagogical concerns." Greater control over student speech was appropriate in school-sponsored events because the school community might reasonably perceive them to bear the school's approval. The valedictory speeches were supervised by faculty and were clearly school-sponsored.

An order to apologize was reasonably related to learning, and did not violate the valedictorian's rights. There was no substantial burden on the valedictorian's free exercise or equal protection rights, as she was held to the same religion-neutral policies as others. The judgment was affirmed. *Corder v. Lewis Palmer School Dist. No. 38*, 566 F.3d 1219 (10th Cir. 2009).

◆   A Rhode Island student and her father sued their school district in a federal district court to prevent an annual graduation prayer performed by clergy members of various faiths. The court held the clergy-led prayers violated the

Establishment Clause of the First Amendment. The defendants appealed to the U.S. Court of Appeals, First Circuit, which also held the prayers violated the Establishment Clause. The First Circuit affirmed the judgment.

On appeal, the U.S. Supreme Court held the district violated the Establishment Clause by selecting clergy members to say prayers as part of an official public school graduation ceremony. **The government may not coerce anyone to support or participate in religion, or otherwise act in any way that establishes a state religion or religious faith, or tends to do so.** In this case, state officials directed the performance of a formal religious exercise. The principal decided that a prayer should be given, selected the clergy participant, and directed and controlled the prayer's content. The district's supervision and control of the graduation ceremony placed subtle and indirect public and peer pressure on attending students to stand as a group or maintain respectful silence during the invocation and benediction. The state may not force a student dissenter to participate or protest. The argument that the ceremony was voluntary was unpersuasive, and the Court affirmed the judgment for the student and her parent. *Lee v. Weisman*, 505 U.S. 577 (1992).

## D.  School Policies

### 1.  The Pledge of Allegiance

*In* Croft v. Perry, *a federal court held recitation of the Texas state pledge is a patriotic exercise, and it is made no less so by the acknowledgment of Texas's religious heritage via the inclusion of the phrase "under God."*

*Nearly 70 years ago, the U.S. Supreme Court held the states cannot compel citizens to recite the Pledge of Allegiance in* West Virginia State Board of Educ. v. Barnette, *319 U.S. 624 (1943). The Court held the First Amendment protects both the right to speak freely and the right to refrain from speaking at all.*

◆   In 2007, Texas legislators added "under God" to the state pledge, which now declares "Honor the Texas flag, I pledge allegiance to thee, Texas, one state under God, one and indivisible." A group of parents sued the governor to challenge inclusion of the phrase "under God" in the pledge. A federal district court upheld the pledge. On appeal, the Fifth Circuit reviewed the legislative history of the bill and found it was intended to mirror the national pledge. The Supreme Court has never ruled on the constitutionality of the national pledge, but the Fifth Circuit has previously found it is a "patriotic exercise designed to foster national unity and pride" and is not a religious exercise.

Using the Establishment Clause tests applied by federal courts, the court found the amendment satisfied each of them. It found the Establishment Clause is not violated by "nonsectarian references to religion." Describing the term "God" as "adequately generic," the court said its use was a "tolerable attempt at acknowledging religion without favoring a particular sect or belief." Under *Lemon v. Kurtzman*, the amendment had a secular purpose. The legislature believed that conformity with the U.S. Pledge was the "safest and smoothest means" to acknowledge "our religious heritage." The court found the bill had permissible secular purposes and was not enacted as a sham to advance

Christianity. **The court found no reasonable observer would understand the purpose of the pledge to be religious endorsement.** Use of the words "under God" acknowledged but did not endorse religion. Applying the test from *Lee v. Weisman*, the court held the pledge did not coerce students to engage in a religious exercise and was not "prototypical religious activity." The court held for the governor, finding even with the addition of "under God," the pledge remained a patriotic exercise with a minimal religious component. *Croft v. Perry*, 624 F.3d 157 (5th Cir. 2010).

◆   California teachers led willing students in daily recitations of the Pledge of Allegiance, as permitted by California Education Code Section 52720. A parent claimed the phrase "under God" in the Pledge offended her disbelief in God, interfered with her parental rights and indoctrinated her child. She filed a federal district court case against the school district, alleging Establishment Clause violations. The court held for the parent, and the district appealed to the U.S. Court of Appeals, Ninth Circuit. On appeal, she pursued only claims based on state law and the school district policy. The court held not every mention of God or religion by the government is a constitutional violation. **Complete separation of church and state was not required.** Instead, the court found **the Constitution "affirmatively mandates accommodation, not merely tolerance, of all religions, and forbids hostility towards any."** The child had never recited the Pledge but was seeking to prohibit others from doing so.

As the Supreme Court found in *Elk Grove Unified School Dist. v. Newdow*, this chapter, "the Pledge is a patriotic exercise designed to foster national unity and pride." Finding that Congress had an "ostensible and predominant purpose" to inspire patriotism, the court held the Pledge was predominantly a patriotic exercise. For this reason, the phrase "one Nation under God" did not convert the Pledge from a patriotic exercise into a religious one. While California Education Code Section 52720 permitted teachers to lead Pledge recitations, the court noted objectors could sit or stand quietly. Under each of the tests used by the Supreme Court in Establishment Clause cases, the court found no violation. "One nation under God" described the Republic, and it was not an expression of the speaker's particular theological beliefs. The court held neither the state law nor the district policy violated the Establishment Clause. *Newdow v. Rio Linda Union School Dist*, 597 F.3d 1007 (9th Cir. 2010).

◆   Florida's Pledge Statute requires Pledge recitation at all public schools and requires that "civilians must show full respect to the flag by standing at attention." The law exempts students from Pledge recitation upon presenting a signed, written statement from a parent. An eleventh-grade student challenged the law in a federal court, asserting speech rights violations. The court agreed with the student. State education officials appealed. The U.S. Court of Appeals, Eleventh Circuit, upheld the student's claim that the "standing at attention" provision of the law could not be enforced. **There is a well-established constitutional right to remain seated and silent during Pledge recitations.** While the "standing at attention" provision was unconstitutional, the remainder of the statute did not violate the First Amendment. Parents had a fundamental right to control their children's upbringing. Thus, they could excuse their children from reciting the Pledge, and school officials would have to honor that request even if the students wished to recite the Pledge. Parents could refuse to excuse their children, and those rights would also be honored. According to the court, parental rights to interfere with the wishes of their children trumped school officials' rights to interfere on behalf of the school's interest. *Frazier v. Winn*, 535 F.3d 1279 (11th Cir. 2008).

◆ Virginia law provides for the daily, voluntary recitation of the Pledge and placement of the U.S. flag in each public school classroom. Loudoun County Public Schools implemented the provision through a policy allowing students to remain seated quietly during Pledge recitation if their parents objected on religious, philosophical or other grounds. An Anabaptist Mennonite parent asserted that the Pledge indoctrinated his children with a "'God and Country' religious worldview" and violated the Mennonite Confession of Faith. He sued the school system, asserting that the inclusion of the words "under God" in the Pledge made it a religious exercise that violated the Establishment Clause. A federal district court dismissed the case, finding recitation of the Pledge was a secular activity that neither advanced nor inhibited religion. On appeal, the U.S. Court of Appeals, Fourth Circuit, stated **the Establishment Clause does not require separation of church and state "in every and all aspects."** It rejected the parent's assertion that Pledge recitation was like a prayer. The Supreme Court ruled "fleeting references to God" in a classroom are not unconstitutional. The Establishment Clause "does not extend so far as to make unconstitutional the daily recitation of the Pledge in public school." The court held for the school system. *Myers v. Loudoun County Public Schools*, 418 F.3d 395 (4th Cir. 2005).

◆ The non-custodial father of a California student sued state, local and federal officials in a federal court, claiming that a 1954 Act of Congress adding the words "under God" to the Pledge violated the Establishment Clause. He also claimed a state law requiring elementary schools to open the day with patriotic exercises and the school district's use of daily Pledge recitations violated the Constitution. The court dismissed the case, but the U.S. Court of Appeals, Ninth Circuit, held the 1954 Act and district policy violated the Establishment Clause.

The court denied a motion by the child's mother to intervene in the case, even though a state family court order granted her the child's exclusive legal custody. She alleged that her daughter was a Christian who did not object to recitation of the Pledge. The Ninth Circuit reconsidered the standing issue and noted that the father no longer claimed to represent his daughter. It held that he retained a state law right to expose her to his particular religious views, even if they contradicted those of the mother. The U.S. Supreme Court then rejected the father's claim to unrestricted rights to inculcate his daughter in his atheistic beliefs. His rights could not be viewed in isolation from the mother's parental rights. Nothing done by the mother or the school board impaired his right to instruct the child in his religious views. **State law did not authorize the father to dictate what others could say or not say to his daughter about religion.** The Court reversed the judgment. *Elk Grove Unified School Dist. v. Newdow*, 542 U.S. 1, 124 S.Ct. 2301, 159 L.Ed.2d 98 (2004).

◆   An Alabama student raised his fist and remained silent while the rest of his class recited the Pledge. The principal told him he could not receive a diploma unless he served three days of detention and apologized to the class. The student sued the teacher, principal and school board in a federal court for First Amendment violations. The case reached the U.S. Court of Appeals, Eleventh Circuit, which noted that *West Virginia State Board of Educ. v. Barnette*, 319 U.S. 624 (1943), established a clear right for students to refuse to say the Pledge. Any reasonable person would have known that disciplining the student for refusing to recite the Pledge violated his First Amendment rights. **Officials may only regulate student expression that materially and substantially interferes with school activities or discipline.** Here, the student was being punished for his unpatriotic views, not for being disruptive. *Holloman v. Harland*, 370 F.3d 1252 (11th Cir. 2004).

## 2.  Other Policies

*Courts have upheld released time programs, policies prohibiting harassment based on sexual orientation, and mandatory anti-harassment training for students. Courts have allowed schools to set limits on the time and manner the Gideons may distribute Bibles at school.*

◆   In 2006, the South Carolina legislature enacted the Released Time Credit Act, which permitted school districts to award high school students "no more than two elective Carnegie units for the completion of released time classes in religious instruction." Prior law authorized districts to release students from school to attend classes in religious instruction conducted by a private entity. The Spartanburg County School District adopted a released time program permitting students to receive instruction in a Bible education program. Their grades were sent to the school district by a private religious school and treated as coming from the school "without further inquiry" for entry on student transcripts.

Parents and a public interest group sued the district in a federal district court for Establishment Clause and equal protection violations. The court found **released time programs allowing students to leave campus during school hours for religious instruction have been upheld as constitutional**, notably by the Supreme Court in *Zorach v. Clausen*, 343 U.S. 306 (1952). While the court denied the district's motion to dismiss the Establishment Clause claim, it found no equal protection violation. There was no evidence that students were treated differently based on participation in the released time program. *Moss v. Spartanburg County School Dist. No. 7*, 676 F.Supp.2d 452 (D.S.C. 2009).

The parents and organization sought to join the state of South Carolina as a party. The court held an absent party must be joined when complete relief cannot be awarded among existing parties or if the absence of a party might impair that party's ability to protect an interest or expose the party to a substantial risk of inconsistent obligations. The court held the state was not a required party because its absence would not preclude the parents and organization from obtaining complete relief. *Moss v. Spartanburg County School Dist. No. 7*, No. 7:09-1586-HMH, 2010 WL 2136642 (D.S.C. 5/25/10).

◆   A Missouri school allowed the Gideons to distribute Bibles to fifth-grade classrooms during the school day in the presence of a teacher or administrator. Objecting parents sued the school district. The school board then passed a new policy on the distribution of literature at school. The case reached the U.S. Court of Appeals, Eighth Circuit, which noted that the amended policy required organizations to obtain approval from the superintendent prior to distributing literature. If material was approved by the superintendent, it could be distributed in front of school offices or at a table in the cafeteria during non-class times. If a request was denied, the policy specified that the organization could appeal to the school board. **The amended policy was reasonable and did not prohibit the district from neutrally facilitating private Bible distributions.** *Roark v. South Iron R-1 School Dist.*, 573 F.3d 556 (8th Cir. 2009).

◆   A Kentucky school board implemented a new speech rights policy after being sued by a group of students who petitioned for a gay/straight alliance club. See *Boyd County High School Gay Straight Alliance v. Board of Educ. of Boyd County*, 258 F.Supp.2d 667 (E.D. Ky. 2003), Chapter Three.

The board then adopted policies prohibiting harassment based on sexual orientation, and providing mandatory anti-harassment training to all students. A student believed it was his Christian responsibility to "tell others when their conduct does not comport with his understanding of Christian morality." He said he refrained from commenting about his beliefs to avoid punishment under the school's anti-harassment policy, then sued the board for speech rights violations. The board revised its policy to allow anti-homosexual speech unless the speech was sufficiently severe or pervasive that it adversely affected a student's education or created a climate of hostility or intimidation. The student appealed to the U.S. Court of Appeals, Sixth Circuit, arguing that he had refrained from telling of his beliefs to avoid discipline, and that the new policy "chilled" speech in violation of the First Amendment. The Sixth Circuit ruled against him. Here, **the student's claim that his rights were chilled under the board policy was insufficient to establish standing in a federal court**. It was speculative whether he would have been punished under the new policy. *Morrison v. Board of Educ. of Boyd County*, 521 F.3d 602 (6th Cir. 2008).

◆   A Louisiana elementary school principal informed fifth-grade teachers at his school that the Gideon society would distribute Bibles to the fifth-grade class outside his office. He said that while students did not have to take a Bible, he was acting on instructions from the school board. A student accepted a Bible but claimed she felt pressured to do so because of potential name-calling and teasing from peers if she refused. Her parent sued the school board. A court ruled that **the Bible distribution violated the Establishment Clause**. The student feared peers would say she did not believe in God and call her a "devil worshipper" or "Goth" if she refused a Bible. Concern for religious coercion in elementary grades is strong, based on the impressionability of young students. Elementary students may not fully appreciate the difference between official and private speech, and a school board policy might be misperceived as endorsement. Allowing the Gideons to have access to an elementary school during a school day to hand out Bibles was "unquestionably religious." The board had no secular purpose for the practice, and it created an impression of religious preference that violated the Establishment Clause. *Roe v. Tangipahoa Parish School Board*, Civ. No. 07-2908, 2008 WL 1820420 (E.D. La. 4/22/08).

◆    A New York school district released Catholic and Protestant students to nearby programs at designated times during the school day. Others remained in classrooms with nothing to do until the released students returned. A family claimed the program led to "abusive religious invective directed against those who did not participate and that the district did not adequately train teachers and principals to protect non-participants from the taunts of program participants."

The family sued the district, asserting the "released time" program violated the Establishment Clause by promoting Christianity over other religions and non-religion. A court held for the school district, and the family appealed. The Second Circuit noted the released-time program authorized by New York Education Law permitted districts to release students, with parental permission, for one hour per week for religious instruction. The U.S. Supreme Court had upheld this law in *Zorach v. Clauson*, 343 U.S. 306 (1952). The Second Circuit noted that the program used no public funds and involved no on-site religious instruction. Schools simply adjusted their schedules to accommodate student religious needs. **The court rejected the argument that the school's imprimatur was placed on a program of religious instruction and that churches used the schools in support of their religious missions.** Nothing here suggested that the released time program was administered in a coercive manner. *Pierce v. Sullivan West Cent. School Dist.*, 379 F.3d 56 (2d Cir. 2004).

### 3.  Immunization

*School districts and state educational agencies have a compelling state interest in requiring the immunization of all students in an effort to prevent and control communicable diseases.*

◆    A New York high school denied a student's request for a waiver allowing him to attend school without undergoing immunization pursuant to New York Public Health Law Section 2164(9). The section exempts students from state immunization requirements if their parents hold "genuine and sincere religious beliefs" which are contrary to immunization. The student appealed the district's decision to forbid him from competing or practicing with the lacrosse team, which he had done in years past without obtaining an immunization. While the appeal was pending before the state commissioner of education, he sued the district for violating his religious free exercise rights. He claimed that the district's policy had a discriminatory impact on students whose religious convictions prohibited immunization. The court disagreed, finding that **the district's responsibility for ensuring student safety was rationally based**. It was "firmly established that there is no constitutional right to participate in extracurricular sporting activities." The district did not violate the student's equal protection or religious free exercise rights. *Hadley v. Rush Henrietta Cent. School Dist.*, No. 05-CV-6331T, 2007 WL 1231753 (W.D.N.Y. 4/25/07).

◆    New York parents refused immunizations based on their religious beliefs, asserting that their genuine and sincere beliefs fulfilled the legal requirements for a state law religious exemption. School officials met with the family to discuss their position. The parents stated that use of aborted fetal tissue made immunization unholy and violated God's supreme authority. However, they cited no biblical authority for this claim. The school district denied the request, and its decision was upheld by the New York State Commissioner of Education.

A federal court noted the parents did not know the basis for their religious objection. The district sought pretrial judgment on that ground. The court found the Second Circuit has emphasized the limited function of the judiciary in determining whether beliefs are to be accorded First Amendment protection. To assess a person's religious sincerity, the Second Circuit used a subjective test under which the person's claim must be given great weight. **So long as the person conceived of his or her beliefs as religious in nature, the subjective test was met.** It was not appropriate to award pretrial judgment when a person's subjective state of mind was at issue. Since the family had presented evidence of a sincerely held religious belief against immunization, the court denied pretrial judgment. *Moses v. Bayport Bluepoint Union Free School Dist.*, No. 05 CV 3808 (DRH) (ARL), 2007 WL 526610 (E.D.N.Y. 2/13/07).

◆    Arkansas law prevented schools from admitting students without a certification of immunization for specified diseases. An exemption was granted to families who objected to immunization on religious grounds if they were members of a "recognized church or religious denomination." Four Arkansas students filed lawsuits against state and local officials, asserting the law violated the Establishment Clause by limiting the exemption from immunization to those who objected on religious tenets and practices of a "recognized" church or denomination. The students claimed they had sincere religious beliefs even though they did not belong to a religion "recognized" by the state. The courts held that the exemption violated the Establishment Clause, agreeing with the students that the exemption had a discriminatory impact on religious groups not officially recognized by the state. But **the unconstitutional part of the law could be separated from the rest of the law** and the students had to be immunized. On appeal, the Eighth Circuit noted the Arkansas legislature had by then amended the law to omit the references to "recognized religions." The exemption was now available to any family with religious or philosophical objections to immunization. As a result, the case was moot and the court dismissed it. *McCarthy v. Ozark School Dist.*, 359 F.3d 1029 (8th Cir. 2004).

## II.  USE OF SCHOOL FACILITIES

*Courts use a "forum analysis" when considering the use of school facilities by students, clubs and non-students. A "limited public forum" exists whenever a government agency voluntarily opens up its facilities or programs for public use. The "forum" may be a bulletin board, public address system, or the use of classrooms for meetings during noninstructional time. Once a district makes the decision to open a limited public forum, any restriction it places on speech must be reasonable in view of the purposes of the forum. There can be no discrimination on the basis of viewpoint. The nature of the forum determines the limits that may be placed on speech by intended users. For cases involving the forum analysis and secular speech, see Chapter Three, Section V.*

The No Child Left Behind (NCLB) Act requires school districts to certify to their state educational agencies "that no policy of the local educational agency prevents, or otherwise denies participation in, constitutionally protected prayer in public elementary schools and secondary schools." The requirement is a condition of receiving federal funds, and is codified at 20 U.S.C. § 7904.

◆ A Tennessee elementary school student said staff members told him not to read and discuss the Bible with his friends on the playground during recess. He said he was told he could discuss the Bible only during his "free time," which staff said did not include recess. The student's parent sued the school board in a federal district court for constitutional rights violations. In pretrial activity, **the court held recess was non-instructional time to which full First Amendment speech protections applied**. And it held the student had a clearly established constitutional right to read and study the Bible in a nondisruptive manner. A jury returned a verdict for the school board and officials. The student sought a post-trial judgment or a new trial, but the court found a jury verdict can be overturned only if the jury had "reached a seriously erroneous result."

According to the court, sufficient evidence supported the verdict. While the student claimed he only wanted to read the Bible with his friends, the school principal testified during the trial that she had rejected a request for an adult-led Bible study class. She said she did not learn of the informal playground Bible study until later. As a result, the court found the principal had misunderstood the student's intent. Testimony by the superintendent corroborated the belief that an adult-led Bible study class was being sought. There was testimony that no parents approached the school about a Bible club. **It was reasonable for the jury to find there had been a misunderstanding about the nature of a Bible club, and the court found no First Amendment violation.** Since the court found the verdict was not a "seriously erroneous result," the court denied the student's request for a judgment in his favor or a new trial. *L.W. v. Knox County Board of Educ.*, No. 3:05-CV-274, 2010 WL 3632208 (E.D. Tenn. 9/9/10).

## A. Assemblies and School-Sponsored Events

◆ A New Jersey school district hosted after-school talent shows called "Frenchtown Idol." The shows were held at 7:00 p.m. in the school auditorium and were entirely voluntary. Students were invited to develop their own performances at home and received no school credit for participating. Three teachers reviewed all song lyrics, skits, and acts. A student submitted "Awesome God" as her talent show selection. The district superintendent found this inappropriate for the show because of its "overtly religious message and proselytizing nature." She found the song was "the musical equivalent of a spoken prayer." The music teacher informed the student that she could not sing "Awesome God" at the show and offered her two songbooks to select a replacement song, even if it was a religious one. The student sued the board in a federal district court for constitutional rights violations. The court found the talent show was not a "school-sponsored production." **Speech taking place in the show "was the private speech of a student and not a message conveyed by the school itself."** The board could not engage in viewpoint discrimination. Any restrictions on speech had to be viewpoint neutral and reasonable in view of the purposes served by the forum. Here, the exclusion of speech simply because it was controversial or divisive was "viewpoint discrimination." The court rejected the school board's argument that it had to exclude the song to avoid an Establishment Clause violation. It was unlikely an audience would perceive the student's song to be the expression of anyone's view but her own. The court awarded pretrial judgment to the student. *Turton v. Frenchtown Elementary School Dist. Board of Educ.*, 465 F.Supp.2d 369 (D.N.J. 2006).

◆ Ohio high school students had a band that performed mostly Christian songs. The father of one student was a school board member and the band's manager. He sought approval for a band performance at a school-wide assembly during school hours. The district superintendent first approved the performance but cancelled it after a school attorney warned her of Establishment Clause problems. The board member appeared in a television interview. He said "together we can bring religion back into the schools." The board then asked another band that performed secular music to perform at the assembly. Band members sued the school district in a federal court, asserting their appearance was cancelled because of disapproval of their Christian message.

The court rejected the band members' claim that the assembly was a public forum in which the district had to maintain viewpoint neutrality. The assembly was not a "forum" of any kind, and for that reason, the district was not subject to any neutrality requirement. The school district "was entitled to exercise editorial control" over it. When the school itself was the speaker, educators were entitled to exercise greater control to assure the views of speakers were not erroneously attributed to the school. **The school district could discriminate against the band members because of their Christian religious identity.** The court awarded pretrial judgment to the school district. *Golden v. Rossford Exempted Village School Dist.*, 445 F.Supp.2d 820 (N.D. Ohio 2006).

### B.  Student Groups

◆ A New York student submitted a request to use school facilities for private religious club meetings after school hours. The superintendent denied the request, stating that this use of facilities amounted to school support of religious worship. The club sued the school in a federal district court, which issued an order preventing the school from prohibiting the club's use of school facilities. The U.S. Court of Appeals, Second Circuit, later held that the school's denial of access was permissible because it was based on content rather than viewpoint.

The club appealed to the U.S. Supreme Court, which observed that **the nature of the forum determines the limits that a school may place on speech taking place in the forum**. The school had established a limited public forum in which it could reasonably seek to avoid identification with a particular religion. While the school was not required to allow all speech, limits on speech could not be based upon viewpoint and had to be reasonable in light of the purpose of the forum. The school's policy broadly permitted speech about the moral and character development of children. The school had excluded the club from its facilities solely because of its religious viewpoint. This resulted in unconstitutional viewpoint discrimination. "Speech discussing otherwise permissible subjects cannot be excluded from a limited public forum on the ground that the subject is discussed from a religious viewpoint." Club meetings took place after school hours and were not school sponsored. No risk of coercion was present, because students had to obtain permission from their parents to attend meetings. The school failed to show any risk of school endorsement of religion. The Court reversed the judgment. *Good News Club v. Milford Cent. School*, 533 U.S. 98 (2001).

◆  A South Carolina school district charged the Child Evangelism Fellowship of South Carolina fees to use its facilities for Good News Club meetings after school. Many other users had free access to school facilities, including parent-teacher and district organizations, booster clubs, political parties, the SADD, 4-H, FFA and FHA. After paying the district over $1,500 during a two-year period, the Good News Club sought a waiver from the fee. The district denied the request, and the club sued it in a federal district court. The board eliminated a "best interest of the district" waiver provision from the policy. A new provision waived fees for organizations that had used its facilities for at least 20 years. Only scouting groups met this requirement. The case reached the Fourth Circuit, which held the provision unconstitutional. The government may not regulate speech based on its content or the message it conveys. **Once government facilities are opened for private speech, an agency may not discriminate based upon the viewpoint of the speaker.** The "best interest of the district" provision was subjective and "a virtual prescription for unconstitutional decision making." And the revised provision incorporated the viewpoint discrimination built into the earlier "best interest" provision, under which the scouting groups initially got access. *Child Evangelism Fellowship of South Carolina v. Anderson School Dist. Five*, 470 F.3d 1062 (4th Cir. 2006).

◆  An Oregon school district let Boy Scout representatives make presentations during school lunch periods when students were required to be present. School employees helped the Scouts by quieting children, directing attention to the Scout representative and helping fasten hospital-style bracelets on students with information on Scout meetings. Staff also distributed Scout flyers in classes and put Scout information in school newsletters. An atheist parent objected to these practices and filed a discrimination complaint against the district under an Oregon statute. The state superintendent of public instruction investigated the complaint, but found no substantial evidence of discrimination. A state circuit court reversed the decision, and the Court of Appeals of Oregon affirmed.

The Supreme Court of Oregon reviewed the case, and noted that the parent did not challenge the decision to allow Boy Scout recruiting at school, but only sought to determine whether the district had discriminated under the statute. Under the statute, there could be no discrimination on the basis of religion or other protected grounds in any public school program, service or school activity. Class time and lunch periods were "school activities." However, handing out Boy Scout flyers and making presentations did not amount to discrimination against the student because it did not treat him differently than others because of religion. **The flyers and other information were distributed to all students, with no mention of a religious affiliation.** The lunchroom presentations were neutral, making no mention of religion. The court reversed the judgment. *Powell v. Bunn*, 341 Or. 306, 142 P.3d 1054 (Or. 2006).

## C. The Equal Access Act

*The federal Equal Access Act (EAA), 20 U.S.C. §§ 4071-4074, governs student use of secondary school facilities during noninstructional time. It makes it unlawful for a public secondary school to deny equal access to facilities, if the school maintains a "limited open forum." A limited open forum exists where student groups have been accorded the right to meet in noncurricular groups on school grounds during noninstructional time.*

◆ A Nebraska high school student wanted permission to begin a Christian Club. The school permitted its students to join, on a voluntary basis, a number of groups and clubs that met after school. Each of these clubs had faculty sponsors. However, the student who wished to start the Christian Club did not have a faculty sponsor. School administrators denied her request because she did not have a sponsor and because they believed a religious club at the school would violate the Establishment Clause. The student sued the school board and administrators in a federal district court. She alleged a violation of the EAA. The district court ruled in favor of the school, holding that the other clubs at the school related to the school's curriculum and thus, the school did not have a "limited open forum" as defined by the EAA.

The student appealed to the Eighth Circuit, which ruled in her favor. The school then appealed to the U.S. Supreme Court, which stated the other clubs did not relate to the school's curriculum. **The school had to provide a limited open forum to all students wishing to participate in groups.** The EAA provided that schools could limit activities that substantially interfered with their orderly conduct. The Court also stated **the EAA did not violate the Establishment Clause because it had a secular purpose and limited the role of teachers who work with religious clubs**. The Court affirmed the decision, holding the school violated the EAA. *Board of Educ. of Westside Community School v. Mergens*, 496 U.S. 226, 110 S.Ct. 2356, 110 L.Ed.2d 191 (1990).

◆ A Minnesota school district classified a gay tolerance organization as "noncurricular." The organization claimed the district violated the EAA by denying it access to school facilities enjoyed by other noncurricular groups like cheerleading and a synchronized swimming club. A federal court granted the organization's request for a preliminary order, finding that cheerleading and synchronized swimming, like the tolerance group, were "noncurricular."

The district appealed to the U.S. Court of Appeals, Eighth Circuit, which explained that a limited open forum exists under the EAA when at least one noncurriculum related group is allowed to meet on school grounds during noninstructional time. The EAA is triggered even if a school permits only one noncurriculum group. The court agreed with the gay tolerance group that cheerleading and the synchronized swimming club were not curriculum-related. The school offered no courses for these activities, and they were not required for a particular course. Accordingly, the gay tolerance group was on the same ground as they were and could use the facilities they enjoyed. **A district could legitimately categorize cheerleading and synchronized swimming classes as "curriculum related" by awarding P.E. credits to participants.** A more drastic option would be to "wipe out all of its noncurriculum related student groups and totally close its forum." The court affirmed the district court's preliminary order for the gay tolerance group. *Straights and Gays for Equality v. Osseo Area Schools-Dist. No. 279*, 471 F.3d 908 (8th Cir. 2006).

The case returned to the lower court, which issued a permanent order for the gay tolerance club to have the same access to meetings, communications and other school facilities as recognized curricular groups. The district appealed again to the Eighth Circuit, which held that the district had violated the EAA by denying the club access to school facilities on the same terms as provided to other noncurricular clubs. And **the placement of favored student groups as student government subgroups did not automatically make them "curriculum related."** This would make it far too easy for a school to circumvent the EAA. The lower court had properly awarded permanent relief to the club, and the judgment was affirmed. *Straights and Gays for Equality v. Osseo Area Schools-Dist. No. 279*, 540 F.3d 911 (8th Cir. 2008).

◆   A Washington school district required student clubs to submit their proposals for official recognition to the Associated Student Body (ASB) council for approval. Students attempted to form a Bible club for several years and submitted three different applications. The ASB denied the application based on the club's proposal to make announcements over the public address system and decorate the school in a biblical theme. The ASB later rejected applications by the club based on its name – "Truth," and its restriction of voting membership to those who professed belief in the Bible and Jesus Christ. After the ASB voted down a second application, the club sued the school district and school officials. A federal court awarded pretrial judgment to the district, finding club membership restrictions were a legitimate reason to deny recognition.

The club appealed to the Ninth Circuit, which ordered the district court to reconsider several claims. It noted that many of the 30 ASB-recognized student clubs had selective membership criteria, including the Earth Club, Gay-Straight Alliance and National Honor Society. Significantly, two honor clubs at the school had gender-exclusive memberships. **The Bible club's membership restrictions inherently excluded non-Christians in violation of the district's non-discrimination policies, making denial of recognition consistent with the EAA.** The club did not show the district's non-discrimination policy restricted ASB status on the basis of religion or the content of speech. To the extent that the district allowed waivers to other groups, there remained an issue of fact to consider. The court reversed and remanded the case for further review. *Truth v. Kent School Dist.*, 542 F.3d 634 (9th Cir. 2008).

◆ A Pennsylvania school district established an "activity period" after homeroom and prior to the first class of the day. During this time, students had to remain on school grounds but could participate in club meetings, go to study hall, attend student activities or relax. The district recognized three student groups as "curriculum-related" and allowed them to meet during the activity period, post signs and use the public address system. When a student Bible Club was not allowed to meet during the activity period, a club member sued the school board for violating the EAA and her First Amendment speech rights. The court denied her request for a preliminary order, finding the activity period was not "noninstructional time" under the EAA.

The student appealed to the Third Circuit, which explained that "noninstructional time" could include the activity period, even though it was neither before the start of the school day, nor after its conclusion. The district had set aside the activity period as noninstructional time. **The court rejected an interpretation of the EAA that would allow districts to evade application of the Act by describing an otherwise "limited open forum" as time that counted toward student instruction.** The district violated the EAA by forbidding Bible club meetings during the activity period. The court remanded the case to determine damages and attorneys' fees. *Donovan v. Punxsutawney Area School Board*, 336 F.3d 211 (3d Cir. 2003).

### D. Non-Student Use

◆ The Good News Club (GNC) held after-school evangelical programs for elementary school students in public schools. Students could only participate if they had prior written parental permission. Meetings were free and students did not raise funds for the GNC. A Virginia school board adopted a new facilities use policy in response to legislation allowing the Boy Scouts to use school facilities. The policy gave the superintendent discretion to waive facilities use fees, and the board waived fees for city or county agencies and groups affiliated with those agencies. All school groups and school-sponsored activities were granted a waiver, as were Boy and Girl Scouts and other patriotic organizations. Local charitable organizations and partners were also exempted from the fee. By contrast, the GNC paid $12.50 per hour to use school facilities. After paying to use school facilities for about six months, the GNC sued.

A federal court noted that the **government does not have to allow all speech on all its property at all times, but once it has opened up facilities to private speech, there can be no discrimination based on the viewpoint of a speaker.** Here, the policy gave the superintendent "complete unfettered discretion in deciding who benefits from the fee-waiver." This improperly allowed the superintendent to decide which organizations could have a fee waiver. As a result, the GNC was entitled to a preliminary order waiving the fees. *Child Evangelism Fellowship of Virginia v. Williamsburg-James City County School Board*, Civ. No. 4:08cv4, 2008 WL 3348227 (E.D. Va. 8/08/08).

◆ A Maryland school district allowed many nonprofit groups to distribute flyers to teachers, who then placed them in student cubbies. The district did not let the Child Evangelism Fellowship distribute flyers for student meetings of the

Good News Club through this forum. The club sued. A federal district court granted the club's request for preliminary relief concerning bulletin boards, open houses and other events, but denied its request to distribute flyers based on the risk of an Establishment Clause violation. On appeal, the U.S. Court of Appeals, Fourth Circuit, reviewed evidence that the district had allowed over 225 groups to distribute flyers in 18 months. Other religious groups, such as the Salvation Army, Jewish Community Center and YMCA were allowed to circulate flyers. **Here, the role of teachers in placing the materials in student cubbies during school hours did not create an Establishment Clause risk.** The risk of religious endorsement was no greater than the risk of a perception of hostility toward religion if the group was not allowed to distribute its flyers. The court reversed the lower court order. *Child Evangelism Fellowship of Maryland v. Montgomery County Schools*, 373 F.3d 589 (4th Cir. 2004).

The board then revised its take-home mail policy. Under the revised policy, materials and announcements of five organizations could be approved for display or direct distribution to students. The case returned to the Fourth Circuit, which found that the new policy gave too much discretion to the school district to control the take-home flyer forum. As the new policy did not require viewpoint neutrality, the court again reversed the judgment. The district could restrict the number or content of messages in the forum in a viewpoint neutral or reasonable manner. It could also eliminate the flyer forum by reserving it solely for government messages. *Child Evangelism Fellowship of Maryland v. Montgomery County Public Schools*, 457 F.3d 376 (4th Cir. 2006).

◆   A New Jersey school district policy reserved the superintendent's right to approve materials from community groups to be sent home with students. Teachers placed approved materials from community organizations in student mailboxes at the close of the school day. Community materials had to meet five requirements, including approval by the superintendent and some relationship to the school or its students. Partisan and election materials were not allowed, nor could students "be exploited" by profit-makers. The policy applied to requests by community groups to post information on school walls, and to "Back to School nights." The district rarely excluded groups from these events.

An evangelical organization sponsored weekly Good News Club meetings after school. The meetings included activities such as Bible lessons and learning games. The superintendent approved the club's request to meet in an elementary school classroom after school hours but rejected its request to distribute flyers and parent permission slips through student mailboxes, citing Establishment Clause concerns. The organization sued the district and its officials for constitutional violations. The case reached the Third Circuit, which held that the district created "limited open public forums" by allowing community groups to use school channels for communication on particular topics. It could not exclude speech unreasonably or discriminate based on viewpoint. The club's materials satisfied all district requirements. The rejection of religious groups which attempted to recruit members was viewpoint discrimination. **Since the district permitted discussion of topics from a secular perspective, it could not shut out speech on the same topics with a religious perspective.** The court rejected the claim that allowing the club to use school facilities would violate the Establishment Clause. *Child Evangelism Fellowship of New Jersey v. Stafford Township School Dist.*, 386 F.3d 514 (3d Cir. 2004).

◆ A New York school district issued regulations allowing social, civic, or recreational uses of its property as well as limited use by political organizations, but provided that the school not be used for religious purposes. An evangelical church sought permission to use school facilities to show a film series on traditional Christian family values. The district denied permission to use its facilities because the film was religious. The church filed a lawsuit in a federal court alleging the district violated the First Amendment. The court found the district's action "viewpoint neutral," and the U.S. Court of Appeals, Second Circuit, agreed. The church appealed to the U.S. Supreme Court, which **held the exclusion of subject matter based on its religious content would impermissibly favor some viewpoints or ideas at the expense of others. Therefore, the regulation discriminated on the basis of viewpoint.**

The exclusion of the church from using school property was not viewpoint neutral. Next, the Court determined that since the film series was not to be shown during school hours and was to be open to those outside the church, the public would not perceive the district to be endorsing religion. Since use of school facilities by the church did not violate the test from *Lemon v. Kurtzman*, permission by the district would not violate the Establishment Clause. The film had a secular purpose, its primary effect did not advance religion, and the showing of the film would not "foster excessive state entanglement with religion." Thus, speech about "family and child related issues" from a religious perspective could be aired on public school grounds. The Court reversed the lower court decisions. *Lamb's Chapel v. Center Moriches Union Free School Dist.*, 508 U.S. 384, 113 S.Ct. 2141, 124 L.Ed.2d 352 (1993).

◆ An Ohio elementary school let community groups place flyers in student mailboxes advertising activities sponsored by the American Red Cross, 4-H Club, sports leagues and local churches. Some of the flyers described religious activities. The principal reviewed the flyers to ensure sponsoring organizations were nonprofit groups serving children in the community, did not advocate any particular religion and did not seek to use flyers as a recruiting tool. Approved flyers were distributed to teachers, who then placed them in student mailboxes with official school papers. Teachers did not discuss the flyers with students. A parent claimed the distribution of flyers advertising religious activities violated the Establishment Clause. He sued the school district in a federal district court.

The court ordered the school to stop distributing flyers that advertised activities at which proselytizing would occur. The district appealed to the Sixth Circuit, which held **no reasonable parent observing the flyers would perceive religious endorsement by the school**. There was no risk of religious coercion, as the activities advertised in the flyers were not school-sponsored and did not take place on school grounds. If the school refused to distribute flyers advertising religious activities while continuing to distribute other flyers, students might suspect disapproval of religion. The court reversed the judgment. *Rusk v. Crestview Local School Dist.*, 379 F.3d 418 (6th Cir. 2004).

### E.  Religious Literature and Symbols

*In* McCreary County v. American Civil Liberties Union of Kentucky, *545 U.S. 844 (2005), the U.S. Supreme Court stuck down the display of the Ten Commandments at county courthouses in Kentucky. In* McCreary County, *the Supreme Court held it would look to the events leading up to a Ten Commandments display to assess its constitutionality. It found substantially religious objectives by the Kentucky counties. In another 2005 case,* Van Orden v. Perry, *545 S.Ct. 677 (2005), the Supreme Court allowed a display of the Ten Commandments on a monument at the Texas Capitol. The Court explained the display was "a far more passable use of those texts than was the case in* Stone, *where the text confronted elementary school students every day."*

◆   A Kentucky statute required the posting of the Ten Commandments on the wall of each public school classroom in the state. A group of citizens sought an injunction against the statute's enforcement, claiming it violated the First Amendment's Establishment and Free Exercise Clauses. The Kentucky state courts upheld the statute, finding it was secular and did not advance or inhibit any religion and did not entangle the state with religion. Utilizing the test from *Lemon v. Kurtzman,* **the U.S. Supreme Court struck down the statute. The Court held the posting of the Ten Commandments had no secular purpose.**

Kentucky state education officials insisted the statute served the secular purpose of teaching students the foundation of western civilization and the common law. The Court stated, however, the pre-eminent purpose was plainly religious in nature. **The Ten Commandments undeniably came from a religious text**, despite the legislative recitation of a secular purpose. The Court noted the text of the Commandments was not integrated into a course or study of history, civilization, ethics, or comparative religion, but simply posted to induce children to read, meditate upon, and perhaps, to venerate and obey them. The Court held it made no difference that the cost of posting the commandments was paid for through private funds and that they were not read aloud. *Stone v. Graham*, 449 U.S. 39, 101 S.Ct. 192, 66 L.Ed.2d 199 (1981).

◆   Four Texas families claimed an elementary school would not let their children hand out religious materials. They sued their school district in a federal court for First Amendment violations. While the case was pending, the school district adopted a new policy that allowed students to distribute materials 30 minutes before or after school, during recess and at annual school parties. Under the new "2005 Policy," middle and secondary school students could hand out literature in hallways and cafeterias during non-instructional time and in cafeterias during lunch. Stated reasons for the policy were to decrease disruption, increase learning time and improve the educational process. After the 2005 Policy was approved, the families sought pretrial judgment.

The court found a challenge to the policy in effect in 2004 was moot and upheld the 2005 Policy. On appeal, the U.S. Court of Appeals, Fifth Circuit, held **a time, place and manner regulation on student speech must be "content and viewpoint neutral,"** be **"narrowly tailored to serve a significant government interest"** and allow ample alternative channels for

**communication**. Under this test, the court upheld the 2005 Policy as content neutral and supported by the district's legitimate interests. Regulation of student speech during and immediately before classes began was intended to facilitate education. Restrictions on hallway and cafeteria distributions of literature were intended to help students move between classes and during lunch and to reduce littering. There was evidence that the 2005 Policy was a positive response to past disruption. Students had ample alternative communication channels under the 2005 Policy. Elementary school students needed more guidance than older students, so it was permissible to limit when they could hand out literature. The court returned claims involving the 2004 policy to the district court for further review. *Morgan v. Plano Independent School Dist.*, 589 F.3d 740 (5th Cir. 2009).

◆   The group of parents from the case summarized above claimed elementary principals "interrogated" their children and searched their gift bags for religious materials. One parent said students were forbidden from using the term "Christmas" for school events. Another claimed a principal threatened to call the police if she tried to hand out religious materials. In pretrial activity, the principals argued they were entitled to qualified immunity. The court denied the request, and the case came before a three-judge panel of the Fifth Circuit.

The panel explained that **qualified immunity shields government officials who are performing discretionary functions from any liability for civil damages if their conduct does not violate clearly established rights of which a reasonable person would have known**. The panel held the principals had "fair warning" that viewpoint-based suppression of student distribution of literature was unconstitutional. It denied immunity to the principals. But the opinion was soon withdrawn and a request for a rehearing before all judges of the Fifth Circuit was granted. *Morgan v. Swanson*, 628 F.3d 705 (5th Cir. 2010).

◆   Las Cruces Public Schools employed an insignia incorporating three crosses that was used on official vehicles and other school district property. A taxpayer challenged the use of the crosses in a federal court, which noted that "Las Cruces" is Spanish for "the crosses." The city had long used crosses in its official insignia, as did non-religious and private entities. The crosses were in a part of the insignia that was less than two inches wide. And the school district did not use the symbol to proselytize. The insignia was locally recognized as having a secular purpose, and it did not advance religion or entangle the government with religion. The taxpayer appealed to the Tenth Circuit, which noted that the insignia was also used by the area chamber of commerce and many private businesses. The **"Establishment Clause enshrines the principle that government may not act in ways that aid one religion, aid all religions or prefer one religion over another."** Of primary importance was whether the government intended to endorse religion or had the effect of endorsing religion. An objective observer would not conclude that the city adopted the logo with the purpose of endorsing Christianity. Compelling evidence established that the symbol was not religious. The policy ensured compliance with Establishment Clause principles, and the court affirmed the lower court judgments. *Weinbaum v. City of Las Cruces, New Mexico*, 541 F.3d 1017 (10th Cir. 2008).

◆ New York City's holiday display policy did not permit creches (nativity scenes). The policy allowed the display of secular holiday symbols, including "Christmas trees, Menorahs, and the Star and Crescent." Displays could not "appear to promote or celebrate any single religion or holiday." The Catholic League for Religious and Civil Rights protested the absence of creches from holiday displays in city schools. After the city refused to change the policy, a Catholic parent of two elementary students sued. She claimed that the policy promoted Judaism and Islam and disapproved of Christianity. After a federal court upheld the policy, the U.S. Court of Appeals, Second Circuit, held the decision to represent Christmas with secular symbols, rather than creches, did not show hostility to Christianity. **The menorah and the star and crescent were religious symbols, but they did not depict a deity while a nativity scene did.** The policy had a secular purpose "to teach the lesson of pluralism." Promoting tolerance and respect for diverse customs did not violate the Religion Clauses of the First Amendment. The policy avoided a religious message by requiring any symbol or decoration to be displayed simultaneously with others reflecting different beliefs or customs. Objective observers would perceive the promotion of pluralism, not religion. The court affirmed the judgment for the city. *Skoros v. City of New York*, 437 F.3d 1 (2d Cir. 2006).

◆ A Florida student painted murals with religious messages or symbols for a school project, without informing the teacher who supervised the project. The student placed them in conspicuous locations in the school, where they caused a commotion. The teacher instructed the student to paint over the overt religious words and sectarian symbols, but allowed other images and messages to remain. Other students were also instructed to edit their murals due to profanity, gang symbols or satanic images. The student complied with the instructions, but sued for First Amendment violations. A federal district court held that the school did not create a public forum when it invited students and staff to paint murals.

The U.S. Court of Appeals, Eleventh Circuit, held that the project was a nonpublic forum. The school did not display an intent to open the project for indiscriminate use, and the principal explicitly forbade profane or offensive content, while the teacher maintained supervision of the project. **The mural project was a nonpublic forum, over which the school could exert editorial control.** Schools can regulate expression in nonpublic forums, so long as their regulations are viewpoint neutral and reasonable in light of the purpose of the forum. The murals were curricular in nature and were "school-sponsored speech" under *Hazelwood School Dist. v. Kuhlmeier*, 484 U.S. 260 (1988). Curricular expression did not have to occur in a classroom. The school had a legitimate pedagogical concern in avoiding disruption, and the court affirmed the judgment. *Bannon v. School Dist. of Palm Beach County*, 387 F.3d 1208 (11th Cir. 2004).

◆ A ministerial association donated monuments inscribed with the Ten Commandments to an Ohio school board and agreed to indemnify the board for any resulting litigation costs. Once the monuments were accepted, the board resolved to dedicate the grounds on which they stood as areas for structures of symbolic history. It erected the monuments at four new high schools and installed signs reciting that the board had incurred no costs and intended no endorsement of religion. Two county residents sued the board to prohibit the display. The board modified the display to add excerpts from the Justinian Code, the Preamble to the U.S. Constitution, the Declaration of Independence and the Magna Carta. The board stated that the Ten Commandments provided the "moral background of the Declaration of Independence and the foundation of our legal tradition." A federal district court held that the display violated the Establishment Clause, and the U.S. Court of Appeals, Sixth Circuit, affirmed. **The original display had no secular purpose. Acceptance of the monuments from a religious organization implied the opposite.** *Baker v. Adams County/Ohio Valley School Board*, 86 Fed.Appx. 104 (6th Cir. 2004).

◆   A New Jersey preschool student tried to distribute pencils stamped with the message "Jesus [heart symbol] The Little Children" at a class party. His teacher confiscated them because of their religious message. The next year, a teacher stopped him from handing out candy canes with a religious story. After the student's mother contacted the school, officials allowed him to distribute candy canes at recess or after school. When the student reached first grade, officials again stopped him from distributing candy canes with a religious story. The student sued the school board and superintendent. The case reached the Third Circuit, which held age and context are key considerations in school speech cases. **A student's age bore an inverse relationship to the degree and kind of control a school could exercise.** Class parties were part of the curriculum, not a place for student advocacy. In an elementary classroom, the line between school-endorsed speech could be blurred for young, impressionable students and their parents. It was appropriate for school officials to set these boundaries, and for the courts to afford them leeway to create an appropriate learning environment and to restrict student messages intending to promote religion. It was within the school's authority to stop the distribution. In any event, the school had allowed him to distribute the message outside class time. *Walz v. Egg Harbor Township Board of Educ.*, 342 F.3d 271 (3d Cir. 2003).

## III.  LIMITATIONS ON EMPLOYEE RELIGIOUS ACTIVITY

*The Free Exercise Clause of the First Amendment provides that Congress shall make no law prohibiting the free exercise of religion. Courts examining the rights of school employees to engage in religious speech follow the First Amendment analysis from* Garcetti v. Ceballos *and* Pickering v. Board of Educ., *discussed in Chapter Three, Section II, with the additional consideration of the employee's right to freely exercise religion. For cases involving religious discrimination against employees, see Chapter Eight, Section V.*

◆   Employees of the Texas Education Agency (TEA) provided support to the state board of education. The board set curricular and graduation requirements for state public schools and determined which textbooks to purchase. TEA staff members were told "not to advocate a particular position on curriculum issues" and to refrain from participating in matters under deliberation. A TEA Director of Science for the Curriculum Division directed the state K-12 science program. Her supervisor instructed her not to communicate with people outside the TEA regarding the state education board's science curriculum deliberations. But she disobeyed the order when she forwarded an email to 36 teachers and teacher organizations concerning a presentation critical of teaching creationism in public schools. Finding the director had violated TEA's neutrality policy, the supervisor recommended employment termination, and she resigned.

The director sued the TEA and state education commissioner in a federal district court, which held for the TEA and the commissioner. On appeal, the U.S. Court of Appeals, Fifth Circuit, held the First Amendment mandates government neutrality among various religions and non-religion. The director claimed the TEA neutrality policy established religion by deeming creationism to be a subject matter for the board to consider in setting the state science curriculum. But the court found no evidence of religious advancement. **A TEA policy against employee speech about possible subjects to be included in the curriculum did not primarily advance religion.** The court held the policy preserved the role of TEA staff to support the board. As the court found no circumstances under which a TEA director's inability to speak about potential subjects for the state curriculum could be perceived as state endorsement of religion, it affirmed the judgment. *Comer v. Scott*, 610 F.3d 929 (5th Cir. 2010).

◆   A Wisconsin guidance counselor prayed with students and destroyed school literature on condom usage without consulting her supervisor. She then ordered literature advocating abstinence. The school superintendent informed her, during her three-year probationary employment contract, that her contract would not be renewed. The counselor sued, asserting that her non-renewal was based on hostility to her religious beliefs in violation of Title VII of the Civil Rights Act and the Free Exercise Clause of the First Amendment. A court awarded pretrial judgment to the school district, and the counselor appealed. The U.S. Court of Appeals, Seventh Circuit, affirmed, noting that the counselor was let go because of her conduct, not her religious beliefs. It was easy to understand the imprudence of retaining a guidance counselor who threw out school materials and substituted her own without asking permission. U.S. Department of Education guidelines prohibit teachers, administrators and other school employees from "encouraging or discouraging prayer, and from actively participating in such activity with students." Finding that **"teachers and other public school employees have no right to make the promotion of religion a part of their job description,"** the court held that the Constitution is not a license for uncontrolled teacher expression. *Grossman v. South Shore Public School Dist.*, 507 F.3d 1097 (7th Cir. 2007).

◆   A South Dakota school district let the Good News Club hold meetings on school grounds under its community use policy. A teacher attended the club's first meeting at her school. The principal told her she could not attend future meetings, warning that her participation might be perceived as an establishment of religion. She sued. A court held that the district had engaged in viewpoint discrimination by excluding her from meetings. While the district could bar the teacher from club meetings at her own school, no Establishment Clause concerns applied to meetings at other schools. The court issued a permanent order allowing the teacher to attend meetings at schools other than her own. The U.S. Court of Appeals, Eighth Circuit, held that **the teacher's participation in after-school club meetings was private speech that did not put the district at risk of violating the Establishment Clause**. Nonparticipants left the building by the time meetings were held, and student participants had parental permission. No reasonable observer would perceive the teacher's presence at club meetings in her own school or any other school to be a state endorsement of religion. The court reversed the decision in part and affirmed it in part, holding for the teacher on all issues appealed. *Wigg v. Sioux Falls School Dist. 49-5*, 382 F.3d 807 (8th Cir. 2004).

◆ A Pennsylvania instructional assistant often wore a small crucifix to work over a six-year period without disruption or controversy. Her supervisor saw her a few times each week but did not notice the crucifix until "someone in the teachers union" reported it. The district suspended the assistant for violating its policy and state law prohibiting public school teachers from wearing religious dress, marks, emblems or insignia while performing their duties. The assistant declined her supervisor's instruction to remove or hide the crucifix.

The school district suspended the assistant, and she sued for reinstatement and a declaration that the policy was unconstitutional. A federal district court noted that although district policy forbade employees from wearing religious symbols, it allowed them to wear nonreligious decorative jewelry. The district's policy was overtly averse to religion, because it punished religious content or viewpoints while "permitting its employees to wear jewelry containing secular messages or no messages at all." **The policy constituted impermissible viewpoint discrimination because it was directed only at religious speech.** It had a discriminatory purpose and effect that was not justified by any countervailing government interest. The court rejected the district's arguments based on potential criminal liability and threatened violations of the Establishment Clause. The section did not apply to the instructional assistant, since she was not a certificated teacher. No reasonable observer would perceive the district as endorsing religion if it allowed employees to wear unobtrusive crucifixes or similar jewelry. The assistant was entitled to reinstatement and an order preventing the district from enforcing its policy. *Nichol v. ARIN Intermediate Unit 28*, 268 F.Supp.2d 536 (W.D. Pa. 2003).

## IV.  FINANCIAL ASSISTANCE AND VOUCHER PROGRAMS

*The U.S. Supreme Court upheld an Ohio law authorizing public funding of a private school voucher program in* Zelman v. Simmons-Harris, *below. The case may be contrasted to cases like* Committee for Public Educ. and Religious Liberty v. Nyquist, *413 U.S. 756 (1973), where the Court held direct aid from states to sectarian schools "in whatever form is invalid."*

*While* Zelman *found no Establishment Clause violation in the Ohio program, the case did not resolve the constitutionality of voucher programs under state constitutional provisions, which is for state courts to decide.*

◆    The Ohio General Assembly adopted the Ohio Pilot Scholarship Program in 1995 in response to a federal court order to remedy problems in the Cleveland School District. The program made vouchers of up to $2,500 available for Cleveland students to attend public or private schools, including schools with religious affiliations. The Supreme Court of Ohio struck down the program on state constitutional grounds in 1999. The general assembly cured the state constitutional deficiencies and reauthorized the program for 1999-2000.

A new lawsuit was commenced in a federal court, which permanently enjoined the state from administering the program. The Sixth Circuit affirmed the judgment, and state officials appealed. The U.S. Supreme Court reversed the judgment, finding no Establishment Clause violation. It held the program allowed government aid to reach religious institutions only because of the deliberate choices of the individual recipients. Any incidental advancement of religion, or perceived endorsement of a religious message, was attributable to the individual recipients, not to the government. The New York program struck down in *Committee for Public Educ. and Religious Liberty v. Nyquist* gave benefits exclusively to private schools and the parents of private school enrollees. Ohio's program offered aid directly to a broad class of individual recipients defined without regard to religion. **Where government aid is religiously neutral and provides direct assistance to a broad class of citizens that in turn directs funds to religious schools through genuine and independent private choices, the program is not readily subject to an Establishment Clause challenge.** *Zelman v. Simmons-Harris,* 536 U.S. 639, 122 S.Ct. 2460, 153 L.Ed.2d 604 (2002).

◆    An Arizona statute provided a tax credit for any corporation contributing cash to a school tuition organization (STO). An STO is a charitable organization exempt from federal tax that allocates 90% of its annual revenue for scholarships or tuition grants to students to attend any qualified school of their parents' choice. A group opposed to the tax credit sued for a declaration that the statute was unconstitutional. A court held for the state, and the opponents appealed. The Court of Appeals of Arizona found that **the statute supported the secular purpose of encouraging Arizona businesses to direct funds to STOs to improve education in the state**. The state had a legitimate interest in facilitating high-quality education for all students, regardless of the school chosen by their parents. As the U.S. Supreme Court has held, "programs of true private choice do not offend the Establishment Clause." The tax credit did not provide direct aid to religious schools, and was neutral with respect to religion, making no distinction between sectarian and nonsectarian schools or STOs. The law created no financial incentive for a student to attend a religious school. As no religious entanglement was present, the law was upheld. *Green v. Garriott,* 221 Ariz. 404, 212 P.3d 96 (Ariz. Ct. App. 2009).

◆    Arizona's Scholarships for Pupils with Disabilities allowed students with disabilities to attend a private school or a school outside their residence school district. Legislators also enacted a Displaced Pupils Choice Grant Program, which permitted children in foster care to attend a private school of their choice. Under the Disabilities Program, parents of a disabled student could apply for scholarships if they were not satisfied with their child's progress in a public school the prior year. After the parents selected a school, they received checks from the state that were restrictively endorsed to their school of choice. The program allowed both sectarian and nonsectarian schools to participate, and schools were "not required to alter their creed, practices or curriculum" to do so. Objectors to the programs sued the state superintendent of public instruction for violating two provisions of the state constitution.

The Supreme Court of Arizona agreed to review the case. It explained that Arizona Constitution Article 9, Section 10, the "Aid Clause," has no equivalent under the U.S. Constitution. The Aid Clause was "aimed at placing restrictions on the disbursement of public funds to specified institutions, both religious and secular." The court distinguished the voucher programs from a state tax credit program for contributions to school tuition organizations. The Aid Clause was primarily designed to protect the public fisc and public schools, and **the scholarship programs provided aid to private schools in violation of the Aid Clause**. *Cain v. Horne*, 220 Ariz. 77, 202 P.3d 1178 (Ariz. 2009).

◆ Opponents of Florida's Opportunity Scholarship Program (OSP) sued state officials in a Florida court for violating three state constitutional provisions. The Supreme Court of Florida held that the OSP was unconstitutional under the "no aid" provision, Article I, Section Three of the Florida Constitution. The OSP violated the state constitution's uniformity requirement by diverting public funds into "separate private systems parallel to and in competition with the free public schools that are the sole means set out in the Constitution for the state to provide for the education of Florida's children." Paying tuition for students to attend private schools was a substantially different manner than the one prescribed in the state constitution. OSP funding was taken directly from each school district's appropriated funds, reducing the funds available to the district. No OSP provision ensured private schools were "uniform." While public schools were held accountable for teaching certain state standards and to teach all basic subjects, private schools were not required to do so and could even hire teachers who did not possess bachelor's degrees. **"Because voucher payments reduce funding for the public education system, the OSP by its very nature undermines the system of 'high quality' free public schools."** The court struck down the OSP program. *Bush v. Holmes*, 919 So.2d 392 (Fla. 2006).

◆ Swan's Island, Maine, had no high school of its own and did not contract with another district to educate resident secondary students as permitted by state law. Two Swan's Island students went to a private religious school at their parents' expense. The Town of Swan's Island then adopted a policy for a monthly tuition subsidy for year-round residents with children enrolled in private high schools. The parents received monthly subsidies for a full school year under the policy, until the Maine Attorney General's Office found the policy violated Maine Revised Statutes Section 2951(2). The town suspended the program, and the parents sued Maine officials in the state court system.

A trial court held for the state, which argued the policy was "nothing more than an attempt to do an end run around the words and the will of the Legislature." On appeal, **the Supreme Judicial Court held Section 2951(2)**

**barred the payment of any public funds, whether state or municipal, from reaching sectarian schools**. The legislature had considered and rejected a bill that would have repealed Section 2951(2) after the court's 2006 decision in *Anderson v. Town of Durham*, below. This reaffirmed the state's public policy against the public funding of sectarian schools. The court affirmed the judgment. *Joyce v. State of Maine*, 951 A.2d 69 (Me. 2008).

◆    Maine law authorizes public funding to pay private school tuition on behalf of students living in school districts that do not operate their own high schools. Districts may contract with other school districts or private schools meeting state criteria to satisfy their obligation to educate resident high school students. In 1980, the state added a provision limiting public funding to nonsectarian schools for school districts that contract with private schools to educate their high school students. The Supreme Court of Maine upheld the provision against a challenge by parents who sought public funding for their children to attend religious schools. *Bagley v. Raymond School Dep't*, 782 A.2d 172 (Me. 1999).

After the U.S. Supreme Court upheld the Ohio voucher program in *Zelman v. Simmons-Harris*, this chapter, a bill to repeal the provision was introduced in the Maine Legislature. The bill failed, and another group of parents seeking public funding for their children to attend religious schools sued. The U.S. Court of Appeals, First Circuit, held that even after *Zelman*, **the Constitution did not require Maine to fund tuition at sectarian schools**. *Eulitt v. State of Maine*, 386 F.3d 344 (1st Cir. 2004).

Another group of parents filed a challenge to the provision in a state court. They sent their children to private schools that were not "nonsectarian schools" under the law. The case reached the Supreme Court of Maine, which noted that the state had decided to exclude sectarian schools from the tuition program based on a 1980 attorney general's opinion. The state was not motivated by religious discrimination, and the provision did not burden or inhibit the free exercise of religion in any constitutionally significant way. The court upheld the provision. *Anderson v. Town of Durham*, 895 A.2d 944 (Me. 2006).

◆    The Colorado Opportunity Contract Pilot Program was enacted to meet the educational needs of low-achieving students in the state's highest poverty areas. Participation was mandatory for any district that had at least eight schools with poor academic ratings. Voucher opponents sued the state in a case that reached the Supreme Court of Colorado. It found local boards retained no authority under the pilot program to determine which students were eligible to participate or how much funding to devote to it. In fact, the program deprived school districts of all local control over instruction. And it violated the local control provision of the state constitution by requiring districts to pay funds, including some locally raised tax revenues, to parents who paid them to nonpublic schools in the form of vouchers. The program violated the state constitution, as **"local control" required school districts to maintain discretion over any instruction paid for with locally raised funds**. *Owens v. Colorado Congress of Parents, Teachers and Students*, 92 P.3d 933 (Colo. 2004).

# CHAPTER FIVE

## Academic Practices

## I.  REFORM LEGISLATION

### A.  The No Child Left Behind Act of 2001

*The No Child Left Behind (NCLB) Act of 2001 reauthorized the Elementary and Secondary Education Act (ESEA) of 1965. It requires the states to use academic assessments to annually review school progress and determine if "adequate yearly progress" (AYP) has been made under state standards. The AYP requirement is a condition for the receipt of Title I funds under the ESEA.*

*Schools that fail to achieve AYP for two consecutive years are designated for "school improvement." If a school does not make AYP after two years of improvement status, it is subject to "corrective action." This may entail replacing teachers or an entirely new curriculum. A school failing to make AYP after a year of corrective action must be "restructured." This involves replacing staff, converting to charter school status or surrendering direct control to state officials. NCLB Act notice and transfer provisions are triggered when schools are identified for improvement, corrective action or restructuring.*

*A federal regulation defining "highly qualified teacher" under the No Child Left Behind (NCLB) Act was declared in violation of Congressional intent because it permitted some California teachers to become highly qualified without obtaining full state certification.*

◆   Under the NCLB Act, alternative-route teachers meet the "highly qualified teacher" designation only by obtaining "full state certification." But a federal regulation, 34 C.F.R. Part 200.56(a)(1)(i), permitted an alternative-route teacher to gain "highly qualified" status without first obtaining "full state certification." Students, parents and two nonprofit organizations claimed the regulation and a parallel California state education regulation allowed a disproportionate number of intern teachers to teach in minority and low-income California schools. The challengers said California intern teachers lacked "full state certification," which is part of the definition of a highly qualified teacher under the NCLB Act.

A federal district court heard evidence that the state's intern teachers were concentrated in schools that served low-income and minority students. But the court upheld the regulation. On appeal, the U.S. Court of Appeals, Ninth Circuit, held **the federal regulation impermissibly expanded the highly qualified teacher definition of 20 U.S.C. § 7801(23) to include alternative-route teachers in the process of obtaining full certification**. Since 34 C.F.R. Part 200.56(a)(2)(ii) was inconsistent with congressional intent, the court invalidated it. The state and federal regulations permitted California and its school districts to ignore the disproportionate number of interns teaching in schools in minority and low-income areas, and the court held the challengers could pursue the case. States could define full certification as they chose, but the NCLB Act required them to take steps to ensure fully certified teachers were proportionately represented in the teaching staffs of minority and low-income schools. The court reversed the judgment and returned the case to the lower court. *Renee v. Duncan*, 623 F.3d 787 (9th Cir. 2010).

◆   A federal appeals court refused to review Connecticut's challenge to federal interpretations of the No Child Left Behind Act. According to Connecticut officials, the NCLB Act's "unfunded mandates provision" required the state to be fully funded for any costs of complying with the NCLB Act. It stated it was currently spending $41.6 million of its own funds to comply with the act. The court ruled against the state, which appealed. The U.S. Court of Appeals, Second Circuit, held arguments regarding the unfunded mandates provision were not ready for judicial review. This claim could be decided once there was an administrative record. The district court was entitled to find the disposition of the proposed plan amendments and request for waivers was not arbitrary or capricious. An NCLB Act provision stated that approval of a state plan should not be declined before a hearing. **But the pending legal issue was the meaning of the unfunded mandates provision, which was not yet ripe for review.** Since the court held that claim was not ready for review, it found no reason to order a hearing on the plan amendments before arguments about the unfunded mandates provision were heard. *Connecticut v. Duncan*, 612 F.3d 107 (2d Cir. 2010).

*As a federal court recently noted, every court to have considered a private claim for relief under the NCLB Act has found the Act does not allow one.*

◆ The number of Newark, New Jersey schools "in need of improvement" under the NCLB Act increased from 37 in 2003-04 to 51 in 2006-07. An audit revealed that the district did not meet its NCLB Act obligation to notify parents of their rights to obtain transfers and supplemental educational services (SES) for their children. A group of Newark parents filed a class action suit against the school system, asserting NCLB Act violations. A federal court held that the Act did not create individually-enforceable rights and dismissed the complaint. On appeal, the U.S. Court of Appeals, Third Circuit, explained that the NCLB Act was enacted by Congress under its Spending Clause powers. As with other Spending Clause legislation, the NCLB Act offered federal money to the states in return for an agreement by the states to perform specific actions. **Unlike federal civil rights legislation, the NCLB Act's "penalties" section did not offer any remedy in the event of noncompliance.** Instead, states that failed to meet the Act's requirements were subject to withholding of funds by the Secretary of the U.S. Department of Education. Thus, the parents lacked a private right of action to enforce the Act's provisions. *Newark Parents Ass'n v. Newark Public Schools*, 547 F.3d 199 (3d Cir. 2008).

◆ The NCLB Act's "Unfunded Mandates Provision" prevents the Act from being construed to authorize an officer or employee of the federal government to mandate that a state or state subdivision spend funds or incur costs not paid for under the Act. School districts from Michigan, Texas and Vermont joined the National Education Association (NEA) and NEA affiliates in a federal action against the Secretary of the U.S. Department of Education, seeking a federal court declaration that she was misinterpreting the Unfunded Mandates Provision. They argued that states need not comply with NCLB Act requirements where federal funding did not cover the increased costs of NCLB Act compliance. A federal court refused to interpret the NCLB Act to excuse states from complying with requirements of the Act that imposed additional costs on states. **The states had to comply with the NCLB Act regardless of any federal funding shortfall.** On appeal, the U.S. Court of Appeals, Sixth Circuit, reached a tie vote, meaning that the lower court's decision stood. As a result, the judgment for the Secretary was affirmed. *School Dist. of City of Pontiac v. Secretary of U.S. Dep't of Educ.*, 584 F.3d 253 (6th Cir. 2009).

◆ Two Illinois school districts and a group of parents sued the U.S. Department of Education in a federal court, arguing that certain NCLB Act requirements were in conflict with those of the Individuals with Disabilities Education Act (IDEA). The court held that the districts and parents lacked legal standing to bring the lawsuit. It also held that the IDEA and the NCLB Act established voluntary programs and that school districts could solve any problem created by the laws by simply turning down federal funds. The districts and parents appealed to the U.S. Court of Appeals, Seventh Circuit.

    The court held that the districts and parents had standing to proceed with the lawsuit because they had no option but to follow the state's lead. Both federal laws required states to opt in or opt out for a year or more at a time. Once a district accepted a grant it had to comply with all program requirements. This condition was sufficient to establish standing. However, the claim of the districts and parents was too weak to pursue any further. **The IDEA had to give way to the NCLB Act if there was truly any conflict between the laws.** The 2004 IDEA amendments were designed in part to conform the IDEA with the NCLB Act, not to displace it. If there was any conflict between the 2001 NCLB Act and IDEA enactments from between 1970 and 1990, NCLB would prevail. The court dismissed the case. *Board of Educ. of Ottawa Township High School Dist. 140 v. Spellings*, 517 F.3d 922 (7th Cir. 2008).

◆ The state of Michigan approved a provider to contract for supplemental educational services (SES) such as tutoring. After the provider served about 1,000 Detroit students during the 2005-06 school year, the Detroit Public School District (DPS) terminated the contract for failing to provide services and not paying its employees. The provider sued DPS in a federal court, asserting state and federal claims. It claimed that the DPS terminated the contract without cause and in retaliation for exercising First Amendment rights.

The court noted that the DPS had taken the action based on failure to provide services and failure to pay its employees. The NCLB Act does not create a private claim for relief. **NCLB simply required districts that fail to make adequate yearly progress to pay for tutoring of low-income students by contracting with SES providers.** The act did not unambiguously create a right for SES providers to enforce claims against a district. The law focused on the rights of children rather than SES providers. The court dismissed the provider's $1 million claim for due process violations. The DPS's decision to remove the provider's name from its approved list did not prevent it from doing business. Being named on a provider list did not amount to a protected property interest. The court dismissed the case. *Alliance For Children, Inc. v. City of Detroit Public Schools*, 475 F.Supp.2d 655 (E.D. Mich. 2007).

◆ Pennsylvania's education secretary identified 13 schools in the Reading School District as failing to achieve AYP. NCLB requires districts to report the test scores of four subgroups when the number of students in the subgroup exceeds a state-designated number. The secretary had established this "N" number at 40, based on several computer studies. The district claimed that the secretary arbitrarily set the N number and did not provide adequate assistance. The district sued the secretary. The Commonwealth Court of Pennsylvania found no evidence to contradict the secretary's selection of the number 40 as appropriate. Plus the secretary provided the district with adequate technical assistance. **The state was not required to provide all the assistance specified in the NCLB Act at the moment a school was identified for improvement.** The secretary did not abuse her discretion. *Reading School Dist. v. Dep't of Educ.*, 855 A.2d 166 (Pa. Commw. Ct. 2004).

The school district then sent the department its plans to bring six schools into compliance. It submitted a cost estimate for the plan in excess of $26 million for 2003-2004. The district estimated it would receive about $8 million in federal funding, and it asked the state education department for the shortfall.

The department did not respond to the request for funds, but found six schools and the district as a whole failed to achieve AYP for 2003-2004 and would be placed on level-one or level-two sanctions for 2004-2005. The district appealed, asserting that the department did not provide federal funds to implement the act, mandatory technical assistance to sanctioned schools, or Spanish language testing on a required statewide assessment. The state education secretary dismissed the district's appeal. The district appealed again to the commonwealth court, which held that the department violated the district's due process rights by limiting the grounds for appeal in its policy. *Reading School Dist. v. Dep't of Educ.*, 875 A.2d 1218 (Pa. Commw. Ct. 2005).

## B.  State Reform Acts

*Before the No Child Left Behind Act of 2001, state legislatures were addressing public school accountability in reform legislation designed to improve student performance. In 2002, the Sixth Circuit upheld the Michigan School Reform Act, which replaced Detroit's elected school board with an appointed one. The Equal Protection Clause did not prevent the legislature from enacting experimental reforms where no suspect class or fundamental right was involved.* Moore v. Detroit School Reform Board, *239 F.3d 352 (6th Cir. 2002).*

*The Pennsylvania Educational Empowerment Act (EEA) was enacted to "fix broken school districts" in urban areas. It placed districts with a history of low test scores on a state list. Although the Pennsylvania Supreme Court struck down the EEA as special legislation in* Harrisburg School Dist. v. Hickock, *563 Pa. 391, 761 A.2d 1132 (Pa. 2000), it upheld amended legislation that expanded the class of cities for which placement on the empowerment district could be waived in* Harrisburg School Dist. v. Zogby, *574 Pa. 121, 828 A.2d 1079 (Pa. 2003). In 2010, the Pennsylvania Supreme Court held a law concerning a financially distressed, poor-performing school district was unconstitutional because it was worded to apply only to that district.*

◆   Due to a history of low test scores, the Duquesne City School District was placed on Pennsylvania's education empowerment list in 2000. It was declared a financially distressed school district, and its management and operations were placed under a special board of control. In 2007, the special board of control eliminated the district's only high school. After the state department of education approved the action, the board laid off 18 district employees. No agreements to enroll high school students were made with neighboring school districts. Six weeks after the school closure, the General Assembly enacted Act 45 of 2007, which gave the state education secretary authority to designate two or more districts to accept high school students from a distressed district. Act 45 required that employees who were furloughed by the closure of a high school be hired on a preferential basis by a district within three miles of the distressed district. Employees of districts located within three miles of Duquesne City School District noted only Duquesne met all of Act 45's requirements. They claimed Act 45 was a "special law" that violated the state constitution.

After the Commonwealth Court held Act 45 was not special legislation, appeal reached the Supreme Court of Pennsylvania. **It held Article III, Section**

**32 of the state constitution prohibits local or special laws regulating school districts.** Duquesne was the only member of the initial class of districts described by Act 45, and no other district could meet Act 45's criteria unless "a highly improbable convergence of events" transpired. The court held the class of districts created by Act 45 was substantially closed to new members. The practical effect of the law was to assure that affected Duquesne staff members would be given preferential hiring treatment. As parts of Act 45 were "special legislation" prohibited by the state constitution, the court reversed the judgment. *West Mifflin Area School Dist. v. Zahorchak*, 4 A.3d 1042 (Pa. 2010).

◆   In 1998, the Missouri legislature passed SB 781 as part of a settlement in a long-running federal lawsuit to desegregate St. Louis public schools. SB 781 created the Transitional School District (TSD) to handle the transition from federal court supervision to local control. SB 781 further provided that if the St. Louis school district lost its accreditation after the restoration of control to the city board, the general authority over the school district transferred back to the TSD. This provision was carried forward into law as Section 162.1100 of the Revised Statutes of Missouri. The St. Louis school district's performance was at or below minimally acceptable levels after 1994, and in 2006, the state board reestablished the TSD. When the district lost its accreditation, it sued the state board. Meanwhile, a special administrative board took control of St. Louis public schools. After a trial, the state board prevailed. The district appealed to the Supreme Court of Missouri, arguing that Section 162.110 was special legislation that violated the state constitution. The court disagreed. While Section 162.1100 created a classification that was characteristic of special legislation, the state constitution was not violated. *Board of Educ. of City of St. Louis v. Missouri State Board of Educ.*, 271 S.W.3d 1 (Mo. 2008).

◆   The Kentucky Education Reform Act (KERA) created site-based councils to provide greater accountability and decentralize school management. A KERA provision, KRS § 160.345(2)(h), required site-based councils to select principals from applicants recommended by the district superintendent. A superintendent fired a high school principal for poor performance. He received nine applications for the resulting vacancy, including one from the former principal. The superintendent forwarded only three applications to the site-based council. The council asked for the others, but the superintendent refused and appointed one of his three candidates as interim principal. A state court ordered the superintendent to forward all nine applications, and the council then recommended rehiring the former principal. The state supreme court consolidated the case with that of an assistant principal who claimed she was passed over for a vacancy due to gender. It held neither superintendent had the authority to limit the pool of "qualified applicants" under Section 160.345(2)(h). **Site-based councils were created in direct response to widespread mismanagement caused by an overly centralized system of school governance.** Superintendents had to send site-based councils the applications of all applicants who met state law requirements, including the assistant principal and the fired principal. *Young v. Hammond*, 139 S.W.3d 895 (Ky. 2004).

◆  In 1993, Maryland's state education board adopted school performance standards that mandated reporting requirements and improvement plans for each public school. Schools that did not meet the standards were placed under the direct control of the local school board. If they failed to improve under local reconstitution, they were designated for "state reconstitution." By 2000, the state board had placed 97 Maryland schools under local reconstitution, 83 of which were in Baltimore. The state board reconstituted three low-performing Baltimore schools, but their performance remained stagnant after three years.

The state board hired a private company to provide the schools curriculum, instructional services, support personnel, teaching tools, special education and related services, educational services for limited and non-English proficient students and other services. The company hired and managed the professional staff for the three schools. The collective bargaining agent (CBA) for school employees sued the state education board in a state court, arguing the board could not adopt regulations creating student performance standards and reconstitution. The court held the board was statutorily authorized to contract with the company. On appeal, the Court of Appeals of Maryland rejected the CBA's claim that state law did not authorize the state reconstitution regulations. Even if the board initially lacked such authority, the general assembly enacted legislation in 1997, 1999 and 2000 showing its awareness and approval for the board to contract with private vendors under the reconstitution regulations. The 1997, 1999 and 2000 laws also recognized that **under state reconstitution, public school teachers might be employed by private entities**. It could be inferred that the legislature approved of and ratified the reconstitution regulations. The court affirmed the judgment. *Baltimore Teachers Union v. Maryland State Board of Educ.*, 379 Md. 192, 840 A.2d 728 (Md. 2004).

## C.  Charter Schools

### 1.  Legislation

*Charter school laws were among the first of the educational reforms of the 1990s to be tested in the courts. They have survived numerous legal challenges asserting violations of state and federal constitutional provisions. But a Florida law shifting the power to authorize charter schools from local boards to a state commission violated a provision of the Florida Constitution.*

◆  In 2006, Florida Statutes Section 1002.335 established the state Schools of Excellence Commission as an independent state entity with power to authorize charter schools throughout the state. Local boards lost their former authority to charter schools. At least 31 local school boards filed resolutions with the state board, seeking to retain their former authority to authorize charter schools. The state board permitted only three local boards to retain this authority. Several boards then appealed. According to a state district court of appeal, article IX section 4 of the Florida Constitution requires school boards to operate, control and supervise all free public schools within their districts. The court held **Section 1002.335 "permits and encourages the creation of a parallel system of free public education escaping the operation and control of local elected** school boards." It vested a commission of state board appointees with the powers of operation, control and supervision that were reserved to local boards. Rejecting the state board's arguments that the new law furthered the goals of systemic uniformity and efficiency, the court found Section 1002.335 in "total and fatal conflict" with article IX, section 4 of the Florida Constitution, and held the act unconstitutional. *Duval County School Board v. State Board of Educ.*, 998 So.2d 641 (Fla. Ct. App. 2008).

◆ An Illinois education association petitioned the state Educational Labor Relations Board to represent charter school employees. The school district that was the governing body of the charter school argued that the labor relations board lacked authority, as the Illinois Education Labor Act (IELA) did not apply to charter schools. The district claimed it was not an "educational employer" as defined by the Act. The board found that charter schools were not exempt from IELA coverage. On appeal, the Appellate Court of Illinois found that **the Charter Schools Law exempted charter schools from "all other state laws and regulations in the School Code governing public schools and local board policies,"** with the exception of seven specific statutes. Among the seven exemptions were laws relating to employee background checks, student discipline, government tort immunity, nonprofit indemnification, abused and neglected children reporting, student record care and report card standards.

Significantly, the Charter School Law did not specify an exemption for the IELA. This indicated the absence of the IELA from the list of Charter School Law exceptions meant the IELA did not apply to charter schools. As the board had incorrectly found that the Education Labor Act applied to charter schools, the decision was reversed. A 2009 amendment to the charter law specified that the governing body of a charter school is an "educational employer." As of January 1, 2010, charter schools must comply with the IELA, but the change did not apply to this case. *Northern Kane Educ. Corp. v. Cambridge Lakes Educ. Ass'n, IEA-NEA*, 394 Ill.App.3d 755, 914 N.E.2d 1286 (Ill. App. Ct. 2009).

◆ A South Carolina academy applied to a school district to open as a charter school for the 2004-05 school year. The district's board gave the academy conditional approval, contingent upon finding a site in the district prior to August 2003. The academy notified the board that it had located a site in the district, and the board paid it over $87,000. But the academy obtained another site, and the state education department approved it. The academy was not ready to open when public schools opened for the 2004-05 school year. It tried to open in a temporary location, but when the school district reported this to the education department, the department directed the academy's closure. The academy obtained a conditional certificate to hold classes in an alternate facility. The school board held a hearing and ruled that the academy had not met four conditions for approval and that it had no contract with the district. The conditions of approval related to space, facility, equipment and personnel.

Although the academy did not meet the conditions, it appealed to the state board of education, which affirmed the local board's decision. On appeal, the Supreme Court of South Carolina reviewed the state Charter School Act and held that **a conditional charter did not confer due process rights on a**

**charter applicant**. Even if there was a lack of due process, the local board had remedied this by holding a hearing. The academy was required to meet the terms of its application. *James Academy of Excellence v. Dorchester County School Dist. Two*, 376 S.C. 293, 657 S.E.2d 469 (S.C. 2008).

◆   A Pennsylvania resident requested an auditor's report and financial statements from a charter school. He also sought information about the written arrangement between the school and a private management entity. The school claimed it was not an agency of the commonwealth and that the state Right-to-Know Act did not apply to it. The management entity denied the resident's request for records on grounds that it was a private company. The resident sued the school for disclosure. A state common pleas court held for the resident and ordered the school to provide copies of the requested records.

On appeal, the Supreme Court of Pennsylvania held that the Right-to-Know Act required "agencies" to make public records accessible for inspection and duplication. Among the agencies required to disclose records were the offices, departments, boards or commissions of the executive branch. **School districts were similar to the entities explicitly listed in the Right-to-Know Act and they qualified as "agencies."** Charter schools were independent public schools created for the essential governmental service of education. As organizations performing essential governmental functions, charter schools were "agencies" covered by the Right-to-Know Act. The court affirmed the judgment. *Zager v. Chester Community Charter School*, 594 Pa. 166, 934 A.2d 1227 (Pa. 2007).

◆   A Wisconsin "virtual academy" was established as a charter school to provide curriculum by Internet and mail to students statewide. Parents had the primary day-to-day responsibility for implementing education. The academy's administrative offices were within the district that established it. The Wisconsin Education Association Council sued the establishing school district, state superintendent of instruction and others, claiming that the school violated state charter school, open enrollment and teacher certification statutes. A court held for the district and state superintendent. On appeal, the state court of appeals found academy students studied and completed assignments under the direction of their parents, who were not licensed. This violated the law. Academy teachers worked from their homes across the state, not just in the district. This also violated the law because **the charter school law prohibited a school board from establishing a charter school located outside the district**. While the academy's offices remained in the district, the statutory term "school" could not be construed to exclude the teachers and students making up the academy. The court also reversed the trial court's decision on the open enrollment issue. As operation of the academy violated three Wisconsin laws, the court reversed the judgment. *Johnson v. Burmaster*, 307 Wis.2d 213, 744 N.W.2d 900 (Wis. Ct. App. 2007), review denied, 749 N.W.2d 662 (Wis. 2008).

◆   Massachusetts law authorized "Commonwealth" and "Horace Mann" charter schools. Horace Mann charter schools were subject to approval by local school committees, but Commonwealth schools were independent of a school committee. The law charged the board of education with the final determination on granting charters and allowed the board to revoke charters. A school committee that served four towns approved an application for a Commonwealth charter school focusing on advanced learning in math and science. The school committees of three towns sued the board, and the case reached the Supreme Judicial Court of Massachusetts. It held the board had the final decision to grant a charter. **No state law or regulation permitted appeals from a board decision.** The trial court had correctly held it lacked authority to review the board's decisions. Public hearings are legislative, not adversary in nature. The legislature did not intend school committees to obtain judicial review in Commonwealth charter school cases. Local school committees could make the process unworkable and unwieldy and played a limited role in the application process. *School Committee of Hudson v. Board of Educ.*, 448 Mass. 565, 863 N.E.2d 22 (Mass. 2007).

◆ The Ohio Federation of Teachers, Ohio Congress of Parents and Teachers, and the Ohio School Boards Association challenged the state's program of community schools, known elsewhere as charter schools. The challengers sought a declaration that community schools violated the Ohio Constitution and sought restoration of funds "diverted" from school districts. The case reached the Supreme Court of Ohio, which found the General Assembly's authority to set educational standards and requirements for common schools allowed it to set different standards for community schools. The General Assembly complied with the constitution by adding flexible, deregulated education opportunities to the school system. Community schools had to administer the standardized tests given in traditional public schools and were monitored by the state education department. The court rejected the claim by community school opponents that the state's funding method diverted funds from school districts. The General Assembly had exclusive authority to spend tax revenues to further a statewide system of schools. There was no violation of state constitutional provisions for local control of city school boards and local tax revenue. **The General Assembly did not intrude upon local powers by creating additional schools that were not part of a school district.** *Ohio Congress of Parents and Teachers v. State Board of Educ.*, 111 Ohio St.3d 568, 857 N.E.2d 1148 (Ohio 2006).

### 2. Applications

◆ An Ohio church sought to sponsor community schools (known elsewhere as charter schools). But the state education department found it ineligible, since neither the church nor its parent, Presbyterian Church USA, was an "education-oriented" entity as required by Section 3314.02(C) of the revised state code. An appeal under Section 119.12 of the state code to a county common pleas court was dismissed, and the state court of appeals then affirmed the judgment.

On appeal, the Supreme Court of Ohio noted Section 3314.015(B) of the state code made "final" a department determination regarding an entity's status as "education-oriented." But as the church argued, another state code provision declared that any decision by the department to disapprove an entity for sponsorship of a community school "may be appealed." Section 3314.015(B)(3) made a department determination regarding "education-oriented" status appealable under state code Section 119.12. Community school provisions did not say department decisions were "not appealable." They only stated that they were "final." **A key to review by appellate courts is that there is a "final" order from which a party may appeal.** "Final" meant the opposite of "not appealable." Since the community school provisions did not prohibit an appeal by the church, the court reversed the judgment and returned the case to the lower courts for further activity. *Brookwood Presbyterian Church v. Ohio Dep't of Educ.*, 127 Ohio St.3d 469, 940 N.E.2d 1256 (Ohio 2010).

◆ A Maryland school board charter review committee rejected a charter application as incomplete. In a 10-page letter, the committee described the deficiencies and sought clarification from the applicant in 50 areas. After the application was resubmitted, the committee found only eight of its concerns had been satisfied. Charter school representatives met with the committee to discuss the school application. Using a county public school "analytical scoring rubric," the board assigned the application only 189 of 530 possible points. After the board voted down the application, it sent the applicants a breakdown of its evaluation criteria, the scoring rubric and the score. Charter school applicants appealed to the Maryland State Board of Education (MSBE), which held the process had been fair. Appeal reached the Court of Special Appeals of Maryland.

The court found **the Maryland Public Charter School Program vested county education boards with primary chartering authority and that the MSBE had broad authority over the administration of public schools.** Prior MSBE rulings permitted local boards to withhold charter application scoring rubrics, so long as the process was otherwise explained. As the MSBE found, the committee explained the deficiencies in a 10-page letter and held four meetings to discuss its action. The court found the MSBE's review of the local decision was consistent with its prior cases. An argument that the local board was "generally opposed to granting a charter" did not show local bias made the board unable to make a fair and impartial decision. As the court found nothing illegal, arbitrary or capricious about the denial of the application, it held for the board. *Board of Educ. of Somerset County v. Somerset Advocates for Educ.*, 189 Md.App. 385, 984 A.2d 405 (Md. Ct. Spec. App. 2009).

◆ A Florida charter school application stated that students who scored at or above the 25th percentile in norm-referenced tests would be considered as having demonstrated acceptable student performance standards. The local board denied the application, finding that this measure would render the school unaccountable and that the 25th percentile was lower than its own standards. Moreover, the academy did not make reasonable enrollment projections and had overestimated its capital budget by $1 million. The academy appealed to the state Charter School Appeals Commission, where it asserted the 25th percentile had been a typographical error and should have been the 51st percentile.

The commission found no requirement that a school grade be a part of a charter application, and no substantial evidence of a deficiency. The state board then granted the application. On appeal, the District Court of Appeal of Florida found the application was not deficient. **There was no state law requirement for a school "A" goal.** The academy offered to correct its typographical error, and the application was sufficient with respect to student assessment and accountability. The academy overcame any reason for denying the application regarding budget and class size. **The state charter school law did not permit the state board to open charter schools.** Once a charter application was granted, the school board had control over the process. The board had authority to revoke a charter, and it still operated, controlled and supervised all free public schools in the district. Rejecting the local board's argument that the state board order violated its authority to control and supervise public schools, the court affirmed the state board's decision. *School Board of Volusia County v. Academies of Excellence*, 974 So.2d 1186 (Fla. Dist. Ct. App. 2008).

◆   South Carolina applicants submitted a charter school application and met with a state Charter School Advisory Committee to review compliance with the state Charter Schools Act. The committee voted to certify the application, but the board for the school district in which the charter school was to be located voted to deny it at a public hearing. The board found the application deficient in at least seven areas; thus, it would adversely affect other students in the district. The state board of education reversed the decision, holding that the local board's factual findings and legal conclusions were not based on substantial evidence. A state court affirmed, and the case reached the Supreme Court of South Carolina, which explained that courts may not substitute their judgment for that of a state agency on the weight of evidence. However, they may reverse or modify decisions that are clearly erroneous.

The Charter School Act permitted the denial of applications that did not meet the specific requirements of S.C. Code Sections 59-40-50 or 59-40-60, that failed to meet the spirit or intent of the act, or that adversely affected the other students in the district. Instead of providing a written explanation of the reasons for denial of the application, and citing specific standards, the local board had only spoken in generalized terms. **The local board had clearly failed to meet the act's requirements.** The judgment for the applicants was affirmed. *Lee County School Dist. Board of Trustees v. MLD Charter School Academy Planning Committee*, 371 S.C. 561, 641 S.E.2d 24 (S.C. 2007).

◆   A Florida charter school concentrated on serving poor children, many of whom had failed at other schools. Its operator applied for two new charters. The board denied the application under a policy that required applicants already having charters from the board to demonstrate a record of success in operating an exemplary charter school for the past two fiscal years. "An exemplary charter school" was one with at least a "B" grade or significant annual learning gains. The school board found the existing charter school to be non-exemplary based on its financial and academic performance. The school received a "D" grade for 2003-04 and was projected for a D or F in 2004-05.

The Florida District Court of Appeal upheld the decision to deny the application. The Charter School Law required applicants to demonstrate how their schools would use "guiding principles" and meet a state-defined purpose. Among other things, charter applicants had to provide a detailed curriculum plan showing how students would be provided with services to meet state standards. The local board's policy of requiring "exemplary performance" was a practical and reasonable approach to testing an applicant's academic and financial abilities. **Competent, substantial evidence indicated that the application was fiscally and academically non-compliant**, and there was good cause to deny it. *Imhotep-Nguzo Saba Charter School v. Dep't of Educ.*, 947 So.2d 1279 (Fla. Dist. Ct. App. 2007).

◆ Illinois charter school applicants submitted a proposal for a school that would offer unemployed high school drop-outs opportunities to earn a diploma while acquiring vocational skills. Participants would divide time between school and work at low-income housing sites. The state board noted that the district had a $32.65 million deficit and faced additional budget cuts if it lost a pending voter referendum. It found the proposal not economically sound. A state court affirmed, as did the Appellate Court of Illinois. The applicants appealed to the Supreme Court of Illinois.

The applicants argued that the state board could not deny a charter school proposal solely because of a school district's financial condition. They asserted that their proposal met 14 of the 15 statutory requirements. Reducing the statutory inquiry into a single question of finance would defeat the purpose of the charter schools law, which was to create educational choice and competition. The supreme court disagreed, explaining that the charter schools law made a district's finances a "legitimate concern." The applicants in this case had refused to accept anything but 100% per capita funding. **The court found that the terms of a proposed charter, including funding issues, must permit both the school and the district to be financially secure.** It agreed with the state board's interpretation of the law as requiring proposals to meet all 15 statutory requirements. As the proposal was not in the best interests of students in the district, the court affirmed the board's decision. *Comprehensive Community Solutions v. Rockford School Dist. No. 205*, 216 Ill.2d 455, 297 Ill.Dec. 221, 837 N.E.2d 1 (Ill. 2005).

## 3.  Operations and Finance

*Florida's highest court held a school board could immediately terminate the charters of two schools based on financial emergency without affording them protections under the state Administrative Procedure Act. Ohio's Supreme Court held community schools seeking to appeal from a sponsor's termination decision are bound to comply with state law procedures. New York's highest court held charter school construction and renovation projects are not public works, meaning the state's prevailing wage provisions are inapplicable to them.*

◆ In 2000, the New York Department of Labor decided that charter schools were generally not considered to be public entities. Thus, a state prevailing wage law for those working on public projects did not apply. But in 2007, the department issued an opinion letter declaring the prevailing wage law should apply to charter school projects. Soon, the state commissioner of labor notified the Charter Schools Institute and state education department that the prevailing wage laws would be enforced for new charter school projects after a specified date. Charter schools and supporting organizations filed a state court action for a declaration that the commissioner's new position exceeded her authority and an order declaring the prevailing wage laws inapplicable to charter schools.

A state trial court held a charter agreement was a public contract and that charter school construction and renovation projects were public works. An appellate division court reversed the judgment, and appeal reached the state's highest court. The New York Court of Appeals found the prevailing wage laws applied to public agency contracts for the employment of laborers, workmen or mechanics on "public works projects." According to the court, a charter agreement was not a contract for public work. **A charter was an authorizing agreement by which an agency determined a charter applicant was competent for state licensure.** While the court held New York charter schools bore some similarities to public entities, the prevailing wage law identified only four covered public entities. None were educational entities such as charter schools. Finding the prevailing wage law did not apply to charter schools, the court affirmed the appellate division's judgment. *New York Charter School Ass'n v. Smith*, 15 N.Y.3d 403, 940 N.E.2d 522, 914 N.Y.S.2d 696 (N.Y. 2010).

◆ A Cincinnati community school sponsor placed a school on probation, then suspended it from operating. The sponsor gave the school a statutory written notice of its right to request an informal hearing within 14 days, but the school sought a direct appeal to the state education department. Asserting the school waived its appeal rights, the sponsor advised the department that the contract was terminated. Unable to continue operating, the school appealed to the state supreme court, which found that the state code permitted a sponsor to terminate a community school contract upon 90 days' written notice. Notice must include reasons for the action and a statement that the school may request an informal hearing within 14 days. A school may appeal from an adverse decision to the state education board. **A community school contract was terminated upon the passage of 90 days after the date of a sponsor's notice.** As the sponsor complied with statutory requirements, the court held that the school was not entitled to relief. *State ex rel. Nation Building Technical Academy v. Ohio Dep't of Educ.*, 123 Ohio St.3d 35, 913 N.E.2d 977 (Ohio 2009).

◆ A 2005 New York Charter School Law amendment directed the state comptroller to audit all school districts and charter schools in the state. Several New York City charter schools filed a state court challenge to the comptroller's authority to do the audits. The case reached the Court of Appeals of New York, which found the legislature designated the state board of regents and chartering entities as the public agents authorized to supervise and oversee charter schools. **Charter school audits could not be construed as "incidental to the audits of school districts."** The state comptroller could not claim the power to conduct the audits on the basis of the receipt of state funds and the performance of a governmental function. Once paid to a charter school, public funds were no longer under state control. As a check on their accountability, charters had to be renewed each five years and could be lost if educational standards were not met. The court ruled for the charter schools. *In re New York Charter Schools Ass'n v. DiNapoli*, 13 N.Y.2d 120, 914 N.E.2d 991 (N.Y. 2009).

◆    A Florida school board voted to terminate two charter schools with long histories of financial mismanagement. The board indicated the action was for "good cause" under Florida law, based on the severity of recent audit findings. Although a charter provision permitted termination upon 24 hours' notice, the school operators claimed the procedural protections of the state Administrative Procedure Act (APA). The state board of education voted to uphold the immediate termination of both charters. Appeal reached the Supreme Court of Florida, which noted that **the law permits the immediate termination of charters for "good cause" shown**, or when the health, safety or welfare of the students is threatened. School boards did not have to follow the APA when there were emergency-type circumstances involving the health, safety or welfare of students, or where other good cause necessitated immediate action. *School Board of Palm Beach County, Florida v. Survivors Charter Schools*, 3 So.3d 1220 (Fla. 2009).

◆    A California non-profit organization called Islamic Relief sponsored a charter school with two Minnesota campuses. For the 2008-09 school year, the academy expected to receive $3.8 million in funds from the state of Minnesota. A vast majority of the academy's students were Somali Muslims. The ACLU claimed that the academy violated the Establishment Clause by permitting prayer sessions during school hours in which parents, volunteers and teachers participated. The academy was accused of endorsing Islamic dress codes and dietary practices, and providing bus transportation only at the end of an after-school religious program. The ACLU asserted that the academy preferred "Muslim" religious practice. A federal court held that while Islamic Relief was not a state actor, it still had potential liability for an Establishment Clause violation due to its role in the traditional function of public education.

Minnesota charter schools are a part of the public school system under state law, and the state Charter School Law (CSL) required each school sponsor to assure compliance with nonsectarian requirements. Therefore, the case required a trial and the court refused to dismiss the lawsuit. For example, **religious entanglement created by the academy's dress code and the busing schedule required a factual inquiry**. The role played by Islamic Relief in the academy's operations also required further scrutiny. *American Civil Liberties Union of Minnesota v. Tarek Ibn Ziyad Academy*, Civil No. 09-138 (DWF/JJG), 2009 WL 2215072 (D. Minn. 7/21/09).

◆    A Texas charter school had a significant enrollment increase after converting a private school to an open enrollment charter school. The charter school board hired the subsidiary of a management company to run the school under a five-year management contract. The parent management company's president signed the contract, which assigned claims to the management company to collect fees owed to the subsidiary. Relations strained between the school operators, the management company and the subsidiary, and the contract was ended after only one year. The company sued for breach of contract, and a state court awarded it a directed verdict of $250,899 and attorneys' fees.

On appeal, the Court of Appeals of Texas affirmed the part of the judgment regarding breach of contract damages for management fees owed to the subsidiary. The court then considered a claim regarding unlawful "advances" by the parent company to the school. **State law prohibited the governing body of an open enrollment charter school from accepting a loan from a management company under contract to manage a charter school.** By law, the "advances" were prohibited loans, voiding the contract. Even if that contract was valid, the parent company could not show a contract existed without proving its own illegal conduct. For this reason, the lower court should have granted the school operators a directed verdict on that claim. *Academy of Skills & Knowledge v. Charter Schools, USA*, 260 S.W.3d 529 (Tex. Ct. App. 2008).

◆   Baltimore's school board rejected applications for funding by three different charter schools. Appeals came before the state board of education (SBE), and then the Maryland Court of Appeals. The court found the SBE's calculation of an "average cost" included students who would receive Title I or special education funds or services. This would in turn require the charter schools to adjust their budgets. The SBE acted within its discretion by deciding the cases. Allowing local boards to decide "what funding is commensurate with the amounts disbursed to the other public schools" risked disparate local methods of implementing a uniform law and undercut the SBE's authority to interpret education law. The legislature must have envisioned that the SBE would have primary authority to interpret the law. **The law's "commensurate funding" language necessarily had a per-student basis, and there was no error in the SBE's use of an average per-student approach.** As a result, the SBE decisions were upheld. *Baltimore City Board of School Commissioners v. City Neighbors Charter School*, 400 Md. 324, 929 A.2d 113 (Md. 2007).

◆   A Texas corporation operated three "distance learning" charter schools in California. Families of students enrolled in the schools claimed the schools did not provide computers, instruction, assessment, review, curriculum, equipment, supplies or services, but collected over $20 million in state funding. The families asserted that the corporation aggressively recruited poor rural districts to approve charter schools. The districts then intentionally failed to perform their oversight duties. The families sued the corporation and chartering districts for breach of contract, misrepresentation, constitutional violations and misuse of taxpayer funds. They added a claim under the California False Claims Act (CFCA) for submission of fraudulent claims and an Unfair Competition Law (UCL) claim for unfair and deceptive business practices. A state court dismissed the CFCA, UCL and breach of contract claims as unrecognizable private claims for "educational malfeasance." The Supreme Court of California reversed. **Charter school operators were "persons" who could be held liable under the CFCA.** And UCL purposes were served by subjecting the school operators to deceptive business practices claims. The case was returned to a lower court for further proceedings. *Wells v. One2One Learning Foundation,* 39 Cal.4th 1164, 48 Cal.Rptr.3d 108, 141 P.2d 225 (Cal. 2006).

◆   The Individuals with Disabilities with Education Act (IDEA) and the Elementary and Secondary Education Act (ESEA) authorize state recipients of federal funds to distribute grant money to local educational agencies (LEAs).

Public charter schools are within the definition of an LEA under both laws. A U.S. Department of Education audit of the Arizona Department of Education (ADE) concluded the ADE had improperly awarded ESEA and IDEA funds to for-profit entities that operated charter schools in the state. The Arizona State Board for Charter Schools and several for-profit charter school operators petitioned for review. A federal court held that the statutes expressed a congressional mandate that in order to receive federal funds, charter schools must be nonprofit. The state board and the schools appealed. The Ninth Circuit affirmed. **Only nonprofit institutional day or residential schools are eligible for federal funding under the ESEA and IDEA.** Congress clearly intended to "prohibit the funding of for-profit schools, charter or otherwise." *Arizona State Board for Charter Schools v. U.S. Dep't of Educ.*, 464 F.3d 1003 (9th Cir. 2006).

◆    A California charter school submitted a facilities request to a school district to serve 223 students in grades K-8. The district rejected the school's request to use a single site that was being used primarily for nonacademic purposes. The district's "final facilities offer" to the school included 9.5 classrooms at five different school sites a total of 65 miles apart. The school sued the district, asserting violation of the state Charter Schools Act. The Court of Appeal of California explained that the **Education Code required districts to allow charter schools to use any facility not currently used by a district**. Charter school facilities had to be "contiguous," and state education department regulations required districts to minimize the number of sites and consider student safety. A charter school should be housed at a single site, if one with sufficient capacity exists. The district had to provide the school with facilities that were both reasonably equivalent and contiguous. Providing five sites did not balance the needs of the charter school and district-run schools. The district's decision was reversed and remanded for an order requiring a new final offer of facilities. *Ridgecrest Charter School v. Sierra Sands Unified School Dist.*, 130 Cal.App.4th 986, 30 Cal.Rptr.3d 648 (Cal. Ct. App. 2005).

◆    The Court of Appeal of California held that state Education Code § 47614 required school districts to make facilities sufficient for a charter school to accommodate all the school's in-district students in a manner similar to other district schools. Charter schools had to provide districts with a reasonable projection of average daily classroom attendance of their in-district students. Section 47614 allowed districts to deny facilities requests for projections of less than 80 students for a year. **Section 47614 did not require charter schools to "demonstrate arithmetical precision" in their projections.** A charter school had to submit reasonable projections for in-district students to the school district by October 1 of the preceding fiscal year. In this case, a charter school had given an incomplete response to a school district's request for information such as student names, dates of birth, grade levels, home addresses and parent names. As a result, there was a rational reason for the district to deny the school's facilities request based on safety concerns. *Environmental Charter High School v. Centinela Valley Union High School Dist.*, 122 Cal.App. 4th 139, 18 Cal.Rptr.3d 417 (Cal. Ct. App. 2004).

## II.  CURRICULUM AND GRADING

*Educators have considerable discretion in academic, curricular and grading matters. Courts do not subject official decisions in these areas to close judicial scrutiny. For religious challenges to curriculums, please see Chapter Four, Section I.B.1. Constitutional challenges on secular grounds appear in Chapter Three, Section IV.B. Testing is considered in Section IV of this chapter. For cases involving students with disabilities, see Chapter Six, Section VII.C.*

### A.  Curriculum

◆   A Washington fourth-grade student was part of his school district's highly capable program. At his parents' request, he was allowed to skip to grade six the next school year. In the next three years, the student completed grades six, seven and eight. His father then objected to a proposal to promote him to grade nine and suggested that he enroll in one eighth-grade class. He asked the school district to designate his son a ninth-grader for academic purposes, and an eighth-grader for athletic and estimated graduation date purposes. After the district denied the father's request, he sued the district in a state court. The court held for the school district, and appeal reached the Court of Appeals of Washington.

On appeal, the father stated the athletic issue had been resolved. His only concern was his son's academics and his wish for a 2013 graduation date. The court found the question was not "ripe" and thus inappropriate for a court order. Under the state constitution, the student had a right to be "amply provided with an education" through a general and uniform system of public schools. While state public schools were open to qualified individuals between ages five and 21, the court found this did not translate into a constitutional right to remain in the public school system until age 18 via grade retention. Graduation depended upon completion of required credits, and many events could affect a district's decision to graduate a student. **School boards were vested with the final responsibility for creating policies to ensure the quality of educational programs and providing student opportunities.** Promotion of the student to grade nine and assigning him an estimated graduation date of 2012 did not violate any constitutional rights. *McColl v. Sequim School Dist.*, 152 Wash.App. 1066 (Wash. Ct. App. 2009).

◆   A Kentucky school offered six weighted classes that were graded on a five-point scale rather than a four-point scale to reflect their difficulty. A student whose goal was to be class valedictorian took all six weighted offerings to improve her chances. Near the end of her senior year, she learned that she did not receive weighted credit for a course she had already completed called "Dual Credit History." A school policy limited the receipt of weighted credit to only five courses. Weighted credit could be obtained for either Political Science or Dual Credit History, but not both. The student argued that she should receive weighted credit for both courses, and she sued the school board, its members and other school officials in a state court. She claimed that the code of conduct created a contract with her, which the board had breached. She also asserted that she was given different advice than that given to other students and that she had been subjected to humiliation, embarrassment and ridicule. She said her lower class standing resulted in lost scholarships and caused emotional distress. The family sought a ruling that would retroactively declare the student valedictorian.

After a hearing, the court dismissed the case, and the family appealed to the Court of Appeals of Kentucky. It held that the lower court had based the judgment on an adequate record. **The interpretation of a written document was a matter of law for a court to decide, not for jurors to resolve.** The trial court had correctly interpreted a disputed phrase in the policy. As the lower court had properly dismissed the case, the judgment for the board was affirmed. *Carnes v. Russell County Board of Educ.*, No. 2007-CA-000273-MR, 2008 WL 4530887 (Ky. Ct. App. 9/17/08), review denied, 6/17/09).

◆  A Connecticut parent challenged the use of "the Responsive Classroom" model by a school her children had attended many years earlier. The Responsive Classroom model was designed to improve cooperation and communication among students and faculty. It involved meetings where students discussed concerns and teachers mediated arguments. The parent claimed the paradigm "encouraged, created and tolerated an atmosphere of chaos, disruptiveness and violence" at the school, interrupted the structure necessary for learning, and increased student tensions and confrontations. She waited until years after her children had left the school to sue school officials, and did not claim any actual violence against her children, but claimed they witnessed bullying of other students. The court found no evidence that others victimized any children, and no evidence of a "culture of violence or chaos," as the parent alleged. Teachers and other staff "described only the usual sorts of school-based problems with none of the dramatic upheaval" she alleged. **The principal had handled disciplinary problems and tried to foster an atmosphere of communication and cooperation.** Students suffered no emotional damage, and there was no extreme or outrageous conduct by school officials. Most of what the parent related in her testimony concerned her own emotional state, and not that of her children. She did not prove any part of her emotional distress claim against the school board and principal. *Bell v. West Haven Board of Educ.*, No. NNH-CV-970399597, 2005 WL 1971264 (Conn. Super. Ct. 2005).

◆  A Texas student was in first place in a race for school valedictorian. She claimed the school principal intentionally scheduled a Spanish III class at an inconvenient time for her that was calculated to assist a classmate's effort to become valedictorian. The student's parents demanded that Spanish III be deleted from the curriculum. When the principal refused, the parents were granted a hearing to discuss removing Spanish III from the curriculum, but they were not allowed to cross-examine witnesses or discuss additional grievances. The parents sued the board for constitutional rights violations. A federal court held that the parents were not entitled to cross-examine witnesses or discuss prior inconsistent decisions by the school administration. The student had no constitutionally protected interest to attend a course of her choosing at a particular time. **Although education is of "unquestioned importance," it has not been recognized as a fundamental right under either the U.S. or Texas Constitution.** The student had no protected property interest in becoming class valedictorian. The property interest recognized in education cases such as *Goss v. Lopez*, 419 U.S. 565 (1975), is the right to participate in the overall educational process, not in a particular course or individual component of the process. The court ruled for the board. *Jeffrey v. Board of Trustees of Bells Independent School Dist.*, 261 F.Supp.2d 719 (E.D. Tex. 2003).

## B. Bilingual Education

*In Lau v. Nichols, 414 U.S. 563 (1974), the U.S. Supreme Court held non-English-speaking students in San Francisco schools could claim protection under Title VI of the Civil Rights Act of 1964. Non-English speakers cannot be denied meaningful opportunities to participate in educational programs.*

◆   As a result of claims by African-American students against nine Texas school districts in 1971, broad aspects of the Texas educational system were placed under federal court supervision. Mexican-American students intervened in the case in 1972, and the nine districts were required to provide them equal educational opportunities. The Texas Education Agency was ordered to study the needs of all minority students in the state. In 1981, the court ordered state officials to offer bilingual instruction to limited-English proficient students, based on "*de jure* discrimination" and violation of the Equal Educational Opportunities Act (EEOA). The U.S. Court of Appeals, Fifth Circuit, reversed the judgment in 1982, expressing concern that no school districts were parties.

In 2006, the Mexican-American intervenors reopened the case, and the court found violations of both the 1971 order and the EEOA. It ordered the state to create a new monitoring system and language programming to fulfill EEOA requirements. State officials appealed to the Fifth Circuit, which found a new monitoring system and secondary LEP language program for all the districts would require an extraordinary effort in a very short time. To prove a violation of the 1971 order, the intervenors would have to show the action flowed from a *de jure* segregated system. This was not shown, as **Texas at no time separated Anglo and Mexican-Americans by law**. Because *de jure* segregation of Mexican-American students was not shown, the 1971 order could not be enforced by the intervenors. As for an EEOA violation, the lower court had failed to address the instructions issued in 1982. At that time, the Fifth Circuit found little reason to resolve the case on a statewide basis. **Problems varied by district and would by necessity present local questions for each individual district.** Since the issues raised by the intervenors could not have been properly addressed in the absence of the individual school districts, the court returned the case to the district court. *U.S. v. State of Texas*, 601 F.3d 354 (5th Cir. 2010).

◆   Nine California school districts challenged a state board policy requiring English language testing of limited English proficient (LEP) students on state tests. According to the districts, English language testing of LEP students was not "valid and reliable" as required by the No Child Left Behind (NCLB) Act, and they faced sanctions for failing to meet adequate yearly progress. The Court of Appeal of California noted that **the NCLB Act did not require native language testing of LEP students**. Students had to be provided reasonable accommodations on assessments. To the extent practicable, assessments were to be "in the language and form most likely to yield accurate data on what such students know and can do in academic concern areas, until such students have achieved English language proficiency." In 1998, California voters had enacted Proposition 227 to require English instruction of public school students with very limited exceptions to promote the rapid development of English for LEP students. The NCLB Act "invites each state to make its own judgment call in fashioning a testing program for its LEP students" consistent with NCLB Act requirements. State board decisions were entitled to deference, and the board had engaged in a deliberative policymaking process to determine how LEP students would be tested. *Coachella Valley Unif. School Dist. v. State of California*, 176 Cal.App.4th 93, 98 Cal.Rptr.3d 9 (Cal. Ct. App. 2009).

◆ After California enacted Proposition 227, LEP students brought a federal court action against state officials, asserting Proposition 227 violated the Equal Protection Clause. The court found no constitutional violation. On appeal, **the Ninth Circuit found nothing in the record indicating that Proposition 227 was race-motivated**. The state's bilingual education system did not operate to remedy identified patterns of racial discrimination but was instead intended to improve the educational system. The reallocation of political authority represented by Proposition 227 addressed educational, not racial issues, and the fact that most of California's LEP student population was Latino did not create a viable equal protection claim. The court affirmed the judgment. *Valeria v. Davis*, 307 F.3d 1036 (9th Cir. 2002).

◆ New Mexico enacted the Bilingual Multicultural Education Act (BMEA) to ensure equal educational opportunities for students by making local school districts eligible for bilingual instruction. To qualify for the program, districts had to provide for the educational needs of linguistically and culturally different students, including Native American students. The Albuquerque Public School District operated the Alternative Language Services (ALS) program pursuant to the BMEA, providing bilingual education for limited English proficient students. The U.S. Department of Education's Office for Civil Rights, which oversees Title VI compliance, reviewed the ALS program and entered into an agreement for corrective action with the district. The agreement established new procedures for identifying and serving limited English proficient students.

A group of Albuquerque students in the ALS program sued the district in a federal court, asserting the BMEA and ALS program were discriminatory, since they classified and placed students on the basis of race or national origin. The case reached the U.S. Court of Appeals, Tenth Circuit. It held **the BMEA did not violate the Equal Protection Clause or Title VI**. There was no evidence that the district violated the agreement with the Office for Civil Rights by forcing students to participate in the ALS program without notice or consent. The ALS program and the BMEA did not violate the federal Equal Education Opportunity Act's mandate to take appropriate action to overcome language barriers that impede equal participation by its students. *Carbajal v. Albuquerque Public School Dist.*, 43 Fed.Appx. 306 (10th Cir. 2002).

## C. Grading

*In* Regents of Univ. of Michigan v. Ewing, *474 U.S. 214 (1985), the Supreme Court held courts may not override academic decisions unless there is "such a substantial departure from accepted academic norms as to demonstrate that the person or committee responsible did not actually exercise professional judgment." An Ohio school did not have to change a student's grades even though the teachers who assigned them deviated from a school policy.*

◆ An Ohio student just missed A grades in two advanced placement classes. She said her calculus teacher improperly averaged grades and claimed her writing teacher incorrectly weighted grades. This violated a general school board policy requiring that full-year grades be weighted and semester grades be averaged. After the teachers declined to change the grades, the student and her father met with the principal and later with the school superintendent, school board and counsel. The board heard the teachers' explanations for assigning the grades and then approved the grades. The state education department denied the student relief, and she filed a state court complaint. Before the court, the calculus teacher said he had used his grading method for years and had told the principal when he began to use it. The writing teacher also stated that she had obtained approval for her grading policy and had been using it for about 10 years.

A judgment was issued for the school district, and the student appealed. The Court of Appeals of Ohio held that to obtain relief, the student had to establish a "clear legal right." But she only cited state laws and rules requiring schools to keep records and issue diplomas. Under either version of the grading guidelines, **the court found teachers had discretion to create alternative grading systems and report them to the principal**. The board had followed its policies by discussing the matter with the family, and the principal and superintendent reviewed the case. Both teachers used the same grading method for all their students and did not treat the student differently from others. As she did not show her grades were unfair or arbitrary, her request for a court order had been properly dismissed. *Hingel v. Board of Educ. of Austintown Local School Dist.*, No. 08 MA 258, 2009 WL 4547721 (Ohio Ct. App. 11/23/09).

◆ An Arkansas middle school student participated in his school's accelerated reader program, in which students could win prizes or awards by reading books and taking tests based on them. He stated that he read four of five books in the *Harry Potter* series because of the high points assigned to the books. After the student scored 100% on each of the tests, his reading teacher accused him of cheating, stating it was impossible to read the books in one week. The student's classroom teacher agreed and confronted him about cheating. The student's mother sought reinstatement of the scores. The school principal permitted only one score to be reinstated, finding no obligation to reinstate the others under program incentive rules. The student sought a court order requiring the principal and teachers to reinstate the cancelled scores, apologize publicly and by letter, and prevent them from "further humiliating and using coercive tactics."

The court dismissed the case and awarded the school district $1,500 in attorneys' fees. The student appealed to the state supreme court, which held that

**no law compelled school officials to reinstate scores in voluntary reading programs**. The court found "a general policy against intervention by the courts in matters best left to school authorities." Reinstatement of test scores was left to the discretion of school officials. As the student had no legal remedy available, the court affirmed the judgment, including the award of attorneys' fees. *T.J. v. Hargrove*, 362 Ark. 649, 210 S.W.3d 79 (Ark. 2005).

◆    A Michigan student ranked first in his class at the end of his junior year. He maintained dual enrollment in his high school during his senior year but took no classes there. The student worked as a paralegal in his mother's law office for an employer-based course taken through a county intermediate district. Although an "A" was the highest possible grade under the intermediate district policy, the student's high school district allowed A+ grades. The student's mother awarded him an A+ for the employer-based course, but his report card indicated an A. The high school district refused the mother's request to change the grade, and the student sued for due process violations. A state court held for the district. Before the state court of appeals, the student argued that a high school district policy allowing grades to be weighted or adjusted did not apply to intermediate district courses. The court stated that **a district's board of education had authority to implement a grading system under Michigan law**. The paralegal training course was administered by the intermediate school district, not the high school, so the highest possible grade was an A. The high school district's policy prevented weighting or adjustment of the grade. Since the student had no vested property interest in an A+ and no legal right to a particular grade, the court affirmed the judgment. *Delekta v. Memphis Community Schools*, No. 249325, 2004 WL 2290462 (Mich. Ct. App. 2004).

◆    **An Ohio school district did not violate a student's rights by suspending her for excessive tardiness** under an attendance policy that assigned students failing grades for poor attendance. An Ohio appeals court upheld the policy as a constitutional means of promoting good attendance. According to the appeals court, under state law, school policies are generally left to the discretion of the school board. The board policy in this case promoted attendance for academic performance and provided sanctions for excessive unexcused absences. It distinguished between excused and unexcused absences and was neither unreasonable nor unconstitutional. *Smith v. Revere Local School Dist. Board of Educ.*, No. 20275, 2001 WL 489980 (Ohio Ct. App. 2001).

◆    A California middle school music teacher assigned three students conduct grades of "needs improvement" or "unsatisfactory." Parents complained about the poor conduct grades, which made the students ineligible for honor society and field trips. The principal then changed the grades to "satisfactory" without consulting the teacher. The teacher filed a grievance that was denied at all three levels, culminating with the school board. The teacher and his collective bargaining association sued the district and principal in the state court system. The California Court of Appeal noted that the state Education Code provides that **a grade assigned by a classroom teacher is final and can be changed only in limited circumstances such as clerical or mechanical mistake**, or where the assignment is characterized by bad faith or incompetency. The court rejected the district's argument that the code section did not apply to citizenship grades. Citizenship grades reflected a teacher's assessment of student performance for cooperation, attitude and effort, and there was no reason to believe the legislature meant to distinguish them from academic marks. Even if citizenship marks were not considered grades, the district had exceeded its authority in changing them. *Las Virgenes Educators Ass'n v. Las Virgenes Unified School Dist.*, 102 Cal.Rptr.2d 901 (Cal. Ct. App. 2000).

## III. STUDENT RECORDS

*Parents and eligible students have rights to access education records and protect their records from access by unauthorized persons under the Family Educational Rights and Privacy Act of 1974 (FERPA), 20 U.S.C. § 1232g. In* Gonzaga Univ. v. Doe, *536 U.S. 273 (2002), this chapter, the U.S. Supreme Court held FERPA does not authorize private lawsuits. Analogous state laws protect student records and may create greater rights than under FERPA.*

*FERPA applies only to "education records," which are records "directly related to a student" and "maintained by an educational agency or institution or by a party acting for the agency or institution." Records that originate from a school, or are created by nonschool entities, may become education records if they are "maintained" by a school. Notes used only as a personal memory aid and kept in the sole possession of the maker are outside FERPA's coverage.*

*Federal regulations interpreting FERPA state when personally identifiable information may be disclosed without consent by a parent or eligible student. "Personal identifiers" may indirectly identify a student, and include date and place of birth, mother's maiden name, or "information that, alone or in combination," may allow identification by a reasonable person in the school community. A FERPA regulation at 34 C.F.R. Part 99.31(a)(1) requires* **educational institutions to "use reasonable methods to ensure that school officials obtain access to only those education records in which they have legitimate educational interests."** *The regulation permits educational agencies to disclose education records without consent to another institution, even after a student has enrolled or transferred, for reasons related to enrollment or transfer.*

**Under 34 C.F.R. Part 99.36 personally identifiable information from an education record may be disclosed to parents and other appropriate parties in connection with "health and safety emergencies."** *A student's social security number or student identification number is personally identifiable information that may not be disclosed as directory information under 34 C.F.R. Part 99.3.*

*The Health Insurance Portability and Accountability Act (HIPAA) was enacted to ensure continued health insurance for persons changing jobs, and to address the problem of health information confidentiality. Under federal regulations, records covered by FERPA are exempt from HIPAA. However, since schools typically provide services deemed to be within HIPAA definitions, schools may be considered "covered entities" under HIPAA in some situations.*

*Several federal court decisions have held HIPAA does not create a private right of action for individuals to bring lawsuits. These include* Dominic J. v.

Wyoming Valley West High School, *362 F.Supp.2d 560 (M.D. Pa. 2005),*
Runkle v. Gonzales, *391 F.Supp.2d 210 (D.D.C. 2005), and* Swift v. Lake Park
High School Dist. 108, *No. 03 C 5003, 2003 WL 22388878 (N.D. Ill. 2003).*

## A. Student and Parental Rights

*An Iowa school superintendent did not violate state law by discussing with
school board members and staff a report by a parent about her daughter's
involvement with a teacher, as the community already knew of the relationship.*

◆    A 21-year-old Iowa teaching assistant and coach exchanged text messages
with a ninth-grader. The two had sexual contact, and the student told a friend.
When her mother learned about the relationship, she met with the district
superintendent. During their meeting, he took a full page of notes, which were
later shown to a school attorney. The coach was placed on administrative leave
and reported to the police, and a criminal investigation was begun. The mother
claimed the superintendent identified the student in discussions with the school
board, administrators and staff and that a board member spoke publicly about
the incident. A lawsuit was filed against the school district for privacy rights
violations. A state court held the superintendent's notes were not a "confidential
public record" under Iowa Code Section 22.7. There was no violation of a state
administrative rule on child abuse investigation procedures, and the school
district was entitled to judgment. Appeal reached the Court of Appeals of Iowa.

The court explained that Iowa Code Chapter 22 establishes a right of access
to governmental records and requires that certain categories of government
records be kept confidential. Since the superintendent's notes were made as part
of his official duties, they were school records. But the court noted he relied on
his memory when speaking with the board and staff, not his notes. It held
**Section 22.7 "is not a general privacy law that prohibits public officials
from discussing information that is neither a record itself nor derived from
a record."** Section 22.7(18) of the state code did not give the mother a cause of
action. Her verbal report was not filed with a designated investigator. There was
no merit to the claim that a state administrative provision governing child abuse
reports by school employees was violated. As a result, the court affirmed the
judgment for the school district. *V.H. v. Hampton-Dumont Community School
Dist.,* No. 09-0364, 2009 WL 5126111 (Iowa Ct. App. 12/30/09).

◆    A divorced New Hampshire mother did not have physical custody of her
child. In addition to claiming lack of appropriate notice when her son missed
school, she claimed an individualized education program (IEP) team member
violated her rights by exchanging confidential medical information with her
son's physician against her wishes. In a federal district court action, the mother
asserted due process violations. The court reviewed evidence that the child's
father had primary residential responsibility for the child. A family court order
directed the school to call both parents in an emergency. The mother had
refused to sign a release for her son's medical records and told IEP team
members not to contact medical providers. But the father had signed a release
that would allow a physician to exchange medical records with the school.

The father had physical custody of the child through legal proceedings that provided full due process to the mother. **There was no constitutional right to notification from the school whenever the child was released to his father.** The mother did not claim interference with her custody rights or a transfer of custody of sufficient magnitude to trigger constitutional concerns. Even if such rights existed, the court held school officials would have immunity based on the absence of any clearly established law supporting the claims. There was no merit to a claim against the father. The court dismissed the case. *Vendouri v. Gaylord*, Civil No. 10-cv-277-SM, 2010 WL 3417921 (D.N.H. 8/27/10).

◆    An Illinois student's parent requested all test questions from honors biology exams. He was offered an opportunity to examine test booklets at school or at home and to hand-copy test questions, so long as they were returned the next day and no photo-copies were made. The parent sued the school district in the state court system, seeking a declaration that the booklet was a "student record" under the state School Records Act. A trial court held that the booklets did not come under the Act, as they were devoid of any student marks or other identifying information. The Appellate Court of Illinois affirmed the decision.

While the case was pending, the parent requested copies of his daughter's algebra exams. The district provided him the parts of exam booklets with the student's answers and calculations, but it blocked the test questions. The parent filed a new action. This time, the appellate court noted the student had written her name, and wrote answers and calculations on the test booklets. **As they contained student markings and other identifying information, the booklets were "student records."** The marked-on algebra test booklets were covered by the Act, so the parent had a right to inspect and copy them. Unlike federal law, the state act allowed parents to "copy" student records, not just "inspect and review" them. *Garlick v. Oak Park and River Forest High School Dist. #200*, 389 Ill.App.3d 306, 905 N.E.2d 930 (Ill. App. Ct. 2009).

◆    Texas school officials claimed that a couple made 2,274 record requests, representing 120,000 pages of documents and 551 open records determinations by the state attorney general's office. The district asserted that the couple's behavior was disruptive and harassing, and claimed it placed a "crippling burden on its office and personnel resources." The couple allegedly made duplicative requests for information, and 162 separate requests for information were "cancelled" after a great deal of time and effort had been spent responding to them. The school district sued the couple for public nuisance and abuse of governmental process under the Texas Public Information Act (PIA). Asserting the cost of prior records requests was $700,000, district officials sought to limit future record requests through a state court-ordered procedure.

The court held that it had no authority to hear the case because the PIA does not create a cause of action for enforcement by the courts. The Court of Appeals of Texas held that **the PIA prohibited a public agency such as a school district from suing a record requestor in a state court**. The only action authorized by the PIA for a governmental body or officer involving public information was an action brought to challenge a decision by the state attorney general's office. In order to bring a proper PIA suit, the school district had to first obtain an attorney general opinion as to whether the disclosures were required. The court rejected the district's argument that there should be an exception in this case because of the extreme burden placed on it by the couple's multiple records requests. The court affirmed the judgment. *Lake Travis Independent School Dist. v. Lovelace*, 243 S.W.3d 244 (Tex. Ct. App. 2007).

◆   A New York school district superintendent told staff members they had a duty to inform parents about student pregnancies. He said a student's disclosure of pregnancy to staff members was unprotected by any privilege and might trigger legal reporting obligations. Staff members who learned of a student's pregnancy "should immediately" report it to a school social worker, who should then "encourage" the student to disclose a pregnancy to her parents. If a student would not inform her parents, the memorandum stated that a social worker "should offer to meet with the parents and the student to help the student inform her parents" and/or offer to inform the student's parents in the student's absence. If a student continued refusing these prompts, the social worker "should inform the student that she/he will inform the parents." The district teachers' association sued the school board and superintendent on behalf of students. A federal court held the association lacked standing to file the action.

On appeal, the U.S. Court of Appeals, Second Circuit, held **the association did not establish any risk of civil liability or professional discipline**. The superintendent stated that he would not discipline staff members for their actions with respect to parental pregnancy notification. The memorandum was non-mandatory, and the court affirmed the judgment for the school board. *Port Washington Teachers' Ass'n v. Board of Educ. of Port Washington Union Free School Dist.*, 478 F.3d 494 (2d Cir. 2007).

◆   An Oklahoma student told his parents and a middle school counselor that he had sex with a high school student who was known to be HIV-positive. Soon, about half his eighth-grade class learned of this. The middle school counselor contacted the principal and the student's father. The student soon noticed graffiti at school stating that he had AIDS, and other students asked him about it. He came to the school principal's office and asked to use the phone "to call his attorney." The principal refused, stating that he could phone his parents. The student's mother then came to school. She said the principal did not cooperate and refused to address incidents of bullying and graffiti. The student did not return to school, but he passed his classes through a home-based program.

The parents sued the school district in a federal court for sexual harassment and other claims. The court held for the school district, finding the student was not targeted for abuse because of his gender. The district did not exclude him from school, as the home-based program was his mother's idea. While unpleasant, the graffiti and rumors were not so unbearable as to deprive the student of a quality public education. The family did not assert valid claims for defamation and negligence. **The complaint only asserted a possibility that school personnel could have spread the rumor of HIV positive status.** *Dawson v. The Grove Public School Dist.*, No. 06-CV-555-TCK FHM, 2007 WL 2874831 (N.D. Okla. 9/27/07).

◆ A Minnesota student told his mother other students had papers about him and were calling him names. She recognized the papers as copies of a report used to determine special education eligibility. The wind had blown the papers out of an open garbage bag at school and students found the report in a parking lot. The mother sued the school district for violating the Minnesota Government Data Practices Act (MGDPA). A jury found the district violated the MGDPA and awarded the student $60,000 in damages for pain, embarrassment and emotional distress, and $80,000 in future damages. On appeal, **the Court of Appeals of Minnesota held that the MGDPA required each school district to establish appropriate security safeguards for all records containing data on individuals**. Evidence indicated that the district did not establish appropriate safeguards. District manuals had no procedures for destroying documents, and employees were not properly trained. There was evidence that the incident would have a devastating effect on the student for a lifetime, and the court affirmed the judgment. *Scott v. Minneapolis Public Schools, Special Dist. No. 1*, No. A05-649, 2006 WL 997721 (Minn. Ct. App. 2006).

◆ New Jersey social service agencies assembled a community group to assess local youth needs. The town education board agreed to survey its students for the community group to understand youth needs, attitudes and behavior, and to better use town programs and resources. The survey sought information about drug and alcohol use, sexual activity, violence, suicide, racial attitudes and parent-child relationships. Some parents expressed concern that explicit questions about drug and alcohol use, sexual activity and suicide suggested "such activity was within normal adolescent experience." Objecting students and parents sued the board and school officials for violations of the FERPA and the U.S. Constitution. Appeal reached the Third Circuit, which found that all students in the district participated in the survey, indicating involuntariness. Parents were not told how they could avoid their child's participation. But the survey protected anonymity. **The constitutional right to prevent disclosure of intimate facts is not absolute, and is balanced against the public interest in health and safety.** Privacy rights did not extend to this survey, as disclosure of personal information occurred in the aggregate and personal data was safeguarded. *C.N. v. Ridgewood Board of Educ.*, 430 F.3d 159 (3d Cir. 2005).

◆ A Pennsylvania school district did not violate the state Right to Know Act by denying a citizen's request for copies of letters to and from the district superintendent. The Commonwealth Court of Pennsylvania held that the letters were not "public records" under the act. Also, **public agencies may charge a reasonable fee when copying public records**. The 25 cents per copy charged by the school district in this case was reasonable. *Weiss v. Williamsport Area School Dist.*, 872 A.2d 269 (Pa. Commw. Ct. 2005).

◆ A Florida superintendent made an 8,000-page investigation report on a school principal accused of misconduct. It referenced other faculty members and included confidential student information. The superintendent notified the principal and other faculty members that they could receive copies of the report with student information blocked to prevent disclosure of identifying material.

Faculty members sued the superintendent to require the district to release the report with no restrictions. A state court directed the board to provide the faculty members the report with all student identifying information blocked. The faculty members appealed to the Florida Court of Appeal, arguing they were unable to respond to the report. The court held that **all student identifying information should be concealed in the report**. State law made all personally identifiable student records and reports confidential and exempt from disclosure. As rights of faculty members to respond to the report did not "trump" the right of students to keep the information confidential, the court reversed the judgment. *Johnson v. Deluz*, 875 So.2d 1 (Fla. Dist. Ct. App. 2004).

◆   A Washington private school student intended to teach in the state's public school system after his graduation. At the time, the state required new teachers to obtain an affidavit of good moral character from the dean of their college or university. When the university's teacher certification specialist overheard a conversation implicating the student in sexual misconduct with a classmate, she commenced an investigation of the student and reported the allegations against him to the state teacher certification agency. She later informed the student that the university would not provide him with the affidavit of good moral character he needed for certification as a Washington teacher. The student sued the university and the specialist under state law and 42 U.S.C. § 1983 for violating FERPA. A jury awarded him over $1 million in damages. The case reached the U.S. Supreme Court, which held that **FERPA creates no personal rights that can be enforced in a court under Section 1983**. Congress enacted FERPA to force schools to respect students' privacy with respect to education records. It did not confer enforceable rights upon students. The Court reversed and remanded the case to a state court for further proceedings. *Gonzaga Univ. v. Doe*, 536 U.S. 273, 122 S.Ct. 2268, 153 L.Ed.2d 309 (2002).

◆   An Oklahoma parent learned that teachers asked students to grade each other's assignments and then call out the results in class. She asserted that the policy was embarrassing to her children and sued the school district and school administrators for violations of FERPA and the Due Process Clause. A federal district court held the policy did not violate any constitutional privacy rights and that the practice of calling out grades did not involve "education records" within the meaning of FERPA. A federal appeals court reversed the judgment.

The U.S. Supreme Court accepted the district's petition to review the case. It observed that an "education record" under FERPA is one that is "maintained by an educational agency or institution or by a person acting for such agency or institution." According to the court, student papers are not "maintained" within the meaning of FERPA when students correct them or call out grades. **The word "maintain" suggested that FERPA records were kept in files or cabinets in a "records room at the school or on a permanent secure database."** The momentary handling of assignments by students did not conform to this definition. The appeals court committed error by deciding that a student acted for an educational institution under FERPA when assisting with grading. Because Congress did not intend to intervene in drastic fashion with traditional state functions by exercising minute control over teaching methods, the Court reversed and remanded the case. *Owasso Independent School Dist. No. I-011 v. Falvo*, 534 U.S. 426, 122 S.Ct. 934, 151 L.Ed.2d 896 (2002).

◆ A Massachusetts student disrupted his special education classroom and directed racial slurs at his teacher. He was suspected of writing racial graffiti on the blackboard in her room and in hallways. The graffiti was photographed and police were provided samples of the student's schoolwork to help determine whether it matched the graffiti. Massachusetts prosecuted the student for malicious destruction of property and violation of civil rights. A trial court held the handwriting samples had been obtained in violation of a state law requiring student or parental consent prior to the release of a "student record." But the Supreme Judicial Court of Massachusetts **rejected the student's argument that his handwriting samples were "student records"** within the meaning of state law. Homework, tests and other assignments were not a part of a student's transcript and were not typically "kept" by schools. The school had a clear obligation to use the student's papers only for educational purposes, but it also had an obligation to prevent racial harassment and property damage. *Comwlth. of Massachusetts v. Buccella*, 434 Mass. 473, 751 N.E.2d 373 (Mass. 2001).

### B. Media Requests

*FERPA's general definition of "education records" is: "those records, files, documents and other materials which – (i) contain information directly related to a student; and (ii) are maintained by an educational agency or institution or by a person acting for such agency or institution." This includes personally identifiable information that may reveal a student's identity.* **Courts have held that records pertaining to a single student meet these criteria, but statistical compilations do not.** *Thus, compiled student disciplinary hearing information could be released to the media under FERPA and the state Open Records Act in* Hardin County Schools v. Foster, *40 S.W.3d 865 (Ky. 2001).*

◆ A Washington student with a severe peanut allergy died on a school field trip after he ate a school lunch with peanut products. The district superintendent revealed that the district had provided the peanut products despite knowing of his severe allergy. The district and family entered into mediation and the family accepted $960,000 in return for a release of all claims. The parties made a joint press release and agreed that the district and staff would decline to comment to the press about the case. The district denied a newspaper publisher's request for 75 documents, including its investigation report, the settlement agreement and investigation notes by the investigator and school attorneys.

The school district, family and student's estate sought a state court order exempting the records from public disclosure. The case reached the Supreme Court of Washington, which held **the Washington Public Records Act requires agencies to make public records available for public inspection and copying, unless an exemption applies**. The documents sought were classified as "work product," prepared in anticipation of the lawsuit and were exempt from disclosure. Teachers and a volunteer nurse chaperone were "clients whose communications with the attorneys were privileged." Even if the documents were not protected from disclosure as "work product," they were protected by the attorney-client privilege. *Soter v. Cowles Publishing Co.*, 174 P.3d 69 (Wash. 2007).

◆ Montana students were disciplined for shooting others on school property with plastic BBs. The school board held a closed hearing to consider their discipline. The board opened the session after deciding on the discipline, then returned to closed session to take the action it discussed. A newspaper publisher noted that the board's previous practice had been to publicly reveal the nature of the student discipline while referencing students with an anonymous number. After the district superintendent refused a further request for information about the discipline, the publisher sued the school district in the state court system.

Appeal reached the Supreme Court of Montana, which found "student records" included student names and addresses, birth days, achievement levels and immunization records. Each school board must maintain a record of any discipline that is educationally related. **Courts in Ohio, Missouri and Georgia have held that disciplinary records are not "education records" as defined by FERPA.** Courts in Indiana and Wisconsin have held that once the names of students are blocked out, they are no longer "education records." The court decided that FERPA did not prevent the public release of student disciplinary records after student names were blocked. As there was no basis for refusing the publisher's request for information under FERPA or state law, the lower court decision was reversed. *Board of Trustees, Cut Bank Public Schools v. Cut Bank Pioneer Press*, 337 Mont. 229, 2007 MT 115, 160 P.3d 482 (Mont. 2007).

◆ The Massachusetts Education Department administered the Massachusetts Comprehensive Assessment System (MCAS) to over 220,000 students in three grades. It contracted with Harcourt Educational Measurement to score the tests. A *Boston Globe* reporter asked the department's commissioner for release of all 2000 MCAS scores, as soon as the department received them. Five days later, the department released statewide test results to the public, but did not include compiled test results for individual schools as they were not yet available. After receiving individual school testing information, the department announced an additional one-week delay in releasing results, to allow local school officials time to correct errors. The *Globe* sought a state court order to require the immediate release of 2000 MCAS test results, but the court denied the request.

The *Globe* appealed to the Massachusetts Supreme Judicial Court, which stated that the state public records law allows the custodian 10 days to comply with a records request. Here, the release of public records within 10 days was presumed reasonable and the department complied with the law by releasing the results in seven days. **As the department had an obligation to release accurate information, it did not unreasonably delay releasing the MCAS scores by allowing local districts to review the raw scores for errors.** The court affirmed the judgment for the department. *Globe Newspaper Co. v. Commissioner of Educ.*, 439 Mass. 124, 786 N.E.2d 328 (Mass. 2003).

◆ A *Chicago Tribune* reporter requested over a million records on current and former Chicago public school students. The request included personal data such as school, medical or special education status, attendance, race, transportation status, free or reduced-cost lunch status, class rank, grade average, bilingual education status, date of birth, and standardized test scores. The board of education denied the request as burdensome and as a high risk of disclosing personal information in violation of federal and state laws including the Freedom of Information Act (FOIA) and Student Records Act. The *Tribune* sued the board, and the case reached the Appellate Court of Illinois. It noted the FOIA required public bodies to comply with record requests unless an exemption applied. **FOIA's student records exemption was a *per se* rule that did not require a case-by-case balancing of the competing interests in public information and individual privacy**. The clear language of the FOIA created an exemption from disclosure for student files. Most of the data requested by the *Tribune* was considered private and confidential. Because the request was entitled to the *per se* exemption, the board had properly denied it. *Chicago Tribune Co. v. Board of Educ. of City of Chicago*, 332 Ill.App.3d 60, 773 N.E.2d 674 (Ill. App. Ct. 2002).

◆   A California school district denied requests to disclose student suspension and expulsion records based on student privacy rights. Statistical information on school discipline was offered instead. The record requestor sued the district, citing Education Code § 48918 and a state attorney general's opinion deeming student names and the reasons for expulsions "public information." The state court of appeal stated student records are generally unavailable to the public. But the Education Code treated expulsion records differently. Although students may opt for a private expulsion hearing, the formal action and expulsion records were public. Under federal law, student disciplinary records are protected from public disclosure as "education records." **Since FERPA conditions the receipt of federal funding on conformity with its provisions, the district risked the withdrawal of federal funds if it disclosed the requested student expulsion records.** The court held it was impossible for the district to obey both laws, so FERPA preempted state law. *Rim of the World Unified School Dist. v. Superior Court*, 104 Cal.App.4th 1393, 129 Cal.Rptr.2d 11 (Cal. Ct. App. 2002).

### C. Electronic and Video Records

*A California school district did not violate state and federal education record requirements by providing parents only printed copies of emails in their child's permanent file, rather than any and all emails in their electronic format that personally identified him. Emails had a "fleeting nature" and were not "education records" unless they were placed in a student's permanent file.*

◆   A California child with autism received special education from a county special education agency. His parents asked for copies of "any and all electronic mail sent or received" by the agency concerning or personally identifying their child. They then clarified that they sought emails in their electronic format. The county sent the parents hard copies of emails that had been printed and placed in their child's permanent file, but it refused to provide electronically formatted emails. The parents complained to the state department of education (DOE) and asserted violations of federal law when the district "unilaterally purged the original electronic files." The DOE held hard copies of emails in the student's files were "pupil records" under state law that had to be provided to parents within five business days of a request. But the DOE held the county did not have to provide emails in an electronic format and found the county was not required to notify parents before purging emails, which were not "educational records."

In a federal district court suit asserting state and federal records violations, the court found the Individuals with Disabilities Education Act (IDEA) required the county to provide parents a child's "education records." IDEA regulations referred to FERPA's definition of "education records." The court held **the DOE correctly found only those emails that personally identified the child and were "maintained" by an educational agency were "education records" under the IDEA and FERPA**. DOE correctly found the county had produced the child's education records by providing hard copies of all the emails that personally identified him and were maintained in his permanent file. Only those emails that were both maintained by the county and which personally identified the student were considered to be "education records." The court held that emails in electronic format were not "maintained" by the county. **Emails had a "fleeting nature" and were not "education records" unless they were placed in a student's permanent file.** The county did not "unlawfully purge" emails without notice to the parents. *S.A. v. Tulare County Office of Educ.*, No. CV F 08-1215 LJO GSA, 2009 WL 3126322 (E.D. Cal. 9/24/09).

◆ A Pennsylvania student discovered webcam photos and screenshots of himself on a school laptop. The school district agreed to disable the security tracking software on the laptop, but the student and others pursued a federal district court case. The court prohibited the district and its agents from remotely activating webcams on laptop computers issued to students. Under the court order, the school district could not remotely capture screenshots of laptops, except for maintenance, repairs or trouble-shooting. **The district could use an alternate means to track lost, stolen or missing laptops.** A global positioning system or other anti-theft device that did not permit the activation of webcams or capture screenshots was permitted. The order prevented the district from accessing any student-created files on laptops, such as emails, instant messages, internet use logs and web-browsing histories. Under the court order, the district was required to adopt official policies governing the use, distribution and maintenance of student laptops. It was further required to issue regulations for student privacy on laptops and to train staff on the oversight and enforcement of the policies. Under the order, the school district would have to provide students and their parents an opportunity to view images already taken from webcams. Such images were to be destroyed when the process was completed. *Robbins v. Lower Merion School Dist.*, No. 10-665, 2010 WL 1976869 (E.D. Pa. 5/14/10).

◆ Parents of students attending the Whitney E. Houston Academy (a performing arts school) signed a form consenting to the videotaping, photographing or sound recording of their children "in classroom, playground, auditorium activities or productions." Consent was given with knowledge that recordings might appear in the media or be used for school exhibits and public relations. The academy PTA presented a play and videotaped it. Copies of the videotape were later made available for sale through the PTA. A student who had a non-speaking role tripped during the show. Although her parent never saw a copy of the videotape, she claimed that it exploited her daughter and sued the PTA for invasion of her daughter's privacy rights. A state court found no evidence that the PTA had received a commercial benefit and that it had acted with a charitable purpose. On appeal, a state appellate court noted that since the PTA was a charitable organization, the parent would have had to show her child's likeness was used for financial or commercial benefit. **An invasion of privacy claim requires proof that a party has used the likeness of another person without consent for commercial benefit, and proof of damages.** It was not sufficient for the parent to simply claim that the recording of her daughter, by itself, established a claim for appropriation of her likeness. The lower court had correctly held for the PTA. *Jeffries v. Whitney E. Houston Academy P.T.A.*, No. L-1389-07, 2009 WL 2136174 (N.J. Super. Ct. App. Div. 7/20/09).

◆ A Tennessee school board approved of the installation of video surveillance cameras throughout a middle school building. There were no specific guidelines for the project. When the school year began, an assistant principal discovered that cameras had been placed to record areas of locker rooms where students dressed for sports activities. Four months later, a visiting girls' basketball coach complained to the school principal after her team members noticed a camera. The principal incorrectly assured the coach that the camera was not activated. The camera was on, and it recorded images of students changing their clothes.

Some of the students and their parents sued the school board, the director of schools, the principal and the assistant principal. The case reached the U.S. Court of Appeals, Sixth Circuit, which held there is a Fourth Amendment "right to shield one's naked body from view by members of the opposite sex." **Even in locker rooms, the students retained a significant privacy interest in their unclothed bodies.** Students using locker rooms had a reasonable expectation that no one would videotape them without their knowledge. Video surveillance is inherently intrusive. A reasonable school administrator would know that students had a privacy right against being surreptitiously videotaped while changing clothes. For this reason, the court held the principal and assistant principal were not entitled to qualified immunity from liability. *Brannum v. Overton County School Board*, 516 F.3d 489 (6th Cir. 2008).

◆ A surveillance video camera on a school bus videotaped a fight by two elementary students. The school district denied a request by the parents of one of the students for a copy of the tape. The district claimed the videotape was exempt from public disclosure under the Washington Public Disclosure Act (PDA). The parents sued, and a court agreed with the district's decision not to disclose the tape. The videotape contained information that would allow a viewer to identify a student, and the tape was "maintained" by the district for potential discipline. The Washington Court of Appeals affirmed.

On appeal, the Supreme Court of Washington explained that the videotape was a "public record" and that the district was an "agency" under the PDA. So the district had to disclose the videotape unless an exemption applied. The student file exemption contemplated the protection of materials in a public student's permanent file, such as student "grades, standardized test results, assessments, psychological or physical evaluations, class schedule, address, telephone number, social security number, and other similar records." Here, the surveillance camera was a means of maintaining security and safety on school buses. The videotape differed significantly from the type of records maintained in student personal files. Because **the videotape could not be legally withheld as a student file document**, the court reversed the judgment. *Lindeman v. Kelso School Dist. No. 458*, 162 Wash.2d 196, 172 P.3d 329 (Wash. 2007).

◆ A New York court held **a videotape of a student fighting with a teacher during school was not an education record under FERPA**. The school district had voluntarily disclosed it to the police. Under FERPA, education records are "records, files, documents and other material which contain information directly related to a student." FERPA is intended to protect records relating to a student's performance and does not apply to a videotape recorded to maintain the school's security and safety. The student's rights to appeal his suspension outweighed the district's interest in protecting the confidentiality of school records. While FERPA does not create a private right of action, the student was not suing the district. He was petitioning the court to have the videotape released so he could appeal the suspension. The court granted the student's request to release the videotape. *Rome City School Dist. Disciplinary Hearing v. Grifasi*, 10 Misc.3d 1034, 806 N.Y.S.2d 381 (N.Y. Sup. Ct. 2005).

◆ A Florida District Court of Appeal held that **videotapes of students on school buses were "records and reports" under the school code**. The court had previously used the definition of "personally identifiable information" from FERPA. But FERPA calls for the denial of eligibility for federal funds only if an educational agency violates federal privacy requirements. The Florida Code went beyond FERPA by protecting the privacy of students against the release of any personal information contained in records or reports permitting the personal identification of a student. The state code protected as confidential even those records or reports that were redacted of any personally identifying information. *WFTV, Inc. v. School Board of Seminole*, 874 So.2d 48 (Fla. Dist. Ct. App. 2004).

◆ A group of Kentucky special education students complained that their teacher mistreated them. The school installed cameras in her classroom to monitor her performance. The principal denied the teacher's request to view class videotapes under the state open records act, stating that they were "education records" under FERPA and its Kentucky counterpart, the KFERPA. The district superintendent claimed that both FERPA and KFERPA prohibited the release of the videotapes to the teacher, and the state attorney general upheld this ruling. A state court held for the district, and the teacher appealed.

The Court of Appeals of Kentucky found that the lower court failed to consider a state Open Records Act exception permitting teachers to inspect "education records." **A FERPA exception exists for school officials, including teachers, who have "legitimate educational interests"** in a student from

**whom consent would otherwise be required.** The lower court erroneously found that the teacher did not qualify for FERPA and KFERPA exceptions. Although the videotapes were "education records" under FERPA and KFERPA, the teacher was not just a "member of the public." Instead, her request had to be judged in view of her position as a teacher who was present in the classroom when the videotapes were recorded. The only way to prevent the teacher from viewing the videotapes under FERPA or KFERPA would be to find that she lacked "a legitimate educational interest." As the board did not show this, the court reversed and remanded the case for a hearing. *Medley v. Board of Educ. of Shelby County*, No. 2003-CA-001515-MR, 2004 WL 2367229 (Ky. Ct. App. 2004).

## IV. TESTING

*Ohio teachers who questioned the validity of student progress examinations were denied access to copies of the exams, which cost the district over $800,000 and were entitled to protection under trade secret laws.*

◆   Cincinnati Public Schools (CPS) spent $809,000 to hire a testing agency to develop exams for students in grades 9 - 11. CPS kept the exams in a secure area at a central location prior to administration. Students and staff members were forbidden from copying exams, and exams were collected immediately after being administered. A CPS teacher grew concerned over the design, implementation and scoring of the exams. About 60 other CPS teachers signed a petition seeking copies of the ninth grade exam. CPS denied the request, arguing that the exams had secure and copyrighted material. After mediation failed, the teacher sought a special order, called a "writ of mandamus," from the Supreme Court of Ohio. The court held that this remedy is available to compel compliance with the Ohio Public Records Act. Since the semester exams were created to fulfill CPS policy decisions, the Public Records Act applied. An exception to the Act applies to trade secrets and copyrighted materials.

**The Ohio Uniform Trade Secrets Act defined "trade secret" to include any information with independent economic value as a result of not being generally known, or which was the subject of reasonable efforts to maintain its secrecy.** CPS had spent a great amount of money in developing the exams, which would have little or no value if they were made public. It would cost a considerable sum to recreate the exams. CPS estimated that replacing just half the questions on the ninth and tenth grade exams would exceed $270,000. It was clear that CPS had taken steps to maintain the secrecy of the exams. Thus, the exams were trade secrets. As the exams were subject to a Public Records Act exception, CPS did not have to disclose them to the teacher. *State ex rel. Perrea v. Cincinnati Public Schools*, 123 Ohio St.3d 410, 916 N.E.2d 1049 (Ohio 2009).

◆   The NCLB Act requires assessment of limited English proficient (LEP) students in English once they have attended school in the U.S. for at least three consecutive years, unless a time extension is warranted. Assessments are to be in the language and form most likely to yield accurate data on student knowledge until English proficiency is attained. Arizona voters approved Proposition 203, which required all children in state public schools to be instructed in English. Proposition 203 specified a standardized, nationally-normed written test of academic subject matter, administered in English at least annually. According to Arizona officials, a verbal agreement was reached between the state education department and the U.S. Department of Education (DOE) regarding the inclusion of LEP student scores in AYP calculations. State officials claimed the DOE agreed to permit appeals of AYP calculations on grounds that LEP student test scores could not be a valid, reliable indicator of academic proficiency due to language deficiencies. A DOE monitoring team found that Arizona improperly used the NCLB Act appeals process to remove LEP assessment scores from AYP calculations.

The DOE ordered the state to cease this use of appeals and to use practices minimizing language barriers to LEP students. The state education department sued the DOE in a federal court for breach of the oral agreement to permit appeals for LEP students. The court agreed with the DOE's argument that **a breach of contract claim could not be based on a claim that the DOE promised to interpret the NCLB Act a certain way**. However, the state could amend its complaint to add an Administrative Procedures Act claim regarding its state plan amendment under the NCLB Act. *Horne v. U.S. Dep't of Educ.*, No. CV-08-1141-PHX-MHM, 2009 WL 775432 (D. Ariz. 3/23/09).

◆   A New York student complained of excessive noise at a state Specialized High School Admissions Test administration site. He was later denied a state court order that would have permitted him to retake the test. A state appellate division court held that the New York City Board of Education's decision was vested with education officials and was not appropriate for review by a court. The case was moot because the test had already been administered. *Tessler v. Board of Educ. of City of New York*, 854 N.Y.S.2d 66 (N.Y. App. Div. 2008).

◆   In 2003, the California state board of education announced that all public school students graduating in spring 2006 would have to pass both the language arts and mathematics parts of the California High School Exit Exam to receive a diploma. Districts had to offer supplemental instruction to all students who did not demonstrate sufficient progress toward passing. The legislature appropriated $20 million in supplemental funding for districts with the highest percentage of students who had not yet passed the exam. The state superintendent of public instruction distributed supplemental funding only to districts in which 28% or more of the class of 2006 had yet to pass the exam.

A lawsuit was filed in Alameda County Superior Court on behalf of 47,000 students who had satisfied other diploma requirements for spring 2006, but had yet to pass at least one part of the exam. The case alleged equal protection and due process violations. The court found that students in poor communities were not provided equal opportunities to learn the materials tested on the exam. Some schools had not fully aligned curriculums to the exam, and the lack of preparation disproportionately affected English language learners. The court issued an order preventing the state from requiring students in the class of 2006 to pass the exam as a condition of graduation. The state court of appeal held that **the superintendent had authority to give priority to the schools with the highest numbers of students who failed both parts of the exam**. The court found nothing arbitrary in the allocation of a limited sum of money to benefit school districts that appeared to have the greatest need. Students failing the exam had nine publicly funded options to continue their education and obtain diplomas. Awarding diplomas without passing the exam would stigmatize these students, deprive them of remedial instruction available to pass the exam, and debase the value of a diploma. Cases holding that education is a fundamental right did not support the finding of a fundamental right to a diploma. *O'Connell v. Superior Court of Alameda County,* 47 Cal.Rptr.3d 147 (Cal. Ct. App. 2006).

◆   A Maryland principal intern was accused of misconduct when taking a Praxis Series School Leaders Licensure Assessment Test. When she took the test, a site administrator submitted irregularity reports citing her for misconduct. The reports were based on alleged failure to stop writing in her test booklet when time was called. The intern challenged the reports in writing, stating that she had conformed completely to the test standards described to her. The Educational Testing Service (ETS) then cancelled her scores and returned her fee. The intern sued the ETS and the site administrator for breach of contract and other claims. The judge awarded pretrial judgment to the ETS on the breach of contract claim and dismissed all of the intern's remaining claims. The intern appealed to the state court of special appeals, which noted that **the ETS reserved the right to cancel a test score for misconduct**. However, the court agreed with the intern that a jury should be allowed to determine if her test scores had been cancelled in bad faith. The court reversed the judgment and remanded the case to the trial court. The intern would have to "surmount a gigantic hurdle" unless she could show that the administrator had some motive to lie. *Hildebrant v. Educational Testing Service,* 171 Md.App. 23, 908 A.2d 657 (Md. Ct. Spec. App. 2006).

◆   A Florida district court of appeal upheld an administrative ruling **rejecting charges that a teacher provided inappropriate assistance to her students during the Florida Comprehensive Assessment Test**. The state education practices commission filed a complaint against the teacher for providing answers and other help to her students on the test. However, after a hearing, an administrative law judge found all of the commission's student witnesses not credible. The judge accepted the testimony of the lone student who testified for the teacher. The commission held another hearing and issued a final order suspending the teacher's certification. The court of appeal held that the commission had improperly modified the judge's findings. As substantial evidence supported the judge's decision, the complaint was dismissed. *Stinson v. Winn,* 938 So.2d 554 (Fla. Dist. Ct. App. 2006).

◆   The Massachusetts Education Reform Act of 1993 specified a comprehensive diagnostic assessment of students in the fourth, eighth and tenth grades, with satisfaction of the tenth-grade examination a high school graduation requirement. Although student failure rates were as high as 53% in some core areas on the first MCAS administration in 1998, the board made the English, math, science and social studies parts of the exam a graduation requirement for students in the class of 2003. The board planned to phase other subjects into the graduation requirement and to raise the threshold scaled score over time. By 2003, about 90% of the state's seniors passed the tenth-grade MCAS and became eligible to graduate. Students who did not pass could receive remediation after grade 12 and further opportunities to take the exam. A group of students from the class of 2003 sued, challenging the regulation requiring them to pass the MCAS exam as a graduation prerequisite. All but one of the students attended public schools, and some of them received special education. The court denied their request for an order prohibiting the state education board from enforcing the regulation.

The students appealed to the Supreme Judicial Court, which held that **the board had the authority to gradually incorporate core areas in the MCAS examination, and to test students in English and math before doing so in other areas.** The regulation largely accomplished the Reform Act goal of holding educators accountable through required academic standards, curriculum frameworks and competency determinations. The legislature twice ratified the MCAS exam appropriating substantial funds for remediation programs. This indicated acceptance of the board's phase-in approach. The court affirmed the lower court decision. *Student No. 9 v. Board of Educ.*, 440 Mass. 752, 802 N.E.2d 105 (Mass. 2004).

## V.  EDUCATIONAL MALPRACTICE

*Claims of educational malpractice have, for the most part, failed. Courts have been reluctant to interfere with a school's internal operations.*

◆  A Florida family obtained an evaluation of their son after he experienced problems in school. He was found eligible for special education and provided with an individual education plan. The family then received information about the Celebration School. The family claimed that Osceola County School Board employees told them Celebration School provided "a quality education based upon a time-tested and successful curriculum known as 'best practices.'" After moving to the Town of Celebration, and enrolling their children in Celebration School, the parents became disenchanted with the school and placed their children in private schools. They sued the school board for misrepresentation. A court dismissed the action, and the parents appealed. A state court of appeal reinstated their claim based on a special education appeal that had been voluntarily dismissed in a federal court.

The court found that the claims for fraudulent inducement and negligent misrepresentation were not "educational malpractice claims," as the trial court had found. The trial court should have allowed the parents to amend their complaint to allege sufficient facts and attempt to prove each element of these claims. However, **the trial court had properly dismissed the family's claim** under the Florida Constitution, which guarantees a high quality free public education. There was no benchmark for determining how to define a "high quality education." This determination was for the legislature to make. *Simon v. Celebration Co.*, 883 So.2d 826 (Fla. Dist. Ct. App. 2004).

◆ A group of parents sued the Denver Public Schools and its superintendent for failing to provide students with a quality education. The complaint asserted that the school system failed to provide course books, failed to impose adequate discipline on students, improperly used credit waivers to inflate graduation rates, maintained a pattern of poorly performing schools, and used "dumbed-down" standards for measuring school performance. It also alleged damages for intellectual and emotional harm, diminution of educational and career opportunities, discrimination, and asserted that parents were forced to send their children to private or alternative schools. A court dismissed the case on grounds that the constitutional and statutory claims were not justiciable. It agreed with the board that the contract claim failed because no contractual relationship existed between public schools and their students.

The state court of appeals agreed to review the contract claim and distinguished it from contract claims against private schools. Contract claims attacking the general quality of public education have been rejected because they are not truly based in contract but instead seek damages for educational malpractice. **Public school students, unlike those attending private schools, have not individually contracted with their school systems for specific educational services and cannot assert breach of contract claims.** There was no legally enforceable promise to provide a curriculum, books or other educational services in this case. The court held the matter was political in nature and not within the power of the courts to decide. No court in the nation has recognized a breach of contract claim rooted in legislative policy. The court affirmed the judgment for the board and superintendent. *Denver Parents Ass'n v. Denver Board of Educ.*, 10 P.3d 662 (Colo. Ct. App. 2000).

# CHAPTER SIX

## Students with Disabilities

## I. THE IDEA

*Each of the states has enacted special education laws that parallel the Individuals with Disabilities Education Act (IDEA) in order to comply with federal standards and become eligible for funding. Unlike Section 504 of the Rehabilitation Act, the IDEA does not prohibit discrimination on the basis of disability. It imposes obligations on the states and requires compliance with IDEA procedures as a condition of receiving federal funds.*

*To receive IDEA funds, states must maintain a policy assuring that all children with disabilities have access to a free appropriate public education (FAPE). "FAPE" refers to special education and related services provided at public expense that meet state educational agency standards in conformity with an individualized education program (IEP). Local educational agencies (LEAs) receiving IDEA funds must make satisfactory assurances they are identifying and providing special education services to resident students with disabilities.*

### A. IDEA Substantive Requirements

*In* Board of Educ. v. Rowley, *this chapter, the U.S. Supreme Court held the IDEA establishes only a basic floor of opportunity for students with disabilities, and imposes no requirement on school districts to maximize student potential.*

**Rowley** *limits a court's inquiry to two things – whether the district has* **complied with IDEA procedural protections, and whether the IEP was** **reasonably calculated to enable the student to receive educational benefits.** *If a school district satisfies this two-part inquiry, the court's analysis is at an end.*

*In recent years, federal appeals courts have suggested a "meaningful benefit" standard. But in* J.L. v. Mercer Island School Dist., *the Ninth Circuit demonstrated it did not intend to deviate from* Rowley. *In* Thompson R2-J School Dist. v. Luke P., *the Tenth Circuit reached a similar result.*

◆   The parents of a Minnesota child sought to have accommodations provided for extracurricular activities in which she might wish to engage. However, they did not identify any specific activity at that time. The student later identified volleyball and after-school clubs as activities she was interested in. Her parents also sought accommodations so she could attend an off-campus fifth-grade graduation party. The district refused to provide accommodations relating to the party since it was a private event sponsored by the parent-teacher organization. In the lawsuit that followed, the state court of appeals held the school district did not have to provide accommodations for the child to attend a private party. But it did have to provide accommodations for the specific activities the student had identified – volleyball and after-school clubs. The case reached the Minnesota Supreme Court, which affirmed the decision in part. **The student did not have to prove that she would receive educational benefits from extracurricular and nonacademic activities in order to qualify for supplemental aides and**

**services.** The IEP team would have to consider whether the extracurricular and nonacademic activities were appropriate. *Independent School Dist. No. 12, Centennial v. Minnesota Dep't of Educ.*, 788 N.W.2d 907 (Minn. 2010).

◆   A New Jersey high school student designated as "other health impaired" received special education and did well in his classes but tested poorly in standardized tests. His parents became concerned with his education and requested a due process hearing, where they noted that his reading skills were at a third-grade level. His teachers and other school employees testified that standardized test scores were unreliable and that academic progress was a better indicator of success, but an administrative law judge disagreed and ruled for the parents. A federal court reversed that decision, but **the Third Circuit held the student's good grades did not indicate that he was making educational progress**. In this case, the school district failed to incorporate necessary recommendations made by the parents' experts and by the student's teachers and evaluators. *D.S. v. Bayonne Board of Educ.*, 602 F.3d 553 (3d Cir. 2010).

◆   A Washington student with learning disabilities attended regular classes and progressed from grade to grade. Her parents became dissatisfied with her education and found an independent evaluator who suggested that no public school in the state could provide her an adequate education. The parents enrolled their daughter in a Massachusetts private school and sought tuition reimbursement from their school district. A federal court held an administrative law judge improperly relied on *Board of Educ. v. Rowley*. According to the court, *Rowley* was superseded by post-1982 IDEA amendments. **The case reached the Ninth Circuit, which held the *Rowley* standard is still appropriate for determining whether a child has received an appropriate education.** Congress never disapproved of *Rowley* in any of the amendments to the IDEA. *J.L. v. Mercer Island School Dist.*, 575 F.3d 1025 (9th Cir. 2009).

◆   A New York student with hearing impairments sought the provision of a sign-language interpreter from her school district. She had residual hearing and was an excellent lipreader, which allowed her to attain above-average grades and to advance through school easily. The student's parents requested the services of a sign-language interpreter at school district expense, arguing that the IDEA required the district to maximize her potential. A federal court held that the disparity between the student's achievement and her potential to perform as she would if not for her disability deprived her of a free appropriate public education. This decision was affirmed by the U.S. Court of Appeals, Second Circuit, and the U.S. Supreme Court agreed to review the case.

The Court found no requirement in the IDEA that public schools maximize the potential of each student with a disability. The opportunities provided to each student by their school varied from student to student. The IDEA was primarily designed to guarantee access to students with disabilities to allow them to meaningfully benefit from public education. The IDEA protected the right to access education by means of its procedural protections, including the annual IEP meeting and review process. In IDEA cases, courts were to limit their inquiry to **whether the district had complied with IDEA procedural**

**protections, and whether the IEP was reasonably calculated to enable the student to receive educational benefits**. If the district satisfied this two-part inquiry, the court's analysis was at an end and the district was entitled to judgment. *Board of Educ. v. Rowley*, 458 U.S. 176 (1982).

◆ Ohio parents disagreed with the IEP prepared for their autistic son and placed him in a private school. They filed a due process hearing request but lost at two administrative levels. Without an attorney, they appealed. A federal court held for the school district, and the Sixth Circuit later held they could not pursue the case without hiring an attorney. **The U.S. Supreme Court heard the parents' appeal, and held the IDEA accorded them independently enforceable rights.** As it would be inconsistent with the statutory scheme to bar them from continuing to assert these enforceable rights in federal court, the Court reversed the judgment, permitting them to pursue their case. *Winkelman v. Parma City School Dist.*, 550 U.S. 516 (U.S. 2007).

◆ A Tennessee school board violated the rights of a student with autism by failing to consider Lovaas programming and improperly staffing his IEP team meetings. The Sixth Circuit held **"meaningful educational benefit" had to be gauged in relation to the student's potential**. The IDEA's legislative history supported exceeding the "meaningful educational benefits" standard where there was a "difference between self-sufficiency and a life of dependence" for a child. *Hamilton County Dep't of Educ. v. Deal*, 392 F.3d 840 (5th Cir. 2004).

The Sixth Circuit returned the case to a federal court, which held that the school district's proposals were substantively appropriate for the student. The court awarded the parents half of their request for reimbursement for Lovaas services, and they appealed. The Sixth Circuit affirmed the decision. As the district's IEPs were reasonably calculated to offer the student a meaningful educational benefit, the reduction in reimbursement was reasonable. *Deal v. Hamilton County Dep't of Educ.*, 258 Fed.Appx. 863 (6th Cir. 2008).

◆ Colorado parents claimed their school district did not address their autistic son's inability to generalize skills he learned at school to other settings. Despite his apparent progress toward IEP goals and objectives, his home behavior was characterized as "unevenly tempered." The child often displayed inappropriate and violent behavior at home and in public places. He had sleep problems, and he sometimes intentionally spread bowel movements around his bedroom. While the child was toilet-trained at school by grade one, he was unable to transfer this skill to his home and other settings. His parents placed him in the Boston Higashi School (BHS) and presented the IEP team with a list of goals from their private therapist's recommendations. After the IEP team proposed an IEP incorporating virtually all the goals sought by the parents, they declined the offer and filed a due process hearing request, seeking reimbursement for the BHS placement. The case reached the U.S. Court of Appeals, Tenth Circuit.

The court held the substantive IDEA standard for the provision of a free appropriate public education is not onerous. **Congress did not impose any greater substantive educational standard than would be necessary to make access to education "meaningful."** *Rowley* rejected "self-sufficiency" as a substantive IDEA standard. The IDEA was not designed to remedy a poor home setting or to make up for some other deficit not covered by the act. Generalization across settings was not required to show educational benefit. The school district did not have to do more than provide an IEP that enabled the child to make measurable and adequate gains in the classroom. *Thompson R2-J School Dist. v. Luke P.*, 540 F.3d 1143 (10th Cir. 2008).

## B.  Procedural Protections

### 1.  IEPs and Team Meetings

*The individualized education program (IEP) is the IDEA's most important procedural protection. The IDEA requires adequate notice to parents and opportunities for parental participation in the development of a student's IEP. A school district "must include the parents of a child with a disability in an IEP meeting unless they affirmatively refuse to attend."*

◆   The parents of a Vermont student with a disability asserted that their school district violated the IDEA because the student's applied media instructor, a regular education teacher, missed some IEP meetings. They claimed that his increased presence might have led to a different placement. After they began due process proceedings, the case reached the Second Circuit, which ruled against them. **The court held the absence of a regular educator at any given IEP meeting is not necessarily a procedural violation of the IDEA.** The instructor's participation in this case was held appropriate under the circumstances. He attended some meetings, and the parents decided to enroll their child in a particular applied media course without regard to the instructor's opinion. Thus, they suffered no harm. *K.L.A. v. Windham Southeast Supervisory Union*, 371 Fed.Appx. 151 (2d Cir. 2010).

◆   The parents of a New York student who had problems in large group settings attended committee on special education (CSE) meetings at which the student's IEP was changed from a classroom of 24 students to a 12:1:1 setting. The parents rejected the proposed IEP and placed the student in a private school and then sought tuition reimbursement. A federal court found the IEP procedurally deficient because the student's special education teacher did not attend the CSE meetings. However, the Second Circuit reversed, noting that **the IEP coordinator at the student's school had attended the CSE meetings along with the student's general education teacher** and that the IEP was reasonably calculated to provide educational benefits. No tuition was awarded. *A.H. v. Dep't of Educ. of City of New York*, 394 Fed.Appx. 718 (2d Cir. 2010).

◆   Parents of an autistic preschool child were denied a ruling that school officials "predetermined" a placement and failed to provide him intensive one-on-one therapy. The U.S. Court of Appeals, Fourth Circuit, affirmed a lower court order finding the school considered information from the parents at IEP meetings. A hearing officer found the parents "derailed the IEP process" by preventing thorough discussions, and many of their own suggestions were adopted in the IEP. **Use of a draft IEP did not show predetermination.** The court affirmed a judgment for school officials under several disability laws. *J.D. v. Kanawha County Board of Educ.*, 357 Fed.Appx. 515 (4th Cir. 2009).

◆   A California school district scheduled an IEP meeting without first checking the parents' availability. The parents had a history of not attending such meetings, and they did not return a signed copy of the IEP meeting notice. The mother asked the district to reschedule the meeting, but the district met in her absence. The parents filed an administrative action against the district for IDEA procedural violations. Eventually the case reached the Ninth Circuit, which held that regardless of the parents' history and the reason for their unavailability on the date in question, the district had an affirmative duty to comply with the IDEA. It held a **school district "must include the parents of a child with a disability in an IEP meeting unless they affirmatively refuse to attend."** By proceeding with the IEP meeting in the parents' absence, the district violated the IDEA. This justified a finding that the student was denied a free appropriate public education for an entire school year. *Drobnicki v. Poway Unified School Dist.*, 358 Fed.Appx. 788 (9th Cir. 2009).

◆   The parents of an autistic student in California claimed that their district violated the IDEA because no teacher from the student's private school attended IEP team meetings. The case reached the Ninth Circuit, which held the district provided a valid IEP. **The court held the exclusion of a private school teacher from IEP team meetings did not result in lost educational opportunities for the student.** However, the school district did have to continue to co-fund an in-home intervention program while the appeals process was completed. The stay-put provision of the IDEA required the district to maintain the student's current educational placement during the appeals process. *Joshua A. v. Rocklin Unified School Dist.*, 319 Fed.Appx. 692, 559 F.3d 1036 (9th Cir. 2009).

◆   The parents of an Ohio student had a contentious relationship with their school district, and they filed numerous administrative complaints. They sought to tape IEP meetings without prior consent and objected to the presence of a school attorney there. As a result of the disputes, the parties were unable to negotiate an IEP. The district filed a due process request and the case reached a federal court, which held that the district's attorney could be present at the IEP meetings. Further, **canceling IEP meetings because of conditions the parents imposed did not deprive them of any due process rights**. *Horen v. Board of Educ. of Toledo City School Dist.*, 594 F.Supp.2d 833 (N.D. Ohio 2009).

◆   A California school district convened an IEP team meeting that included a student's adaptive physical education (PE) teacher from three years earlier. Given the student's disabilities, adaptive PE was one of his most significant IEP components. The PE teacher had recently visited his school to evaluate his needs and was familiar with his current situation. His parents claimed an IDEA violation because his most current special education providers did not attend the meeting. The Ninth Circuit held **the IDEA does not require the most current teacher to attend an IEP meeting. Rather, it requires a special education**

**teacher or provider who has actually taught the student.** Not all a student's special education teachers need to attend the IEP meeting. *A.G. v. Placentia-Yorba Linda Unified School Dist.*, 320 Fed.Appx. 519 (9th Cir. 2009).

◆   A Connecticut student with serious emotional disturbance had increasing behavioral problems as he entered middle school. He was transferred to a state-approved special education day school, where he achieved good grades. His parents sought a private school placement, fearing he was not being sufficiently challenged. After an evaluation, the school board adopted several of the parents' suggested changes to the IEP, and offered a placement in a regional school for students with emotional and behavioral difficulties. The parents rejected the IEP and challenged it in an IDEA due process proceeding. The case reached the Second Circuit, which held that schools comply with the IDEA when parents have adequate opportunities to participate in the development of the IEP. **Nothing in the IDEA requires that parents consent to an IEP.** Because the initial and revised IEPs were sufficient, the board had offered an appropriate IEP. *A.E. v. Westport Board of Educ.*, 251 Fed.Appx. 685 (2d Cir. 2007).

◆   A Virginia student with Asperger's syndrome and a nonverbal learning disability was subjected to teasing and assaults by other students. At the IEP meeting for his ninth-grade school year, the discussion focused on his levels of performance and goals and objectives. The team decided the student would be placed at an unspecified private day school even though the student's mother believed neither of two suggested schools was appropriate for him. The family sought placement in a residential school, and the Fourth Circuit ultimately agreed. **Failure to identify a particular school in the IEP was an IDEA violation.** *A.K. v. Alexandria City School Board*, 484 F.3d 672 (4th Cir. 2007).

The case returned to the district court, which held that the district had to pay the parents over $135,000 in tuition and transportation costs. *A.K. v. Alexandria City School Board*, 544 F.Supp.2d 487 (E.D. Va. 2008).

◆   A California student with ADHD and reactive detachment disorder was expelled from three preschool programs for classroom misconduct. In first grade, the district declared her ineligible for special education under the IDEA, but eligible for accommodation under Section 504. She continued to have behavior problems in elementary school. Her mother placed her in a private residential facility in Montana, then sought tuition reimbursement. The school convened an IEP team meeting, but no representative from the facility attended. After the team again found the student ineligible for special education, the family initiated an IDEA proceeding. A federal court and the Ninth Circuit held **any procedural error by the district in failing to properly staff the IEP team meeting was harmless because the student failed to show that she had a qualifying disability under the IDEA.** *R.B. v. Napa Valley Unified School Dist.*, 496 F.3d 932 (9th Cir. 2007).

◆   An Ohio student began experiencing disciplinary problems in sixth grade and his IEP was then changed twice. His mother rejected his seventh-grade IEP on the grounds that it had been predetermined by the IEP team. She eventually sued, and the case reached the Sixth Circuit. The court of appeals held that predetermination is not the same as preparation and that the **IEP team members could prepare reports and come to meetings with pre-formed opinions about the best course of action for a student**. Here, the parties had met 16 times over a two-year period and had daily communications about homework. The school district's preparation work prior to the IEP meeting did not violate the IDEA. *Nack v. Orange City School Dist.*, 454 F.3d 604 (6th Cir. 2006).

## 2.  Notice and Hearing Requirements

*Local educational agencies must provide parents with notices of their procedural rights once a year, and upon an initial referral or evaluation for special education and related services, the filing of a due process complaint, or other parental request. Schools and school districts may place procedural safeguard notices on their websites. The reauthorized IDEA sets a two-year limitation period on the filing of IDEA complaints. A party appealing from an adverse due process hearing decision must appeal within 90 days from the date of the hearing officer's decision, unless the state has its own limitation period.*

◆  A Maryland student with learning disabilities and a speech impairment attended private schools for years. His parents then sought to place him through the Montgomery County Public Schools. The district evaluated him and drafted an IEP that would have placed him in one of two district middle schools. The parents rejected the offer, and requested a hearing. An administrative law judge (ALJ) found the evidence was close, and held the parents had the burden of persuasion in the case. As a result of this allocation of the burden, the district won. The case reached the U.S. Supreme Court, which explained that the party filing the lawsuit, who seeks to change the state of affairs, should be expected to bear the burden of proof. This was the case, for example, in cases arising under Title VII of the Civil Rights Act of 1964 and the Americans with Disabilities Act. Congress has repeatedly amended the IDEA to reduce its administrative and litigation costs. **The Court held parents who challenge their children's IEPs in special education due process hearings have the burden of proving the IEPs are inappropriate.** The Court affirmed the judgment, holding the burden of proof in an administrative hearing to challenge an IEP is on the party seeking relief. *Schaffer v. Weast*, 546 U.S. 49 (2005).

When the case returned to a federal district court, the parents challenged the student's eighth-grade IEP by presenting evidence of the changes made to his tenth-grade IEP. The school district countered with evidence that the student had graduated with a 3.4 grade point average. The court ruled for the school district, and the Fourth Circuit affirmed the judgment. **Using the tenth-grade IEP to challenge the eighth-grade IEP would promote a hindsight-based review that conflicted with the IDEA's structure and purpose.** *Schaffer v. Weast*, 554 F.3d 470 (4th Cir. 2009).

◆  While incarcerated, the father of a child with a disability attempted to challenge a decision that the student did not need additional special instruction. The board denied his request to review assessment materials and obtain an impartial due process hearing because he had no custodial rights over the child. A federal district court held that **non-custodial status did not automatically divest the father of all parental rights**. On appeal, the Second Circuit ruled that the lower court would have to decide whether the mother should be joined as a necessary party by examining state law and the divorce decree. *Fuentes v. Board of Educ. of City of New York*, 136 Fed.Appx. 448 (2d Cir. 2005).

The case was then returned to the district court, which again held the father lacked legal standing to pursue the case. He filed another appeal. The Second Circuit rejected the father's claim that the case should be resolved under the IDEA. **Amendments to the IDEA in 2004 did not create a presumption that biological parents have a right to sue under the IDEA**, so long as a custody or divorce decree did not restrict those rights. As state law would determine the answer to the parental rights questions, the court certified a question to the state's highest court. It asked: "[w]hether, under New York law, the biological and non-custodial parent of a child retains the right to participate in decisions pertaining to the education of the child where (1) the custodial parent is granted exclusive custody of the child and (2) the divorce decree and custody order are silent as to the right to control such decisions." *Fuentes v. Board of Educ. of City of New York*, 540 F.d 145 (2d Cir. 2008).

The New York Court of Appeals accepted the question from the Second Circuit. **It held that although a non-custodial parent has the right to participate in a child's education, that parent does not have the right to "control educational decisions" absent an express provision in the custody agreement.** Thus, the father could not challenge the district's provision of educational services to the student. *Fuentes v. Board of Educ. of City of New York*, 12 N.Y.3d 309, 907 N.E.2d 696 (N.Y. 2009).

## C. Implementation of IEPs

*In a Texas case, the U.S. Court of Appeals, Fifth Circuit, described a test for assessing whether a school district has adequately implemented an IEP. The court assessed whether education was being provided in a coordinated and collaborative manner by key stakeholders and whether the student was receiving positive academic and nonacademic benefits. **A student challenging the adequacy of an IEP must demonstrate that school authorities failed to implement substantial or significant IEP provisions.*** Houston Independent School Dist. v. Bobby R., *200 F.3d 341 (5th Cir. 2000).*

◆   The mother of a Washington student with autism believed that the in-home ABA therapists provided by her district were not properly trained. She began taking him to a private therapist. The school district then began offering ABA therapy and discontinued paying for the private therapist. The mother refused to let her son attend an extended school year program because she believed the staff was improperly trained. She rejected another IEP offer and sought due process. The case reached the Washington Court of Appeals, which noted that the IEP offered a free appropriate public education even though the IEP team ultimately rejected the mother's position that she had been denied an adequate opportunity to participate in IEP meetings. She had attended the meetings with an advocate and an autism consultant and rejected several attempts to evaluate the student. **The IEP was flexible enough to allow the modifications offered by the district to address the mother's concerns after the IEP was adopted.** *Hensley v. Colville School Dist.*, 148 Wash.App. 1032 (Wash. Ct. App. 2009).

◆   A New Jersey student's IEP called for a personal aide for the full school day as well as 10 hours of at-home tutoring a week at school board expense. Aides were to be trained in Lovaas methodology, which is also known as applied behavioral analysis. When the school district could not find a Lovaas-trained aide, the student's mother did so and the district then hired him. The aide resigned, and it took the school district a while to replace him. During this time, the mother kept her son at home and hired another Lovaas-trained aide, whom the district also hired. She made extra payments to the aides the district provided, then sought reimbursement for those payments. However, a federal district court and later the U.S. Court of Appeals, Third Circuit, ruled for the school board. It found the school board had no idea she was making the payments. Further, the **delay in finding a replacement aide did not amount to a denial of a free appropriate public education**. *Fisher v. Stafford Township Board of Educ.*, 289 Fed.Appx. 520 (3d Cir. 2008).

◆   A severely autistic Oregon student transitioned from elementary to middle school, where his father claimed the school district failed to implement key parts of his IEP. He requested a due process hearing, and an administrative law judge held the district was adequately implementing the student's IEP, except for math instruction. She ordered the district to remedy that aspect of the IEP. A federal court affirmed her ruling, and the Ninth Circuit then largely upheld the decision in favor of the district. It noted that **minor failures in implementing an IEP are not automatic violations of the IDEA. Only a material failure to implement an IEP violates the IDEA.** "A material failure occurs when the services a school provides to a disabled child fall significantly short of the services required by the child's IEP." Because the district had remedied the math instruction deficiency, there were no substantive IDEA violations. *Van Duyn v. Baker School Dist. 5J*, 481 F.3d 770 (9th Cir. 2007).

## II.  DISCIPLINE OF STUDENTS WITH DISABILITIES

### A.  Discipline as a Change in Placement

*In* Doe v. Todd County School Dist., *this chapter, the U.S. Court of Appeals, Eighth Circuit, held the change of a student's placement "is primarily an educational, not a disciplinary, decision." But the IDEA states that disciplinary removals of over 10 school days, or a pattern of removals that exceeds 10 days in a school year, may constitute a "change in placement." See 20 U.S.C. § 1415(k)(G). Students who violate a student code of conduct may be placed in an appropriate interim alternative setting. The IDEA allows schools to "consider any unique circumstances on a case-by-case basis when determining whether to order a change in placement" for a student with disabilities who violates a student code of conduct. See 20 U.S.C. § 1415(k). It specifies the "special circumstances" in which schools may remove a student to an interim alternative educational setting for up to 45 days, regardless of whether the behavior leading to discipline is a manifestation of a disability.*

*The "special circumstances" are: weapons possession, the sale, use or possession of drugs; or infliction of serious bodily injury while at school, on school grounds, or at a school event. A hearing officer reviewing a disciplinary removal may return the child to his or her placement, or order a change in placement to an appropriate interim alternative setting for not more than 45 school days. To do so, the hearing officer must find maintaining the current placement is "substantially likely to result in injury."*

*In* Honig v. Doe, *below, the U.S. Supreme Court held that while a school district cannot unilaterally change the placement of a disabled student it feels is be dangerous,* **the district can use "its normal procedures for dealing with children who are endangering themselves or others," such as "time-outs, detention, the restriction of privileges," or suspension.**

◆   Two emotionally disturbed children in California were each suspended for five days for misbehavior that included destroying school property and assaulting and making sexual comments to other students. Pursuant to state law, the suspensions were continued indefinitely during the pendency of expulsion proceedings. The students sued the school district in U.S. district court contesting the extended suspensions on the ground that they violated the "stay-put" provision of the IDEA, which provides that a student must be kept in his or her "then-current" educational placement during the pendency of proceedings which contemplate a change in placement. The district court issued an injunction preventing the expulsion, and the school district appealed. The U.S. Court of Appeals, Ninth Circuit, held the indefinite suspensions constituted a prohibited "change in placement" without notice under the IDEA. There was no "dangerousness" exception to the IDEA's "stay-put" provision.

On appeal, the U.S. Supreme Court held the intended purpose of the "stay-put" provision was to prevent schools from changing a child's educational placement over parental objections until all IDEA proceedings were completed. While the IDEA provided for interim placements where parents and school officials were able to agree on one, there was no emergency exception for dangerous students. **Where a disabled student poses an immediate threat to the safety of others, school officials may temporarily suspend him or her for up to 10 school days.** The Court affirmed the court of appeals' decision that indefinite suspensions violated the "stay-put" provision of the IDEA. It modified the decision by holding that suspensions up to 10 rather than up to 30 days do not constitute a change in placement. Significantly, the Court held that **a school district can use "its normal procedures for dealing with children who are endangering themselves or others," such as "time-outs, detention, the restriction of privileges," or suspension**. The Court also upheld the court of appeals' ruling that states could be required to provide services directly to disabled students where a local school district fails to do so. *Honig v. Doe*, 484 U.S. 305, 108 S.Ct. 592, 98 L.Ed.2d 686 (1988).

## B. Manifestation Determinations

*A manifestation determination review is required when disciplinary action would result in a disabled child's removal from school for over 10 days in a school year.* **The student's IEP team must perform the review.** *Parents and IEP team members are to determine "if the conduct in question was caused by, or had a direct and substantial relationship, to the child's disability." If so, the team must determine if the conduct was a direct result of failure to implement the IEP.* **If the team finds the child's behavior is not a manifestation of a disability, the disciplinary procedures applied to nondisabled children may be applied to the child.** *A student whose misconduct is not a manifestation of a disability is still entitled to regular disciplinary procedures. If the team finds the misconduct is related to the child's disability, it may still seek the parents' agreement to change the placement. A local education agency (LEA) that disciplines a student with disabilities must continue to provide the student with a free appropriate public education if a placement is changed. This is irrespective of whether the child's behavior is found to manifest a disability.*

◆   A South Dakota student fought with another student and brought a knife to school. After being suspended, a manifestation determination meeting was held, and the IEP team found his misconduct was not a manifestation of his learning disability. After missing four days of school, he was placed in an alternative educational setting. His grandmother asked for a school board hearing but was informed that was not possible because the student was no longer suspended. In his alternative placement, the student received two hours of instruction four days a week instead of his usual 30 hours per week. In a federal court action, the court held the alternative placement amounted to a long-term suspension that exceeded 10 days. It held the student was entitled to a hearing before the school board, just like any other student facing similar discipline. On appeal, the U.S. Court of Appeals, Eighth Circuit, agreed with the school district that the student had only been suspended for four days. The assistant principal had explained the charges to the student and given him an opportunity to respond. **As suspensions of 10 days or less trigger only minimal due process protection, due process had been satisfied.** The IEP team could have removed the student from school for up to 45 school days under a section of the IDEA allowing schools to place a student in an interim alternative educational setting. The team also had the option to place him in an alternative educational setting with parental consent. This is what had actually occurred, as the grandmother agreed to the change to obtain counseling and instructional services. **Federal law expressly provided that IEP teams must determine any interim alternative educational placement.** Once the IEP team changed the student's placement with the grandmother's consent, the team, and not the school board, "became the decision-maker authorized to change his placement" under 34 C.F.R. Part 300.530(d)(5). By agreeing to the change in placement, the grandparent "gave the IEP team, rather than the District's school board, control of the situation." As the district did not violate the student's rights, the judgment was reversed. *Doe v. Todd County School Dist.*, 625 F.3d 459 (8th Cir. 2010).

◆   A District of Columbia student who was eligible for special education taunted a substitute teacher and refused to follow instructions. Because he had two prior infractions in the same school year, he was suspended for 54 days and placed in an alternative educational setting. A manifestation determination review found his behavior was not a manifestation of his disability. After a hearing officer reduced the suspension to 10 days, an assistant district superintendent increased it to 45 days. Another hearing officer found that the alternative placement was not appropriate under the IDEA and reduced the suspension to 11 days. **When the district challenged that decision, the D.C. Circuit upheld it because the alternative placement denied the student a FAPE.** The hearing officer did not exceed his authority in modifying the suspension. *District of Columbia v. Doe*, 611 F.3d 888 (D.C. Cir. 2010).

◆   An Ohio student with ADD received interventions in grades one and two but was determined not to need an IEP. In third grade, she became physically aggressive and was referred to a mental health agency. Later, she was suspended for threatening behavior. Her mother requested a manifestation determination review and an evaluation, which found her eligible for special education. Her mother then filed a due process request for various IDEA violations. A hearing officer awarded compensatory education for the delay in identifying the student as IDEA-eligible. **A federal court agreed that the district should have conducted a manifestation determination before suspending the student.** It also ordered the discipline wiped from her record. *Jackson v. Northwest Local School Dist.*, No. 1:09-cv-300, 2010 WL 3452333 (S.D. Ohio 8/3/10).

◆   Along with several friends, an emotionally disabled Virginia student vandalized his school by shooting the building and some school buses with paintball guns. The principal recommended that he be expelled, which triggered an IDEA manifestation determination review. The review committee found his behavior was not a manifestation of his disability. A hearing officer recommended suspending the student for the rest of the year. His parents objected and sought due process. The hearing officer found no IDEA violation, and a federal court agreed. **There was no IDEA requirement that the review committee members know the student personally.** And the student was not drawn into the vandalism by his friends. Rather, he had been an instigator. *Fitzgerald v. Fairfax County School Board*, 556 F.Supp.2d 543 (E.D. Va. 2008).

◆   A Pennsylvania student who was eligible for a Section 504 plan but not an IEP under the IDEA caused a bomb scare at his school. The school district denied his parents' request for a manifestation determination hearing and expelled the student. The parents sued the school district in a federal court, which held **a manifestation determination is required for discipline under the IDEA, but not Section 504**. While a manifestation determination is one way to comply with Section 504 requirements, the law does not mandate this. As a result, the student had not been denied due process by the failure to conduct a manifestation determination. *Centennial School Dist. v. Phil L.*, 559 F.Supp.2d 634 (E.D. Pa. 2008).

◆  Classmates called a learning disabled New York student "faggot" and "PLC," which stood for "prescriptive learning class." A fight broke out between the student and a classmate, and the student was suspended for five days. The district notified him of a hearing to consider a longer suspension. The superintendent accepted the hearing officer's recommendation for another five-day suspension pending a manifestation hearing. The school's committee on special education found the student's behavior was not a manifestation of his disability, and the superintendent then planned to suspend him for the rest of the year. The student sued the school district in a federal district court, which found that **"PLC" was a reference to his learning disability, making the incident "related to" his disability**. Also, the district treated the manifestation determination "dismissively" and did not afford adequate due process. *Coleman v. Newburgh Enlarged City School Dist.*, 319 F.Supp.2d 446 (S.D.N.Y. 2004).

After the student graduated, he sued the district for his attorneys' fees. The Second Circuit held he had to exhaust his administrative remedies and was not entitled to fees. He had no right to graduate at a particular time from a particular school, even if he was a superior athlete on the verge of graduation. *Coleman v. Newburgh Enlarged City School Dist.*, 503 F.3d 198 (2d Cir. 2007).

## C.  Delinquency and Juvenile Justice

*A federal regulation at 34 C.F.R. Part 300.535(a) explains that special education protections do not shield students who commit crimes or juvenile offenses from law enforcement efforts. The regulation states "[n]othing in this part prohibits an agency from reporting a crime committed by a child with a disability to appropriate authorities or prevents [s]tate law enforcement and judicial authorities from exercising their responsibilities with regard to the application of Federal and State law to crimes committed by a child with a disability." In the following case, the Court of Appeals of Michigan rejected a student's claim that this regulation violated his due process rights.*

◆  A Michigan student had Tourette's Disorder and related disabilities. He received special education services and had a behavioral plan. After the school district issued him several suspensions, it petitioned a state court to find him guilty of school incorrigibility under Section 712A.2 of the state code. This section made school incorrigibility an offense for juveniles who were "willfully and repeatedly" absent or who repeatedly violated school rules and regulations.

The court upheld the petition, and the student appealed to the Court of Appeals of Michigan. The court held the petition was properly filed and that the prosecutor had been neutral. **Despite the provision of behavioral plan services, the court found the student engaged in repeated and escalating misconduct** that disturbed others. It was not error for the county court to assume jurisdiction over the student, and the agency did not have to provide his special education and disciplinary records prior to filing a juvenile petition. In a separate proceeding, an administrative law judge had found the juvenile petition was not a change in placement. Since the student did not appeal from that finding, he could not attack it later. In any event, he was never removed from school for more than 10 consecutive school days or a series of removals totaling more than 10 school days in one school year. So the court found a manifestation determination hearing was unnecessary. Section 712A.2 did not require evidence of willful violations and did not exempt violations based on a juvenile's disability. **The IDEA does not prevent schools from reporting crimes by disabled students to appropriate officials.** As sufficient evidence supported an adjudication of guilt, the judgment was affirmed. *In re Nicholas Papadelis*, No. 291536, 2010 WL 3447892 (Mich. Ct. App. 9/2/10).

◆   A Georgia school district assigned a one-on-one assistant to an aggressive autistic student for an after-school daycare program and also devised a behavior intervention plan for him. A custodian with a special needs son received training and served as the assistant, but often had to be away to attend to his own child. On a day when the custodian was absent, the student became agitated and left the building. Eventually, several staff members placed him in his time-out room, where he hit the window and kicked the walls. A police officer handcuffed him until his father could come and pick him up. The father later sued for disability discrimination under Section 504 and the ADA, but **a federal court found no evidence of intentional discrimination against the student**. At most, staff members acted negligently. *J.D.P. v. Cherokee County, Georgia School Dist.*, 735 F.Supp.2d 1348 (N.D. Ga. 2010).

◆   A New Mexico student with a specific learning disability skipped classes 136 times in a semester, used drugs and alcohol, was arrested for attacking family members and sent to a juvenile detention center. The center evaluated her and recommended "placement in reg-ed with support." The student's school district accepted the form as an "interim IEP" when the student returned to school in fall, where she was to repeat grade nine. The district did not revise the "interim IEP" prior to the school year and did not update her last functioning IEP. During the next term, the student had serious disciplinary problems and 65 unexcused absences. The school suspended her for fighting, and she failed all her fall classes. A hearing officer found that the district did not deny the student a FAPE. The student enrolled in ninth grade at a different high school. This time, she consistently attended school and earned a 4.0 grade point average for the school year. But the student resumed skipping classes, and she used drugs and alcohol. She stopped attending school when her mother kicked her out of the house. The student appealed the administrative decision to a federal court.

The court held **any loss of educational opportunity suffered by the student was the result of her own behavior and not school errors**. On appeal, the U.S. Court of Appeals, Tenth Circuit, held any IDEA violation was immaterial because of her truancy and behavioral problems. The student had largely rejected the services offered to her, and the district was bound to provide her a FAPE if she decided to return to school. *Garcia v. Board of Educ. of Albuquerque Public Schools*, 520 F.3d 1116 (10th Cir. 2008).

◆   An Illinois student who received special education and related services was charged with lighting fireworks and throwing them at others. A juvenile court adjudicated him delinquent and placed him on probation. When he violated probation, his probation officer recommended a residential placement. His mother moved to a new school district, which was notified that it should appear in juvenile court regarding its potential liability for funding the student's placement. The juvenile court agreed with the probation officer that the student should be residentially placed, and ordered the district to fund the placement. The district challenged the decision in a state court and won. The Illinois Supreme Court held that **the student's placement was not made under the School Code, but under the Juvenile Court Act**. It was made to remedy a probation violation, not the student's educational needs. Also, the district was not given the opportunity to show that it could educate the student. The state had to fund the placement. *In re D.D.*, 819 N.E.2d 300 (Ill. 2004).

◆   A New York principal initiated a family court proceeding to determine if a student was in need of supervision based on 16 unexcused absences from school during a two-month period. The family court ordered the school's committee on special education to conduct an evaluation. It found that the student was emotionally disturbed and had a disability. After the court placed the student on probation for a year, he appealed. The New York Supreme Court, Appellate Division, ruled that the **adjudication of the student as a child in need of supervision did not constitute a change in placement** under the IDEA. The student's placement was not changed. He was simply ordered to attend school and participate in his IEP. *Erich D. v. New Milford Board of Educ.*, 767 N.Y.S.2d 488 (N.Y. App. Div. 2003).

## III. PLACEMENT OF STUDENTS WITH DISABILITIES

*The IDEA requires each local education agency to identify and evaluate students with disabilities in its jurisdiction. After a district identifies a student as disabled, it must develop and implement an individualized education program (IEP). The IEP must be reasonably calculated to provide educational benefits and where possible, to include the student with nondisabled students.*

### A. Identification and Evaluation

*Parents may request the initial evaluation of a child for special education and related services, as may the state or the local educational agency (LEA). An evaluation is to take place within 60 days of receiving parental consent, or within a time frame established by the state. LEAs are exempt from the 60-day requirement in transfer cases or if a parent "repeatedly fails or refuses to produce the child for the evaluation."*

*Parents who have not allowed an evaluation of their children, or have refused special education and related services, will be barred from later asserting IDEA procedural protections in disciplinary cases. A special rule for eligibility determinations states that lack of appropriate instruction in reading or math may not be used to make an IDEA eligibility determination.*

*Lack of English proficiency is also specifically excluded from entering into eligibility determinations. When determining whether a child has a specific learning disability, LEAs may not consider a severe discrepancy between achievement and intellectual ability in oral expression, listening comprehension, written expression, basic reading skill, reading comprehension, mathematical calculation or mathematical reasoning.*

◆   The parents of a New York preschool student obtained three evaluations showing that their son had either an autism spectrum disorder, ADHD or serious social issues. They sought special education for him even though his teachers maintained that he made academic progress and his behavior problems were manageable. A due process hearing officer noted that the student's behavior did not adversely impact his education to a degree that indicated a need for special education. A federal court agreed, ruling that **all the parents could show was that because their son needed frequent redirection, he was not reaching his full academic potential**. But achievement of full academic potential is not the IDEA eligibility standard. And the record in this case did not demonstrate that the student's educational performance was adversely affected by his Asperger's syndrome. *A.J. v. Board of Educ., East Islip Union Free School Dist.*, 679 F.Supp.2d 299 (E.D.N.Y. 2010).

◆   After an evaluation, a Pennsylvania second-grader was thought to have ADHD. But there was no discrepancy between his ability and his achievement, so he was not placed in special education. By the seventh grade, the student's performance declined and at the end of the eighth grade, he was evaluated again and found to have ADHD. His performance continued to decline over the next two years, and he dropped out of school. The student's parents filed an IDEA action against the school district for failing to timely identify him as disabled. A federal court, and later the Third Circuit ruled against the parents, finding that **the school district did not rely solely on an ability/achievement analysis in determining that the student did not need special education at an earlier age**. The district did not violate its child-find duty under the IDEA. *Richard S. v. Wissahickon School Dist.*, 334 Fed.Appx. 508 (3d Cir. 2009).

◆   A California student had Pachygyria, a disorder associated with seizures, developmental delays and neuropsychiatric dysfunction. School evaluators, though highly experienced, had never before assisted a child with Pachygyria. They recommended a public school placement and determined that the student's behaviors and anxieties did not disrupt her ability to learn and participate in school activities. The parents, desiring a private school placement, sought due process and appealed an adverse decision to a federal court. **The court ruled that the evaluators' lack of familiarity with Pachygyria did not violate the IDEA and that the district offered the student an adequate academic program.** *Marcotte v. Palos Verdes Peninsula Unified School Dist.*, No. CV 08-1671 PSG (PLAx), 2009 WL 1873024 (C.D. Cal. 6/29/09).

◆   A New York student with ADHD was sexually abused by a cousin and was later suspended for fighting and drug possession. His grades dropped out of the honor roll range, but he continued to pass his classes. His parents placed him in a boarding school for troubled students. The committee on special education met and determined the student did not meet the IDEA criteria for severe emotional disturbance. His parents appealed, and the case reached the Second Circuit. The court held for the school district, ruling that **even if the student exhibited some of the symptomology for an emotional disturbance, his symptoms did not affect his academic performance**. Instead, drug use appeared to be at the root of his school problems. *Mr. and Mrs. N.C. v. Bedford Cent. School Dist.*, 300 Fed.Appx. 11 (2d Cir. 2008).

◆   A Pennsylvania student with autism spectrum disorder had a behavioral crisis while in a private school funded by the district. **A reevaluation led to an evaluation report that used boilerplate language, listing generic goals and principles that might work for any child rather than specifying the student's needs and issues.** The IEP also contained much of that boilerplate language. When the parents sought due process, a hearing officer determined that both the IEP and the private school placement were inappropriate. The case reached a federal court, which agreed that the IEP and the private school were inappropriate. A new IEP would have to be developed. *A.Y. and D.Y. v. Cumberland Valley School Dist.*, 569 F.Supp.2d 496 (M.D. Pa. 2008).

◆   A California student spent three years in foster care before reuniting with his mother as a five-year-old, just before beginning kindergarten. He acted out at school and was disciplined by his teacher four times in less than four months at a Los Angeles public school. His mother requested an initial special education assessment, which the district denied because of the student's limited school experience and the lack of general education interventions. The family moved out of the district, and the mother requested due process. A hearing officer held that the district had to pay for an independent educational evaluation, and a federal court agreed. **Although the district did not have to assess the student itself, it had an obligation to fund the independent evaluation.** *Los Angeles Unified School Dist. v. D.L.*, 548 F.Supp.2d 815 (C.D. Cal. 2008).

◆   A Texas student with ADHD received special education services until the fourth grade, after which he no longer needed them. He performed well in school but had behavioral problems through the seventh and eighth grades. He nevertheless passed all his classes and met the statewide standards required by the Texas Assessment of Knowledge and Skills. After he robbed a school concession stand he was placed in an alternative setting. His mother requested a due process hearing, alleging that the district failed to identify him as a student with a disability. The case reached the Fifth Circuit Court of Appeals, which held that even though the student had a qualifying disability (his ADHD), he did not need special education services as a result. **His behavioral problems resulted from non-ADHD occurrences, such as family problems.** *Alvin Independent School Dist. v. Patricia F.*, 503 F.3d 378 (5th Cir. 2007).

◆   A Maine elementary school student excelled academically but began having problems with peers and depression. She stayed in public school until sixth grade, when she skipped school, inflicted wounds on herself and had more peer problems. After attempting suicide, she was hospitalized and later diagnosed with Asperger's Syndrome. A school pupil evaluation team identified her as a qualified individual with a disability under Section 504, but determined she was ineligible for special education under the IDEA. She was offered 10 hours of weekly tutoring. Instead, her parents enrolled her in a private school. In the lawsuit that arose over her education, **the First Circuit held that even though the child did not have academic needs, she could still be eligible for special education under the IDEA**. Here, the student's condition adversely affected her educational performance in nonacademic areas. Accordingly, the student was entitled to compensatory education for the period during which she was deemed ineligible. However, she was not entitled to tuition reimbursement for the private school placement. *Mr. I. v. Maine School Administrative Dist. No. 55*, 480 F.3d 1 (1st Cir. 2007).

◆   The foster parents of an HIV-positive Maryland student told her about her condition for the first time just before her fifth-grade year. Her behavior deteriorated sharply over the next two years. She cut herself, heard voices telling her to stab herself, and was hospitalized at five institutions, finally being diagnosed with a psychotic condition. She missed a lot of school, and her academic performance declined during sixth grade. Her mother requested an IEP meeting to determine her eligibility under the IDEA. The IEP team found that although the student engaged in inappropriate behavior or had inappropriate feelings, she did not qualify for special education because her condition caused no adverse educational impact. Eventually the dispute reached the Fourth Circuit, which held the student was eligible for special education. **Her emotional disturbance affected her educational performance**, despite contrary testimony from school district experts. *Board of Educ. of Montgomery County, Maryland v. S.G.*, 230 Fed.Appx. 330 (4th Cir. 2007).

◆   A Kentucky student was diagnosed with ADHD near the end of his fourth-grade year. His mother claimed the district should have identified him as IDEA-eligible earlier and requested a due process hearing. A hearing officer awarded the student 125 hours of compensatory education. A state appeals board affirmed the decision, but decided that the student's IEP team should determine how much compensatory education he should receive. On appeal, the Sixth Circuit held that the IEP team should not have been granted the authority to decide how much compensatory education the student was due. However, it rejected the mother's claim that the district should have referred the student for special education as early as kindergarten. **Children have different development rates and referring a child for special education too early can be damaging.** The court remanded the case for a re-determination of the compensatory education award. *Board of Educ. of Fayette County, Kentucky v. L.M.*, 478 F.3d 307 (6th Cir. 2007).

◆   The mother of a Florida student attending regular classes under a Section 504 plan sought other accommodations for him. After his fourth-grade year, she requested a due process hearing. After consenting to a less-than-full evaluation of her son, she agreed to a full evaluation. However, a school psychologist conducted only intellectual and process tests, based on his supervisor's instructions. These tests found the student had normal intelligence and did not qualify as an exceptional student. An administrative law judge found that the board had done all that could be expected to define the student's needs. **A Florida District Court of Appeal held the school district violated the IDEA and state law by making insufficient efforts to evaluate the student. His IDEA rights were not "extinguished by his mother's failure immediately to accede to the School Board's every suggestion."** The case was remanded with instructions to order the board to perform a complete evaluation of the student. *M.H. v. Nassau County School Board,* 918 So.2d 316 (Fla. Dist. Ct. App. 2005).

## B.  Child Find Obligation

*The IDEA's "child find" obligation requires the states, through their local educational agencies (LEAs), to "identify, locate, and evaluate all children with disabilities residing within their boundaries." The child find obligation is triggered as an individualized duty to a child when an educational agency "has knowledge" that the child has a disability. Under the pre-2004 IDEA, students who were not declared eligible for IDEA services often made successful claims for IDEA procedural protections when their schools sought to discipline them.*

*Under current 20 U.S.C. § 1415(k)(5)(b), a school may be deemed to have knowledge that a child is disabled only if: (i) before the behavior leading to discipline, the child's parent "has expressed concern in writing" to a teacher or to supervisory or administrative personnel that the child is in need of special education or related services; (ii) the child's parent has requested an individual initial evaluation to determine if the child has a disability; or (iii) the child's teacher, or other school personnel, "has expressed specific concerns about a pattern of behavior demonstrated by the child, directly to the director of special education of such agency or to other supervisory personnel of the agency."*

*The "child find" duty of each state applies to children with disabilities who are homeless or wards of a state. LEAs must "conduct a thorough and complete child find process" to determine the number of parentally placed students with disabilities attending private schools in the LEA.*

*The child find process must be designed to ensure the equitable participation of parentally placed private school children. Local educational agencies must "undertake activities" for parentally placed private school students similar to activities for public school students. Services to parentally placed students may be provided at private schools, including religious schools, "to the extent consistent with law." Under the IDEA, LEAs and private schools must have "timely and meaningful consultation" for that purpose.*

◆   A California ninth-grade student had poor grades and scored below the first percentile on standardized tests. A school counselor attributed her performance to "transitional year difficulties." At the end of the student's 10th-grade year, she had failed her academic classes. Teachers said she was "like a stick of furniture" in class and said that her work was "gibberish and incomprehensible." They also reported the student played with dolls, colored with crayons and sometimes urinated on herself in her classroom. As the student's mother was "reluctant to have the child looked at," the school district "decided not to push" a special education evaluation. A third-party counselor recommended that the district test the student for learning disabilities, but she was instead promoted to grade 11. Early in the school year, the mother requested an assessment and an IEP meeting. Later, the district found the student IDEA-eligible. The parent sought a due process hearing, resulting in a decision in her favor. After a federal court upheld the decision, the case reached the U.S. Court of Appeals, Ninth Circuit.

On appeal, the district asserted there was no parental right to file a claim unless an IDEA notice provision specifically applied. The court reviewed 20 U.S.C. § 1415(b)(6)(A) and held **a party may present a complaint to a court or hearing officer with respect to any matter relating to identification, evaluation or placement of a child**. As a result, the court held the child-find claim advanced by the parent was recognizable under the IDEA. *Compton Unified School Dist. v. Addison*, 598 F.3d 1181 (9th Cir. 2010).

◆   The parents of a Connecticut student with a nonverbal learning disability believed their school district should have diagnosed their son as IDEA-eligible for the fourth grade. However, the district did not find him eligible until it created an IEP for his sixth-grade year. The parents placed their son in a private school and eventually sued for tuition reimbursement. A federal district court held they failed to prove that district officials "overlooked clear signs of disability and were negligent in failing to order testing." **The IDEA child find provision does not impose liability for every failure to identify a child with a disability, and nonverbal learning disabilities are difficult to identify.** On appeal, the Second Circuit found the student's Connecticut Mastery Test scores indicated he was performing at goal in math and reading and was "proficient" in writing. And his lowest grade before being removed for a private school placement was a C+. The judgment for the school board was affirmed. *A.P. v. Woodstock Board of Educ.*, 370 Fed.Appx. 202 (2d Cir. 2010).

◆   The mother of Nevada preschool twins with speech and other developmental difficulties took them to a free screening session at a private learning center, which referred them to their school district. The district referred the mother to a "Child Find Day" about six weeks later and did not give her a copy of her IDEA procedural safeguards. The children were not responsive at the Child Find Day, and assessments were scheduled for two months later. Meanwhile, the private center determined that the children had autism. The district eventually agreed with that diagnosis. A hearing officer determined that the district had failed to timely evaluate the children, but on appeal, the Ninth Circuit held that **the delay between when the twins were evaluated and began receiving services was reasonable**. As a result, the mother was entitled to be reimbursed only for the $1,670 she spent on private evaluations. *JG v. Douglas County School Dist.*, 552 F.3d 786 (9th Cir. 2009).

◆   A student moved with her family to Delaware from New York. She had an accommodation plan under Section 504. At the end of her third-grade school year, she failed math and did not meet requirements for promotion to grade four. Upon learning the student would be retained in grade three, her parents sought a full range of assessments. One indicated a severe discrepancy in reading comprehension. Although an IEP was offered, the parents placed the child in a

Christian school and requested a due process hearing for reimbursement from the district for their costs. The case reached the U.S. Court of Appeals, Third Circuit. It found the evidence at the time the parents sought an evaluation did not show their child's Section 504 plan was failing. Her grades were improving in all subjects. School officials could not have known that the student would later fail to advance in grade and fail a state test. While some of her programs were available to others, it appeared to the court that her curriculum was tailored to her needs. Her teacher "provided extra support at every turn."

Although the parents argued that the IEP put into place by the district was deficient, the court disagreed. **A lower court had properly found the student had no other IDEA-qualifying disabilities in math and writing,** as the parents claimed. And the district court found the IEP addressed her reading comprehension and had "significant provisions" devoted to her non-qualifying areas of concern, including math. Since the IEP was adequately drafted to provide a free appropriate public education, the court affirmed the denial of private school tuition reimbursement. *Anello v. Indian River School Dist.,* 355 Fed.Appx. 594 (3d Cir. 2009).

◆  An Ohio student was diagnosed with ADD, ADHD, oppositional defiant disorder and absence seizures. He was finally diagnosed with Asperger's syndrome in eighth grade. A dispute arose over the student's IEP, and his parents filed an IDEA action, asserting that the district's failure to diagnose Asperger's syndrome amounted to a violation of the act. **A federal court held that the district's failure to correctly label the student's disabilities did not violate the IDEA.** The student received special education from his second-grade year to the present. **The IDEA does not require schools to place students in specific categories. It only requires that they be given an appropriate education,** which the student received. *Pohorecki v. Anthony Wayne Local School Dist.,* 637 F.Supp.2d 547 (N.D. Ohio 2009).

◆  A federal court held **the IDEA child find obligation is triggered whenever a school has reason to suspect a child has a disability and requires special education to address it**. But discussions about a District of Columbia student did not satisfy the IDEA's requirement of a written request for an evaluation. Oral expressions of concern by parents about the educational performance of their children do not trigger a school's child find duty. *Reid v. District of Columbia,* 310 F.Supp.2d 137 (D.D.C. 2004).

### C. Least Restrictive Environment

*The IDEA requires placing students with disabilities with non-disabled peers to the extent possible. This is known as the least restrictive environment (LRE) requirement. Each IEP must explain the extent to which a child will not participate in regular education classes. In analyzing the LRE requirement, many courts rely on* Oberti v. Board of Educ. of Borough of Clementon School Dist., *995 F.2d 1204 (3d Cir. 1993).* Oberti *evaluated whether the district made reasonable efforts to accommodate a student in regular classes, whether appropriate supplemental aids and services were made available, and the possible negative effects for other students if the student remained in regular education classes. While the IDEA has a strong preference for placements in the LRE, the U.S. Court of Appeals, Seventh Circuit, held in* Beth B. v. Van Clay, *282 F.3d 493 (7th Cir. 2002), that the Act does not require a regular classroom placement that would provide an unsatisfactory education.*

*In* McLaughlin v. Holt Public Schools Board of Educ., *320 F.3d 663 (6th Cir. 2003), the Sixth Circuit found an IDEA regulation requiring placement "as close as possible to the child's home" did not apply if a necessary program was unavailable at a neighborhood school.*

◆ An 18-year-old Pennsylvania student with multiple disabilities was non-verbal and not toilet trained. Her district proposed placing her in a full-time life skills class and in mainstream school assemblies, lunch, homeroom and recess. Her parents requested a due process hearing, asserting the placement was too restrictive. A hearing officer agreed with them and ordered compensatory education, but an appeals panel held that the student required a regular education setting only for lunch, recess, physical education, homeroom, music, art and a single academic class. The award of compensatory education was reversed. A federal district court and later the Third Circuit upheld that decision, noting that **the student was making progress in her life skills class and her frequent loud vocalizations had a negative effect on other students.** A.G. v. Wissahickon School Dist., 374 Fed.Appx. 330 (3d Cir. 2010).

◆ A New Hampshire student with mental retardation, orthopedic impairment and other disabilities attended a rehabilitation day center for four years under an IEP. When she was 19, the IEP team recommended a continued placement there. But her parents refused to consent to the IEP and withdrew her from school. They sought a home- and community-based program to help her with basic life skills and community interaction. The case reached the First Circuit, which ruled for the school district. It found **the student's behavior appeared to be improving and the day center was a less restrictive placement than the home service setting the parents wanted.** Further, the IEP called for a significant increase in services in the area of pre-vocational skills. Lessard v. Lyndeborough Cooperative School Dist., 592 F.3d 267 (1st Cir. 2010).

◆ A 14-year-old Arizona student suffered a traumatic brain injury that confined him to a wheelchair and made him dependent on caregivers for daily activities. He was considered the most severely disabled student in his school district. His IEP team determined that he had a better chance of achieving his IEP goals if he were placed at a particular private day school 35 miles away. His parents objected, seeking instead to keep him in his neighborhood school with his non-disabled peers. A special education hearing officer found that the student failed to respond despite the district's best efforts and that the private day placement was best for him. The Arizona Court of Appeals agreed. **The student's severe disability made continued mainstreaming inappropriate.** Stallings v. Gilbert Unified School Dist. No. 41, No. 1 CA-CV 08-0625, 2009 WL 3165452 (Ariz. Ct. App. 10/1/09).

◆  A Connecticut school district behavioral consultant notified the parents of a student with Down syndrome and other impairments that because of his behavior problems it was becoming more difficult to keep the student in a regular classroom. A performance and planning team drafted an IEP that called for only 60% regular classroom placement instead of the 80% urged by the parents. The district hired a consultant who recommended gradually increasing the student's time in regular classrooms to 80%, and the district agreed to increase the time to 74%. However, the parents were determined to achieve 80% time in regular classrooms. A federal district court and the Second Circuit eventually upheld the IEP, noting that while mainstreaming is an important objective, it has to be weighed against the need for an appropriate education. **Mandating a percentage of time in regular classes would be inconsistent with the individualized approach of the IDEA.** *P. v. Newington Board of Educ.*, 546 F.3d 111 (2d Cir. 2008).

◆  The mother of a Kansas student with Down syndrome challenged the IEP proposed for his entry into high school, as it would require a long bus ride to a high school in another town. She sought to place him in the high school in their town. An educational cooperative serving eight school districts ran a "level program" or "cluster system" using a functional educational approach. A hearing officer and a federal court found that the Level IV program at the distant high school was the least restrictive placement and that the neighborhood school had no teachers qualified to teach the student. The student's inability to focus in regular classrooms was documented, and the Level IV program provided a continuum of placements and support services. **Although neighborhood placements are preferred under the IDEA and implicate the least restrictive environment, they are not an enforceable right.** *M.M. v. Unified School Dist. No. 368*, No. 07-2291-JTM, 2008 WL 4950987 (D. Kan. 11/18/08).

◆  A New York student with autism-spectrum disorders began to withdraw from reality. Her mother removed her from the private day school placement specified by her IEP and placed her in an unapproved private school in Connecticut. The following year, the district recommended a public school placement. The mother rejected the IEP and sought tuition reimbursement. A federal court found the IEP inadequate. But the Second Circuit reversed, finding considerable evidence to support the school district. **The student's recent social progress indicated she could make educational progress in an environment consistent with the IDEA's preference for mainstreaming.** *Cabouli v. Chappaqua Cent. School Dist.*, 202 Fed.Appx. 519 (2d Cir. 2006).

◆  A New Jersey school district placed a student with profound sensorineural hearing loss in a public school for deaf children outside the district. The next year, it proposed placing her in a self-contained school for the deaf located in the neighborhood school she would have attended if not for her special needs. It did not explain why it failed to propose that placement previously, or what now made it appropriate. The case reached the Third Circuit, which **found the school district's emphasis on least restrictive environment misplaced**. The district did not show the new placement would provide meaningful educational benefit. As the neighborhood school would offer only minimal mainstreaming opportunities, the school district was not allowed to change the placement. *S.H. v. State-Operated School Dist. of City of Newark*, 336 F.3d 260 (3d Cir. 2003).

### D. Change in Placement and the 'Stay-Put' Provision

*The IDEA requires school districts to provide parents of students with disabilities prior written notice of any proposed change in placement. If the parents wish to contest the change in placement, a hearing must be granted. During the pendency of review proceedings, the child is to remain in the "then-current" educational placement. This is the IDEA "stay-put" provision.*

◆   The parents of a Texas student with disabilities disagreed with the district's proposed IEP for grade two and placed her in a private school. They sought due process and obtained a ruling from the hearing officer that the district did not make an appropriate placement. Thus, the parents were entitled to tuition reimbursement. **By the time the administrative ruling was issued, the school year was nearly over.** When the district appealed to a federal court, the parents did not ask for tuition reimbursement for another school year. As a result, when the court ruled on the case over a year later, it held that they were not entitled to tuition reimbursement. However, the Fifth Circuit reversed, finding that **another year of tuition was due under the stay-put provision**. *Houston Independent School Dist. v. V.P.*, 582 F.3d 576 (5th Cir. 2009).

◆   A Pennsylvania student had a specific learning disability. His parents and the school district disagreed on a placement after his third-grade year. Over the next two years, his third-grade IEP became his stay-put placement under the IDEA. The district proposed providing itinerant learning support primarily in a regular classroom instead of the daily hour of resource room support specified in the third-grade IEP. The parents rejected that proposal, arguing that it amounted to a change in placement. In the lawsuit that followed, the Third Circuit held that the district provided the same services to the student in the inclusive setting, on a daily basis and with the same special education teacher. Thus, **providing the itinerant learning support was not a change in placement that violated the IDEA's stay-put provision**. *In re Educ. Assignment of Joseph R.*, 318 Fed.Appx. 113 (3d Cir. 2009).

◆   A Virginia special education student with an emotional disability attended a gifted and talented program in an elementary school. He persuaded a classmate to place a threatening note in another student's computer file stating "death awaits you." The district assembled a manifestation determination review committee, which found no relationship between the student's disabilities and the threatening note. It recommended expelling the student, but the district instead transferred him to a gifted and talented program at a nearby school for the remainder of the year. His parents objected to the transfer decision and requested a due process hearing. The hearing officer ruled against the parents, and the Fourth Circuit affirmed, noting that **the student's transfer to a nearly identical program at a nearby school did not implicate the**

**IDEA's stay-put provision**. The court also held his IEP was appropriate. *A.W. v. Fairfax County School Board*, 372 F.3d 674 (4th Cir. 2004).

The student later used his cell phone to take pictures up a classmate's skirt without her knowledge. The school suspended the student for 10 days and recommended expelling him. The IEP team determined his misconduct was not a manifestation of his disability. A hearing officer then ruled he should be suspended for 18 days and reassigned to another school. The school board agreed and offered interim services, but the parents appealed to a federal court, seeking money damages. The court dismissed their lawsuit, noting that they failed to exhaust their administrative remedies. *A.W. v. Fairfax County School Board*, 548 F.Supp.2d 219 (E.D. Va. 2008).

◆   Florida triplets with autism received IDEA Part C services from the state's early intervention program until they turned three. When they "aged out" of Part C eligibility and the responsibility for their special education needs passed to IDEA Part B, their school district became obligated to provide them with IEPs. Because their school district did not have their IEPs in place, their parents sought to use the IDEA's stay-put provision to continue their individual family service plans (IFSPs). A federal court held **a student's Part C placement is not his or her current educational placement for stay-put purposes**. The Eleventh Circuit later affirmed the judgment, ruling the IDEA did not provide for the continued provision of services to the triplets pursuant to their IFSPs. *D.P. v. School Board of Broward County*, 483 F.3d 725 (11th Cir. 2007).

◆   An Ohio school district made addendums to a student's IEP in three consecutive months during his sixth-grade year. The third addendum sought to phase out a point reward system used to reinforce his behavior. The addendum also stated if the target behavior was not maintained, the original IEP would be reinstated. The parents did not learn that the addendum was being implemented until the district sent them a certified letter several days after the IEP meeting. A due process hearing officer found that the student's sixth-grade IEP included the third addendum, rendering it the student's "stay-put" placement pending the outcome of the due process hearing. A state appeals court held that the district did not provide adequate notice that the final addendum would be implemented. The court remanded the case for a determination of **whether the addendum fundamentally changed the student's IEP and whether the stay-put provision was implicated**. *Stancourt v. Worthington City School Dist. Board of Educ.*, 841 N.E.2d 812 (Ohio Ct. App. 2005).

After further consideration by the trial court, the case returned to the Ohio Court of Appeals. It noted the addendum was neither a fundamental change in nor an elimination of a basic element of the IEP. The original IEP called for a behavior plan that would eventually thin reinforcers. The court affirmed the judgment for the school district, holding that **not every change to an IEP constitutes a change in placement**. *Stancourt v. Worthington City School Dist.*, Nos. 07AP-835, 07AP-836, 2008 WL 4151623 (Ohio Ct. App. 9/9/08).

◆   The parents of a Michigan student with disabilities asserted the IEP offered by their school district denied him a free appropriate public education. They requested a hearing to challenge the IEP, then placed their son in a private school. The hearing officer dismissed the case upon learning of the unilateral placement. A state-level review officer upheld that decision, as did a federal district court. The court noted that the school district did not violate the IDEA by failing to annually update the student's IEP. **Once an IDEA action has been commenced, the student's most recent IEP continues to operate under the stay-put provision until conclusion of the appeal or litigation.** *Kuszewski v. Chippewa Valley School Dist.*, 56 Fed.Appx. 655 (6th Cir. 2003).

◆  In a Missouri case, the Eighth Circuit found the stay-put provision requires that a student remain in his or her "then-current educational placement" during the pendency of any IDEA action. **The transfer of a student to a different school building for fiscal reasons did not constitute a change of placement.** *Hale v. Poplar Bluff R-I School Dist.*, 280 F.3d 831 (8th Cir. 2002).

### E.  Other Placement Issues

#### 1.  Behavior Problems

◆  A Texas student with autism and other disorders regressed significantly in the summer before her ninth-grade year. Her IEP was revised, but her behavior and academic problems increased. She ran away from school and had sexual contact with other students in a lavatory. Her parents sought to place her at a residential school and a hearing officer agreed with their decision. A federal district court also affirmed the residential placement, awarding over $110,000 in tuition plus $36,000 in attorneys' fees to the parents. But the Fifth Circuit found **the parents had not yet shown that the residential placement was necessary for educational (rather than medical or behavioral) reasons**. The court returned the case to the lower court for further proceedings. *Richardson Independent School Dist. v. Michael Z.*, 580 F.3d 286 (5th Cir. 2009).

◆  A New York school district offered an autistic student support from a special education teacher for part of the day and a program assistant for the rest of the day. However, he had behavioral and lack-of-focus problems and his parents placed him in a private school. They sued for tuition reimbursement, alleging that the district violated the IDEA because it failed to offer a functional behavioral assessment (FBA). A hearing officer found that the district should have offered an FBA, but a state review officer reversed. The case reached the U.S. Court of Appeals, Second Circuit, which observed that three key district officials had testified that an FBA was not necessary. **The IEP adequately addressed the student's behavior, and the parents were not entitled to tuition reimbursement.** *A.C. and M.C. v. Board of Educ. of Chappaqua Cent. School Dist.*, 553 F.3d 165 (2d Cir. 2009).

◆  A Pennsylvania student with worsening psychological problems attended private schools at the district's expense. After she was kicked out of a residential school in New Mexico, her parents placed her in a psychiatric residential treatment center that provided no educational services. Her parents sought reimbursement for the costs. The case reached the Third Circuit, which held that **the district did not have to pay for the treatment center placement because her admission there was necessitated by her acute medical condition.** And her medical and educational needs could be separated. Further, once the student's condition stabilized, the district began providing services again. *Mary v. School Dist. of Philadelphia*, 575 F.3d 235 (3d Cir. 2009).

◆   The mother of a New York student with Asperger's disorder signed him up for a private school before the school district prepared an IEP for the upcoming year. The IEP, when completed, maintained his "other health impaired" classification, but placed him in a more restrictive special education class. The mother sought tuition reimbursement and a hearing officer found that the district's failure to obtain a functional behavior analysis (FBA) entitled the mother to tuition reimbursement. A review officer reversed, and a federal court agreed that the lack of an FBA was not fatal to the IEP. **School districts must consider using positive behavioral interventions and supports as well as other strategies to address behavior, so the mere failure to conduct an FBA did not violate the IDEA.** *Connor v. New York City Dep't of Educ.*, No. 08 Civ. 7710 (LBS) 2009 WL 3335760 (S.D.N.Y. 10/13/09).

◆   A Minnesota student with emotional and behavioral disabilities was suspended several times for fighting with other girls. Her suspensions added up to more than 10 days out of class. The district offered home schooling services, but the student's mother rejected the offer. After conducting a functional behavioral assessment, the district offered to place the student in an emotional behavioral disability setting that included boys. The mother rejected this placement as well, preferring an all-girl setting. An administrative law judge held the district denied the student an appropriate education because of the suspensions and the district's failure to modify her IEP. But the Eighth Circuit found **the mixed-gender setting was appropriate given that all the student's serious behavior problems involved altercations with girls.** *M.M. v. Special School Dist. No. 1*, 512 F.3d 455 (8th Cir. 2008).

◆   A Minnesota student with a behavior disorder was escorted by paraprofessionals to a separate room when he needed to calm down. His IEP called for a written behavior intervention plan (BIP), but none was created by the relevant deadline. The dispute reached the Eighth Circuit, which held that **nothing in state or federal law required a written BIP in a student's IEP.** The school responded to the student's behavioral incidents using set procedures, and there was no substantive or procedural violation of the IDEA. *School Board of Independent School Dist. No. 11 v. Renollett*, 440 F.3d 1007 (8th Cir. 2006).

## 2.   Extended School Year Services

◆   A dispute arose between a New Jersey school district and the parents of a student over extended school year services (ESY) and transportation. A federal court ruled for the district on the ESY and transportation claims, but it awarded 17 days of compensatory education due to the district's failure to serve the student for the same number of days at the start of his fifth-grade year. The family then sought costs and attorneys' fees of $118,787. The court modified the award but still granted them all their costs and $71,850 in attorneys' fees. Even though they were successful on only one claim, their claims were all related. *L.T. v. Mansfield Township School Dist.*, No. 04-1381 (NLH), 2009 WL 1971329 (D.N.J. 7/1/09).

◆   A Pennsylvania school district offered an incoming kindergartner with autism an IEP that included applied behavioral analysis (ABA) therapy and verbal behavior (VB) services in an autistic support class. But the IEP reduced the student's ABA therapy from his early intervention IEP and also reduced his occupational therapy. His parents challenged the IEP and reached a settlement in which the student was to receive two hours of ABA and VB therapy a day. The district then provided three hours of therapy a day, exceeding interim IEP requirements. Later, the district proposed reducing the ABA/VB therapy for the rest of the school year and a summer extended school year program. A federal court held the district could provide less than three hours of ABA therapy a day and did not have to provide over 1.5 hours a day in the summer. **It had already provided more ABA therapy than the interim IEP required.** *Travis G. v. New Hope-Solebury School Dist.*, 544 F.Supp.2d 435 (E.D. Pa. 2008).

◆   A multiply disabled 11-year-old Massachusetts student had attended a seven-week summer program called "Active Healing" at district expense since her kindergarten year. But the program was not approved by the state. After a seizure caused the student to regress, her mother sought a 12-week extended evaluation at Active Healing. The district refused to pay for the evaluation because the program was unapproved, and the mother sought administrative review. A hearing officer ruled that the district had to pay for the evaluation, but a federal court disagreed. **Despite the past history of the district funding the summer program, it could not be ordered to pay for the extended evaluation at an unapproved program.** *Manchester-Essex Regional School Dist. v. Bureau of Special Educ. Appeals*, 490 F.Supp.2d 49 (D. Mass. 2007).

◆   The IEPs for a Kentucky student with cerebral palsy and delayed cognitive development addressed his ongoing behavior issues. His parents believed he was regressing and sought direct occupational therapy for him as well as a summer placement. Ultimately, the district rejected extended school year (ESY) programming for the student's next school year. The parents unilaterally placed the student in a residential facility that offered summer programs and requested a due process hearing. A hearing officer ruled for the district, but an appeals board and a federal district court reversed his decision. On further appeal, **the Sixth Circuit reversed the lower court decision, holding ESY programming was the exception, not the rule.** The parents would have to show that ESY was necessary to avoid something more than "adequately recoupable regression." *Kenton County School Dist. v. Hunt*, 384 F.3d 269 (6th Cir. 2004).

◆   A Virginia student with autism received ESY services prior to entering kindergarten. In kindergarten, he progressed in all but two of the 27 goals stated in his IEP. His parents sought to continue the one-on-one services he received during the summer, but were unable to agree with their school district on an IEP. A hearing officer and a federal court both ruled that the purpose of ESY services was to make reasonable progress on unmet goals. The court found that the district's IEP was adequate. The Fourth Circuit Court of Appeals held that **ESY services are necessary only when the regular school year benefits to a student will be significantly jeopardized in the absence of summer programming**. The court remanded the case to the hearing officer for a redetermination of the appropriateness of ESY services using the correct standard. *J.H. v. Henrico County School Board,* 326 F.3d 560 (4th Cir. 2003).

### 3. Transfer Students

*The IDEA allows schools to conduct an evaluation of any student who transfers from a school outside the state before becoming obligated to develop a new IEP. When parents repeatedly refuse a school's efforts to conduct an individual evaluation of a child, the school is relieved of the obligation to convene an IEP meeting and is not considered in violation of the IDEA.*

◆ A New Jersey couple moved to Montana after a doctor determined that their child's performance had an autistic component. An IEP had been crafted to provide the child with speech/language therapy while he was in New Jersey. The IEP team at his new school refused to consider a New Jersey doctor's evaluation and reduced the student's speech/language therapy. After two months, the IEP team referred the student to a child development center for free autism testing. Five months later, a report came back confirming that his behavior was consistent with autism spectrum disorder. At this point, the school year was almost over. The IEP team met to develop an IEP for the next year and determined that the student did not need extended school year services. The parents brought an IDEA challenge that reached the Ninth Circuit. The court of appeals held that the **referral of the student to the child development center did not comply with the IDEA. The school district failed to meet its obligation to evaluate the student.** *N.B. and C.B. v. Hellgate Elementary School Dist.,* 541 F.3d 1202 (9th Cir. 2008).

◆ A California student with a cochlear implant received one-on-one deaf and hard of hearing services in his family's home. When his family moved to Nevada, the school district there offered the services in his neighborhood school under an interim IEP. His parents objected, asserting the location violated the California IEP. They hired a private service provider and sought reimbursement from the Nevada school district. A hearing officer and then a federal district court held that the school district had offered comparable services to the transfer student. **The IDEA did not require the Nevada district to adopt the California IEP in its exact form.** *Sterling A. v. Washoe County School Dist.,* No. 3:07-CV-00245OLRH-RJJ, 2008 WL 4865570 (D. Nev. 11/10/08).

◆ A Louisiana school district transferred a student with deafness from his neighborhood school to a cluster school located about four miles farther away from his home. His parents claimed the transfer was a change in placement under the IDEA that required the district to give them prior written notice. They requested a due process hearing. A federal court upheld the decision to transfer the student. The parents appealed. The U.S. Court of Appeals, Fifth Circuit, held that **the change in a school site at which an IEP is implemented is not a "change in placement" under the IDEA**. The few changes the student experienced as a result of the transfer to the new school did not amount to a change in placement. Riding a special bus for disabled students instead of a regular school bus and sharing a transliterator with another student instead of having his own were not fundamental changes to his IEP. *Veazey v. Ascension Parish School Board*, 121 Fed.Appx. 552 (5th Cir. 2005).

◆    When a student with autism moved to Rhode Island, his new school district assembled an IEP team and proposed an interim IEP within two weeks of the parents' first contact. The district wanted to place the student in a newly established self-contained classroom that used a modified version of the TEACCH method. The parents asserted that only DTT methodology was appropriate. They rejected the IEP and notified the district that they would be placing their son in a private school. They then rejected a second IEP developed by the district. A due process hearing officer ruled for the parents, but the First Circuit Court of Appeals ruled for the district, noting that **the IDEA did not require the best possible education for students with disabilities**. Here, the IEP was reasonably calculated to provide an appropriate education. The classroom was half the size of the student's previous placement, and the teachers had extensive experience and training with autistic children. Further, many of the elements of DTT would be available through the use of the TEACCH method, including considerable one-on-one instruction. *L.T. on Behalf of N.B. v. Warwick School Committee*, 361 F.3d 80 (1st Cir. 2004).

◆    A Seattle first-grade student with mild mental retardation and Down syndrome was assigned to a unique classroom combining special education and general education students. Just before the start of the next school year, her mother moved and sought a regular education placement for her daughter. The new district offered a temporary placement in a self-contained special education class until it could perform an evaluation. Two months into the school year, the student had yet to attend class, and the district offered a temporary placement of four hours of special education with at least an hour of regular education. It proposed increasing time in the regular education classroom as appropriate.

A due process hearing officer upheld the district's temporary placement as the closest approximation to the student's last IEP. A federal court and the Ninth Circuit agreed with the hearing officer that the district's placement was appropriate. **The temporary placement was not a "take it or leave it" proposition, but was rather designed to get as close to the student's previous unique placement as possible pending an evaluation.** The temporary IEP conferred educational benefits on the student. *Ms. S. and her Daughter G. v. Vashon Island School Dist.*, 337 F.3d 1115 (9th Cir. 2003).

◆    A California school district that became responsible for the education of a student with autism when he turned three years old did not have to replicate the individualized family service plan designed for him by the regional center that was formerly responsible for his education. The Ninth Circuit held that the status quo necessarily changed when responsibility for his education shifted to the district. According to the Ninth Circuit, the hearing officer and district court had properly analogized the case to that of an incoming transfer student. **When a student transfers from one public agency to another, the receiving agency is required only to provide a program that conforms with the last agreed-upon placement, not provide the exact same program.** *Johnson v. Special Educ. Hearing Office*, 287 F.3d 1176 (9th Cir. 2002).

## F.  Residency Issues

*The IDEA mandate to provide a free appropriate public education extends to all children with a disability residing in the area served by a local educational agency. Disputes among school districts and other agencies are generally resolved through interagency agreements. Occasionally, parents fail to establish a clear domicile, raising residency issues.*

◆  A Kansas school district provided two children special education for some time. It determined they were not district residents because they did not sleep at their mother's rental unit. As a result, the district demanded the immediate withdrawal of the children from school. The parent requested an IDEA hearing and submitted an affidavit of residency. When it was learned that the children again stopped sleeping within district boundaries, the district filed a state court action against the parent and her boyfriend for fraud, seeking to recover the costs of serving the children while they were nonresidents. The mother sued the school district and special education director in a federal district court under the IDEA, Rehabilitation Act, and constitutional provisions. The court held for the district on a challenge to the district admissions policy and the constitutional claims. It found the boyfriend had no standing to maintain any claims pertaining to the children and the district's special education services director was entitled to qualified immunity. After a trial, the court dismissed the IDEA claim.

On appeal, the U.S. Court of Appeals, Tenth Circuit, affirmed the judgment on the IDEA claim but vacated the judgment on all the others. The district court again held for the district and director, and a second appeal went to the Tenth Circuit. It found the parent had abandoned the IDEA claims. The lower court had correctly held she lacked standing to challenge the nonresident admissions policy, since **she never actually sought admission for the children as nonresidents**. Even if the parent had standing, there was evidence that her children were absent from school due to illness and not due to the district's conduct. *D.L. v. Unified School Dist. No. 497*, 596 F.3d 768 (10th Cir. 2010).

◆  The mother of a Michigan special education student sought to enroll him in a neighboring school district, which had accepted 67 applications from nonresidents under the state's school choice law. However, because the process was less streamlined for special education students due to the higher costs, the two districts were unable to reach an agreement and the neighboring district rejected the student's application. His mother sued for discrimination and the case reached the Sixth Circuit. The court of appeals held that the school choice law did not violate equal protection. **There was a rational reason for the stricter transfer requirements for special education students.** *Clark v. Banks,* 193 Fed.Appx. 510 (6th Cir. 2006).

## IV. RELATED SERVICES

*Related services include the provision of sign-language interpreters, transportation, speech pathology, psychological and counseling services, and physical and occupational therapy. The IDEA requires school districts to provide services that are necessary for students with disabilities to receive educational benefits, but excludes medical services from coverage except where required for evaluation or diagnostic purposes. See 20 U.S.C. § 1402 (26).*

### A. Generally

◆ An Iowa student suffered a spinal cord injury that left him quadriplegic and ventilator dependent. For several years, his family provided personal attendant services at school. A family member or nurse performed catheterization, tracheostomy suctioning, repositioning and respiratory observation during the school day. When the student entered the fifth grade, his mother requested that the district provide him with continuous, one-on-one nursing services during the school day. The district refused, and the family filed a request for due process. An administrative law judge held the school district was obligated to reimburse the family for nursing costs incurred during the current school year and to provide the disputed services in the future. The case reached the U.S. Supreme Court, which held that the requested services were related services, not medical services. The court based its decision in the IDEA definition of related services, its holding in *Irving Independent School Dist. v. Tatro,* and the IDEA purpose of making special education available to all disabled students. Adopting a bright-line, physician/non-physician standard, the Court held that **since the disputed services could be performed by someone other than a physician, the district was obligated to provide them**. *Cedar Rapids Community School Dist. v. Garret F. by Charlene F.,* 526 U.S. 66 (1999).

◆ A West Virginia student with medical problems suffered abuse and neglect at the hands of his parents. He was placed in foster care. A state court conducted a review of his pending abuse and neglect petition and ordered his school board to provide and pay for a full-time nurse even though the board received no notice or opportunity to appear at the review hearing. The Supreme Court of Appeals of West Virginia issued an order for the board, finding that it should have been given notice and an opportunity to help shed light on the best interests of the student. **School records showed that the student had not suffered a seizure in two years and that he had not had a full-time nurse assigned to him for four of his 11 years in the school system.** *State of West Virginia v. Beane,* 680 S.E.2d 46 (W. Va. 2009).

◆  **The U.S. Supreme Court ruled that clean intermittent catheterization (CIC) is a related service not subject to the "medical service" exclusion of the IDEA.** The parents of an eight-year-old girl born with spina bifida brought suit against their local Texas school district after the district refused to provide CIC for the child while she attended school. The parents pursued administrative and judicial avenues to force the district to train staff to perform the simple procedure. After a U.S. district court held against the parents, they appealed to the U.S. Court of Appeals, Fifth Circuit, which reversed the district court ruling. The school district then appealed. The U.S. Supreme Court affirmed the court of appeals' ruling that CIC is a supportive related service, not a medical service excluded from the IDEA. *Irving Independent School Dist. v. Tatro*, 468 U.S. 883, 104 S.Ct. 3371, 82 L.Ed.2d 664 (1984).

◆  A Tennessee student with profound bilateral hearing loss received a cochlear implant at the age of 14 months. Her school district later developed an IEP for her, offering to place her in a new collaborative program that was being developed with Head Start. The program also served low-income students, many of whom did not have disabilities. The school district also proposed to discontinue the mapping service (optimization of the implant) it had been providing for the student. The parents objected and requested a hearing. A hearing officer held that the district's placement met IDEA requirements, but ruled that it had to continue the mapping services. **A federal court held that the 2004 IDEA Amendments excluded the mapping of a cochlear implant as a related service under the IDEA.** The regulations clarified that position in October 2006, so the district had to pay for mapping the implant until that time. *A.U. v. Roane County Board of Educ.*, 501 F.Supp.2d 1134 (E.D. Tenn. 2007).

◆  **A Virginia school board did not have to reimburse a disabled student for hospitalization costs that were paid years earlier by his father's group health insurance,** even though the payments counted against the lifetime medical benefits limit of the policy. The father made several requests to recover the $200,000 cost of the hospitalization from the board, but he did not request a due process hearing for almost 10 years. The hearing officer held the action was barred by a one-year Virginia statute of limitations. A federal district court affirmed. The Fourth Circuit agreed that the action was untimely. Also, the student was now an adult and was no longer covered by his father's insurance policy. He had his own Medicaid coverage, and this insurance was not affected by the decrease in lifetime medical benefits to his father's plan. *Emery v. Roanoke City School Board*, 432 F.3d 294 (4th Cir. 2005).

## B.  Level or Location of Services

◆  A Pennsylvania student with learning disabilities received special education in reading, math and writing. In the sixth grade, his parents placed him in a private school and sought tuition reimbursement as well as compensatory education for the prior two years. After a federal court upheld the student's sixth-grade IEP, the U.S. Court of Appeals, Third Circuit, agreed that it addressed his deficiencies. **A lack of occupational therapy in the student's**

**seventh-grade IEP was attributable to the delay by the parents in providing an occupational therapy evaluation.** Once they did so, a revised IEP provided for reevaluation of his potential needs within 30 days of his return to a district school. *Souderton Area School Dist. v. J.H.*, 351 Fed.Appx. 755 (3d Cir. 2009).

◆  A California student with multiple disabilities could not swallow food, instead receiving nutrition through a surgical opening in his stomach called a gastrostomy tube or "G-tube." His mother claimed he developed a severe reflux disorder from liquids, necessitating that he be fed only pureed foods. She used a syringe plunger even though standard medical practice called for using a gravity methodology. A dispute arose over the method of feeding her son. She kept him at home for a while, then sought compensatory education. A federal district court ultimately ruled that the mother could not dictate the method to be used to feed her son. **No doctor prescribed the plunge method, and the mother never provided evidence that the gravity method would not work.** No compensatory education was due. *C.N. v. Los Angeles Unified School Dist.*, No. CV 07-03642 MMM (SSx), 2008 WL 4552951 (C.D. Cal. 10/9/08).

◆  A Maryland student with disabilities received two types of medication from the school nurse under an agreement signed by her treating/prescribing psychiatrist. When teachers and other staff members observed that the student was lethargic and drowsy, the psychiatrist prescribed another medication. However, the student's fatigue continued. The nurse sought clarification from the doctor on giving the student medication when symptoms contraindicated further drug administration. The parents told the doctor not to provide further information to the nurse or other district employees regarding the student's medical condition and treatment. The district then refused to continue medicating the student. When the parents challenged that decision, they lost. The Court of Appeals of Maryland held that the dispute was about medical treatment and not special education. **The nurse could not be forced to medicate the student without free communication with the doctor.** *John A. v. Board of Educ. for Howard County*, 400 Md. 363, 929 A.2d 136 (Md. 2007).

◆  A Georgia student with a disability complained that words became fuzzy or three dimensional when he tried to read. A behavioral optometrist diagnosed accommodative and convergence disorder and recommended visual therapy to reduce vision loss. The district refused to pay for such therapy on the grounds that the student was receiving a free appropriate public education. The parents paid for the therapy, then sought due process. An administrative hearing officer and a federal court found that the parents were entitled to reimbursement for the therapy as a related service. The Eleventh Circuit agreed. **Although the student's condition had not yet caused poor academic performance, it did prevent him from receiving a free appropriate public education.** *DeKalb County School Dist. v. M.T.V.*, 164 Fed.Appx. 900 (11th Cir. 2006).

◆  The IEP of an Illinois third-grade student with Down syndrome called for 30 minutes of weekly direct occupational therapy (OT). The therapist who provided OT services to the student received her master's degree before the start of the school year, but did not obtain her license until near the end of the year. Using the results of the student's triennial evaluation, the district proposed an IEP for the student's fourth-grade year that called for 30 minutes of monthly OT consultation and less physical therapy than the parents desired. They rejected the IEP and obtained independent evaluations. A due process hearing officer agreed with the district's denial of reimbursement for the independent evaluations. Although she rejected the parents' claims of IEP deficiencies for 9 of 11 areas identified, she held the district should provide 60 minutes weekly of direct OT services as compensatory services during the fourth grade because the occupational therapist was unlicensed and improperly supervised. A federal court upheld the IEP, but ordered the district to provide OT services.

The Seventh Circuit agreed that **60 minutes of direct OT services each week was appropriate given the failure of the district in the third-grade year to properly supervise the unlicensed occupational therapist**. However, the parents were not entitled to reimbursement for the independent evaluations because the district's evaluations had been appropriate. *Evanston Community Consolidated School Dist. No. 65 v. Michael M.*, 356 F.3d 798 (7th Cir. 2004).

◆  A hearing-impaired Louisiana student attended a public school with the assistance of a cued speech transliterator to supplement spoken information in his classes. Although other hearing-impaired students in the district who used American Sign Language attended their neighborhood schools, the cued speech transliterator served at a centralized location. The student achieved substantial academic benefit there, but his parents decided he should attend his neighborhood school for social reasons. The school district denied a transfer request by the parents. A hearing officer upheld the decision, but a federal district court held the student was entitled to attend his neighborhood school with the transliterator. The Fifth Circuit reversed the judgment. The student's IEP satisfied the IDEA, and his parents were seeking the neighborhood placement for primarily social reasons. **They did not have veto power over the district's decision to provide the transliterator only at the central location.** *White v. Ascension Parish School Board*, 343 F.3d 373 (5th Cir. 2003).

◆  A South Dakota student who suffered epileptic seizures was provided transportation to and from school by her district as a related service under the IDEA. She was accompanied by a nurse during the ride. Although parents could designate different pick-up and drop-off sites within a specific school area boundary, students were not transported outside the boundary unless it was necessary to obtain an educational benefit under an IEP. The district denied a request by the student's mother to drop her off at a day care center outside the boundary. The state Office of Special Education ordered the district to pay for transportation to the day care center, but a hearing examiner ruled it was not necessary. A federal court agreed, and the Eighth Circuit affirmed the decision that **the district did not have to provide transportation to the day care center**. The request was for the mother's own convenience and was not necessary to provide the student with educational benefit. *Fick v. Sioux Falls School Dist. 49-5*, 337 F.3d 968 (8th Cir. 2003).

## C.  Provision of Related Services at Private Schools

◆    A New York first-grader with ADHD sought a 1:1 aide at his private school, and administrative rulings agreed that the aide would be sent to the private school. The district then sought a court ruling that the aide should be provided only at the public school. The Supreme Court, Appellate Division, held state law permitted a school district to provide services at a private school. It ruled that the decision must be made on a case-by-case basis, with the student's needs in the least restrictive environment serving as a guide. The New York Court of Appeals affirmed the judgment, finding **the state's dual enrollment statute was intended to offer private school students with disabilities "equal access to the full array of specialized public school programs."** *Board of Educ. of Bay Shore Union Free School Dist. v. Thomas K.*, 14 N.Y.3d 289 (N.Y. 2010).

◆    The parents of a student at the Delaware School for the Deaf became concerned when he began performing below grade level. They requested a general education placement with a full-time American Sign Language interpreter and a private school placement with a small class size. The school district responded that a sign-language interpreter would be provided only if the student attended district schools. After the parents placed their son in a private school, a hearing officer held that the district should have provided a sign-language interpreter. A federal district court reversed the judgment. **Nothing in the IDEA or its regulations conferred upon parentally placed private school students an individual right to receive special education and related services that they would receive in public schools.** The IDEA only required school districts to allocate a proportional share of IDEA funds to private schools, which the district had done here. *Board of Educ. of Appoquinimink School Dist. v. Johnson*, 543 F.Supp.2d 351 (D. Del. 2008).

◆    An Arizona student attended a school for the deaf from grades one through five and a public school from grades six through eight. During his public school attendance, a sign-language interpreter was provided by the school district. The student's parents enrolled him in a parochial high school for ninth grade and asked the school district to continue providing a sign-language interpreter. The school district refused, and the student's parents filed an IDEA action.

The case reached the U.S. Supreme Court, which held the Establishment Clause did not exclude religious institutions from publicly sponsored benefits. If this were the case, religious groups would not enjoy police and fire protection or have use of public roads and sidewalks. Government programs that neutrally provide benefits to broad classes of citizens are not subject to Establishment Clause prohibition simply because some religiously affiliated institutions receive an attenuated financial benefit. **Providing a sign-language interpreter under the IDEA was part of a general program for distribution of benefits in a neutral manner to qualified students.** A sign-language interpreter, unlike an instructor or counselor, was ethically bound to transmit everything said in the way it was intended. The Court reversed the decision. *Zobrest v. Catalina Foothills School Dist.*, 509 U.S. 1 (1993).

## V.  TUITION REIMBURSEMENT

*If a school district is unable to provide special education services to a student with a disability in its own facilities, it must locate an appropriate program in another district, hospital or institution. When a private placement is required, the district may become responsible for tuition and other costs.*

### A.  Private School Tuition Claims

◆   A student attended Oregon public schools through grade 11. He had problems paying attention and finishing work, but he was able to pass his classes with help at home from family members. The school district evaluated him but found him ineligible for special education and related services. After he experienced multiple behavioral problems, a psychologist determined that he had ADHD, depression and other issues. His parents enrolled him in a three-week wilderness program and then a private residential school. They then requested a due process hearing. A hearing officer found the student was eligible for special education under the IDEA but held the school district only had to pay for the residential placement, not the wilderness program or the evaluation.

On appeal, the Ninth Circuit agreed with the student that he was not categorically barred from seeking tuition reimbursement. The U.S. Supreme Court agreed to review the case and took the opportunity to reaffirm its ruling in *Burlington School Committee v. Dep't of Educ.*, this chapter. In *Burlington*, the Court first approved of private school tuition reimbursement awards as a special education remedy. In this case, the Court found the district's failure to provide an IEP of any kind was at least as serious a violation of its IDEA responsibilities as a failure to provide an adequate IEP. **The Court rejected the district's argument that the student had to receive special education and related services from the district before advancing any claim for tuition reimbursement.** The 1997 IDEA amendments did not mandate a different result from *Burlington*, and the judgment was affirmed. *Forest Grove School Dist. v. T.A.*, 129 S.Ct. 2484 (U.S. 2009).

The case was returned to a federal court, which held the district did not have to pay the student's tuition. It reasoned that the parents had failed to notify the district of their private school selection until well after making it. Moreover, the district had found that the student did not need special education or even a Section 504 plan. And the parents seemingly chose the private school because of the student's drug use and behavioral problems. *Forest Grove School Dist. v. T.A.*, 675 F.Supp.2d 1063 (D. Or. 2009).

◆   An adopted student in Maryland with learning disabilities and emotional disturbance exhibited suicidal tendencies and clinical depression. Her IEP team placed her in a private special education day school. She later self-mutilated and attempted suicide. Her parents placed her in a residential school, even though a school psychologist found that she should be placed in a therapeutic school for students with serious emotional issues. The parents sought reimbursement, but a federal court and later the Fourth Circuit ruled against them. **The placement was based on the parents' desire to ensure the student did not harm herself.**

**It was not made for educational reasons and was not the least restrictive environment** because she made progress in the day school when her mental health issues stabilized. *Shaw v. Weast*, 364 Fed.Appx. 47 (4th Cir. 2010).

◆   An Oregon student with ADHD and depression made progress in school but engaged in defiant and risky behavior at home. Her parents sought a more restrictive placement for her, but the school district ruled it out because she was earning good grades when she did her work. Her parents unilaterally placed her in a residential facility, but she was expelled for having sex with another student. Her parents then placed her in an out-of-state facility and sought tuition reimbursement, which the Ninth Circuit denied. It held **the student did not require residential placement for any educational reason. She was not disruptive in class and was well regarded by teachers.** *Ashland School Dist. v. Parents of Student R.J.*, 588 F.3d 1004 (9th Cir. 2009).

◆   A Virginia student with autism and a significant communication disorder made little progress in public schools, mastering only one IEP objective in six years. His parents requested a due process hearing, suggesting a one-on-one Lindamood-Bell Center placement. After a hearing, the school board acknowledged the student should be classified as having multiple disabilities but refused to provide one-on-one instruction. The parents placed him in the Lindamood-Bell program for four years and then sought tuition reimbursement. A hearing officer found three of the IEPs were invalid but also found the center to be an inappropriate placement. **A federal court agreed, but the Fourth Circuit vacated and remanded the case for a year-by-year IEP analysis.** If the center was appropriate, tuition reimbursement might be awarded. *M.S. v. Fairfax County School Board*, 553 F.3d 315 (4th Cir. 2009).

◆   The parents of a Colorado three-year-old with autism rejected the draft IEP offered by their school, which would have placed their son in an integrated setting, and kept their son at home with the one-on-one therapy program he had been receiving. The district failed to finalize the IEP for that year. The next year, the parents again rejected the district's IEP calling for an integrated placement with five hours of discrete trial training a week. The school district finalized that IEP, but the parents selected a private school, then sought tuition reimbursement. A hearing officer held for the school district, but a federal court found the parents entitled to tuition for the first year because the district failed to finalize the IEP. The Tenth Circuit reversed the judgment, noting that IDEA procedural violations were not sufficient for the parents to prevail in this case. **A procedural violation must result in lost educational opportunities to justify an award of tuition.** The court remanded the case (returned it to the district court) for further consideration of that issue. *Sytsema v. Academy School Dist. No. 20*, 538 F.3d 1306 (10th Cir. 2008).

When the case returned to the district court, it held that the unfinished IEP failed to offer the student needed one-on-one services. As a result, the parents were entitled to an award of their tuition costs. *Sytsema v. Academy School Dist. No. 20*, No. 03-cv-2582-RPM, 2009 WL 3682221 (D. Colo. 10/30/09).

◆   A Georgia school district failed to assess a student for special education for four years despite requests from his teachers. When it finally did evaluate the student, it determined that he had an IQ of 63. A reevaluation of the student when he turned 16 found his IQ was 82 – the low end of average. However, the student was still at a third-grade level in reading and math. Eventually, his parents obtained an independent educational evaluation diagnosing dyslexia. The parents pursued a due process proceeding under the IDEA, and a hearing officer gave them a choice of additional support at the public school or a private school placement with reimbursement limited to $15,000 a year. The parents chose the private school, and the district appealed. A federal district court removed the tuition cap and ordered the school district to pay annual tuition of $34,150. On further appeal, the Eleventh Circuit held that **while the IDEA has a preference for public school placements, a private school placement may be an appropriate compensatory education remedy where a school denies a student a FAPE.** *Draper v. Atlanta Independent School System*, 518 F.3d 1275 (11th Cir. 2008).

◆   A South Carolina ninth-grader with a learning disability attended special education classes. Her parents disagreed with the IEP devised by their school district. The IEP called for mainstreaming in regular education classes for most subjects. The parents requested a due process hearing and unilaterally placed the student in a private school. A hearing officer held that the IEP was adequate. After the student raised her reading comprehension three full grades in one year at the private school, the parents sued the district for tuition reimbursement. A U.S. district court held the educational program and achievement goals of the proposed IEP were "wholly inadequate" under the IDEA. Even though the private school was not approved by the state education department, it provided the student with an excellent education that complied with IDEA substantive requirements. The parents were entitled to tuition reimbursement.

   **The U.S. Supreme Court held that the failure of the school district to provide an appropriate placement entitled the parents to tuition reimbursement, even though the private school was not on any state list of approved schools.** This was because the district denied the student FAPE and the private education provided to her was found appropriate by the district court. South Carolina did not release a list of approved schools to the public. Under the IDEA, parents may unilaterally place children in private schools at their own risk. To recover tuition costs, parents must show that the placement proposed by the school district violates the IDEA, and that the private school placement is appropriate. The Court upheld lower court decisions for the parents. *Florence County School Dist. Four v. Carter*, 510 U.S. 7 (1993).

◆   The U.S. Supreme Court held that the parents of a child with a disability did not waive their claim for reimbursement of the expenses involved in unilaterally placing their child in a private school during the pendency of proceedings to review the child's IEP. The case involved a learning disabled child who was placed in a public school special education program against the wishes of his parents. The parents requested a due process hearing and, prior to the resolution of their complaint, placed their child in a private residential school recommended by specialists. The parents then sought reimbursement for their expenses. A federal appeals court found the IDEA stay-put provision to be "directory" rather than "mandatory." It decided that this "status quo" provision did not bar claims for reimbursement. The U.S. Supreme Court held that to bar reimbursement claims in cases of unilateral parent placement was contrary to the IDEA, which favors proper interim placements for disabled children. However, **parents who unilaterally change a child's placement during the pendency of proceedings do so at their own financial risk**. If the courts ultimately determine a child's IEP is appropriate, the parents are barred from obtaining reimbursement for any interim period in which the placement violated the IDEA. The Court affirmed the appellate court ruling. *Burlington School Committee v. Dep't of Educ.*, 471 U.S. 359, 105 S.Ct. 1996, 85 L.Ed.2d 385 (1985).

## B. Parental Conduct

*The IDEA discourages unilateral conduct by school districts and parents alike. The IDEA allows for the reduction or denial of reimbursement to parentally placed private school students, if the parents fail to give at least 10 days notice of the intended placement, do not make the child available to designated school employees for an assessment and evaluation before the child's removal from public school, or if a judge so rules.*

*In* M.C. ex rel. Mrs. C. v. Voluntown Board of Educ., *226 F.3d 60, 68 (2d Cir. 2000), the U.S. Court of Appeals, Second Circuit, found that "courts have held uniformly that reimbursement is barred where parents unilaterally arrange for private educational services without ever notifying the school board of their dissatisfaction with their child's IEP." And in* Frank G. v. Board of Educ. of Hyde Park, *459 F.3d 356 (2d Cir. 2006), the court held it is inequitable to permit reimbursement when parents have not timely requested it.*

◆   The mother of a Delaware student with disabilities placed him in a private school after a dispute about his IEP. The district agreed to fund the placement for one year and began the formal IEP process for the next year. However, the mother failed to return a form requesting permission to evaluate her son until midway through the summer. She also claimed she could not attend an IEP meeting because of scheduling conflicts. She then returned her son to the private school and refused to further participate in the IEP process, asserting that a free appropriate public education (FAPE) was denied because the IEP was not in place at the start of the school year. A federal district court ultimately ruled against her when she sued for tuition reimbursement, noting that **the delays were at least partly her fault and did not deny her son FAPE**. On appeal, the Third Circuit affirmed, noting that not all procedural violations of the IDEA result in a denial of FAPE. Here, the parents' non-cooperation caused the delay. *C.H. v. Cape Henlopen School Dist.*, 606 F.3d 59 (3d Cir. 2010).

◆   A New York school department's committee on special education developed an IEP for a student with autism. The IEP stated that the student would attend school in District 75 (a group of schools for students with disabilities) but did not specify which school he would attend. Instead, a citywide placement officer would make that determination. The student's parents objected to the school that was eventually proposed, but instead of visiting a second school they enrolled their son in a private school. When they sought tuition reimbursement, a federal court and later the Second Circuit ruled against them. Under the circumstances, **the IDEA did not require the school district to name the particular location for receiving special education services**. *T.Y. v. New York City Dep't of Educ.*, 584 F.3d 412 (2d Cir. 2009).

◆ The parents of a New Hampshire student became concerned that she needed special education, and their school district found she had a learning disability in math. An IEP team suggested a private school placement, which the parents agreed to. The following year, the parents requested due process, claiming the district had denied her a free appropriate public education (FAPE) for the past five years. They withdrew the student from school and began home-schooling her. The district threatened to file truancy charges against them unless they registered her as a home-schooled student. When the case finally reached a federal district court, **the court held that the parents acted unreasonably during the IEP process; thus, any delay in developing an IEP did not violate the IDEA**. Also, the truancy threat did not amount to a denial of FAPE. *Kasenia R. v. Brookline School Dist.*, 588 F.Supp.2d 175 (D.N.H. 2008).

◆ The parents of a Maine student placed her in a private residential facility before the district could evaluate her. They then demanded a due process hearing and met with the district to consider her eligibility for IDEA services. The hearing was delayed while an independent evaluation was conducted. At an IEP meeting, the parents insisted on a therapeutic residential placement while the district asserted that a nonresidential public school setting would be appropriate. The parents challenged the district's placement, claiming it failed to offer the student a finalized IEP. A federal district court and the First Circuit ruled for the district, noting that the IEP was never finalized because the parents disrupted the IEP process. **Their fixation on a residential placement at district expense caused the breakdown of the IEP process.** *C.G. and B.S. v. Five Town Community School Dist.*, 513 F.3d 279 (1st Cir. 2008).

◆ A New York student began to experience anxiety about school after being bullied there. He was diagnosed with severe anxiety and depression, and the school's committee on special education found him eligible under the IDEA with emotional disturbance. The district developed an IEP specifying individualized counseling, resource room services and test modifications. The parents later withdrew their consent for the IEP and sought home tutoring. The district then recommended several alternative high school placements. The parents unilaterally placed their son in an unapproved private school without informing the district, then rejected the district's recommendations. When they sought tuition reimbursement, the Second Circuit ruled against them. **The private school lacked a therapeutic setting and an administrative hearing officer had found it inappropriate.** *Gagliardo v. Arlington Cent. School Dist.*, 489 F.3d 105 (2d Cir. 2007).

## VI. TRANSITION AND GRADUATION

*Transition services describe "a results-oriented process, that is focused on improving the academic and functional achievement of the child with a disability ..." The IDEA requires a statement of a student's transition service needs for the IEP of each student with a disability no later than the age of 14, or earlier if appropriate. See 34 C.F.R. Part 222.50. Introductory language in the 2004 IDEA Amendments declared an increased emphasis on the provision of effective transition services for disabled students, in view of their increasing graduation rates.*

### A. Transition Plans

◆   A New York preschooler received 30-35 hours per week of home-based Applied Behavioral Analysis (ABA) therapy from his school district, with speech and occupational therapy. The committee on special education (CSE) recommended a special education placement but without the ABA sessions. His parents rejected the IEP and sought due process. A hearing officer ruled for the school district, and the Second Circuit held the district did not have to provide home-based ABA therapy. **Appropriate supports and services were included in the IEP to ease the student's transition to school.** And the parents failed to show that the CSE had predetermined a kindergarten placement. *T.S. and S.P. v. Mamaroneck Union Free School Dist.*, 554 F.3d 247 (2d Cir. 2009).

◆   A New Hampshire school district prepared an IEP for an 18-year-old student that was nearly 60 pages long and contained nine pages of transition services. The parents rejected the IEP but refused to make any modifications to the plan or even to specify which parts of it were objectionable other than to say they disagreed with the behavior aspects of the IEP. The district unsuccessfully tried to put the rest of the IEP into effect and then filed an administrative due process request. A hearing officer ruled for the school district, and a federal district court affirmed the judgment, ruling **the district did not have to comply with the parents' unspecified vision of a perfect IEP.** The district had offered the student a detailed and comprehensive IEP that more than adequately addressed his needs. The mother appealed to the U.S. Court of Appeals, First Circuit. The court agreed with school officials that the student's IEP should be put into effect. **The IDEA does not require transition plans to be articulated as a separate component of an IEP. Nor were behavior plans necessary unless certain disciplinary actions had been taken.** Thus, the first proposed IEP, which discussed a behavior plan, did not violate the IDEA. *Lessard v. Wilton Lyndeborough Coop. School Dist.*, 518 F.3d 18 (1st Cir. 2008).

◆   After a Pennsylvania student with disabilities turned 16, his new IEP left sections of his mandatory transition plan largely blank, instead noting that he would meet with a school counselor to discuss his prerequisites for college and other issues. At the next IEP team meeting, the district offered the student an alternative special education day placement at an in-state private school. His parents instead opted for a residential school in New York. When they sought tuition reimbursement, the district failed to submit the due process request for more than three months. However, a hearing officer still ruled in favor of the district, finding the proposed placement appropriate. A federal court and the Third Circuit affirmed the judgment. **The dispute over the transition plan and the delay in submitting the due process request did not add up to an IDEA violation where the proposed IEP was appropriate.** *Sinan v. School Dist. of Philadelphia*, 293 Fed.Appx. 912 (3d Cir. 2008).

♦   An Illinois student with Rett Syndrome engaged in self-injurious behavior and sometimes struck others. In her first year of high school, she head-butted two staff members, breaking their noses. The district sought a special education setting, but the parents objected, instead settling for keeping the student at home. Eventually she was returned to her neighborhood school, where she made limited academic progress. When the district again tried to place the student in a special education setting, the parents requested a hearing, asserting that the IEP meeting was a sham to mask a "predetermined placement." A hearing officer, a federal court and the Seventh Circuit all ruled for the district. The parents received a meaningful opportunity to participate in the development and review of their daughter's IEP. **While the district did not include a transition plan in the IEP, the student was unable to benefit from one at the time**, so the lack of a transition plan did not violate the IDEA. *Board of Educ. of Township High School Dist. No. 211 v. Ross*, 486 F.3d 267 (7th Cir. 2007).

## B.  Graduation

*The 2004 IDEA amendments relieved schools of a duty to seek an evaluation before terminating the eligibility of a student who has graduated with a regular diploma or become too old to be eligible for a free appropriate public education (FAPE). When an eligible child graduates or "ages out" of school, the school district must give the child a summary of his or her academic achievement and functional performance, with recommendations for assistance in meeting the child's postsecondary goals.*

♦   An Indiana school district offered special education to a learning disabled student until his parents decided to home-school him. They sought to reintegrate him into public schools and obtained private evaluations showing that he had autism. But the school district did not identify an autism spectrum disorder until the student was 17 and awarded him a diploma at age 19. His parents challenged the graduation, asserting he should continue to receive special education. A federal court, using the stay-put provisions of the IDEA, ordered the district to continue educating the student in a college preparatory program. **The parents' challenge to the validity and good faith of the decision to graduate their son warranted a stay-put placement.** *Tindell v. Evansville-Vanderburgh School Corp.*, No. 309-cv-00159-SEB-WGH, 2010 WL 557058 (S.D. Ind. 2/10/10).

♦   An Illinois sophomore with Type 1 diabetes and a social anxiety disorder began missing school and took classes at a community college. She sought reimbursement for her tuition there, but a federal court and the Seventh Circuit ruled against her. The student had a Section 504 plan in place for her diabetes but was not IDEA eligible. **There was no medical evidence that she stopped attending high school because her anxiety had worsened, and she was unable to establish a medical basis for her better attendance and performance at the community college.** As a result, the parents' request for community college tuition reimbursement was properly denied. *Loch v. Edwardsville School Dist. No. 7*, 327 Fed.Appx. 647 (7th Cir. 2009).

◆   The parents of a California student waited until after he graduated to file a Section 504 claim against the school district. Appeal reached the Ninth Circuit. It held that despite differences between Section 504 and the IDEA, **a party seeking relief that is also available under the IDEA must exhaust administrative remedies to the same extent as for IDEA claims.** *Fraser v. Tamalpais Union High School Dist.*, 281 Fed.Appx. 746 (9th Cir. 2008).

◆   An Oregon student with a Section 504 plan had ADHD but did not qualify for an IEP. He was suspended for accessing a school database to change his grades. A hearing was conducted to consider expulsion, but his father claimed he received improper notice and thought the meeting was just for fact-finding. The school district agreed to further investigate, and the family filed a Section 504 complaint, challenging the suspension and seeking restoration of class credit. A hearing officer ordered the district to give the student the opportunity to recover lost credits. The student graduated with a regular diploma but sued the district under Section 504 and the IDEA, seeking to modify his final grades and requesting money damages. A federal court dismissed the case, holding that **even though he had graduated, he should still have pursued administrative remedies** before suing. *Ruecker v. Sommer*, 567 F.Supp.2d 1276 (D. Or. 2008).

◆   A 19-year-old Florida student had Asperger's syndrome and was non-verbal. His senior-year IEP identified writing as a priority need. At an IEP meeting held three months before the end of the year, the district proposed eliminating goals requiring him to complete written work. It also advised the parents their son would graduate at the end of the year, if he received all of his academic credits. The parents rejected the proposal to graduate their son and to eliminate his written work. They requested a new IEP meeting or mediation and new evaluations. Days before graduation, the board advised the parents it would hold an IEP meeting to discuss a diploma and review the IEP. It then informed them the graduation ceremony was the day before the IEP meeting.

   An administrative law judge rejected the parents' request for stay-put relief, but a federal district court held their due process request before graduation triggered the stay-put provision. The board appealed to the Eleventh Circuit. It rejected the district court's finding that the board had misled the parents by scheduling an IEP meeting the day after their son's graduation. There was no evidence that the board did not intend to hold the meeting if the student failed to graduate. **The district court should not have back-dated a stay-put injunction.** The court vacated the decision and instructed the district court to decide if a preliminary order should be issued. *Sammons v. Polk County School Board*, 165 Fed.Appx. 750 (11th Cir. 2006).

   The case returned to the district court, which held that the student, now 22, was not entitled to stay-put protection or compensatory education. *Sammons v.*

*Polk County School Board*, No. 8:04-cv-2657-T-24-EAJ, 2007 WL 4358266 (M.D. Fla. 12/10/07).

◆   A Washington student became pregnant as a high school senior. She failed a quiz near the end of the year and was barred from the graduation ceremony. The district superintendent later met with the family and suggested a Section 504 plan to increase the student's point total for the failed course. A resulting increase in points for the class allowed her to graduate. She and her family sued the district and school officials, alleging discrimination and due process violations. A jury found that the district violated the student's due process rights and awarded her $5,000, with over $31,000 in attorneys' fees and costs. However, the jury found no discrimination. On appeal, the Court of Appeals of Washington found that **no state or federal law created an entitlement for students to attend graduation ceremonies**. The student received an opportunity to meet with the principal to resolve her grievance prior to the ceremony. She was not deprived of any interest protected by the Constitution. *Nieshe v. Concrete School Dist.*, 128 Wash.App. 1029 (Wash. Ct. App. 2005).

◆   The parents of a Pennsylvania student with dyslexia, memory disorder and ADHD agreed with their school district on a 12th-grade IEP that called for transition services in a college preparatory program in Maryland. The district did not provide the transition services, but at the end of the year, it recommended that the student be graduated. The parents objected, and the IEP team met without the parents to finalize an IEP for a thirteenth year of services that also did not include transition services. A due process hearing officer found that the student had received a free appropriate public education, but a state special education appeals panel reversed. The Commonwealth Court of Pennsylvania upheld the panel's decision. **The district had failed to provide agreed-upon transition services, then scheduled the student's graduation.** The court ordered the district to provide the student with a year of compensatory education in the college preparatory program. *Susquehanna Township School Dist. v. Frances J.*, 823 A.2d 249 (Pa. Commw. Ct. 2003).

◆   A federal district court held that an Illinois school district improperly decided to graduate a high school student with multiple disabilities on the basis of his accumulation of required credits instead of his progress toward his individualized goals. As the district committed several violations of the IDEA with respect to the student's educational program and IEPs, it was required to reimburse him for private school costs and provide compensatory education at a private school until he reached age 22. The violations included designing IEPs with vague and immeasurable goals, not changing IEP goals from year to year despite regression, and failure to develop a timely transition plan. **To be eligible for graduation, the student had to meet general graduation requirements and make progress on his IEP goals and objectives.** *Kevin T. v. Elmhurst Community School Dist. No. 205*, 2002 WL 433061 (N.D. Ill. 2002).

## VII. SCHOOL LIABILITY

### A. IDEA Claims

#### 1. Compensatory Education

*Compensatory education is the belated provision of necessary educational or related services to a student to which the student was entitled, but which the education agency failed to provide. Compensatory education may be awarded to students who are over the statutory age of entitlement (usually 21) to prohibit education agencies from indefinitely delaying the provision of necessary services until the student is beyond school age.*

◆ The parents of an 11-year-old Pennsylvania student who had never attended public schools requested an evaluation for special education after obtaining a private evaluation. They did not sign the consent forms for a public evaluation, instead enrolling the student in a private school recommended by their evaluator. Eventually the district was able to conduct an evaluation and prepare an IEP, which the parents rejected. They sought compensatory education for the delay, claiming that they had asked for an evaluation during the student's kindergarten year. The case reached the Third Circuit, which ruled against the parents. It noted that **they were not entitled to compensatory education because they had no intention of placing their son in public school. There was no evidence they had asked for an evaluation during kindergarten.** *P.P. v. West Chester Area School Dist.*, 585 F.3d 727 (3d Cir. 2009).

◆ A Texas student with multiple disabilities had an IEP that included a goal to initiate communications about his need to go to the bathroom. The district used a voice-output device for him to communicate this need and gave a device to the parents for home use, explaining its proper use to his mother. The student regressed in his ability to use the device at home and in his extended school year program, and he wet the bed every morning. His parents challenged the IEP's schedule of in-home and parent training. A hearing officer noted that the district provided only four of ten scheduled training sessions, and ordered 150 minutes of compensatory training. But a federal district court ruled that **the student's regression in toilet training was not a failure to implement a significant portion of the IEP.** The award of compensatory training was reversed. *Clear Creek Independent School Dist. v. J.K.*, 400 F.Supp.2d 991 (S.D. Tex. 2005).

◆ A District of Columbia student with multiple disabilities had received special education for some time. An evaluation team determined that he was making progress but that he required new evaluations. However, they were not performed. After six months, the student's mother requested a due process hearing. A hearing officer determined the district failed to provide the student with a FAPE, but limited compensatory education to the two-month period prior to the hearing request. The mother appealed. A federal court noted that **the district had failed to show it was providing the services required by the IEP and did not conduct a reevaluation required by the IDEA.** Accordingly, the court held the student was entitled to compensatory education for the entire three-year period at issue. *Argueta v. Government of District of Columbia*, 355 F.Supp.2d 408 (D.D.C. 2005).

◆   A 19-year-old Tennessee student with no hands, one foot and cerebral palsy was dropped while school district attendants were attempting to move him from his wheelchair. His parents received his complete academic record for the first time and filed a due process complaint. A federal district court held the system violated the IDEA by not relaying information from the student's assessments. After he received a special education diploma, the Sixth Circuit ordered the district court to decide whether the case was moot. The district court held **the compensatory education claim was based on an assertion that the school system had denied a FAPE at a time when the student remained eligible for services.** Though he was now 24 and had a special education diploma, his compensatory education request involved past violations and the case was not moot. On appeal, the Sixth Circuit agreed, and found an IDEA procedural violation. *Barnett v. Memphis City Schools*, 113 Fed.Appx. 124 (6th Cir. 2004).

## 2.  Monetary Damages, Costs and Fees

*In* Ortega v. Bibb County School Dist., *397 F.3d 1321 (11th Cir. 2005), the Eleventh Circuit restated a longstanding rule that tort-type personal injury claims for damages are unavailable under the IDEA. But attorneys representing students often add claims alleging disability discrimination and tort damages to IDEA actions. Claims involving any matter relating to the identification, evaluation or placement of a child, or the provision of a free appropriate public education, are subject to the IDEA's administrative exhaustion requirement.*

◆   The parents of a New York student with disabilities sought private school tuition reimbursement. After winning at administrative and federal court levels, they sued to recover $29,350 in fees for assistance provided by an educational consultant throughout the process. A federal court awarded only $8,650 in fees, allowing only those charges accumulated between the hearing request and the administrative ruling. Appeal reached the U.S. Supreme Court. It found that nothing in the IDEA made clear to the states that accepting federal funds would make them responsible for reimbursing parents for expert witness fees. Expert witness fees could not be deemed costs so as to be reimbursable. *Arlington Cent. School Dist. Board of Educ. v. Murphy*, 548 U.S. 291 (2006).

◆   A Pennsylvania student had academic difficulty during her school career. By the fifth grade, she was receiving 45 minutes of daily learning support. In the second half of the year, the district reevaluated her and found her ineligible for special education. A due process hearing officer ruled that the district violated the IDEA and ordered compensatory education as well as reimbursement for an independent education evaluation. A review panel largely affirmed the decision. When the district appealed to a federal district court, the parents sought money damages. **The court ruled that the IDEA does not permit compensatory damages but ruled they might be available under**

**Section 504.** The case would move forward. *Breanne C. v. Southern York County School Dist.*, 665 F.Supp.2d 504 (M.D. Pa. 2009).

◆ The mother of a Nevada student with autism took her son to a childhood autism program ordered by a hearing officer as compensatory education. The district was required to pay "all out-of-pocket expenses" – nearly $65,000. When the mother sought an additional $26,515 to fully compensate her for wages and benefits she lost while transporting her son to the program, the Supreme Court of Nevada held that she was not entitled to them. **Out-of-pocket expenses did not include lost income.** *Gumm v. Nevada Dep't of Educ.*, 113 P.3d 853 (Nev. 2005).

## B. Discrimination Claims

*The Americans with Disabilities Act (ADA), 42 U.S.C. § 12101, et seq., and Section 504 of the Rehabilitation Act of 1973, 29 U.S.C. § 794, are federal statutes prohibiting discrimination against persons with disabilities. Both acts require schools and their employees to make "reasonable accommodations" for qualified individuals with disabilities, but no institution is required to lower its academic standards in order to do so. As the Eighth Circuit Court of Appeals held in* Sonkowsky v. Board of Educ. for Independent School Dist. No. 721, *327 F.3d 675 (8th Cir. 2003),* **to create liability under Section 504 or the ADA, there must be evidence of bad faith or gross misjudgment by school officials.**

◆ Hawaii sisters were diagnosed as autistic when they were pre-schoolers. According to their parent, the Hawaii Department of Education (DOE) found the girls eligible for special education but did not implement or design IEPs for them. He alleged the school system "warehoused" them in their first years of school. A federal district court dismissed the family's discrimination case, finding Section 504 of the Rehabilitation Act created no private right of action to enforce the requirement to provide a free appropriate public education (FAPE), and no evidence of intentional discrimination based on disability.

On appeal, the U.S. Court of Appeals, Ninth Circuit, noted a distinction between FAPE under the IDEA and Section 504. **To establish Section 504 liability, the family had to show the DOE intentionally discriminated against the students or was deliberately indifferent to their rights.** Evidence supported the claim that the girls could not access the benefits of a public education without autism-specific services. There was evidence that the DOE was on notice that they required services but failed to provide them. Failure to act despite knowledge of the likelihood of harm was evidence of deliberate indifference. Rejecting the DOE's arguments regarding claims under Section 504 and regulations published under Section 504, the court returned the case to the district court. *Mark H. v. Hamamoto*, 620 F.3d 1090 (9th Cir. 2010).

◆ A Kentucky student with diabetes attended her neighborhood school, which did not have a nurse working there. Because the student required insulin shots, her mother arranged to have someone give them to her. However, the mother then sought to have the school district hire a nurse for the neighborhood school. The district instead offered to transfer the student to a nearby school where a nurse worked. The mother rejected this option because of the extra transportation time it would involve. She later sued the district in a federal district court for Rehabilitation Act and ADA violations. The court ruled against her, noting that **the school district had offered a reasonable accommodation, which the mother had refused.** *B.M. v. Board of Educ. of Scott County, Kentucky*, Civ. No. 5:07-153-JHM, 2008 WL 4073855 (E.D. Ky. 8/29/08).

◆   A disabled Wisconsin student with physical deformities endured verbal attacks and mockery by other students. Two boys in shop class also threw pieces of wood at him, causing injury. After they were suspended, he was allowed to leave classes early to avoid them. A third shop student then threw safety glasses at the student, causing a concussion and cracked teeth. That student was also suspended. The disabled student sued the school board and the shop teacher in a federal district court for violating his equal protection and due process rights by failing to protect him from his fellow students. **The court held he could not prove intentional discrimination by the board or teacher.** The shop teacher did not treat him differently than non-disabled students. There were also no ADA or Rehabilitation Act violations. *Werth v. Board of Directors of the Public Schools of City of Milwaukee*, 472 F.Supp.2d 1113 (E.D. Wis. 2007).

◆   A Pennsylvania student began having behavioral problems in elementary school and was diagnosed with ADHD and oppositional defiant disorder. He took medication that helped him in class, and he performed at grade level in reading, writing, math, science and social studies. In grade seven, the district found him eligible for a Section 504 accommodation plan. The student's behavior deteriorated; he threatened to shoot a teacher and burn down the school, and he was suspended. His parents asserted that the district had failed him under both the IDEA and Section 504. After a hearing officer found the school district had adequately addressed the student's attention and organization problems, the parents sued. **A federal court held that the student did not have a serious emotional disturbance so as to be entitled to IDEA disciplinary protections like a manifestation determination.** He understood the consequences of his behavior, and the school district accommodated his needs. *Brendan K. v. Easton Area School Dist.*, No. 05-4179, 2007 WL 1160377 (E.D. Pa. 4/16/07).

◆   A Massachusetts student with Asperger's syndrome applied for admission to an agricultural high school, seeking entry into its landscaping program. He scored only 32 of 55 possible points under the school's admissions policy and was placed on the waiting list. The school admitted 16 other students with IEPs, and at least 25 other students with IEPs ranked ahead of him on the waiting list. His claimed the school discriminated against him on the basis of his disability. A federal district court found no discrimination. **The school's admissions policy was neutral,** and other disabled students had been selected under its criteria. The school did not have to modify its admissions requirements because that would constitute a fundamental change in its program. *Cordeiro v. Driscoll*, No. 06-10854-DPW, 2007 WL 763907 (D. Mass. 3/8/07).

◆   The parents of an Arkansas student with mental retardation and serious heart disease said a group of non-disabled students pretended to befriend their son, then confined him in a dog cage and forced him to eat dog feces. They also stole from him, sexually abused him and exposed him to non-disabled peers. The parents claimed they discussed the bullying with school officials repeatedly, but that the district did nothing to stop the abuse. In the family's federal district court lawsuit, the district sought to have the claims dismissed for failure to exhaust administrative remedies, but a federal district court refused to do so. **As there was some evidence that the district acted with bad faith or gross misjudgment, the court held the case should proceed.** *R.P. v. Springdale School Dist.*, No. 06-5014, 2007 WL 552117 (W.D. Ark. 2/21/07).

◆   A Wyoming student with cerebral palsy attended school in a district that initially did not have accessible buildings. The district hired a full-time aide to assist her during the school day. During her entire school career, the student continued to have accessibility issues. The district did not make accessible seating in the school gym available, and locked her out of a school building because an accessible door was not working. Also, during her senior year, her aide frequently missed school due to a personal situation. When the student sued the district under Section 504 and the ADA, the district sought to have the case dismissed. The court refused to do so, noting that **the mere hiring of the full-time aide did not mean that the district had not intentionally discriminated against the student**. A trial would have to be held. *Swenson v. Lincoln County School Dist.*, 260 F.Supp.2d 1136 (D. Wyo. 2003).

## C.  Negligence and Civil Rights Claims

*In order to hold school districts liable for negligence, there must be some act or omission that creates a foreseeable risk of harm. Civil rights actions require an injured party to show violation of a clearly established right, and often, "conscience-shocking" conduct. Many of these cases are decided on the basis of immunity, a concept more fully discussed in Chapter Twelve.*

◆   A New York student with a history of behavior problems that included aggression at home, setting fires, stealing and threatening others attended school under an IEP. He made better social progress after being placed in a community residence and displayed no aggressive behaviors for two years. When he was 11 years old, he called a kindergartner his girlfriend while on a school bus. Her mother asked that they be separated. Later, he exposed himself to the kindergartner and forced her to touch him. Her mother sued the district for negligence. The Court of Appeals of New York ruled that she could not recover for her daughter's injuries because **the molestation by the 11-year-old was not foreseeable**. His past conduct did not indicate any sexually aggressive behavior. *Brandy B. v. Eden Cent. School Dist.*, 934 N.E.2d 304 (N.Y. 2010).

◆   An Illinois autistic student had daily tantrums, an eating disorder and episodes of running on impulse. A doctor prescribed a service dog, which was obtained two years later. This calmed the student greatly. However, at a preschool IEP meeting, district officials told his mother the service dog could not accompany him to school because even though the dog was hypoallergenic, another student was highly allergic to dogs. The family sought a preliminary injunction to temporarily allow the student to bring the dog to school. **The Appellate Court of Illinois agreed with the family that the student would suffer irreparable harm if he could not have the service dog in class, and it issued an order in his favor based on state law.** *Kalbfleisch v. Columbia Community Unit School Dist., Unit No. 4*, 920 N.E.2d 651 (Ill. App. Ct. 2009).

Later, the family sought an order that would allow the dog to accompany the student to school. The Appellate Court of Illinois held **the dog met the state's definition of a "service animal" even though the commands to assist the student came from staff members and not the student himself.** The student could bring the dog to school. *K.D. v. Villa Grove Community Unit School Dist. No. 302*, 936 N.E.2d 690 (Ill. App. Ct. 2010).

◆   A New York City special education teacher initiated a Type Three referral to remove an aggressive student from her class, and she contemplated quitting because of his behavior. Her supervisors told her to "hang in there" because referral could take up to 60 days. Forty-one days after initiating the referral, the student attacked another child and the teacher intervened, sustaining injuries. She sued the city for negligence, alleging that a "special relationship" supported her claim. A jury awarded her over $512,000, and appeal reached the state's highest court. **According to the New York Court of Appeals, no special relationship existed between the teacher and the board that would create a cause of action for negligence.** *DiNardo v. City of New York*, 13 N.Y.3d 872, 921 N.E.2d 585, 893 N.Y.S.2d 818 (N.Y. 2009).

◆   An assistant principal in North Carolina called a disabled student's mother to report some sexual experimentation between the student and another boy. The mother believed the contact was not consensual and she sued the school board for negligence, also asserting state constitutional claims. The school board sought immunity, but the North Carolina Supreme Court held the lawsuit could proceed. **Sovereign immunity was created by the courts, but constitutional rights trumped them.** And granting immunity to the board would leave the student and his mother without an adequate state remedy. *Craig v. New Hanover County Board of Educ.*, 678 S.E.2d 351 (N.C. 2009).

◆   A North Carolina teacher's aide allegedly force-fed a student to the point of choking on several occasions, used abusive language and pulled his hair. The student stopped eating and had to be hospitalized. His parents sued the aide, the school board, administrators and a teacher for claims including infliction of emotional distress. The teacher sought immunity, but the state courts rejected her claim. Her job was not created by the state constitution or laws, so she was denied public official immunity. While teachers served a vital role in public education, they did not meet the test for public official immunity.

Turning to the federal claims, **the court held the test for public official immunity starts with an inquiry into whether the official has violated clearly established rights of which a reasonable person would have known**

**at the time of the violation**. Under both the state and U.S. Constitutions, the court found there is a liberty interest in the integrity of the human body. A right to be free from state-created brutal, harmful or demeaning intrusions into personal privacy and bodily security was recognized in 1980 by the Fourth Circuit. The complaint alleged the teacher knew of and might have witnessed the repeated abuse of the student. As there was evidence of the teacher's continued inaction in the face of widespread abuse, and the claims involved clearly established constitutional rights of which she would have known, the court held she could not claim immunity for the federal law claims. *Farrell v. Transylvania County Board of Educ.*, 682 S.E.2d 224 (N.C. Ct. App. 2009).

◆   The mother of a Virginia child with cerebral palsy and a seizure disorder became concerned that the student's teacher was improperly confining her to a wheelchair for most of the day. She hid recording equipment in the child's wheelchair, got information that corroborated her concerns and then sued the teacher, the school board and the superintendent for violating her child's right to bodily integrity under the Due Process Clause. The defendants sought immunity, but the Fourth Circuit held that they were not entitled to it. **The student had a clearly established right to be free from bodily restraint, and the mother alleged that the confinement was intentional and excessive.** If staff members indeed restrained the child for hours at a time as alleged, they would have violated clearly established law. The court remanded the case for further proceedings. *H.H. v. Moffett*, 335 Fed.Appx. 306 (4th Cir. 2009).

◆   A disabled California student had an IEP that called for full-time adult supervision. She had held hands with a male student on more than one occasion and went with him unsupervised to a greenhouse on campus, where he made sexual advances towards her. Her family sued the district for negligence and lost. The California Court of Appeal held that **the student's IEP did not require the district to supervise her every minute she was on campus**. Further, the hand-holding did not make it foreseeable that the male student would make sexual advances towards her during one brief, unsupervised period. *M.P. v. Chico Unified School Dist.*, No. 138462, 2009 WL 226005 (Cal. Ct. App. 2/2/09).

◆   A Minnesota student with an emotional-behavioral disorder and a history of sexually inappropriate behavior was supposed to sit alone behind the bus driver, and his transportation form included that directive. However, the form did not detail his past history. He was allowed to move back in the bus at some point, and he sexually assaulted another student. When the other student sued the district, the Minnesota Court of Appeals held that **the district had immunity with respect to its decision to withhold the student's prior history of sexual misbehavior.** But as for the failure to follow directions and keep the student in the seat behind the driver, the bus service had no immunity. *J.W. v. 287 Intermediate Dist.*, 761 N.W.2d 896 (Minn. Ct. App. 2009).

◆   A disabled female student in Ohio rode the bus home every afternoon with three disabled male students. No bus aide accompanied them because none was required by any of the students' IEPs. The student was abused by a male student during the rides home. A bus aide present on the morning drive eventually discovered the abuse, and the parents ultimately sued the district for her injuries. They claimed that the motor vehicle exception to immunity allowed them to sue, while the district asserted that the exception applied only to the action of driving the bus. On appeal, the Ohio Supreme Court held **immunity protected the school district. The motor vehicle exception applied only to the driving of the bus and not the supervision of students by the driver.** *Doe v. Marlington Local School Dist. Board of Educ.*, 907 N.E.2d 706 (Ohio 2009).

◆   A 15-year-old Tennessee student with depression, ADHD, bipolar disorder and schizophrenia jumped off a moving school bus after the driver refused to allow him to get off at a location that was not designated as a bus stop. The student died from the fall. His mother sued school officials, claiming disability discrimination and civil rights violations. A federal district court and the U.S. Court of Appeals, Sixth Circuit, ruled against her. The Sixth Circuit held **the school board had no policy or custom of deliberate indifference to student rights, and its conduct was not the moving force or cause of the death.** *Hill v. Bradley County Board of Educ.*, 295 Fed.Appx. 740 (6th Cir. 2008).

◆   A learning-disabled Colorado high school student told her mother she did not want to attend school anymore because boys teased her. The mother told the principal that certain boys were "bothering" her daughter. Later, the student told a school counselor that one boy had repeatedly called her to ask for oral sex and that two boys had coerced her into sexual conduct. The school resource officer then investigated, but the mother refused to cooperate on "advice of counsel." The district attorney then declined to prosecute the case because of the difficulty of proving the activity was not consensual and because of the trauma to which the student would be subjected. The student had a psychotic episode that required hospitalization. The family moved away, and they sued the school district under Title IX. A federal court and the Tenth Circuit ruled for the district, finding that **the district did not have actual knowledge of the sexual harassment until the student told the counselor about it**. Nor did the district have a policy of allowing student-on-student sexual harassment. Finally, the district was not required to discipline the boys for sexual harassment. *Rost v. Steamboat Springs RE-2 School Dist.*, 511 F.3d 1114 (10th Cir. 2008).

◆   An Ohio school aide supervised an autistic student who had previously injured fellow students on the bus. The aide rode with the student on the bus, and was hit and bitten by the student on one occasion. Later, the aide accompanied the student on a field trip to a bowling alley, where the aide intervened to protect another student from the autistic student's attack. The aide was injured. She sued the school board for negligence and civil rights violations, asserting a "state created danger" theory. A federal court and the Sixth Circuit ruled in favor of the school board, noting that **the school district did not create the danger or increase the risk to the aide**. The board was simply attempting to discharge its duties under the IDEA. *Hunt v. Sycamore Community School Dist. Board of Educ.*, 542 F.3d 529 (6th Cir. 2008).

◆   A Kentucky special education student with profound mental disabilities fell while wearing roller skates during a field trip and broke his ankle. The parents then sued the school board and the teacher. A state trial court held the board and teacher were entitled to immunity. The Court of Appeals of Kentucky agreed. **Public employees have qualified immunity where they perform acts involving the exercise of discretion and judgment, if those acts are taken in good faith and within the scope of employment authority.** In this case, the teacher had to exercise discretion and her personal judgment a number of times during the day, including on how to implement the student's IEP and how to supervise him. She also acted in good faith and within the course and scope of her employment. *Pennington v. Greenup County Board of Educ.*, No. 2006-CA-001942-MR, 2008 WL 1757209 (Ky. Ct. App. 4/18/08).

◆   A Michigan student with multiple disabilities, including a seizure disorder, had to be harnessed into seats when traveling in a vehicle or a wheelchair. During a field trip, the student suffered a seizure and became unresponsive on a school bus. Later, he suffered another seizure on the bus, and neither the attendant nor the driver could perform CPR. Emergency responders arrived 10 minutes later and took the student to a hospital, where he died the next day. Litigation in the state court system reached the Michigan Court of Appeals. It found **the board was entitled to immunity because school officials did not act with "gross negligence," which is defined as conduct so reckless as to amount to a disregard for safety.** *Lofton v. Detroit Board of Educ.*, No. 276449, 2008 WL 4414255 (Mich. Ct. App. 9/30/08).

◆   A Nevada student had tuberous sclerosis, which is a neurological disease that causes tumors. He also had autism and was non-verbal. An IDEA lawsuit was brought on his behalf against his school district and teacher. In it, he alleged that his teacher slapped him repeatedly and body-slammed him into a chair. The student also claimed that school officials knew about his teacher's violent conduct but did nothing to prevent it. The teacher and the school district asked for qualified immunity, but a federal court and the Ninth Circuit refused to grant it. **The court held that no reasonable special education teacher would believe it was lawful to seriously beat a disabled four-year-old.** The case was allowed to proceed. *Preschooler II v. Clark County School Board of Trustees*, 479 F.3d 1175 (9th Cir. 2007).

### D.  Abuse and Neglect

◆   A Minnesota student took a student to her resource room as a result of a behavior incident, as specified in her IEP. On the way, she denied the student lavatory use, causing the student to have an accident. An investigation found that the lavatory incident was merely a lapse in judgment, so the teacher was not disciplined. The student's mother sued the school district for claims including child abuse and neglect. A federal court and the Eighth Circuit ruled against her, noting that the mother failed to allege anything done by the teacher that was "shocking to the contemporary conscience" and that there was no due process or Fourth Amendment violation. **The student's IEP, which included a**

**behavior intervention plan, stated she was to be taken to her resource room if she had a behavior incident.** The teacher was complying with this instruction at the time of the accident. *C.N. v. Willmar Public Schools, ISD No. 347*, 591 F.3d 624 (8th Cir. 2010).

◆   A Georgia student with emotional and behavioral issues and ADHD made suicidal comments to staff members but told a school psychologist he was just kidding. He was hospitalized for two weeks and released. The school placed him in its time-out room for most of two days due to disruptive behavior. He made suicidal threats again. After picking a fight with another student, the student was sent to the time-out room again, and he hanged himself. His parents sued the school system and state department of education, but the Georgia Court of Appeals found **no official disregarded his rights in a manner that could be deemed deliberately indifferent.** *King v. Pioneer Regional Educ. Service Agency*, 688 S.E.2d 7 (Ga. Ct. App. 2009).

◆   The family of an Ohio student with Down Syndrome sued their district and several employees, alleging that a substitute teacher did not monitor their child's classroom on many occasions and that the student was assaulted by a known abuser as a result. The Court of Appeals of Ohio granted the district immunity because the **failure to monitor was within the scope of the employees' official job duties.** But the individual employees might be liable for their "recklessness." The court returned the case to the trial court for consideration of that issue. *E.F. v. Oberlin City School Dist.*, No. 09CA009640, 2010 WL 1227703 (Ohio Ct. App. 3/31/10).

◆   A Florida student with autism sued his former teacher and school board based on five incidents of corporal punishment. He claimed that she violated his due process rights and the Rehabilitation Act by abusing him in class, and he pointed to her suspension and later conviction on one count of child abuse. But the court found four of the incidents were related to the student's refusal to go to a "cool-down room" or his calling the teacher names or threatening her. The fifth incident involved her tripping him, which was not corporal punishment. In each case of corporal punishment, **the teacher used restraint on the student only until he calmed down or agreed to comply with her instructions.** *T.W. v. School Board of Seminole County, Florida*, 610 F.3d 588 (11th Cir. 2010).

◆   A Minnesota student's IEP team determined she was ineligible for extended school year services, but it provided curb-to-curb transportation and an aide for one summer. The next summer, it required the student to use general education transportation without an aide. A driver sexually abused her, and the parents sued the school district for violating Section 504. A federal district court and the Eighth Circuit held for the district, as **discontinuation of the aide and abuse by the driver did not amount to discrimination. The district did not act with bad faith or gross misjudgment.** School officials had followed the IEP, which stated that the student was ineligible for ESY and related services. *M.Y. v. Special School Dist. No. 1*, 544 F.3d 885 (8th Cir. 2008).

# CHAPTER SEVEN

## Employment Practices

## I. EMPLOYEE PRIVACY

*In O'Connor v. Ortega, 480 U.S. 709 (1987), the Supreme Court held public employees have a reasonable expectation of privacy in their workspaces, desks and file cabinets. Courts reviewing public employee privacy cases balance legitimate personal interests against the government interest in supervision, control and workplace efficiency. In* City of Ontario, California v. Quon, *below, the Supreme Court held a California police department did not violate an officer's privacy rights by reviewing text messages on his department-owned pager. In so ruling, the Court held* **cases applying to government searches of employee offices, including O'Connor, applied in the electronic sphere**.

◆ A California police department informed employees that they had "no expectation of privacy or confidentiality when using" department-owned pagers capable of sending and receiving text messages. An officer's monthly pager usage soon exceeded his text message character allotment under the department's contract with the pager service. To find out why, a supervisor investigated. He found many messages on the officer's pager were not work-related and some were sexually explicit. The officer sued the department for Fourth Amendment violations. The U.S. Supreme Court agreed to review the case and noted that a public employer's search was reasonable if justified at its inception and not excessively intrusive in light of the reasons for the search.

The search in this case was justified at its inception, as there were reasonable grounds for investigating pager use. The supervisor ordered the search to see if the character limit on pagers was sufficient for department needs. As this was a legitimate, work-related reason, the Court found no Fourth Amendment violation. Review of the text messages was not excessively intrusive. Supervisors took care to investigate only pager usage that took place during work hours. The officer and others had received no assurances of privacy and had limited privacy expectations. **The text-message search did not violate the officer's rights or the rights of those with whom he communicated.** The Court noted "the judiciary risks error by elaborating too fully on the Fourth Amendment implications of emerging technology before its role in society has become clear." *City of Ontario, California v. Quon*, 130 S.Ct. 2619 (U.S. 2010).

## A. Employee Search and Seizure

*Searches and seizures conducted by school authorities implicate the Fourth Amendment. Because these searches are not carried out to enforce criminal laws, the courts consider them "administrative searches," which may be justified by the need to protect student safety and ensure order in schools.*

### 1. Drug Testing

◆ A Texas teacher claimed her principal took her to a drug-testing facility because he believed she was under the influence of an illegal substance. Testing reflected no substance use, and she filed an incident report with the local police concerning the principal. After the incident, the teacher claimed the principal humiliated her in front of students and colleagues, placed her on a performance improvement plan and reprimanded her for no reason. When the district superintendent notified the teacher that her contract would not be renewed, she filed a grievance against the district. She later filed a lawsuit against the district, principal and other officials. A federal district court held the school officials were entitled to immunity for the teacher's state law false imprisonment claim. This was because she was also asserting the claim against the school district itself. Immunity applied to claims against the school district for punitive or exemplary damages. **A school district could only be liable for civil rights violations based on actions for which it was actually responsible.** The teacher claimed that an official district policy or custom was the moving force in the violation of her federally protected rights. If her claims were true, the teacher raised a valid question of her right to relief. As a result, the court denied the district's motion to dismiss the federal claims. *Catlett v. Duncanville Independent School Dist.*, No. 3:09-CV1245-K, 2010 WL 2217889 (N.D. Tex. 5/27/10).

◆   A West Virginia school board implemented a random, suspicionless drug-testing policy on employees in 47 "safety-sensitive positions," including teachers, coaches, cabinetmakers, handymen, plumbers and the district superintendent. Teachers and their employees' association sought to prevent implementation of the policy. A 19-year veteran teacher testified that he never witnessed a school employee coming to work in an impaired state. And the district superintendent admitted there had been no instances of any student injuries due to a drug- or alcohol-impaired teacher. A federal court found drug testing is a "seizure" under the Fourth Amendment. When a state agency conducts a search, there must ordinarily be individualized suspicion of wrongdoing. The U.S. Supreme Court has found that special safety needs outweigh employee privacy interests where there are major safety concerns such as a risk of great harm to people and property. But **the teachers and other school employees in this case did not have a reduced privacy interest by virtue of their public employment**. They were not in "safety-sensitive" positions. The risk of harm stated by the board was speculative and it did not outweigh the employees' privacy interests. The court issued a preliminary order preventing implementation of the policy. *American Federation of Teachers - West Virginia, AFL-CIO v. Kanawha County Board of Educ.*, 592 F.Supp.2d 883 (S.D. W.Va. 2009).

◆   A Kentucky school district randomly tested 25% of its employees in "safety-sensitive" positions, including teachers. A tenured teacher with 14 years of experience in district schools sued the district in a federal court, arguing the policy violated the Fourth Amendment and the Americans with Disabilities Act (ADA). The court noted that state law required teachers to submit to certain duties, responsibilities and licensing requirements. Those entering the profession understand it is heavily regulated and have a reduced expectation of privacy in comparison with others. Here, the Kentucky district was in a location experiencing extensive drug problems. Given the high concentration of drugs in the area, it was reasonable to assume drug use was an imminent threat to students and faculty. **Random testing would significantly enhance the board's ability to ensure teachers remained drug free.** The court held drug testing was not a "medical examination" under the ADA. The court denied the teacher's request for injunctive relief. *Crager v. Board of Educ. of Knott County*, 313 F.Supp.2d 690 (E.D. Ky. 2004).

### 2.  Individualized Searches

*The special need of public employers to protect the public safety allows them to avoid the Fourth Amendment warrant and probable cause requirement. In O'Connor v. Ortega, 480 U.S. 709 (1987), the Supreme Court held the search of a public employee's office was reasonable when the measures adopted were reasonably related to the objectives of the search and not excessively intrusive.*

◆   A Massachusetts high school electronics shop teacher admitted to police investigators that he let students leave pornographic materials in a drop folder on his computer. He also admitted storing copyrighted movies and computer viruses on his computer, along with a collection of porn. The teacher told police that he "could not guarantee there were not any child pornographic images stored in electronic format within his computer." A detective executed a search warrant and found files on the teacher's computer with pirated movies, hacking tools and child pornography. The teacher appealed a conviction for possessing child pornography to the Supreme Judicial Court of Massachusetts. The court held the seizure was reasonable. Computer files can easily be destroyed and the school search was less intrusive than searching the teacher's home for evidence. He had no reasonable expectation of privacy in the computer's open share files, which were accessible to all network users. **There was no probable cause to search the teacher's private computer files** based on items found on an unauthorized computer that a student had connected to the school computer network. The fact that pirated movies had been passed from the student's computer to his did not suggest the teacher's private files had child pornography. The court reversed the conviction. *Comwlth. v. Kaupp*, 453 Mass. 102, 899 N.E.2d 809 (Mass. 2009).

◆ Maryland law officers charged a 26-year-old teacher with sex crimes after a 17-year-old student at his high school reported their sexually oriented text, telephone and instant message communications. The teacher had emailed the student sexually explicit pictures of himself. She came to his classroom, where he exposed his penis to her. A few weeks later, the student reported the teacher's conduct, and police persuaded her to place a one-party consent call to him. In the course of the call, the teacher admitted exposing himself. Police then obtained a search warrant for his residence, vehicle, cell phone and computers. A state court denied his motion to suppress evidence found through the warrant. A jury found him guilty of sexual abuse of a minor, indecent exposure and telephone misuse. The teacher appealed to the Court of Special Appeals of Maryland, which held that **the search warrant application identified reasonable grounds to believe that evidence of crime could be found in his house**. Enough evidence was present to reasonably infer that the teacher used home computers to communicate with students and that this evidence remained in the house. As a result, the court affirmed the judgment. *Ellis v. State of Maryland*, 185 Md.App. 522, 971 A.2d 379 (Md. Ct. Spec. App. 2009).

◆ A longtime New York teacher was found guilty of having an inappropriate relationship with a female student in 1990. In 1998, he was accused of sexually harassing a student, and was later arrested for stalking the student from the 1990 incident. The district suspended the teacher without pay and reassigned him to an administrative job. He was instructed to remove his personal belongings from his classroom so it could be used by another teacher. Administrators and custodians cleaned out the classroom. When the teacher came to retrieve his property, he claimed some items were missing, including tests, quizzes and other teaching materials. He sued the district for constitutional rights violations. The case reached the Second Circuit, which ruled for the district. Many persons had access to the classroom, and the teacher acknowledged that his property was commingled with school materials. **His suspension greatly reduced, if not eliminated, any reasonable expectation of workplace privacy he might have had,** and the district's demand that he remove personal items put him on notice that he had no remaining expectation of privacy in the classroom. Further, tests, quizzes and homework problems stored in the classroom and file cabinet were the district's property. *Shaul v. Cherry Valley Springfield Cent. School Dist.*, 363 F.3d 177 (2d Cir. 2004).

### 3. Employee Examinations

◆   Students, parents and colleagues complained that a Connecticut teacher used foul language, made sexual remarks to students, yelled and "breached school security." The district placed him on paid administrative leave, pending an investigation. The board later found that the teacher violated its standards of conduct, but could return to work under a remediation plan that included an independent psychiatric evaluation and the release of unrestricted medical records from 13 years earlier. Instead, the teacher obtained three medical and psychiatric opinions stating he was able to return to work. He sued the board for a court order allowing his return. A federal court held for the school board. After the teacher agreed to an examination by a board psychiatrist and released his medical records to the psychiatrist, but not to the board, he returned to his job. He nevertheless appealed, and the Second Circuit held that **a person's psychiatric health data and substance abuse history is intimate information protected by a right of confidentiality.** The teacher had a protected privacy right in his medical records and did not have to disclose them without sufficient justification. The board's demand for medical records was arbitrary. The court remanded the case for a determination of whether his substantive due process rights were violated. *O'Connor v. Pierson*, 426 F.3d 197 (2d Cir. 2005).

◆   A Florida assistant middle school principal became involved in a loud and angry dispute with a uniformed school resource officer in front of students. He was suspended and later discharged after protesting a reprimand by the school board. The board required him to undergo a psychological examination. The assistant principal claimed race and disability discrimination, speech rights violations and retaliation by his school board. He commenced a federal discrimination lawsuit. **A federal district court found the examination was job-related and necessary and was not a violation of federal disability law.** Moreover, the assistant principal did not establish a claim because he did not suffer an "injury-in fact," which is required to recover monetary damages in any lawsuit. The Eleventh Circuit affirmed the judgment for the school board. *Mickens v. Polk County School Board*, 195 Fed.Appx. 928 (11th Cir. 2006).

### B. Technology and Surveillance

*Louisiana law requires each public school to have policies requiring that all employee electronic communications regarding educational services to students enrolled at their schools use a means provided (or made available) by the school system. Employees cannot use school systems to electronically communicate with students for a purpose unrelated to education. This includes voice and text communications and refers to Internet-based social networks.*

◆   Parents of severely disabled Illinois students claimed a special education teacher and classroom aide verbally and physically abused their children. They claimed their children were screamed at, degraded, force-fed, pushed, slapped and abandoned in a time-out room or a lavatory. An investigation forced the resignation of the teacher and aide, but the parents raised new concerns. To help prevent future abuse incidents, the school board proposed installing security cameras with both audio and video in classrooms. A group of special education teachers sued the board under the Illinois Eavesdropping Act and the Fourth Amendment. A federal district court held a "search" occurs under the Fourth Amendment when an expectation of privacy that society would consider reasonable is infringed upon. Teachers had no reasonable expectation of privacy in a classroom, and the court found nothing private about the communications taking place there. It held instead that a **"classroom in a public school is not the private property of any teacher,"** and held for the board. *Plock v. Board of Educ. of Freeport School Dist. No. 145*, 545 F.Supp.2d 755 (N.D. Ill. 2007).

After the federal case was dismissed, a state court held the audio-taping of classrooms violated the Illinois Eavesdropping Act. On appeal, the Appellate Court of Illinois held "eavesdropping" occurred when a person knowingly and intentionally used a device to hear or record a conversation, or when a conversation was intercepted, retained or transcribed without the consent of all parties. A "conversation" was defined as "any oral communication between two or more persons." This definition applied regardless of whether one or more of the parties intended a communication to be "private under circumstances justifying that expectation." The court found this broad language defeated the board's claim that teaching did not constitute a "conversation" as defined in the Act. **As the Act defined "conversation" to include any oral communication, the trial court had ruled correctly for the teachers.** *Plock v. Board of Educ. of Freeport School Dist. No. 145*, 920 N.E.2d 1087 (Ill. App. Ct. 2009).

◆   A New Mexico assistant principal's wife installed a recording device on her home phone. She recorded a graphic, sexual conversation between her husband and his secretary. The school district obtained the tape, then non-renewed the assistant principal's contract, offering him a teaching job instead. He accepted an administrative job in another New Mexico school district, then sued his former school district's board, superintendent and other officials for defamation and violations of federal law. A court held for the board and officials, and the assistant principal appealed to the U.S. Court of Appeals, Tenth Circuit. He asserted a liberty interest that was violated by use of an illegally obtained recording of his phone conversation. However, the assistant principal's employment was not terminated. **His one-year contract was fulfilled, and he found a better paying job in another school district. This defeated a claim that his opportunities were foreclosed.** The court affirmed the judgment. *Castillo v. Hobbs Municipal School Board*, 315 Fed.Appx. 693 (10th Cir. 2009).

◆   A Connecticut principal had a history of conflict with her superintendent. When she returned from a medical leave, she learned that he had used her computer, accessed her email and sent a copy of a letter from her attorney to his own email inbox. The principal sued the superintendent for speech and privacy rights violations. In pre-trial activity, the court noted that while email carried risks of unauthorized disclosure, **confidential information may generally be communicated through un-encrypted email with a reasonable expectation of confidentiality and privacy**. The school district's acceptable use policy (AUP) notified system users of a "limited privacy expectation in the contents of their personal files on the district system."

AUP language prohibited users from unauthorized access to the system, including logging onto another person's account or using an open account to access another person's files. This prompted the court to find that the principal had a reasonable expectation of privacy in her work emails. The superintendent's use of the principal's email did not appear to be the type of "routine monitoring" permitted by the AUP. As a result, since his conduct was not objectively reasonable, he would not enjoy immunity in further proceedings. *Brown-Criscuolo v. Wolfe*, 601 F.Supp.2d 441 (D. Conn. 2009).

◆  A California teacher submitted a workers' compensation claim for a back injury. She underwent disc replacement surgery and was married while still on disability leave. The School Insurance Program for Employees (SIPE) and the teacher's school district hired an investigator to surreptitiously attend her wedding and obtain videotape of her. The investigator went to the wedding and represented himself as a guest. He videotaped the ceremony and the reception. The day after the wedding, the investigator videotaped the teacher and her husband while they sunbathed on the balcony of a rented room. The teacher sued the school district, SIPE and others for invasion of privacy and negligence. The court dismissed the case, and the teacher appealed.

The Court of Appeal of California rejected the teacher's claim that SIPE and her district "intended to harass her," not to conduct an investigation or disciplinary action. The investigation was part of a judicial or administrative proceeding that was "cloaked in immunity" because it was an essential step to an administrative proceeding. For this reason, **the district and SIPE were entitled to immunity** and there was no liability for either agency under the Government Code. The court also ruled against the teacher on her claims for invasion of privacy. The conduct of the district and SIPE was within the scope of Government Code immunity. *Richardson-Tunnell v. School Insurance Program for Employees (SIPE)*, 157 Cal.App.4th 1065, 69 Cal.Rptr.3d 176 (Cal. Ct. App. 2007).

◆  A 2006 Michigan law required the state education department to use all available technology to compare registered educational personnel with conviction records maintained by the state police department. The education department attempted a database comparison before the law went into effect. A state official sent a letter to local school officials identifying teachers with criminal convictions. The letter said that teachers having a "listed offense" must be dismissed. The state official later stated that it was expected that the comparison would result in some "false hits" because some data fields, such as social security numbers, might match. The Michigan Education Association (MEA) claimed the department was releasing inaccurate criminal history records, and it sued state officials to prohibit the release of information.

The court issued an order for the MEA that would prevent the department from releasing the comparison data to local school officials. Despite the order, the state distributed lists of convicted teachers to local officials. A teacher who was an MEA member sued, asserting a host of negligence claims on behalf of all certified teachers with criminal convictions. The case reached the Michigan Court of Appeals, which held the state governmental tort liability act conferred immunity on state officials acting within the scope of their authority. **The officials were attempting to comply with school safety legislation.** *Frohriep v. Flanagan*, 275 Mich.App. 456, 739 N.W.2d 645 (Mich. Ct. App. 2007).

On review, the Supreme Court of Michigan held a chief academic officer and supervisor of client services did not qualify for immunity, reversing part of the appellate decision. *Frohriep v. Flanagan*, 480 Mich. 962 (Mich. 2007).

◆ A California school resource specialist notified supervisors of her suspicion that a school custodian was using a computer after hours. Without informing the specialist and another employee who used the computer office, supervisors began after-hours surveillance of the office with a hidden video camera and VCR. Surveillance continued even after the custodian was videotaped using a computer. The computer employees sued the school district for invasion of privacy. A state trial court found the surveillance was reasonable and furthered district goals. On appeal, the Court of Appeal of California observed that the employees had a reasonable expectation of privacy in the computer office. But the intrusion on privacy was not highly offensive. Surveillance occurred after school hours, when the only person expected to be present was the custodian. The videotaping was confined to the area where misconduct was occurring and did not include audio surveillance. **The district had a strong, legitimate reason for conducting surveillance.** While the better practice would have been for the school district to notify the computer employees about the surveillance, their privacy rights were not absolute. *Crist v. Alpine Union School Dist.*, No. D044775, 2005 WL 2362729 (Cal. Ct. App. 2005).

## C. Personnel Records

*State data privacy acts protect the confidentiality of public employee personnel files. Common law rules of defamation may also provide a basis for legal action against a school district or its officers for wrongful disclosure of private facts or erroneous factual statements. For additional cases involving open meeting laws, see Chapter Fourteen, Section IV.C. of this volume.*

### 1. Media Access

◆ An Illinois resident asked for a copy of a school district superintendent's employment contract under the state Freedom of Information Act (FOIA). A school district record-keeper denied the request on the grounds that the contract was part of the superintendent's personnel file. The resident sued in an Illinois circuit court, which held that employment contracts found in personnel files were "per se" exempt from disclosure under the FOIA. On appeal, the Supreme Court of Illinois explained that the FOIA intends to open governmental records to public scrutiny. A superintendent's contract was a "public record" under the

FOIA, but an exemption existed protecting "information, that if disclosed, would constitute a clearly unwarranted invasion of personal privacy." The court found that the district was incorrect in asserting that the superintendent's contract was *per se* exempt from disclosure. Since any employment contract contained terms and conditions of employment, "by its very nature, **the superintendent's employment contract, as a whole, constitutes 'information that bears on his public duties.'"** Accordingly, the superintendent's contract had to be disclosed. Placement of a contract of employment within a personnel file did not insulate it from public disclosure. *Stern v. Wheaton-Warrenville Community Unit School Dist. 200*, 233 Ill.2d 396, 910 N.E.2d 85 (Ill. 2009).

◆   A Pennsylvania court granted a preliminary order prohibiting the public release of school employee home addresses. While the state Open Records Law did not specifically exempt employee home addresses from public release, the court relied on a state constitutional right of privacy. Independent constitutional rights of privacy protected individuals from the disclosure of personal matters in which there was a "legitimate privacy expectation." Legitimate privacy expectations are those that society recognizes as reasonable. The court found **it is generally accepted that persons have privacy interests in their home addresses**. It added that "disclosure of personal information, such as home addresses, reveals little, if anything about the workings of government." *Pennsylvania State Educ. Ass'n v. Wilson*, 981 A.2d 383 (Pa. Commw. Ct. 2009).

◆   An Alabama teacher could not appeal an adverse Open Records Act ruling after a state circuit court held that **her school board had to disclose disciplinary information in her personnel file to a newspaper**. Her position that the Alabama Open Records Act did not require disclosure to the newspaper was not being contested by her school board. On appeal, the Supreme Court of Alabama found no live controversy between the teacher and board. Unless parties have conflicting interests, the case is likely to yield an advisory opinion and the controversy is academic. As there was no controversy between the teacher and board, the court vacated the judgment and dismissed the appeal. *Fenn v. Ozark City Schools Board of Educ.*, 9 So.3d 484 (Ala. 2008).

◆   A Wisconsin school board held a public hearing to consider discharging a teacher for viewing adult website images on his work computer. After the board voted for discharge, a Milwaukee newspaper requested access to the exhibits presented at the hearing. The teacher's union filed a grievance to challenge the discharge action. In preparation for the grievance, the district assembled the images viewed on his work computer and put them on a CD. The newspaper filed an Open Records Request for the CD. The teacher sought a court order prohibiting release of the requested information. He argued that the materials sought by the newspaper were off limits as part of a current investigation and because they had copyrighted images. The court noted that the Open Records Law has a presumption of complete public access that is overcome only in exceptional cases. An exception exists for "materials to which access is limited by copyright."
  The newspaper claimed that the teacher could not raise the copyright

objection, since he did not own the copyrights. The Supreme Court of Wisconsin held that the teacher could assert the copyright exception. But the board's release of the memorandum and CD was a "fair use" of the copyrighted materials, and the records could be disclosed. **The state's "presumption of complete public access" to records outweighed the teacher's privacy and reputation interests.** *Cedarburg Educ. Ass'n v. Cedarburg School Dist.*, 300 Wis.2d 290, 731 N.W.2d 240 (Wis. 2007).

◆  A newspaper asked three Washington school districts for copies of records relating to teacher sexual misconduct in the prior 10 years. The districts notified 55 current and former teachers that their records had been gathered. Thirty-seven of the teachers asserted that the disclosure of records identifying them as subjects of sexual misconduct violated their privacy rights. A state court ordered the districts to disclose the identities of all the teachers whose misconduct was substantiated, or had resulted in some discipline, and where a district's investigation was inadequate. The court held that 15 teachers could claim exemption from disclosure of their names, but the 22 others could not. "Letters of direction" to the teachers did not have to be disclosed.

On appeal, the Supreme Court of Washington explained that allegations of sexual misconduct by a teacher were "personal information" under the state's Public Records Act (PRA). **Disclosing a public school teacher's identity for an unsubstantiated sexual misconduct allegation was a violation of privacy rights under the PRA.** On the other hand, no privacy rights were violated when complaints about specific misconduct were substantiated after an investigation. Letters of direction had criticisms and observations of teachers and thus constituted personal information. They could not be released to the public if they simply guided future conduct and did not identify incidents of substantiated misconduct. The court ruled that a teacher's identity should be released only when an allegation of sexual misconduct was substantiated or when the misconduct resulted in discipline. *Bellevue John Does 1-11 v. Bellevue School Dist. #405*, 189 P.3d 139 (Wash. 2008).

◆  A New York City principal was notified that she would have to improve her unsatisfactory performance to gain tenure and keep her job. She negotiated an agreement by which she received a satisfactory employment review and gained tenure. In return, she retired from the New York City Department of Education (DOE) and agreed not to seek future employment there. Within two weeks, the DOE issued a press release announcing the removal of 45 DOE principals. After being served with a state Freedom of Information Law (FOIL) request by the media, the DOE released the names of the principals. Various newspapers then published articles naming the principal as one of the removed principals. She claimed the articles portrayed her in an unflattering light and "made finding new employment impossible." She sued the DOE for depriving her of a liberty interest in her reputation, alleging the DOE was "complicit in the media's publication." The court rejected her claim. Nothing indicated that the DOE was involved with the publication of the unflattering articles. The DOE press release communicated on matters of public concern, and the DOE made no stigmatizing comments. **It did not damage the reputation of any principal**

**and provided names to the media as required under the state FOIL.** *Jones v. Dep't of Educ.*, No. 05-cv-3075, 2008 WL 3836122 (E.D.N.Y. 8/13/08).

◆ A Maine school committee went into executive session to discuss the handling of a budget shortfall by senior staff members. Some notes were taken, and the superintendent wrote a memorandum presenting her management philosophy. A newspaper publisher sought all notes, minutes, transcripts or other documents reflecting discussions during the closed session. The school committee denied the publisher's request under the state Freedom of Access Act (FOAA), and the publisher sued to obtain the records. The case reached the Supreme Judicial Court of Maine, which noted that the FOAA allows executive sessions in employment-related cases, such as assignments, duties, promotions, demotions, evaluations and discipline. **An executive session may be held only if public discussion could be reasonably expected to cause damage to an individual's reputation or rights to privacy.** In this case, the finance questions raised in the meeting were limited, and the school attorney said they should not be answered. The court found the executive session did not violate the FOAA, and the documents and notes used there were not public records. *Blethen Maine Newspapers v. Portland School Committee*, 947 A.2d 479 (Me. 2008).

◆ The Supreme Court of South Carolina held that a school board violated the Freedom of Information Act (FOIA) by refusing to provide information sought by a publisher during the selection process for a superintendent. The publisher sought all materials gathered by the district "relating to not fewer than the final three applicants under consideration," as permitted by the FOIA. But the board released information on only two finalists, citing privacy concerns. The court rejected the claim that state law mandated the disclosure of material only for "final applicants," even if this was less than three persons. **FOIA' language was not subject to limitation by a district seeking to avoid disclosure** by naming less than three "finalists." *New York Times Co. v. Spartanburg County School Dist. No. 7*, 374 S.C. 307, 649 S.E.2d 28 (S.C. 2007).

◆ A Montana newspaper sought documents relating to employee disciplinary actions under the "right to know" provisions of the Montana Constitution and state law. A state court held that the employees had no reasonable expectation of privacy in their conduct as public employees and that any interest was exceeded by the interest in disclosure. The employees appealed, and the Supreme Court of Montana dismissed the appeal as premature. The trial court then dissolved the stay and ordered the district to release designated documents to the newspaper. The district released the documents, and the teachers appealed to the supreme court a second time. They did not request a stay and the documents were released to the newspaper, which published them. **The supreme court refused to consider the teachers' claim that they had reasonable expectations of privacy in the documents. The issue was moot in view of the publication of the documents by the newspaper.** *In re Petition of Billings High School Dist. No. 2*, 335 Mont. 94, 149 P.3d 565 (Mont. 2006).

◆  Thirteen people complained about verbal abuse and sexual harassment by a California school superintendent. The school board hired an investigator to draft a report on the complaints. She interviewed students, parents, employees and former students, prepared summaries of the interviews and presented them to the board. The board shared copies of interview summaries with some of the complaining parties. Although they were marked "confidential," they were leaked to a newspaper. The board accepted the superintendent's resignation in return for a financial settlement and a promise to keep the report confidential.

The report exonerated him of all serious misconduct, but 40 tort claims were filed regarding his conduct. The public and media demanded release of the report and related documents. In a case that reached the state court of appeal, the court explained that state law defined "pupil records" as any information directly related to an identifiable pupil that was maintained by a school district. The Family Educational Rights and Privacy Act (FERPA) defined "education records" in nearly the same way. **The Supreme Court has held "education records" are institutional records maintained by a single custodian, not individual assignments handed in by students in separate classes.** The investigatory report in this case did not directly relate to student educational interests and was not a "pupil record" under state law. The public interest in the board's actions far outweighed the superintendent's interest in keeping them quiet. The court ordered the board to release the report, with the names of students and others blocked. *BRV, Inc. v. Superior Court*, 143 Cal.App.4th 742, 49 Cal.Rptr.3d 519 (Cal. Ct. App. 2006).

## 2.  Disclosure to Third Parties

◆  A Vermont school superintendent recommended discharging a principal during his contract term based on performance issues. After a public hearing, the school board decided to retain the principal but also voted to investigate his job performance. Several months later, the superintendent assigned the principal a poor performance evaluation and again recommended discharge. This time, the board met in executive session with the principal and superintendent. After the principal refused to resign, the board placed him on paid administrative leave. At a later school board meeting, many citizens turned out to speak on his behalf. Instead of revealing the reasons for the decision, board members explained the decision was based on performance and a prior investigation. After a hearing, the board voted against renewing the principal's contract. He sued the board for due process and contract violations, race discrimination and defamation. The court held for the board, and the principal appealed. The Supreme Court of Vermont affirmed. **A decision not to rehire a non-tenured employee does not implicate a protected interest.** Evidence supported the trial court's findings that the principal was not stigmatized by the board action. He showed only vague allegations by board members about his unspecified incompetence. *Herrera v. Union No. 39 School Dist.*, 975 A.2d 619 (Vt. 2009).

◆  The Michigan Federation of Teachers submitted a Freedom of Information Act (FOIA) request to the University of Michigan (UM) for employee names, home addresses, home phone numbers, job titles, pay rates, and work contact information. The UM provided most of the information, including home addresses and phone numbers for about 21,000 employees who had given permission to publish this information in a staff and faculty directory. As for the remaining 16,406 employees, the UM denied the request on privacy grounds.

The Federation sued the UM, seeking the remaining addresses and phone numbers. The court held employee home addresses and phone numbers were personal information and not likely to contribute to the public's understanding of how the government works. The case reached the Supreme Court of Michigan, which explained that **public entities may refuse to disclose a public record, if the record includes information of a personal nature and disclosure "would constitute a clearly unwarranted invasion of an individual's privacy."** Disclosure of home addresses and phone numbers could subject employees to potential abuse, and place some in danger if the information fell into the wrong hands. Disclosure would reveal little or nothing about the conduct of the university and would do nothing to advance the public policy behind the FOIA. *Michigan Federation of Teachers and School Related Personnel v. Univ. of Michigan*, 481 Mich. 657, 753 N.W.2d 28 (Mich. 2008).

◆  A New Jersey school employee suffered a concussive brain injury after a speaker fell off a wall and struck him on the head. He began having "profound, incapacitating fatigue" and difficulty with concentration and memory. An incident report describing his injury was accidentally stuffed into an envelope with another teacher's contract. Later, the employee walked into a meeting and found some teachers laughing. One of them joked that he had gotten the results of the employee's CAT scan and said "and as we all knew, there was nothing there." The employee sued the school board, asserting that it had failed to accommodate his disability and unlawfully disclosed medical information. The case reached the Third Circuit, which stated that the employee was not protected by the Americans with Disabilities Act because his impairment was not substantially limiting. And although **medical information is entitled to privacy protection against disclosure, the Due Process Clause was not implicated by an official causing an accidental disclosure of data**. The CAT scan joke did not create a constitutional violation. The comment did not reveal anything about the employee's medical condition. *Weisberg v. Riverside Township Board of Educ.*, 180 Fed.Appx. 357 (3d Cir. 2006).

◆  A Texas school district received a request for all records on a teacher. It provided some documents but withheld others, including one memorializing a meeting with the principal. The district sought a ruling from the state attorney general, who found the memorandum was not a "document evaluating the performance of a teacher" and thus not "confidential" under the state Public Information Act. The district then asked for the opinion of a state court, which found the memorandum was confidential and exempt from disclosure. The case reached the Court of Appeals of Texas. It held that to withhold information under the Public Information Act, the government must show the requested information is either not subject to the Act or is exempt under one of the Act's exceptions. **Teacher evaluations are exempt from public disclosure under Section 21.355 of the act.** The memorandum touched on performance issues discussed at the meeting. It gave the teacher corrective direction and referred her to school policies. The court held the memorandum "evaluated" the teacher because it reflected the principal's judgment, gave her correction and provided for further review. The judgment for the school district was affirmed. *Abbott v. North East Independent School Dist.*, 212 S.W.3d 364 (Tex. Ct. App. 2006).

## 3.  Electronic Communications

*Courts in Arizona, Arkansas, Colorado, Florida, Idaho, Ohio, Tennessee, Washington and Michigan have found the contents of public employees' personal emails are not public records. A Florida court held that although digital in nature, "there was little to distinguish a personal email from personal letters delivered to public employees through a government post office box and stored in a government-owned desk."* Times Publishing Co. v. City of Clearwater, *830 So.2d 844 (Fla. Dist. Ct. App. 2002).*

◆  A Wisconsin taxpayer sought the contents of all emails sent by teachers on school computers over 13 months to see if anyone was violating school district policy. After the district advised teachers it intended to reveal their emails to the requester – without regard to content – the teachers filed a state court action to block the disclosure. A state circuit court held the personal emails sent on the school district system were "records" under the Wisconsin Public Records Law. Appeal reached the Supreme Court of Wisconsin, which noted the district's Internet use policy permitted employees to make occasional personal use of their school email accounts. **The court found no other state court has held that personal emails should be released to members of the public.**

To be a "record" under the Public Records Law that was available for public inspection, the court held the content of the document must have a connection to a government function. The court found the personal emails in this case had no such connection and were not "records" under the Public Records Law. Personal emails were not "records" simply by virtue of being sent or received on government email and computer systems. Flexible workplace policies allowing occasional personal email use were "in line with the mainstream of professional practice." Agreeing with the teachers, the court held that the public disclosure of their personal email was neither a proper nor intended effect of the law. *Schill v. Wisconsin Rapids School Dist.*, 786 N.W.2d 177 (Wis. 2010).

◆  During heated collective bargaining negotiations reported by the media, a Michigan individual sought all emails sent to and from three teachers who also served as officers for the local education association. The teachers and their unions sued to block the district from complying with the request for emails. A state court held emails generated through the school's email system and retained or stored by the district were public records under the state Freedom of Information Act (FOIA). The Court of Appeals of Michigan held that under the FOIA, a "public record" is a "writing prepared, owned, used, in the possession of, or retained by a public body in the performance of an official function."

But the court explained that "mere possession of a record by a public body does not render the record a public document." Emails have to be stored or retained by the school in performance of an official function to come within the FOIA's definition of "public record." The personal emails in this case had nothing to do with school operations. Retention of emails by the school system was a "blanket saving of all information" that did not distinguish among personal and official purposes. The email system backup was not an "official function" which made all emails public records. As union communications by the teachers did not concern their official capacities as public employees, the court held **the union-related emails were not "public records" under the FOIA**. *Howell Educ. Ass'n MEA/NEA v. Howell Board of Educ.*, 287 Mich.App. 228 (Mich. Ct. App. 2010).

◆   A Florida high school teacher was suspended for exchanging emails and instant messages with students that were sexually explicit and made derogatory comments about staff members and school operations. An administrative law judge allowed a board expert to inspect the hard drives of the teacher's home computers to discover if they had relevant data for use in a formal termination hearing. The teacher appealed, arguing that production of the home computer records would violate his Fifth Amendment right against self-incrimination and his privacy rights. The court agreed with the teacher that the request for wholesale access to his personal computers would expose confidential communications and extraneous personal information such as banking records. There might also be privileged communications with his wife and his attorney.

An earlier Florida decision held that **a request to examine a computer hard drive was permitted "in only limited or strictly controlled circumstances," such as where a party was suspected of trying to purge data**. Other courts had permitted access to a computer when there was evidence of intentional deletion of data. There was no evidence that the teacher was attempting to thwart the production of evidence in this case. The broad discovery request violated the teacher's Fifth Amendment rights and his personal privacy, as well as the privacy of his family. The court reversed the order allowing unlimited access to the teacher's home computers. *Menke v. Broward County School Board*, 916 So.2d 8 (Fla. Dist. Ct. App. 2005).

◆   A Tennessee citizen sought to view and inspect a county education board's digital records of Internet activity, including emails sent and received, websites visited, and the identity of Internet service providers conducted during school hours or stored on school-owned computers. A judge reviewed the requested records privately, and found they were not accessible under the state Public Records Act (PRA). The citizen appealed to the Court of Appeals of Tennessee, asserting that the digital records or documents were open to public inspection because they had been made during business hours or were stored on the school's computers. The court found the PRA favored disclosing public records, including documents, papers, electronic data processing files and other material "made or received pursuant to law or ordinance or in connection with the transaction of official business by any governmental agency."

**The PRA did not limit access to records based on the time a record was created or the place the record was produced or stored.** The citizen's argument that the material he sought was produced during business hours and on school-owned computers was not relevant. The trial judge properly inspected documents in private to decide if they were "made or received pursuant to law or ordinance or in connection with the transaction of official business." Placement of a document in a public employee's file did not make it a "public record." The judgment was affirmed. *Brennan v. Giles County Board of Educ.*, No. M2004-00998-COA-R3-CV, 2005 WL 1996625 (Tenn. Ct. App. 2005).

## II.  EMPLOYEE QUALIFICATIONS

### A.  Certification and Licensure

*In* Morrison v. State Board of Educ., *1 Cal.3d 214, 82 Cal.Rptr. 175, 461 P.2d 375 (1969), the California Supreme Court found "before any act could be deemed a ground for discharge, it must bear directly on the teacher's fitness to teach and must cause a clearly discernible detriment to the school and to its students." Michigan and California courts relied on* Morrison *in recent cases involving teacher misconduct off school grounds. Arizona and Pennsylvania courts have upheld decisions to revoke professional licenses based on misconduct that relates to a teacher's fitness to teach, even for misconduct that did not result in a conviction or that occurred off campus.*

◆   A California teacher was subject to suspension of her teaching credential after her third DUI conviction. While the third incident resulted in a 30-day jail sentence, the court allowed her to fulfill the time at home and at work in the classroom by wearing an ankle bracelet. She was placed on probation and ordered to participate in an alcohol education program. Two years later, the California Commission on Teacher Credentialing found cause to suspend the teacher's credential for 60 days. An administrative law judge (ALJ) held the commission did not prove unprofessional conduct and recommended dismissal of the charge. In doing so, the ALJ relied on a test for the discipline of teachers created by the state supreme court in *Morrison v. State Board of Educ.*, above.

But the commission rejected the ALJ's decision, also relying on *Morrison*. A state trial court denied the teacher's challenge, and she appealed. The Court of Appeal of California approved of the lower court's consideration of six of the seven *Morrison* factors, including the "adverse effect upon students and teachers" of the misconduct. **The court held any conduct used as a ground for the suspension of a professional license must demonstrate unfitness to practice that profession.** Statutory terms such as "immoral or unprofessional conduct" and "moral turpitude" are almost unlimited in scope. The court found the legislature did not grant the commission power to let employers dismiss employees on the basis of personal, private conduct that might be deemed objectionable. Students might observe the teacher's ankle bracelet, so it was likely her conviction had an adverse affect on them. As the lower court order was correct, it was affirmed. *Broney v. California Comm'n on Teacher Credentialing*, 184 Cal.App.4th 462, 108 Cal.Rptr.3d 832 (Cal. Ct. App. 2010).

◆   A Kentucky teacher injured her head in a bicycling accident and had post-concussive syndrome, memory and attention problems, sleep loss, depression, anxiety, irritability and outbursts of anger. She later confronted students playing basketball outside her school and a parent filed a complaint against her, stating she had threatened to kill them. After an investigation, her contract was terminated for conduct unbecoming a teacher. There was evidence of 31 other infractions. A teacher tribunal affirmed the termination action, as did the state court system. The Kentucky Education Professional Standards Board (KEPSB) then revoked the teacher's teaching certificate for 10 years. Based on the basketball incident, the teacher was also convicted of terroristic threatening.

The threatening charges were upheld by a state court, which fined the teacher $4,500 and ordered her to refrain from abusive conduct with the victims. She appealed the decision to revoke her teaching license to a state court, which held terroristic threats were reason enough for revocation. On appeal, the state court of appeals affirmed the judgment. **State law permitted the revocation, suspension or refusal to renew or issue a teaching certificate for reasons including physical or mental incapacity** preventing a teacher from performing duties with "reasonable skill, competence or safety." The KEPSB and circuit court had found the teacher lacked the capacity to safely carry out her duties. *Macy v. Kentucky Educ. Professional Standards Board*, Nos. 2008-CA-002234-MR, 2008-CA-002293-MR, 2010 WL 743668 (Ky. Ct. App. 3/5/10).

◆   An Arkansas teacher pleaded no contest to a charge of misappropriation of about $36,000 from a county conservation district. She was ordered to repay the money and serve a 60-month probationary term. The Arkansas State Board of Education then denied the teacher's request to obtain licensure. Two years after the conviction, the court expunged (erased) the offense from her record. The teacher again sought certification, and the board again denied her request for a waiver that would allow her to obtain it. She petitioned a state court for review, but the court affirmed the decision. The state court of appeals found that under Section 6-17-410 of the Arkansas Code, an "individual's underlying conduct shall be deemed as a matter of law never to have occurred" when an offense is expunged. An individual may also state that no such conduct ever occurred.

While the teacher claimed the statute prevented the board from considering the offense, the court disagreed. **A state licensure and renewal law prohibited licensure of a person who has a report in the Child Maltreatment Central Registry or has pled guilty (or no contest) to, or has been found guilty of offenses including felony theft.** It appeared to the court that the state General Assembly intended to make ineligible for licensure those whose records were expunged. There was no abuse in the board's decision to deny the teacher licensure or to deny a request for a waiver. *Landers v. Arkansas Dep't of Educ.*, 2010 Ark.App. 312 (Ark. Ct. App. 2010).

◆   A Florida teacher attempted suicide at her school. The state commissioner of education brought a complaint against her, and she asked for a hearing after sanctions were sought against her teacher's certificate. An administrative law judge (ALJ) found insufficient evidence to show others were present at the time of the suicide attempt. Although the school superintendent asked that the ALJ order the teacher to participate in a recovery network program for counseling, the request was rejected. Instead, the ALJ found the teacher guilty of misconduct and recommended a reprimand and two years of probation. A final order required her to enter counseling. A Florida district court of appeal agreed with the teacher that the reasons for modifying the ALJ's order were not stated. It returned the case to the education practices commission for review and to complete the record by stating the particular reasons for the modification and decide if the penalty was warranted. **Failure by the commission to state its reasons for modifying the ALJ order was a fundamental error and a due process violation.** *Withers v. Blomberg*, 41 So.3d 398 (Fla. Dist. Ct. App. 2010).

◆ A Texas teaching intern had a one-year probationary contract as part of a program that required a favorable principal evaluation and a continued offer of employment in order for her to obtain alternative certification. But the principal recommended that she repeat her internship and be assigned to another school district. It was recommended that certification be denied and that the intern repeat her internship. After filing unsuccessful grievances, she appealed to the state commissioner of education. The commissioner ruled that he lacked the authority to review the grievances, and the intern appealed. On appeal, the state court of appeals noted state law limited the commissioner's authority to review school board decisions to actions that violated the school laws of the state or contractual provisions. The court rejected the claim that the principal's failure to recommend certification violated the school rules of Texas. It held the law did not impose a duty on the school board, principal or course provider. Nor did it confer any rights or privileges on the intern. There was no merit to the intern's breach of contract claim. **Her employment was conditioned on satisfactory participation in the certification program.** The court held the commissioner had properly dismissed the case. *McCandless v. Pasadena Independent School Dist.*, No. 03-09-00249-CV, 2010 WL 1253581 (Tex. Ct. App. 4/2/10).

◆ A Florida school board learned that teachers were obtaining college credits from "Eastern Oklahoma State College" for which no work was done. A teacher reported earning credits from this entity and used them to obtain his teacher certification. After discovering that his transcripts were fraudulent, the board suspended him and initiated employment termination proceedings. The teacher requested a hearing before the state department of administrative hearings. An administrative law judge (ALJ) recommended termination, and the school board adopted the recommendation. The teacher appealed to a Florida District Court of Appeal, claiming the board had recently suspended, rather than fired, another teacher for a similar violation. He argued the board should issue disciplinary guidelines establishing ranges of permissible punishment for school employees for specified violations and that lack of guidelines yielded inconsistent results. The court found no statutory requirement for the board to issue guidelines and affirmed the decision. **State law permitted discharge for "just cause," which included incompetency, gross insubordination, willful neglect of duty, or conviction of certain crimes.** The court affirmed the order. *Mitchell v. School Board of Miami-Dade County*, 972 So.2d 900 (Fla. Dist. Ct. App. 2007).

◆ A California school board classified teachers and counselors holding less than a regular teaching credential as "temporary employees." It voted to lay off 225 employees classified as probationary or temporary for budget reasons, and most of them pursued their hearing rights. An administrative law judge upheld the layoffs and the teachers association sued the district. A state court invalidated the policy of classifying employees solely on the basis of their certification and ordered the misclassified employees reinstated. On appeal, the state court of appeal held **employees who were qualified to teach were not "temporary employees" simply because they were not yet fully accredited**.

The court rejected the district's claim that it had the discretion to classify employees as "temporary," based on their certification status. The district had to classify as "probationary employees" teachers employed in positions requiring certification qualifications, unless they were classified as permanent employees or substitutes. **Teachers holding emergency permits and satisfying other conditions of state law could be classified as probationary employees.** Probationary employees with emergency or specialist permits accrued no credit toward permanent status. As state law required interns who were reemployed in a succeeding school year to be classified as "permanent," the court affirmed the judgment. *Bakersfield Elementary Teachers Ass'n v. Bakersfield City School Dist.*, 145 Cal.App.4th 1260, 52 Cal.Rptr.3d 486 (Cal. Ct. App. 2006).

◆ A California teacher worked for a school district for one year under a pre-intern certificate, then obtained a university intern credential. She continued teaching in a job requiring certification. After two years, she obtained a clear teaching credential. At the end of the school year, the district issued a summary performance evaluation stating the teacher met her employment objectives and was an asset to her school. But a letter dated May 27 said she would not be rehired. The teacher claimed a notice of non-reelection had to be sent by March 15. The district stated that she had only worked as a probationary employee for one year, and her employment under an internship credential did not count toward a state law consecutive two-year requirement. A state superior court ordered the district to reinstate the teacher as a permanent, certificated teacher.

The state court of appeal found **state law deems a probationary teacher reelected for the next year, if she is employed for two consecutive years** in a position requiring certification qualifications and is not given a contrary notice by March 15. The teacher was not denied probationary employee status by virtue of her final year of internship work. The court rejected the district's assertion that work under a university intern credential did not count toward the two-year tenure requirement. The teacher had finished her second complete consecutive school year of employment in a position requiring certification qualifications at the time she received the late non-reelection notice. *Peoples v. San Diego Unified School Dist.*, 41 Cal.Rptr.3d 383 (Cal. Ct. App. 2006).

◆ A Delaware school district employed a media specialist who had originally worked as a librarian. Over time, her duties came to include teaching reading and language skills to students. Eight evaluations of the specialist's classroom performance found her instructional planning and strategies unsatisfactory. District officials held post-evaluation conferences but notified her she would be discharged for incompetence and neglect of duty. After a hearing, the board discharged the specialist. She appealed to a state superior court, which found it was proper to evaluate her using a Lesson Analysis Form based on the Delaware Performance Appraisal Standards for teachers. The evaluations were properly conducted during appraisal periods. She declined opportunities to change her improvement plan and remained uncooperative while superficially complying with her plan. On appeal, the Supreme Court of Delaware affirmed the decision. It found **library functions had changed from an emphasis on cataloging to providing complementary teaching of reading and language skills**. The district required its librarians to teach, and it was reasonable to evaluate the specialist in instructional situations. *Squire v. Board of Educ. of Red Clay Consolidated School Dist.*, 911 A.2d 804 (Table) (Del. 2006).

◆   A white male saw the statement "Need to be minority," on a job intake form at an Illinois college career placement office. He complained to the state human rights department, which filed a complaint on his behalf. A placement office secretary testified that she had been directed to indicate "minority encouraged to apply" on the form. But as the office was very busy, she mistakenly indicated "Need to be minority" instead. A white female teacher was hired for the job. The applicant was not endorsed to teach music full time and was not accredited in music. He had no relevant teaching experience and had never applied for substitute work. The Appellate Court of Illinois held the person hired for the job had superior qualifications. The board showed it would not have hired the applicant in any event, because he was not qualified. **If an Illinois teacher's certificate does not contain an endorsement for a subject, the teacher is not legally qualified to teach it.** That was the case here. *Board of Educ. of City of Chicago v. Cady*, 307 Ill.Dec. 872, 860 N.E.2d 526 (Ill. App. Ct. 2006).

◆   The Iowa Department of Human Services found a child abuse complaint was well-founded against a teacher who had her 11-year-old daughter help her avoid an auto interlock ignition device. The Iowa Board of Educational Examiners held a hearing at which the teacher denied ordering her daughter to blow into her car's interlock ignition device so that she could drive the vehicle while intoxicated. She admitted asking her to blow into the device to avoid a false reading after she smoked cigarettes or used mouthwash. She also admitted using marijuana, but not in her daughter's presence. The board suspended her certification for not less than three years, and a state court affirmed the judgment. On appeal, the Court of Appeals of Iowa held **the board only needed proof of a founded child abuse report to suspend or revoke a teaching certificate**. The board did not have to determine if a teacher actually committed the acts substantiating a founded report. The court rejected her assertion that the abuse complaint was unrelated to her fitness to teach because it only involved her own child. The report against the teacher involved illegal activities that threatened the health and safety of a child and set an extremely poor example. As any founded child abuse report against a teacher had some relevance to licensure, the court affirmed the judgment. *Halter v. Iowa Board of Educ. Examiners*, 698 N.W.2d 337 (Table) (Iowa Ct. App. 2005).

◆    The U.S. Supreme Court held that **the non-renewal of a tenured teacher's contract because of her failure to earn certain continuing education credits was not a deprivation of her due process and equal protection rights**. The teacher persistently refused to comply with her district's continuing education requirements. After several years, the Oklahoma Legislature mandated certain salary increases for teachers regardless of compliance with the continuing education requirements. The district then threatened the teacher with dismissal unless she fulfilled the requirements. The teacher failed to do so, and the district fired her. The Supreme Court held in favor of the school board, noting the desire of the district to provide well-qualified teachers was not arbitrary, especially when it made every effort to give the teacher a chance to meet the requirements. There was no deprivation of equal protection since all teachers were obligated to obtain the credits, and the sanction of contract non-renewal was rationally related to the district's objective of enforcing the continuing education obligation of its teachers. *Harrah Independent School Dist. v. Martin*, 440 U.S. 194, 99 S.Ct. 1062, 59 L.Ed.2d 248 (1979).

## B. Testing and Reform Legislation

*The No Child Left Behind Act required all teachers of "core academic subjects" to be "highly qualified" by the end of the 2005-2006 school year. A "highly qualified" teacher holds a bachelor's degree, is fully licensed by the state, and demonstrates knowledge in the subject area taught. The "full state certification" requirement does not include emergency, temporary or provisional licenses. The states are responsible for devising rigorous tests for current teachers in their academic subject areas, and subject knowledge and teaching skills for basic curriculum areas for new elementary teachers.*

◆    A No Child Left Behind (NCLB) Act provision permits alternative-route teachers to meet the "highly qualified teacher" designation only by obtaining "full state certification." But a federal regulation, 34 C.F.R. Part 200.56(a)(1)(i), permitted alternative-route teachers to gain "highly qualified" status without obtaining "full state certification." Students, parents and nonprofit organizations claimed the regulation and a California state education regulation allowed a disproportionate number of intern teachers to teach in minority and low-income schools. They said state intern teachers lacked "full state certification," which is part of the NCLB Act's definition of a highly qualified teacher. A federal court upheld the regulation, despite evidence that intern teachers were concentrated in California schools serving high numbers of low-income and minority students. On appeal, the Ninth Circuit held **the federal regulation impermissibly expanded the highly qualified teacher definition of 20 U.S.C. § 7801(23)** to include alternative-route teachers in the process of obtaining full certification. The court found 34 C.F.R. Part 200.56(a)(2)(ii) was inconsistent with Congressional intent, and so invalidated it. As state and federal regulations permitted the state and its districts to ignore disproportionate numbers of interns teaching in minority and low-income areas, the court held the challengers could pursue the case. *Renee v. Duncan*, 623 F.3d 787 (9th Cir. 2010).

◆   An Ohio teacher gave her students a worksheet with problems similar or identical to those on a current Ohio Achievement Test (OAT). She reviewed the math portion of the OAT while students worked on the reading portion, changed the directions on a practice worksheet and distributed copies to other teachers. When doing so, the teacher said "don't let the students take this home," and "destroy this when you are done." She later said this was sarcasm. Similarities in the worksheet and the actual test problems were noted and the principal questioned the teacher. The Ohio State Board of Education notified the teacher of its intent to suspend her teaching certificates for violating a state statute and regulations regarding test security. A hearing officer recommended suspending her teaching certificates for one year. The case reached the Court of Appeals of Ohio, which noted that **state law forbade revealing to any student specific questions known to be part of a statutory student achievement test**.

The statute prohibited persons from helping a student to cheat in "any way." According to the teacher, sixth grade math concepts could only be tested in a limited number of ways. Materials created by teachers to teach standardized concepts were necessarily similar to the standardized test. The teacher also said the practice worksheet questions were not taken verbatim from the OAT. The court rejected her argument that the statute only prohibited verbatim disclosure of OAT questions and affirmed the decision to suspend her teaching certification for a year. *Luscre-Miles v. Dep't of Educ.*, No. 2008P-0048, 2008 WL 5330522 (Ohio Ct. App. 12/19/08).

◆   The Educational Testing Service (ETS) administers the Praxis Series School Leaders Licensure Assessment Test. Test takers acknowledge in writing all ETS testing policies. An ETS bulletin addresses the consequences of violating testing rules and procedures. The document states that ETS "reserves the right to cancel any test score when, in ETS's judgment, a testing irregularity occurs." Scores could be invalidated for misconduct, which included working on a test after time had been called. A principal intern paid ETS $465 to take the test and she agreed to the testing conditions. When she took the test, a proctor noted that she twice failed to stop writing when the allotted time had passed and she was told to stop writing. The proctor submitted an "irregularity report" to ETS, which cancelled the intern's Praxis scores. She sued ETS for "malicious defamation" and breach of contract. The court held for ETS, finding the contract reserved to ETS the right to make judgment calls. There was no evidence of defamation or negligence. On further appeal, the Court of Appeals of Maryland agreed that **under the terms of the contract, ETS had the right to rely on the proctor's report and to cancel test scores**. *Educational Testing Service v. Hildebrant*, 399 Md. 128, 923 A.2d 34 (Md. 2007).

◆   **A Florida district court of appeal upheld an administrative ruling rejecting charges that a teacher provided inappropriate assistance to her students during the Florida Comprehensive Assessment Test.** The state education practice commission filed a complaint against the teacher for providing answers and other help to her students on the test. But after a hearing, an administrative law judge found all of the commission's student witnesses not credible. The judge accepted the testimony of the lone student who testified for the teacher. The commission held another hearing and issued a final order suspending the teacher's certification. The state court of appeal then held that the commission had improperly modified the judge's findings, and it dismissed the complaint. *Stinson v. Winn*, 938 So.2d 554 (Fla. Dist. Ct. App. 2006).

## C.  Residency, Anti-Nepotism and Patronage Policies

◆   A certified Massachusetts school business administrator claimed he was passed over for several jobs in favor of applicants who lacked certification. He claimed the commissioner of the department of education granted hardship waivers to numerous uncertified applicants without scrutinizing them. According to his state court complaint, hardship waivers were automatically granted electronically. A trial court found the commonwealth and department of education had immunity and the claims were barred under the Massachusetts Tort Claims Act. On appeal, the state court of appeals found the Education Reform act of 1993 allowed a school district to hire only certified school business administrators. Waivers of certification were permitted if a district established that compliance would be a great hardship.

The court held the practice was not an exercise of discretion, because the commissioner divested himself of discretion and "no discretion was involved." According to the complaint, the waiver practice was automatic and violated the act. Discretion for granting waivers should entail "weighing alternatives and making choices with respect to public policy." The administrator claimed due process and equal protection violations, noting that in some cases, friends of appointing authorities were rewarded. The trial court did not rule on the constitutional claims but if true, such actions would be an abuse. The court returned the case to the trial court for further activity. *Nordberg v. Massachusetts Dep't of Educ.*, 76 Mass.App.Ct. 216 (Mass. App. Ct. 2010).

◆   An investigation of a Kentucky school superintendent revealed he resided in Ohio in violation of KRS Section 160.350(2). The school board, district and superintendent sued commonwealth officials for a declaration that the law violated equal protection principles and restricted a fundamental right to travel. After a Kentucky circuit court ruled for the commonwealth, the case came before the state court of appeals. It held that KRS Section 160.350(2) **imposed a permissible residency requirement**. There was no requirement that superintendents reside in Kentucky for a certain number of years. Kentucky residence became a condition of employment that could occur even after hiring, undercutting the claim that the law improperly restrained rights to travel. There was a rational basis for requiring superintendents to live in the commonwealth, and no equal protection violation. *Newport Independent School Dist./Newport Board of Educ. v. Comwlth. of Kentucky*, 300 S.W.2d 216 (Ky. Ct. App. 2009).

◆   A Texas teacher claimed she was denied a promotion because her children attended private schools. The district superintendent stated that the school district required the children of all school administrators to attend public schools. In the teacher's federal action, a court awarded qualified immunity to the superintendent, but the Fifth Circuit reversed. Meanwhile, the teacher was promoted twice and became a high school principal. The case returned to the district court, which found that the delayed promotions deprived her of future salary increases, since she would have earned a higher salary in future years had her administrative career begun earlier. Here, the superintendent had enforced an illegal patronage policy. However, the teacher failed to prove her claims against the district. The case returned to the Fifth Circuit, which held that **school districts have no vicarious liability for federal civil rights violations under 42 U.S.C. § 1983. They are liable only for unconstitutional conduct by policymakers,** and the superintendent was not a policymaker. *Barrow v. Greenville Independent School Dist.*, 480 F.3d 377 (5th Cir. 2007).

The court then awarded the teacher over $654,000 in attorneys' fees and costs. The superintendent appealed to the Fifth Circuit for the third time. The court rejected his claim that the lower court had applied an improper standard in analyzing his actions. Public school employees have a protected right to place their children in private schools. The court refused to reduce the damage award and upheld the award of attorneys' fees. *Barrow v. Greenville Independent School Dist.*, No. 06-10123, 2007 WL 3085028 (5th Cir. 10/23/07).

◆   A New Jersey school board's anti-nepotism policy applied to the immediate families of school board members, school administrators and board employees. However, the policy stated that it "shall have no effect on tenured employees." The board notified an untenured teacher that her one-year teaching contract would not be renewed after she married a tenured teacher in the district. Both teachers sued the board under the state Law Against Discrimination (LAD). They added federal due process and equal protection claims. The board presented evidence that the policy had the legitimate purpose of eliminating conflicts of interest that could arise when employees were married to each other. A state court agreed with the board, and the teachers appealed. A New Jersey appellate court held **the untenured teacher's contract was not renewed because of her relationship to a tenured teacher, not on the basis of her marital status.** The LAD was not designed to prohibit discrimination based on specific family relationships, even though the relationship itself existed by reason of a marriage. The teacher's due process claim failed. She was not tenured and had no right to continued employment beyond her current contract. There was a rational basis for the policy, and it was reasonably related to avoiding conflicts of interest, discord and favoritism. *Wowkun v. Closter Board of Educ.*, 2006 WL 1933475 (N.J. Super. Ct. App. Div. 2006).

◆   An Ohio principal told a substitute teacher that the district's new superintendent would not allow him to work full-time unless his son attended a district school. During the teacher's interview for full-time work, he told the superintendent that his son would remain at the Catholic school he had attended since kindergarten. The teacher was not hired full time. The superintendent later told him the school board wanted teachers to enroll their children in public schools because it "looked good to parents." After the superintendent discharged the teacher for being "disloyal," the teacher sued. A court held for the district and board on some claims, but denied qualified immunity to the superintendent. On appeal, the Sixth Circuit held that the teacher stated a claim for a violation of his constitutional right to direct the education of his children. The right of parents to direct the education of their children was clearly established in *Meyer v. Nebraska*, 262 U.S. 390 (1923). The teacher could not be denied public employment for exercising a fundamental right. **Since existing law clearly established the unlawfulness of denying employment based on constitutionally protected conduct**, the superintendent was not entitled to immunity. *Barrett v. Steubenville City Schools*, 388 F.3d 967 (6th Cir. 2004).

◆   The U.S. Supreme Court addressed the issue of citizenship requirements for certification of non-U.S. citizens lacking a manifest intent to apply for citizenship. Two teachers who consistently refused to seek citizenship despite their eligibility to do so challenged the law under the Due Process Clause of the Fourteenth Amendment to the U.S. Constitution. In upholding the state law, the U.S. Supreme Court held that **teaching in the public schools is a state function so bound up with the operation of the state as a governmental entity as to permit exclusion from that function of those who have not become part of the process of self-government**. The Constitution requires only that a citizenship requirement applicable to teaching in the public schools bear a rational relationship to a legitimate state interest. Here, a rational relationship existed between the educational goals of the state and its desire that citizenship be a qualification to teach in the state. *Ambach v. Norwick*, 441 U.S. 68, 99 S.Ct. 1589, 60 L.Ed.2d 49 (1979).

## III.  VOLUNTARY EMPLOYEE LEAVE

### A.  Family and Maternity Leave

*The Family and Medical Leave Act (FMLA), 29 U.S.C. §§ 2601–2654, grants eligible employees 12 weeks of leave in a one-year period for specific disabling health problems of employees and their families, including a family member's serious illness or a childbirth. It requires employers to issue two forms of notice to employees: (1) a generalized notice posted in the employer's premises; and (2) a customized notice of FMLA rights and procedures for employees who indicate a need to take leave for an FMLA purpose.*

*In* Hunter v. Valley View Local Schools, *the U.S. Court of Appeals, Sixth Circuit, examined an FMLA regulation at 29 C.F.R. Part 825.220 which forbids employers from using the taking of FMLA leave as a negative factor in actions like hiring, promotion or discipline.* **FMLA leave cannot be counted under "no fault" attendance policies.** *The FMLA authorizes damage awards against violating employers, and an employee taking FMLA leave is entitled to return to his or her job (or an equivalent) unless he or she is unable to perform an essential function of the position.*

*The federal Pregnancy Discrimination Act, 42 U.S.C. § 2000e(k), prohibits employers from discriminating against employees on the basis of pregnancy and requires them to treat pregnancy the same as any other disabling illness for all employment-related purposes, including health benefits.*

◆   A Pennsylvania teacher asked her school district for an 11-month maternity leave. About six months after delivering her child, she asked to return to work early due to financial obligations. The district denied the request, stating it had hired a long-term substitute. The teacher filed a grievance. In deciding it, the district applied a childrearing leave provision of the parties' collective bargaining agreement (CBA), rather than a childbearing provision. Under the childbearing provision, a return to work was permitted in emergencies. There was no similar language in the childrearing provision. An arbitrator found leave was taken under the CBA childbearing provision and that there was a financial emergency. He held the district should have allowed the teacher to return to work early. Appeal reached the Commonwealth Court of Pennsylvania, which rejected a district claim that the CBA's separate sections were discriminatory.

The district had negotiated the terms of the CBA and was legally barred from arguing that the arbitration award violated a public policy against sex discrimination. The arbitrator found the childbearing leave provision had been in all the CBAs of the parties since 1977. The district recognized that the term "emergency" included a financial emergency. Even if the court allowed the district to advance its public policy arguments for disallowing the teacher's early return to work, the court found **male teachers could take child-rearing leave under that provision of the CBA**. The court affirmed the judgment for the teachers association. *West Allegheny School Dist. v. West Allegheny Educ. Ass'n*, 997 A.2d 411 (Pa. Commw. Ct. 2010).


◆   A Chicago teacher was a probationary assigned teacher (PAT) at a high school. Due to budgetary reasons, the school lost 1.2 special education positions during the teacher's second year. The principal identified the teacher as "the least effective special education PAT" at the school and recommended contract nonrenewal. The teacher claimed she had already told the principal of her pregnancy by this time. Later in the month, the recommendation was approved by the school board. The teacher filed a federal agency discrimination charge against the board and principal. The teacher was rehired following her pregnancy, but she was again found deficient in her methods of instruction and classroom management. The principal recommended that she not be rehired, and she filed another agency complaint against the board and principal. She then filed a federal district court action, asserting pregnancy discrimination and violations of the Family and Medical Leave Act (FMLA), among other claims.

The court explained that claims filed under Title VII of the Civil Rights Act of 1964 may be based on indirect evidence. Although the teacher challenged the principal's reasons for finding her "the least effective PAT," the court rejected this claim. As the Seventh Circuit has held, **the fact that an employer was mistaken or based its decision on bad policy is irrelevant to whether the stated reason for an action is a pretext**. Since courts do not sit in review of an employer's appraisal of an employee's qualifications, the teacher was unable to show pregnancy discrimination. Her FMLA claim failed because the board rehired her after she took her pregnancy leave. As none of the teacher's claims had merit, the court held for the board and principal. *Silverman v. Board of Educ. of City of Chicago*, No. 08 C 2220, 2010 WL 3000187 (N.D. Ill. 7/26/10).

◆ An Ohio custodian missed significant time from work after an auto injury in 2003. Over the next three years, she took intermittent periods of FMLA leave and underwent three rounds of surgery. When the custodian returned to work, her doctor imposed permanent work restrictions on her. The school district placed her on involuntary unpaid medical leave. The district superintendent stated the leave was based on the doctor's restrictions and "excessive absenteeism." The custodian sued. Following another period of involuntary leave, she returned to work. The court held for the district, finding that regardless of any FMLA violation, the custodian would have been placed on involuntary leave due to her work restrictions. On appeal, the U.S. Court of Appeals, Sixth Circuit, noted that **employers cannot discriminate or retaliate against an employee for taking FMLA leave**. The court found that the school district had used the custodian's leave as a negative factor in its decision. This violated the FMLA. Testimony by the superintendent admitting that involuntary leave had been imposed due to her excessive absenteeism was direct evidence of a retaliatory motive. The court remanded the case for a determination of whether the district would have inevitably laid off the custodian. *Hunter v. Valley View Local Schools*, 579 F.3d 688 (6th Cir. 2009).

◆ A part-time Massachusetts school employee worked as a school monitor for several years. Her husband became ill, and she requested FMLA leave to help him. According to the employee, the deputy superintendent said she did not have to "worry about rushing to return." But soon after the death of her husband, her job was terminated, for the stated reason that monitors were no longer needed. Although the employee had not worked enough hours in the prior 12 months to be covered under the FMLA, she sued, asserting that she could pursue FMLA claims based on the deputy superintendent's assurances. A federal district court held for the school district, and the employee appealed.

On appeal, the First Circuit explained that **to be eligible under the FMLA, an employee must have worked at least 1,250 hours in a 12-month period before taking leave**. The employee here had worked only 554 hours in the previous 12 months. While she claimed she received assurances by the deputy superintendent that she could take leave, she never sought written confirmation. Even if the employee was unaware that she was ineligible for FMLA leave, she "let matters lie," without insisting on written confirmation. The court noted that as of January 16, 2009, employers must provide employees with written rulings on their FMLA requests. See 29 CFR Part 825.300(d). But the amended FMLA regulation did not apply to this case, since the events occurred in 2004-05. *Nagle v. Acton-Boxborough Regional School Dist.*, 576 F.3d 1 (1st Cir. 2009).

◆ A Louisiana school employee worked as an assistant supervisor of school accounts. She helped school principals and staff with bookkeeping, working directly with school staff at various school sites. When the employee took maternity leave, the school board reorganized her department and revised her job description. Upon her return to work, she was no longer required to travel to various schools or to work directly with principals and staff. Instead, she audited the books of schools from a central office location. The employee claimed the change in her job title and her duties violated the FMLA and sued the school board. A court found her new position was equivalent to her former one and held for the board. On appeal, the Fifth Circuit stated that **employees returning from FMLA leave must be restored to their same job, or a comparable one with equivalent pay, benefits and working conditions**. Minimal, intangible changes in an employee's position do not violate the FMLA. In this case, the employee's duties before and after her leave both involved school accounting responsibilities. The court held the board offered her an equivalent position upon her return to work and affirmed the judgment. *Smith v. East Baton Rouge Parish School Board*, 453 F.3d 650 (5th Cir. 2006).

◆   An untenured New Jersey teacher accused his district superintendent of being homophobic, then stopped coming to work and submitted a doctor's statement excusing him from work for at least four weeks due to severe anxiety and stress. The school district informed him that his paid sick leave had been exhausted and that he was "entitled to protect his health benefits under the FMLA." But a school attorney wrote that he could not return to work without first providing doctors' "diagnoses, prognoses and medical opinions" regarding his fitness for duty. The teacher showed school officials a doctor's note clearing him to return to work, but the superintendent rejected it as too "generic." The teacher sued the board and superintendent in a federal court. It said **federal regulations create a lenient standard for what constitutes FMLA notice. Employees do not have to mention the FMLA to obtain protection.** They need only state a qualifying reason for leave. The doctor's note complied with FMLA notice requirements. The court rejected the board's claim that it could require additional psychiatric or physical examinations of any employee who deviated from normal, physical or mental health. *Curcio v. Collingswood Board of Educ.*, No. Civ.A. 04-5100 (JBS), 2006 WL 1806455 (D.N.J. 2006).

◆   A federal court held **employees must provide employers with enough information to place them on notice that FMLA-qualifying leave is needed** and submit medical certification establishing a qualifying condition. An Illinois teacher provided her superintendent a note from her physician describing her hypertension. The court held she showed she had a "serious health condition" qualifying for FMLA protection. The school board made no genuine effort to determine whether she qualified for leave, and it did not show she violated a policy or failed to cooperate. She could prevail if she provided medical evidence that she would have been able to return to work at the end of her leave. Employers must provide employees general and individualized notice of FMLA rights. The FMLA imposes fines for not conspicuously posting FMLA notices, but it does not allow private lawsuits for not doing so. The board was awarded judgment on this claim. *Holmes v. Board of Educ. of West Harvey-Dixmoor School Dist. No. 147*, No. 03 C 6897, 2006 WL 1843393 (N.D. Ill. 2006).

◆   An Arkansas employer exceeded FMLA minimum requirements by allowing employees to take 30 weeks of unpaid leave. It denied an employee's request for additional time off for treatment of Hodgkin's disease. The employer never notified the employee that 12 of her 30 weeks of leave were considered "FMLA leave." The employer discharged her when she did not return to work after she exhausted 30 weeks of leave. The employee sued, alleging violations of a U.S. Department of Labor regulation that does not count leave taken against an employee's FMLA entitlement if the employer does not designate it as "FMLA leave." Appeal reached the U.S. Supreme Court, which held that the regulation imposed a penalty on employers that was contrary to the law's remedial design, without regard to harm the employee might suffer from lack of notice. **A "categorical penalty" was incompatible with the FMLA and invalid because it fundamentally altered the law.** The court struck down the regulation and affirmed a judgment for the employer. *Ragsdale v. Wolverine World Wide Inc.*, 535 U.S. 81, 122 S.Ct. 1155, 152 L.Ed.2d 167 (2002).

◆ The U.S. Supreme Court held that **a school board rule requiring maternity leaves at mandatory and fixed time periods violated the Due Process Clause**. Two cases were involved in this appeal to the Supreme Court. In both cases school district rules required mandatory leaves at a fixed time early in pregnancy. The Court said that the rules were unconstitutional. The test in this case and other similar cases is that the maternity policy, in order to be valid, must bear a rational relationship to legitimate school interests. If there is a relationship, the rules pass constitutional examination; if not, they are unconstitutional and cannot be enforced. *Cleveland Board of Educ. v. LaFleur,* 414 U.S. 632, 94 S.Ct. 791, 39 L.Ed.2d 52 (1974).

### B. Compensatory, Vacation and Sick Leave

◆ A Maine principal worked in his capacity for a district for 17 years. His final employment contract stated that upon retirement from the school system, he would be paid for up to 30 days of accumulated vacation time. At the end of the school year, the principal retired, and the district paid him for 30 days of unused vacation time. The principal filed a state court action against the school department, asserting he had "accumulated" 178 days of vacation time when he retired. He sought to be paid for 148 days of unused vacation time under 26 M.R.S. Section 626, a state wage payment statute. A state court ruled for the school department, and the principal appealed to the Supreme Court of Maine.

The court held that while Section 626 created a statutory right for former employees to seek payment for unpaid wages, the "entitlement to payment is governed solely by the terms of the employment agreement." Section 626 did not modify or supercede the terms of an employment agreement, as the court had found in prior cases. Since the employment agreement set the amount of wages or vacation time a former employee was owed, the court examined the principal's contract. The principal claimed his contract allowed him to accrue unlimited amounts of vacation time because of the use of the word "accumulated" in the relevant provision. Under that theory, he was entitled to be paid for all 178 days of vacation he had accumulated. Instead, the court found **the plain language of the contract limited the principal to 30 days of vacation pay upon retirement**. Since the lower court did not commit error in finding he was not entitled to further payments, the court affirmed the judgment. *Richardson v. Winthrop School Dep't*, 983 A.2d 400 (Me. 2009).

◆   A Louisiana teacher was unintentionally hit and knocked unconscious by one of two students who rushed out of their computer lab to fight each other in a hallway. The school board placed him on leave without reduction in pay for a year. The teacher later sued the board for refusing to pay him sick leave benefits for longer than one year. He claimed benefits under the "assault" provision of La. R.S. Section 17:1201(C), which would entitle him to leave without a reduction in pay for the duration of his disability. A state court awarded pretrial judgment to the school board, and the teacher appealed.

The Court of Appeal of Louisiana explained that Section 17:1201(C) has different leave provisions for teachers who are injured on the job, depending on the cause of injury. The "assault pay" provision of Section 17:1201(C) permits a teacher to remain on sick leave without a pay reduction and with no reduction in sick leave days while disabled by an assault or battery. **The section has a "physical contact" provision that permits teachers to receive unreduced sick leave for up to one calendar year, if they are injured while helping to prevent a student injury.** The board argued that the teacher had simply stepped between the students to break up the fight. Neither of the students had intended to hit him. The court held the "assault pay" provision applied whenever a teacher was the victim of a battery by a student. The provision was not limited to situations when a teacher was the intended victim of an assault. The board had to pay for his leave during the duration of his disability. *Stoshak v. East Baton Rouge School Board*, 959 So.2d 996 (La. Ct. App. 2007).

◆   A group of Texas county deputy sheriffs agreed individually to accept compensatory time off in lieu of cash compensation for working overtime. The county implemented a budgetary protection policy under which supervisors set a maximum number of hours that could be accumulated by an employee. Employees were advised of the maximum and asked to take voluntary steps to reduce compensatory time accumulations. Supervisors could require employees to take their compensatory time at scheduled times. The deputies sued, alleging that the compelled use of compensatory time violated the Fair Labor Standards Act (FLSA). The case reached the U.S. Supreme Court, which noted that the FLSA guaranteed that an employee could make some use of compensatory time upon request. However, **the FLSA did not expressly or impliedly limit a public employer from scheduling employees to take time off work with full pay**. Because the FLSA was silent on employer-compelled compensatory time use, the Court ruled for the county. *Christensen v. Harris County*, 529 U.S. 576, 120 S.Ct. 1655, 146 L.Ed.2d 621 (2000).

◆   A Washington education employees' union required field representatives to use sick leave and vacation time in partial-day increments for any absence during a regular work week. After the union deducted leave from one field representative's employee leave bank 79 times, he sued it under the Washington Minimum Wage Act (MWA) and the FLSA for failure to pay him time-and-a-half for overtime. A federal court held that the representative was exempt from the MWA and FLSA as an administrative employee. He appealed to the Ninth Circuit, which affirmed the decision concerning the FLSA claim but remanded the case for reconsideration of the state law claim under the MWA.

The court asked the Washington Supreme Court to answer certain state law questions. The supreme court held that the MWA exempted executive, administrative and professional employees from its overtime pay requirements by allowing the payment of fixed salaries. To qualify as an exempt employee under both state and federal law, employees must meet both a "duties test" and a "salary basis test." Employees must show their pay is "subject to improper deductions" to prove they are not paid on a salary basis. An employer's single improper salary deduction did not prevent a finding that an employee was paid on a salary basis. **The partial-day deductions from accrued leave banks did not create an automatic violation of the MWA**, but could be considered by the district court in determining whether the representative was exempt from its requirements as an administrative employee. *Webster v. Public School Employees of Washington Inc.*, 60 P.3d 1183 (Wash. 2003).

◆   After working for an Arkansas school district for almost 20 years, a teacher quit to work as a school counselor in Missouri. She sought payment for 90 days of unused sick leave, but the district refused because she did not meet either of the criteria for such a payment – retirement or being hired by another Arkansas school district. The teacher sued, and the Arkansas Supreme Court held that the terms of her employment provided for payment for unused sick leave only in the two circumstances identified. While the state allowed payments for unused sick leave, **such a payment was not required, as the teacher was ineligible for retirement and had not been reemployed by another Arkansas district**. *Turnbough v. Mammoth Spring School Dist. No. 2*, 78 S.W.2d 89 (Ark. 2002).

## IV. REASSIGNMENTS, TRANSFERS AND SUSPENSIONS

*Subject to state laws and the terms of any applicable collective bargaining agreement, courts have evaluated reassignment, transfer and suspension cases on the basis of whether the action violates the law or contract, or is arbitrary and capricious or an abuse of discretion.*

◆   A tenured Tennessee teacher served for 17 years as head coach of a high school girls' basketball team. Parents and players complained about his use of profanity, sexually suggestive remarks and racial slurs. The school principal and director of schools removed the teacher from his coaching duties, though he retained his tenured teaching status. The teacher's collective bargaining organization filed a grievance on his behalf. An arbitrator found that the coaching assignment had to comply with the bargaining agreement as the position was a "professional advantage." Thus, the teacher should be paid for his coaching supplement for 2001-02. Rather than pursuing another grievance, the teacher sued the board. The case reached the Supreme Court of Tennessee.

The court noted the state's 1992 Educational Improvement Act (EIA) had implemented a corporate model under which school directors had authority to assign, suspend, dismiss or transfer teachers. **Directors retained the power to transfer teacher coaching responsibilities without regard to a collective bargaining agreement.** The term "teacher" did not extend to contracts for coaching duties, as there was no certification of coaches in the state. State labor law protections related only to a person's status as a "professional employee," and not to non-licensed positions. The teacher's coaching job was unprotected by the collective bargaining agreement. *Lawrence County Educ. Ass'n v. Lawrence County Board of Educ.*, 244 S.W.3d 302 (Tenn. 2007).

◆   A Pennsylvania school board hired a superintendent under a five-year contract. Within two years, an administrative assistant formally complained to the school board president of a pattern of inappropriate sexual behavior. She claimed the superintendent retaliated against her for refusing his advances by demoting her, increasing her workload, imposing unreasonable deadlines, interfering with her duties and treating her differently than other employees.

The district suspended the superintendent with pay and hired an attorney to investigate the complaint. The attorney interviewed witnesses and then held an informal hearing, where he questioned the superintendent about the allegations in the presence of his counsel. The attorney advised the board there was sufficient evidence for termination. The board suspended the superintendent without pay or benefits. He sued for reinstatement with salary and benefits. The case reached the state supreme court, which held that **the Pennsylvania School Code's removal provision did not divest school boards of their implied authority to suspend superintendents accused of serious misconduct**. Action could be taken against superintendents without pay and benefits, within the constraints of procedural due process. *Burger v. Board of School Directors of McGuffey School Dist.*, 839 A.2d 1055 (Pa. 2003).

◆   A Rhode Island teacher was placed on paid administrative leave near the end of a school year, pending an investigation into a sexual harassment charge. Over three months later, the district superintendent issued him a reprimand letter stating the language he used had been unprofessional and in violation of the department's harassment policy. The teacher was allowed to resume his teaching duties upon completing a course. His union requested a grievance to have the reprimand letter removed from district records. Because of various delays, the teacher then petitioned a state court, asserting that he should have received a pre-suspension hearing prior to being placed on paid administrative leave. The case reached the Rhode Island Supreme Court, which held that **the teacher was not entitled to a hearing as a "suspended" employee because he continued to be paid while on administrative leave and thus was never suspended**. *Martone v. Johnston School Committee*, 824 A.2d 426 (R.I. 2003).

◆   A Colorado administrator had worked for a school district for almost 20 years when an employee complained to the administrator's supervisor that he treated women less favorably than men, was abusive to all employees and had physically bumped her. The district superintendent for human resources began an investigation. The administrator admitted some of the allegations, and the district placed him on administrative leave, pending completion of the investigation. Although district policies did not mention "administrative leave," they permitted the suspension of an employee pending an investigation. Six months after the incident, the district placed the administrator on paid leave.

The state Public Employees' Retirement Association found him eligible for permanent disability retirement benefits. The administrator sued the district for due process and equal protection violations. A federal court and later the Tenth Circuit ruled for the district. The administrator had voluntarily retired and **there was no due process violation in placing him on "administrative leave."** District policy allowed suspensions during investigations and there was no distinction between "suspension" and "administrative leave." The administrator had received ample opportunity to present his version of the facts and respond to the allegations. There was also no equal protection violation. *Bartell v. Aurora Public Schools*, 263 F.3d 1143 (10th Cir. 2001).

## V.  REPORTING ABUSE AND NEGLECT

*State laws require the reporting of suspected child abuse or neglect by teachers and other mandatory reporters and afford immunity for good-faith reports. New York recently amended its child abuse reporting law to clarify that mandated reporters who work for a school must report suspected child abuse or maltreatment* **themselves.** *Schools are not to designate an agent to make reports on behalf of a mandated reporter and are prohibited from putting any conditions upon child abuse or maltreatment reports by mandated reporters. New York's highest court has suggested that teachers and other state-mandated reporters of child abuse and neglect "ought to err on the side of caution and make a report" if they reasonably suspect child abuse or neglect.*

◆    A Texas court acquitted a teacher of charges of indecency with a child. He then sought expunction (erasure) of records relating to the charges. Some of the records were in the possession of the Texas Education Agency (TEA). A court ordered the TEA to return all files and records pertaining to the teacher "arising out of the transaction of indecency with a child" and his subsequent arrest. The Court of Appeals of Texas noted that an agency may possess and retain documents related to an acquitted defendant that are not subject to expunction. Child abuse reports and internal investigations were subject to expunction if they referenced police records and files relating to the arrest. **The TEA could have files pertaining to the teacher that were separate from those relating to his criminal investigation, arrest and prosecution.** State law did not intend to erase all evidence of underlying misconduct. While evidence of a criminal investigation, arrest and prosecution was to be expunged, TEA documents from its internal investigation were not. *Texas Education Agency v. T.G.F.*, 295 S.W.2d 398 (Tex. Ct. App. 2009).

◆    California first-graders claimed a substitute molested them at a Central School District (CSD) school. The students sued CSD and three other school districts that formerly employed the substitute, claiming each failed its mandatory duty to report suspected child abuse. One of those districts argued that it had no duty to protect students not in its district from potential abuse in the future. The district argued the Supreme Court of California refused to find such a broad duty under the state Reporting Act in *Randi W. v. Muroc Joint*

*Unified School Dist.*, 14 Cal.4th 1066, 60 Cal.Rptr. 263 (1997). After considering 2000 amendments to the Reporting Act, the court held that the legislature did not intend to overcome the *Randi W.* rule that "**future victims were not within the class of persons intended to be protected by the statute.**"

On appeal, the Court of Appeal of California noted that the first-graders did not attend the former district at the time of the misconduct. Nor was the substitute under the former district's supervision at that time. The Reporting Act protected children in the custodial care of the person charged with abuse, not all those who might be abused by the same offender in the future. According to the court, *Randi W.* was not intended to extend liability to all children who might conceivably be harmed, even years later, for a reporter's failure to report suspected injury to a child. *P.S. v. San Bernardino City Unif. School Dist.*, 94 Cal.Rptr. 788 (Cal. Ct. App. 2009).

◆  A Kentucky kindergartner reported to her mother that another girl in her class had "put her finger up my butt" while they were at school. The mother called the teacher, who assured her the girls would be separated. But the kindergartner later reported that the other girl had been "up my butt" during a classroom reading group. The teacher immediately questioned the other girl, who admitted touching the kindergartner. The teacher was unable to find an administrator for advice at this time, so she carried on with her instructional duties. That evening, the kindergartner told her aunt that the girl had fingered her genitals. The kindergartner's mother reported the improper touching to the school principal the next day. After a conference, the other girl admitted she had "accidentally touched" the kindergartner between the legs.

The principal deemed the incidents to be accidents and did not report them to child protection authorities. The kindergartner reported more conduct by the other girl of a sexual nature. A physical examination of the kindergartner found she had some irritation of the vagina. Medical personnel then reported their observations to the police. The mother sued the school district, teacher and district's insurer for negligently failing to report and investigate. A state court found the teacher's supervision of the children was in good faith and was a discretionary function. The board and teacher were entitled to state law immunity. On appeal, the Court of Appeals of Kentucky held that **it is well-established state law that public school teachers may be held liable for negligent supervision of students**. As the lower court had given no analysis of the discretionary acts issue, the court vacated the judgment and returned the case to the trial court. *Nelson v. Turner*, 256 S.W.3d 37 (Ky. Ct. App. 2008).

◆  New York parents sought the names of school employees who reported them for suspected child abuse and maltreatment to the statewide central register. In response to the report, the parents sued the school district and an employee in a state court, asserting claims for defamation and intentional infliction of emotional distress. They sought to compel the disclosure of the names of the persons who reported the incidents. The court granted the motion and the district appealed. The New York Supreme Court, Appellate Division, stated Social Services Law Section 422 makes reports to the central register confidential and available only to persons and agencies listed by statute.

The court stated the parents, as the subjects of the report, were entitled to see the report, but not the names of the reporters. It rejected the trial court's reasoning that because a court could obtain these names, it had an implied right to release them to the subject. While the parents might encounter difficulty in bringing their civil action against the reporters, **Social Services Laws Sections 419 and 422 did not permit the release of reporter names based on allegations that the reporters acted with wilful misconduct or gross negligence.** This holding was consistent with the intent of Section 422 to protect the confidentiality of reporters of suspected child abuse. Disclosure of the names might have a chilling effect on reporting and hamper agency efforts to help families. The court reversed the trial court order. *Selapack v. Iroquois Cent. School Dist.*, 794 N.Y.S.2d 547 (N.Y. App. Div. 2005).

◆ A student who attended a private school in Massachusetts claimed the 22-year-old brother of a classmate forced her to have sex with him when she was 15. The incident occurred off school grounds. The brother had previously sexually abused another student and his own sister. The student sued the school in a Massachusetts court for negligently failing to report the brother's history of sexually abusing other students to the state Department of Social Services. The court held for the school, and the student appealed. The Court of Appeals of Massachusetts held that to prove the school was negligent, the student had to first show it had a duty to protect her. She was not on school property and was under her parents' control at the time of the assault. **The state child abuse reporting statute created no duty for the school to protect unnamed, potentially at-risk children in the abstract.** It was instead intended to protect specific children that a reporter had reasonable cause to believe were at risk. The court affirmed the judgment for the school. *S.I. v. Sennott*, 65 Mass. App. Ct. 1102, 836 N.E.2d 350 (Table) (Mass. App. Ct. 2005).

◆ An Ohio teacher was investigated for inappropriately touching and making sexual remarks to a ninth-grader. The principal determined the student was lying and took no action. The allegation was not reported to the police or a child services agency. Three years later, the teacher sexually assaulted another ninth-grader in a school athletic equipment room. The student and her parents sued the school board, alleging that its failure to report the first incident violated mandatory state abuse and neglect reporting requirements. A court held that the board was entitled to sovereign immunity. The Court of Appeals of Ohio affirmed the sovereign immunity ruling and determined that state law created a duty only to a specific child. Failure to report the 1996-97 incident could result in liability to that child, but not a different one. The Supreme Court of Ohio found that **teachers and school officials have a special responsibility to protect students committed to their care and control.** They should appreciate that all students are in danger when an abuse report is received about a teacher. A school board could be held liable for failing to report sexual abuse of a minor student by a teacher, when the failure caused the abuse of another minor student by the same teacher. *Yates v. Mansfield Board of Educ.*, 102 Ohio St.3d 205, 808 N.E.2d 861 (Ohio 2004).

◆   A New Jersey principal covered his school office windows in violation of a state law and always kept the door locked. The district superintendent did not monitor this and other violations, and the school board took no action to ensure he complied with the law. A school secretary frequently heard the principal taking pictures of students in his office but failed to report it because he was her "superior." Other staff observed many questionable incidents involving the principal and male students, but no one reported him. Law enforcement investigators arrested the principal for suspected child abuse and found 176 photographs in his office of male students with their legs spread in a chair. The parents of two student victims sued him, and a jury returned a verdict of $275,000 for each student, adding over $100,000 for their parents.

The court entered a judgment of over $775,000 against the board, and the case reached the Supreme Court of New Jersey, which upheld the trial court's liability finding against the board. Here, the **board did not fulfill its most basic obligation of protecting students and did not implement even rudimentary reporting procedures**. The board "grossly disregarded critical information" requiring scrutiny of the principal's activities. School nurses and others breached their independent state law obligation to report child abuse to the appropriate state agency. *Frugis v. Bracigliano*, 827 A.2d 1040 (N.J. 2003).

◆   A South Dakota elementary school counselor met several times with a third-grader, who said that her father had asked her to touch his penis. The counselor discussed the student's statements with a high school guidance counselor and decided the third-grader's reports were probably untrue, based on the student's tendency to fabricate or exaggerate. District policy forbade employees from speaking with parents about abuse allegations, but the counselor discussed the child's statements with the parents. Over a year later, the father pled guilty to sexually assaulting a neighbor child.

The sheriff's office questioned the counselor, who admitted contacting the parents. The state then brought criminal charges against the counselor for failing to report child abuse. The charges were eventually dismissed, but the district notified the counselor of its intent to fire her. The Supreme Court of South Dakota found no evidence to support the district's conclusion that the failure to report child abuse was a breach of the counselor's contract. When the board nevertheless voted to discharge the counselor without making additional findings of fact, the supreme court noted that the board failed to make the required findings of fact in support of its decision. **In the absence of a finding in the record that the counselor suspected child abuse, the board action was arbitrary, capricious and an abuse of discretion.** *Hughes v. Stanley County School Dist.*, 638 N.W.2d 50 (S.D. 2001).

# CHAPTER EIGHT

## Employment Discrimination

## I. EQUAL PROTECTION

*The Equal Protection Clause of the Fourteenth Amendment to the U.S. Constitution commands that no state shall "deny to any person within its jurisdiction the equal protection of the laws." The Equal Protection Clause is the foundation for all anti-discrimination laws, including the Civil Rights Act of 1964 and state human rights acts. The Supreme Court has refused to recognize an employee's claim to equal protection rights under a "class of one" theory.*

◆ A Michigan school district retained a married male and laid off an unmarried female when budget problems required combining their duties into a single position. The female worked as a district director of transportation, while the male was the building and grounds supervisor. The district deemed the male better qualified to hold the consolidated position. It noted that the building and grounds job required considerable training, while the director of transportation job did not. The female sued the district in a state court for discrimination under the state civil rights act. The court held for the district, and she appealed to the state court of appeals. It found statements by administrators that the married employee was a "head of household" with "a family to support" did not amount to age, sex or marital status discrimination. Many heads of household are unmarried, and they may also be female. And the building and grounds position required specialized knowledge and training that the unmarried employee could not quickly obtain. **Concerns for the budget and the belief that the married employee was better qualified for the job were found to be legitimate, nondiscriminatory reasons for hiring him.** As a result, the judgment for the district was affirmed. *Swartz v. Berrien Springs Public School Dist.*, No. 286285, 2009 WL 4163539 (Mich. Ct. App. 11/24/09).

◆   An Ohio educational service center (ESC) employee said she was injured in an on-the-job traffic injury. The Ohio Industrial Commission decision found no fraud in her workers' compensation claim. The ESC did not appeal to the court system. Instead, it asked the state industrial commission to find fraud and terminate the employee's participation in the compensation fund. Two hearing officers found no evidence of fraud and the commission denied further appeal. The ESC appealed to a state trial court, which dismissed the case. The case then came before the Supreme Court of Ohio, which noted that the commission had found no evidence of employee fraud. The ESC argued that employers did not receive equal protection under the law because only a claimant whose right to participate in the fund had been terminated could appeal an administrative decision to the court system. The court held that when an employee's right to participate in the fund was granted, an employer had a right to appeal, and when the right was terminated, an employee had a right to appeal. **There was no equal protection violation, because both employers and employees had appeal rights from an adverse commission ruling.** *Benton v. Hamilton Educational Service Center*, 123 Ohio St.3d 347, 916 N.E.2d 778 (Ohio 2009).

◆   An Oregon state employee complained that a co-worker subjected her to repeated problems over a long time period. A supervisor directed the co-worker into diversity and anger management training, but he was eventually promoted into a job the employee also wanted. After the employee's position was eliminated, she sued the state agency, co-worker and a supervisor. The court held against the employee on some of her claims, but allowed a jury to hear her equal protection claim based on a "class of one" if she could prove she was irrationally singled out due to animosity by the co-worker and supervisor, and treated differently than others who were similarly situated to her. A jury found that the co-worker and supervisor intentionally treated her differently than similarly situated employees for improper reasons and awarded her $425,000 in damages. Appeal reached the U.S. Supreme Court, which noted that persons may advance equal protection claims based on a "class of one" if there is intentional government conduct that treats a person differently than other similarly situated persons without any rational basis. But that kind of protection did not apply in public employment cases. **The "class of one" theory was simply a poor fit in the public employment context.** The theory was contrary to the presumption of at-will employment and would "constitutionalize the employee grievance." *Engquist v. Oregon Dep't of Agriculture*, 553 U.S. 591 (2008).

◆   A part-time Colorado drama teacher was hired for a one-year employment term at a higher pay grade than her qualifications required. After being rehired for a second year, she declared herself a school board candidate. According to the teacher, the superintendent combed through her personnel file, then initiated a review of her salary and qualifications. After the board voted to reduce the teacher's salary to the level her experience and education supported, it complied with a media request for her personnel files under the state Open Records Act.

Voters elected another candidate for the board, and at the end of the year, the teacher's part-time position was changed to a full-time language arts, speech and drama position. She was not qualified for the job and was not rehired when her contract expired. A federal court awarded pretrial judgment to the district. On appeal, the Tenth Circuit considered the teacher's equal protection claim in view of *Engquist v. Oregon Dep't of Agriculture*, above. **Her equal protection argument failed under *Engquist*. "Government offices could not function if every employment decision became a constitutional matter."** There was no merit to the teacher's claim that she was not rehired based on an improper motive. Evidence indicated she was unqualified for the new position. All the information furnished to the media had to be disclosed under Colorado law. *Pignanelli v. Pueblo School Dist. No. 60*, 540 F.3d 1213 (10th Cir. 2008).

## II. RETALIATION

*Title VII and other laws protecting employees from workplace discrimination have anti-retaliation provisions that attempt to prevent employer interference with employee efforts to "secure or advance enforcement of the Act's basic guarantees," including freedom from discrimination.* Burlington Northern & Santa Fe Railway Co. v. White, *548 U.S. 53 (2006). Disability retaliation claims filed under the Americans with Disabilities Act (ADA) and Section 504 of the Rehabilitation Act use the analytical framework that is used in Title VII cases.*

*The U.S. Supreme Court has given a broad interpretation to the anti-retaliation provision of Title VII of the Civil Rights Act of 1964. Retaliation claims are not limited to employment-related activity or to discrimination claims that the employee has initiated. Retaliation is a separate offense from discrimination, and an employee "need not prove the underlying claim of discrimination for the retaliation claim to succeed."* Sullivan v. Nat'l R.R. Passenger Corp., *170 F.3d 1056, 1059 (11th Cir. 1999).*

◆   A Florida teacher who resigned after filing a Title VII discrimination lawsuit against her school board could also bring a Title VII claim for retaliation against the board for denying her volunteer opportunities. Some time after filing her initial discrimination case against the board, the teacher resigned. She continued participating in a volunteer mentoring program in the county school district for six months, after which the board prohibited her from continuing as a volunteer. She alleged violations of Title VII. After a trial court held for the board, the District Court of Appeal of Florida held that the lower court correctly found volunteers are not protected by Title VII, which applies to employment relationships. **Title VII applied in this case because of the prior relationship of the parties.** Under *Robinson v. Shell Oil Co.*, 519 U.S. 337 (1997), former employees enjoy Title VII protection when they can establish the elements of a Title VII claim. The lower court committed error in dismissing the claim, as the teacher's status as a former employee qualified her for coverage. The case was returned to the lower court for further proceedings. *Gates v. Gadsen County School Board*, 45 So.3d 39 (Fla. Dist. Ct. App. 2010).

◆ The U.S. Court of Appeals, Ninth Circuit, rejected an Arizona teacher's retaliation claims based on her advocacy for Native American students at her school. The court noted that **the school board had offered her a new contract immediately after her criticisms were published** by the local news media. This precluded an inference that the nonrenewal was retaliatory. School administrators correctly argued that the teacher's conduct was insubordinate. This included taking a day off without permission and referring supervisors to her lawyer in response to their lawful directions. The teacher also threatened to call the police if her immediate administrator spoke to her. The court found no retaliatory motive. *Avent v. Tempe Union High School Dist. No. 213*, 359 Fed.Appx. 744 (9th Cir. 2009).

◆ A 30-year Tennessee school human resources officer was asked, during an internal investigation, if she had witnessed any inappropriate behavior by the district's employee relations director. She described several instances of his sexually harassing behavior. The officer stated that the director had repeatedly grabbed his crotch and once pulled her head there. Two other employees reported that the director sexually harassed them. While the government took no action against the employee relations director, it fired the HR officer and the two others who reported sexual harassment. The HR officer sued the school agency for violating Title VII. A federal court awarded pretrial judgment to the agency, finding that Title VII did not protect persons answering questions during internal investigations, but only protected those who initiated claims.

Appeal reached the U.S. Supreme Court, which explained that Title VII makes it an unlawful employment practice for an employer to discriminate against any employee who has opposed any practice made unlawful by Title VII. Another provision made it unlawful for an employer to retaliate against an employee who participated in a Title VII investigation. A person could "oppose" conduct by responding to someone else's questions. A contrary rule would undermine protection from workplace discrimination. **The anti-retaliation provisions of Title VII extended to employees who answered questions during an internal investigation.** The Court reversed the judgment. *Crawford v. Metropolitan Government of Nashville and Davidson County, Tennessee*, 555 U.S. 271 (2009).

◆  A Tennessee railway employee complained about her supervisor's sexually harassing comments. The company disciplined the supervisor but also transferred the employee to a less desirable position. A superior said her reassignment reflected complaints by co-workers that a "more senior man" should have the "less arduous and cleaner job of forklift operator." The employee filed a Title VII complaint, and the company suspended her without pay for insubordination. The employee sued, and the case reached the Supreme Court, which explained that Title VII's anti-retaliation provision was created to prohibit a wide variety of employer conduct intended to restrain employees in the exercise of protected activities. **Although Title VII does not create a general civility code for the workplace, the jury properly found that the reassignment and suspension amounted to retaliation.** The reassignment was "materially adverse" to the employee, who went unpaid for 37 days during which she was uncertain of her employment status. *Burlington Northern & Santa Fe Railway Co. v. White*, 548 U.S. 53 (2006).

◆  An African-American who applied for a transportation department job was unable to prove that an Arizona school district passed him over for a job based on retaliation for his earlier complaint about the district's lack of African-Americans in supervisory positions. The U.S. Court of Appeals, Ninth Circuit, agreed with a lower court that **a nine-month period between his prior complaint and the decision not to hire him into a transportation supervisory position was not close enough in time to be relevant** for the district to be held liable under federal anti-discrimination laws. *Williams v. Tucson Unified School Dist.*, 316 Fed.Appx. 563 (9th Cir. 2008).

## III.  SEX DISCRIMINATION

### A.  Title VII of the Civil Rights Act

*Title VII prohibits employment discrimination based on race, color, sex, religion or national origin. To show discrimination in a Title VII case, an employee must show some "adverse employment action." This occurs if there is "a materially adverse change in the terms of employment." The Supreme Court held an adverse impact or effect is not sufficient to show a violation of the Equal Protection Clause. Proof of intent to discriminate is required. Since it is difficult to prove intentional discrimination, civil rights statutes such as Title VII are a more common basis for employment discrimination claims.*

◆  A Texas school district outsourced the management of its custodial services department, resulting in the loss of five field supervisor positions. The private service that contracted to run the department eliminated the field supervisor position and replaced it with an area custodial supervisor (ACS) position. A female administrator with 20 years of experience in the district obtained an interview, but claimed she was told that only men would be hired for the job. Each of the eight ACS positions went to a male applicant. The administrator was the only former field supervisor not selected for an ACS position. She was reassigned to a facility supervisor position, and her supervisory duties were reduced. She filed a discrimination charge against the school district with the EEOC. She then received her first negative performance review. When she sued for discrimination and retaliation, a court held for the district.

The U.S. Court of Appeals, Fifth Circuit, found no direct evidence of discrimination. The district claimed that the administrator was not hired due to her low scores and lack of relevant skills. However, she raised an inference of discrimination regarding the first ACS offering based on the former supervisor's statement. There was evidence that the decision-maker had relied on the former supervisor's recommendations. The court noted evidence that the administrator had received satisfactory or better ratings on all her performance reviews and was a field supervisor for three years in a position nearly identical to the ACS jobs. Three of the men hired for ACS jobs lacked the district's minimum education and experience requirements. **As the administrator raised sufficient doubt about the district's stated reasons for not hiring her, the judgment was reversed and the case was returned to the district court.** *Gillaspy v. Dallas Independent School Dist.*, 278 Fed.Appx. 307 (5th Cir. 2008).

◆   An African-American employee served as a secretary to several Mississippi school superintendents over a 10-year period. After a superintendent resigned, no immediate replacement was hired. The employee claimed she assumed many of the superintendent's duties for the next two years, when a white male became a "central office administrative coordinator." She said the coordinator performed substantially the same job she did, but for a higher salary. She quit and sued the school system for race and gender discrimination under Title VII, and for violating the Equal Pay Act (EPA). A jury returned a verdict for the school district, and the court found the case baseless and frivolous. It ordered the employee to pay the school district's fees and costs, which exceeded $154,000. On appeal, the U.S. Court of Appeals, Fifth Circuit, found nothing to indicate the employee's working conditions were so intolerable that she was forced to quit. Instead, she was disgruntled that a white, high-level administrator received greater benefits than she did. **The coordinator had greater responsibilities than the employee, such as supervising several departments and managing grants.** The lower court did not abuse its discretion by ruling for the district on the EPA claim. But as the action was not frivolous or unfounded, the award of attorneys' fees and costs was reversed. *Stover v. Hattiesburg Public School Dist.*, 549 F.3 985 (5th Cir. 2008).

◆   A teacher/coach and his wife worked for a Texas school district. He sued the district in 1999, claiming Title VII violations. The action was settled, but the district did not rehire him for 2000-01, based on complaints about his coaching. The district did not fill his position. Instead, the girls' coaching staff was made up of the teacher/coach's wife and a male employee, whom the district later placed on administrative leave. It then brought in high school coaches to help coach the middle school girls' teams. The teacher/coach submitted an unsolicited application for the vacant job, and the athletic director allegedly told his wife that he could not hire her husband because of his previous lawsuit. The teacher/coach sued the district for not rehiring him. He asserted retaliation by the district based on his prior lawsuit. A jury agreed with the teacher/coach and found he should receive $5,400. The U.S. Court of Appeals, Fifth Circuit, found that the teacher/coach did not suffer an "adverse employment action." **An employer does not discriminate or retaliate against an employee if there is no job vacancy.** The athletic director was not responsible for deciding if an available position existed at the middle school at the time of his statement. The fact that a position had become vacant did not make it "available." The jury verdict was not supported by the evidence, and the court reversed the decision. *Adams v. Groesbeck Independent School Dist.*, 475 F.3d 688 (5th Cir. 2007).

◆ After teaching high school Spanish for three years, a Tennessee teacher expected to gain tenure. She claimed her principal sexually harassed her, and filed a complaint against him with the EEOC. Soon, the district notified her of her employment termination. With the help of her union, the teacher appealed to a school administrator. The administrator found the election to non-renew the teacher's contract would stand, but said she would be rehired and gain tenure if she met evaluation requirements. After teaching another year, she received tenure. The teacher sued the school district for sex discrimination under Title VII. A jury found the delay in granting tenure was not an "adverse employment action." The teacher appealed to the Sixth Circuit, which found **the teacher did not lose any tangible benefits or income as a result of the initial denial of tenure**. While she was initially denied tenure, she had another chance to prove herself. She was no worse off with respect to seniority, income or benefits despite being granted tenure after her fourth year, rather than her third. As the teacher lost no income or benefits and did not claim her job had been materially changed, the judgment was affirmed. *Shohadaee v. Metropolitan Government of Nashville and Davidson County*, 150 Fed.Appx. 402 (6th Cir. 2005).

◆ A Texas bus driver asked another driver to punch in his time card at work the morning after the two had been drinking at a bar. The other driver did so, but the driver later called in sick and never showed up for work. The school board accepted a review committee's recommendation to discharge both drivers for misconduct. They sued the school district for gender discrimination, claiming the district did not fire female employees who had also clocked in for their co-workers. After a trial, the court awarded the drivers lost wages and $175,000 each for mental anguish. The state court of appeals affirmed the judgment, and the district appealed to the Supreme Court of Texas.

**The court found that the law deemed employees "similarly situated if their circumstances are comparable in all material respects."** To prove the discipline was discrimination based on sex, the drivers had to show time clock violations by female employees of comparable seriousness to their own. While female employees had been reprimanded for time card violations, and some incidents went unpunished, there was no incident in which a female employee did not show up for work. The court refused to find the male and female employees were "similarly situated," as their misconduct was not of comparable seriousness. The court reversed the judgment for the drivers. *Ysleta Independent School Dist. v. Monarrez*, 177 S.W.3d 915 (Tex. 2005).

## B. Pregnancy Discrimination

*The Pregnancy Discrimination Act, 42 U.S.C. § 2000e(k), is an amendment to Title VII prohibiting employment discrimination on the basis of pregnancy. The act requires employers to treat pregnancy the same as disabling illnesses for purposes of health benefits programs and all other employment-related purposes. For more cases involving health-related leaves of absence, please see Chapter Seven, Section III. Title VII states that it is not an unlawful employment practice for an employer to apply "different standards of compensation ... pursuant to a bona fide seniority ... system ... provided that such differences are not the result of an intention to discriminate because of ... sex."*

◆ A private corporation based pension calculations on a seniority system that relied on years of service, less uncredited leave. Under the plan, employees who took pregnancy leave earned less retirement credit than was available for other kinds of medical leave. A group of California employees sued the corporation, and the case reached the U.S. Supreme Court. It observed that the Pregnancy Discrimination Act (PDA) (added to Title VII in 1978) made "clear that **it is discriminatory to treat pregnancy-related conditions less favorably than other medical conditions.**" On the effective date of the PDA, the corporation replaced its old plan with a new one providing the same credit for pregnancy leave as for others in the future. But the plan did not retroactively adjust pre-PDA credits. Each of the employees thus received less service credit for a pre-PDA pregnancy leave than she would have for general disability leave, as well as a lower pension benefit. The Court held that the employer did not violate the PDA by paying disparate benefits calculated in part under an accrual rule that applied only to pre-PDA leave. Because the corporation's pension payments were in accord with a *bona fide* seniority system, they were insulated from the present challenge. *AT & T Corp. v. Hulteen*, 129 S.Ct. 1962 (U.S. 2009).

◆ A Washington custodian who was her district's only full-time custodial employee took maternity leave in 1998. The district's family leave policy stated employees need not be reinstated to a specific job if the job was eliminated by a restructuring or reduction in force. The custodian took maternity leave again in 1999, and experienced complications with twins. The district superintendent allowed her to structure a leave of over nine months through the use of sick days, family leave, holidays and unpaid leave time. The district demolished buildings and built new ones during the custodian's second maternity leave. It reduced daily custodial hours from 13 to nine district-wide and reallocated this time between the two part-time custodians. The district later hired a full-time custodial employee from another school system. The custodian sued the district for gender, pregnancy and family status discrimination. The state court of appeals held **the district did not need to reinstate an employee whose job was eliminated by a restructuring or reduction in force caused by a lack of funding or work**. The district showed the nonrenewal decision was based on the construction project, not discrimination. *Ackerman v. Quilcene School Dist. No. 48*, 117 Wash.App.1087 (Wash. Ct. App. 2003).

◆   A Maine school district hired a teacher on a probationary basis after she served as a long-term substitute for most of one school year. Although she experienced classroom management issues, her performance improved during the year and she received a second probationary contract. At the time the teacher received the second contract, she was pregnant. She missed the first weeks of her second probationary year due to her pregnancy. Upon resuming her duties, she received a poor evaluation due to her messy and disorganized classroom. The teacher showed improvement during the year, and she eventually received recommendations for a continuing contract. She became pregnant again during her second probationary year and, without explanation, the board replaced her with a teacher who was not pregnant.

The teacher sued the board in a federal district court. The court refused to dismiss the case, noting **Title VII prevents an employer from discharging an employee on the "categorical fact of her pregnancy," or in retaliation for taking an authorized maternity leave**. Here, the board asserted that the teacher was not good enough to deserve tenure. But the principal and superintendent had given her good evaluations when her case came up for review. And a board member who was alleged to be unaware of the teacher's pregnancy saw her frequently when the signs of her advancing pregnancy were unmistakable. The teacher pointed out inconsistencies and weaknesses in the statements of four board members, and she showed a financial motive for her termination. The court held she produced sufficient evidence to make a trial necessary. *Johnson v. School Union No. 107*, 295 F.Supp.2d 106 (D. Me. 2003).

## C.  Equal Pay and Gender

*The Equal Pay Act requires employers to pay males and females the same wages for jobs involving "equal skill, effort, and responsibility, and which are performed under similar working conditions, except where such payment is made pursuant to (i) a seniority system; (ii) a merit system; (iii) a system which measures earnings by quantity or quality of production; or (iv) a differential based on any other factor other than sex." The act has been interpreted to require only that the jobs under comparison be "substantially" equal. Strict equality of the jobs under comparison is not required. Claimants may also bring sex-based wage claims under the Equal Protection Clause.*

◆   A Georgia school board began to receive complaints about the varsity softball coach. Administrators notified her in writing of the need to improve her performance and advised her of specific behavior to avoid, such as making disparaging remarks about team members. When complaints continued, the school board fired the coach. She sued, asserting she was fired in violation of Title VII. She also asserted a violation of the Equal Pay Act (EPA). The court ruled for the school system, and the coach appealed. The U.S. Court of Appeals, Eleventh Circuit, explained that an EPA claimant must show that the employer paid persons of different genders different wages for equal work in jobs requiring similar skill, effort and responsibility and under similar conditions. The lower court had agreed with the school system that the softball coach could not compare her job with that of the varsity boys' baseball coach, as his team played 13 more games and had five to 10 more players than the softball team. The court of appeals held **reasonable minds could differ as to whether the coaching jobs were substantially similar**. So the district court had incorrectly dismissed that part of the case. But since the coach did not present any evidence that she was fired because of her gender, her Title VII claim failed. *Hankinson v. Thomas County School System*, 257 Fed.Appx. 199 (11th Cir. 2007).

◆   A Massachusetts school district hired a female teacher in its technical division in 1993. She began at a salary level for employees with five years of experience, and she had the highest starting salary of any teacher hired by the division up to that time. Five years later, the district hired a male technology teacher with four years of teaching experience and 18 years of contracting experience. His starting wage was the same as that earned by an employee with seven years of teaching experience. The employee and a female colleague believed the district paid them lower starting wages than males. They filed a complaint with the state commission against discrimination, then sued the district. A court awarded over $60,000 to the employee and over $115,000 to the female colleague, plus their attorneys' fees and costs.

On appeal, **the Supreme Judicial Court of Massachusetts noted that the state equal pay act allowed for variations in rates of pay based on seniority**. In this case, the collective bargaining agreement authorized the superintendent to set the salaries of new teachers. And the superintendent did not use her discretion in any clear or consistent way to set initial salaries for either men or women. There was evidence that four male technical teachers who were hired before the females all received three years of credit, even though their relevant work experience varied from over six years to 17 years. Thus, when compared with male teachers, the female employees were not subjected to wage discrimination based on gender. As the lack of uniformity in starting salaries did not establish wage discrimination, the court reversed the judgment. *Silvestris v. Tantasqua Regional School Dist.*, 446 Mass. 756 (Mass. 2006).

◆   Two female Pennsylvania school employees claimed they were paid less than male teachers with less seniority. Both males received full credit for their past employment history, and one had insisted on a certain starting wage. Although a female teacher had 13 years of experience at the time she was hired, and a female librarian had 12, they did not receive full credit for this time, based on lapses in their employment history. The females sued the school district for violating the Equal Pay Act. A jury unanimously held for the district, and the employees appealed. The U.S. Court of Appeals, Third Circuit, affirmed. Here, the district introduced sufficient evidence that **the disparity in pay was not caused by gender, but by the particular certification possessed by one male teacher, his salary demand, and the collective bargaining agreement**. *Henderson v. Chartiers Valley School*, 136 Fed.Appx. 456 (3d Cir. 2005).

◆   A female Michigan coach served for 10 years as a girls' varsity basketball coach. She also coached the boys' junior varsity for eight years and was an assistant coach of the boys' varsity team for eight years. The coach applied for the boys' varsity head coaching position when the incumbent retired. The only other applicant was a less experienced male teacher who had coached the boys' freshman team for two years. District hiring committee members expressed concerns about complaints from the community if it hired her for the boys' varsity job. The school board president voiced similar concerns, and the male teacher was hired for the job. The coach sued the school district for sex discrimination under Title VII and the state's Elliott-Larsen Civil Rights Act.

A jury returned a verdict of $455,000 for the coach. The court ordered the district to name her coach of the boys' varsity basketball team, but it reduced the award by $210,000. On appeal, the Sixth Circuit Court of Appeals **rejected the district's assertion that it had legitimate, nondiscriminatory reasons for not hiring the coach**. It found direct evidence that gender was a factor in its decision. The board president and the superintendent made similar comments about hiring a female coach, and the superintendent admitted that board members opposed her application. The court affirmed the judgment. *Fuhr v. School Dist. of City of Hazel Park*, 364 F.3d 753 (6th Cir. 2004).

### D.  Sexual Harassment

*Sexual harassment is a form of sex discrimination that violates Title VII. Harassment creating a hostile work environment entails discriminatory behavior if a reasonable person, as well as the victim, would find it hostile. See* Harris v. Forklift Systems, Inc., *510 U.S. 17 (1993).*

*The Supreme Court held Title VII is violated if an employee is "exposed to disadvantageous terms or conditions of employment to which members of the other sex are not exposed." In* Burlington Industries, Inc. v. Ellerth, *524 U.S. 742 (1998), and* Faragher v. City of Boca Raton, *524 U.S. 775 (1998), **the Court held Title VII creates employer liability for sexual harassment by supervisors**. Where no adverse employment action occurs, the employer may avoid liability by showing it used reasonable care to prevent and promptly correct harassment, and the employee unreasonably failed to use available employer remedies.*

◆   A Virginia instructional aide was admonished by school administrators for hugging students, smoking in a parking lot, submitting incorrect timesheets, and leaving a cigarette lighter in a special education resource room. According to the employee, the school had an official "zero-tolerance" hugging policy that was only enforced against males. He claimed to be an undercover FBI agent and said he wished to videotape "little burning children coming out of the school." A school board personnel supervisor met with him and offered to let him resign. When the employee refused, the supervisor fired him for charges including failure to meet expectations, inappropriate conduct with students and inability to comply with an improvement plan. The employee sued the school board in a federal court, asserting it enforced an anti-hugging policy only against males. Apart from the employee's own statements, the court found no evidence of any discriminatory policy. **There was no evidence that he was performing his job duties at a level that met the board's legitimate expectations**, and the court held for the school board. *Schroeder v. Roanoke County School Board*, No. 7:08cv00468, 2008 WL 5043474 (W.D. Va. 11/25/08).

◆  An executive secretary had a long-term sexual relationship with a future Mississippi school superintendent. After his election, the superintendent created a job for her. The secretary claimed the superintendent began to sexually harass her shortly after she began her job. In his second year as superintendent, she claimed he raped her in his office. The incident was reported, as were phone harassment charges, but the case was not prosecuted. The secretary took an extended medical leave and returned to work in an elementary school. She claimed this was in retaliation for reporting the assault and harassment, and she sued the school district and superintendent. A federal court dismissed the Title VII claim against the district, noting the secretary was not an "employee" under Title VII's "personal staff exception." **The Fifth Circuit held the statutory term "employee" excluded a person chosen by an elected official to be on the officer's personal staff.** As the superintendent was an elected official and he had hand-picked the secretary, she did not meet the statutory definition of "employee." The court rejected the secretary's arguments that she was not a part of the superintendent's personal staff. He had created the job for her and did not interview anyone else for it. The secretary was hired outside the normal hiring process, and the Title VII exception applied. The court affirmed the judgment. *Saddler v. Quitman County School Dist.*, 278 Fed.Appx. 412 (5th Cir. 2008).

◆  A South Dakota school employee claimed that a male co-worker made suggestive comments to her and asked her to feel his penis. She did not report the misconduct. After three years, a female co-worker complained about the male to a supervisor. The female employee then made a written complaint of the harassment. After an investigation, the district suspended the male without pay and directed him into counseling, threatening to fire him if he did not stop his harassment. When he continued his harassment, he was suspended again, but with no threat of termination. Again he continued his harassing behavior. The female employee resigned, and at a farewell party, she told the superintendent that harassment was a factor in her resignation. She later sued the school district for sexual harassment. A court awarded pretrial judgment to the school board.

The U.S. Court of Appeals, Eighth Circuit, explained that **an employer may be liable for sexual harassment under Title VII if it knew or should have known of misconduct, but failed to take proper remedial action**. The court found sufficient evidence that sexual harassment continued after the district took remedial action in this case. And the second remedial action had "backtracked" from the threat to immediately terminate his employment. Thus, the female employee was due further consideration of her claims that decreasing the threat of sanctions was a negligent response that increased the harassment. The court reversed and remanded the case. *Engel v. Rapid City School Dist.*, 506 F.3d 1118 (9th Cir. 2007).

◆  A California teacher said she was victimized by sexual harassment due to being exposed to the pages of an underground student publication. She claimed the district was required to take steps to prevent harassment directed at her by students. She sued. A jury found for the teacher on her hostile work environment claim, but the court ordered a new trial. While the case was pending before a state court of appeal, the California Legislature amended state law, clarifying that **employers could be liable for sexual harassment of employees by non-employees**. The court of appeal held that the trial court failed to apply the new standard and gave the jury vague instructions about non-employee harassment that were inconsistent with the new law. The Supreme Court of California reviewed the case and ordered the court of appeal to reconsider it. The court of appeal then remanded the case for a new trial where the jury would be told the correct standard for evaluating the district's potential for liability based on harassment by the students. *Adams v. Los Angeles Unified School Dist.*, No. B159310, 2007 WL 68104 (Cal. Ct. App. 1/11/07).

◆   A Michigan counselor worked full time for the Detroit Board of Education and part time at a vocational center. She had a long-term sexual relationship with her supervisor at the vocational center. When it ended, he became involved with another employee. The counselor claimed the supervisor threatened her with adverse employment action if she did anything to interfere with his new relationship. She stated that the other employee taunted and embarrassed her. The vocational center discharged the counselor, and she sued the school board for sexual harassment, breach of contract and intentional infliction of emotional distress. The court granted the board's motion for pretrial judgment, but the state court of appeals held there were grounds for a sexual harassment claim.

The board appealed to the state supreme court, which explained that when submission to **unwelcome sexual advances, requests for sexual favors, or other verbal or physical conduct or communications of a sexual nature** is used as a factor in decisions affecting a person's employment or education, the person may prevail in a "quid pro quo" harassment action. Sexual conduct or communication substantially interfering with employment or education may create grounds for a "hostile environment" sexual harassment claim. Here, the conduct and communication alleged by the counselor fell short of this definition. The supervisor's threats were not inherently sexual, but were instead based on the consequences of interfering with his new relationship. State law did not prohibit personal animosity between romantic rivals, even if it involved sexual competition. The court affirmed the ruling for the board *Corley v. Detroit Board of Educ.*, 470 Mich. 274, 681 N.W.2d 342 (Mich. 2004).

◆   A Nevada employee met with two male supervisors to review psychological evaluation reports from job applicants. She alleged that one supervisor read a report that an applicant commented to a co-worker, "I hear making love to you is like making love to the Grand Canyon." The employee claimed one supervisor then said, "I don't know what that means." According to the employee, the other supervisor responded, "Well, I'll tell you later," and the two males chuckled. The employee was transferred to another job 20 months later.

The employee sued the district for sexual harassment. A federal court held for the district, but the Ninth Circuit reversed. On appeal, the U.S. Supreme Court held no reasonable person could have believed the single incident giving rise to the lawsuit violated Title VII. Sexual harassment is actionable only if it is so severe or pervasive as to alter the conditions of the victim's employment and creates an abusive working environment. The supervisor's comment and the other male's response was "an isolated incident" that could not be considered serious. There was "no causality at all" between the job transfer and the employee's complaint. The Court reversed the judgment, stating **there must be a close proximity in time between an employer's knowledge of an employee's protected conduct and an adverse employment action, if this is the employee's only evidence of retaliation.** *Clark County School Dist. v. Breeden*, 532 U.S. 268, 121 S.Ct. 1508, 149 L.Ed.2d 509 (2001).

## E. Sexual Orientation

*In* Oncale v. Sundowner Offshore Services, *523 U.S. 75 (1998),* **the U.S. Supreme Court held that same-sex harassment is a violation of Title VII.** *Title VII is not a general code of workplace civility, but covers conduct that is severe or pervasive enough to create an objectively hostile or abusive work environment. No language in Title VII bars a sex discrimination claim when the complaining party and alleged perpetrators are of the same sex.*

◆ Two female Wyoming school administrators lived as a couple and were employed by the same school district as middle school assistant principals. A student claimed she saw them holding hands and walking into a Victoria's Secret store during a school field trip. Both administrators denied the report, but the district superintendent discussed the complaint with them. Both administrators lost their jobs during a school district reorganization the next school year, and they sued the school board and the superintendent for employment discrimination on the basis of sexual orientation. The court found the superintendent's actions were unconstitutional, but that the law on sexual orientation discrimination was not clearly established when his conduct was at issue. A jury awarded the administrators $160,515. The court held the district liable, but not the superintendent. The U.S. Court of Appeals, Tenth Circuit, held the superintendent was not the final policy-maker for the district. So the district was not liable for his wrongdoing. And **since the law on sexual orientation discrimination was not clearly established at that time, the superintendent was not liable to the administrators either**. The court ruled against the administrators. *Milligan-Hitt v. Board of Trustees of Sheridan County School Dist. No. 2*, 523 F.3d 1219 (10th Cir. 2008).

◆ A Minnesota teacher was placed on administrative leave near the end of his probationary period, then discharged. He sued the school district in a state court, asserting that he had reported many incidents of bad behavior by students during his three years with the district, including taunts that he was homosexual. The teacher claimed a right to be free from any abuse or harassment by students in the school environment under a state statute and the district's own policies.

The court held for the district, and the teacher appealed to the Court of Appeals of Minnesota. The court rejected the teacher's argument that the statute created an absolute legal duty for school districts. The section required the commissioner of education to maintain a model policy on discrimination, harassment and violence. **School boards were required to adopt and conspicuously post their policies and verify they conformed to state requirements.** The teacher did not argue that the school district violated a particular part of the statute. Here, the district investigated three incidents of student harassment, two of which involved students who implied he was homosexual. The district disciplined the students and informed the parents. District policymaking and enforcement required discretion. The trial court had properly held that the district was protected by discretionary immunity. The court affirmed the judgment. *Malone v. Special School Dist. No. 1*, No. 2004 CA 00347, 2005 WL 3289468 (Minn. Ct. App. 2005).

## IV.  RACE AND NATIONAL ORIGIN DISCRIMINATION

### A.  Race Discrimination

*As the Supreme Court noted in* St. Mary's Honor Center v. Hicks, *509 U.S. 502 (1993), intentional discrimination can be inferred from a disbelief of the employer's stated reason for adverse employment action. Title VII's bona fide occupational qualification (BFOQ) exception allows employers to use sex, religion or national origin as a hiring criterion if one of those characteristics is a "bona fide occupational qualification necessary to the normal operation of that particular business or enterprise." A BFOQ defense will fail unless the qualification at issue is a matter of "necessity," not merely employer convenience. Successful assertion of a BFOQ defense will result in dismissal of a discrimination claim. Race can never be a BFOQ.*

*The Equal Protection Clause prohibits intentional discrimination by government entities. An intent requirement was imposed by the Supreme Court in* Washington v. Davis, *426 U.S. 229 (1976), which involved a written verbal skills test required for employment as a police officer. The test resulted in the rejection of a disproportionately high percentage of African-Americans.*

◆   A Mississippi coach at a predominately African-American high school was promoted to principal and held both positions for two years. During this time, he used school facilities for a private summer track training program, to which white private school students were invited. He claimed this prompted the board to adopt a policy restricting school administrators from holding more than one position in the district. Electing to keep his principalship, the principal stepped down as coach. The next school year, the superintendent began investigating his conduct, and later proposed discharging him for failing to account for funds, inaccurate record-keeping, removing a class from the curriculum, failing to complete student schedules and not fulfilling other duties. After the school board voted to discharge the principal, he filed an employment discrimination case against the board for violations of Title VII and other federal laws. He claimed his discharge was racially motivated based on his inclusion of white students in the track program. The case reached the U.S. Court of Appeals, Fifth Circuit, which denied his claim. Here, the principal had no personal relationship with the white students. **He showed only that any bias was directed against the white students, not against himself.** The court ruled for the school district. *Floyd v. Amite County School Dist.*, 581 F.3d 244 (5th Cir. 2009).

◆ An Arkansas school district employee sought a promotion from a lower-level purchasing job to a buyer position. Job requirements included a college degree and five years of public purchasing experience. None of the candidates for the job had a college degree, but all were granted interviews. Before any interviews, the superintendent withdrew the job announcement. A second job announcement was issued that deleted the college degree requirement and changed the title to "buyer/fixed asset administrator." A supervisor later said that the new title reflected actual job responsibilities, which included the duties of a fixed asset administrator position that had been unfunded for several years.

A candidate with 20 years of purchasing experience was selected for the new position. The employee believed she was denied an interview based on race discrimination, and also believed the new title was "phony" and specifically tailored for the selected candidate. She sued the district, and the case reached the U.S. Court of Appeals, Eighth Circuit. According to the court, the selected candidate had over 20 years of public purchasing experience, some at senior levels. **Even if the employee met the minimal job requirements, the district had a legitimate non-discriminatory reason for not hiring her.** As for the revision of the job description, the court found no evidence of discrimination. It appeared that the new job qualifications accurately represented the position. *Dixon v. Pulaski County Special School Dist.*, 578 F.3d 862 (8th Cir. 2009).

◆ An African-American teacher was suspended for five days for calling a referee "the n-word" at a Virginia high school basketball game. While the teacher was initially told the referee and the NAACP had filed a complaint against her, she later learned no complaint was actually filed. **She filed a grievance, then a federal district court action against the school district, claiming "use of the 'n-word' between African-Americans is culturally acceptable."** The court rejected her due process and related claims that the NAACP charge had been used to coerce an admission of guilt. In a brief order, the U.S. Court of Appeals, Fourth Circuit, affirmed the judgment. *Parker v. Albemarle County Public Schools*, 332 Fed.Appx. 111 (5th Cir. 2009).

◆ An African-American Missouri teacher was hired to tutor a homebound student. The principal later offered her a substitute teaching job. The teacher claimed that within days of her hiring, the principal began making racial remarks. She reported this to a school administrator, but no action was taken. After a few months, the district discharged the teacher, stating the student with whom she had been working was ready for a classroom setting. She claimed she was not assigned additional homebound and substitute work. She reported the principal's conduct to an administrator and sought reemployment. She was then reinstated to the list of substitute teachers, but claimed the district assigned her less frequently than white substitutes. The district maintained that this was because some schools had complained about her personality. She sued the principal and the school district for race discrimination and retaliation. The court awarded pretrial judgment to the principal and district.

The teacher appealed to the U.S. Court of Appeals, Eighth Circuit, which reversed the judgment for the principal, finding that his remarks were direct evidence of discrimination. **As a jury could find that a discriminatory**

**attitude by the principal was a motivating factor in his decisions, the claims against him were remanded for further consideration.** The lower court would also have to reconsider the teacher's claim that she was denied a pay increase because of her race, as there was evidence that she qualified for a raise under the school district's salary schedule. However, she did not raise a valid claim regarding substitute work. There was evidence of complaints about her, and she did not show that any white teachers with similar conduct were retained on the substitute list. *King v. Hardesty*, 517 F.3d 1049 (8th Cir. 2008).

◆    An African-American teacher was repeatedly denied a promotion by her Arkansas school district, despite good performance reviews, a master's degree and administrative certification. She was denied promotional applications at least five times. Twice, the district hired a white female applicant with less teaching experience for the position. The teacher said she was not notified about one job and not interviewed for another. According to the district, one of the jobs remained vacant because it would have been difficult to fill a vacancy if an internal applicant received the job. Claiming the district's repeated failure to promote her was racially motivated, the teacher sued the school district.

A federal court held for the school district, and the U.S. Court of Appeals, Eighth Circuit, affirmed the judgment. It found **no evidence that the district gave inconsistent reasons for failing to promote the teacher** in 2000 and 2005. In the 2000 case, both applicants lacked relevant experience. In the 2005 case, the selected applicant had prior administrative experience. The teacher had failed to meet a filing deadline for the 2005 promotion. This, coupled with the selected applicant's relevant experience, provided legitimate, non-discriminatory reasons to deny the teacher's application. *Moore v. Forrest City School Dist.*, 524 F.3d 879 (8th Cir. 2008).

◆    A New Mexico special education teacher of African-American heritage accused the principal of treating him more harshly than others. The teacher's classroom was observed as being out of control and disorganized. The principal placed him on a professional growth plan and sent independent observers to his class. The teacher rejected the growth plan. He claimed the principal yelled at him and suggested he might be involved in the theft of a laptop. He also stated he was treated more harshly and assigned a bigger workload than other teachers. The teacher sued the district, superintendent and principal in a federal district court for race discrimination. The court held for the district and officials.

The case reached the U.S. Court of Appeals, Tenth Circuit, which held that the placement of an employee on a professional growth plan is not by itself evidence of race discrimination. **An adverse employment action is one that significantly changes an employee's status.** Examples of this include hiring, firing, failing to promote, reassignment, or a significant change in benefits. While placement on a growth plan and a reprimand may have angered and embarrassed the teacher, they did not affect his compensation or employment terms. The teacher failed to prove that his performance was not the genuine reason for the reprimand and performance plan. *Anderson v. Clovis Municipal Schools*, 265 Fed.Appx. 699 (10th Cir. 2008).

◆ School officials did not violate federal law by discharging a human resources administrator after only two months of work. The U.S. Court of Appeals, Fourth Circuit, affirmed a judgment for school officials, finding no evidence of race discrimination. The administrator was African-American, as was a supervisor who interviewed and hired her. Soon after her hiring, the supervisor admonished her for not working long enough hours and failing to communicate about district human resources needs. The administrator based her race discrimination claims in large part on the district's decision not to hire an African-American candidate she had solicited for a director of elementary education position. The candidate admitted she had a pending job offer elsewhere, and the district hired a qualified assistant director of elementary education for the position. **The Fourth Circuit agreed with the school board that there was no evidence to rebut the legitimate, nondiscriminatory reasons for the firing.** *Coleman v. Loudon County School Board*, 294 Fed.Appx. 778 (4th Cir. 2008).

## B. National Origin Discrimination

*Title VII of the Civil Rights Act of 1964 creates liability based on a supervisor's conduct. To prevail in a Title VII case, there must be evidence of an "abusive working environment" that is sufficiently severe or pervasive to alter the conditions of employment.*

◆ An Iowa Spanish teacher claimed that her contract was not renewed because parents complained that her students could not understand her English. She asserted that emails complained about her accent and use of Spanish language in class. A student told her "she should be dead, and should not be in America." Near the end of her first year, the principal advised her that her contract would not be renewed. She sued the district, arguing that she was forced to resign due to a hostile work environment. The court noted that none of the claims of discriminatory or harassing conduct involved alleged conduct by the district. Instead, parents and students were the perpetrators. **The teacher did not establish there was a hostile work environment or that the district knew of any harassment.** She did not report any harassment based on national origin. By contrast, there was substantial evidence that the teacher had classroom management issues. The court awarded pretrial judgment to the district. *Lizama Lidon v. Anamosa Community School Dist.*, No. C08-45 EJM, 2010 WL 2293387 (N.D. Iowa 6/7/10).

◆ A school security officer did not show the U.S. Court of Appeals, Fifth Circuit, that he was discharged based on his Hispanic origin in violation of federal anti-discrimination law. **As he was replaced by another Hispanic person, he could not make out a valid case of discrimination.** In addition, the lower court had found that his discharge was based on frequent tardiness, absences, unprofessional remarks, insubordination and the attempted improper adjustment of time sheets. *Moore v. Duncanville Independent School Dist.*, 358 Fed.Appx. 515 (5th Cir. 2009).

◆   A teacher from Poland began working in the English as a Second Language (ESL) program of the Chicago Public Schools. For the 2005-06 school year, she worked as a full-time probationary teacher under a one-year contract. When the teacher complained that Hispanic students at the school were treated better than Polish students, she said the principal made anti-Polish remarks and gave her a cautionary notice for insubordination based on her refusal to follow the ESL teaching schedule. After a confrontation where the principal allegedly called her a "stupid Polack," the teacher complained to administrators about the principal's mismanagement of the school. The principal assigned the teacher to a classroom with mostly Spanish-speaking students. At the end of the school year, the teacher's contract was not renewed and she sued the school board in a federal court. It held for the school board on each the teacher's claims.

On appeal, the U.S. Court of Appeals, Seventh Circuit, found no evidence that the board knew of any retaliatory basis for non-renewal. But the court held the national origin discrimination claim under Title VII should not have been dismissed. **Unlike constitutional claims, Title VII creates liability based on a supervisor's conduct and does not require action by a final policy-maker.** The teacher made a sufficient case for national origin discrimination based on anti-Polish comments to avoid pretrial judgment. A jury would have to decide if her account of the principal's derogatory remarks was to be believed. *Darchak v. City of Chicago Board of Educ.*, 580 F.3d 622 (7th Cir. 2009).

◆   A Texas teacher of Mexican ancestry claimed he was not provided a new computer and that his class sizes were increased until they were "probably the largest in the school and probably in violation of fire safety norms." He also said his classrooms were not cleaned for days at a time. After the teacher raised his concerns to the school board, he received a warning letter about failing to submit attendance rosters. He claimed there were accusations about his ability to teach and negative treatment by staff. The teacher claimed the school tried to cancel a Hispanic Heritage Festival that he had organized over the prior 13 years. After being denied a transfer, he sued. The case reached the U.S. Court of Appeals, Fifth Circuit, which held that the teacher did not prove national origin discrimination. While he cited examples of discriminatory conduct, **he did not explain how they were motivated by national origin, and did not show that other Hispanics were treated differently than white employees.** Here, the incidents alleged by the teacher were not severe or threatening. *Garza v. Laredo Independent School Dist.*, 309 Fed.Appx. 806 (5th Cir. 2009).

◆   Persons of Arab descent are protected from racial discrimination under 42 U.S.C. § 1981. A Pennsylvania college professor, born in Iraq, was a U.S. citizen and a Muslim. He sued St. Francis College under Title VII and Section 1981 after St. Francis denied his tenure request. A federal court ruled that Section 1981 did not cover discrimination based on Arab ancestry. On appeal, the U.S. Supreme Court noted that Section 1981 states: "[a]ll persons ... shall have the same right to make and enforce contracts ... as is enjoyed by white citizens..." In affirming the decision, the Court noted that although Section 1981 does not use the word "race," the statute forbids all racial discrimination in the making of private as well as public contracts. The Court cited several dictionary and encyclopedic sources to support its finding that under Section 1981, Arabs, Englishmen, Germans and certain other ethnic groups are not to be considered a single race. Based on the history of Section 1981, it concluded Congress "intended to protect from discrimination identifiable classes of persons who are subjected to intentional discrimination solely because of their ancestry or ethnic characteristics." The Court affirmed the decision. **If the professor could prove he was subjected to intentional discrimination because he was Arab, rather than solely because of his place of origin or religion, he could proceed under Section 1981.** *St. Francis College v. Al-Khazraji*, 481 U.S. 604, 107 S.Ct. 2022, 97 L.Ed.2d 749 (1987).

◆   A Utah school district hired a Native American teacher on a provisional basis. She claimed the principal discriminated against her, but not others, for returning late from lunch. She asserted that the principal told her she was "geographically, racially, culturally, and socially out of place" at the school. He gave her bad evaluations and eventually recommended her contract not be renewed. The teacher asked the superintendent to evaluate her performance. He came to the school three times to observe her, but was unable to ever see her actively teaching her class. The superintendent reviewed critical letters from parents and other teachers, and he met with the teacher twice to discuss her effectiveness and her discrimination claims. He decided the teacher should not be rehired. The teacher claimed the principal made a racially derogatory remark to her on her last day, and she sued the district in a federal court.

The court held for the district. On appeal, the U.S. Court of Appeals, Tenth Circuit, held that **a supervisor's statement may show a discriminatory motive in a Title VII case**. Under certain circumstances, the employer may be held liable if a decisionmaker who discharges the employee "merely acted as a rubber stamp, or the 'cat's paw' for a subordinate employee's prejudice," even if the supervisor had no discriminatory motive. The "cat's paw doctrine" did not apply if the decisionmaker made an impartial investigation, as had occurred in this case. The court affirmed the judgment. *Natay v. Murray School Dist.*, 119 Fed.Appx. 259 (10th Cir. 2005).

## C.  Affirmative Action

*Government entities, including school districts, must comply with the Equal Protection Clause, as well as Titles VI and VII when devising affirmative action programs. The U.S. Supreme Court struck down a no-minority-layoff (or "affirmative retention") clause in a teacher collective bargaining agreement in* Wygant v. Jackson Board of Educ., *below. In* Ricci v. DeStefano, *below, the Court held Connecticut municipal officials improperly discarded promotional exam test results taken by firefighters based solely upon racial considerations.*

◆   A Connecticut city used both written and oral exams to fill vacancies for lieutenant and captain firefighter jobs. It ranked and then promoted applicants by the "rule of three." It also hired a company to design its tests so that minority candidates would not be disadvantaged. However, after a lieutenant exam, all 10 of the top-scoring candidates were white. Also, under the rule of three, seven whites and two Hispanics were eligible for promotion, while none of the black candidates reached that level. The city threw out the test results, and the formerly eligible white firefighters sued for race discrimination. The case reached the U.S. Supreme Court, which held that **the city could not intentionally discriminate against one group so as to avoid a lawsuit for unintentional discrimination by another group,** unless it could show that the test was not job-related. *Ricci v. DeStefano,* 129 S.Ct. 2658 (U.S. 2009).

◆ An affirmative action (or "affirmative retention") plan implemented by the Jackson, Michigan, Board of Education called for the layoff of non-minority teachers with greater seniority than some minority teachers. A federal court held that the importance of providing minority teachers as "role models" for minority students as a remedy for past "societal discrimination" justified the layoff provision. Appeal reached the U.S. Supreme Court, which held the non-minority teachers had been unfairly discriminated against in violation of the Equal Protection Clause. It rejected the "role model" justification for retaining minority teachers on the ground that such a theory would allow racially based layoffs long after they were needed to cure the ills of past discrimination. Even if the Jackson school board had sufficient justification for engaging in remedial or "benign" racial discrimination, laying off white teachers was too drastic and intrusive a remedy. **While hiring goals and promotion policies favorable to minorities are acceptable under the Equal Protection Clause, the actual laying off of a certain race of employees was unconstitutional.** "Denial of future employment is not as intrusive as loss of an existing job," observed the Court. *Wygant v. Jackson Board of Educ.,* 476 U.S. 267, 106 S.Ct. 1842, 90 L.Ed.2d 260 (1986).

◆ A Los Angeles high school physical education teacher sought a transfer to a similar position at a magnet school located on the same campus. According to the teacher, the principal of the high school told him he need not apply for the transfer, because the teacher was of "the wrong ethnic origin." The teacher did not formally apply for the transfer, instead relying on this statement. In fact, the district's policy allowed employment transfers that did not cause a school's percentage of minority faculty to deviate more than 15% below or 25% above the overall percentage of minority faculty in Los Angeles Unified School District (LAUSD) schools. The transfer policy did not apply to hiring or firing decisions, and provided that its goals could be modified as a result of the qualifications of available applicants, to meet student instructional needs, or to meet other school requirements. The teacher sued the principal, school district, school board, district superintendent and union for equal protection violations.

A federal district court held that the policy did not violate the teacher's equal protection rights, and he appealed. The U.S. Court of Appeals, Ninth Circuit, found it uncertain if the transfer policy would have even affected the teacher. The principal's statement might be "wholly irrelevant" if he lacked decision-making power. He was the principal of the high school, not the magnet school where the teacher sought to work. **The transfer policy could be modified based on the qualifications of applicants. LAUSD might have accepted the teacher's application based on need, his qualifications, or**

**another reason.** Since there were many unanswered questions about the transfer policy and whether the teacher had standing to pursue the action, the case was returned to the district court. *Friery v. Los Angeles Unified School Dist.*, 448 F.3d 1146 (9th Cir. 2006).

In *United Steelworkers of America v. Weber*, 443 U.S. 193 (1979), the U.S. Supreme Court held that a voluntary affirmative action in employment plan could withstand a Title VII challenge if: 1) there was a statistical disparity between the races or sexes in a job category, or if the institution was guilty of discrimination in the past; 2) the affirmative action plan did not "unnecessarily trammel" the rights of non-minority employees; 3) the plan did not stigmatize non-minority employees; and 4) the plan was temporary in nature and scheduled to terminate upon the achievement of its goals.

## V.  RELIGIOUS DISCRIMINATION

*Title VII prohibits employment discrimination on the basis of religion, but exempts religious employers from coverage. The U.S. Supreme Court has held that an employer discharges its duty under Title VII by making a reasonable accommodation of an employee's religious needs, but no duty to accommodate arises where it would work an undue hardship upon the employer.*

◆   A New York teaching assistant had problems with co-workers, was found unreceptive to supervision and was reassigned twice. A principal denied his request to leave school for prayers and then allowed him to use personal time. He greeted Muslim students in Arabic with a traditional greeting meaning "peace be upon you." At a parent-teacher conference, the employee greeted a young Muslim child by picking her up, hugging her and kissing her on the forehead. The child's mother believed this was inappropriate, and the principal issued the employee a counseling memorandum advising him not to speak Arabic at school or to bring a Quran into classrooms. A school building committee issued a memorandum to the staff stating that only English should be spoken, as the school was an English-as-a-second-language facility. The employee posted a copy of the memorandum and discussed it in non-school internet discussion groups. After the employee received a poor evaluation, he was denied tenure.

In a federal district court suit against the school district and administrators, the court found the posting of the counseling memorandum was not a matter of public concern that was entitled to constitutional protection. Legitimate reasons existed for denying tenure, as conflicts with staff members led to reassignments and the employee was unreceptive to supervision. Posting the memorandum disregarded confidentiality concerns relating to the Muslim child's family. **A Title VII religious discrimination claim failed, as the district offered the employee reasonable accommodations for prayers.** He was allowed to use personal time and lunch breaks to attend Friday prayers. As the district provided nondiscriminatory reasons for denying tenure, the court held in its favor. *Mustafa v. Syracuse City School Dist.*, No. 5:05-CV-813, 2010 WL 4447774 (N.D.N.Y. 11/1/10).

◆   A New York City school employee was denied Supreme Court review of his religion and national origin discrimination lawsuit. According to the employee, the school board took adverse employment actions against him, and ultimately discharged him. The U.S. Court of Appeals, Second Circuit, held that the board had legitimate, nondiscriminatory reasons for adverse action. There was evidence that he slapped and restrained students, gave them standardized test answers and sexually harassed colleagues. As a lower court held, **"no reasonable jury could have found that plaintiff was discriminated against because he is Egyptian or because he is Muslim."** *Raheim v. New York City Board of Educ.*, No. 09-5610, 130 S.Ct. 293 (U.S. Cert. den., 10/05/09).

◆   An Indiana elementary school principal argued with a Jewish teacher on her staff and allegedly said "Heil Hitler" with her arm outstretched to several staff members who had raised their hands in a meeting. The principal also did not excuse the teacher from an "All Student Sing-Along" with Christian carols, or the school's first ever "Staff Ham Breakfast." Conflict between the principal and teacher escalated, and the teacher filed a religious harassment complaint against her. A new superintendent notified the principal that her contract would not be renewed based on her "minimal leadership skills and inability to accept constructive criticism." She sued the school system for unlawful termination and religious discrimination. The court found no religious discrimination. On appeal, the U.S. Court of Appeals, Seventh Circuit, found that **when an employer has a legitimate, nondiscriminatory reason for firing an employee, "it simply doesn't matter" if the employee presents allegations of discrimination.** The school system had a legitimate, nondiscriminatory reason for not rehiring the principal. She had minimal leadership skills, could not accept or understand suggestions, and treated supervisors as adversaries. As the principal did not show the action was based on a pretext for religious discrimination, the judgment was affirmed. *Larson v. Portage Township School Corp.*, 293 Fed.Appx. 415 (7th Cir. 2008).

◆   An Arkansas school district required a teacher to attend in-service trainings at a Christian college where an opening prayer was said. He objected to mandatory prayers at teacher training meetings and the display of a Bible and scriptural quotes in the superintendent's office. The superintendent refused to remove the displays. The teacher sued the district, superintendent and other school officials in a federal court, which held that prayers at mandatory faculty meetings and in-service trainings violated the Establishment Clause. However, the Bible and framed scripture displays, as well as religious jewelry and T-shirts worn by students and staff, were protected by the Speech and Free Exercise Clauses. The case reached the Eighth Circuit, which noted that the Constitution forbids the government from conveying a message that it endorses a particular religious position. **The prayers at mandatory meetings and trainings unconstitutionally conveyed religious endorsement.** The court precluded prayers at mandatory meetings, regardless of whether the teacher was present. *Warnock v. Archer*, 380 F.3d 1076 (8th Cir. 2004).

The teacher later attended a baccalaureate ceremony at a district high school that included an invocation and benediction by ministers. The court granted his motion for contempt, finding that school employees had planned and supervised the ceremony where prayers were offered. The school district appealed to the Eighth Circuit, which affirmed the order, based on ample evidence that school employees were involved in almost every aspect of the event. *Warnock v. Archer*, 443 F.3d 954 (8th Cir. 2006).

◆   The U.S. Court of Appeals, Seventh Circuit, held that a Wisconsin school district did not retaliate against an employee on the basis of his religion. He was disciplined numerous times and eventually suspended for violating school policies he knew about and had promised to follow. The misconduct included making inappropriate comments, touching female students, offering students rides home and recruiting students for his nonprofit organization. The court held that **the discipline was not evidence of discrimination, as the employee was not performing his job satisfactorily**. *Mohammed v. Racine Unified School Dist.*, 206 Fed.Appx. 543 (7th Cir. 2006).

◆   A New York school board had a collective bargaining agreement with the union representing its teachers with a clause allowing teachers up to three paid days of leave for religious observance. Any additional time was charged to an employee's personal leave or unpaid leave. The board denied requests by two teachers for paid leave under the religious observance clause and directed them to take personal leave time instead. The union sued the board on their behalf for an order compelling compliance with the leave clause. After the court held the clause violated the Establishment Clause, the union appealed. The New York Supreme Court, Appellate Division, rejected an argument that the religious leave clause impermissibly advanced religion. It imposed no requirements on teachers to pick the religious holidays that could be invoked for leave. **The clause was better viewed as a reasonable accommodation of teachers' religious beliefs than an impermissible advancement of religion.** The U.S. Constitution mandates religious accommodation, not mere tolerance. The court reinstated the union's petition and remanded the case for further proceedings. *In re Maine-Endwell Teachers' Ass'n v. Board of Educ. of Maine-Endwell Cent. School Dist.*, 771 N.Y.S.2d 246 (N.Y. App. Div. 2004).

◆   A Connecticut high school teacher belonged to a church that required members to refrain from secular employment on designated holy days. He missed about six school days each year for religious purposes, but the relevant collective bargaining agreement allowed only three days of paid leave for religious observation. Although the agreement allowed three days paid leave for "necessary personal business," the district said it could not be used for religious purposes. The teacher repeatedly asked for permission to use three days of his "necessary personal business" leave for religious purposes. He offered to pay for a substitute if the school board would pay him for the extra days that he missed. The board rejected this, and the teacher sued the board, alleging the policy on "necessary personal business" leave was religious discrimination.

   Appeal reached the U.S. Supreme Court, which held that the school district did not need to accept the teacher's proposals, even if this would not cause "undue hardship." **The board was only bound to offer a fair and reasonable**

**accommodation of her religious needs.** The collective bargaining agreement policy of allowing three days paid leave for religious purposes, but excluding additional days of "necessary personal business" leave for religious purposes, would not be reasonable, if paid leave was provided "for all purposes *except* religious ones." Because the lower courts had not decided whether the "necessary personal business" leave policy had been administered fairly in the past, the Court remanded the case for resolution of that question. *Ansonia Board of Educ. v. Philbrook,* 479 U.S. 60, 107 S.Ct 367, 93 L.Ed.2d 305 (1986).

On remand, the Second Circuit held that the accommodation was reasonable. *Philbrook v. Ansonia Board of Educ.,* 925 F.2d 47 (2d Cir. 1991).

## VI. AGE DISCRIMINATION

*The federal Age Discrimination in Employment Act of 1967 (ADEA), 29 U.S.C. § 621 et seq., is part of the Fair Labor Standards Act. It prohibits the use of age as a criterion for employment with respect to persons age 40 and over, and applies to institutions with 20 or more employees that "affect interstate commerce." The ADEA contains an exception allowing the use of age as an employment criterion "where age is a bona fide occupational qualification reasonably necessary to the normal operation of the particular business."*

### A. Employment Decisions

*In* Jones v. Oklahoma City Public Schools, *below, the Tenth Circuit held the ADEA, like other federal anti-discrimination laws, has a "causation requirement." While age need not have been the only factor in an employment decision, it must be shown that "age was the factor that made a difference." The Supreme Court held the "ADEA's requirement that an employer take adverse action 'because of' age [means] that age was the 'reason' that the employer decided to act."* Gross v. FBL Financial Services, Inc., *129 S.Ct. 2343 (U.S. 2009).*

◆   An Oklahoma school district eliminated a longtime administrator's job and reassigned her to an elementary principal job at a similar pay rate. Her vacation benefits were immediately affected and the next year, her salary went down by about $17,000. A month after the administrator was reassigned, a new position called "executive director of teaching and learning" with job duties similar to the administrator's former job was created. At the time of her reassignment, the administrator was nearly 60 years old. A 47-year-old employee was hired for the newly created job. The administrator sued the school district in a federal district court for violating the ADEA. After the court held for the district, she appealed to the U.S. Court of Appeals, Tenth Circuit. It found the ADEA requires an employee to show that "age was the factor that made a difference" in an "adverse employment action." **The requirement was satisfied in this case because the administrator lost salary and went to a job with significantly a different status and different duties.** Once an employee has shown a factual dispute regarding the truth of an employer's reason for taking action, a jury can infer the employer acted for a discriminatory reason. According to the Tenth Circuit, the lower court should have allowed the case to go before a jury. Since it did not, the judgment was reversed. *Jones v. Oklahoma City Public Schools*, 617 F.3d 1273 (10th Cir. 2010).

◆ A 54-year-old claims administration director for an Iowa financial service was reassigned to a claims project coordinator job. The company transferred many of his responsibilities to a newly created position and gave the job to a woman in her early forties whom the coordinator had previously supervised. He sued the company for discrimination under the ADEA, presenting evidence that he was reassigned in part because of his age. The company claimed the reassignment was part of corporate restructuring. The case reached the U.S. Supreme Court, which held that **an employee can only win an ADEA claim by proving that age was the sole motivating factor for adverse employment action**. *Gross v. FBL Financial Services, Inc.*, 129 S.Ct. 2343 (U.S. 2009).

◆ A Maryland teacher with extensive experience teaching English, Spanish, German and French was turned down for a foreign language teaching position. After learning that younger teachers were hired to fill vacancies for which she qualified, she sued the school board for age discrimination. A state court found the teacher's ADEA claim was barred by Eleventh Amendment immunity. On appeal, the state court of special appeals reversed the judgment, finding the board had waived its Eleventh Amendment Immunity. The Court of Appeals of Maryland held a state statute barred county education boards from raising a sovereign immunity defense to any claim of $100,000 or less. The court refused to interpret the phrase "any claim" as excluding certain categories of claims. **As the state expressly waived its immunity for any and all claims of $100,000 or less, the teacher could pursue claims against the board.** *Board of Educ. of Baltimore County v. Zimmer-Rubert*, 409 Md. 200, 973 A.2d 233 (Md. 2009).

◆ A demoted 63-year-old Louisiana special education director was not forced from her job based on age, race or sex, according to the Fifth Circuit Court of Appeals. Although the director claimed she was replaced by a younger man of a different race, the school board stated that she mishandled the reporting of her school system's special education to state authorities. **Her only evidence of age bias was the superintendent's remark that the board sought to project an image of youth and vitality when recruiting new teachers.** A state law claim was returned to a lower court so it could explain its reason for dismissal. *Crary v. East Baton Rouge Parish School Board*, 340 Fed.Appx. 239 (5th Cir. 2009).

◆ A New York school district defeated an age discrimination case by explaining that **the person selected for a teaching job had a better interview than the complaining party**. The complaining party was rejected for two teaching jobs and claimed this was based on age discrimination. The U.S. Court of Appeals, Second Circuit, affirmed a lower court finding that she did not make out a preliminary showing of age discrimination. The district's non-discriminatory reason was sufficient to avoid further proceedings in the case. *Boyer v. Riverhead Cent. School Dist.*, 343 Fed.Appx. 740 (2d Cir. 2009).

◆   An atomic power laboratory in New York was ordered to reduce its workforce and had to cut 31 jobs. It did so in part by ranking employees on job performance, flexibility and criticality. The flexibility factor assessed whether the employees' skills were transferable to other assignments. The criticality factor assessed the importance of the employees' skills to the lab. When 30 of the 31 people laid off were age 40 or older, an ADEA lawsuit ensued. A jury ruled that the layoff process had a disparate impact on older employees, but the Second Circuit reversed, finding the employees should have been required to prove that the selection process was unreasonable. The Supreme Court vacated and remanded the case. In doing so, the Court held **the burden should have been on the employer to prove that its layoff process used reasonable factors other than age**. *Meacham v. Knolls Atomic Power Laboratory*, 554 U.S. 84 (2008).

◆   A 60-year-old Nebraska teacher worked full time from 1969 through 1977, then began working only 24 hours per week. She earned her master's degree in education and assumed a part-time paraeducator job in the school district in addition to her teaching duties in 2000. While the teacher's evaluations were proficient, she did not earn "distinguished" performance ratings. She lacked special education certification and was not working toward it. The paraeducator position was discontinued when the district's Title I grant ended. The teacher sought a full-time teaching job and applied for four vacancies. Two of the jobs required special education certification, and one included coaching duties. The district hired younger female candidates for each of the four jobs.

The teacher sued the school district, asserting age discrimination and a violation of her First Amendment rights. The court held for the district. On appeal to the U.S. Court of Appeals, Eighth Circuit, the district argued that it had legitimate, nondiscriminatory reasons for not hiring the teacher into any of the full-time jobs. The four persons who were hired were all better qualified than she was, despite their youth. The court agreed. Here, **no inference of discrimination arose when younger applicants were more qualified than or similarly qualified to an older candidate**. The teacher's First Amendment claims also lacked merit, as she did not raise any issue of public concern. *Wingate v. Gage County School Dist. No. 34*, 528 F.3d 1074 (8th Cir. 2008).

### B.  Wages and Benefits

*In* Gross v. FBL Financial Services, *this chapter, the U.S. Supreme Court held age discrimination claimants must show age was the sole reason for an employer's adverse action under the Age Discrimination in Employment Act (ADEA). Relying in part on* Gross, *the U.S. Court of Appeals, Tenth Circuit, held a 54-year-old Utah teacher did not show her contract was non-renewed solely because of her age in* Reeder v. Wasatch County School Dist., *below.*

◆   A 54-year-old Utah provisional teacher finished out a school year for a teacher who resigned, then worked two more years as a provisional teacher under one-year contracts. As the teacher had served less than three years, the school district believed it only had to give her a notice at least two months prior to the end of her contract year if her contract would not be renewed. The district provided this notice, stating no reason for not rehiring her. When the teacher asked why she was not being offered a new contract, the school principal stated it was her incompetence in the classroom. She learned three other teachers over 40 were also not offered new contracts. She claimed "student interns who had almost no teaching experience" were being hired as replacements. In a federal district court lawsuit, the teacher claimed ADEA violations and conspiracy by the district and its officials. The court held for the district, and she appealed.

According to the U.S. Court of Appeals, Tenth Circuit, the teacher had to show the stated reason for non-renewal was a pretext for discrimination and that age was the sole reason for adverse action. The teacher complained of "an institutional, systemic and intentional system to rid the District of teachers who were due to become tenured," but due to age "would not be as profitable" to retain. **The court held "the desire to save money is not a motive prohibited by the ADEA."** While interns were paid half the salary of a regular teacher, nothing indicated this related to age. The court found any savings would be "age-neutral." There was no evidence linking the teacher's age with eligibility for retirement or the cost of benefits. As she did not show a correlation between the district's desire to save money and her age, the court affirmed the judgment. *Reeder v. Wasatch County School Dist.*, 359 Fed.Appx. 920 (10th Cir. 2009).

◆   Near the end of his 23-year career, a custodian and building operator at a Kansas school district was diagnosed with a ruptured aneurysm and took three months of Family and Medical Leave Act (FMLA) leave. Two years later, the employee had a heart attack and underwent bypass surgery, which forced him to take 12 weeks of FMLA leave plus three weeks of unpaid leave. Later, he had an abdominal hernia at work and missed additional months of work time. According to the employee, the district's human resources director told him "he was too old" and was "getting on in age." Another administrator discussed health and early retirement options with the employee, and he filed age and disability discrimination charges against the district with the state human rights commission and the U.S. Equal Employment Opportunity Commission.

The employee sued the district in a federal district court for violating the FMLA, ADEA, the Americans with Disabilities Act (ADA) and state workers' compensation law. After the court held for the district, the employee appealed. The U.S. Court of Appeals, Tenth Circuit, noted that **the employee was not discharged or demoted but had retired**. While he could bring a lawsuit based on "constructive discharge," he did not show he was forced into retirement, and only asserted undesirable treatment. There was contrary evidence that administrators made no threats, but only suggested that he retire. There was no merit to the employee's remaining arguments regarding federal law, and he did not comply with state requirements for commencing a workers' compensation claim. *Lara v. Unified School Dist. # 501*, 350 Fed.Appx. 280 (10th Cir. 2009).

◆   Kentucky created a disability pension plan that favored county and state "hazardous" workers who took disability retirement before they became eligible for a pension. A sheriff's department employee became eligible for normal or disability retirement at age 55. He continued to work until he became disabled at age 61, at which point the pension plan calculated his retirement pay as if he had retired without a disability. He sought to obtain the higher benefits available for employees who retired with a disability and sued under the ADEA when he was unsuccessful. The case reached the U.S. Supreme Court, which held that **Kentucky's disability retirement pension plan could favor younger workers because the plan did not discriminate against employees on the basis of age**. The plan had a clear non-age-related rationale for its disparity – to treat a disabled employee as if he became disabled after, rather than before, he became eligible for normal retirement. Age factored into the calculation only because the normal retirement rules permissibly included age as a consideration. *Kentucky Retirement Systems v. EEOC*, 554 U.S. 135 (2008).

◆   An Iowa school district offered an early retirement incentive package to teachers who had worked for 20 years and had reached the age of 55. The plan was announced as a way to show appreciation for services rendered and save the district funds. Among other things, teachers had to be at least age 55 and have 20 years of experience of continuous contract service in the district by the end of the current school year to qualify. A teacher with 30 years of experience in the district would not reach 55 until three months after the end of the school year. The school board found her ineligible for the plan, and she sued for age discrimination in violation of the Iowa Civil Rights Act (ICRA).

The case reached the Supreme Court of Iowa, which noted that state law expressly allowed early retirement plans with minimum age requirements. It held **ICRA provisions relating to age discrimination did not apply to retirement plans or benefit systems unless they were a subterfuge to avoid the ICRA**. There was no evidence of age-related discrimination by the district, as it had a legitimate reason for setting the minimum age for plan participants at 55. The district committed no ICRA violation by expanding the pool of qualified employees when it later lowered the years of service requirement to 15. Iowa law gave school districts discretion to set the age for early retirement benefits and did not require them to offer the same plan each year, or to offer plans at all. As a result, the court held for the district. *Weddum v. Davenport Community School Dist.*, 750 N.W.2d 114 (Iowa 2008).

◆   A group of veteran Mississippi police officers challenged their city's revised pay policy because it gave proportionately higher raises to officers with less than five years of tenure. They claimed that the revised policy had a disparate or discriminatory impact on them. In other words, a facially neutral policy had an adverse effect on them. The case reached the U.S. Supreme Court, which held that **the officers could sue for disparate impact discrimination under the ADEA**. To win, the officers would have to identify a "specific test, requirement, or practice with the pay plan that ha[d] an adverse impact on older workers." The city claimed that the differential was justified by the need to make junior officers' salaries competitive with comparable positions in the market. In this case, the Court determined that the policy was based on reasonable factors other than age and therefore did not violate the ADEA. *Smith v. City of Jackson*, 544 U.S. 228 (2005).

◆   An Iowa school district offered employees an early retirement incentive plan (ERIP), which included the payment of health insurance premiums until the age of 65, plus a one-time cash payment equal to 30% of the employee's annual salary. In 2001, the plan was amended so eligible teachers could receive a $200 credit for each unused sick leave day they had accumulated as of their date of retirement. A teacher who had reached age 65 was denied benefits under the ERIP. He sued the district for violating the ADEA and Iowa's Wage Payment Collection Law. A federal district court held the ERIP conflicted with the purposes of the ADEA, and the teachers were entitled to judgment. The school district appealed to the Eighth Circuit, which stated that because under the district's ERIP, an employee age 65 or older was ineligible for early retirement benefits, the plan was discriminatory on its face. It was not unlawful for an employer to offer an ERIP, but **it was unlawful to condition or reduce early retirement benefits on the basis of age**. The district had done this by offering the amended ERIP. The amount of an employee's early retirement benefits dropped to zero upon the attainment of age 65. The court agreed that the ERIP violated the ADEA. The judgment for the teachers was affirmed. *Jankovitz v. Des Moines Independent Community School Dist.*, 421 F.3d 649 (8th Cir. 2005).

## VII. DISABILITY DISCRIMINATION

### A.  Federal Law

   *Rehabilitation Act Section 504 bars any federal funding recipient from discriminating against an "otherwise qualified individual with a disability." An otherwise qualified person with a disability can perform the "essential functions" of the job "with reasonable accommodation" of a disability. But employers need not accommodate a disability if it creates an undue hardship.*
   *Congress enacted the Americans with Disabilities Act (ADA) in 1991 to extend disability protection to most public and private employees who worked for employers with at least 15 employees. In Bragdon v. Abbott, 524 U.S. 624 (1998), the Supreme Court held an individual with HIV was entitled to the protections of the ADA, despite the fact that she was not yet symptomatic.*
   *In enacting the ADA, Congress contemplated that the same legal analysis was to apply in Section 504 and ADA cases. But Congress found in 2008 that the U.S. Supreme Court was interpreting the ADA differently from Section 504, and it acted to broaden certain ADA definitions. The 2008 Amendments defined the term "disability" to mean "a physical or mental impairment that substantially limits one or more major life activities" of an individual.*
   *In 2010, the U.S. Department of Justice amended ADA regulations for public entities. A key provision requires use of design standards consistent with guidelines published by the U.S. Architectural and Transportation Barriers Compliance Board. A new rule defines "service animal" as a dog that has been individually trained to do work or perform tasks for the benefit of an individual with a disability. Apart from a limited exception permitting use of trained miniature horses, only individually trained dogs qualify as "service animals."*

◆ A teacher sought accommodations for part of the New York State Teacher Certification Examinations. She sought accommodations for a written assignment known as the LAST, identifying herself as dyslexic and seeking a dictionary, extra time, frequent breaks and an oral examination. The National Evaluation Systems (NES), which contracted with the state to administer the LAST, rejected the requests. The teacher underwent a full neuropsychological evaluation and made later attempts to gain accommodations from the NES. By the time the NES agreed to provide her accommodations such as a reader, extended time and breaks, and a separate testing room, she lost had her teaching position. A federal court explained that an employer or service need not make an accommodation if doing so would fundamentally alter the nature of the service, program or activity. **If an examinee seeks an accommodation that would preclude accurate evaluation of abilities measured by the test, it is not unlawful to deny the accommodation.** The ability to spell, punctuate, capitalize and write a paragraph was an inherent part of the LAST. As exempting the teacher from the LAST writing, spelling and punctuation requirements would not put her on a level playing field with non-disabled persons, the court held for the department and the NES. *Falchenberg v. New York State Dep't of Educ.*, 567 F.Supp.2d 513 (S.D.N.Y. 2008).

◆ A Kentucky teacher suffered a head injury in a bicycling accident. She suffered various ailments, including outbursts of anger. At one point, she confronted a group of students playing basketball unsupervised outside the school. The students claimed that she threatened to kill them and made inappropriate comments about their families and their sexual activity. After an investigation, the school superintendent notified her that her contract was being terminated for conduct unbecoming a teacher. The state court system upheld the decision, and the state Education Professional Standards Board then revoked her teaching certificate for 10 years. The state convicted the teacher on criminal charges of terroristic threatening as a result of the basketball incident. She sued the school board for civil rights violations. A federal court held for the board, and the teacher appealed to the Sixth Circuit. The court held that **an employer may fire an employee for disqualifying conduct, even if that conduct occurs as a result of a disability**. As the board fired the teacher for threatening the group of boys and making inappropriate remarks, it had a legitimate, nondiscriminatory reason for firing her. So the court affirmed the judgment. *Macy v. Hopkins County School Board of Educ.*, 484 F.3d 357 (6th Cir. 2007).

◆ A Texas school district employee worked as a buyer. He claimed depression sometimes prevented him from accomplishing simple tasks like mowing the lawn and working on his car. The district placed him on a deficiency plan and granted him a four-month FMLA leave. Less than one month into his leave, the employee obtained a note from his doctor indicating that he could return to work without restrictions. The employee stated that he might need additional time off "to balance his medication." Five weeks later, the district discharged him for failing to complete his deficiency plan. He sued the district, asserting that it violated the Rehabilitation Act and the FMLA. The case reached the Fifth Circuit, which stated that **the employee was not an individual with a disability**

**under the Rehabilitation Act because he did not show that his depression limited him in the major life activity of working**. He also did not prove he was discharged for any other reason than poor job performance. Further, he did not give the district adequate notice of the need to take additional leave before being discharged, and his physician did not indicate he needed additional time. This undercut his FMLA claims. *Prejean v. Cypress-Fairbanks Independent School Dist.*, 97 Fed.Appx. 480 (5th Cir. 2004).

◆ A New York guidance counselor with serious medical problems received satisfactory performance evaluations and was recommended for tenure. She described pain she had experienced to a colleague and joked that she could commit suicide with a gun belonging to her husband: a police officer. The colleague later described the conversation as "entirely in jest" but still reported it to school officials. The principal called the police department to secure the husband's gun. The counselor was reassigned to administrative duties and instructed to see two psychiatrists and a neurologist. The psychologists and neurologist provided documentation that the counselor could return to her job, but the principal told her she would not receive tenure due to her performance.

The counselor sued the district, principal and superintendent for disability discrimination and defamation. A federal court held for the district and officials. On appeal, the Second Circuit stated that the counselor's evidence was sufficient to show that **the district perceived her as having a mental illness that made her suicidal**. Rehabilitation Act regulations, published at 29 C.F.R. Part 32.3(b)(1)(ii), recognize emotional or mental illness as an "impairment" that may bring an individual under the act's protection. The lower court had incorrectly dismissed the case on the basis of the counselor's failure to show she was perceived to be incapable of working in a broad range of suitable jobs. There was sufficient evidence that she was limited in her ability to care for herself, which is recognized as a major life activity. The court reversed the judgment on the Rehabilitation Act and state law claims. It affirmed the judgment for the principal on the counselor's defamation claim. *Peters v. Baldwin Union Free School Dist.*, 320 F.3d 164 (2d Cir. 2003).

◆ A Georgia school bus driver who suffered panic attacks was not protected by the Americans with Disabilities Act (ADA). She could be discharged since she could not perform her job without a reasonable accommodation. The driver claimed her school board had to accommodate her disability, but a federal court found that the board did not commit any discrimination against her. The U.S. Court of Appeals, Eleventh Circuit, upheld the ruling, finding that **the driver did not have a disability as defined in the ADA**. *Albright v. Columbia Board of Educ.*, 135 Fed.Appx. 344 (11th Cir. 2005).

◆ A Missouri teacher worked as an exceptional education case manager. This required frequent visits to several schools, extensive walking and stair-climbing and repetitive handwriting. She was injured in a car accident and two slip-and-fall incidents, one of which occurred at a high school. The teacher went on medical leave, returning to her case manager position after four months, but she was unable to perform physical tasks required by the job. The district assigned her to part-time, light-duty clerical work. She made a formal request for a medical assessment and job accommodations. Her physician determined that she was still recovering from her injuries and needed restrictions. A district physician determined her impairments were resolved with no lasting effects.

An independent medical examiner later found the teacher did not need accommodations. The school district transferred her to an alternative middle school for students with mental and behavioral disorders. The teacher objected to the assignment and was soon injured when a student kicked a chair in which she was sitting. She obtained an extended medical leave of absence and did not return to work for nearly a year. After again requesting a long-term leave of absence, the teacher sued the school district. A court held for the district, and the teacher appealed to the Eighth Circuit. The court held that **temporary impairments with little or no long-term impact are not disabilities under the ADA.** There was no evidence that the teacher had a long-term or permanent disability or could not perform a broad range of jobs in various classes. The district court had properly held for the district on the ADA claim. *Samuels v. Kansas City Missouri School Dist.*, 437 F.3d 797 (8th Cir. 2006).

◆   An Illinois high school principal received excellent evaluations before being transferred to a communication academy. Once there, parents and teachers accused him of being unavailable to help and mishandling discipline. The principal claimed he got no support from the school board, causing stress and depression. In response, the board sought a performance improvement plan. Before it could be implemented, he took a leave for work-related stress and produced a doctor's note in support of it. The principal sought reduction to six-hour work days, and to be excused from special projects. The board declined these restrictions as unreasonable. After the principal returned from leave, the board reassigned him to a teaching position, citing budgetary reasons. He sued and lost. The U.S. Court of Appeals, Seventh Circuit, found evidence that the principal functioned well in teaching and administrative positions after leaving the academy. His depression was not permanent or even long term. He soon returned to public school administration, becoming a principal in Chicago public schools. **Isolated incidents of depression do not qualify an individual for ADA coverage.** The school board did not regard the principal as disabled, and he did not tell any board members he was being treated for depression. *Cassimy v. Board of Educ. of Rockford Public Schools, Dist. 205*, 461 F.3d 932 (7th Cir. 2006).

◆   A Texas teacher was hospitalized for depression in a mental institution during her third year of probationary employment for a school district. She took medical leave for over three months. When the school board voted not to rehire her for the following school year, she asserted ADA violations based on having a record of depression or being regarded by the district as disabled. She sued the district in a federal court, which ruled for the district. On appeal to the U.S. Court of Appeals, Fifth Circuit, she argued that her leave and hospitalization proved a record of disability. The court disagreed. Hospitalization itself does not establish a record of mental disability. A presumption that temporary hospitalization is disabling would be contrary to ADA goals. Here, the teacher's condition did not cause a substantial limitation in a major life activity. She was not disabled within the meaning of the ADA. The evidence showed that **the teacher's depression was treatable with medication and did not prevent her from working**. Her leave and hospitalization did not establish a disability and did not prove that the district regarded her depression as preventing her from performing her job. The court affirmed the judgment. *Winters v. Pasadena Independent School Dist.*, 124 Fed.Appx. 822 (5th Cir. 2005).

◆  Congress exceeded its authority by allowing monetary damage awards against the states in ADA cases, according to a 2001 U.S. Supreme Court decision. The Court held that Congress did not identify a history and pattern of irrational employment discrimination against individuals with disabilities by the states when it enacted the ADA, and therefore, states were entitled to Eleventh Amendment immunity from such claims. As a result, **two state employees were unsuccessful in their attempt to recover money damages under the ADA from their state employer** for disability discrimination they claimed to have been subjected to. *Board of Trustees of Univ. of Alabama v. Garrett*, 531 U.S. 356, 121 S.Ct. 955, 148 L.Ed.2d 866 (2001).

◆  A Wisconsin teacher with 30 years of experience in her school district had arthritis, bursitis, degenerating spinal discs, scoliosis and spondylitis. She took increasingly more time off school, arrived late and required others to cover her class while she rested. Several months before the end of a school year, the superintendent of schools recommended not renewing her contract. The teacher retired, then sued the school district for violating the ADA and forcing her retirement. A federal court held for the district and the teacher appealed to the U.S. Court of Appeals, Seventh Circuit. It rejected her constructive discharge claim, since she was not subjected to "unendurable working conditions." There was no evidence that the district had given the teacher demeaning assignments or forced her to resign. She kept her job for six months after the superintendent proposed non-renewal. **The court rejected the teacher's argument that the district's efforts at accommodating her meant it regarded her as being disabled.** An employer that offered accommodations to an employee for other reasons could not be said to have regarded the employee as "disabled." As the district did not force her to resign, the judgment was affirmed. *Cigan v. Chippewa Falls School Dist.*, 388 F.3d 331 (7th Cir. 2004).

◆  The U.S. Supreme Court held that tuberculosis and other contagious diseases may be considered disabilities under Section 504. The case involved a Florida elementary school teacher who was discharged because of the continued recurrence of tuberculosis. She sued her school board under Section 504 in a U.S. district court. The case reached the U.S. Supreme Court, which held **tuberculosis is a disability under Section 504 because it affects the respiratory system and the ability to work, which is a "major life activity."** The Court reasoned the teacher's contagion and physical impairment resulted from tuberculosis. It would be unfair to allow employers to distinguish between a disease's potential effect on others and its effect on the employee to justify discriminatory treatment. Discrimination based on the contagious effects of a physical impairment would be inconsistent with the purpose of Section 504. The case was returned to a lower court to determine whether the teacher was otherwise qualified for her job and if the board could reasonably accommodate her. *School Board of Nassau County v. Arline*, 480 U.S. 273 (1987).

The district court then held the teacher was "otherwise qualified," as **she posed no threat of transmitting tuberculosis** to others. The court ordered her reinstatement or $768,724 in wages, representing her earnings until retirement. *Arline v. School Board of Nassau County*, 692 F.Supp. 1286 (M.D. Fla. 1988).

## B. State Statutes

*State civil rights laws including the Florida Civil Rights Act and California Fair Employment and Housing Act are construed by courts in a similar manner as the Americans with Disabilities Act and Section 504 of the Rehabilitation Act. They all bar discrimination against individuals based on a disability.*

◆  **A Michigan school social worker with fecal incontinence could not convince the Sixth Circuit that her employer violated state and federal laws protecting people with disabilities.** The social worker had exhausted a three-year cap on her leave, and there was evidence that she could not perform her job even with accommodations. It was not error for a lower court to have permitted questioning of the social worker on the potential danger to students of abruptly leaving them alone while she used a lavatory, and the risks that they could come into contact with germs. The court did not give improper jury instructions or commit error by allowing evidence that the social worker had obtained disability benefits. It was also not error to refuse to overturn a jury verdict for the school district. The judgment was affirmed. *Hubbard v. Detroit Public Schools*, 372 Fed.Appx. 631 (6th Cir. 2010).

◆  A Washington school employee who wore hearing aids was hired as a part-time assistant cook at a high school but soon transferred to a middle school to work more hours. However, she did not get along with her supervisor, and she returned to the high school after only nine days. She filed a complaint with the school district, but it investigated and found no harassment or discrimination. Dissatisfied, the employee sued the school district for violating the Washington Law Against Discrimination. She then transferred to a school where she could work full-time. There, the employee disregarded the food services director's instruction to use sick time to have a hearing aid repaired. The director claimed the employee had to leave for safety reasons, and escorted her out of a training session. She quit and added retaliation and constructive discharge claims.

A state court held for the school district, and the employee appealed. The state court of appeals noted that **when using her hearing aids, the employee's impairment did not have a substantially limiting effect on her abilities**. Evidence indicated that her disability was easily accommodated. The brief conflict with the middle school supervisor was investigated immediately and resolved. Each of the employee's transfer requests had been granted. An undesirable work situation alone did not support a claim for constructive discharge. Nothing supported the employee's claim that the safety-based order to repair her hearing aid was a deliberate act that had forced her to quit. *Townsend v. Walla Walla School Dist.*, 196 P.3d 748 (Wash. Ct. App. 2008).

◆ A Florida school district conducted a criminal background check on a teaching applicant and learned he had misrepresented his record. Without revealing that the applicant was twice convicted of driving under the influence, the district human resources director notified a school principal and vice principal that the application was inaccurate. A school district committee decided the teaching applicant would need to provide proof of treatment to qualify for employment. The job was reposted, and a qualified candidate with many years of teaching experience was soon hired. The day after she was hired, the teaching applicant gave the district his treatment records. The human resources director advised him that he had been requalified as an applicant, but the applicant made an administrative complaint against the district, asserting that he was not hired based on his "perceived disability" of alcoholism.

After an administrative hearing, the case reached a Florida District Court of Appeal. It noted that **to be "perceived" as having a disability, the teacher had to show his perceived disability involved a major life activity that was "substantially limiting."** There was no evidence that the district perceived him as "disabled." Once the applicant provided proof of treatment, he was requalified for job vacancies. The district had a neutral policy and did not discriminate against the applicant based on a perception of disability. *St. Johns County School Dist. v. O'Brien*, 973 So.2d 535 (Fla. Dist. Ct. App. 2007).

◆ A California school district offered employee health coverage from several group health maintenance organizations, including PacifiCare. Although the PacifiCare plan specifically excluded in vitro fertilization (IVF) treatment from coverage, it covered many other forms of infertility treatment. A teacher's wife was unable to become pregnant due to polycystic ovarian disease. One of her doctors requested pre-authorization for IVF, despite being aware that it was not covered by the teacher's PacifiCare plan. The teacher and his wife began IVF treatment at their own expense and filed a discrimination charge against the district, alleging a violation of the California Fair Employment and Housing Act (FEHA). A state superior court awarded judgment to the district.

The state court of appeal affirmed. It held that broad distinctions applying to the treatment of dissimilar conditions, and pertaining to individuals with and without disabilities, are not "distinctions based on disability." While the distinctions might have a greater impact on certain individuals, they were not intentional disability discrimination and did not violate the ADA. **The discrimination alleged by the teacher was not genuinely based on fertility, because the plan covered many other forms of infertility treatment.** IVF was an expensive treatment used only when others failed. The court explained that if the FEHA and the similar ADA prohibited treatment-based distinctions, they would mandate comprehensive health coverage for all job-related disabilities. This was not the intent of FEHA. Federal case law interpreting the ADA did not prohibit treatment-based distinctions. *Knight v. Hayward Unified School Dist.*, 132 Cal.App.4th 121, 33 Cal.Rptr.3d 298 (Cal. Ct. App. 2005).

◆   An Ohio school bus driver who had worked for a district for 22 years tested positive for marijuana use after driving disabled children to school. A district supervisor met with her two days later and denied her request for leave to enter a rehabilitation program. He stated that school policy required discharge, but allowed her to resign. The supervisor rejected the driver's request to retire instead of resign, and she submitted her written resignation the same day. The school board approved the resignation at a special meeting held six days later. The driver's grievance was denied through the first three steps. Her employee association declined to take the grievance to arbitration. The district denied efforts by the driver to withdraw her resignation and later refused to rehire her. She sued the board and supervisor for disability discrimination and due process violations. A federal court awarded pretrial judgment to the board and supervisor, and the driver appealed. The Sixth Circuit affirmed. **A disease or condition caused by illegal drug use is not a disability unless the individual has successfully completed a supervised rehabilitation program and no longer uses illegal drugs.** Here, the driver presented little medical evidence of drug addiction and failed to show that she had a disability. There was also no indication that the district regarded her as a drug addict. *Rhoads v. Board of Educ. of Mad River Local School Dist.*, 103 Fed.Appx. 888 (6th Cir. 2004).

## VIII. DISCRIMINATION AGAINST VETERANS

*State veterans preference acts prohibit discrimination against veterans, but do not require the hiring of unqualified preference-eligible veterans. The Uniformed Services Employment and Reemployment Rights Act (USERRA) prevents employers from using an applicant's membership in a branch of the uniformed services as a motivating factor in employment decisions.*

◆   An Alabama school board did not violate the federal Uniformed Services Employment and Reemployment Rights Act by failing to hire a National Guard member as an administrator. The U.S. Court of Appeals, Eleventh Circuit, held the board hired the most qualified candidate for the job and stated **an employer violates the act if an applicant's membership in a branch of uniformed service is a motivating factor in an employment decision**. In this case, the board had legitimate reasons for not hiring the guardsman. *Gambrill v. Cullman County Board of Educ.*, 395 Fed.Appx. 543 (11th Cir. 2010).

◆   A New York elementary principal who was an Army reservist submitted six requests for brief military service leave in one year. During leaves, she could not perform her duties as principal, and board members and the superintendent expressed displeasure over her absences. The principal refused to comply with a board member's request to place his child in a "looping class" so the child could remain with the same teacher for the next grade. The superintendent then told her to place the child in the looping class. Later, the superintendent notified the principal he would recommend her employment termination to the board for inaccessibility to staff and parents, failure to meet with clerical staff, and failure to timely complete class lists. The board discharged her, and she sued the school district under the Uniformed Services Employment and Reemployment Rights Act (USERRA), the state Military Law, and the First Amendment. A federal court dismissed the claims against the board under USERRA and the New York Military Law. On appeal, the U.S. Court of Appeals, Second Circuit, held that **the principal could not pursue her USERRA action against individual board members under 42 U.S.C. § 1983**. The court dismissed the appeal and remanded the case to the district court for further proceedings. *Morris-Hayes v. Board of Educ. of Chester Union Free School Dist.*, 423 F.3d 153 (2d Cir. 2005).

◆   An untenured Kansas teacher and Vietnam-era veteran worked for a school district for three years. After learning he would not be rehired due to performance deficiencies, he followed the recommendation of his principal to submit a resignation letter in lieu of non-renewal. He then sued the district and superintendent for violating the Kansas Veteran's Preference Act (VPA), his federal due process rights and defamation. The court held for the district on all claims, and the teacher appealed. The Court of Appeals of Kansas stated that the VPA pertained to appointments and reductions in force, not resignations. Resignation could not be considered a reduction in force. The teacher did not show he was equally qualified to any employee retained by the district.

The teacher admitted the principal's recommendation for non-renewal was based on performance deficiencies. **As the VPA provided no relief for untenured school employees who resigned under the threat of non-renewal, the court affirmed the judgment on the VPA claim.** The teacher also failed to prove defamation, as no defamatory information was communicated to a third party. And he could not prove that his contract was not renewed in retaliation for promoting or endorsing his teacher's association, in violation of his First Amendment speech rights. Key district officials were not even aware of his advocacy for the association. The trial court had correctly held for the district and superintendent. *Richardson v. Dietrich*, 105 P.3d 279 (Kan. Ct. App. 2005).

◆   A Pennsylvania school district twice rejected a veteran for employment. The second time, he advanced to the fourth step of the district's five-step hiring process. A letter sent by the district informed the veteran he was not selected, but did not state a reason. He sued the district in a state court, which held that the district was a "local agency" under the Pennsylvania Local Agency Law. The letter informing the veteran of its decision was an "adjudication" by a local agency that had to be appealed within 30 days. Since the veteran did not file suit for 90 days after the date of the letter, the court dismissed the case. The case reached the Supreme Court of Pennsylvania. It found the Veterans' Preference Act created vested rights. But to enjoy a preference, a veteran had to possess the minimum job qualifications. **The act did not require the hiring of unqualified preference-eligible veterans.** As no decision had been made concerning the veteran's qualifications, the court reversed the judgment and returned the case to the trial court to assess whether the district was trying to circumvent the act. *Merrell v. Chartiers Valley School Dist.*, 855 A.2d 713 (Pa. 2004).

# CHAPTER NINE

# Employment Termination, Resignation and Retirement

## I. BUDGET REDUCTIONS AND REDUCTIONS IN FORCE

*State legislatures across the nation are addressing seniority-based tenure systems. A 2011 Florida act links instructional employee retention and compensation with student performance and prohibits prioritizing the retention of employees based on seniority. Florida school boards will be required to retain employees based on program needs and performance evaluations during reductions in force. Within programs being reduced, employees will be released by the order of their evaluations, with the lowest-rated employee going first.*

*A landmark 2010 Colorado act tied tenure decisions to student performance. Provisions of the law phase in through 2013-14 and will make it possible for teachers to lose tenure by receiving consecutive poor evaluations.*

*Traditional tenure laws recognize seniority principles and prohibit the replacement of tenured teachers by probationary teachers. Courts in Montana and New Mexico permit the retention of junior teachers if retaining more senior teachers would seriously affect educational programs. And the California Education Code permits the retention of junior teachers with "special skills and competence," even if more senior teachers are similarly certified.*

◆  Clay County, Nebraska, reduced a veteran art teacher's job to .5 full-time equivalency (FTE) in 1997 due to low student enrollment. She kept her .5 FTE job in Clay County and taught .5 FTE in Aurora Schools. In 2008, an art teacher resigned from Clay Center School District, and that district agreed to share an art position with Clay County. Clay Center advertised the job, but the veteran teacher did not apply for it. A probationary teacher was hired to work .5 FTE for Clay Center and Clay County, and Clay County advised the veteran teacher that her position would be eliminated. It voted to reduce its art program to 0 FTE and to contract with Clay Center for an art teacher. At a hearing, the school board found a reduction in force was necessary due to changed circumstances related only to the teacher, who was unqualified for any other district position.

At a hearing, Clay County's superintendent admitted the only change in the district's art program was the identity of the art teacher and a savings of $8,785 via sharing the probationary teacher with Clay Center. A Nebraska county court vacated the decision, and appeal reached the Supreme Court of Nebraska. It held a teacher's contract may be terminated only for the reasons stated in Nebraska law. **A "reduction in force" had been previously held to involve contract termination "due to a surplus of staff."** The county court had correctly found no reduction in force due to a surplus in staff. Clay County simply planned to replace the veteran teacher. The district was not reducing its staff based on reduced need. It only changed the method by which it secured the services of a .5 FTE art teacher to save money. This was not by itself a legal basis for terminating a tenured teacher's contract. *Miller v. School Dist. No. 18-0011 of Clay County, Nebraska*, 278 Neb. 1018, 775 N.W.2d 413 (Neb. 2009).

◆  A New Mexico teacher was in her third year of employment with a school district and had a good record. However, the superintendent notified her that he was recommending her discharge under a reduction in force (RIF) because of shortfalls in state funding and the discontinuation of federal grant money. The school board discharged the teacher, and an arbitrator found that the RIF constituted "just cause" under state law. On appeal, the Supreme Court of New Mexico explained that unless there were personal grounds for discharging a teacher, a school board had to affirmatively show that no position was available for which the teacher was qualified to support discharge by RIF. So the board had to affirmatively show that no position was available for the teacher. Nothing indicated the board had considered whether any other positions were available. Discharge, unlike contract non-renewal, resulted in job loss in the middle of a school year. Given this hardship, **a board had to show it could not financially endure the school year to justify a mid-year discharge.** *Aguilera v. Board of Educ. of Hatch Valley Schools*, 139 N.M. 330, 132 P.3d 587 (N.M. 2006).

◆ An Iowa school district terminated the contract of a longtime elementary principal due to declining enrollment, budget problems, a reduction of positions and a realignment of the school organization. The grade 7-12 principal became superintendent and the new superintendent's brother was hired as the grade 7-12 principal. When the ousted principal challenged the realignment, the school board upheld her discharge, and a state court affirmed the decision. On appeal, the Supreme Court of Iowa had to decide if termination was supported by "just cause" for the reasons stated. It held **"just cause" under state law included legitimate reasons relating to personnel and budgetary requirements**. Here, the district showed enrollment had declined over 25 percent since 1999. Projections indicated further reductions, and the district had lost about $1 million in annual revenues. As the evidence substantiated a district strategy to gradually reduce its administrative staff, the judgment was affirmed. *Martinek v. Belmond-Klemme Community School Dist.*, 772 N.W.2d 758 (Iowa 2009).

In a separate case, the state supreme court held neither state law nor the contract allowed termination prior to the end of the contract term. *Martinek v. Belmond-Klemme Community School Dist.*, 760 N.W.2d 454 (Iowa 2009).

◆ A Montana school superintendent recommended budget cuts for the district and devised reduction in force (RIF) criteria that stated a preference for multiple endorsements "due to the versatility of using teachers in more than one area." The school board voted to discharge a teacher who was endorsed to teach only social studies, based on his lack of multiple-subject endorsements. He filed for arbitration under the collective bargaining agreement (CBA). He argued that two less experienced teachers were rehired, including one who was untenured. The arbitrator held for the board, and the case reached the Supreme Court of Montana. It held **teacher tenure rights must be balanced against a school board's authority to manage the district in a financially responsible manner**. A reduction in revenue was "good cause" for the RIF. The board had considered alternatives and was not required to take actions that negatively affected operations and educational programs to preserve a teacher's bumping rights. The court noted that a teacher with multiple endorsements is especially valuable to a small rural district which needs teachers to teach in many subjects and to differing age groups. The teacher's dismissal was upheld. *Scobey School Dist. v. Radakovich*, 332 Mont. 9, 135 P.3d 778 (Mont. 2006).

## II.  IMMORALITY AND OTHER MISCONDUCT

*In* Broney v. California Comm'n on Teacher Credentialing, *108 Cal.Rptr.3d 832 (Cal. Ct. App. 2010), the court held statutory terms such as "immoral or unprofessional conduct" and "moral turpitude" are almost unlimited in scope. To avoid arbitrary results, the court looked to* Morrison v. State Board of Educ., *1 Cal.3d 214 (1969). In* Morrison, *the California Supreme Court found **"before any act could be deemed a ground for discharge, it must bear directly on the teacher's fitness to teach"** and cause a clearly discernible detriment to a school and its students. Michigan and California courts have relied on factors listed in* Morrison *in recent cases involving teacher misconduct off school grounds.*

## A. Sexual Misconduct

◆   Kentucky employees did not show they were forced to quit when they were suspended and had "sexually charged allegations" raised against them. One was a middle school principal who was reassigned to a teaching position pending the investigation. The other was charged with "moral turpitude" involving students and possibly employees. While the employees claimed the charges were false and designed to humiliate them, the state court of appeals found no objective person would believe they were subjected to intolerable working conditions. Both were advised that they would be reinstated if the investigations did not lead to charges, but both resigned. The employees failed to show they were defamed or subjected to hostile work environments. In fact, **the district superintendent was legally required to report any action against their teaching certificates**. The appeal was dismissed as without merit. *Cvitkovic v. Freeman*, No. 2008-CA-001647, 2010 WL 3292906 (Ky. Ct. App. 8/6/10).

◆   A Delaware art teacher had worked for a school district for eight years when he had sexual relations with a 17-year-old former student who no longer attended district schools. On one occasion, he called in sick and met the student at his home. She later told a friend about the relationship, and her parent reported it to state police. The teacher was charged with fourth degree sexual rape based on the student's age and his position of trust, authority or supervision over her. But the charge was dropped. The board discharged the teacher for immorality, noting that his conduct interfered with his function as a role model, threatened the moral and social orientation of students, and reflected a serious lack of judgment. The teacher appealed to the Supreme Court of Delaware, arguing that his positive employment evaluations indicated he was still able to teach. The court found that substantial evidence supported the school board's decision. **There was a nexus between the sexual relationship and the teacher's fitness to teach.** His positive work reviews predated the disclosure of his misconduct and he discounted the sexual nature of the relationship. It made no difference to the court that the student no longer attended school in the district. The teacher had compromised his position of trust and his status as a role model, and the court upheld the teacher's firing for immorality. *Lehto v. Board of Educ. of Caesar Rodney School Dist.*, 962 A.2d 222 (Del. 2008).

◆   A New Jersey teacher resigned after the end of his one-year contract. The next school year, two students who had been in his class told a school guidance counselor the teacher had accessed pornographic websites on his classroom computer. The district superintendent ordered an investigation, and a school technology director found some sites viewed on the teacher's computer that might be pornographic. Three students corroborated earlier reports. A detective obtained arrest warrants for the teacher, who admitted viewing adult websites on his school computer, but said students did not see any nudity. A grand jury indicted the teacher on four counts of endangering the welfare of a child and one count of official misconduct. He pleaded guilty to reduced charges of unauthorized computer use and was sentenced to a year of probation. The teacher sued the detective, school board, district superintendent, administrators and families for malicious prosecution and negligence. A federal district court ruled against him, finding **the officials and others were entitled to qualified immunity for the malicious prosecution claims**. The teacher did not show school officials played any role in a constitutional violation, and their actions were reasonable in response to the allegations. There was no evidence that students lied or their parents consented to lying. *Grendysa v. Evesham Township Board of Educ.*, No. Civ.A. 02-1493 (FLW), 2005 WL 2416983 (D.N.J. 2005).

◆ A Wisconsin teacher had conflicts with a principal. Several female students later filed complaints against the teacher for touching them, referring to them as "honey, dear or sweetheart," refusing to let them wear sweatsuits over their swimsuits while doing calisthenics, and related conduct. After suspending the teacher with pay, the school board terminated his employment for just cause. An arbitrator reinstated the teacher but suspended him for a year without pay. A state court vacated the arbitration award and the teacher's employee association appealed. The Court of Appeals of Wisconsin held the relevant collective bargaining agreement gave the arbitrator authority to determine discipline and to craft a remedy. The arbitrator's findings were not reviewable by the trial court because he did not exceed his authority or violate public policy in making the award. **There was no evidence of any flaw in the arbitrator's finding of no just cause to terminate the teacher's employment.** *Greendale Educ. Ass'n v. Greendale School Dist.*, 259 Wis.2d 481, 655 N.W.2d 546 (Wis. Ct. App. 2002).

## B. Immoral Conduct and Moral Turpitude

*Misconduct that may lead to employment termination includes immoral or criminal conduct, moral turpitude, and neglect of duty. A Florida court has held moral turpitude requires an "intent to defraud or deceive." In* Beebee v. Haslett Public Schools, *239 N.W.2d 724 (1976), Michigan's Supreme Court held that if a teacher's off-campus conduct is at issue, there must be some link between the out-of-school acts and in-school behavior to justify employee discipline.*

◆ A Michigan teacher was photographed while simulating oral sex with a mannequin at a bachelor/bachelorette party. The pictures were taken without her knowledge and posted on a website. Two years later, students at her school accessed the photos, which were then removed from the website. But the teacher was suspended and then discharged for engaging in lewd behavior contrary to the moral values of her community. The school board found the teacher's conduct had undermined her authority and professional responsibilities as a role model for students. But the state tenure commission ordered her reinstatement.

On appeal, the Court of Appeals of Michigan found the discipline of a tenured teacher must be based on reasonable and just cause under state law. **Just cause must be shown by significant evidence proving unfitness to teach.** As a teacher's essential function is to impart knowledge, the court found the focus of the evidence is the effect of the questioned activity on the teacher's students. Courts in Michigan, California and other states with similar tenure laws have focused on incompetence and inefficiency, since they have a direct effect on students. The court found that where a teacher's conduct, outside school and not involving students, was the basis for discipline, a serious question existed as to whether a school could impose discipline without showing the conduct had **"an adverse effect upon the educational process."** The photos created gossip, but there was testimony that parents had not lost respect for the teacher. As the commission did not abuse its authority in finding a lack of reasonable cause for discharge, the court affirmed its decision. *Land v. L'Anse Creuse Public School Board of Educ.*, No. 288612, 2010 WL 2135356 (Mich. Ct. App. 5/27/10).

◆   A Delaware school board charged a special education teacher with four incidents of misconduct and/or immorality, including selling grades to students for cash, sleeping during the day and swearing in front of students at a school football game. The most serious charge against the teacher was that he asked one of his students for a ride to a dangerous area to purchase drugs. At the time, the teacher' driving privileges were suspended due to a DUI conviction. A hearing officer found his statements were "incredible." Grade books supported charges that the teacher had raised the final grades of two students for cash.

A state court upheld the decision to discharge the teacher for immorality and misconduct. He appealed to the Supreme Court of Delaware. **The court found state law permitted the admission of any evidence pertinent to the written reasons for a teacher's dismissal.** As the board could hear all evidence that could conceivably throw light on a controversy, a due process claim failed. All the incidents considered by the hearing officer were related to the grounds provided in the termination notice. State law permitted the board to consider evidence of a teacher's performance throughout the entire employment term. Board procedures satisfied due process requirements, and substantial evidence supported the board's decision. *Bethel v. Board of Educ. of Capital School Dist.*, 985 A.2d 389 (Table) (Del. 2009).

◆   A Washington student participated in a harassment charge involving an openly gay teacher at his high school. The student and teacher had differing accounts, but they admitted calling each other names and using profanity. After school officials investigated the student's complaint, the teacher was issued a letter of probable cause for discharge. A hearing officer found the teacher lied but found no probable cause for discharge, as the conduct cited in the termination letter would have no adverse impact on the teacher's effectiveness.

A Washington court denied the district's appeal and awarded the teacher $38,774 in attorneys' fees. When the district appealed to the Court of Appeals of Washington, the teacher withdrew his request for reinstatement and waived his attorneys' fees award. Asserting the case was settled, he asked to dismiss the appeal as moot. The court found not all the issues had been settled and held the case was not moot. In ruling on sufficient cause for discharge, the lower court had to consider if the teacher's deficiencies were "unremediable" and if they materially and substantially affected his performance. Reversing the judgment and award of attorneys' fees, **the court found the teacher's dishonesty during an investigation was misconduct that "lacks any professional purpose and is sufficient cause for termination as a matter of law."** *Federal Way School Dist. v. Vinson*, 154 Wash.App. 220, 225 P.3d 379 (Wash. Ct. App. 2010).

◆    A California school district began termination proceedings against a high school teacher for inappropriate conduct. One incident involved his decision to remove a high school student from his classroom for wearing a shirt that said "Israeli Police." Before a district commission on professional competence (CPC), officials claimed he made disparaging remarks about Israel, used physical force upon students, made inappropriate sexual comments to female students, and used profanity and threats. The CPC found the teacher engaged in unprofessional conduct, but dismissal was not warranted. A state superior court affirmed, as did the Court of Appeal of California. As the CPC had found, the teacher incorrectly believed a student's "Israeli Police" shirt violated the school dress code. However, his demands to remove the shirt were rooted in the desire to maintain classroom order. Also, the CPC did not find that the teacher used force or profanity. Sexual comments to female students were found by the CPC to be "friendly banter," and the comments were not reported as "unwelcome" or upsetting to students. The teacher's conduct after being transferred did not show such unfitness to teach as to warrant dismissal. Finally, **the teacher acknowledged his misconduct, was unlikely to repeat it and was not a danger to students**. *Santa Barbara School Dist. v. Commission on Professional Competence*, No. B199525, 2009 WL 73621 (Cal. Ct. App. 1/13/09).

◆    A Florida school hired a teacher six months after he was involved in an accident in which a seven-year-old child was killed. A highway patrol arrest affidavit stated he was driving recklessly and jockeying for position in traffic at a high speed when he lost control of his van. The teacher pleaded no contest and was found guilty of vehicular homicide. He was placed on probation for five years and assigned 500 hours of community service. For unstated reasons, the teacher's school board waited more than four years to initiate dismissal proceedings for committing a "crime of moral turpitude." The board dismissed the teacher, and the action was upheld by an administrative law judge. On appeal, the District Court of Appeal of Florida noted that while the teacher had operated his vehicle in a reckless manner that was likely to cause death or great bodily harm, his actions were not deemed "moral turpitude." **Moral turpitude had the essential element of intent to defraud or deceive.** Since the school board failed to prove moral turpitude, the court reversed the judgment and reinstated the teacher. *Cisneros v. School Board of Miami-Dade County*, 990 So.2d 1179 (Fla. Dist. Ct. App. 2008).

◆    A Missouri teacher brought her children, ages 2, 10 and 11, to a casino and left them in her car for 45 minutes while she went inside. When she returned to her car, the police had arrived, and she was charged with a class A misdemeanor of endangering the welfare of a child in the second degree. The teacher pleaded guilty and completed a year of probation. The school board rehired her, even after it learned about the incident. The state education department filed a complaint to suspend the teacher's teaching certificate, but it offered no further evidence about the incident. The teacher claimed that the weather was mild, and that she went into the casino to contact a friend and did not gamble.

    The state education commissioner recommended a 90-day suspension of her teaching certificate. The state board found the discipline was appropriate, based on a guilty plea to a crime involving moral turpitude. A Missouri county circuit court reversed the decision. The board appealed to the Court of Appeals of Missouri, which explained that the board could discipline the teacher only if her offense involved "moral turpitude." **Moral turpitude has been defined as "an act of baseness, vileness, or depravity in the private and social duties" which a person owes others or society.** As the teacher did not plead guilty to a crime that necessarily involved moral turpitude, and because the education department presented no evidence on the issue, the court held that the board should have dismissed the case. *Brehe v. Missouri Dep't of Elementary and Secondary Educ.*, 213 S.W.3d 720 (Mo. Ct. App. 2007).

◆   An Oregon teacher served a school district for 19 years with no disciplinary problems. Her husband left her for a girlfriend and sought a divorce. The teacher drove to the girlfriend's house and argued with him. She attempted suicide by taking prescription medications, then rammed her vehicle into her husband's vehicle and damaged the house. The teacher voluntarily committed herself for psychiatric treatment. The incident was reported in local newspapers. Law officials charged the teacher with four crimes, three of which were dropped via plea bargain. She pleaded no contest to a criminal mischief charge, which provided for dismissal with no charges if she completed her term of probation.

The school board voted to dismiss the teacher, and she appealed to the Oregon Fair Dismissal Appeals Board (FDAB). An FDAB hearing panel heard testimony from a psychologist who said the teacher's conduct was isolated and unlikely to reoccur. The board had previously let two teachers return to work after suicide attempts, and another had returned after entering into a diversion agreement for domestic violence charges. The FDAB panel found the dismissal had been "unreasonable." The board overreacted to an isolated incident and had to reinstate the teacher. The Court of Appeals of Oregon reversed the panel's decision, and the teacher appealed. **The Supreme Court of Oregon stated that contract teachers may be dismissed only for immorality or neglect of duty.** The FDAB failed to determine whether the board had applied an excessive remedy. The court returned the case to the panel for further consideration. *Bergerson v. Salem-Keizer School Dist.*, 341 Or. 401, 144 P.3d 918 (Or. 2006).

◆   A 14-year-old Illinois student gave birth to a child in 1986. Blood tests indicated a 99.99% probability that her junior high school assistant principal (AP) was the child's father. The school district dismissed the AP, but he was later acquitted of aggravated criminal sexual assault. A hearing officer reversed the action dismissing him in 1991, finding the district did not prove he had sexual contact with the student. A state court affirmed the AP's reinstatement, as did the Appellate Court of Illinois. In 1997, a paternity case was opened and a court ordered the AP to submit to DNA testing. Testing indicated a 99.9% probability that the AP was the child's father, and the court entered a judgment of paternity and ordered him to pay child support. The state superintendent of education advised the AP of an action to suspend his administrative and teaching certificates for immoral conduct. A hearing officer upheld the action.

On appeal, the Appellate Court of Illinois held that the action to suspend the AP's certificates was not barred by the district's effort to dismiss him years earlier. The employment dismissal and the certificate suspension proceedings were distinct and were brought by entirely different entities. **And the assistant principal's acquittal from criminal charges did not prevent the state superintendent from suspending his certificates.** The 1998 DNA test results were "evidence of immorality" permitting suspension. *Hayes v. State Teacher Certification Board*, 359 Ill.App.3d 1153, 835 N.E.2d 146 (Ill. App. Ct. 2005).

◆    An Oklahoma teacher who was threatened with discharge returned to work after he settled his state court lawsuit. When the superintendent stated he would "write him up for not reporting to his assigned area," the teacher said "if you do, I'll beat the shit out of you" in a threatening manner. The superintendent left to obtain a witness, and the teacher again threatened him. The teacher then said he was sick and left school for the day. The school board voted to terminate his contract for moral turpitude, and he sued it in a state court. The court affirmed the board's finding that his conduct was moral turpitude justifying employment termination. On appeal, the Oklahoma Supreme Court held **"moral turpitude" under state law involved a level of conduct that was more than "mere impropriety."** It was not a catch-all for all offensive, inappropriate or unprofessional conduct. While the teacher's threats were "unprofessional, unwise and unacceptable," there was no moral turpitude. *Ballard v. Independent School Dist. No. 4 of Bryan County, Oklahoma*, 77 P.3d 1084 (Okla. 2003).

### C. Criminal Conduct

*Utah's highest court upheld the firing of a school maintenance supervisor after a police investigation confirmed he performed contracting work for his private business and used a school district vehicle during work hours.*

◆    A Utah school district maintenance supervisor was a salaried employee who considered himself on duty at all times and kept a cell phone to respond as needed. No district policy prohibited outside employment, and he operated a contracting business. Co-workers reported that he was performing personal work during normal work hours, and one subordinate reported he could not reach him by phone. Local police investigated, and confirmed that the supervisor left work early on most days. He also used his school district vehicle to visit non-district work sites during work hours. After the supervisor was suspended without pay, he pled no contest to misdemeanor charges of communications fraud. The district terminated him for misuse of his vehicle, time card falsification, and neglect of professional obligations in violation of the classified agreement that governed his employment. The supervisor sued the school district and officials, and the case reached the Supreme Court of Utah.

The court found it "disingenuous" for the supervisor to argue that as long as he had his cell phone with him, he was still working for the district. **The supervisor's misrepresentations regarding work hours were sufficient grounds for termination for cause.** The school district was not contractually required to provide any prior notice, hearing, or progressive discipline prior to termination, as the action was "for cause" and not for "unsatisfactory conduct." *Oman v. Davis School Dist.*, 956 F.3d 956 (Utah 2008).

◆   An Oklahoma special education teacher accused a student of typing the word "jackass" on his computer, which the student denied. The student then left the classroom, as he had often done in the past. The teacher went to look for him, fearing the student might leave school grounds. He found the student in the school office and slapped him twice on the face. A school secretary later testified that the slaps were not very hard. The teacher stated that he did not intend to harm the student, and he went to the student's home to apologize to the family. The school district discharged the teacher under the state Teacher Due Process Act, asserting physical or mental abuse of a child. A state court held that he did not violate the act and ordered him reinstated. The school district appealed to the Supreme Court of Oklahoma, which noted that the student was often a disciplinary problem at school. He was on medication and had social interaction problems. The teacher had apologized to family members, who said they would be satisfied if he taught the student again. **He had begun counseling, and his counselor testified that the incident was unlikely to ever be repeated.** The court affirmed the judgment for the teacher. *Hagen v. Independent School Dist. No. I-004*, 157 P.3d 738 (Okla. 2007).

◆   A South Carolina teacher was arrested for possessing crack cocaine in 1988, but authorities dismissed his case. In 2000, the teacher was arrested "in his car in a well-known drug area" while his passenger attempted to buy crack. Charges against the teacher were dropped when the passenger pled guilty. After the 2000 incident, the teacher was placed on administrative leave, pending an investigation into the arrest and "similar behavior in the past." The superintendent advised him by letter his contract was being terminated. At the teacher's school board hearing, the superintendent said the termination was based solely on the teacher's unfitness. The board upheld the discharge, and the teacher appealed. A state court held that being arrested but not convicted for two criminal charges was not substantial evidence of unfitness to teach. The case reached the state supreme court, which noted that **two drug arrests, 12 years apart, neither resulting in charges, did not support a finding of unfitness to teach**. This was especially true when the district did not contend the teacher ever used, possessed or sold illegal drugs. The teacher was entitled to reinstatement with back pay and benefits from the date of his suspension. *Shell v. Richland County School Dist. One*, 362 S.C. 408, 608 S.E.2d 428 (S.C. 2005).

◆   New York's highest court upheld the dismissal of two school mechanics for misconduct. They sold untaxed cigarettes on school grounds while driving a school-owned vehicle. The mechanics stored the cigarettes in school vehicles. After a hearing, each was found guilty of disciplinary charges and discharged. The mechanics appealed to a state court, where they argued the evidence was insufficient to support a finding of misconduct. The court agreed, ruling that employment termination was too severe a penalty for their offenses. The school district appealed to a state appellate division court, which affirmed. At most, the mechanics acted inappropriately during work hours and misused school facilities. The court reduced their punishment to two years of suspended pay and benefits. On appeal, the New York Court of Appeals held that the district did not abuse its discretion in discharging the mechanics. **The misconduct took** place over several months, involved misappropriation of work time and violated the district's trust as well as district policy. *In re Maison Scahill v. Greece Cent. School Dist.*, 2 N.Y.3d 754, 778 N.Y.S.2d 771 (N.Y. 2004).

## D.  Neglect of Duty

*Court review of tenure proceedings is limited to an inquiry into whether the school board or state agency has complied with statutory requirements and whether the administrative findings are supported by substantial evidence.*

◆   A Louisiana teacher served her district for 16 years before being assigned to teach social studies and language arts at a middle school. The principal repeatedly explained that if teachers needed to send students to his office for discipline, they were to call him to have the students escorted to the office. The principal reprimanded the teacher twice during the opening weeks of the school year for sending students unescorted to his office for discipline. The principal sought to discipline the teacher, who refused to sign reprimand forms related to her policy violations. The school board found substantial evidence to support her discharge. A state trial court upheld the board's decision, and the teacher appealed. The case reached the Supreme Court of Louisiana, which noted that state law permitted the removal of a tenured teacher for willful neglect of duty. Here, the principal's warnings to the teacher against sending unescorted students to the office for discipline adequately explained school policy. There was substantial evidence to support the board's decision that her **repeated failure to follow these directions constituted willful neglect of duty**. The court upheld the board's action dismissing the teacher. *Wise v. Bossier Parish School Board*, 851 So.2d 1090 (La. 2003).

◆   A Louisiana teacher was a tenured vocational instructor whose only area of certification was shop mechanics. He was suspended with pay after he reported the theft of a loaded gun from his wife's car – which he had parked outside his classroom. A state trial court affirmed the board's decision to fire the teacher for willful neglect of duty, as did the state court of appeal. The Supreme Court of Louisiana reversed the lower courts, finding **no rational basis to discharge the teacher for neglect of duty simply because of the theft of the loaded gun from his wife's car**. It ordered the board to reinstate him to his former position, with all salary and benefits. Instead of rehiring the teacher, the board notified him it had discontinued shop mechanics from the curriculum. As this was his only area of certification, the board terminated his employment, retroactive to a date four years earlier. The teacher again appealed to the supreme court, which found no evidence that the board had complied with its mandate to reinstate the teacher to his former position with all salary and benefits. The teacher should have been considered reinstated as of the date of his last paycheck until the date of the board's notice of reduction in force, when he was formally advised of employment termination. The court amended the judgment to require the board to pay him for this four-year period, with interest. *Howard v. West Baton Rouge Parish School Board*, 865 So.2d 708 (La. 2004).

◆   A Texas teacher checked out a district vehicle for a soccer clinic. Before he went to the clinic, a witness saw him leaving a store with beer and getting into the vehicle. When the principal confronted him about it, the teacher admitted buying beer while using the vehicle. He submitted his resignation after being formally reprimanded, but he later rescinded it. The superintendent recommended not renewing his contract, and the school board voted for non-renewal after a hearing. The state education commissioner affirmed the decision, finding substantial evidence that **the teacher was "in the course and scope of his employment while he was in possession of alcohol."** A Texas court affirmed the decision, and the teacher appealed. The Court of Appeals of Texas held it could not substitute its judgment for the commissioner's and could only review it to determine if it was supported by substantial evidence. The teacher had admitted his error and stated that he was acting within the scope of his duties to attend the clinic. The teacher agreed it was reasonable to assume he was acting for the school when the school day began. As the commissioner's decision was supported by substantial evidence, the court affirmed it. *Simpson v. Alanis*, No. 08-03-00110-CV, 2004 WL 309297 (Tex. Ct. App. 2004).

### E.  Misuse of Technology

*A Florida case held requests to examine employee computer hard drives were permitted "in only limited or strictly controlled circumstances," such as where a party was suspected of trying to purge data.* Menke v. Broward County School Board, *916 So.2d 8 (Fla. Dist. Ct. App. 2005). Other courts have upheld such access only when there was evidence of intentional deletion of data.*

◆   Ohio school administrators placed a junior high school teacher on leave of absence after investigating charges that he accessed sexually oriented websites on school computers and viewed them with students. The school board resolved to suspend him without pay or benefits, but agreed to delay his hearing until criminal proceedings were complete. The teacher was convicted of several felonies, fined $5,000 and jailed for nearly a year. When the state education department sought to revoke his teaching certificate, he alleged due process violations. A hearing officer found the teacher had sexually abused students, provided them with alcohol and sexually explicit books and movies, let a student view sexually oriented websites on a school computer and "brutalized" at least two students. This conduct was criminal, immoral and unbecoming to a teacher under state law. The state board revoked the teacher's eight-year teaching certificate, and his permanent certification. On appeal, the Ohio Court of Appeals held **he could not be employed as a teacher because he was convicted of one of the crimes listed as disqualifying under state education law**. After his teaching certificates were revoked, the board could not maintain his contract. *Huntsman v. Perry Local School Dist. Board of Educ.*, No. 2004 CA 00347, 2005 WL 1519344 (Ohio Ct. App. 2005).

◆   A Texas teacher found a "Teacher Evaluations" icon on a classroom computer. Students later discovered documents involving employee reprimands on the computer's hard drive. The teacher recognized some of the information as confidential and inappropriate for students, but he read it with them. A student saved the personnel documents on floppy disks, and the teacher gave them to his attorney without telling school administrators. The district discharged the teacher, and the Court of Appeals of Texas upheld the discharge. It noted that the state education commissioner had defined **"good cause" as the failure to perform employment duties that a "person of ordinary prudence would have done under the same or similar circumstances."** The court upheld the commissioner's finding of good cause. The teacher did not dispute that he discovered confidential records and allowed students to review and download them. *Tave v. Alanis*, 109 S.W.3d 890 (Tex. Ct. App. 2003).

## III. INCOMPETENCE

### A. Teaching Deficiencies

*An Ohio court has held that recommendations in teacher evaluations "must be specific enough to alert a reasonable person to the need for change." California law authorizes the midyear dismissal of a teacher only if specific instances of unsatisfactory performance are not timely corrected. And Nevada law requires school administrators to notify employees in writing whenever it is necessary to admonish the employee, along with the reasons. Reasonable efforts to assist the employee must be made to correct the deficiency.*

◆ A California probationary teacher's evaluations indicated her performance could be "refined," but she was not told it was unsatisfactory, or that failure to improve would result in dismissal. After her second evaluation, the principal told her the school board had discussed her discharge, which came as a surprise to her. He gave the teacher a report which lauded her for creating a "pleasant feeling tone" in classes, but criticized her for allowing students to spend too much time off task. Eight days after the second observation, the district notified the teacher of her dismissal for unsatisfactory performance. The school board finalized the dismissal at a hearing, and the teacher sued. The court held that the district did not comply with the state Education Code and ordered the teacher reinstated with lost wages and benefits. The Court of Appeal of California affirmed. Dismissal of probationary employees during a school year for unsatisfactory performance required a written notice to the teacher identifying particular instances of unsatisfactory performance 90 days prior to any notice of dismissal. **Here, the district did not provide the teacher a timely written notice of unsatisfactory performance or an opportunity to correct specified deficiencies.** *Achene v. Pierce Joint Unified School Dist.*, 176 Cal.App.4th 757, 97 Cal.Rptr.3d 899 (Cal. Ct. App. 2009).

◆ A Nevada school district admonished a teacher for failing to follow district procedures for testing English language learners. She was provided training and mentoring, and her caseload was reduced by 50%. After a second admonition, the district provided the teacher one-on-one training and feedback on testing procedures. After a third admonition, the district suspended the teacher and advised her that her contract would not be renewed. She sought arbitration, claiming the district violated state law by dismissing her only eight days after the last admonishment. The arbitrator upheld the non-renewal. On appeal to the Supreme Court of Nevada, the teacher argued that she should have been allowed to improve her job performance after the final admonition. The court held the law required a "reasonable time for improvement, which must not exceed three months for the first admonition." **The teacher was admonished many times for the same unprofessional conduct.** There was no violation of the law since all the admonishments were for the same type of conduct. The district provided the teacher assistance for over a year to correct her deficient performance, including training, mentoring and reduction of her workload. She received a reasonable time to improve her performance, but was unable to do so. *Clark County Educ. Ass'n v. Clark County School Dist.*, 131 P.3d 5 (Nev. 2006).

◆  An Ohio trial court ordered a school board to rehire a teacher. It held her evaluations did not give her specific recommendations for improvement and the means to obtain assistance. Comments such as "see me before next observation" did not satisfy state law. The principal found that the teacher lost control of one class, and noted many of her students wandered around, slept or otherwise failed to participate in classes. The state court of appeals held that the board had to rehire her. **Recommendations in teacher evaluations "must be specific enough to alert a reasonable person to the need for change."** The state supreme court refused to review the case. *Cox v. Zanesville City School Dist. Board of Educ.*, 105 Ohio St.3d 1466, 824 N.E.2d 93 (Ohio 2005).

◆  A Missouri school district discharged a resource teacher whose individualized education programs were incomplete. District administrators had worked with her before and after issuing her a notice of deficiencies. The district special education director met with the teacher at least once weekly and made additional efforts to assist her. She received extensions for job target deadlines. In her state court action, the state court of appeals held the district complied with each of the state Tenure Act's requirements. There was no merit to the teacher's claim that her termination was improperly based on "non-teaching, non-substantive processing of burdensome administrative paperwork." **Missouri case law defines "incompetency and inefficiency" as the "inability to perform professional teaching duties in a manner acceptable to the Board."** Timely completion of special education paperwork was "inextricable from a special education teacher's professional teaching duties." Failure to comply with paperwork requirements could result in the denial of an appropriate education to a student. *Hellmann v. Union R-XI School Dist.*, 170 S.W.3d 52 (Mo. Ct. App. 2005).

## B.  Procedural Problems

*Even before the sweeping amendments to Florida law in 2011, the state required that assessment procedures for instructional personnel be "primarily based on the performance of students assigned to their classrooms." Assessments had to "primarily use data and indicators of improvement in student performance assessed annually.*" *In* Sherrod v. Palm Beach County School Board, *a board that did not primarily base its decision on the performance of students in a teacher's classroom was held in violation of law.*

*In* Buchna v. Illinois State Board of Educ., *an Illinois court held state law clearly specified a three-tiered, mandatory rating system, which a district was not free to ignore in negotiating a collective bargaining agreement.*

◆   A Florida school nurse left a seizure-prone, quadriplegic student to assess whether another child was having a seizure. At the time he was called by a teacher to assess the other child, the nurse was tube-feeding the quadriplegic student. The school board sought to fire the nurse for not following safe procedures and failing to provide first aid. In termination proceedings, it was learned that the teacher who sought his help did not know he was tube-feeding the quadriplegic student. Although an administrative law judge (ALJ) recommended a written reprimand, the board terminated the nurse's employment. On appeal, a state district court of appeal held the ALJ's findings were improperly modified. There was no proof that the nurse failed to provide appropriate nursing care or fell asleep on the job, as the board claimed. As **the board could not modify the ALJ's findings unless they were not based on competent substantial evidence**, the court reversed the decision with directions to adopt the ALJ's order. *Resnick v. Flagler County School Board,* 46 So.3d 1110 (Fla. Dist. Ct. App. 2010).

◆   A Florida school board brought formal discharge proceedings against a career contract teacher with many classroom and communication problems. The teacher was then transferred to a different school. There were new complaints about excessive and inappropriate use of R-rated videos, failure to timely post and enter grades into the system, and failure to provide timely instruction on covered materials. The teacher was charged with failing to properly control students and was put on probation. He was transferred to another school, where he failed to follow lesson plans and had no required text for students. After a formal hearing, the school board fired the teacher. He appealed to the Florida District Court of Appeal, which explained that under state law, the assessment procedure for instructional personnel must be primarily based on the performance of students. Assessments **"must primarily use data and indicators of improvement in student performance assessed annually."** Here, the school board did not primarily base its decision on the performance of students in the teacher's classroom. The court rejected the board's argument that a teacher may be discharged if factors other than student performance are "properly deemed more crucial." The statute required primary reliance on standardized tests and left no discretion for teacher assessment. The court ruled for the teacher. *Sherrod v. Palm Beach County School Board,* 963 So.2d 251 (Fla. Dist. Ct. App. 2006).

◆   A Michigan teacher was transferred after getting unsatisfactory performance ratings. When her performance was again rated unsatisfactory, she sought help from her teachers union. The union declined the teacher's request to process her grievances against the school board. A hearing officer found that the teacher failed to plan, prepare, develop and provide appropriate lessons and educational activities for students and did not effectively control them or maintain a proper learning atmosphere. The board discharged the teacher, and the state court of appeals affirmed the decision. She filed unfair labor practice charges against the union and board with the Michigan Employment Relations Commission (MERC). A MERC hearing officer recommended dismissing the charge against the union. The court of appeals affirmed the MERC decision. The teacher filed a new action against the district for age discrimination, conspiracy, breach of contract, and discharge against public policy. She included claims against the union for breach of its duty of fair representation and intentional infliction of emotional distress. The case reached the state court of appeals, which held **the teacher's issues were addressed in the prior action**. Accordingly, her lawyer was fined $500 for filing a frivolous action. *Knubbe v. Detroit Board of Educ.*, No. 240076, 2003 WL 22681553 (Mich. Ct. App. 2003).

◆    The Illinois Education Code requires school districts to evaluate employees and take remedial action where necessary. The law establishes three categories for employment ratings: excellent, satisfactory and unsatisfactory. Despite this mandatory language, a school district negotiated a collective bargaining agreement establishing two evaluation categories: "does not meet district expectations" and "meets or exceeds district expectations." A district found a teacher deficient in 10 areas and placed her on a one-year remediation plan. She then received "does not meet district expectations" ratings in two consecutive quarterly reports. The district fired the teacher, and she appealed to the Appellate Court of Illinois, which noted that the statute clearly indicated a three-tiered, mandatory rating system. The legislature used unmistakable language, which the district was not free to ignore. **The remediation and dismissal provisions of the law applied only to teachers who received "unsatisfactory" ratings.** Since the teacher never received that designation, she was not subject to remediation and her discharge was improper. The court reversed the judgment. *Buchna v. Illinois State Board of Educ.*, 795 N.E.2d 1045 (Ill. App. Ct. 2003).

◆    A newly tenured Nebraska high school principal claimed he was fired and denied due process because he was not evaluated as frequently as specified by state law. The Nebraska Court of Appeals rejected his argument concerning the number of evaluations he had. The discharge occurred after he acquired tenure, and the district had properly evaluated him during the year. There was evidence that the district had thoroughly evaluated the principal and offered to assist him, but that he did not respond professionally. He was advised of his deficiencies and given an opportunity to correct them. The court reviewed evidence that the principal misled the superintendent about an incident that required police intervention. He was also dishonest to parents, students and police concerning another incident, and he was slow to discipline a teacher for accessing pornographic websites at school. **The court found substantial evidence of incompetence, neglect of duty and performance issues that supported the finding of just cause for termination.** *Montgomery v. Jefferson County School Dist. No. 0008*, No. A-01-1018, 2003 WL 1873713 (Neb. App. 2003).

## IV. INSUBORDINATION AND OTHER GOOD CAUSE

*In* Barnes v. Spearfish School Dist., *the Supreme Court of South Dakota defined "insubordination" as "a willful disregard of an employer's instructions" or an "act of disobedience to the proper authority," such as "refusal to obey an order that a superior officer is authorized to give." The Court of Appeals of Tennessee reached a similar conclusion in* Ketchersid v. Rhea County Board of Educ., *holding the term "insubordination" included the refusal to carry out specific assignments made by a principal.*

◆ An Ohio middle school teacher was reprimanded and placed on leave for misconduct, disrespect and insubordination. It was reported that he said he would slash the principal's tires, and he signed a "last chance" agreement with the school board. After the board suspended the teacher, a hearing referee found he had grabbed a student by the arm or shirt during a video presentation. He pulled the student, put him in front of the screen and pointed his face at it. The referee found this use of physical force violated a board policy against corporal punishment. It was also found that he had twisted hair and pulled ears of some students several times that year. The board voted to terminate his contract.

A state court upheld the decision, and the teacher appealed to the Court of Appeals of Ohio. He argued his use of corrective actions had been appropriate and necessary to maintain a productive and safe learning environment. The court disagreed, finding physical intervention with a student to redirect his attention was a violation of the board's policy and disproportionate to the misbehavior involved. Significantly, the court found **the dismissal was based on the teacher's cumulative misconduct over the previous three years, not just the last incident**. Agreeing with the board that his repeated misconduct constituted "good and just cause" for employment termination, the court affirmed the lower court's decision. *Lanzo v. Campbell City School Dist. Board of Educ.,* No. 09 MA 154, 2010 WL 3835868 (Ohio Ct. App. 9/24/10).

◆ After 27 years of teaching in a Kentucky school district, a teacher was suspended pending termination proceedings for knocking a banana from a student's hands. A school tribunal found the teacher had violated a prior written directive instructing him to exhibit professional and appropriate behavior, make only professional comments to students and refrain from touching them. Among the tribunal's findings was that the teacher "had flown into a rage" and "initiated aggressive physical contact with a student." It further found that he had misrepresented the incident and violated the state teachers' professional ethics code by lying and not taking reasonable measures to protect students. The tribunal found contract termination appropriate, and a Kentucky circuit court upheld the decision. The teacher appealed to the Court of Appeals of Kentucky.

According to the court, the insubordination charge was unsupported by a proper written record, as required by state law. **Section 161.790(1) of the state revised statutes requires supervisors to support charges against a teacher with a written record of performance.** The record "must be specific to the individual teacher and the circumstances leading up to the charge." The court found no evidence that the teacher had touched the student. It found the "banana incident" involved a student who took a banana from the teacher, disobeyed his instructions to put it down, and then tried to eat it. The teacher knocked the banana down without touching him. He was not advised of any deficiencies as required by school policy, and he received no directive regarding expected behavior. The judgment was reversed due to lack of notice, the administration's failure to comply with its own procedures and other errors. *Raley v. Ohio County Schools*, No. 2009-CA-001358-MR, 2010 WL 3361125 (Ky. Ct. App. 8/27/10).

◆   A California high school teacher had a single subject teaching credential in music and was her school's only music teacher. A 2002 state audit found her district out of compliance with state law because some teachers without an English Language Learners (EL) certification were assigned to teach EL students. The district created a plan for all teachers to obtain EL certification. A collective bargaining agreement (CBA) provision required all certificated staff to obtain EL certification by the end of 2005 or face employment termination. Under the CBA, the district paid for EL training, plus a $400 stipend to each teacher. The music teacher repeatedly refused to sign a commitment to receive EL training. After the district fired her, a court upheld her discharge. She appealed to the Court of Appeal of California.

The court held that **the teacher's arguments trivialized the dilemma faced by the district, which was subject to penalties if it assigned an EL student to an improperly certified teacher**. The Legislature recognized that EL students have the same rights to quality education as all other California students. The district could discharge the teacher for unprofessional conduct, evident unfitness for service, and persistent refusal to obey reasonable district regulations. The teacher was not guaranteed employment or tenure, and she remained authorized to teach music by another district that might hire her. Since EL certification was reasonably related to the hours, wages and conditions of employment, it was an appropriate subject of collective bargaining. *Governing Board of Ripon Unified School Dist. v. Commission on Professional Conduct*, 177 Cal.App.4th 1379, 99 Cal.Rptr.3d 903 (Cal. Ct. App. 2009).

◆   A South Dakota teacher's first evaluation noted "excellent" performance. But she disagreed with other comments on the evaluation and did not sign it. She submitted a written response challenging each of the principal's comments, except the observation that she was an excellent teacher. During the next three years, she refused to sign evaluations and responded to them in writing. The school board later deemed these responses "confrontational" and "insolent."

The next school year, the principal grew concerned that the teacher was talking about personnel issues with other staff. He informed her this was inappropriate and had to stop. The teacher responded that the principal "undermines his own authority and imposes a low morale on the teachers by his own inappropriate actions." The teacher was reprimanded in writing for performance deficiencies and her intentional and willful failure to heed warnings or to follow performance expectations. After the teacher's fourth year in the district, her contract was not renewed because of her insubordination. The teacher appealed, and the Supreme Court of South Dakota noted that **insubordination is "a willful disregard of an employer's instructions" or an**

**"act of disobedience to the proper authority,"** such as refusal to obey a superior's order. The hearing had produced a wealth of testimony and documentation supporting the board's action. The court affirmed the judgment. *Barnes v. Spearfish School Dist. No. 40-2*, 725 N.W.2d 226 (S.D. 2006).

◆   The Supreme Court of North Carolina declined to review lower court decisions that upheld a school board's decision not to rehire a teacher who squirted her principal with a water pistol at a school-sponsored event. The state court of appeals found no evidence that the principal was biased. The action was based on several instances of misconduct and was not arbitrary. **The record indicated that the teacher's contract was not renewed because she was a counterproductive force to faculty morale at her school.** *Davis v. Macon County Board of Educ.*, 360 N.C. 645, 638 S.E.2d 465 (N.C. 2006).

◆   A Tennessee teacher with over 10 years of experience did not meet the requirements of an improvement plan while teaching a kindergarten class. She was transferred to another school and assigned to a classroom of third-graders needing remedial education. A few weeks into the school year, a student reported that the teacher had "smacked her on the face." The principal and assistant principal met with the teacher, stressing the importance of being positive with children and admonishing her that "she was not, under any circumstances, to put her hands on the students." Later in the school year, the parents of another student reported that the teacher had slapped their child.

The district conducted an investigation, and she admitted slapping five of seven students in the class "when she was angry and when the children were being disrespectful." The district immediately suspended the teacher for "complete insubordination." The school board upheld the recommendation to discharge the teacher for insubordination, incompetence, and inefficiency. A state court upheld that decision, and the teacher appealed. The Court of Appeals of Tennessee held that **"insubordination" included the refusal to carry out specific assignments made by the principal.** In this case, the teacher refused to follow a specific directive. As there was evidence of unfitness, as well as inefficiency and insubordination, the judgment was affirmed. *Ketchersid v. Rhea County Board of Educ.*, 174 S.W.2d 163 (Tenn. Ct. App. 2005).

◆   A Kentucky principal experienced considerable conflict with staff members and a small group of parents. The district superintendent issued charges against her and advised her she was immediately suspended. He proposed terminating her continuing contract. The charges included insubordination, conduct unbecoming a teacher, inefficiency and incompetence. A three-member tribunal upheld two of the six charges. It found that she carried a loaded gun onto school property and failed to accurately report the number of students attending school. The tribunal held the appropriate sanction for the two violations was a reprimand and a two-year suspension without pay. The school board appealed to a Kentucky circuit court, which upheld the decision. The state court of appeals affirmed, and the board and superintendent appealed.

The Supreme Court of Kentucky explained that **state law had been amended several times to remove the authority of school boards and**

**district superintendents to discipline teachers and provide for hearings by tribunals**. The administrative tribunals had the implied authority to reduce the sanctions proposed by a superintendent. The court rejected the superintendent's additional arguments. The principal was a "teacher" under Section 161.790 since she required certification to hold her position. As the tribunal was entitled to reduce the discipline, the court affirmed the judgment. *Fankhauser v. Cobb*, 163 S.W.3d 389 (Ky. 2005).

◆   A Florida teacher had several incidents involving contact with students and was then directed to report physical confrontations and avoid the appearance of intimidating students. He tried to pass candy out to his students in a class, but they became disruptive and rushed toward him. The teacher refused repeated attempts by one student to take more candy. When the student persisted, the teacher struck or shoved him, causing him to fall back or step back against some lockers. The school board filed an administrative complaint against the teacher. An administrative law judge (ALJ) conducted a hearing and determined that the student was disruptive and had put his hands on the teacher. The ALJ found that the teacher's use of force was reasonable and lawful. The board modified the ALJ's findings and rejected the recommendation to reinstate the teacher.

The board discharged him, and he sued it for reinstatement. A state district court of appeal observed that a school board may not reject a hearing officer's findings unless it finds they were not based on competent, substantial evidence or did not comply with essential requirements of law. Evidence indicated that students crowded the teacher into a small locker area and that the student persisted in attempting to get more candy after the teacher told him he could have no more. **The teacher did not violate the board's previous directive against touching students in a manner that served no educational purpose.** As his actions were not misconduct, gross insubordination, willful neglect of duty, or conduct unbecoming a teacher, the court reversed the board's decision. *Packer v. Orange County School Board*, 881 So.2d 1204 (Fla. Dist. Ct. App. 2004).

◆   A Missouri teacher answered a series of questions from one student on controversial subjects including abortion and interracial relationships. She stated that interracial couples "should be fixed" so that they could not have children and said that such children were "mixed" and "racially confused." Two biracial students attended her class. Later in the day, she made further disparaging remarks about biracial children. The district superintendent placed her on administrative leave. The school board terminated the teacher's indefinite contract for willfully violating its policies on equal opportunity, anti-discrimination and harassment. A state court affirmed the judgment.

On appeal, the Court of Appeals of Missouri found **sufficient evidence showed the teacher had willfully violated board policy**. Her statements regarding marriage and the ability to have children solely based on race were disparaging and discriminatory. The court rejected the teacher's claim to First Amendment protection because her comments did not address a matter of public concern. Even had the comments been deserving of First Amendment protection, they seriously disrupted the school environment. Because the district interest in efficiently operating a school free from racially discriminatory speech outweighed any personal speech rights held by the teacher, the court affirmed the judgment. *Loeffelman v. Board of Educ. of Crystal City School Dist.*, 134 S.W.3d 637 (Mo. Ct. App. 2004).

## V.  RESIGNATION AND RETIREMENT

*An employee's resignation ends contractual and tenure rights. It may not be withdrawn if the school board has relied on it and hired a replacement. In the next case, a Minnesota teacher who resigned after earning continuing-contract (tenured) status in a school district did not regain this status when he resigned, worked elsewhere for a year, then returned to the district.*

### A.  Resignation

◆   A Minnesota teacher worked for a school district from 2000 to 2007. He earned continuing-contract status under state law when he completed his third consecutive year of teaching in the district. After the teacher worked for another employer in 2007-08, he returned to the district for the 2008-09 school year. His contract did not refer to continuing-contract status, stating that its duration was subject to Section 122A.40 of Minnesota Statutes. In April 2009, the school board non-renewed the teacher's contract, effective at the end of the school year. He filed a state court action against the district, arguing he had continuing contract status and was entitled to a hearing prior to any non-renewal action.

The case reached the Court of Appeals of Minnesota, which held that under Section 122A.40, teachers are initially subject to a three-year probationary period. During this period, a school board may renew or non-renew a teacher's contract as it sees fit. Upon completion of a probationary period, a teacher had a "continuing contract" with the district that could be terminated only for cause after a hearing or by a written resignation. After completing a probationary period in a district, "the probationary period in each district in which the teacher is thereafter employed shall be one year." According to the court, the phrase "each district in which the teacher is thereafter employed" included the district in which a teacher completed a three-year probationary period. When a teacher resigned, taught elsewhere and then returned to a district, it was reasonable for the district to want to reevaluate him. **A teacher was subject to an additional one-year probationary period of state law upon resignation** and was subject to a one-year probationary period upon returning to the same district. *Montplaisir v. Independent School Dist. No. 23*, 779 N.W.2d 880 (Minn. Ct. App. 2010).

◆   After a Kansas Spanish teacher had worked at a high school for eight years, the principal notified her of his intent to recommend not renewing her contract. Prior to a meeting of the school board, the teacher and her union representative met with the superintendent to discuss a settlement. During the meeting, the board held several executive sessions, while the superintendent communicated offers between the parties. After some negotiating, the teacher agreed to retire or resign and apply for disability benefits. In exchange, the board agreed to extend her salary for seven months, pay her medical insurance or a lump-sum equivalent for five years, and pay her $20,000. The agreement was reduced to writing, but she refused to sign it. When the board resolved not to renew her contract, it declared it had an oral contract with her, and sued to enforce the agreement. The court rejected her arguments that she did not enter into a binding oral contract, and she appealed to the state court of appeals. It held that **the parties reached a complete and binding oral agreement with all essential separation terms**. *Unified School Dist. No. 446, Independence, Kansas v. Sandoval*, 214 P.3d 1225 (Table) (Kan. Ct. App. 2009).

◆   A Colorado teacher had an annual contract that permitted her school district to recover "all damages provided by law" for job abandonment or breach of contract. The district could withhold up to one-twelfth of her annual salary to pay the cost of finding a replacement if she did not provide notice of resignation 30 days prior to a school year. The teacher learned of a personal conflict and advised the district she could not maintain her assignment. The district withheld the teacher's final paycheck. In a state court action, she asserted the district was limited to recovering its actual costs rather than her full paycheck. The case reached the Colorado Supreme Court, which held **the law intended to reimburse districts for their actual cost outlays, not the cost of salaries they would have had to pay in any event**. The teacher tried to resolve a personal conflict in good faith, and had tried to comply with district procedures when she resigned. As a result, the district was entitled only to its actual cash outlay. *Klinger v. Adams County School Dist. No. 50*, 130 P.3d 1027 (Colo. 2006).

◆   Certificated Maryland public school employees generally have to provide written notice of a contract termination by May 1. Two teachers submitted written resignations after this deadline. The school board withheld their last paychecks for violating their contracts and replaced them with substitutes. The superintendent upheld the forfeiture provisions, and the board affirmed her decision. A state board upheld the provision, finding it was designed to further the legitimate public purpose of deterring late resignations that deprived local boards of the time needed to recruit and hire replacements at the last minute. It also defrayed some recruiting and hiring costs and the costs of hiring substitute teachers. Appeal reached the Court of Appeals of Maryland, which noted that **the forfeiture provision in the teaching contracts was a reasonable forecast of just compensation, and was binding and could not be altered to correspond to actual damages**. As no evidence indicated the enforcement of the forfeiture provision was arbitrary, the court affirmed the action. *Board of Educ. of Talbot County v. Heister*, 392 Md. 140, 896 A.2d 342 (Md. 2006).

◆   A Kentucky court held an agreement to conditionally reemploy a teacher who was reprimanded pending an evaluation did not violate state law provisions on voluntary termination of contracts. The teacher had written a letter to stop the pending termination as a last resort. There was no evidence of fraud, conspiracy or duress by the district. **A threat to fire an employee unless she resigns did not amount to duress.** *Keeling v. Jefferson County Board of Educ.*, No. 2002-CA-000528-MR, 2003 WL 1860539 (Ky. Ct. App. 2003).

◆   The Arkansas Supreme Court **rejected a school board's argument that its vote to accept a teacher's oral resignation converted the action into a vote to terminate or not renew his contract**. This was because the board was not required to take any action in response to an oral resignation. The teacher was not required to commence an action within 75 days, but the court held the teacher's assertion that the board vote to accept his resignation was itself void. *Williams v. Little Rock School Dist.*, 66 S.W.3d 590 (Ark. 2002).

## B. Retirement

*As in resignation cases, an employee's notice of retirement is typically binding as it cuts off the employee's contractual rights. A school board may not have to rehire an employee who tries to rescind a valid retirement notice.*

◆   A South Dakota teacher had worked for her district for 39 years when she learned her position would be reduced from full time to half time the next school year. She retired at the end of the year, took pay for her unpaid sick leave and began receiving benefits from the state retirement system. She came out of retirement before the start of the next school year and signed a one-year probationary contract for the half-time position she had previously rejected. Near the end of the school year, the board did not renew her contract and did not provide her a hearing. The teacher claimed she had no break in service and thus retained her continuing contract status, entitling her to due process protections. She sued the board, and the Supreme Court of South Dakota held that her arguments overlooked her voluntary retirement and her acceptance of a one-year probationary contract. **Her resignation was "a complete termination of her employment relationship" with the district**, and terminated her tenure rights. *Wirt v. Parker School Dist. #60-04*, 689 N.W.2d 901 (S.D. 2004).

◆   The Ohio Supreme Court held that **a retired bus mechanic was entitled to reinstatement after his school board illegally abolished his position**, laid him off and outsourced his duties to a private company. Since the board acted illegally, his retirement was considered involuntary. The mechanic retired because of the board's illegal action to abolish his position and outsource his work to a private company. His conduct in applying for retirement benefits did not indicate an intent to give up his continuing public employment rights, and he reapplied for his position as soon as he became aware of his potential right to reinstatement. The court remanded the case for resolution of the mechanic's claim for back wages and benefits. *State of Ohio, ex rel. Stacy v. Batavia Local School Dist. Board of Educ.*, 779 N.E.2d 216 (Ohio 2002).

◆   After 20 years of service, a Minnesota teacher submitted a notice of his retirement. He soon changed his mind and applied for the vacancy he created, resuming work without missing a school day. The district superintendent wrote the teacher that he was now a probationary teacher subject to employment termination on the last day of the school year. The letter noted the teacher's seniority date was the first day he resumed teaching and that he was entitled to benefits for new hires as of that date. He signed a document designating him as a long-term substitute, and the district approved his employment as a probationary teacher. Near the end of the school year, the school board resolved not to renew his contract. The teacher petitioned the Minnesota Court of Appeals, which rejected his claim to continuing contract status. A substitute teacher cannot attain continuing contract status without first being offered, then accepting, a continuing contract. The teacher signed a document advising him he was a long-term, probationary substitute with no continuing contract rights. He was clearly advised that he could regain continuing contract rights only if he were hired for the following school year. **As the teacher had terminated his own contractual rights by retiring and did not reactivate them by resuming his duties, the court affirmed his employment termination.** *Thomas v. Independent School Dist. No. 2142*, 639 N.W.2d 619 (Minn. Ct. App. 2002).

◆ Three Indiana teachers told their district in 1997 that they would retire the next year and accept early retirement benefits under a 1995-1997 master contract. The board and teachers association negotiated a master contract for 1997-2000 that dramatically reduced early retirement benefits. The retirees sued the association for breach of the duty of fair representation, and the board for breach of contract for failing to pay benefits under the 1995-1997 contract.

The court dismissed the complaint, ruling that it should have been filed with the Indiana Education Employment Relations Board (IEERB). The case reached the state supreme court, which held the retirees had to file their unfair representation claims with the IEERB. The state Certificated Educational Employee Bargaining Act recognized a right of school employees to organize and collectively bargain, creating a method to resolve labor disputes through the IEERB. But this ruling did not mean that the trial court had no jurisdiction over the breach of contract claim. **The IEERB had no power to consider a breach of contract claim concerning the board's liability for early retirement benefits.** By dismissing the breach of contract claim, the trial court had denied the retirees the only forum in which the claim could be heard. The trial court was ordered to retain the breach of contract claim. No action was to be taken until the IEERB decided the unfair representation claim. *Fratus v. Marion Community Schools Board of Trustees*, 749 N.E.2d 40 (Ind. 2001).

## C. Retirement Benefits

*The 2010 Patient Protection and Affordability Act and the Healthcare and Education Reconciliation Act are expected to have implications on school district compensation policies, retirement plans and collective bargaining agreements. The acts have timelines that will eventually require public school retirement plans to comply with requirements of the Employee Retirement Income Security Act (ERISA). Well-publicized provisions extending insurance coverage of dependents up to age 26, prohibiting insurer exclusions for preexisting health conditions and establishing state health insurance exchanges do not take full effect until 2014. A Patient Protection and Affordability Act provision applies to group health plans and health insurance coverage in which an individual was enrolled on March 23, 2010, the date of enactment of the act.*

◆   An Oklahoma school district offered an early retirement plan to encourage highly paid senior employees to retire so they could be replaced by lower-paid employees. Eligible retirees were to receive 10% of their salaries plus healthcare benefits. A provision said the plan could end "because of lack of funds." However, plan documents did not explain the nature or extent of "lack of funds" that would justify termination. In 2002, the district declared a financial crisis that would likely eliminate plan benefits. The school board then voted to terminate payments to retirees but to continue paying for their health insurance. Seventy-nine retirees sued the school district in the state court system for breach of contract. A jury found the retirees proved the district had sufficient revenues to continue paying them benefits and returned a $1.4 million verdict in their favor.

On appeal, the Supreme Court of Oklahoma noted that the state constitution required political subdivisions, such as school districts, to carry all "corporate operations on a pay-as-you-go basis." Indebtedness was prohibited beyond a current year. Under state law, **a party demonstrating municipal liability in a contract action had to prove the municipality's ability to pay the claim so that any judgment did not exceed constitutional debt limits**. Since the retirees did not submit evidence proving the district's legal indebtedness for the fiscal year in which the judgment was issued, a lower court had correctly found lack of compliance with state law. So the judgment was void. But the court held failure to present proof of indebtedness for the relevant year did not affect the verdict, which was supported by competent evidence. The trial court would have to consider evidence establishing the district's actual indebtedness for the year the judgment was issued. *Ahlschlager v. Lawton School Dist., Independent School Dist. 008 of Comanche County*, 242 P.3d 509 (Okla. 2010).

◆   A Pennsylvania school district employee pension plan based retirement benefits on years of service and the employee's average salary in the final years of employment. The plan was administered by the Public School Employees Retirement System (PSERS). Two district employees were approved for leaves of absence to serve in executive union positions for five years. They received pay that was between 44% and 55% higher than what they would have received in their regular school district employment. When the employees filed retirement applications with the PSERS, the PSERS did not include the increased salaries they were paid by the union in calculating their retirement benefits. Instead, the PSERS calculated retirement benefits based on salary levels corresponding to their school district positions. This sharply reduced the retirement benefits the employees expected. The employees appealed to the public school employees' retirement board, which denied their request to use wages earned as union executives in their retirement calculations. They petitioned the state court system for relief, and appeal reached the Supreme Court of Pennsylvania.

The supreme court affirmed the retirement board's decision. It found **state law did not suggest that union employees should receive greater retirement benefits than others who chose to stay in their school positions**. It appeared that the law intended to equalize the playing field by providing retirement benefits for school employees without regard to union service. *Kirsch v. Public School Employees' Retirement Board*, 985 A.2d 671 (Pa. 2009).

◆ An Ohio school janitor suffered an on-the-job fall from a ladder, resulting in back and nerve injuries. After the janitor's treating physician certified her as unable to perform her job duties for 12 months, the state School Employees Retirement System (SERS) ordered a medical examination. It found that nothing precluded her from continuing her custodial work. A SERS medical advisory committee granted her a personal appearance to present her case, but then found that she was not permanently disabled. It denied her application for disability-retirement benefits. The janitor obtained a second medical opinion stating that she could not return to work. The SERS committee denied the janitor's request for a second personal appearance before it, and determined that **the janitor was able to perform her employment duties and was not incapacitated for a period of at least 12 months**. Some 12 years after the fall, the case reached the Supreme Court of Ohio, which found no denial of due process. Despite being denied a second personal appearance before the SERS, the janitor was allowed reconsideration of the decision. The evidence failed to show a disabling condition during the 12 continuous months after the application for benefits. *VanCleave v. School Employees Retirement System*, 120 Ohio St.3d 261, 898 N.E.2d 33 (Ohio 2008).

◆ An Ohio teacher worked as a special education teacher for over 18 years. During the 1989-90 school year, he applied for disability retirement benefits due to an inner eyelid infection that caused a film over his eyes. The medical review board of the state teachers retirement system certified the teacher as having an "ongoing" disability. In 2006, an ophthalmologist selected by the board found that he was not capable of resuming regular full-time service, and that his benefits should continue. The board questioned these findings, and he clarified that it was unreasonable to expect the teacher to return to his duties after a 17-year absence. But he did not consider the teacher to be totally and permanently disabled based on his medical examination. The medical review board terminated then the teacher's disability retirement benefits.

The case reached the Supreme Court of Ohio, which found that the retirement board did not abuse its discretion by convening a review board panel. State law provided that if the board agreed with an examining physician's report that a recipient was no longer incapable of returning to work, disability benefits should be terminated. **The ophthalmologist's examination revealed no incapacitating medical disability.** His conclusion was not based on medical factors, but on the passage of time since the initial disability determination. The board's determination was upheld. *Ackerman v. State Teachers Retirement Board*, 117 Ohio St.3d 268, 883 N.E.2d 445 (Ohio 2008).

◆ A New York school superintendent served a school district for about seven years under employment contracts that provided for lifetime health insurance coverage "upon his retirement from the District." He notified the district of his intent to retire from the district, but took a job as a superintendent of another New York district for a salary increase. The district deemed the separation to be a "resignation," then informed the superintendent that because he had resigned, he was not entitled to lifetime health benefits. The superintendent sued the district in a state court for breach of contract, seeking over $450,000.

The court dismissed the complaint, and the superintendent appealed to the New York Supreme Court, Appellate Division. The court found that the contract permitted termination by either retirement or resignation, making it clear the terms were not synonymous. **While health insurance benefits would be provided in the event of retirement, no reference was made to resignation. The superintendent did not change his status by applying for retirement benefits.** Instead, he took a similar position in a neighboring county. As this action was within the recognized definition of "resignation," the court affirmed the judgment for the school district. *Bauersfeld v. Board of Educ. of Morrisville-Eaton Cent. School Dist.*, 846 N.Y.S.2d 809 (N.Y. App. Div. 2007).

◆ A Montana school superintendent obtained assurances from his school board that he could retire with lifetime health insurance premiums for himself and his wife under a contract addendum. Six years later, a board made up of all new members voted to terminate the superintendent's premium payments. He sued the school district in a federal court, asserting violations of state law and due process. The case reached the U.S. Court of Appeals, Ninth Circuit, which held that **the district's arguments to void the contract failed**. The former superintendent had provided adequate consideration for the contract addendum by continuing to work for the district for six weeks after its execution. *McCracken v. Lockwood School Dist. #26*, 208 Fed.Appx. 513 (9th Cir. 2006).

◆ The Michigan Public School Employees' Retirement Board began providing health care benefits for public school retirees in 1975. Over the years, health insurance deductibles and prescription copays were gradually increased through amendments to the health care plan. Six retirees sued the state, the retirement board and state officials in a Michigan trial court, asserting that the increases violated the state constitution, and that plan amendments violated state and federal constitutional provisions prohibiting the impairment of existing government contracts. The case reached the Michigan Supreme Court. Although the Michigan Constitution prohibits the state from diminishing or impairing the accrued financial benefits of any state pension plan or retirement system, health care benefits did not qualify as "financial benefits" so as to be protected by the state constitution. The legislature expressed no intent to be contractually bound by enacting health care plan legislation for public school retirees. **Health care benefits legislation reflected only a policy decision, and did not create contractual rights.** *Studier v. Michigan Public School Employees' Retirement Board*, 472 Mich. 642, 698 N.W.2d 350 (Mich. 2005).

## VI. UNEMPLOYMENT BENEFITS

*School employees are not entitled to unemployment benefits between academic years, if there is a reasonable assurance of teaching for the school the next year. An employee must work a minimum amount of time to qualify for benefits, but if the employee has committed misconduct resulting in dismissal or left a job without good cause, benefits will typically be denied.*

## A. Eligibility Requirements

◆ A Pennsylvania teacher earned $126.34 per day with 10 sick days for her work as a long-term substitute for a school district. At the end of the school year, she accepted placement on the day-to-day substitute list and applied for unemployment compensation benefits. The state department of labor and industry denied benefits, but the state Unemployment Compensation Board of Review (UCBR) reversed the decision, finding the teacher had no reasonable assurance of returning to work under the Unemployment Compensation Act.

On appeal, the state supreme court noted that state law specified **a school employee is not entitled to unemployment benefits between academic years, if there is a reasonable assurance of performing services in an instructional, research or administrative capacity for the school in the second year**. In this case, the UCBR had found the teacher did not have reasonable assurance of returning to work for the district. Her terms and conditions of employment as a day-to-day substitute teacher were substantially less favorable than those applicable to a long-term substitute. State law was not intended to "eliminate the payment of benefits to school employees during summer months," as the district argued. The decrease in the teacher's income was not caused by the summer vacation, but by the district's decision to offer her a position with fewer wages, hours and benefits. As a result, the court reinstated the UCBR's decision to award the teacher unemployment benefits. *Slippery Rock Area School Dist. v. Unemployment Compensation Board of Review*, 603 Pa. 374, 983 A.2d 1231 (Pa. 2009).

◆ A Missouri school district responded to a loss in revenue by assigning a tenured teacher who was certified in music and English to teach two band classes for which she claimed to have no experience or expertise. She resigned after informing the school board by letter that the assignment required considerable time beyond classroom instruction and constituted an excessive teaching load. She filed a claim for unemployment compensation benefits in which she stated that her employment separation was caused by lack of work. Her claim was initially approved, but an appeals board reversed, finding that she had voluntarily separated from work without good cause attributable to her work or employer. The state labor and industrial relations commission affirmed the decision, and the Missouri Court of Appeals adopted the commission's order, reasoning that **claimants have an affirmative obligation to attempt to resolve work-related problems prior to abandoning employment**. A claimant must act in good faith before a finding of good cause to leave employment may be found. *Standefer v. Missouri Division of Labor and Industrial Relations Comm'n*, 959 S.W.2d 479 (Mo. Ct. App. 1998).

◆ A Rhode Island teacher was laid off after three years of employment and began receiving unemployment compensation benefits. She accepted substitute teaching assignments from two school districts, which partially set off some of her unemployment benefits. She filed a claim for additional benefits based on the lack of available work during the school Christmas break, which was denied by the state Department of Employment and Training (DET). Her later claim for additional unemployment benefits for the summer was also denied on the basis of a state law preclusion for the payment of benefits to school employees during holidays and summer breaks. A Rhode Island trial court found that the claims for additional benefits had been properly denied, but it reversed the decision concerning previously awarded benefits. DET appealed to the Supreme Court of Rhode Island, arguing that the acceptance of substitute teaching work resulted in the denial of unemployment benefits, even for benefits previously awarded for prior full-time work. The court disagreed with the DET, finding that **the teacher's substitute teaching income had been properly deducted from her unemployment compensation benefits**. She was not precluded from receiving previously awarded benefits based on her prior full-time employment, since she was still eligible for them. *Brouillette v. Dep't of Employment and Training Board of Review*, 677 A.2d 1344 (R.I. 1996).

◆   A West Virginia custodian worked for his school district during the summer as a painter for several years. The school board did not offer him employment for the summer one year, and he filed a claim for unemployment compensation benefits. The West Virginia Department of Employment Security declared the employee disqualified from benefits on the basis of the existence of reasonable assurances that he would be working for the school board that fall. The department's board of review reversed this decision, finding that he was entitled to benefits since he had worked for the school district in prior summers and was effectively laid off. The case reached the Supreme Court of Appeals of West Virginia, which held that **service personnel employed by school boards are ineligible for unemployment unless they hold a second, separate contract for the summer months or show the existence of a continuing contractual relationship**. Since the employee failed to show he had a continuing contract for the summer break, he was not entitled to receive benefits. *Raleigh County Board of Educ. v. Gatson*, 468 S.E.2d 923 (W. Va. 1996).

## B.  Misconduct

*While the Supreme Court of Florida has found an employee's absence without authorization is "inherently detrimental to the employer's interests," a Virginia court has held "mere absence without leave is not disqualifying misconduct." In the next case, a North Dakota teacher was unable to collect unemployment benefits after being removed for poor evaluations, complaints by the community, and performance issues such as not following the curriculum.*

◆   A newly hired North Dakota teacher reported that two students had been raped. She was assured that the report was unfounded. An evaluation of the teacher noted she required improvement in several areas. Midway through the school year, the district superintendent placed her on administrative leave for continuing to talk about alleged rapes of students at school. She returned to work with directives to refrain from discussing personal matters, teach only the curriculum, follow the chain of command and stop making false accusations about student rapes, but was soon found in violation of the directives. The superintendent advised her that her contract would not be renewed. The school board voted not to renew the teacher's contract, but it later called a special meeting to remove her prior to the end of the school year. She filed a claim for unemployment benefits, which was denied based on her non-renewal for misconduct. Appeal reached the Supreme Court of North Dakota.

The court explained that state law disqualified an employee who was discharged for misconduct in connection with employment. **"Misconduct" included the deliberate violation or disregard of standards of behavior which an employer had a right to expect.** Under North Dakota law, non-renewal of a teaching contract ordinarily did not rise to the level of misconduct. But in this case, there was evidence that the teacher was discharged for reporting unsubstantiated conduct, and for repeatedly and deliberately violating directives. She was also the subject of complaints from the community. The teacher's own writings indicated she was insolent and unwilling to yield to reasonable employer directives. As the evidence indicated she deliberately disregarded her employer's interests, the court affirmed the denial of benefits. *Schmidt v. Job Service North Dakota*, 756 N.W.2d 794 (N.D. 2008).

◆   A Nevada school district fired an in-school suspension teacher for being absent without leave eight times in five weeks. She filed an unemployment compensation claim, which was granted. The district challenged the award of benefits, maintaining that it admonished the teacher and that excessive absences amounted to misconduct. The teacher stated that her absences were required to see a doctor and to take care of a sick child, whose illness was the result of a continuing medical condition that the school knew about. A hearing referee found the principal more credible than the teacher and held that the discharge was based on attendance problems and failure to notify the district of her absences, in violation of a district policy. A review board reversed the decision, and appeal reached the Supreme Court of Nevada.

According to the court, an employee's absence will be misconduct in unemployment compensation cases "only if the circumstances indicate that the absence was taken in willful violation or disregard of a reasonable employment policy" or lacked an appropriate notice. The court found that the school district had the burden to show the teacher's conduct disqualified her from benefits. **An absence without leave was not disqualifying misconduct. The district would have to show that the teacher's absences were excessive.** Since the board failed to consider whether the absences were "excessive" and whether the first five absences were justifiable, the case was returned to the board for further activity. *Clark County School Dist. v. Bundley*, 148 P.3d 750 (Nev. 2006).

◆   A discharged teacher received unemployment benefits while appealing her dismissal. The Oregon Fair Dismissal Appeals Board held that the dismissal was unlawful and ordered the school district to reinstate her with back pay. The district asserted a right to set off unemployment benefits received by the teacher against her back pay award. It claimed the quarterly payments it made to the state employment department for the Unemployment Compensation Trust Fund justified the offset. The board agreed with the district, finding the district's contributions to the trust fund made it a reimbursing employer. The case reached the Supreme Court of Oregon, which reviewed ORS § 342.905, the statute under which setoff was approved. The court found the board could reinstate a teacher if the charges were untrue or there were inadequate grounds for dismissal. **While Section 342.905 authorized back pay awards for wrongfully discharged employees, nothing permitted the board to set off unemployment compensation against back pay** with money received under an unrelated benefit program. The district had not itself paid unemployment compensation benefits to the teacher. Any such issue was between the teacher and the employment department. As the district did not pay the compensation benefits it now sought to set off, the judgment was reversed. *Zottola v. Three Rivers School Dist.*, 342 Or. 118, 149 P.3d 1151 (Or. 2006).

◆   A Pennsylvania school district suspended a substitute teacher without pay for violating its policy prohibiting weapons on school property. She submitted a claim for unemployment benefits that was denied by a state unemployment compensation referee, who found no justification for inadvertently bringing guns to school when called to work as a substitute on short notice. The case reached the Supreme Court of Pennsylvania, which explained that **a finding of "willful misconduct" was necessary to disqualify unemployment compensation benefits**. Section 402(e) of the Unemployment Compensation Law did not define "willful misconduct," but previous state court decisions characterized it as disregard for an employer's interests, deliberate violation of employer rules, or disregard for the employer's standards of behavior. Employee negligence could result in a finding of willful misconduct only when it showed intentional disregard for the employer's interest or an employee's duties or obligations. Since the district could not show the teacher's actions were intentional or deliberate, she was not disqualified from benefits. *Grieb v. Unemployment Compensation Board of Review*, 827 A.2d 422 (Pa. 2003).

◆   The Court of Appeals of Minnesota upheld the **denial of unemployment compensation benefits to a custodian who did not lock the exterior doors to his school several times**. After being suspended with a written warning, he yelled at a supervisor and threatened her when she complained about him. The court of appeals held the custodian was properly denied unemployment benefits. His repeated failure to lock exterior doors and his insubordination was misconduct showing both a substantial lack of concern for his employment and a violation of reasonable standards of behavior. *Ashong v. Independent School Dist. #625*, No. A04-1623, 2005 WL 1432203 (Minn. Ct. App. 2005).

## VII. WRONGFUL DISCHARGE

*Employees who claim to be discharged for reasons that violate state law or public policy may have recourse against employers under "whistleblower" protection acts, and may bring actions for wrongful or retaliatory discharge. In the next case, Missouri's highest court held that teachers who are employed under contracts can sue their employers for wrongful discharge, extending a state law protection that was previously only available to "at-will" employees.*

◆   A teacher at the Missouri Military Academy observed bruises on a cadet's arms and insisted that school officials make a report of evidence of physical abuse to the state Division of Family Services. The teacher asserted that the academy not only refused to report the evidence but fired him on the same day as he reported his suspicions to supervisors. In a state court action for wrongful discharge and breach of contract, the teacher sought punitive damages and claimed emotional distress. The court dismissed the wrongful discharge and emotional distress claims but held a trial on the breach of contract claim. As a result of the trial, the court awarded the teacher $13,300 in damages.

Appeal reached the Supreme Court of Missouri, which explained that **a teacher who is employed "at-will" (without a contract) may sue an employer for wrongful discharge if an employment termination violates a clear mandate of public policy**. But the cause of action had not been extended to contract employees such as the teacher in this case. The court found compelling reasons for allowing a contract employee to pursue a wrongful discharge claim. Allowing contract employees to pursue wrongful discharge claims put them on the same footing as "at-will" employees. The availability of the claim would discourage employers from making employees choose between earning a living and reporting misconduct. The teacher was under a statutory mandate to report suspected child abuse and could pursue a wrongful discharge claim. *Keveney v. Missouri Military Academy*, 304 S.W.3d 98 (Mo. 2010).

◆   A Texas middle school earned "academically unacceptable" test results on the Texas Assessment of Knowledge and Skills (TAKS). The school was the only one in the district to earn this rating. The district superintendent and a human resources director discussed reassigning the principal to an assistant principal job. The next day, the principal called the Texas Education Agency (TEA) to report his belief that 38 fifth-graders at his school had been socially promoted to grade six. A day later, the superintendent reassigned the principal to an elementary school assistant principal position. His contract was not renewed at the end of the school year and he retired. He sued the school district, superintendent and other officials for violating the Texas Whistleblower Act and Constitution. A state court ruled against the principal, and he appealed.

On appeal, the state court of appeals held **the Texas Whistleblower Act requires an employee to show that the employer's only reason for discharge was retaliation or discrimination**. According to the school district, the principal would have been reassigned as the result of his school's performance regardless of any TEA report. The superintendent and human resources director said that a reassignment was being considered three months earlier. Parents had previously expressed concern about the principal, and he had twice been placed on growth plans following reported incidents of racial insensitivity and biased comments. *Dardeau v. West Orange-Cove Consol. Independent School Dist.*, No. 09-08-00167-CV, 2009 WL 2253245 (Tex. Ct. App. 7/30/09).

◆   A Missouri teacher designed the "Out of Area Program" for use by teachers to respond to student disruptions. He claimed he developed and implemented the program during his employment with the school district. The teacher asserted that the district continued using materials he developed after it discharged him. He sued the district for copyright infringement. A court dismissed the case, finding the teacher's program was a "business idea" that was excluded from federal copyright protection. The teacher appealed to the U.S. Court of Appeals, Federal Circuit, which noted that general concepts and ideas are beyond the protection of federal copyright law. According to the court, copyright law protected the expression of an idea, but not the ideas themselves. Although a hall pass used at the school during the relevant time period had the same language as the teacher's program, the school's hall pass was not otherwise like the teacher's materials. The court found that **the limited use of similar functional language did not constitute copyright infringement,** even if the district had deliberately copied it. Fragmentary words and phrases are not protected by copyright law. Forms of expression directed solely at functional considerations do not exhibit the level of creativity to warrant federal copyright protection. The court ruled for the school district. *Clark v. Crues,* 260 Fed.Appx. 292 (Fed. Cir. 2008).

◆  An Arizona assistant principal claimed she was given the choice to quit or accept demotion to a teaching position in retaliation for trying to "resolve several illegalities and deficiencies involving counselors at the high school." She submitted a letter to the district claiming she lost her salary of $68,000 per year and an additional $7,000 for summer school. The letter claimed she would earn only $36,800 as a teacher, and would suffer economic damages of approximately $35,000 per year "or more" over the next 18 years. She also asked for compensatory damages for emotional distress of "no less than $300,000," plus general damages of "no less than $200,000." The school district did not respond to the letter, and the assistant principal sued it for wrongful termination. The case reached the Arizona Supreme Court, which noted that the assistant principal failed to comply with the statute governing the notice of claims. **Her letter lacked both the specific amount for which the claim could be settled and the facts supporting that amount.** Further, she could no longer pursue her claim because more than 180 days had passed since the alleged wrongful discharge. *Deer Valley Unified School Dist. No. 97 v. Houser,* 214 Ariz. 293, 152 P.3d 490 (Ariz. 2007).

◆  A ninth-grade Pennsylvania student was hospitalized after a suicide attempt. A special education teacher had ongoing talks with the student's mother about the student's problems. The teacher found a note by the student expressing suicidal thoughts and later suggested that the student see a therapist, but the student refused to see the therapist unless the teacher went with her. The student's mother's granted permission, but the principal later directed the teacher to stop attending therapy sessions with the student. The district superintendent advised the teacher she had engaged in willful neglect of duty, insubordination, incompetency, persistent negligence, willful violation of laws and improper conduct. After a hearing, the superintendent sent the teacher a letter describing district policies and limiting her interactions with at-risk students. The teacher claimed the letter was designed to stifle her protected speech and punish her for helping special education students. She sued the district in a federal court for First Amendment and Rehabilitation Act violations.

The court held the letter was necessary to assure she was in compliance with special education law and district policy. The U.S. Court of Appeals, Third Circuit, held **the teacher's conduct in attending therapy sessions with the student was unprotected by the First Amendment or the Rehabilitation Act**. Disability laws do not protect persons who simply provide assistance to students with disabilities. There must be some advocacy, or some protest against discrimination or other unlawful conduct. As the teacher's conduct was not expressive or communicative, the court affirmed the judgment. *Montanye v. Wissahickon School Dist.*, 218 Fed.Appx. 126 (3d Cir. 2007).

◆   A teacher in a rural Utah school district claimed the district superintendent retaliated against her for reporting sexual misconduct and favoritism toward polygamist families by her colleagues. She claimed that the superintendent threatened her, wrote adverse employment reports and ordered her to undergo a psychological examination intended to discredit her reports, and also induced her daughter to fabricate a sex abuse charge. The district refused to renew the teacher's contract, and she sued the district, superintendent and a colleague for constitutional rights violations, wrongful termination, and whistleblower claims under the Utah Protection of Public Employees Act. A jury awarded the teacher identical sums of $65,000 against both the superintendent and district for the whistleblower claims. It awarded $55,000 against the district and $32,500 against the superintendent for the civil rights claims. On appeal, the U.S. Court of Appeals, Tenth Circuit, held the teacher did not receive an "impermissible double recovery," as the district and superintendent argued. She was properly denied her claim for punitive damages against the district, but was entitled to proceed with a claim for punitive damages against the superintendent. **Punitive damages are available in civil rights actions against officials with an evil motive or intent, or who demonstrate reckless indifference to federally protected rights.** *Youren v. Tintic School Dist.*, 343 F.3d 1296 (10th Cir. 2003).

## VIII. WORKERS' COMPENSATION

*Workers' compensation is typically the exclusive remedy for an employee injured in the course and scope of employment. A significant part of the litigation in this area focuses on whether an injured employee may assert tort claims for more money than what is available under workers' compensation law by showing intentional conduct or a deliberate or conscious failure to act for the employee's safety.*

◆   An Ohio county educational service center (ESC) employee said she was injured in a work-related auto accident. The state Bureau of Workers' Compensation later granted her claim to participate in the state workers' compensation fund. However, the ESC did not file an appeal to the court system. Instead, it asked the state industrial commission to find fraud and terminate the employee's participation in the workers' compensation fund.

Hearing officers found no evidence of fraud, and the commission denied further appeal. The ESC appealed to a state court of common pleas, which dismissed the case. The case came before the Supreme Court of Ohio, which held **only commission decisions involving employee participation rights can be appealed to the court system**. In this case, the commission had found no evidence of employee fraud and the employer did not appeal from this finding. As the commission had refused to reconsider the claim, the employee's right to participate in the fund had been conclusively determined. Since the case did not involve the right of a claimant to participate in the workers' compensation fund, the court of common pleas had correctly dismissed the case. *Benton v. Hamilton Educ. Service Center*, 123 Ohio St.3d 347, 916 N.E.2d 778 (Ohio 2009).

◆    A Washington custodian was ordered to clean up the remains of a student who shot himself to death in a school entryway and help search the school for a bomb he claimed to have placed in the school. She did not finish cleaning the suicide site until 4:15 a.m., and became distraught and physically ill. For several days, the custodian was ordered to clean up candles and cards left by students and others at the scene of the suicide. Claiming this was emotionally disturbing, she sued the school district and the superintendent in a state court for infliction of emotional distress. A state court held that the action was barred by the exclusivity provisions of workers' compensation. The Court of Appeals of Washington explained that **the custodian was engaged in her employment duties when she was ordered to clean up the suicide site, which took until 4:15 a.m.** However, the custodian correctly asserted that the workers' compensation act did not bar her post traumatic stress disorder claims because they were not based on an "injury" or an "occupational disease." Her post-traumatic stress disorder resulted from traumatizing duties over a period of days. Any such injury was excluded from the definition of occupational disease in workers' compensation law. The custodian's symptoms appeared in the weeks after the suicide, and were not the result of exposure to a single event. *Rothwell v. Nine Mile Falls School Dist.*, 206 P.3d 347 (Wash Ct. App. 2009).

◆    A North Carolina teacher had consistent problems managing her classroom and maintaining order. After negative performance evaluations and failed action plans, the teacher missed a meeting with her principal to address her performance problems. She refused to sign a warning letter, left school, and did not return to work. A psychologist diagnosed her with generalized anxiety disorder (GAD) and medically excluded her from work. The teacher submitted a workers' compensation claim, asserting GAD was an occupational disease caused by her "hostile and abusive" classroom. The state industrial commission found that **the teacher failed to show that her GAD was due to causes and conditions characteristic of her job**. It denied her claim. Appeal reached the Supreme Court of North Carolina, which held that an employee satisfies the workers' compensation statute by showing work exposed the employee to a greater risk of contracting an occupational disease than members of the general public. Here, the commission determined that her psychologist's report was not believable, and she did not bring him to testify on her behalf. Without his testimony, the teacher had no expert medical evidence to support her claim. *Hassell v. Onslow County Board of Educ.*, 661 S.E.2d 709 (N.C. 2008).

◆    A Georgia school bus driver's family had a history of asthma, and one of her sisters had died at age 21 after a severe asthma attack. The driver was diagnosed with asthma after two years of work in the district. She suffered an asthma attack on her special needs school bus, and claimed that fumes and chemicals caused it. Doctors soon released her to work without restrictions, but she did not return. A workers' compensation panel physician and a pulmonologist released her to work without restrictions, but the driver did not feel safe driving special needs children. A clinical psychologist diagnosed her with adjustment disorder and depression and stated that she had too much anxiety about driving a bus to return to work. A school psychologist found inconsistent symptoms suggesting she had "a severe somatization disorder and/or malingering." The board discharged her for job abandonment. A state administrative law judge found the driver suffered a compensable injury. The state court of appeals affirmed the judgment for the driver. It held **a claimant is entitled to workers' compensation benefits for mental disability and psychic treatment arising out of an accident in which a compensable physical injury was suffered**. There was evidence that the driver's psychic problems were based on a real fear of her death from an asthma attack and her concern for special needs children on her bus. *DeKalb Board of Educ. v. Singleton*, 294 Ga.App. 96, 668 S.E.2d 767 (Ga. Ct. App. 2008).

◆    A California student established a pattern of pushing others and making sexual innuendos to girls. His parents repeatedly rejected any special placement as they did not want their son "labeled." The student later told classmates he wanted to "put a bullet in the head" of his teacher, the teacher's wife and baby. The student was out of school for weeks. When he returned, the school psychologist recommended placing him in a program for emotionally disturbed students. The mother again insisted he remain in a regular classroom. On a day when the student had knocked down a classmate on the playground, a teacher accompanied him to the school bus. The student charged into her and knocked her down on the bus. The teacher received workers' compensation benefits of over $91,000, but sought additional benefits for serious and willful misconduct.

The state Workers' Compensation Appeals Board found that the school district engaged in "serious and willful misconduct" by failing to permanently remove the physically and verbally aggressive student from the teacher's classroom. It awarded her an additional $45,785. The Court of Appeal of California held that **the school district did not deliberately or consciously fail to take action for the teacher's safety**. It had been trying to place the student in a behavior-based placement since third grade, but the parents had repeatedly refused to consent. The district had found the student eligible for an emotionally disturbed program, put him on a daily contract and suspended and counseled him several times. As a result, the court annulled the award of additional benefits. *Elk Grove Unified School Dist. v. Workers' Compensation Appeals Board*, No. C052945, 2007 WL 1169336 (Cal. Ct. App. 4/20/07).

◆    An Idaho behavioral counselor worked for a behavioral support division and traveled to different schools in Idaho Falls School District No. 91. She also spent two days each week at an alternative school in Bonneville County Joint School District No. 93. The school was attended by students from both school districts. The counselor went on a field trip with students and District 93 employees to a former ski lodge leased from the U.S. government. She was injured while helping to catch a student during a "trust fall" exercise. The counselor received workers' compensation benefits from District 91, but filed a personal injury lawsuit against District 93 in the state court system, claiming negligence. The court held she was a statutory employee of District 93, making the district immune from personal injury lawsuits. The counselor appealed.

The Supreme Court of Idaho held that **if the counselor was either a statutory employee or a "borrowed employee," District 93 was entitled to immunity** from personal injury damages. Since District 93 did not operate a "business" as defined in state law, it could not be the counselor's statutory employer. But the trial court had incorrectly held that the counselor was not a "borrowed employee," as it remained unclear whether District 91 or District 93 had the right to control her. The court remanded the case for a determination of whether the counselor was a borrowed employee. *Cordova v. Bonneville County Joint School Dist.*, 144 Idaho 637, 167 P.3d 775 (Idaho 2007).

◆   A New Jersey teacher was knocked down and injured when a student bolted from his seat and charged at another student. She sued the school district and officials for negligence, based on the student's history of behavioral problems and inadequate discipline. She claimed school administrators should not have allowed him to remain in a general education setting. A state court awarded judgment to the district and officials, and the teacher appealed. The Superior Court of New Jersey, Appellate Division, noted that most of the student's disciplinary incidents involved skipping detention. **A board-certified psychiatrist had evaluated the student and concluded he was not a threat to peers.** The court found that "student fights cannot be said to be so totally unexpected or unusual as to allow an injured teacher to recover outside the Workers' Compensation scheme." Teachers often supervise students in non-teaching settings, and there was always a chance that a student altercation might erupt. The teacher might have been knocked down by a normally behaved student. The court affirmed the judgment. *Kibler v. Roxbury Board of Educ.*, 392 N.J. Super. 45, 919 A.2d 878 (N.J. Super. Ct. App. Div. 2007).

◆   A disabled Washington student inflicted frequent injuries on students and staff. In one school year, he caused over 200 documented injuries. The student pushed his teacher as she tried to intervene during one of his attacks, knocking her unconscious. The next day, he bit an aide on her breast as she tried to distract him from other students. Despite these incidents, the student remained in his class with the same staff for most of the year. Both employees received workers' compensation benefits, but sought additional damages and sued the school district. The case reached the Supreme Court of Washington, which stated that **while workers' compensation is typically the exclusive remedy for an injured employee, a limited exception applies to employers who intentionally injure employees**. An employer's gross negligence or failure to observe safety laws and procedures does not constitute deliberate intent to injure. An employee had to show that an employer had actual knowledge injury was certain to occur before the employer could be liable in a tort case. The behavior of a child with special needs was far from predictable. The district had tried increasingly restrictive strategies to address his behavior. The employees did not show the district was certain its strategies would fail. There could be no liability for the district based on simple negligence. *Vallandigham v. Clover Park School Dist. No. 400*, 109 P.3d 805 (Wash. 2005).

◆ A Florida school bus attendant was injured when a wheelchair lift fell on him. He claimed that a maintenance worker negligently repaired or adjusted the lift twice in a four-month period before the accident. He sued the school board for negligence, arguing that he and the maintenance employee were involved in "unrelated work" under the workers' compensation law. The court held that the exception for unrelated work did not apply, and held for the board. The Supreme Court of Florida explained that **workers' compensation law created an exception to immunity for cases involving employees of the same employer when each was assigned primarily to "unrelated works."** The attendant and mechanics were both employed by the board, worked in the same facility and were involved in the same transportation services. The unrelated works exception applied only if an employee who caused injury was clearly engaged in works unrelated to the injured employee. The trial court had correctly held the employees had the common goal of providing safe transportation. *Taylor v. School Board of Brevard County*, 888 So.2d 1 (Fla. 2004).

◆ The Supreme Court of South Dakota upheld an administrative decision denying workers' compensation benefits to a school bus driver injured while snow skiing on a school field trip. She was receiving "down time" pay during the student activity and was free to do whatever she wanted when she accepted a free lift pass. Here, the driver's injury was not "work-related" because it did not arise out of her employment. She was not expected to supervise students after they left the bus. **The driver had "stepped aside from her employment purpose when she went skiing,"** and was not entitled to benefits. *Norton v. Deuel School Dist. #19-4*, 674 N.W.2d 518 (S.D. 2004).

◆ Michigan school custodians claimed that exposure to asbestos from a school carpeting project caused respiratory irritation, post-traumatic stress disorder and other medical and psychological problems. They sued the district and school officials in a federal court for violations of federal environmental laws, due process violations and state law negligence. The case reached the U.S. Court of Appeals, Sixth Circuit. It rejected the due process claims, as the custodians did not show that the carpeting assignment was so punitive or retaliatory that it shocked the conscience. The Michigan workers' compensation act is the exclusive remedy for occupational injuries, except where an employer has actual knowledge that an injury was certain to occur, yet willfully disregards that knowledge. **The custodians did not show that the administration intended to injure them or knew that an injury was certain to occur.** *Upsher v. Grosse Pointe Public School System*, 285 F.3d 448 (6th Cir. 2002).

# CHAPTER TEN

## Tenure and Due Process

## I. STATE TENURE STATUTES

### A. Tenure Status

#### 1. Contract Renewal by Operation of Law

*Failure to comply with statutory notices may confer tenure on an employee by operation of law. For example, under Section 16-24-12 of the Alabama Code, a public school teacher is deemed to have received an offer of reemployment for the next school year at the same salary unless the board provides written notice on or before the last day of the school term in which the teacher is employed.*

*After three years of full-time employment, non-teaching Ohio school employees are deemed to be employed pursuant to a continuing contract. New York's highest court held a teacher was entitled to 28 days of pay due to a school district's failure to send him timely notice of employment termination.*

◆ During a summer break, a New York school board voted to terminate the contract of a probationary teacher in 30 days. But the board did not provide him written notice until two days before the action was to take effect. The teacher sued the board in a state court for 28 days of pay, plus a name-clearing hearing

381

and attorneys' fees based on violation of federal due process principles. The court held for the board, as did a state appellate division court. On appeal, the New York Court of Appeals observed that state Education Law Section 3019-a required school officials to give probationary teachers a 30-day written notice before the effective date of employment termination. **If a probationary teacher was being denied tenure, written notice had to be provided no later than 60 days before the probationary period expired.** While the law did not specify a remedy for failure to provide teachers required notices, the court had held in a 1993 case that a teacher was entitled to a day's pay for each day a termination notice was late. This was true here, even though the failure to comply occurred over the summer vacation. Ruling the teacher was entitled to 28 days of pay plus attorneys' fees, the court reversed the judgment. *Vetter v. Board of Educ., Ravena-Coeymans-Selkirk Central School Dist.*, 14 N.Y.3d 729 (N.Y. 2010).

◆   An Ohio school district's part-time Safe and Drug Free Schools coordinator position was funded entirely by grants. A licensed substitute teacher was hired for the job. She lacked an Ohio teacher's certificate and was unauthorized to teach full time. After seven years of part-time employment, the school board employed the coordinator full time under successive two-year contracts. The board then approved a five-year contract that did not specify it was contingent on funding. The state auditor declared the school district to be in a fiscal emergency, and the coordinator position was abolished based on declining enrollment and the loss of grant funding. The school board suspended the coordinator's contract prior to the 2005-06 school year. An arbitrator rejected her grievance, finding that her position was not within the bargaining unit. The coordinator petitioned the Supreme Court of Ohio, seeking her reinstatement.

The court found that **after three years of full-time employment, non-teaching school employees were deemed to be employed pursuant to a continuing contract**. The coordinator had been employed full time in a non-teaching position for three years when the board approved her five-year contract. She was a continuing contract employee under state law, and this status was not contingent on grant funding. As the coordinator had continuing contract status, the board of education was not authorized to abolish her position and lay her off. The court ordered the board to reinstate her. *State ex rel. Couch v. Trimble Local School Dist. Board of Educ.*, 120 Ohio St.3d 75, 896 N.E.2d 690 (Ohio 2008).

◆   The Colorado Teacher Employment Compensation, and Dismissal Act (TECDA) requires written notice to probationary teachers of a contract non-renewal by June 1. In April 2004, a school board held a meeting to discuss contract renewal for probationary teachers. It moved into an executive session, where it decided not to rehire a teacher for the 2004-05 school year. The district superintendent sent him a "letter of intent," stating that the board did not intend to offer him a teaching contract for the next year. The board did not ratify its decision in a public session until September 2004. The teacher sued, and his case reached the Supreme Court of Colorado. It held the vote in executive session violated the state Open Meetings Law and was not binding. **Failure to provide timely written notice to the teacher of a non-renewal vote resulted**

**in automatic reemployment under the TECDA.** As the board did not advise the teacher of his non-renewal by June 1, he was automatically reemployed for 2004-05. *Hanover School Dist. No. 28 v. Barbour*, 171 P.3d 223 (Colo. 2007).

◆ An Indiana school district hired a biology teacher under a one-year contract, even though he lacked a standard teaching license. The principal emailed him on May 7 of the school year that he would meet with him the next day to discuss his employment. The principal then orally notified the teacher his teaching contract would not be renewed. The teacher sued, claiming the law required him to be notified by May 1 or else his contract would automatically be renewed. The case reached the Court of Appeals of Indiana, which rejected the district's argument that the teacher's limited teaching license relieved it of the statutory notice requirements. There was no exception for teachers who held limited licenses. Although non-permanent teachers were entitled to only minimal due process protections, school officials were required to comply with statutory procedures when informing them about contract renewal. **Since the school district did not give the teacher the written notice he was due by May 1 of the school year, his contract was automatically renewed for the next year.** *Pike Township Educ. Foundation v. Rubenstein*, 831 N.E.2d 1239 (Ind. Ct. App. 2005).

◆ A California teacher completed a one-year contract under an emergency teaching permit and then received a professional clear teaching credential. The district classified him as a probationary employee. The teacher worked the full school year for the district. On May 23, he was sent a notice of non-reelection of employment for a third year. He sued the district, arguing that he had completed two years of service in a teaching position requiring certification qualifications, and that he had a right to notice of non-reelection of employment by March 15. The court found that the May 23 notice of non-reelection was timely and that the district had no duty to reemploy him.

The Court of Appeal of California stated that if the board does not give notice to a permanent employee by March 15, the employee is deemed re-elected. **However, notice applied only to those eligible to become permanent employees under tenure rules.** Here, the teacher was ineligible for permanent employment and could not insist on notice. The case was unlike *California Teachers Ass'n v. Governing Board of Golden Valley Unified School Dist.*, 98 Cal.App.4th 369, 119 Cal.Rptr.2d 642 (2002), where a teacher who served under an emergency credential was held to qualify as a probationary employee. That case did not involve a claim to permanent employment. Accordingly, the court affirmed the judgment for the district. *Culbertson v. San Gabriel Unified School Dist.*, 121 Cal.App.4th 1392, 18 Cal. Rptr.3d 234 (Cal. Ct. App. 2004).

◆ A Louisiana teacher with 18 years of experience became a probationary special education teacher at a correctional center for youth. She signed two consecutive annual teaching contracts. At the end of the second year, the center's principal recommended her contract not be renewed. The state board of education approved the recommendation, but the director's summary did not state the reasons for the action, as required by law. The teacher sued the board, alleging that it tried to circumvent the law by disguising her discharge as a non-renewal. The case reached the state supreme court, which explained that probationary teachers who do not receive written notification of discharge from their school board automatically become regular or permanent teachers if they have completed their three-year probationary terms. **The board had to state the valid reasons for a recommendation of discharge or dismissal at any time during a teacher's probationary period, even at the conclusion of a school year.** Here, the board violated state law by failing to provide the teacher with valid reasons for its action. It should have provided the teacher with valid reasons for the non-renewal of her contract during the probationary period. *Palmer v. Louisiana State Board of Elementary and Secondary Educ.*, 842 So.2d 363 (La. 2003).

*In* Williams v. Lafayette Parish School Board, *533 So.2d 1359 (La. Ct. App. 1989), the Court of Appeal of Louisiana held voluntary resignation breaks the continuity of state tenure law. In* Brubaker v. Hardy, *5 Ohio St.2d 103, 214 N.E.2d 79 (Ohio 1966), the Supreme Court of Ohio held the acceptance of a teacher's resignation, and his subsequent acceptance of a one-year teaching contract, resulted in waiver of the right to a continuing employment contract.*

## 2.  Temporary and Probationary Assignments

*The Supreme Court of Tennessee held that generally, a non-tenured, non-licensed employee was only entitled to notice of the charges against him, an explanation of the administration's evidence and an opportunity to respond in writing. If dismissal then followed, the employee could have a full hearing.*

◆   A non-licensed, non-tenured Tennessee high school teaching assistant (TA) had a one-year contract to supervise an in-school suspension program. A student filed a sexual harassment complaint against him. The next year, a teacher claimed the TA emailed her about her appearance in jeans, and she filed a sexual harassment complaint against him. The director of the school district suspended the TA for 10 days with pay, pending an investigation. A day after sending the TA notice of his hearing rights, the director sent him another letter advising him that he was dismissed as of that date for improper conduct. The TA's attorney appeared on his behalf at a personnel hearing. A school personnel hearing authority upheld the dismissal. Instead of appealing to the school board as specified by the district's policy, the TA appealed to the state court system.

The court awarded judgment to the school board and awarded the board attorneys' fees based on filing a frivolous case. On appeal, the Supreme Court of Tennessee held **Section 49-2-301 of the state code gave the director authority to non-renew an unlicensed staff member such as the TA before the end of his contract for insubordination, neglect of duty, incompetence, inefficiency, or improper conduct**. There was a clear difference in termination procedures for unlicensed employees and for those who held licenses. Neither Section 49-2-301 nor board policy conferred rights on the TA to a full hearing. He chose not to appeal to the school board after his hearing before the personnel authority, defeating his due process and related claims. But since the trial court had failed to consider any non-due process claims, they would have to be reconsidered. This included a wrongful discharge claim. The court held the trial court had erroneously assessed the TA attorneys' fees for filing a frivolous lawsuit. *Bailey v. Blount County Board of Educ.*, 303 S.W.3d 216 (Tenn. 2010).

◆   A New York school district hired a teacher to serve as an administrator under a three-year contract. Six months into the contract, the district decided to eliminate the position for financial reasons. The administrator sued for breach of contract, and a state court ruled in her favor. An appellate division court affirmed, and the case reached the New York Court of Appeals. On appeal, the school district argued that a breach of contract claim could not be maintained, as New York Education Law prohibits school districts from entering contracts that guarantee employment to non-tenured administrators for a specific term. The district claimed the contract did not guarantee any set duration, but only established the terms and conditions of the administrator's probationary employment. The court noted that the Education Law at issue allowed school districts to end probationary appointments at any time during the probationary period. The law did not prohibit a school board from entering into a durational, three-year contract of employment with a probationary school administrator. However, **absent an express waiver, a school district retained the right to discharge teachers during a probationary term**. Here, the language of the contract was too equivocal to establish a conscious waiver by the district. Thus, the judgment was reversed. *Consedine v. Portville Cent. School Dist.*, 12 N.Y.3d 286, 907 N.E.2d 684, 879 N.Y.S.2d 806 (N.Y. 2009).

◆   A Kentucky school board did not violate state law by passing over a special education teacher for promotion to a special education teacher/director position. It hired a qualified applicant who had emergency certification for the job. After a state trial court ruled for the school board, the Court of Appeals of Kentucky noted evidence that **the teacher was unqualified for the promotion**. A former employer "absolutely did not recommend him for employment," and he was under review by the state Professional Standards Board. *Hicks v. Magoffin County Board of Educ.*, 292 S.W.3d 335 (Ky. Ct. App. 2009).

◆   A South Dakota school board rehired two retired teachers under one-year probationary contracts for 2004-05. In April 2005, the school board discussed in an executive session whether to renew the contracts of 34 teachers. After meeting in executive session, the board reconvened in open session and voted to renew the contracts of 30 teachers. The two probationary teachers were among the four who were not offered new contracts. The superintendent sent them written notices of non-renewal before April 15, as required by state law. The probationary teachers claimed they were entitled to an affirmative vote of non-renewal by the board. They sued the school district in a state court, which held that the notices satisfied state law.

On appeal, the Supreme Court of South Dakota noted that **the superintendent or board had to give written notice of non-renewal by April 15, but was not required to give further process or a reason for non-renewal**. Nothing in state law required an affirmative school board vote. The law authorized the board to renew the contract by a vote or to non-renew by refusing to vote. The board's refusal to vote to offer new contracts was within its statutory right to "not renew." *Scheller v. Faulkton Area School Dist. #24-3*, 731 N.W.2d 914 (S.D. 2007).

◆   A Texas school district suspended a continuing contract teacher for verbally harassing a six-year-old student. The teacher agreed to work as a probationary employee under a single-year contract. Before the end of the year, the school board voted to terminate her probationary contract and sent her a timely notice of the action. She then filed a grievance, which was dismissed. On further appeal, the Texas Commissioner of Education noted that the district failed to give the teacher proper notice of the termination of her continuing contract prior to the change in her status. But because the teacher failed to contest the change in an administrative proceeding, she could not pursue the matter further.

The Court of Appeals of Texas upheld that decision. **The Education Code allowed the re-designation of a continuing contract teacher as a "probationary teacher" in lieu of discharge**, after providing written notice of a proposed discharge, termination or non-renewal of contract. Here, the teacher agreed to the terms of her probationary contract, despite having a right to file a grievance over the change in her status. By accepting the probationary contract until she received notice that it would be terminated, she waived her right to complain about any lack of notice from the board. *Wittman v. Nelson*, 100 S.W.3d 356 (Tex. Ct. App. 2002).

◆   A Florida school administrator received continuing contract status as a teacher in 1972. He was promoted to an assistant principal position in 1974 and later became a principal. He was employed under annual employment contracts, and his school board specified that neither he nor the board of education owed any further obligation to the other party after expiration of the contract. Near the end of the 2000-2001 school year, the board accepted a supervisor's recommendation not to offer the administrator a new contract. The administrator's appeal reached the Florida Court of Appeal, which noted that he was entitled to continuing employment as a teacher by virtue of the status he had obtained in 1972. However, **his continuing contract status as a teacher did not automatically confer that same status to his subsequent promotions to administrative positions**. Continuing contract status in the position of assistant principal or principal would have to be earned. The plain language of his annual contracts indicated that he had no such entitlement to continued employment beyond the term of each individual contract year. He was not entitled to a hearing under state law or the Due Process Clause. *Jones v. Miami-Dade County Public Schools*, 816 So.2d 824 (Fla. Dist. Ct. App. 2002).

◆   A post-probationary music teacher in Nevada, who had been accredited in California and taught there for years, received a notice that he would be discharged unless he remedied a technical defect in his teaching license application in four days. He failed to remedy the defect in time and was fired. The district rehired him a few days later, after he provided the necessary documentation and reapplied for his position. But the district reclassified the teacher as probationary for the rest of the school year and the next year. He filed a lawsuit, asserting that his Nevada school employment never terminated and that he was entitled to post-probationary status. He claimed that the district never terminated his employment because it failed to follow state notice and hearing requirements when it gave him only four days to correct the defective certification forms. The court agreed, and the district appealed.

The Supreme Court of Nevada held that the teacher had post-probationary status. Under state law, he was entitled to 15 days' notice prior to employment termination, plus notice of the right to a hearing. The district had given him only four days of notice with no opportunity for a hearing. Without regard to whether the teacher was properly licensed, **the district had employed him as a post-probationary teacher for over a year**. The teacher was not effectively terminated and thus did not lose his post-probationary teaching status. *Clark County School Dist. v. Riley*, 14 P.3d 22 (Nev. 2000).

### 3.  Special Programs

*States have established separate laws for teachers in special programs such as California's regional occupational program (ROP). The Court of Appeal of California recognized a legislative purpose to exclude service as an ROP instructor from the computation of service required for attaining permanent status in a school district. The rationale was to "avoid the prospect of having to retain teachers who were 'virtually untransferable' to other assignments."*

*According to the Supreme Court of Alabama, teachers who were employed under the federally funded Head Start program were entitled to state tenure law protections. They were deemed school board "employees" under state law, because local officials controlled their selection and work assignments.*

◆   An Alabama teacher and a teaching assistant were employed under the federally funded Head Start program. After being discharged, they attempted to contest the action pursuant to guidelines in the Head Start policy manual. After this failed, they sued the school board, asserting that they were school board employees entitled to the statutory protections applicable to city and county employees under the Alabama Fair Dismissal Act. The case reached the Supreme Court of Alabama, which explained that whether the teacher and assistant were considered "employees" of the school board depended upon the extent to which the board had a right to select and control them while they worked at Head Start. The board had delegated its authority to approve policies and procedures for Head Start operations in the county to a "policy council." Federal Head Start regulations state that there is a "partnership" between school boards and Head Start policy councils regarding the hiring and firing of Head Start personnel. Policy councils are encouraged to work with school boards to reach employment decisions. Here, the school board had control over the Head Start director's employment. His involvement with the policy council indicated that the board could influence or control the employment of other Head Start employees. Therefore, **the teacher and the assistant were employees**. *Peterson v. Lowndes County Board of Educ.*, 980 So.2d 975 (Ala. 2007).

◆ A California teacher taught agricultural maintenance in a school district's regular education program as a .57 full-time equivalent (FTE) employee. He also worked as a .43 FTE maintenance employee in a regional occupational program (ROP). After the district notified him that it was not going to rehire him for either position the following year, he sought a court order that the district had to reelect him for both positions. He claimed that he was a regular teacher who was "subsequently assigned" to the ROP position. A court agreed and ordered the district to reinstate the teacher to both jobs. The Court of Appeal of California upheld the decision concerning the .57 FTE position. The district's conduct in not reelecting the teacher was arbitrary and capricious. However, **the period of time (.43 FTE) that the teacher spent in the ROP position did not count toward his attainment of permanent status** because he was "not assigned out from a regular teaching position into an ROP position," but was assigned to a second, concurrent position in the ROP. The court reversed the judgment concerning the .43 FTE ROP assignment, as this service did not count toward permanent status. *Reis v. Biggs Unified School Dist.*, 126 Cal.App.4th 809, 24 Cal.Rptr.3d 393 (Cal. Ct. App. 2005).

◆ A California teacher served eight years in a reading specialist position that was categorically funded under California Education Code § 44909. The district then hired her for a full-time position in its regular education program supported by the district's general funds. The district classified the teacher as a second-year probationary employee. It notified her by March 15 that she would not be rehired and then discharged her at the end of the school year. The teacher claimed she was improperly classified. A state court held that the district had an unqualified right to discharge her at the end of the school year.

The Court of Appeal of California agreed. Service under Section 44909 was not "included in computing the service required as a prerequisite to attainment of, or eligibility to, classification as a permanent employee" unless the person was subsequently employed as a probationary employee in a position requiring certification qualifications. This required employment for an entire school year. Otherwise, a teacher serving in a categorically funded program might never serve as a probationary employee. **Section 44909 was intended to prevent a person from acquiring permanent status solely through categorically funded programs.** *Schnee v. Alameda Unified School Dist.*, 125 Cal.App.4th 555, 22 Cal.Rptr.3d 800 (Cal. Ct. App. 2004).

◆ Two Massachusetts teachers worked as public school teachers in the 1950s and 1960s, before leaving their jobs to raise families. Both held elementary education teaching certificates from the state education department. The teachers returned to work in the 1980s, taking jobs in a federally funded Chapter I supplemental instruction program. One worked in the program for 15 years and the other for eight years before being laid off due to budget cuts. They claimed to have "professional teacher status," with the right to bump non-tenured teachers from elementary teaching positions. The district superintendent denied their requests, and after holding separate arbitration hearings, arbitrators issued a joint decision for the school committee. The arbitrators held that the teachers had no bumping rights because they were not "teachers" as defined by state law.

The teachers appealed to a state court, which vacated the arbitration award as a violation of public policy. The school committee appealed to the Supreme Judicial Court of Massachusetts, which noted the strong public policy in favor of arbitration. Courts may vacate arbitration awards only in limited circumstances. Here, the arbitrators had analyzed the teachers' conditions of employment and job functions in resolving whether they were "teachers" under the state professional teacher status provision. Accordingly, the decisions were not subject to judicial review. **The teachers had no bumping rights.** *Lyons v. School Committee of Dedham*, 440 Mass. 74, 794 N.E.2d 586 (Mass. 2003).

## B. Tenure Rights

### 1. Reductions in Force

*Under traditional tenure laws, a tenured teacher may not be laid off and bumped by a non-tenured teacher if the tenured teacher is properly licensed for the position. However, state legislatures are considering legislation to base teacher retention decisions on performance, rather than seniority. Florida and Colorado have already enacted such legislation.*

◆ A California school district reduced or discontinued five positions, including a full-time equivalent (FTE) psychologist position. Instead of rehiring two part-time psychologists for the new full-time job, the district hired a less senior full-time certificated school psychologist. A state court denied relief to the part-time employees, and they appealed. The Court of Appeal of California found that **state law permitted a school board to make assignments and reassignments in such a way that employees were retained to render services for which their seniority and qualifications made them fit**. The Education Code did not compel the district to split positions in the event of layoffs. School districts had broad discretion to define job positions and establish employment requirements. The court found little reason why the district could not define the position as "full time," if it found the job duties could not be performed by two part-time employees. The district needed to employ a full-time psychologist for several reasons. Since the part-time psychologists did not have the right to force the district to divide the duties of a full-time position to accommodate their wishes, the court affirmed the judgment. *Hildebrandt v. St. Helena Unified School Dist.*, 172 Cal.App.4th 334, 90 Cal.Rptr. 855 (Cal. Ct. App. 2009).

◆ A South Dakota computer science teacher had worked for a school district for 17 years. The district employed three other computer teachers, including one who had taught in the district for over 30 years. Another teacher had 10 years in the district, while another was in his first year there. The collective bargaining agreement (CBA) between the board and teachers had a two-part method for determining if seniority could be used. This included appropriate certification and the courses taught by a teacher in the preceding seven years. The school board determined that the 30-year veteran teacher could use her seniority only for the areas in which she had taught during the previous seven years. As a result, she was allowed to bump only into a computer science position. The 30-year veteran could not bump the 10-year veteran, who also taught business classes. Nor could the 30-year veteran teacher satisfy the seniority requirements for the first-year teacher's assignments because he taught technology modules that were heavily weighted on math and science. The computer science teacher was unable to bump the 10-year and first-year teachers for the same reasons that the 30-year veteran could not. Her contract was not renewed, and the district denied her grievance. The case reached the South Dakota Supreme Court.

The court held that **the teacher lacked the certification and recent experience of the less-senior teachers whose positions she was trying to assume**. She could not partially bump other teachers by assuming parts of their job assignments. The district had properly followed the CBA policy, and its contract non-renewal action was upheld. *Hanson v. Vermillion School Dist. No. 13-1*, 727 N.W.2d 459 (S.D. 2007).

◆   A New York board of cooperative educational services (BOCES) provided student occupational programs in several districts. Teaching assistants (TAs) supplemented the services of classroom teachers. The BOCES laid off nine TAs due to declining student enrollment. Layoffs were not in accord with seniority. Five of the laid off TAs sued the BOCES in a state court, which allowed the state education commissioner to determine if TAs were "teachers" as defined by New York Education Law. The TAs claimed they could only be dismissed according to seniority under a tenure provision addressing the appointment of "teachers and members of the teaching staff." The BOCES asserted that TAs were like vocational teachers, without specific educational, certification, or licensure requirements. The commissioner disagreed and reinstated the TAs with back pay and benefits. The case reached the Court of Appeals of New York, which agreed with the commissioner that **the TAs should be included in the tenure system**. As the BOCES appeared to be going against its own policies, the court ruled that the TAs were entitled to be laid off by seniority. *Madison-Oneida Board of Cooperative Educ. Services v. Mills*, 4 N.Y.3d 51, 823 N.E.2d 1265, 790 N.Y.S.2d 619 (N.Y. 2004).

◆   An Ohio school district laid off a teacher with seven years of experience as part of a reduction in force. The board employed her the next year as a substitute for a teacher on sick leave, and she worked in the position for 180 days during the school year. The board compensated the teacher according to the minimum salary under its salary schedule for teachers with a bachelor's degree and zero years of teaching experience. The next school year, the board rehired the teacher for full-time work, crediting her with eight years of experience on the salary scale. The teacher sued the board in a state court, seeking the salary and benefits that would reflect nine years of teaching experience. The trial court held for the school board, and appeal reached the Supreme Court of Ohio. It held that a state statute confers certain "local privileges" upon long-term substitutes, including salary not less than the minimum on the current adopted salary schedule. **School boards were required only to pay the minimum amount to substitutes** under the plain language of the statute. The court agreed with the board and Ohio School Boards Association that the legislature would have stated in the law if it intended that long-term substitutes earn additional service credit or be entitled to additional amounts beyond the minimum. The court affirmed the judgment for the board. *State ex rel. Antonucci v. Youngstown City School Dist. Board of Educ.*, 87 Ohio St.3d 564, 722 N.E.2d 69 (Ohio 2000).

◆   Minnesota law prohibits a teacher with continuing contract rights from being placed on unrequested leave while probationary employees kept positions for which a continuing contract teacher was licensed. But **bumping rights did not require districts to make unlimited staffing changes. A teacher had no right to demand that a board create a new position.** Seniority rights normally do not apply to the supervision of study halls. Instead, the court found this depended on the past practices of the school district. In this case, the school board did not consider study hall assignments in finding there was no existing position from which a teacher could bump anyone else. As a result, a state court held the district had appropriately placed her on leave. *Moe v. Independent School Dist. No. 696, Ely, Minnesota*, 623 N.W.2d 899 (Minn. Ct. App. 2001).

### 2.   Other Substantive Rights

*A Minnesota school administrator was not entitled to state law continuing contract protections after a year of service as an interim principal.*

◆   Before being appointed interim principal of a middle school, a Minnesota administrator served for three years as the district's activities director. The job posting for the activities director position required candidates to either hold a principal licensure or be in the process of obtaining one. The administrator held a K-12 principal's license and was hired as an interim principal. Near the end of the school year, the school board voted to terminate his contract without a hearing or other statutory procedures for continuing contract teachers. Although the administrator filed a grievance against the district, it was denied because he did not complete a three-year probationary term as a "teacher" under the state continuing contract statute. He then sued the board in the state court system.

The case reached the Court of Appeals of Minnesota, which found that an employee who is deemed a "teacher" under state law can be discharged only if specified procedural protections, such as a hearing, are provided. Under the continuing contract statute, a "teacher" was defined as "a principal, supervisor, and classroom teacher and any other professional required to hold a license" from the Minnesota Department of Education (MDE). Significantly, **MDE licensure requirements determined a school employee's "teacher" status, not any requirements that might be set by a district**. Otherwise, the court found that school districts could create continuing contract rights that did not exist by law. Since the MDE did not require an activities director to be licensed, the administrator's years of work in that job did not count toward continuing contract rights. As the administrator was not a continuing contract employee at the end of his year as interim principal, the board was entitled to discharge him without a hearing or other continuing contract protections. *Emerson v. School Board of Independent School Dist. 199*, 782 N.W.2d 844 (Minn. Ct. App. 2010).

◆   A Wyoming school district hired a guidance counselor in 1990, under a contract describing her as a "qualified certified employee." According to the contract, she had no continuing contract status. She continued to work for the school district under a series of non-teaching contracts. In 2003, the school district advised the counselor that her position was being cut for budgetary reasons. She asked for a hearing, but the request was denied as the district deemed her to have no contract or statutory rights. She sued, claiming protection under the Wyoming Teacher and Employment Law (WTEL). A state court held for the school district, and the counselor appealed to the Supreme Court of Wyoming. According to the court, the WTEL defined a "teacher" as any person employed under contract by a school board as a "certified professional employee." The counselor argued that her professional certification required treating her as a "teacher," since she was a "certified professional employee." She also noted that she instructed students in various skills.

The court held that the WTEL had to be read with other parts of the Wyoming Education Code. **While the WTEL required all teachers to be certified employees, not all certified professional employees were teachers.** Several Education Code provisions recognized a distinction between teachers and other certified professional employees. Instruction of non-academic skills and studies did not make the counselor a "teacher." *Luhm v. Board of Trustees of Hot Springs County School Dist. No. 1*, 206 P.3d 1290 (Wyo. 2009).

◆   Birmingham (Alabama) hired public school teachers for non-teaching duties under supplemental contracts to serve as coaches, football workers and support activity sponsors. Positions were not reserved for teachers and no teaching certification was required for them. In 2004, 2005 and 2006, the board failed to notify some teachers before the end of the school year of the non-renewal of supplemental contracts for the following school years. Teachers sued the board for improperly cancelling the contracts. The case reached the Supreme Court of Alabama, which found that state law defined "teacher" to include all persons regularly certified by the state as instructors, principals or supervisors in the public schools. **Coaches and other employees under supplemental contracts were not certified by the state to perform duties of an instructor, principal or supervisor.** For this reason, the court declined to afford state law protections to teachers performing supplemental duties independent of their teaching functions. As a result, the court ruled for the board. *Boone v. Birmingham Board of Educ.*, 45 So.3d 764 (Ala. 2009).

◆   A Mississippi school guidance counselor learned her contract would not be renewed at the end of her first year. She requested the factual basis for non-renewal and a hearing before the school board. The board upheld the action, and the counselor appealed to a state chancery court under the Education Employment Procedures Act of 2001, Mississippi Code Sections 37-9-101 to 37-9-113. The court held that the act unconstitutionally conferred jurisdiction on chancery courts. The parties appealed to the Supreme Court of Mississippi.

The court held chancery court jurisdiction was limited. Several decisions prior to enactment of the 2001 act made it clear that school board and other agency decisions were "matters in equity," which the state constitution allowed chancery courts to hear. **The court held Mississippi Code Sections 37-9-111 allowed an aggrieved school employee to appeal a final board decision to a chancery court.** The scope of a chancery court's review was limited to determining if the board action was supported by substantial evidence, was arbitrary or capricious, beyond the board's authority, or in violation of the employee's statutory or constitutional rights. As the chancery court committed error by holding the Education Employment Procedures Act unconstitutional, the court reversed and remanded the case with instructions for the court to decide if the action complied with Mississippi Code Sections 37-9-101 to 37-9-113. *Lawrence County School Dist. v. Bowden*, 912 So.2d 898 (Miss. 2005).

◆ **An Alabama principal employed under a probationary contract was not entitled to an evaluation and 90 days' notice prior to termination of his contract.** The Alabama Court of Civil appeals held that the Teacher Accountability Act distinguished between contract principals and probationary principals. As the principal was not entitled to the statutory protections he claimed, the court affirmed a lower court judgment for the school board. *Holmes v. Macon County Board of Educ.*, 11 So.3d 205 (Ala. Ct. App. 2006).

◆ A New York teacher had served a school district for parts of two school years when the district contracted with a board of cooperative educational services (BOCES) to operate its alternative education program. He accepted a full-time job with the BOCES teaching mathematics, but his employment there was terminated prior to the conclusion of his extended probationary period. The district refused to hire the teacher to fill a vacancy created by another teacher's retirement, and he sought review by the state education commissioner. The commissioner held that once the BOCES took over the district's alternative education program, the probationary teacher was automatically considered a BOCES employee with no preferred eligibility rights with the district. The teacher appealed, and the state's highest court held that **a qualified teacher whose position has been abolished during a BOCES takeover of a district program has a right to be placed on a district's preferred eligibility list for seven years**. *Bojarczuk v. Mills*, 746 N.Y.S.2d 450 (N.Y. 2002).

### C.  Collective Bargaining Agreements

*California courts do not allow greater contract protections for probationary teachers than those created by law. In* Board of Educ. of Round Valley Teachers Ass'n, *13 Cal.4th 269, 52 Cal.Rptr.2d 115, 914 P.2d 193 (1996), the Supreme Court of California held that parties cannot negotiate greater protections for probationary teachers than what is afforded by statute. A decision not to reelect a teacher cannot be collectively bargained.*

◆ A California school district refused to reelect a teacher after his second year as a probationary teacher, denying him tenure. His teachers' association filed a grievance, claiming retaliation for his participation in association activities. An arbitrator held the action came in retaliation for the teacher's exercise of rights protected by the collective bargaining agreement and the state Educational

Employment Relations Act. The arbitrator ordered reinstatement of the teacher with lost wages and other relief. A state court held the district had an absolute right to decide whether or not to reelect a probationary teacher under state law. On appeal, the Court of Appeal of California noted that the association had filed its grievance under a collective bargaining provision repeating substantive rights and duties of the EERA. **For that reason, the arbitrator exceeded his powers by enforcing a collective bargaining provision that conflicted with the statutory scheme.** The state supreme court has held that parties cannot negotiate greater protections for probationary teachers than afforded by statute. A decision not to reelect a teacher cannot be collectively bargained. Since the association's interpretation would grant a probationary teacher a grievance procedure prohibited by state law, the decision could not be challenged as a breach of the collective bargaining agreement. *Sunnyvale Unified School Dist. v. Jacobs*, 171 Cal.App.4th 168, 89 Cal.Rptr.3d 546 (Cal. Ct. App. 2009).

◆ A New Jersey school district employed a custodian under one-year employment contracts containing no language granting tenure or guaranteeing reemployment. It sought to discharge him at the beginning of his third year due to his "attitude, inefficiency" and "lack of cooperation." The custodian's employee association filed a grievance on his behalf that was denied by the district superintendent. An arbitrator for the state Public Employment Relations Commission found that no just cause existed for termination because the board did not provide him with progressive discipline. The district reemployed the custodian for the last month of the school year and then notified him it would not renew his contract. He followed district procedures for an informal board hearing and was informed that the district would not reemploy him.

The custodian pursued a second grievance, but the board maintained that a custodian does not acquire tenure and may not grieve the non-renewal of an annual contract. The case reached the Supreme Court of New Jersey, Appellate Division, which noted that the non-renewal decision was a contractual prerogative of the board, not "discipline." **The custodian had no contractual rights of reemployment or any right to grieve the non-renewal of his employment.** The reinstatement of the custodian for the final month of his contract did not give him additional rights to reemployment. The non-renewal action was an independent matter from the previous arbitration, which was limited to the term of that contract. *Cresskill Board of Educ. v. Cresskill Educ. Ass'n*, 826 A.2d 778 (N.J. Super. Ct. App. Div. 2003).

◆ The collective bargaining agreement (CBA) between a South Dakota district and its teachers association set out mandatory procedures for reductions in force. Teachers with less than full certification would be released first, followed by those without continuing contract status, then those with continuing contract status, according to "length of service." The board voted for a work force reduction because of budgetary constraints, and it notified a teacher and a teacher/coach that they were subject to release. The teacher/coach had three years of continuous service to the district, but the teacher had more than five years of overall service. She had worked as a substitute for one school year, taught summer school and worked as a substitute for two years before becoming a full-time contract teacher two years earlier. The board decided that since the teacher/coach would reach continuing contract status first, he had seniority over the teacher. However, the state labor department held that the CBA bound the district. The reduction-in-force policy measured seniority by "length of service," not "continuous service." Because the teacher's overall service was greater, the board had to retain her. A state trial court affirmed the decision, and the district appealed.

The South Dakota Supreme Court held that **the district had to abide by the CBA's terms and could not add words that the parties left out**. The agreement enumerated the protocol for implementing a reduction in force, using a principle of seniority measured by length of service within the school system. The board was not permitted to insert or delete contract language. The contract included no language such as "continuous" or "uninterrupted" to define length of service. Since the teacher should have been retained under the plain language of the agreement, the court affirmed the department's decision. *Gettysburg School Dist. 53-1 v. Larson*, 631 N.W.2d 196 (S.D. 2001).

## D.  State Regulatory Authority

*In the next case, a Florida school board that delegated its investigatory powers to an office of professional standards was bound to comply with an administrative law judge's order to comply with an investigation by the office.*

◆   A Florida teacher was investigated for possible misconduct with a student. An investigator for the school board's office of professional standards (OPS) directed the teacher to appear for an investigatory interview. When she advised him the interview would take place with no attorney, the teacher declined. Due to the teacher's refusal to appear before the OPS investigator, the superintendent recommended his suspension pending termination for misconduct, gross insubordination and violation of a school policy requiring employees to cooperate with the OPS. An administrative law judge (ALJ) found the teacher had been compelled to appear before the OPS investigator in the course of an official investigation. For that reason, **he was entitled to be accompanied by counsel at his own expense under Florida Statutes Section 120.62(2)**. The board rejected the ALJ's decision and fired the teacher. A Florida District Court of Appeal agreed with the ALJ that the board had delegated its investigatory powers to the OPS. The court agreed with the ALJ that the teacher was ordered to appear before the OPS investigator in the course of an official investigation. As a result, the court reversed the board's decision. *Raven v. Manatee County School Board*, 32 So.3d 126 (Fla. Dist. Ct. App. 2009).

◆   An Alabama teacher was discharged after two students accused him of cursing at them and soaking their pants with water. Discharge was based on the most recent discipline and 11 others over the past four school years. At a hearing, the school board sought to prevent the teacher from offering any evidence about the underlying events for the 11 prior incidents documented in his file. The hearing officer allowed him to present evidence beyond what was in his personnel records, including the argument that many of the prior incidents were the result of bias. The hearing officer then reinstated the teacher and ordered nine of the 11 disciplinary actions expunged (erased) from the teacher's personnel file as either unwarranted or the result of personal bias.

The Supreme Court of Alabama held that a "hearing officer may consider the employment history of the teacher, including, but not limited to, matters occurring in previous years." **Hearing officers had discretion to accept testimony and exhibits, and the court found nothing in the Act to limit this discretion.** However, the Tenure Act did not grant hearing officers authority to alter prior disciplinary actions or expunge them from a teacher's employment records. The case was returned to the hearing officer to vacate the part of his order altering past disciplinary action and expunging the teacher's employment records. *Ex parte Webb*, 53 So.3d 121 (Ala. 2009).

◆   A Texas school counselor was accused of violating district policies and Section 261.101 of the Texas Family Code by failing to report suspected child abuse or neglect, and only minimally cooperating with a police investigation. After a hearing, a hearing examiner recommended non-renewal of his contract. The school board voted to accept the recommendation. Instead of appealing to the state commissioner of education under the Texas Term Contract Nonrenewal Act, the counselor sued the district in a state district court for retaliation. He asserted he was discharged in retaliation for cooperating in good faith with a child abuse or neglect investigation. The court denied the district's motion to dismiss the case, and it appealed to the Court of Appeals of Texas.

The court explained that the Term Contract Renewal Act specified procedures for teachers employed under term contracts to obtain review of adverse decisions. Teachers who were aggrieved by a board's decision could appeal to the commissioner of education. Those who were dissatisfied with a ruling by the commissioner could then appeal to a district court. **An aggrieved party had to first exhaust all administrative remedies if the subject matter of an action concerned the administration of school laws and involved questions of fact. The court held that the termination of the counselor involved questions of fact that must be appealed to administrative authorities before resort to the courts.** It rejected his claim that the case was excused from exhaustion as a retaliation suit under the Family Code. The counselor was a term contract employee. The board had properly notified him of its non-renewal decision and his next step was to appeal to the commissioner. The court reversed the judgment, holding the counselor could not maintain a retaliation suit and had to comply with state administrative procedures. *Ysleta Independent School Dist. v. Griego*, 170 S.W.3d 792 (Tex. Ct. App. 2005).

## II.  DUE PROCESS REQUIREMENTS

*Due process protects property and liberty interests that arise from state laws, contracts and expectations. For example, a collective bargaining agreement creates a "property interest" in employment for the term of the contract. State tenure and continuing contract laws create property interests in the procedures described in the laws. Teachers have a "property interest" in their employment under these laws. At a minimum, due process means that the government will give an individual notice and an opportunity to be heard when it threatens the individual's liberty or property interests. In a pair of landmark cases, the U.S. Supreme Court found pre-termination hearings are designed to be an "initial check" against a mistaken employment decision.*

Two U.S. Supreme Court decisions, *Board of Regents v. Roth* and *Perry v. Sindermann*, below, help define the due process rights of teachers. The cases emphasize there must be an independent source for a liberty or property interest as such interests are not created by the Constitution, but arise by employment contract or by operation of state tenure laws. If a liberty or property interest is not established, no requirement of due process exists under the Fourteenth Amendment. If a teacher has a liberty or property interest in employment, then due process protections are required. An untenured teacher has an interest only in the term of his or her contract.

◆   A Wisconsin university hired a teacher for a fixed contract term of one year. At the end of the year, he was informed he would not be rehired. No hearing was provided and no reason was given for the decision not to rehire him. In dismissing the teacher's due process claims, the U.S. Supreme Court held no liberty interest was implicated because in declining to rehire him, the university made no charge such as incompetence or immorality. Such a charge would have made it difficult for the teacher to gain employment elsewhere and thus would have deprived him of liberty. **As no reason was given for the non-renewal of his contract, the teacher's liberty interest in future employment was not impaired and he was not entitled to a hearing on these grounds.** The Court stated as he had not acquired tenure, he had no property interest in continued employment at the university. To be sure, the teacher had a property interest in employment during his one-year contract term, but upon its expiration his property interest ceased to exist. The Court held **"to have a property interest in a benefit, a person clearly must have more than an abstract need or desire for it. He must have more than a unilateral expectation of it. He must, instead, have a legitimate claim of entitlement to it."** *Board of Regents v. Roth*, 408 U.S. 564, 92 S.Ct. 2701, 33 L.Ed.2d 548 (1972).

◆   The *Sindermann* case involved a teacher employed at a Texas university for four years under one-year contracts. When he was not rehired for a fifth year, he brought suit contending that due process required a dismissal hearing. The Supreme Court held "a person's interest in a benefit is a 'property' interest for due process purposes if there are such rules and mutually explicit understandings that support his claim of entitlement to the benefit that he may invoke at a hearing." **Because the teacher had been employed at the university for four years, the Court felt that he might have a protectable property interest in continued employment.** The case was remanded to the trial court to determine whether there was an unwritten "common law" of tenure at the university. If so, the teacher would be entitled to a dismissal hearing. *Perry v. Sindermann*, 408 U.S. 593, 92 S.Ct. 2694, 33 L.Ed.2d 570 (1972).

## A. Property Interest

*A school employee must have a liberty or property interest in employment to have procedural due process rights. A common source for creating a property interest arises from state tenure statutes. Notice and an opportunity to respond are the essential requirements of due process. In the following case, the Court of Appeals of Tennessee held that while the state teacher tenure act did not list "conduct unbecoming a teacher" as a ground for discharge, the charge was included in the Act as a ground for an employee's suspension.*

◆ A tenured Tennessee teacher was suspended for kissing a student in class and sending love notes to some students. After a hearing, the board of education voted to suspend him, impose a three-year probationary period and require sensitivity training. Grounds for the suspension were insubordination, conduct unbecoming a teacher and unprofessional conduct. A state chancery court affirmed the suspension, and appeal reached the Court of Appeals of Tennessee.

The court held "conduct unbecoming to a member of the teaching profession" included disregard for the state education association code of ethics "in such a manner as to make one obnoxious as a member of the profession." There was sufficient evidence to support a charge of unprofessional conduct. **The teacher's right to due process was not violated when the board charged him with "conduct unbecoming to a member of the teaching profession" as well as with "unprofessional conduct."** There was no deficiency of the notice to him under the state Teacher Tenure Act. The teacher received a full set of charges as required by the act. While "unprofessional conduct" was not a statutory ground for dismissal or suspension under the Tenured Teachers Act, the court found it was a ground for teacher discipline. Evidence showed the teacher was unprofessional and violated the state educational association's code of ethics. Since the board did not violate his due process rights and he created an atmosphere that was harmful to student learning, the suspension was affirmed. The court held the teacher was entitled to be paid only after the date of the lower court's order. This meant he was not paid for most of two school years. *Taylor v. Clarksville Montgomery County School System*, No. M2009-02116-COA-R3-CV, 2010 WL 3245281 (Tenn. Ct. App. 8/17/10).

◆ After about two years of work at a Connecticut technical high school, an untenured teacher began posting profiles on MySpace.com. He used a profile called "Mr. Spiderman" to communicate with students for school and private discussions. A school guidance counselor learned of the teacher's MySpace profile and found pictures of naked men and "inappropriate comments" posted on it. After the counselor complained to the teacher about his profile, he took it down and created a new one. School officials viewed the profile and found it was nearly the same as the "Mr. Spiderman" profile. They placed the teacher on leave with pay and eventually informed him that his contract would not be renewed. The teacher sued, alleging Due Process Clause violations. The court found the teacher had no protected property interest in his employment, as he did not have tenure under the state Teacher Tenure Act. **The employment relationship was governed by the collective bargaining agreement, not the**

**Teacher Tenure Act.** School officials complied with the collective bargaining agreement by providing timely written notice of the contract non-renewal, and there was no due process violation. The agreement did not require "just cause" to terminate an untenured teacher's contract. The court agreed with the officials that the teacher was disruptive. It was reasonable to expect him to maintain a professional, respectful association with his students and not communicate with them as if they were peers. Accordingly, the court upheld the non-renewal. *Spanierman v. Hughes*, 576 F.Supp.2d 292 (D. Conn. 2008).

◆   An Arizona school district determined that a teacher had improperly taken a college-level Spanish test for another person. The school board met in closed session but did not consider the teacher's statement. He was later allowed to read a prepared statement at a public meeting. The board then voted not to renew the teacher's contract. A non-renewal letter was placed in his file, but it was later removed. The board reported its action to the state board of education. The teacher completed the remainder of his contract, then sued the school district and board for due process violations under the state and federal constitutions. A federal court noted that **non-tenured teachers do not have a property right in continued employment under Arizona law**. The teacher's contract stated that his employment would end with the school year. The court rejected his claim that he had a "reasonable expectation of future employment" that was protected by the Due Process Clause. A teacher's subjective expectation that he would receive tenure due to performance did not create a property interest. There was also no deprivation of a constitutional liberty interest in reputation, honor and dignity. The board complied with state law by voting not to renew the teacher's contract in a public meeting and allowing him to work through the end of the school year. *Murdock v. Mingus Union High School Dist.*, No. CV 04-2313-PHX-DGC, 2006 WL 1328817 (D. Ariz. 2006).

◆   A Mississippi Junior ROTC instructor worked for a school district for three school years, left for a year, then returned to his job for a week. The U.S. Court of Appeals, Fifth Circuit, held that he had no protected property interest in employment. The school board never approved a recommendation by the principal to rehire the instructor. State law codified the procedures for hiring teachers and limited the role of principals to recommending candidates. **Any expectation for reemployment held by the instructor was based on statements allegedly made by the principal.** This was not enough to create a property interest in employment, and the district was entitled to judgment. *Watson v. North Panola School Dist.*, 188 Fed.Appx. 291 (5th Cir. 2006).

◆   An Iowa teacher was reprimanded in writing for pushing students into their seats. The assistant principal issued a reprimand letter. Parents called the school, and two of them filed a police report. The principal met with the teacher, and a district administrator investigated the incident. He wrote a report concluding that the teacher had used unreasonable force in violation of board policy. The district suspended the teacher for two days, then held a hearing. The teacher appeared with counsel, testified on his own behalf, introduced exhibits and called witnesses. The principal testified and answered questions from the board. The board upheld the suspension without pay and denied the teacher's request for reconsideration. When the teacher sued, a federal court commented that the board provided a prompt post-suspension hearing, and there was no interruption in benefits or harm to reputation. **The board satisfied the fundamental requirement of due process**, which is to provide an opportunity to be heard at a meaningful time and in a meaningful manner. As the teacher received due process, the court held for the board. *Oswald v. Waterloo Board of Educ.*, No. C02-2050, 2003 WL 22284654 (N.D. Iowa 2003).

◆   A Texas school administrator served a district for over 30 years with generally good performance appraisals. The district proposed his termination for sexual harassment, using district resources for personal benefit, obstructing an investigation into his behavior and falsifying school asbestos records. Under the Texas Education Code, employees were entitled to a pre-termination hearing if they filed written requests with the state education commissioner within 15 days of receiving a termination notice. The administrator submitted a written hearing request to the commissioner 12 days after he received notice of his termination. The board received the notice in two days, but the commissioner did not receive it until 18 days after the administrator received his notice. The commissioner found the hearing request untimely, stating it had to be "received," not "filed," within 15 days. The administrator sued the school district in a federal court, which found that he had filed a timely hearing request, and that **the board violated his due process rights by discharging him without a hearing**. The court awarded the administrator over $215,000 in damages, and the district appealed to the Fifth Circuit, which affirmed. *Coggin v. Longview Independent School Dist.*, 337 F.3d 459 (5th Cir. 2003).

◆   A Wisconsin principal called the police when a group of five or six students violently and aggressively assaulted a fellow student. After she suspended the students, some of their parents began to denounce her. The district administrator initially recommended renewal of the principal's contract. When a complaining parent reported that the closed board vote renewing the principal's contract violated the state open meetings law, the board rescinded its action and held a second meeting. By the time the board met again, it was bound by state law to renew the contract. But all district employees were notified that the board had revised the principal's title and job description.

The principal resigned from her position, stating that the removal of her main job duties amounted to a constructive discharge. Her federal civil rights action reached the U.S. Court of Appeals, Seventh Circuit, which noted that state law and the principal's contract did not encompass any right to perform particular job duties. The district did not transfer her, and she retained her title and salary. **An expectation of retaining certain job duties did not create a protectable property interest.** The principal's constructive discharge claim failed because she had abruptly resigned. There was no violation of her liberty interest in reputation because a charge of mismanagement or incompetence does not rise to a constitutionally protected level. *Ulichny v. Merton Community School Dist.*, 249 F.3d 686 (7th Cir. 2001).

## B. Notice

*Due process requires the government to provide notice and an opportunity to be heard at a relevant time when a liberty or property interest is at stake. To determine the specific notices and timelines for a school employee, districts must look to relevant state laws and collective bargaining provisions.*

◆ An Arkansas school district complied with state law when it discharged a teacher who was arrested in an ex-boyfriend's driveway with her minor child. She was allegedly under the influence of and in possession of chemical substances. The teacher did not appear at her termination hearing, and the board voted to discharge her. She claimed the board gave her a faulty notice, and she received a new hearing. The board again voted to fire the teacher. On appeal, **the Court of Appeals of Arkansas held that a subsequent hearing cures any notice defect from a prior hearing**. The board based its action on the record before it, and the teacher received ample opportunity to address the charges. The discharge was supported by a police report. While the teacher had been found competent in the classroom, her arrest with her child while intoxicated and stalking an ex-boyfriend justified her firing. *Harter v. Wonderview School Dist.*, No. CA 06-1254, 2007 WL 3276989 (Ark. Ct. App. 11/7/07).

◆ A Maryland school board did not violate the due process rights of an instructional assistant who was discharged for his inappropriate relationships with students. He invited student mentees to his house and individual lunches, causing suspicion of misconduct. The board placed the instructional assistant on leave with pay, contacted police and initiated an investigation. He had an opportunity to meet with investigators and respond to the charges. The assistant went through a grievance procedure and had two hearings. The case reached the U.S. Court of Appeals, Fourth Circuit, which found no U.S. Supreme Court case making detailed notices of possible discipline a formal requirement. The instructional assistant got a written suspension notice, alerting him that the charges against him were serious. **As he was on notice of serious consequences, he received all the process he was due.** *Curtis v. Montgomery County Public Schools*, 242 Fed.Appx. 109 (4th Cir. 2007).

◆ An Arkansas district superintendent informed a high school principal he was not going to recommend renewal of his contract. Almost one month later, the principal requested a hearing. The board scheduled a hearing more than 10 days after the principal's request, despite the state Teacher Fair Dismissal Act's (TFDA) requirement for a hearing between five and 10 days after a request is made. The principal objected to the delay, arguing that it resulted in the automatic renewal of his contract. The board voted not to renew his contract. A state court agreed with the principal's assertion that the district's failure to strictly comply with the act voided its attempted contract non-renewal. Thus, the contract was automatically renewed, and the principal was entitled to a year of pay. The Arkansas Supreme Court affirmed, noting that **the TFDA required strict compliance. A noncomplying contract non-renewal, termination, suspension or other disciplinary action was void**. Here, the district failed to comply with the TFDA's timing requirements. Because the attempted non-renewal was void, the trial court had properly found the district in breach of contract and liable for the principal's salary during the next school year. *Foreman School Dist. No. 25 v. Steele*, 61 S.W.3d 801 (Ark. 2001).

◆ A Washington teacher fired for misconduct with a student was not denied due process protections at her discharge hearing, according to the state court of appeals. The district gave her proper notice of misconduct charges including sexual relations with the student, giving him alcohol and staying with him in a hotel. The notice complied with state law and nothing indicated the hearing officer improperly assigned the burden of proof to the district. **The teacher had no constitutional right to counsel, which is limited to cases in which a fundamental liberty interest is at stake.** *Powell v. Cascade School Dist. No. 228*, No. 22831-2-III, 124 Wash.App. 1055 (Wash. Ct. App. 2004).

◆ During a Nebraska teacher's third year of employment, her principal sent her a letter stating that he would not recommend renewing her contract due to classroom management problems. After an informal hearing, where the teacher appeared with her attorney, the board deliberated in a closed session, then recessed. The board held another closed session, then returned to open session to vote against renewal. When the teacher appealed, the Nebraska Supreme Court found the principal had evaluated her, provided a written growth plan for the year, and notified her of her classroom management problems. There was no state requirement that a probationary teacher receive notice that a performance deficiency is of such magnitude that failure to remedy it could lead to non-renewal. **The board complied with statutory observation and evaluation requirements, and state law notice and hearing requirements by providing written notices of both hearings.** State law did not require board deliberations in open session. The court affirmed the judgment. *McQuinn v. Douglas County School Dist. No. 66*, 259 Neb. 720, 612 N.W.2d 198 (Neb. 2000).

## C. Hearing

### 1. Minimum Requirements

*Tenured employees must be given a fair and impartial hearing, conducted in accordance with statutory procedures, as they have a property interest in their continuing employment.*

◆ The master agreement between an Idaho school district and the association representing its teachers permitted paid professional development leave with a school principal's prior written approval. A teacher's request for a day off work to defend his final project in a master's degree in educational administration was denied by the school principal. A grievance on behalf of the teacher was denied, and the association sued the district and its board in a state court for breach of contract. The court held for the district, and the association appealed to the Supreme Court of Idaho. It found that while the master agreement seemed to give a principal the discretion to authorize professional leave, all contracts are subject to a "covenant of good faith and fair dealing." It was clear to the court that the contract required teachers to obtain the principal's written approval before taking paid professional leave. Nothing in the master agreement created an entitlement to take professional leave. Instead, the school district was vested with discretion to allow teachers two days of paid leave.

So long as this was done in good faith, the principal had authority to deny a request for professional development leave. A reason stated for denying leave was that **the master's program was not pedagogical in nature but instead prepared teachers for administrative careers**. The principal and district could have interpreted the agreement in good faith as permitting leave only for activity within a teacher's particular academic area. As the agreement did not require the district to offer professional development leave to pursue a degree in a field unrelated to a teacher's academic area, the lower court had correctly awarded judgment to the district. *Potlatch Educ. Ass'n v. Potlatch School Dist. No. 285*, 148 Idaho 630, 226 P.3d 1277 (Idaho 2010).

◆ An untenured Tennessee teacher was suspended for 10 days without pay for making sexually inappropriate remarks to a female student. The next school year, two teachers complained that he emailed them inappropriate comments. The teacher hired a lawyer and requested a chance to be heard before any discipline was imposed. Instead, the director of schools for the district sent the teacher a letter discharging him as of the date of the letter and notifying him that he could request a hearing with a personnel hearing officer. The teacher requested a hearing, but the discharge decision was upheld. Appeal went before the Court of Appeals of Tennessee. It held **the state code required notice of the charges and an opportunity for a full and complete hearing prior to the dismissal of any non-tenured, licensed employee**. There was no opportunity for a hearing until after the teacher was dismissed, since the director's letter stated he was dismissed as of that date. But on further appeal, the Supreme Court of Tennessee found the teacher was allowed to respond in writing to the charges being investigated. As an untenured teacher, he was not specifically entitled to a post-dismissal hearing under state law. And the teacher waived his claim that he was dismissed prematurely. Although there was no due process violation, the case was returned to the trial court to review his remaining claims. *Bailey v. Blount County Board of Educ.*, 303 S.W.3d 216 (Tenn. 2010).

◆ The Supreme Court of North Carolina decided not to review lower court decisions that found a probationary teacher was not entitled to a school board hearing regarding her contract non-renewal. The school board did not make an arbitrary decision based on evidence that she hit students with a ruler and used profanity in her classroom. **State law required notice to probationary teachers of non-renewal decisions, but it did not provide them with rights to evidentiary hearings.** *Moore v. Charlotte-Mecklenburg Board of Educ.*, 185 N.C. App. 566, 649 S.E.2d 410 (N.C. cert. denied 362 N.C. 360, 4/10/08).

◆ The U.S. Court of Appeals, Fifth Circuit, upheld the firing of a bilingual education teacher who was accused of improperly helping students during an administration of the Texas Assessment of Knowledge and Skills reading test. Colleagues observed her making erasures on tests and making comments to students beyond the test script. After a hearing, the teacher was fired. She sued the school district for due process violations. The court held for the district, and she appealed to the Fifth Circuit. The court of appeals affirmed, noting that **she had received a trial-like hearing that satisfied due process requirements**. As the teacher had opportunities to address the school board before it made any decision, there was no merit to her due process claim. *Rodriguez v. Ysleta Independent School Dist.*, 217 Fed.Appx. 294 (5th Cir. 2007).

◆  An untenured Missouri teacher was suspended for grabbing a student by the throat, pushing him into a wall and threatening to hit him. He also directed "threatening, intimidating, erratic and/or potentially violent behavior" at district personnel. After the district superintendent notified him he would propose the termination of his one-year contract, the teacher requested a public hearing, which began with testimony by eight district witnesses. His attorney cross-examined them, but due to the lateness of the hour, the hearing was adjourned. The teacher later sought two continuances and rejected a settlement offer by the district. When the hearing reconvened, the district sought to close it and hold an executive session to hear testimony from students, due to perceived intimidation by the teacher. The teacher sought a state court order requiring the board to keep it open. The board voted not to renew his contract, and he sued it in a federal court, asserting due process violations. The court held that he was entitled to a hearing to "clear his name." The school district appealed to the Eighth Circuit, which observed that the teacher had received his full pay for the school year. The failure to complete a termination hearing did not implicate a property interest. **Under Missouri law, probationary teachers have a property interest in employment for only the duration of the school year.** The teacher completed the school year, and there was no due process violation. *Gibson v. Caruthersville School Dist. No. 8*, 336 F.3d 768 (8th Cir. 2003).

◆  A Texas middle school principal served as a secondary school principal in Houston for 21 years before coming to the Ft. Bend Independent School District at the request of an area superintendent. The superintendent gave the principal an excellent performance review at the end of her first year, and she received a two-year contract. The next year, the district superintendent abruptly sought her termination, stating he did not like her and that she "was not keeping the parents of her students under control." The superintendent reassigned the principal to the maintenance department, then to a staff development position in which she had no contact with parents. The principal pursued an unsuccessful grievance, then resigned and sued the school board, district superintendent and area superintendent. The Fifth Circuit rejected the principal's claim of entitlement to a pre-termination hearing. **Pre-termination hearings were required only when an employee was forced to choose between resignation and discharge.** The principal received written notice of the reasons for her reassignment, and two grievance hearings. Reassignment to minimize her interaction with parents appeared rational, and the superintendents were entitled to qualified immunity. *Finch v. Fort Bend Independent School Dist.*, 333 F.3d 555 (5th Cir. 2003).

◆ A police officer employed by a Pennsylvania state university was arrested in a drug raid and charged with several felony counts related to marijuana possession and distribution. State police notified the university of the arrest and charges, and the university's human resources director immediately suspended the officer without pay pursuant to a state executive order requiring such action where a state employee is formally charged with a felony. Although the criminal charges were dismissed, university officials demoted the officer because of the felony charges. The university did not inform him it had obtained his confession from police records and he was unable to fully respond to damaging statements in the police reports. He sued university officials for failing to provide him with notice and an opportunity to be heard before his suspension without pay. The case reached the U.S. Supreme Court, which held that **the university did not violate due process by refusing to pay a suspended employee charged with a felony pending a hearing**. Any pre-suspension hearing would have been useless, since the filing of charges established an independent basis for believing that the officer had committed a felony. The Court noted that the officer faced only a temporary suspension without pay, and not employment termination. *Gilbert v. Homar*, 520 U.S. 924 (1997).

◆ In two consolidated cases, the U.S. Supreme Court considered what pre-termination process must be afforded a public employee who can be discharged only for cause. A security guard hired by a school board stated on his job application that he had never been convicted of a felony. Upon discovering that he had in fact been convicted of grand larceny, the board summarily dismissed him for dishonesty in filling out the job application. He was not afforded an opportunity to respond to the dishonesty charge or to challenge the dismissal until nine months later. In the second case, a school bus mechanic was fired because he had failed an eye examination. The mechanic appealed his dismissal after the fact because he had not been afforded a pre-termination hearing. The Court held that **the employees had a property right in their employment and were entitled to a pre-termination opportunity to at least respond to the charges against them**. The pre-termination hearing need not fully resolve the propriety of the discharge, but should be a check against mistaken decisions. In this case, the employees were entitled to a pre-termination opportunity to respond, coupled with a full-blown administrative hearing at a later time. *Cleveland Board of Educ. v. Loudermill*, 470 U.S. 532 (1985).

## 2. Hearing Procedures

*State tenure and dismissal laws determine the applicable hearing procedures for tenured teachers. The Court of Appeal of California has held that while school boards "are not expected to observe meticulously all of the rules of evidence applicable to a court trial, common sense and fair play dictate certain basic requirements for the conduct of any hearing."*

◆ A California school board employee worked for a district as a plumber for over 21 years. The district put him on administrative leave pending an investigation of charges that he used paid sick leave on five days when he was not actually sick. The district asserted that the employee performed plumbing services in a private home on work days he had claimed to be ill and received sick pay. The board held a hearing to consider discharge. It relied on videotapes of the employee apparently working in private homes on the days he called in sick. The person who made the videotapes did not attend the hearing. The videotapes had time lapses, and dates on them "skipped around." A human resources officer who introduced the videotapes had no knowledge of who made the tapes, did not know if they had been edited, and could not state whether their dates were accurate. The board found the tapes proved the employee was not ill on the days he called in sick, and it dismissed him for dishonesty, falsifying information, and contract violations.

The state court of appeal noted that **while school boards "are not expected to observe meticulously all of the rules of evidence applicable to a court trial, common sense and fair play dictate certain basic requirements for the conduct of any hearing."** Here, the unauthenticated videotapes were not properly admitted as evidence and were irrelevant. The trial court had incorrectly allowed the case to return to the board for a new chance to authenticate the videotapes. The state code did not permit reconsideration of new evidence in this situation. The court disallowed a second hearing. *Ashford v. Culver City Unified School Dist.*, 29 Cal.Rptr.3d 728 (Cal. Ct. App. 2005).

◆   An Indiana special education aide claimed two 16-year-old students came to a party at his house without being invited and brought alcohol with them. The students stated that the aide offered them alcohol and sexually propositioned them. The aide claimed that he asked the students to leave several times and denied propositioning them or providing them with liquor or illegal drugs. School officials found that "he had engaged in improper conduct with the minors." The superintendent suspended him and barred him from school grounds. The aide claimed that the union representative did nothing to help him, and that he was never told of his hearing or grievance rights.

The board discharged the aide, who did not attend the board meeting, as he had been excluded from school grounds. The aide sued the school board in a federal court, which rejected the board's assertion that the meetings with the aide and the hearing satisfied his due process rights. **He was excluded from school grounds and reasonably believed he could not attend the meeting where his discharge was discussed.** He was never presented with the evidence against him, or allowed to cross-examine the two students or present his own evidence. The board did not allow the aide to respond to the charges of sexual impropriety, and denied him due process of law. The aide's negligence and due process claims could proceed. *Badger v. Greater Clark County Schools*, No. 4:03-CV-0101 SEB-WGH, 2005 WL 645152 (S.D. Ind. 2005).

◆   An Alabama school board unanimously voted to fire an elementary teacher. She appealed to the state tenure commission for a hearing and asked the school to send all documents it intended to present at the hearing. It did so in a timely manner. While many documents were retrieved from the teacher's personnel file, some had been kept elsewhere. The teacher did not know before the request that the files outside her personnel file even existed. She argued that the board did not give her proper notice of those documents. The commission rejected her argument and ruled in the board's favor. A state court held that the board did not provide adequate notice of the grounds for dismissal, but the state civil appeals court found the notice sufficient and reversed the trial court's decision. The teacher appealed to the state supreme court.

The teacher claimed that the documents outside her personnel file were "illegally obtained," and that their admission at the hearing violated her due process rights. The court held that due process requires only notice and a hearing at a relevant time. **The board gave the teacher advance notice of all documents it intended to present and provided a hearing.** The court affirmed the judgment, finding that even if it accepted the teacher's argument that the board could not collect and use the information from outside her personnel file, she did not allege any injury from the retention of these documents. *Ex parte Jackson*, No. 1021330, 2003 WL 22753456 (Ala. 2003).

◆   The Florida commissioner of education sought to permanently revoke a high school teacher's teaching certificate based on charges that he battered his wife and frequently used his school computer to access pornography on the Internet. The teacher requested an informal hearing before the state Education Practices Commission (EPC). The commissioner presented evidence that he had accessed "teenage oriented pornography" and that the battery of his wife had adversely affected her ability to work. The teacher admitted accessing inappropriate Internet sites but denied accessing teenage pornography. The EPC permanently revoked his certificate, and he appealed to the Florida Court of Appeal. He asserted that the commissioner's EPC evidence amounted to new claims that should have been referred for a formal administrative hearing. The court disagreed with his assertion that evidence of teenage pornography and adverse impact on his wife's employment were new charges of wrongdoing. These issues were properly presented to the EPC. **The teacher failed to timely raise the request for a formal hearing before the EPC during the administrative hearing and had thus waived his right to this relief** on appeal. The court affirmed the permanent revocation of his certificate. *Stueber v. Gallagher*, 812 So.2d 454 (Fla. Dist. Ct. App. 2002).

◆   An Iowa teacher hosted a party on her property at which high school students consumed alcohol. She claimed she did not know the students were drinking, and she took car keys from some of them. Four students were killed when their car hit a tree on the night of the party. The district superintendent recommended terminating the teacher's contract for unprofessional conduct, failure to effectively monitor a party where students used alcohol illegally, failure to protect student safety and welfare, ineffective leadership, inability to be effective as a teacher, and being a poor role model. The teacher requested a hearing, which was held in a private special session. The board voted to terminate her contract, and she appealed to an adjudicator. She then petitioned a state court, seeking to introduce additional evidence that was not included in the board's findings of fact. The case reached the Supreme Court of Iowa, which held that **since the adjudicator had yet to consider the teacher's appeal, there was no final decision to review**. The legislature intended the administrative process to be the exclusive means of challenging a board action. *Walthart v. Board of Directors of Edgewood-Colesburg Community School Dist.*, 667 N.W.2d 873 (Iowa 2003).

### 3. Impartiality

◆ A California math teacher was hired under the assumption that he would learn the nationwide college preparatory mathematics (CPM) curriculum the district used. The teacher participated in CPM training sessions, but shortly after the start of the school year objected to using CPM materials and allegedly pursued a course of argumentative, rude and arrogant behavior with students, staff and supervisors. The principal placed the teacher on administrative leave, and the district held a dismissal hearing, appointing an attorney who represented the district to serve as hearing officer. The teacher noted that the attorney's wife worked for the district and claimed bias. The attorney declined to recuse himself. The board voted to discharge the teacher for dishonesty, unfitness for service and persistent refusal to obey administrative directions. The board decision was upheld by a state trial court. The state court of appeal upheld the dismissal. The teacher's due process claim was based on alleged bias by the hearing officer/attorney and superior court judge. Courts have held that **there must be more than an appearance of bias to establish a due process violation. There was no showing of any actual bias or dishonesty.** The district did not have to bring in a hearing officer from outside the area to avoid bias or prejudice. *Regan v. Governing Board of Sonora Union High School Dist.*, No. F037765, 2002 WL 31009412 (Cal. Ct. App. 2002).

◆ A Pennsylvania high school principal received satisfactory evaluations but was assigned areas of concern during his first three years of employment. The district superintendent issued him an unsatisfactory rating at the end of his fourth year, and the board voted to demote him. He petitioned the state secretary of education for review, arguing that a board member was married to a district secretary who had testified against him and that potential bias existed because of their relationship. The secretary held that the decision was justified and that while allowing the board member to participate in the voting was imprudent, it did not violate the school code. The secretary's *de novo* review of the case cured any potential for bias in the board proceedings.

The Commonwealth Court of Pennsylvania ruled that the principal had been denied due process because of the appearance of bias created by the board member's presence in board deliberations. On appeal, the Supreme Court of Pennsylvania observed that although school board proceedings have an inherent potential for bias because of a board's dual prosecutorial and judicial roles, **independent review by the secretary ensured that the requirements of due process were satisfied**. Since the principal received all the process he was due, the court reversed and remanded the commonwealth court's decision. *Katruska v. Bethlehem Center School Dist.*, 767 A.2d 1051 (Pa. 2001).

# CHAPTER ELEVEN

## Labor Relations

## I. PROFESSIONAL ASSOCIATIONS

### A. Representation

*Union members are entitled to representation during an "investigatory interview" under NLRB v. J. Weingarten, Inc., 420 U.S. 251 (1975). But the Supreme Court of Illinois held a probationary teacher was not entitled to union representation at remediation meetings under state law or the relevant collective bargaining agreement. This was because the meetings were intended to help her correct her performance deficiencies, not to impose discipline.*

◆ An Illinois teacher was placed on a corrective action plan to improve her classroom performance and communication skills. She asked for her union representative to sit in on remedial meetings with the principal to discuss her progress. The principal refused, but the representative told him that *NLRB v. J. Weingarten, Inc.*, above, permitted union representatives at an "investigatory meeting" if an employee reasonably believed the meeting may involve disciplinary action. The representative was permitted to attend meetings but was not allowed to speak. The principal later advised the teacher that her union representative could not attend the meetings. After the teacher earned poor ratings for her instructional presentation and professional communications, she was advised that her contract would end with the school year. Her union filed a successful unfair labor practice charge with the Illinois Educational Labor Relations Board (IELRB). Appeal reached the Supreme Court of Illinois, which noted that remediation was a required "preliminary step" under state law. **But the state supreme court held no right to union representation automatically attached to "post-observation conferences" such as a remediation meeting.**

The relevant collective bargaining agreement (CBA) did not state a right to union representation at remediation meetings. Under the CBA, teachers were entitled to union representation "at any meeting leading to disciplinary action." Post-observation conferences were not disciplinary, and were required by the state board. And the CBA expressly gave supervisors discretion over evaluative conclusions and remediation decisions. While remediation meetings "had the potential of resulting in adverse action," the court held the CBA did not require representation. As neither the law nor the CBA assured a right to union representation, the judgment was reversed. *SPEED Dist. 802 v. Warning*, No. 108785, 2011 WL 681131 (Ill. 2/25/11).

◆ A Tennessee teacher was employed as a varsity basketball coach under a separate contract from his regular teaching contract. He became embattled due to complaints about his conduct, and the school principal and the district's director of schools removed him from his coaching duties. While he retained his tenured teaching status, another teacher was named head basketball coach. The teacher's collective bargaining organization (CBO) filed a grievance on his behalf. The arbitrator found the master contract covered teaching assignments, and that the coaching assignment had to comply with it since the position was a "professional advantage." The case reached the Supreme Court of Tennessee, which held that the teacher's coaching assignment was not protected by the parties' CBO covering his regular employment as a teacher. Instead, he had a year-to-year coaching appointment. **His education association was precluded from representing teachers in their capacities as non-licensed coaches**, and the arbitrator had incorrectly found a master teachers contract governed the renewal of the coaching contract. But as the board had approved of the arbitrator's recommendations, it could not avoid paying for additional duties during the final year of the teaching contract. *Lawrence County Educ. Ass'n v. Lawrence County Board of Educ.*, 244 S.W.3d 302 (Tenn. 2007).

◆ **The U.S. Supreme Court upheld a collective bargaining agreement between an Indiana school board and a teachers union which gave the union exclusive access to the school district's internal mail system.** A rival union challenged the denial of access to the mail system on grounds that the restriction violated free speech rights under the First Amendment and the Equal Protection Clause. The Supreme Court held that since the inter-school mail system was not a public forum generally available for use by the public, access to it could be reasonably restricted without violating either free speech or equal protection rights. The Court noted the special responsibilities of the exclusive bargaining representative and the fact that other channels of communication remained available to the rival union. *Perry Educ. Ass'n v. Perry Local Educators' Ass'n*, 460 U.S. 37, 103 S.Ct. 948, 74 L.Ed.2d 794 (1983).

◆   A Minnesota law required public employers to engage in official exchanges of views only with their professional employees' exclusive representatives on certain policy questions. By law, public employers were required to bargain only with the employees' exclusive bargaining representative. The statute gave professional employees rights to "meet and confer" with the employer on matters outside the scope of a collective bargaining agreement. Community college faculty members sued the state board for community colleges, claiming the law violated the First Amendment. The faculty members objected to the "meet and confer" provision, saying that rights of professional employees within the bargaining unit who were not union members were violated. The U.S. Supreme Court held the "meet and confer" provision did not violate the faculty members' constitutional rights. **There was no constitutional right to force public employers to listen to employees' views.** The fact that an academic setting was involved did not give the faculty members any special constitutional right to a voice in the employer's policy-making decisions. The state had a legitimate interest in ensuring that public employers heard one voice presenting the majority view of its professional employees on employment-related policy questions. *Minnesota Community College Ass'n v. Knight*, 465 U.S. 271, 104 S.Ct. 1058, 79 L.Ed.2d 299 (1984).

◆   Some professional employees of a Kansas school district defected from membership in the Olathe National Education Association (ONEA) and joined the Association of American Educators (AAE). The AAE openly solicited ONEA members and proclaimed its interest in replacing the district's existing seniority-based compensation system with one based on merit. The district declined several AAE requests to use the district's internal mail system to distribute recruiting materials, noting the ONEA had negotiated this exclusive right through collective bargaining. The dispute reached the Kansas Supreme Court, which explained that while the state Negotiations Act allowed more than one professional employees' association per district, only one association could be a district's exclusive collective bargaining representative. **Since the ONEA had bargained for the privilege of using the school district's mail system, the district was legally prohibited from granting the privilege to any other association.** *Unified School Dist. No. 233, Johnson County, Kansas v. Kansas Ass'n of American Educators*, 275 Kan. 313, 64 P.3d 372 (Kan. 2003).

## B. Agency Fees

*Expenditures of employee associations fall into two categories: chargeable expenses, which relate directly to collective bargaining and representation; and nonchargeable expenditures, which include funding of political causes. The U.S. Supreme Court has held that employee financial support of collective bargaining representatives implicates the First Amendment.*

◆   Detroit teachers elected a labor association to become their exclusive collective bargaining representative, and it instituted an agency shop agreement. A group of teachers filed a class action lawsuit in a Michigan trial court, stating that they would not pay dues or agency fees because of their opposition to collective bargaining in the public sector. They specifically disapproved of the union's political and social activities, which they claimed were unrelated to the collective bargaining process. The teachers argued that the agency shop agreement violated state law and the First and Fourteenth Amendments. A state court dismissed the case, and appeal reached the U.S. Supreme Court on federal constitutional issues. The Court agreed with the teachers that **compelled agency fees should not be used to support political views and candidates that were unrelated to collective bargaining issues**. Because the state court had dismissed the case without a trial, the teachers had not received the opportunity to make specific allegations that their contributions were being used to support activities with which they disagreed. There was no evidentiary record, and the Court remanded the case. If the teachers could prove a First Amendment violation, they were entitled to relief in the form of an injunction or a *pro rata* refund of fees being used for such purposes. *Abood v. Detroit Board of Educ.*, 431 U.S. 209 (1977).

◆  The Supreme Court later held the Chicago Teachers Union did not adequately protect the speech rights of nonunion teachers. In 1982, the Chicago school board and the teachers' union agreed to deduct "proportionate share payments" from the paychecks of any nonunion employee. The deduction was fixed at 95% of the dues for union members, and no explanation was given as to how that figure was reached. This method of deduction was held to violate First Amendment freedom of speech protections. **To guard against the possibility of nonunion teachers' service fee payments being used for political purposes disagreeable to the nonmembers**, the Supreme Court ruled that there must be an adequate accounting and explanation of the basis for the deduction. In case of a challenge, there must be an opportunity for a reasonably prompt decision by an impartial decisionmaker as to whether any part of the service fee deduction has gone to fund political causes. Any amount that was reasonably in dispute must be held in escrow during the pendency of the challenge. *Chicago Teachers Union v. Hudson*, 475 U.S. 292 (1986).

◆  Washington law permitted public employee unions to negotiate agency shop agreements. Unions could charge nonmembers who were in a collective bargaining unit an "agency fee" that was equivalent to full union membership dues. In 1992, state voters approved an initiative that prohibited unions from spending the agency fees collected from union nonmembers for election-related purposes unless this was "affirmatively authorized" by the individual nonmember. The Washington Education Association (WEA) sent nonmembers biannual notices of their right to object to paying fees for expenditures that were spent on items unrelated to collective bargaining. The options included paying fees under objection and applying for a rebate. In 2001, the state and a class of nonunion public school employees sued the WEA, claiming the union had used nonmember fees to make political expenditures without the affirmative authorization of union nonmembers. The state supreme court held that the affirmative authorization requirement violated the First Amendment.

On appeal, the U.S. Supreme Court held a state could require its public-sector unions to receive affirmative authorization from a nonmember before spending that nonmember's agency fees for election-related purposes. **Unions had no entitlement to the fees of nonmember employees.** Therefore, the law requiring that nonmember employees affirmatively opt in to political spending of their agency fees did not violate the First Amendment. *Davenport v. Washington Educ. Ass'n,* 551 U.S. 177 (2007).

◆ The exclusive bargaining representative of the faculty at a state college in Michigan entered into an agency-shop arrangement with the college requiring nonunion bargaining unit employees to pay a service or agency fee equivalent to a union member's dues. Employees who objected to particular uses by the unions of their service fee brought suit under 42 U.S.C. § 1983, claiming that using the fees for purposes other than negotiating and administering the collective bargaining agreement violated their First and Fourteenth Amendment rights. A federal court held that certain collective bargaining expenses were chargeable to the dissenting employees. The case reached the U.S. Supreme Court, which held **chargeable activities must be "germane" to collective bargaining activity and be justified by the policy interest of avoiding "free riders" who benefit from union efforts without paying for union services**.

A local union could charge the objecting employees for their pro rata share of costs associated with chargeable activities of its state and national affiliates, even if those activities did not directly benefit the local bargaining unit. The local could even charge the dissenters for expenses incident to preparation for a strike that would be illegal under Michigan law. However, lobbying activities and public relations efforts were not chargeable to the objecting employees. The Court affirmed in part and reversed in part the lower court decisions and remanded the case. *Lehnert v. Ferris Faculty Ass'n,* 500 U.S. 507 (1991).

## C. Payroll Contributions

*In 2009, both the U.S. Supreme Court, and the U.S. Court of Appeals, Tenth Circuit, held states were not required to assist employee associations in the funding or expression of their political ideas though payroll deductions.*

◆ Idaho's Voluntary Contributions Act (VCA) amended the Right to Work Act in 2003 to permit all employees of the state and its political subdivisions to continue authorizing payroll deductions for general union dues. But they could not authorize payroll deductions for "political activities," which were defined as "electoral activities, independent expenditures, or expenditures made to any candidate, political party, political action committee or political issues committee in support of or against any ballot measure." The Idaho Education Association and Pocatello Education Association sued state officials in a federal court, asserting that the VCA violated employee rights. The court upheld the prohibition on political payroll deductions for state level employees, since the state incurred costs to set up and maintain the payroll deduction program. But the court found the VCA prohibition was not valid at local levels.

Appeal reached the U.S. Supreme Court, which held that **while the government must accommodate expression in some contexts, it is not required to assist in the funding of political expression**. Both sides agreed that the state did not need to provide payroll deductions. And Idaho was not obligated to assist unions with their political causes. Unions remained free to engage in political speech, but were "simply barred from enlisting the State" for that purpose. The VCA ban on political payroll deductions furthered a government interest in distinguishing between government operations and private speech. According to the Court, "Idaho does not suppress political speech but simply declines to promote it through public employer checkoffs for political activities." As the VCA ban on political deductions helped to separate public employment from political activities, the Court reversed the judgment. *Ysursa v. Pocatello Educ. Ass'n*, 555 U.S. 353 (2009).

◆   Utah's Voluntary Contributions Act (VCA) was enacted in 2001 to end voluntary payroll contributions to labor union political funds. The legislation prompted the Utah Education Association (UEA) and other public employee unions to file a federal court action, seeking to nullify the Act on First Amendment grounds. According to the unions, the VCA restricted member employee rights. The court agreed, as did a three-judge panel of the U.S. Court of Appeals, Tenth Circuit. After the U.S. Supreme Court upheld a similar Idaho statute in *Ysursa v. Pocatello Educ. Ass'n*, above, the Tenth Circuit held that **a state was not required to assist a union in the funding or expression of political ideas**. When a state declined to subsidize speech, it did not infringe upon individual First Amendment rights. Here, there was a rational basis for the VCA that survived limited judicial scrutiny. Like the Idaho VCA, Utah's VCA did not suppress political speech, but simply declined to promote it through a system of public employee payroll deductions. *Utah Educ. Ass'n v. Shurtleff*, 565 F.3d 1226 (10th Cir. 2009).

## II.   COLLECTIVE BARGAINING AGREEMENTS

*Federal labor law imposes a duty on employers to bargain with duly elected collective bargaining representatives over the terms and conditions of employment. School districts and employees become bound by the terms of their agreements, and failure to abide by them constitutes an unfair labor practice.*

### A.  Compensation

◆   A California school district paid its teachers for working 185 days during the 2006-07 school year. This included 180 instructional days, two days before classes started and three staff development days when students did not attend school. Classified employees (including paraeducators, instructional assistants and special education assistants) were not paid for staff development days when no students attended school. The union representing the classified employees petitioned a state court for a special order, asserting the district violated state law by not paying them on staff development days when they did not work.

A state superior court denied the petition, and the union appealed to the Court of Appeal of California. It explained an order called a "writ of mandate" was available to compel a public entity to perform a legal and ministerial duty.

The order was typically unavailable in wage disputes but would be a proper remedy in this case if state law created an official duty to pay the wages. A review of Education Code Section 45203 revealed that the classified employees were not entitled to the relief sought by the union. The section required payment of classified personnel on school days when pupils would otherwise have been in attendance but were not, and for which certificated teachers received regular pay. **Agreeing with the school district, the court held the staff development days were not "schooldays" during which pupils would otherwise have been in attendance.** As the district argued, staff development days were in addition to, not in lieu of, the 180 days of instruction required by state law. *California School Employees Ass'n v. Torrance Unified School Dist.*, 182 Cal.App.4th 1040, 106 Cal.Rptr.3d 375 (Cal. Ct. App. 2010).

◆ A South Dakota school district and the association representing its teachers reached impasse in negotiations for a contract for the 2006-07 school year. The 2005-06 agreement stated that it would remain in effect until a new contract was approved, and it provided for implementation of contract terms under Section 3-18-8.2 of the state code. While contract negotiations were in progress, the district hired 15 new teachers for 2006-07 and paid them on the 2005-06 salary schedule. South Dakota law did not permit teacher strikes, and after impasse, the Section 3-18-8.2 provisions took effect. Under this law, the school board's last offer had to be implemented "as a minimum," and the offer became the relevant agreement between the parties. The board's last offer for 2006-07 had a new salary schedule that departed significantly from the 2005-06 schedule. Without notifying the teachers association, the district unilaterally declined to adjust the salaries of the 15 new teachers downward. When the association learned of this, it filed a grievance with the state department of labor (DOL).

After the DOL held the district committed a grievable offense, a state trial court reversed the decision. The association appealed to the state supreme court. It held **agreements imposed when an impasse is reached are legally binding on the parties.** The district's last salary offer was based on a formula that tied increases to teacher degrees and a pool of money referred to as the Average Daily Membership Advancement Pool. Statutory language did not require the district to honor individual teacher contracts that were more favorable than the last offer, as the district contended. To interpret the "as a minimum" language of Section 3-18-8.2 as the district urged would undermine the entire collective bargaining process. **Collective bargaining statutes did not allow districts to negotiate with individual members of the bargaining unit.** The case was returned to the lower court for an appropriate award of relief. *Spearfish Educ. Ass'n v. Spearfish School Dist. # 40-2*, 780 N.W.2d 481 (S.D. 2010).

◆ Washington's highest court rejected a lawsuit asserting that legislative funding formulas which allowed differing salaries among employees in various school districts violated the state constitution. **Local salary variations were permitted, since the legislature was aware of the relevant political and economic issues.** *Federal Way School Dist. No. 210 v. State of Washington*, 219 P.3d 941 (Wash. 2009).

◆   A Wisconsin school district hired a teacher in 2002 who qualified for salary at the BA +8 lane of the collective bargaining agreement (CBA). However, the district accidentally put her at the BA + 0 level, where she remained for three school years. At the end of the 2004-05 school year, the teacher finally realized she was being underpaid and submitted a formal request to change lanes for the 2005-06 school year. The change was approved and she was paid at the BA + 8 lane, but nothing was done to remedy the underpayment of her wages during the prior years. When the teacher sought back wages to reflect the BA + 8 pay rate for her first three years of employment, the district refused the request. She filed a formal grievance, and an arbitrator found her grievance timely under a CBA provision requiring employees to give written notice to their immediate supervisor 15 days after learning the facts upon which a grievance was based.

Among the arbitrator's findings was that initial placement on the incorrect pay lane did not trigger the grievance. The case reached the Supreme Court of Wisconsin, which held that **the arbitrator permissibly found that the teacher did not know she had a grievance with the district until it made the decision to deny her back wages**. The teacher was challenging the denial of back wages, not her initial placement in the BA + 0 lane. Since this construction of the CBA had a foundation in reason, the award had to be upheld. *Baldwin-Woodville Area School Dist. v. West Cent. Educ. Ass'n - Baldwin-Woodville Unit*, 317 Wis.2d 691, 766 N.W.2d 591 (Wis. 2009).

◆   A Nebraska school district designated a long-term certificated teacher as a "substitute" and assigned her to take the place of a teacher who had resigned. The substitute was the only applicant with proper certification for the job. But a school administrator wanted to avoid hiring her as a permanent employee, so he designated her a "long-term substitute" instead of offering her a probationary contract. Later, the district re-posted the position and hired one of the previous applicants for the job, who had by then obtained proper certification. The district then told the substitute her services were not needed. Her union filed a grievance on her behalf, but the district denied the grievance and took her name off its list of active substitute teachers. The union filed an action with the Nebraska Commission of Industrial Relations, which ordered the district to reimburse the substitute by the amount she would have otherwise received under the collective bargaining agreement. On appeal, the Supreme Court of Nebraska found that **the district improperly hired the teacher as a long-term substitute**, even though she was a certificated teacher replacing a teacher who had resigned and did not plan to return. The district unilaterally altered the wages of a bargaining unit member, which was prohibited. *South Sioux City Educ. Ass'n v. Dakota County School Dist. No. 22-0011*, 278 Neb. 572, 772 N.W.2d 564 (Neb. 2009).

◆   A California school district and a teachers association agreed to a collective bargaining agreement (CBA) provision "compressing" teacher salaries to keep its salary rates competitive. The former 27-step schedule was compressed into 24 steps. All teachers with 17 to 20 years of service were placed into step 17. New step 20 was renumbered step 17, and all subsequent steps were renumbered. As a result, steps for teachers with at least 17 years of service did not correspond to their years of experience. Some teachers were moved three steps back. Aggrieved teachers sought a state court order recognizing uniform credit for each year of teaching experience, plus compensation and corresponding benefits they would otherwise have. A state court ordered the district to restore the teachers' lost compensation and retirement contributions.

The Court of Appeal of California noted the state Education Code mandates uniform teacher salary schedules when they are based on years of experience and training. Moreover, a uniform salary schedule meant one in which teachers were compensated invariably according to seniority and education. **The step reassignment in this case caused non-uniform treatment of teachers with equal experience.** The CBA's salary schedule treated more experienced teachers as "second-class employees" by requiring them to work longer than others to obtain the same salary increases. This violated the Education Code requirement that salaries be wholly commensurate with years of experience and training. And although parties could negotiate CBAs based on criteria other than a uniform allowance for years of training and experience, there were no such criteria in this case. The court affirmed the judgment. *Adair v. Stockton Unified School Dist.*, 162 Cal.App.4th 1436, 77 Cal.Rptr. 62 (Cal. Ct. App. 2008).

◆   **A Texas school administrator who did not follow her school district's procedure for addressing wage and earnings grievances could not pursue a due process claim** in federal court. The U.S. Court of Appeals, Fifth Circuit, affirmed a judgment for the district, which cut the administrator's pay when it involuntarily transferred her from a regular high school to an alternative school. The district later notified her that the reduction was in error and paid her for back wages. The administrator could not show a due process violation, as she did not use the district's grievance procedure prior to filing suit. *Vicari v. Ysleta Independent School Dist.*, 291 Fed.Appx. 614 (5th Cir. 2008).

◆   The Waterloo (Iowa) Education Association (WEA) submitted an overload pay proposal for the teachers it represented. The proposal would have required extra compensation for elementary teachers who taught over 300 minutes daily as part of a regular work assignment. The district maintained that the proposal was not a mandatory subject of collective bargaining under the state Public Employment Relations Act (PERA). The state Public Employment Relations Board (PERB) held that the proposal was not a mandatory subject of collective bargaining under PERA, and the WEA appealed. After an Iowa court affirmed the result, the case reached the Supreme Court of Iowa.

The court explained that the PERA listed 17 topics that were subject to collective bargaining. It required public employers and employee associations to negotiate in good faith regarding wages, hours, vacations, insurance, holidays, leaves of absence, overtime compensation, supplemental pay, seniority, transfers and the other listed mandatory collective bargaining topics. Here, **the overload compensation proposal was within the statutory definition of "wages," and it was a mandatory subject of collective bargaining**. The parties were required to bargain over the proposal. *Waterloo Educ. Ass'n v. Iowa Public Employment Relations Board*, 740 N.W.2d 418 (Iowa 2007).

◆   A Nebraska school district and the collective bargaining association representing its teachers failed to reach a negotiated agreement for the 2002-03 school year. The parties disputed the inclusion of a deviation clause in the agreement that was part of their 2001-02 contract. The deviation clause permitted the school board to deviate from the agreement if this was necessary to hire teachers for particular positions. The association petitioned the state Commission of Industrial Relations (CIR), which held for the association, finding that the deviation clause should be excluded. The Supreme Court of Nebraska then noted that **each district with a deviation clause had the ability to depart or deviate from the salary schedule**. Since this commonality among contracts was consistent with the definition of "deviation," the CIR had incorrectly struck down the deviation clause. The court reversed the judgment with instructions to include the clause in the parties' 2002-03 contract. *Hyannis Educ. Ass'n v. Grant County School Dist. No. 38-0011*, 274 Neb. 103, 736 N.W.2d 726 (Neb. 2007).

◆   A Montana school superintendent agreed to pay a prospective teaching candidate $2,000 in moving expenses as an inducement. The school board later offered the candidate a teaching position. Two weeks later, the board voted to hire another teaching candidate who also sought moving expenses. However, her request was denied on grounds that this would exceed the salary specified in the collective bargaining agreement (CBA). The teachers' association filed an unfair labor practice charge with the state Board of Personnel Appeals (BOPA).

After a hearing, the BOPA held the incentive was additional compensation and a condition of employment that was the subject of mandatory collective bargaining. The Supreme Court of Montana rejected the board's argument that the payment was made before the candidate accepted employment. Terms and conditions offered by an employer to a non-employee may still be subject to mandatory bargaining if they "vitally affect" the terms and conditions of employment for current employees. The $2,000 inducement materially or significantly affected the terms and conditions of employment for association members. **The board circumvented the collective bargaining process by bargaining directly with and agreeing to pay the candidate compensation beyond what was stated in the CBA.** The timing of the decision to issue the check was irrelevant. The supreme court affirmed the BOPA's decision. *Ekalaka Unified Board of Trustees v. Ekalaka Teachers' Ass'n, MEA-MFT, NEA*, 335 Mont. 149, 149 P.3d 902 (Mont. 2006).

◆   An Oregon assistant principal signed a three-year contract with a school district requiring him to work 220 days each year. During the first year of the contract, the district adopted a new employee compensation plan for the next five school years. Under the plan, the assistant principal's salary remained the same, but his work days were increased from 220 to 230 each year. The assistant principal appealed to the state Fair Dismissal Appeals Board, contending that the action amounted to an unauthorized "reduction in pay." The board ruled against him, as did the Court of Appeals of Oregon. **The addition of 10 work days to the administrator's workload was not an "assignment or reassignment" under state law.** A "reduction in pay" meant a decrease in the amount of money paid under a contract. School administrators could be paid on a salary basis and were exempt from overtime laws. The legislature intended the term "pay" to mean "salary." The administrator did not receive a reduction in pay, as his salary remained the same as before the salary plan. *Folkers v. Lincoln County School Dist.*, 205 Or.App. 619, 135 P.3d 373 (Or. Ct. App. 2006).

◆   In 1993, the Washington Legislature authorized a pilot program allowing school districts to assign educational employees to non-instructional "learning improvement days" for additional training. Learning improvement days were not a part of the "basic education" required by the Washington Constitution. The program became permanent, and most districts took advantage of learning improvement days. In 2000, Washington voters approved Initiative 732, which mandated an annual cost-of-living increase for all school employees. When the legislature responded to a significant budget deficit in 2002 by reducing the annual learning improvement days from three to two, educational employees lost about one-half of a percent of their annual pay. A coalition of teachers, districts and others challenged the reduction. The case reached the Supreme Court of Washington, which stated that learning improvement days were not part of the constitutionally mandated basic education. Thus, **the legislature's decision to fund only two learning improvement days rather than three did not result in a lower cost-of-living increase than was required by Initiative 732**. *Brown v. State of Washington*, 119 P.3d 341 (Wash. 2005).

◆   The South Carolina General Assembly enacted a law to pay teachers a $7,500 annual bonus for obtaining national board certification. A school district supplemented this incentive by offering a 10% pay increase for obtaining the certification. The superintendent discussed the program at some meetings, but the board reduced the incentive to $3,000 per teacher due to a budget shortfall. Five teachers sued the district in a state court, alleging that the reduced incentive was a breach of contract and a violation of the state Payment of Wages Act. The court awarded pretrial judgment to the district, and the teachers appealed. The state supreme court **rejected the breach of contract claim. The district was not bound to the 10% incentive program as initially described.** The teachers had no equitable claim to a 10% pay increase. They did not show they reasonably relied on a promise by the district superintendent. He informed teachers on several occasions that the pay incentive was subject to the board's approval. The board had acted to reduce its budget, and did not act in bad faith or with malice. It also complied with the South Carolina Payment of Wages Act by informing the teachers well in advance of a seven-day statutory notice requirement. *Davis v. Greenwood School Dist. 50*, 620 S.E.2d 65 (S.C. 2005).

◆   Florida pre-school instructors in a federal Head Start program claimed they consistently worked over 40 hours per week. The local school board did not pay them overtime for working excess hours, and they sued the board for violating the Fair Labor Standards Act (FLSA). A court considered the board's argument that an FLSA professional exemption for teachers applied to the instructors, exempting them from any overtime pay. In exempting teachers from FLSA overtime provisions, Congress and the U.S. Department of Labor realized that a teacher's usual weekly time commitment exceeds 40 hours per week. Head Start instructor duties closely paralleled those of regular teachers. They shared a common job description and did everything done by the certified teachers in the district. **The instructors were within the FLSA's professional teacher exemption and not entitled to overtime pay.** *Ramos v. Lee County School Board*, No. 2:04 CV 308FTM-33SPC, 2005 WL 2405832 (M.D. Fla. 2005).

◆  An Ohio bus mechanic worked for a school board for 13 years. The board laid off all its drivers and mechanics, and contracted with a private transportation service to operate its buses. Its contract required the service to offer employment to laid-off employees with a 3% pay raise and comparable benefits, including continued participation in the School Employees Retirement System (SERS). The mechanic rejected a job offer and received retirement and social security benefits for three years, without seeking other employment. The union representing the drivers and mechanic sued the school board in a state court. In 2000, **the state supreme court held that the board had unlawfully laid off the drivers and outsourced their jobs.** *State ex rel. Ohio Ass'n of Public School Employees/AFSCME, Local 4, AFL-CIO v. Batavia Local School Dist. Board of Educ.*, 89 Ohio St. 191, 729 N.E.2d 743 (Ohio 2000).

When the school board denied the mechanic's request for reinstatement, he filed a separate action for reinstatement with back pay and lost benefits. His case reached the state supreme court, which held that the mechanic's failure to accept employment by the private service was a failure to mitigate his lost wages. As a result, **he was not entitled to any back pay.** *Stacy v. Batavia Local School Dist. Board of Educ.*, 105 Ohio St.3d 476, 829 N.E.2d 298 (Ohio 2005).

◆  A union collective bargaining agent who represented the employees of two schools owned and operated by the U.S. Army submitted proposals asking for mileage reimbursement, paid leave, and salary increases on behalf of school employees. The schools refused to negotiate, stating that under Title VII of the Civil Service Reform Act of 1978 they were not required to negotiate these matters. The union filed a complaint with the Federal Labor Relations Authority (FLRA), which held that the union's proposals were negotiable. The U.S. Supreme Court noted that **Title VII of the Civil Service Reform Act defines conditions of employment as matters "affecting working conditions"** but excludes matters relating to prohibited political activities, classification of positions, and those specifically provided for by federal statute. The Court determined that the union's proposals were "conditions of employment," and it affirmed the district court decision. The schools were required to negotiate salary increases and fringe benefits. *Fort Stewart Schools v. Federal Labor Relations Authority*, 495 U.S. 641, 110 S.Ct. 2043, 109 L.Ed.2d 659 (1990).

## B.  Positions

◆  A non-tenured, part-time New Jersey teacher/secretary worked under an individual employment contract that could be terminated by either party upon 60 days' notice. Only a month into her job, the district superintendent began receiving complaints about her. He observed her in the classroom and found she was "unsatisfactory" or "needed improvement" in 22 of 25 relevant areas. Her contract was terminated for "serious deficiencies" in performance and she asked her union to file a grievance on her behalf. It did so, asserting the action was not supported by "just cause" under the collective bargaining agreement (CBA). The board sought to prevent arbitration and the case reached the Supreme Court of New Jersey. It found that **despite language recognizing employee rights to grievance procedures, the CBA recognized the existence and enforceability of individual employment contracts, like the employee's**. The CBA stated that grievances were inapplicable when the board decided not to renew a non-tenured employee's contract. The board had reserved its rights to terminate any non-tenured employee when this was in the best interest of the school district. The court rejected the union's arbitration request. *Northvale Board of Educ. v. Northvale Educ. Ass'n*, 192 N.J. 501, 933 A.2d 596 (N.J. 2007).

◆ An Ohio school board employed an unlicensed non-teacher as a girls' high school basketball coach for many years. A middle school teacher who was an assistant varsity coach and junior varsity head coach applied for the high school varsity coaching job. However, the high school's athletic director rehired the non-teacher coach. The middle school teacher grieved the board's decision, asserting that the collective bargaining agreement required the board to award a certificated employee a supplemental coaching contract over a non-teacher. An arbitrator found no collective bargaining provision directly addressing the selection of coaches. The arbitrator then determined that state education law required the hiring of the middle school teacher over the non-teacher coach.

The Court of Appeals of Ohio agreed with the arbitrator that **the board had to offer the position to the middle school teacher before it could give the job to the non-teacher**. In the absence of a collective bargaining provision about a matter, public employers and their employees were subject to state laws or local ordinances pertaining to wages, hours and terms and conditions of employment. Under state education law, the board could employ a non-licensed coach only if it offered the job to licensed employees of the district and none of them accepted the position. *Eastwood Local School Dist. Board of Educ. v. Eastwood Educ. Ass'n*, 172 Ohio App.3d 423, 875 N.E.2d 139 (Ohio Ct. App. 2007).

◆ A Florida teacher qualified for a veterans' preference as the spouse of a disabled veteran. When the district rejected her application for employment in 2001, she filed an administrative complaint with the state Public Employees Relations Commission (PERC). The district hired the teacher under a settlement agreement that ended the 2001 challenge. She signed a one-year contract and began the 2003-04 school year as a fourth-grade teacher. The school's vice principal gave her a good employment evaluation early in the school year but later observed her without prior notice and issued her a poor evaluation. The teacher responded with a 146-page packet that included a transcript of her veterans' preference hearing. The principal advised her that she would not be rehired. She called in sick the next day and was placed on administrative leave for the rest of her contract term. The teacher filed a second PERC complaint against the district, claiming it discharged her and retaliated against her through a series of unfair labor practices, including an unlawful suspension. The PERC dismissed the claims, and the Florida District Court of Appeal affirmed the judgment. A claimant has the burden of proving an unfair labor practice charge. **Here, the teacher did not show retaliation was a motivating factor in the adverse employment decisions.** *Cagle v. St. Johns County School Dist.*, 939 So.2d 1085 (Fla. Dist. Ct. App. 2006).

## C.  Other Terms and Conditions

*The "terms and conditions of employment" are matters that must be negotiated in collective bargaining agreements. Tennessee law defines the term as "those fundamental matters that affect a professional employee financially or the employee's employment relationship with the board." By contrast, inherently managerial subjects such as a school calendar cannot be bargained over.*

*Employers cannot unilaterally change any collective bargaining provision involving a mandatory subject of bargaining. A Tennessee court held a dress code had fundamentally affected teachers, and required mandatory bargaining.*

◆   A Minnesota school district that had 24 approved vendors for its employee 403(b) retirement plans began using a single vendor. The district declined the employee association's demand to meet and negotiate over the issue, and the association sued, claiming the district's unilateral decision was an unfair labor practice under the state Public Employee Labor Relations Act (PELRA). A court held that 403(b) retirement contributions and benefits are not mandatory subjects of negotiation under the PELRA. The association then appealed to the Court of Appeals of Minnesota, arguing that retirement benefits were within the PELRA's definition of "terms and conditions of employment" and thus a mandatory subject of negotiation. The court explained that "terms and conditions of employment" includes subjects such as hours of work, compensation and fringe benefits. But the PELRA specifically excluded "retirement contributions or benefits" unrelated to health insurance coverage.

While the court found the selection of a 403(b) plan vendor was a "fringe benefit," the PELRA excluded certain fringe benefits, and the exception for retirement contributions or benefits unambiguously covered the selection of vendors for 403(b) plans. The primary purpose of such plans was unquestionably to help employees save for retirement. **The PELRA excluded the selection of 403(b) plan vendors as a subject of mandatory negotiation.** *Educ. Minnesota-Osseo v. Independent School Dist. No. 279, Osseo Area Schools*, 742 N.W.2d 199 (Minn. Ct. App. 2007).

◆   Michigan taxpayers sent letters to school board members, requesting them to stop providing medical benefits to same-sex domestic partners of school employees. The letters claimed the practice was illegal. The taxpayers later sent copies to the attorney general, then sued the Ann Arbor School District. The Ann Arbor Education Association intervened. A state court held that the letters were not sufficient to be considered a "demand" upon public officials under a state statute. Since a demand under the statute is a prerequisite to filing suit, the case was dismissed. The state court of appeals affirmed the decision, and the taxpayers appealed. The Supreme Court of Michigan first noted that the letters were sufficient to create a "demand" under the statute. The purpose of the demand requirement was to inform the appropriate party that legal action was forthcoming. A letter to the state attorney general was a demand on the state's top legal officer. However, the court then held that the taxpayers lacked standing to pursue the lawsuit. **The taxpayers did not stand to suffer any injury based on the provision of benefits to partners of school employees.** The court affirmed the judgment of the lower courts. *Rohde v. Ann Arbor Public Schools*, 479 Mich. 336, 737 N.W.2d 158 (Mich. 2007).

◆ The New Jersey state health benefits plan was revised to increase the minimum weekly work hours required for employees to qualify for paid health insurance coverage. A local school board increased the minimum weekly hours for coverage from 20 hours to 32 to qualify for paid coverage. The union representing its teachers objected, but the parties did not refer to the elimination of health insurance benefits for part-time employees during negotiations for collective bargaining agreements (CBAs) until five years later, when a special education teacher who worked at least 20 hours per week complained that she was not receiving paid health insurance. But the new CBA for 2002-04 again did not resolve the issue of paid insurance benefits for part-time employees. An arbitrator held **the board committed a "continuing violation" of the CBA, based on the elimination of benefits for part-time employees without notice and without negotiating a change in the CBA**. The award required the board to provide paid health insurance benefits to the teacher and another certificated part-time employee who worked over 20 hours per week. On appeal, the state supreme court upheld the award. *Board of Educ. of Borough of Alpha, Warren County v. Alpha Educ. Ass'n*, 188 N.J. 595, 911 A.2d 903 (N.J. 2006).

◆ A Florida school board believed its employee health insurance plan was in danger of becoming insolvent after running deficits for many years. It notified the teachers union of the financial urgency and approved modifications to address the deficit. The sides failed to coordinate negotiations. The board then unilaterally changed employee health care benefits and notified the state Public Employees Relations Commission (PERC) of an impasse in negotiations. It also requested a bypass of statutory special master proceedings. The board then reached agreement with the teachers union. However, negotiations between the board and the noninstructional employees union were fruitless. The board declared an impasse and notified the union of its intent to skip mediation and related proceedings. After a hearing, it implemented the proposed changes.

The union filed a grievance, alleging that unilateral modification of health insurance benefits violated the parties' collective bargaining agreement (CBA). An arbitrator held that the board violated the CBA by failing to raise health care issues during contract negotiations. On appeal, the District Court of Appeal of Florida held **the board's unilateral modification of the employee health insurance plan was pursuant to statutory law and was not a breach of the collective bargaining agreement**. The arbitrator was preempted by the PERC, which had exclusive jurisdiction over the matter. The solvency of the employee health insurance plan was a compelling interest, and the fact that the board did not strictly follow the statutory collective bargaining process did not divest the

PERC of its exclusive authority. As a result, the court vacated the arbitration award. *Communications Workers of America, Local 3180 v. Indian River County School Board*, 888 So.2d 96 (Fla. Dist. Ct. App. 2004).

◆ A Tennessee school board adopted a dress code for all instructional personnel without first negotiating over it with the association representing district teachers. The association filed a grievance against the board and sought arbitration. The case reached the state court of appeals, which considered a state statutory amendment defining "working conditions." The amendment defined the term as "those fundamental matters that affect a professional employee financially or the employee's employment relationship with the board." The court observed that the board's managerial prerogatives had to be balanced with employee rights to negotiate the terms and conditions of their employment. It did not appear that the dress code had fundamentally affected teachers so as to require mandatory collective bargaining. While the dress code was not so restrictive that teachers would be forced to buy new wardrobes, it was silent regarding sanctions, enforcement and implementation. **The court found enforcement of the dress code policy could fundamentally impact the teachers' employment relationships**, which had to be bargained for. The court declared the dress code policy a "working condition." *Polk County Board of Educ. v. Polk County Educ. Ass'n*, 139 S.W.3d 304 (Tenn. Ct. App. 2004).

◆ A Rhode Island school committee distributed an internet access policy that limited staff Internet use to research and/or instructional purposes. Violations could lead to discipline or criminal prosecution. The state labor relations board determined that the policy affected disciplinary practices and was a mandatory subject for collective bargaining. Implementation of the policy by the committee without submitting it to collective bargaining constituted direct dealing with employees. A state court rejected the committee's argument that it unilaterally implemented the policy in the exercise of its statutory duty to safeguard children. The policy's limitations on conditions of employment did not concern the general obligations of state law, but were limited to ensure teacher rights to collective bargaining. The court also rejected the committee's argument that the policy was an attempt to comply with the federal Children's Online Protection Act (COPA). The COPA did not restrict casual personal use of the Internet by school employees. Thus, implementation of the policy was a mandatory subject of collective bargaining because it affected employee discipline. **Employers cannot unilaterally change any collective bargaining provision involving a mandatory subject of bargaining.** *Johnston School Committee v. Rhode Island State Labor Relations Board*, No. Civ.A. PC 03-0141, 2004 WL 877619 (R.I. Super. 2004).

◆ An Ohio school board and the union representing teachers in the district had a collective bargaining agreement (CBA) with no tuition reimbursement provision. The board offered to reimburse teachers up to $1,200 for 12 credits toward a master's degree at Xavier University. The union did not want the program, and it sought an order from the state employment relations board (SERB) to stop the board from unilaterally approving it. The SERB held the board committed an unfair labor practice, and the Ohio Court of Appeals agreed. It found the union might have believed it could negotiate a better plan during the next bargaining period and had the right to reject the offered benefit. The court held **the reimbursement plan was covered as a wage or a term and condition of employment**. As the plan had to be negotiated, the court upheld the SERB decision. *Oak Hills Educ. Ass'n v. Oak Hills Local School Dist. Board of Educ.*, 158 Ohio App.3d 662, 821 N.E.2d 616 (Ohio Ct. App. 2004.)

◆   **A South Dakota union could not convert the school calendar into a negotiable item for collective bargaining.** The state supreme court held that the calendar was a matter of general public interest that affected the community and an inherently managerial subject that could not be bargained over. Requiring the board to negotiate the school calendar would significantly interfere with the exercise of its inherent management prerogatives. Most other jurisdictions that have addressed the issue have held that the school calendar is an inherently managerial subject that is not a mandatory topic of negotiation. The school calendar affected teachers, other school employees, students, parents, taxpayers, other school districts and entire communities. If the union was allowed to bargain the issue, none of the other community interests would be represented. Determination of the calendar by collective bargaining substantially interfered with an inherent managerial prerogative pertaining to government educational policy. *West Cent. Educ. Ass'n v. West Cent. School Dist. 49-4*, 655 N.W.2d 916 (S.D. 2002).

## III.  GRIEVANCES AND ARBITRATION

### A.  Arbitrability

*By including arbitration clauses in collective bargaining agreements, the parties agree to an arbitrator's interpretation of the agreement. If an arbitrator resolves a dispute concerning the interpretation of contract terms and the award draws its essence from the agreement, a court may not disturb the award.*

◆   A New Jersey high school custodian disobeyed his supervisor's instruction to knock and announce himself before entering female changing areas on the night of a school dance recital. He entered a classroom where female students were changing, and ignored their pleas for him to leave. A teacher said he should not be in a classroom when females were changing and also told him to leave. By his account, he hesitated and asked her "what's the big deal" before leaving. After suspending the custodian, the school board reported the incident to the state division of youth and family services. A division investigation was closed without action, but the board investigated and voted to discharge the custodian. A grievance was filed on his behalf under a collective bargaining agreement that specified tenured employees were not to be disciplined, discharged or not reappointed without just cause. But the agreement did not define the term "just cause." An arbitrator held progressive/corrective discipline was an integral part of the "just cause" concept. As this was the custodian's first offense, the arbitrator imposed a two-week suspension without pay. After a state court confirmed the award, appeal reached the Supreme Court of New Jersey.

The court noted that New Jersey law emphasizes that **courts are bound by a presumption in favor of arbitration of collective bargaining agreements**. When the parties to a collective bargaining agreement agree to arbitrate their disputes, they agree to an arbitrator's interpretation of the agreement. In promoting finality, the court found a strong preference for judicial confirmation of arbitration awards. Vacation of awards was allowed in limited circumstances such as corruption, fraud, partiality or misconduct by an arbitrator. In this case, **the agreement did not define "just cause," making it necessary for the arbitrator to give meaning to the term**. In the court's view, the arbitrator had reached a decision that was "reasonably debatable." Since the court found that the arbitrator acted in full compliance with the submission of the parties, the trial court's decision confirming the arbitration award was affirmed. *Linden Board of Educ. v. Linden Educ. Ass'n*, 202 N.J. 268, 997 A.2d 997 (N.J. 2010).

◆ The Classified Employees Association (CEA) was the representative of many Alaska school district employees. No collective bargaining agreement (CBA) provision dealt with outsourcing, but the subject was much discussed in negotiations. While the CEA claimed the district gave assurances that work would not be outsourced, the CBA did not reflect this. During the term of the CBA, the district contracted for custodial services and maintenance for specified facilities. The CEA sought a grievance, then sued to compel the district to participate in the grievance proceeding. It claimed a state law prohibited outsourcing school custodial work. Agreeing with the district, the court held the CBA did not apply to disputes over decisions to privatize work.

On appeal, the Supreme Court of Alaska found a presumption in favor of arbitrability of disputes when parties intend arbitration. But **the court found no CBA provision on outsourcing, nor any management clause that could be misinterpreted or inequitably applied**. Alaska law required written collective bargaining agreements, foreclosing the CEA's claim that there had been an oral agreement not to outsource work. And state law did not provide for interest arbitration for the class of employees represented by the CEA. As the lower court had correctly found arbitration improper, and state law did not bar outsourcing, the judgment was affirmed. *Classified Employees Ass'n v. Matanuska-Susitna Borough School Dist.*, 204 P.3d 347 (Alaska 2009).

◆ Soon after accepting employment as a non-tenured employee under a one-year contract, a New Jersey school custodian was accused of hitting a coworker. The school board held a disciplinary hearing the same day and fired him. The custodian's union filed a grievance, claiming the collective bargaining agreement (CBA) required arbitration. The board sued to restrain arbitration, based on the argument that the custodian's contract had a 14-day notice period for termination and was not subject to arbitration. A state court agreed and restrained arbitration. A New Jersey appellate court affirmed. But it emphasized that the custodian could still request reasons for the discharge and obtain a board hearing under the CBA  The Supreme Court of New Jersey held that a

CBA generally superseded an individual contract. **If individual contract provisions conflicted with a CBA and diminished rights granted under the CBA, the individual contract had to yield.** Here, the custodian's individual contract conflicted with and diminished his CBA rights. So the contract had to yield to the CBA. Also, state law adopted a presumption in favor of arbitration of public employee CBAs. And a clause of the CBA entitled the custodian to a statement of reasons and a hearing for discipline. The judgment was reversed with instructions to send the case to arbitration. *Mt. Holly Township Board of Educ. v. Mt. Holly Township Educ. Ass'n*, 972 A.2d 387 (N.J. 2009).

◆ A Wisconsin teacher's union filed a grievance to challenge his discharge for viewing adult images on his school computer. An arbitrator reinstated him, finding that the board violated a collective bargaining provision which required "just cause" to discharge a permanently employed teacher. The board refused to honor the arbitration award, and a state court held that the award violated public policy. The court vacated the award, and the union appealed to the state court of appeals. The court held that the arbitration award "ignored the fact that immoral conduct provides grounds for license revocation." **The Wisconsin Supreme Court has noted that courts may only vacate arbitration awards that are illegal or in violation of a strong public policy.** The arbitrator in this case had held that immoral behavior was not grounds for termination, which was at odds with Wisconsin law. The teacher had turned off a computer "safe search" function and then purposefully searched for pornography. Protection of children and the promotion of a safe educational environment was a clear, compelling public policy, requiring vacation of the arbitration award. *Cedarburg Educ. Ass'n v. Cedarburg School Dist.*, No. 2007AP852, 2008 WL 2812714, 756 N.W.2d 809 (Table) (Wis. Ct. App. 2008).

◆ A Massachusetts teacher was suspended for 10 days for closing a door on a student's arm. The union representing the teacher filed a grievance, claiming it was harmed in its representation of the teacher by the school committee's failure to provide the names of student witnesses to the incident. An arbitrator held that the school committee's blocking of student identification was not supported by any practice or policy, or by any law or the relevant collective bargaining agreement. The school committee appealed to a Massachusetts superior court, which held that the award did not require the committee to violate a law or public policy. On appeal, **the Appeals Court of Massachusetts affirmed the decision. The legislature had narrowly limited the grounds for vacating an arbitration award.** As the lower court had found, the school committee did not show that the arbitration award violated any law or public policy. *School Committee of Boston v. Boston Teachers Union*, No. 07-P-518, 71 Mass.App.Ct. 1121, 885 N.E.2d 173 (Table) (Mass. App. Ct. 4/23/08).

◆ A Tennessee school board did not renew a probationary teacher's contract after three years as an in-school suspension teacher. The collective bargaining agreement (CBA) between the board and teachers association applied to all teachers with certificates, including those without tenure. The teacher filed a grievance against the board, alleging that the non-renewal was discriminatory. The board sought a court order to avoid binding arbitration. A state court found that the teacher had no right to continued employment beyond a one-year term.

The CBA extended additional rights to all teachers. This included the right to written notice of any employment deficiencies, a chance to correct them, the right to be represented when being reprimanded, warned or disciplined, and other rights. The CBA limited the board's right to lay off teachers to cases in which there was a substantial drop or change in the student population, or unavoidable budget problems. The court held the parties had agreed to submit the case to arbitration. On appeal, the Court of Appeals of Tennessee found that **the teacher, though not tenured, was certificated and entitled to the due process protections of the bargaining agreement**. His individual contract was limited to one year, yet the CBA expressly limited the board's authority to lay off teachers. The trial court should have further considered whether the teacher was entitled to binding arbitration. The court returned the matter to the trial court for further consideration. *Cannon County Board of Educ. v. Wade*, No. M2003-02260-COA-R3-CV, 2005 WL 195106 (Tenn. Ct. App. 2005).

◆ A New Hampshire school district reassigned an elementary teacher to a middle school. He claimed this was based on his pro-union activity, and his union first filed a grievance, then arbitration. The association also filed an unfair labor practice complaint with the state public employee labor relations board (PELRB). The PELRB ordered the parties into arbitration, unless a party requested an additional hearing within 30 days of an arbitration decision. The arbitrator upheld the grievance and ordered the district to reassign the teacher to his former position. The district requested a new hearing before the PELRB, asserting the arbitration decision was improper and inconsistent with the collective bargaining agreement. The PELRB denied the request. The district appealed to the Supreme Court of New Hampshire, which **rejected the district's claim that the PELRB was obligated to consider an appeal from the arbitration award**. Once arbitration was concluded, the PELRB lacked authority to review the award unless there was a filing of a subsequent unfair labor practice complaint by the association alleging district failure to implement the award. As there had been no such filing, the arbitration award was final. *Appeal of Laconia School Dist.*, 840 A.2d 800 (N.H. 2004).

◆ A Washington teacher's full-time teaching certificate expired at the end of his second year of employment in a district. He earned the academic credits he needed for renewal during the summer, but he did not obtain his certificate by the first day of school. The district superintendent notified the teacher that his failure to possess a valid full-time certificate invalidated his employment contract. The teachers association filed a grievance on the teacher's behalf, which was denied through the first three steps of the procedure. The district notified the teacher of his right to request arbitration as the final step of the grievance process, then sued for a declaration that he had no contract and an order prohibiting arbitration. **The Supreme Court of Washington stated that its duty was to determine if the parties had agreed to arbitrate a dispute, not to decide the merits of the controversy.** The district itself had processed the grievance through the first three steps, and arbitration had been scheduled prior to the filing of the court action. It could not be said with "positive assurance" that the bargaining agreement precluded arbitration. The grievance had to be arbitrated. *Mt. Adams School Dist. v. Cook*, 81 P.3d 111 (Wash. 2003).

## B. Procedures

*Parties to a collective bargaining agreement are required to exhaust the remedies of their agreement. Court review of an arbitration award is extremely limited. In Wisconsin, an arbitration award may be overturned only if it is a "perverse misconstruction," a "manifest disregard of the law," is illegal, or violates a strong public policy. Pennsylvania courts may only vacate an award that has no foundation or does not flow from a collective bargaining agreement.*

◆    A Wisconsin teacher was involved in a disciplinary grievance proceeding in which she provided a union-appointed attorney a copy of a student's IEP. The district reprimanded the teacher in writing for releasing the student record to an unauthorized third party without consent. The reprimand matter was submitted to an arbitrator, who found that the teacher could provide the IEP to her union attorney. The Court of Appeals of Wisconsin noted that the disclosure violated two school board policies intended to comply with state law and the federal Family Educational Rights and Privacy Act (FERPA). One policy prohibited the disclosure of personally identifiable student information from a school's education records without prior written consent from parents. The court held **an arbitration award may be overturned only if it is a "perverse misconstruction" or "manifest disregard of the law," is illegal or violates a strong public policy**. A mistake of fact or law is not grounds for setting aside an award. The arbitrator did not make any finding that the teacher had violated state and federal privacy laws. There was a considerable discussion of FERPA, but this was to explore whether the teacher had violated the board's policy rather than the laws themselves. The court rejected the board's argument that the award violated a strong public policy favoring limited disclosure of student records, and affirmed the award. *Madison Metropolitan School Dist. v. Madison Teachers*, 308 Wis.2d 395, 746 N.W.2d 605 (Table) (Wis. Ct. App. 1/31/08).

◆    Pennsylvania's highest court reversed an appellate decision that would have reinstated an arbitration award for a maintenance employee who tested positive for use of marijuana shortly after a workplace injury. An arbitrator interpreted the district's drug-free workplace policy to prohibit drug usage only on school grounds. He found the employee's off-school conduct beyond the control of the school district. A trial court held the arbitrator exceeded his authority. The state supreme court vacated the decision and ordered the trial court to reconsider the case in view of *Westmoreland Intermediate Unit #7 v. Westmoreland Intermediate Unit #7 Classroom Assistants Educ. Support Personnel Ass'n*, 939 A.2d 855 (Pa. 2007), this chapter. **Courts may only vacate an award that has no foundation or does not flow from a collective bargaining agreement.** *Loyalsock Township Area School Dist. v Loyalsock Custodial Maintenance, Secretarial and Aide Ass'n*, 957 A.2d 231 (Pa. 2008).

◆   A New Hampshire teacher had worked for the same school district since 1986. She remained seated and refused to participate in recitals of the Pledge of Allegiance by her class. In 2003, a new principal began work at the teacher's middle school, and he expressed displeasure with her non-participation. She said the principal and school district then began to retaliate against her. From 2004 to 2007, the teacher filed four grievances relating to her retaliation claims. None of them raised a First Amendment claim, and she did not appeal under the grievance process from the applicable collective bargaining agreement (CBA).

Nor did the teacher file a complaint with the state Public Employee Labor Relations Board. She sued the school district and principal in a federal court for retaliating against her based on her refusal to participate in Pledge recitals. The court held **employees may invoke rights independent of the collective bargaining process on their own behalf and not as members of a collective bargaining organization**. Significantly, "the mere existence of a collective bargaining agreement does not waive those separate statutory rights." A union-negotiated waiver of employee rights must be clear and unmistakable from the language of the CBA. Here, since the CBA contained no clear waiver of employee rights to pursue constitutional claims, the teacher's failure to appeal her grievances under the CBA did not bar the lawsuit. *Dunfey v. Seabrook School Dist.*, No. 07-cv-140-PB, 2008 WL 1848655 (D.N.H. 4/24/08).

◆   A Washington school employee's union sued school administrators and her school district for harassment by a supervisor. The claims included infliction of emotional distress and federal civil rights violations. The employee and union claimed the supervisor interfered with her collective bargaining rights, and that the district failed to disclose information about him in violation of a state public disclosure act. The court dismissed the claims, finding that they should have first been filed with the district under the state claims filing statute. The public disclosure act claims should have been pursued under the relevant collective bargaining agreement. The case reached the Supreme Court of Washington, which held that the state claims filing statute was inapplicable in cases against individuals for acts committed in the scope of their employment. The trial court had erroneously dismissed claims against the supervisors under the claims filing statute. The lower court improperly held state law applied to federal civil rights claims filed under 42 U.S.C. § 1983. The union's unfair labor practice claim was not a "tort" (personal injury-type) claim and was not subject to the claims filing statute. **An action for unfair labor practices was to be filed either with a state court or the Public Employment Relations Commission.** The case was returned to the lower courts. *Wright v. Terrell*, 170 P.3d 192 (Wash. 2007).

◆   A Virginia superintendent suspended a principal without pay and advised him of his right to a hearing before the school board. The principal instead sought a hearing before a fact-finding panel under a state board grievance procedure, seeking immediate reinstatement. The superintendent informed the principal that suspension with pay was not grievable. The school board upheld the decision and demoted the principal to a teaching position, with a reduction in pay. He appealed to a Virginia circuit court, arguing that the suspension presented a grievable issue. The court held that the principal's suspension was grievable under the state board procedure and had to be timely resolved. But the state supreme court reversed, finding that **the principal's only recourse was the very process he had rejected when the superintendent offered him a hearing.** *Tazewell County School Board v. Brown*, 591 S.E.2d 671 (Va. 2004).

◆ **The Oregon Court of Appeals held that the Portland Public Schools (PPS) could privatize its custodial force,** resolving two conflicting agency decisions. The Employment Relations Board (ERB) upheld a PPS proposal to contract out custodial work due to a budget crisis, and found that the proposal was not a prohibited subject of bargaining. The Custodians Civil Service Board then held that the PPS violated a state civil service law. The appeals court held that the ERB decision precluded the Civil Service Board from later ruling on the same question. *Scherzinger v. Portland Custodians Civil Service Board*, 196 Or.App. 384, 103 P.3d 1122 (Or. Ct. App. 2004).

◆ The Vermont Department of Education erroneously issued a teacher an elementary teaching certificate. She was previously certified by the state of New Jersey to teach high school. After the teacher informed the superintendent of the error, he advised her that he had obtained a state waiver allowing her to teach elementary grades. The teacher suffered multiple allergic reactions and took two sick leaves, but the board denied her request for additional leave. It voted to discharge her. She filed grievances, and an arbitrator ordered the district to reinstate her to her former position as a sixth-grade teacher or to an equivalent one. The district instead offered her a kindergarten position. The teacher learned that she could not accept the position because, contrary to the superintendent's statement, she had no waiver to teach elementary classes. She appealed the arbitration award. The state supreme court held that **the denial of the teacher's contractual protections was evidence of retaliation against her for filing grievances** and complaints. In addition, the district had offered her a position that it knew she could not accept. The superintendent failed to request a waiver of state licensing requirements, despite his statement to the contrary. In view of this evidence, the lower court should have held that there was a genuine issue for trial. *Mellin v. Flood Brook Union School Dist.*, 790 A.2d 408 (Vt. 2001).

### C. Standard of Review

*A court may vacate an arbitration award on the basis of fraud, corruption or procedural irregularities, or if the arbitrator exceeds his or her powers. Arbitration awards may be vacated if they do not draw their essence from a collective bargaining agreement, are not based on a plausible interpretation of the agreement, disregard a contract provision or reach an irrational result.*

◆ A Cambodian refugee began teaching in Massachusetts public schools in 1992. Her annual evaluations earned the highest ratings until 2002, when a new principal began evaluating teachers for English proficiency. He assigned her an unsatisfactory rating. Due to post-traumatic stress disorder, the teacher took a two-year medical leave. During her leave, she failed two English fluency assessments. She claimed she was experiencing symptoms of post-traumatic stress disorder at the time. When the teacher advised the superintendent she could return to work, she was again told her English was insufficient. A review hearing was held in 2005, but the superintendent again found her insufficiently fluent in English. The school committee dismissed the teacher, but an arbitrator held reliance on the English fluency assessments alone violated due process. Evaluation by the principal was held invalid because the teacher was not informed that her fluency was being evaluated. A state court agreed with the school committee that the arbitrator exceeded his powers and violated state law.

The Supreme Judicial Court of Massachusetts explained that **state law placed the burden upon the school committee to prove that "just cause" existed for her dismissal**. State law permitted vacating an arbitration decision only if the arbitrator exceeded his powers or if the award required a person to commit an act prohibited by law. The court found nothing in state law or regulations required the superintendent to rely on the principal's assessment. It held the lower court neglected arbitration findings that the principal's evaluation did not incorporate state standards defining sufficient fluency. And the teacher was not informed that her fluency was being observed or evaluated at the time. Medical evidence indicated the teacher's condition negatively affected her ability to demonstrate her English ability. As the lower court was not authorized to review this finding, the court reinstated the award. *School Committee of Lowell v. Robishaw*, 456 Mass. 653, 925 N.E.2d 803 (Mass. 2010).

◆   A New York teacher began exchanging emails and instant-messaging one of her students. Eventually, he reported the conversations to the principal, and the case was referred to a school investigatory office. When confronted, the teacher admitted making inappropriate communications. She entered therapy to cope with the situation. Later, the student discovered postings to an online journal by the teacher under an alias. They discussed the teacher's desire to be close to him and kiss him. At the conclusion of the investigation, the school department recommended employment termination. A hearing was held, and the teacher was found guilty of three charges. The hearing officer noted she was remorseful and that she had entered therapy. He found that she had learned her lesson about inappropriate relationships with students and believed she would not repeat the conduct. Rejecting the recommendation to discharge the teacher, the hearing officer imposed a 90-day unpaid suspension and assigned her to a different school. A state court reinstated the school department's decision.

Appeal reached the New York Supreme Court, Appellate Division. **It held arbitration awards may only be vacated based on evidence of misconduct, bias, an excess of arbitrator authority, or a procedural defect.** There was no basis for disturbing the hearing officer's decision. Arbitration awards may be vacated if they are contrary to public policy. The public policy must be "more than a general societal concern." The lower court had violated this rule by scrutinizing the facts. The court also held the penalty imposed was not so lenient as to be arbitrary and capricious. Since there was a rational basis for the hearing officer's decision, and a strong basis for concluding the teacher could be trusted again, the court reinstated the arbitration award. *City School Dist. of City of New York v. McGraham*, 905 N.Y.S.2d 86 (N.Y. App. Div. 2010).

◆ A Pennsylvania classroom assistant was found unconscious in a school lavatory. She later admitted wearing a narcotic Fentanyl patch. As she had no valid prescription for it, this was a misdemeanor. The school intermediate unit fired her, but an arbitrator found no "just cause" to do so under the Pennsylvania School Code. Her conduct did not rise to the level of "immorality," and she had a previously unblemished 23-year career. A Pennsylvania court reinstated the discharge. The case reached the Supreme Court of Pennsylvania, which held that broad judicial review of arbitration awards would undercut the value of arbitration. An award could be vacated if it violated a well-defined public policy. The court found the award was rationally derived from the collective bargaining agreement. It returned the case to the lower court for a determination of whether public policy precluded the award. *Westmoreland Intermediate Unit #7 v. Westmoreland Intermediate Unit #7 Classroom Assistants Educ. Support Personnel Ass'n, PSEA/NEA*, 939 A.2d 855 (Pa. 2007).

The case was returned to a lower court. It noted evidence of the assistant's "extensive history of abuse of pain pills." **While the arbitrator's attempts to rehabilitate the assistant were "admirable," immediate reinstatement to the classroom violated public policy.** Fentanyl is a controlled substance with effects more potent than heroin. To reinstate an employee charged with caring for children after being at work under the influence of this drug "defies logic and violates public policy." As an elementary classroom was "no place for a recovering addict," the court vacated the arbitration award for violating a dominant public policy to protect children. *Westmoreland Intermediate Unit #7 v. Westmoreland Intermediate Unit #7 Classroom Assistants Educ. Support Personnel Ass'n, PSEA-NEA*, 977 A.2d 1208 (Pa. Commw. Ct. 2009).

◆ An Alabama coach and tenured teacher taught physical education and was the cheerleading sponsor for a high school. Following a complaint from a parent whose child was removed from the cheerleading squad, an investigation revealed 14 grounds for discharge, many involving the improper use of funds. The coach allegedly violated school board fundraiser and cheerleader fund policies, resulting in the loss of almost $6,000 in cheerleading funds in one year. The board voted to discharge the coach, but she received a new hearing before a hearing officer under the Alabama Teacher Tenure Act. The hearing officer reversed the board's decision and ordered no discipline. The case reached the Supreme Court of Alabama, which held that the 2004 Tenure Act amendments did not strip school boards of their authority to discharge teachers. The discretion to determine good and just cause for discharge remained with local school officials. Also, **the hearing officer had improperly applied employment law standards from collective bargaining agreements** rather than applying the amended Teacher Tenure Act. The court ruled against the coach. *Ex Parte Wilson*, 984 So.2d 1161 (Ala. 2007).

◆ A Rhode Island school committee eliminated a longstanding practice of assigning high school English teachers a composition period for budgetary reasons. Instead of filling two newly vacated English teaching positions, the superintendent of schools hoped to eliminate the composition periods and redistribute English classes among remaining teachers. The school committee adopted the superintendent's plan and voted to eliminate the composition periods. A grievance was denied, and the case was put before an arbitrator.

After a hearing, the arbitrator upheld the union's claim that the composition period amounted to a past practice of the parties. Eliminating the practice thus violated a savings clause in the parties' agreement. The case reached the Supreme Court of Rhode Island, which explained that review of arbitration awards was limited in scope. Public policy favors the finality of arbitration awards, which may be overturned only if irrational or manifestly in disregard of the law. In this case, the arbitrator had found the school committee made its decision based on workload, and did not make an educational policy choice involving a management prerogative. **As the arbitrator had noted, work load decisions were "always subject to negotiation."** Since the arbitrator did not exceed his powers or manifestly disregard the law, the award was upheld. *North Providence School Committee v. North Providence Federation of Teachers, Local 920, American Federation of Teachers*, 945 A.2d 339 (R.I. 2008).

◆   A New York school district filed formal charges against a teacher who engaged in a relationship with a 16-year-old student over the course of her senior year of high school. A hearing officer determined that they had been in "virtually constant telephone contact" during the year. The student visited him in his office and they spent time in private. And the teacher tried to conceal the relationship from the student's family. School administrators informed the family of the relationship and told the teacher to stay away from the student. The teacher continued the relationship in private and left school early without permission to take her to his house. An investigator observed the two together for six hours. Despite this evidence, the hearing officer declined to find they had a romantic relationship. The hearing officer found the teacher guilty of insubordination, neglect of duty and conduct unbecoming a teacher. The hearing officer imposed a one-year, unpaid suspension on the teacher, but the New York Supreme Court, Appellate Division, vacated the award. It held the award violated a strong public policy to protect children from the harmful conduct of adults, particularly in an educational setting. **Vacating the award on public policy grounds was justified by the teacher's insubordination and lack of remorse.** *In re Arbitration Between Binghamton City School Dist. and Peacock*, 33 A.D.3d 1074, 823 N.Y.S.2d 231 (N.Y. App. Div. 2006).

◆   A New Hampshire school district issued several teachers renewal letters requiring them to prepare improvement plans before the end of the 2003-04 school year. The teachers' association claimed the letters were a unilateral change to procedures in the collective bargaining agreement concerning teacher evaluation and performance reviews. The agreement specified that tenured teachers would be observed at least once a year and evaluated in writing. The association filed a complaint with the New Hampshire Public Employee Labor Relations Board (PELRB), which held that the district committed an unfair labor practice by using new procedures to communicate teacher deficiencies.

The district appealed to the Supreme Court of New Hampshire, which found that collective bargaining agreement procedures for evaluating teachers and communicating deficiencies were clear. When the district issued renewal letters with reservations and required improvement plans, it did not follow the procedures of the agreement. **The use of renewal letters with reservations and requirements for teacher improvement plans violated the collective bargaining agreement.** The district had no reserved right to implement different procedures for addressing teacher performance and evaluation than those specified in the agreement. The court upheld the PELRB's decision. *Appeal of White Mountain Regional School Dist.*, 908 A.2d 790 (N.H. 2006).

## IV.  STRIKES

*The purpose of state legislation to prohibit or limit strikes by public employees is to protect the public and not to circumvent meaningful collective bargaining. Courts have upheld punitive actions taken against unlawfully striking teachers and their unions.*

◆   A Massachusetts law prohibits public employees and unions from inducing, encouraging or condoning a strike, work stoppage, or slowdown, and from withholding services by public employees. This law requires public employers to petition the Commonwealth Relations Board (CRB) to investigate violations, and it governs relations between the Boston Teachers Union and the Boston School Committee. After a collective bargaining agreement expired in 2006, the parties unsuccessfully and acrimoniously negotiated for a new one. Union leaders announced a meeting to consider a one-day strike, and notified the school superintendent regarding a pending strike vote. Anticipating that union members would vote to strike, the school committee petitioned the CRB to investigate as specified by the law. After an investigation and hearing, the CRB found that a strike was about to occur. The union did not comply with the CRB's order to rescind and disavow the strike vote. A Massachusetts court enforced the CRB order and ordered the union to pay a $30,000 fine for contempt. On appeal, the Court of Appeals of Massachusetts held that **the union violated the law by encouraging and inducing a strike**. Any incidental limitation of First Amendment freedoms was justified. *Comwlth. Employment Relations Board v. Boston Teachers Union, Local 66, AFT, AFL-CIO*, 908 N.E.2d 772, 74 Mass. App. Ct. 500 (Mass. Ct. App. 2009).

◆   A Minnesota school district violated an agreement not to take action against teachers who participated in a lawful strike when it failed to rehire a probationary Spanish teacher who participated in the strike. The district and union resolved the dispute that led to a two-month teacher strike and agreed to a memorandum of understanding (MOU). The MOU bound the district not to take reprisal, punishment or other action against teachers due to lawful participation in the strike. The district later refused to renew the contracts of four of the five probationary teachers it employed, including the Spanish teacher. An arbitrator sustained a grievance in her favor, and the case reached the Court of Appeals of Minnesota. It found the district had agreed to include probationary teachers under the MOU. **State law placed a school district's right to select staff beyond the scope of collective bargaining, but the**

**district had waived this right.** Having entered into an agreement that clearly stated it would not retaliate against strikers, the district could not rely on rights it had waived. *Independent School Dist. #182, Crosby-Ironton v. Educ. Minnesota Crosby Ironton, AFL-CIO, Local 1325*, No. A07-0745, 2008 WL 933495 (Minn. Ct. App. 4/8/08, Minn. review denied 6/18/08).

◆  Wisconsin education law prohibited strikes by teachers, and gave school boards sole authority over hiring and firing decisions. Boards were required to negotiate the terms and conditions of employment with collective bargaining representatives. When contract negotiations between teachers and a local school board became protracted, the teachers called a strike. The board attempted to end the strike, noting that it was in direct violation of state law. When the teachers refused to return to work, the board held disciplinary hearings and fired the striking teachers. The teachers appealed to the Wisconsin courts, arguing that the board was not an impartial decisionmaker and that the discharges had violated their due process rights. The state supreme court held due process required an impartial decisionmaker. The board was not sufficiently impartial to make the decision to discharge the teachers.

The board appealed to the U.S. Supreme Court, which found no evidence that the board could not make an impartial decision in determining to discharge the teachers. The fact that the board was involved in negotiations with the teachers did not support a claim of bias. **The board was the only body vested with statutory authority to employ and dismiss teachers, and participation in negotiations with the teachers was required by law.** This involvement prior to the decision to discharge the teachers was not a sufficient showing of bias to disqualify the board as a decisionmaker. *Hortonville Joint School Dist. No. 1 v. Hortonville Educ. Ass'n*, 426 U.S. 482 (1976).

◆  The collective bargaining agreement between an Ohio school board and the union representing its bus drivers expired without a new agreement. The board contracted with a private company for transportation services and abolished its driver and mechanic job classifications. Union members declared a strike, but within days most of them notified the superintendent of their intention to return to work under their continuing contract rights. The company agreed to hire district drivers. Eight of the district's drivers retired, but four reported to work at the district's bus garage. The board assigned them to new positions for which their wages and daily work hours were reduced. The four drivers sought an order compelling the board to recognize their continuing contract rights. The case reached the state supreme court, which held that the drivers were entitled to the relief they requested. **State law did not authorize the board to lay them off by abolishing their positions and hiring nonpublic employees.** The contracting out of the drivers' jobs was invalid. The drivers were entitled to recognition as continuing contract employees of the board and could not be reclassified as general public employees. The court ordered the board to reinstate the drivers with back pay. *State ex rel. Boggs v. Springfield Local School Dist. Board of Educ.*, 757 N.E.2d 339 (Ohio 2001).

# CHAPTER TWELVE

## School Liability and Safety

## I. NEGLIGENCE

*Negligence is the failure to use reasonable or ordinary care under the circumstances. In order for a school district to be liable for negligence, it must have a duty to the person claiming negligence. If a reasonably prudent person cannot foresee any danger of injury, there is no duty, and thus no negligence. A school district may be held liable for the acts or omissions of a negligent employee. A pattern of negligence showing a conscious disregard for safety may be deemed "willful or wanton misconduct," a form of intentional conduct.*

### A. Elements

*The elements of a negligence lawsuit are: 1) the existence of a* **legal duty** *to conform conduct to a specific standard in order to protect others from unreasonable risks of injury, 2) a* **breach** *of that duty that is, 3) the direct* **cause of the injury***, and 4)* **damages***. In short, negligence consists of a duty of care, followed by a breach of that duty which causes injury and damages. The foreseeability of harm is also a prerequisite to liability in negligence cases, as explained by the Supreme Court of Montana in the case that follows.*

◆  A Montana student submitted a list of resolutions with violent themes for a school assignment. Among the themes were to "get a drivers license so I can do those horrible things people like to read about in the paper," and "kill the tooth fairy." A teacher reported the list, and his parents were contacted. In a meeting, the principal stated that although the list was inappropriate, the student was "a normal kid." Meeting attendees felt the list was "a teenage attempt at black humor" that he knew was inappropriate, so no action was taken. While driving near the high school some 17 months later, the student intentionally ran over a jogger. Before doing so, he told a passenger he planned to run her over and commit necrophilia with her corpse. The jogger sued the district for negligence.

A Montana court found no "special relationship" between the district and the jogger so as to give rise to liability. The Supreme Court of Montana rejected the jogger's argument that she did not need a special relationship with the school district for it have a duty of ordinary care to protect her from the student. She was not a "foreseeable plaintiff." **Foreseeability is of primary importance in establishing the existence of a legal duty of care.** If a reasonably prudent person cannot foresee any danger of direct injury, there is no duty, and thus no negligence. It was not foreseeable that 17 months after writing the list, the student would deliberately run over a jogger, after school hours and off school grounds. The court affirmed the ruling for the district. *Emanuel v. Great Falls School Dist.*, 351 Mont. 56, 209 P.3d 244 (Mont. 2009).

◆ A California teacher applied for work at the La Habra City School District. His application indicated that he had never been convicted of a felony or misdemeanor, but he noted that another school district had asked him to resign midway through a school year. After a criminal background check revealed no sexual misconduct, La Habra hired him. Seven years later, the teacher was arrested for child molestation. He pleaded guilty to 12 offenses occurring while at La Habra. One victim sued La Habra, seeking to hold it liable for negligent investigation, hiring, training and supervision. A state court found that the school did not have evidence that the teacher posed a risk of harming students.

On appeal, the Court of Appeal of California stated that public entities are liable for injuries caused by the negligence of employees if the employees act within the scope of their employment. If district officials responsible for hiring or supervising the teacher knew (or should have known) of prior misconduct toward students, or of a reasonable risk to students, they had a duty to protect the students. However, **simple knowledge of the teacher's prior struggles with classroom control did not make it foreseeable that he might sexually abuse students.** Liability could only be imposed for a molestation if La Habra officials knew or should have known about prior sexual misconduct toward students. As no evidence indicated that the teacher might sexually abuse students, the court affirmed the judgment for La Habra. *Ryan W. v. La Habra City School Dist.*, No. G040704, 2009 WL 1581499 (Cal. Ct. App. 6/5/09).

◆ A California student was attacked by eight males while he walked past the school gymnasium. Another student was assaulted by a group of three others while approaching a school exit. Both students suffered substantial injuries, and their guardian sued their school district, board of education and school principal for negligence. She also asserted violation of a duty to supervise students, claiming that officials were indifferent to reports of threats against the students, and that daily brawls and rampant gang activity were present at the school. The court held for the district and officials, and the guardian appealed to the Court of Appeal of California. It noted that "causation" is one element of a negligence claim. The court agreed with the school district that the guardian had failed to show that officials caused the injuries to the students arising from the third-party attacks. She did not show it was more probable than not that additional security precautions would have prevented the attacks. **School districts are not**

**the insurers of the physical safety of students.** To hold a district liable for negligence, a student must prove the elements of the claim, including causation. Claims of abstract negligence cannot survive. The court affirmed the judgment for the district and officials. *Castaneda v. Inglewood Unified School Dist.*, No. B198829, 2008 WL 2720631 (Cal. Ct. App. 7/14/08).

## B.  Defenses

◆   An 11-year-old New York student fell from a banister at school while unsupervised and suffered serious injuries. When his parents sued the district for negligence, it asserted that he had assumed the risk of harm by engaging in horseplay when he slid down the banister. The case reached the Court of Appeals of New York, which found that **assumption of risk is typically raised in cases involving athletic and recreational activities**. Allowing the defense here would have unfortunate consequences and could not be used to nullify the district's duty. If assumption of risk was allowed, students would be deemed to consent in advance to the risks of their own misconduct. Children often act impulsively and without good judgment. This does not mean they consent to assume the resulting danger. If the student's injury was attributable to his own conduct, this could be handled by allocating comparative fault. The court returned the case to a lower court for more proceedings. *Trupia v. Lake George Cent. School Dist*, 927 N.E.2d 547 (N.Y. 2010).

### 1.  Immunity

*Immunity protects school districts and their employees from liability in many cases. Sovereign or "governmental" immunity precludes district liability in cases where school employees are performing "discretionary duties" within the scope of their employment. State laws define the scope of school and official immunity in specific cases. "Discretionary" or "official" immunity protects school employees and officials from liability when they perform "discretionary" (as opposed to "ministerial") duties. A "ministerial act" leaves nothing to discretion and is a simple or definite duty. Public officials whose duties require them to exercise judgment or discretion are not personally liable for damages unless they act intentionally. Discretionary or official immunity ensures that public officials who are charged by law with duties calling for the exercise of judgment or discretion are not held personally liable for damages, if they act in the scope of their employment and not intentionally, wilfully or with malice.*

◆   On a February day, an Indiana teacher took her students to a middle school for enrichment classes. She slipped and fell on a walkway. While there had been no precipitation for at least two days, a witness later described the area as "slick and wet looking." The teacher sued the district for negligence, and a jury awarded her $90,000. The Supreme Court of Indiana upheld the verdict. It held **the state tort claims act confers immunity on government units for injuries caused by temporary conditions on "a public thoroughfare" resulting from weather**. However, there is a common law duty to maintain roads and sidewalks in a reasonably safe condition. In this case, the school district claimed that the accident was due to normal thawing and freezing of a thin layer of ice. But because there had been no precipitation for a few days before the accident, the court found there was no "temporary conditions" immunity. *Gary Community School Corp. v. Roach-Walker*, 917 N.E.2d 1224 (Ind. 2009).

◆ A Kansas parent entered a school gymnasium to pick up his stepson. He then left the gym through double doors leading to a commons area. One of the doors came off a closing mechanism and fell on the parent's head. He sued the school district in the state court system for negligence. A trial court agreed with the district that the Kansas Tort Claims Act (KTCA) provided immunity. It applied the KTCA's "recreational use exception" to liability. After the state court of appeals affirmed the decision, the Supreme Court of Kansas agreed to hear the case. It held the legislative purpose of the KTCA was to immunize government entities to encourage them to build recreational facilities without fear of lawsuits. The court found that while the commons was not exclusively used for recreational purposes, it was an integral part of the gymnasium's use.

The commons was used to sell tickets and concessions during events and was not "incidentally connected to the gymnasium." And the court found the commons was necessarily connected to the gymnasium as a principal means of access and for purchasing tickets and concessions. **A school would be discouraged from opening a gymnasium for recreational use if liability was permitted in an area that was an integral part of its recreational usage.** Accordingly, the school district was immune from liability under the recreational use exception to the KTCA. *Poston v. Unified School Dist. No. 387, Altoona-Midway, Wilson County*, 189 P.3d 517 (Kan. 2008).

◆ An Illinois eighth-grader participated in an extracurricular tumbling class during lunch periods in his school gymnasium. The teacher who supervised the class had a physical education degree, but little mini-trampoline experience. After taking a forward flip off the mini-trampoline, the student seriously injured his neck and became quadriplegic. He and his mother sued the school board and teacher. They claimed that the teacher failed to provide any spotters and did not watch students while they used the mini-trampoline. The complaint also named the Chicago Youth Centers (CYC), which ran the tumbling class. The family asserted that use of a mini-trampoline was a hazardous recreational activity, and that the CYC and the teacher could not claim state law immunity because they acted willfully and wantonly. The trial court granted immunity to the teacher, the CYC and the board. Appeal reached the Supreme Court of Illinois. It held the Illinois Local Governmental and Governmental Employees Tort Immunity Act contained exceptions to immunity for hazardous recreational activities.

**Trampolining was listed in the act as a hazardous recreational activity.** The risk of spinal cord injuries from the improper use of a mini-trampoline was well known. Evidence indicated the CYC tumbling/trampoline program was not supervised by an experienced instructor and was not taught properly, as trained spotters and safety equipment were often not provided. Genuine issues of fact existed regarding whether the board, CYC and teacher were guilty of willful and wanton conduct, and the case required a trial. *Murray v. Chicago Youth Center*, 224 Ill.2d 213, 864 N.E.2d 176 (Ill. 2007).

## 2. Comparative and Contributory Negligence

*Under comparative negligence principles, courts may apportion negligence among parties by their degree of fault. For example, a jury may find a student who slipped on a bar of soap in a school locker room 40% negligent, and the district whose employee left out the bar of soap 60% negligent. If the damages were $10,000, the student would recover $6,000 from the district.*

*"Contributory negligence" is a defense barring any recovery by a plaintiff in a negligence case when the plaintiff is at fault in any measure for the injury. A 1985 Indiana amendment adopted a "modified comparative fault system." In* Penn Harris Madison School Corp. v. Howard, *861 N.E.2d 1190 (Ind. 2007) below, the Indiana Supreme Court held contributory negligence principles still applied in actions against school districts. State law recognized a presumption that children between the ages of seven and 14 are incapable of contributory negligence.*

◆   A 13-year-old Indiana student blacked out during a basketball practice. Later, his mother told the coach he could walk through plays but could not run or perform strenuous activities. The student attended school for the next two days without incident. Although a doctor did not clear him to practice, he did so without restrictions at a practice two days after the blackout. During a running drill, the student collapsed and died. His parents sued the school district in the state court system. There, the district argued the student's own negligence was a contributing factor in his death. A jury returned a verdict for the parents, and the district appealed. The case reached the Supreme Court of Indiana, which held **a child between ages seven and 14 is required to exercise due care for his or her own safety**. Indiana law recognized a presumption that children between ages seven and 14 are incapable of contributory negligence. In this case, the district failed to overcome that legal presumption. *Clay City Consolidated School Corp. v. Timberman*, 918 N.E.2d 292 (Ind. 2009).

◆   A deaf Florida student left her school bus near her home on a two-lane residential street with a 25 mile-per-hour speed limit. The bus driver activated the bus' flashing lights and waited for her to cross the street. The driver heard a pickup truck speeding down the street and tried to signal the student. However, the pickup struck the student and knocked her to the ground. The pickup truck driver pleaded no contest to criminal conduct and was sentenced to five years in prison for reckless driving. The student's family sued the school board for negligence. In pre-trial activity, the bus driver said, "in my heart, yes, I feel like I hurt her a lot." A jury found the board 20 % at fault for the student's injuries, the pickup driver 70 % at fault, and the student 10 % at fault. The family appealed to a Florida District Court of Appeal, arguing that the pickup driver acted intentionally (removing him from the negligence calculations), and that the school board should have been liable for a greater share of liability. The court of appeal affirmed, noting that **although the pickup driver had been fleeing police, he never intended to injure the student**. The percentage of fault had been properly calculated. *Petit-Dos v. School Board of Broward County*, 2 So.3d 1022 (Fla. Dist. Ct. App. 2009).

◆   An Indiana high school student helped an elementary school music teacher produce the play "Peter Pan." He had rock climbing experience, and he designed and built a pulley mechanism to allow the Peter Pan character to "fly." The teacher held a ladder for the student as he connected himself to the mechanism during a dress rehearsal for the play. When the student jumped from the ladder, the mechanism failed and he fell to the gym floor, suffering serious injuries. He and his mother sued the school district for negligence. A jury awarded him $200,000, but the Court of Appeals of Indiana held that the trial court gave the jury improper instructions. The student appealed. The Supreme Court of Indiana reinstated the jury's award. Although the jury instruction had been inaccurate, it hadn't prejudiced the school. **Under contributory negligence principles, the school could not defend its negligence by asserting the student's negligence.** *Penn Harris Madison School Corp. v. Howard*, 861 N.E.2d 1190 (Ind. 2007).

◆   A Washington student and her family sued a teacher, district and principal for sexual abuse by the teacher. The claims included negligent supervision and hiring. The principal and district sought to have any potential damage award reduced in part based on the student's alleged consent to have sexual relations with the teacher. The case reached the Supreme Court of Washington. It noted that the state Tort Reform Act required comparing the fault of the parties in negligence cases. However, contributory fault did not apply in this case. **Washington schools have a "special relationship with students" and a duty to protect them from reasonably anticipated dangers.** Because of the vulnerability of students, they had no duty to protect themselves from sexual abuse by teachers. This result was consistent with cases from Indiana, South Carolina, Colorado, Oregon, and Pennsylvania. The school district could not rely on the defense of contributory negligence. *Christensen v. Royal School Dist. #160*, 156 Wash.2d 62, 124 P.3d 283 (Wash. 2005).

## II.  SCHOOL ATHLETICS

*Student-athletes assume the inherent risks of sports participation. Absent a showing of gross negligence or intentional conduct by a coach, league or school, they may not recover damages. The cases in this section involve district or school board liability. For more cases attempting to hold coaches personally liable for student injuries, please see Chapter Thirteen, Section III.C.*

### A.  Participants

#### 1.  Duty of Care

◆   An Iowa high school basketball player elbowed an opposing player on the court. The opponent suffered from postconcussion syndrome, and his family sued the player in a state court for assault and battery, adding a claim against the player's district for negligent supervision. The court awarded damages against the player but refused to award the opponent's family any punitive damages. It also dismissed the claims against the district. The Supreme Court of Iowa found no error in the compensatory damage award against the player. **Under Iowa law, school districts have a duty of reasonable care. But there was no foreseeable risk in this case.** The assaulting player had only committed one previous technical foul, and it was for using profanity. While he was regarded as an intense player, his school district was not held liable because it could not have foreseen he would commit a battery during a game. *Brokaw v. Winfield-Mt. Union Community School Dist.*, 788 N.W.2d 386 (Iowa 2010).

◆    A California community college baseball player was hit in the head by a pitch, possibly in retaliation for a pitch thrown by his teammate the previous inning. After being hit, the student staggered, felt dizzy, and was in pain. His manager told him to go to first base. The student did so, but complained to his first-base coach, who told him to stay in the game. Soon after that, the student was told to sit on the bench. He claimed no one tended to his injuries. The student sued the host college for breaching its duty of care by failing to supervise or control its pitcher and failing to provide umpires or medical care. The court dismissed the case, and appeal reached the Supreme Court of California. It noted that in sports, the doctrine of assumption of risk precludes liability for injuries deemed "inherent in a sport." **Athletic participants have a duty not to act recklessly or outside the bounds of the sport.** Coaches and instructors have a duty not to increase the risks inherent in sports participation. Being hit by a pitch is an inherent risk of baseball. Colleges are not liable for the actions of their student-athletes during competition. The failure to provide umpires did not increase risks inherent in the game. The student's own coaches, not the host college, had the responsibility to remove him from the game for medical attention. The court reversed the judgment. *Avila v. Citrus Community College Dist.*, 38 Cal.4th 148, 41 Cal.Rptr. 299, 131 P.3d 383 (Cal. 2006).

◆    A Louisiana football player injured his back in a weight training session. His physician diagnosed him with a lumbar strain and dehydrated disc, and gave him a medical excuse from football for a week with instructions for "no weightlifting, squats or power cleans." Coaches interpreted the weightlifting limitation to be for only one week, and a coach instructed the student to do a particular lift. He did the lift, suffered severe back pain, and was diagnosed with a disc protrusion and a herniated disc. He lost interest in school, failed classes and transferred to an alternative school. He sued the school board for personal injury. A state trial court awarded him less than $7,500 for medical expenses, but awarded him $275,500 for pain and suffering, future medical expenses and loss of enjoyment of life. On appeal, the Louisiana Court of Appeal reviewed testimony that the student continued to experience severe back pain and often could not sleep. It held the trial court did not commit error in awarding the student damages for pain and suffering. **Evidence supported the trial court's findings that he had been severely injured and would experience recurring pain that would limit his daily activities indefinitely.** The court affirmed the damage award for loss of enjoyment of life, based on evidence that the student lost the opportunity to play varsity baseball and football. *Day v. Ouachita Parish School Board*, 823 So.2d 1039 (La. Ct. App. 2002).

## 2. Governmental Immunity

*Wisconsin's Supreme Court held a cheerleading spotter and his school district were entitled to immunity in an action by a cheerleader who was injured while practicing a stunt. Wisconsin Statues Section 895.525 had a legislative purpose to decrease uncertainty in recreational liability issues and helped to assure the continued availability of school recreational activities.*

◆ A 17-year-old Mississippi student collapsed during football practice on a hot August day. Emergency responders were unable to revive him, and he later died at a hospital. His survivors sued the school district for negligence. A state trial court denied pretrial judgment on the negligence claim. On appeal, the Supreme Court of Mississippi noted the Mississippi Tort Claims Act (MTCA) is the exclusive remedy in a negligence action against a governmental entity or employee. The MTCA provides immunity to state and political subdivisions whose employees act in the course and scope of their employment while performing discretionary acts. **Acts are discretionary if they require officials to use their own judgment and discretion. Coaching is a discretionary act.** Nothing indicated that the district or its coaches violated any statute, ordinance or regulation concerning practices, and the district was entitled to immunity. *Covington County School Dist. v. Magee*, 29 So.3d 1 (Miss. 2010).

◆ An Illinois school district operated a summer football camp. A student was hurt when he tripped over a grass-concealed shot-put bumper on the route he was told to take. His parent sued the district in a state court for over $50,000 in damages for negligence and willful and wanton conduct. Applying a recreational immunity provision of Illinois law, the court dismissed the action against the district. Before the Appellate Court of Illinois, the parent argued that the football facility was educational and not recreational in nature. This would preclude a recreational immunity defense. **The appellate court noted that immunity depended upon the character of the property, not the activity performed.** The property was on school grounds and was being used for a summer camp – by inference an educational purpose. As the lower court did not fully explore the property's character, dismissal was improper. *Peters v. Herrin Community School Dist. No. 4*, 928 N.E.2d 1258 (Ill. App. Ct. 2010).

◆ A Wisconsin varsity basketball cheerleading squad practiced a stunt in their high school commons area without mats. A spotter failed to stop a cheerleader from falling backward and striking her head. The cheerleader sued the spotter and school district for negligence. Evidence indicated that the cheerleaders were practicing a stunt they had not previously performed together, and that the spotter was not positioned to prevent the injury. The cheerleading coach was working with others about ten feet away at the time of the fall. The court held that the spotter and the school district were entitled to immunity, but the state court of appeals reversed the judgment against the spotter. On appeal to the state supreme court, the cheerleader argued that state law gave immunity only to athletes in "contact sports," and that cheerleading was neither a team nor a contact sport. However, the court held that cheerleading was a "contact sport."
The court found no evidence that the spotter was "reckless," which would

defeat his claim to statutory immunity. He was simply standing in the wrong place. His conduct was characterized as "discretionary," not ministerial. In this case, the cheerleading squad operated under "spirit rules" that did not eliminate the coach's discretion. Spirit rules did not mandate a spotter for this exercise, and the coach had discretion to use mats. **The district was entitled to immunity.** *Noffke v. Bakke*, 315 Wis.2d 350, 760 N.W.3d 156 (Wis. 2009).

◆   A disagreement arose between a Texas faculty cheerleading sponsor and a principal over the punishment of varsity cheerleaders who were accused of disrespect, leaving school grounds, violating the school dress code and making obscene gestures toward staff. They were also accused of drinking at off-campus parties and being photographed in suggestive poses. After the cheerleading sponsor lost her job, she sued the school district, superintendent, principal and others for breach of contract, wrongful termination and defamation. The principal claimed sovereign immunity. After amending her petition to add claims for interference with her contract and denial of due process, the cheerleading sponsor filed a notice of non-suit, which had the effect of voluntarily dismissing her case. Before entering a non-suit order, the court held for the principal, based on her defense of immunity. It also awarded her $14,071 for her attorneys' fees and costs. The court then dismissed the case.

The cheerleading sponsor appealed to the Court of Appeals of Texas, asserting that her non-suit notice mooted the case and relieved her from paying the principal's attorneys' fees. **The court agreed that the notice of non-suit made the principal's claim to immunity moot.** But she was still entitled to her attorneys' fees under the state Education Code, since she was acting within her discretionary authority regarding student punishment. *Ward v. Theret*, No. 08-08-00143-CV, 2009 WL 2136299 (Tex. Ct. App. 7/15/09).

◆   An Ohio student injured his forehead and wrist during a pole vault at a high school track meet. He landed on improper padding near the landing pad that was later identified as in violation of National Federation of State High School Associations rules. The student sued the school district, coach and other officials for negligence. A state court held for the district and officials. The Court of Appeals of Ohio held the trial court had improperly granted immunity under the state recreational user statute. The student was not a "recreational user." The trial court also committed error by finding he assumed the risk of injury by the inherent dangers of pole vaulting. The court held **the sponsor of a sporting event has a duty not to increase the risk of harm over and above any inherent risks of the sport**. The court rejected the district's claim to immunity, as there was no discretionary, policy-making, planning or enforcement activity. But the coach was entitled to immunity under state law, as he did not act recklessly, with malice, or in bad faith. *Henney v. Shelby City School Dist.*, No. 2005 CA 0064, 2006 WL 747475 (Ohio Ct. App. 2006).

◆   A Maine high school wrestling team ran timed drills in school hallways in its warm-up routine. A wrestler was seriously injured after being bumped into a window by a teammate during a drill. The school had no policy prohibiting athletic training in school hallways at the time. The student sued the school district in the state court system for personal injury. A court held that the district and officials were protected by discretionary immunity. The Maine Supreme Judicial Court agreed, and held **government entities are generally entitled to absolute immunity from suit in any tort action for damages**. An exception to this rule imposes liability on government entities for the negligent operation of a public building. Here, allowing relay races in the school hallway was not the "operation of a public building." To impose liability under the public building exception to immunity, the claim must implicate a building's physical structure. The district and officials were protected by discretionary immunity. *Lightfoot v. School Administrative Dist. No. 35*, 816 A.2d 63 (Me. 2003).

◆  A Kansas school football team held its first practice on a hot August day. A student reported feeling ill after completing his first two stations. An assistant coach instructed him to drink some water, which he did. He then asked to sit out further drills and was told again to get water. As the team left practice, the student collapsed and was taken to a hospital, where he died the next day. His estate sued the school district and head coach for negligence. A state court granted the estate's motion to prevent the district and coach from relying on the "recreational use" exception to the Kansas Tort Claims Act (KTCA). On appeal, the Supreme Court of Kansas found a rational basis existed for distinguishing between injuries occurring on public recreational property and those occurring elsewhere. **The discretionary function exception protects government entities and employees from claims based on the exercise of discretion or the failure to exercise it.** The recreational use exception eliminated liability for ordinary negligence and barred all the claims. The court reversed the judgment and returned the case to a lower court for a determination of whether the district or coach acted with gross or wanton negligence. *Barrett v. Unified School Dist. No. 259*, 32 P.3d 1156 (Kan. 2001).

### 3. Assumption of Risk and Waiver

*The New York Supreme Court, Appellate Division, recently restated the general rule that "by engaging in a sport or recreational activity, a participant consents to those commonly appreciated risks which are inherent in and arise out of the nature of the sport generally and flow from such participation."*

◆  A New York student said he contracted herpes in a school wrestling match. He sued his school district, high school, wrestling opponent and the opponent's school in a state court for negligence. The case reached the New York Supreme Court, Appellate Division, which explained that **athletes consent to commonly appreciated risks inherent in the sport**. Athletes indicate their consent to injury-causing events by participating in them when risks are known, apparent or reasonably foreseeable, and are not assumed, concealed or unreasonably increased risks. Wrestling involved close contact between athletes, and diseases transmitted through skin-to-skin contact could result. The wrestling coach had identified communicable diseases as an "inherent danger of the sport." Even the student's expert admitted that herpes may exist in 29.8 % of high school wrestlers. And the lower court had found that the possibility of contracting communicable diseases such as herpes is well known to coaches and officials.

Contrary to the student's argument, school officials informed him of the specific risk of contracting herpes, as well as the general risk of contracting skin diseases through wrestling. He was instructed to shower after each practice, and to use strong soap and shampoo to limit the possibility of contracting skin diseases including staph, ringworm, impetigo and herpes simplex virus. The court rejected all the student's arguments and reversed the judgment. *Farrell v. Hochhauser,* 65 A.D.3d 663, 884 N.Y.S.2d 261 (N.Y. App. Div. 2009).

◆   An Indiana student-athlete who weighed over 250 pounds had "dry heaves" early in a morning school football practice session. He stopped his activity for a minute, then told two coaches he felt better. The student ate lunch during a team rest period. He spent time lying on the locker room floor. The head coach asked the student how he felt, and the student again said he was okay. Near the end of the afternoon session, the student told a coach he did not feel well. The coach told him to get water, but he soon collapsed. The coaches took him to the locker room and placed him in a cool shower. He lost consciousness and the coaches called for an ambulance. He died at a hospital the following day. His parents sued the school district in the state court system for negligence.

After a trial, a jury returned a verdict for the school district. The parents appealed to the Court of Appeals of Indiana, which held that they did not submit sufficient evidence to find the district negligent as a matter of law. The head coach responded to hot weather by shortening parts of the schedule and adding more water breaks. Coaches emphasized the importance of drinking fluids, and several of them checked on the student. They had no indication that he was ill until he collapsed, when they called 911. **To negate a legal duty of care and avoid any finding of negligence, a participant must have "actual knowledge and appreciation of the specific risk involved and voluntarily acceptance of that risk."** But the release forms did not refer to "negligence." Since the release forms did not contain the word "negligence," the district was not released from negligence claims. The trial court should have granted the parents' request for a jury instruction stating that they had not released the district from negligence. The court reversed the judgment and remanded the case for a new trial. *Stowers v. Clinton Cent. School Corp.*, 855 N.E.2d 739 (Ind. Ct. App. 2006).

◆   A Massachusetts school district required a signed parental release for all students seeking to participate in extracurricular activities. For four years, the father of a high school cheerleader signed a release form before each season. During her fourth year, she was injured during a practice. When the cheerleader reached age 18, she sued the city in a state court for negligence. She added claims for negligent hiring and retention of the cheerleading coach. The court held for the city on the basis of the parental release, finding the father had released the city from any and all actions and claims. The cheerleader appealed to the Massachusetts Supreme Judicial Court, asserting the release was invalid. The court held that **enforcement of a parental release was consistent with Massachusetts law and public policy**. There was undisputed evidence that the father read and understood the release before signing it, and that the form was not misleading. It was not contrary to public policy to require parents to sign releases as a condition for student participation in extracurricular activities. To hold the release unenforceable would expose public schools to financial costs and risks that would lead to the reduction of extracurricular activities. *Sharon v. City of Newton*, 437 Mass. 99, 769 N.E.2d 738 (Mass. 2002).

## B. Spectators, Employees and Parents

*A Louisiana court has held that to impose liability on a public entity, the entity must know of "a particular vice or defect" that causes damage, yet fail to fix the defect after having a reasonable opportunity to do so. In Alabama litigation, numerous claims against county school boards have been barred by an absolute immunity provision of the state constitution.*

◆   The Supreme Court of Delaware denied a request for relief from a pretrial order that required a private cheerleading organization to defend and indemnify a school district for injuries to a spectator who was attending a cheerleading event at a district high school. The organization had leased the school gymnasium from the school district for a cheerleading competition. After the spectator fell from the bleachers, the organization claimed gross negligence by school staff who failed to install guard rails. In pretrial proceedings a state trial court dismissed negligence claims against the school board and officials but allowed the claims for gross or wanton negligence to proceed. As the supreme court found no reason to allow an appeal at this stage of the case, **the organization had to provide legal defense to the school board and indemnify it for any loss.** *Diamond State Wildcats v. Boyle*, 986 A.2d 1164 (Table) (Del. 2010).

◆   A patron at an Alabama high school basketball game fell from the bleachers where he had been sitting, and was injured. He sued the school board for negligence and contract claims. A trial court held for the school board on the negligence claims, but allowed a breach-of-implied contract claim to survive. On appeal to the Supreme Court of Alabama, the patron argued that county education boards can be sued for an implied breach of contract for failing to provide safe premises for athletic contests. In contrast, the board argued that it was an agency of the state entitled to the same immunity as any state agency enjoyed. The court found that immunity was conferred by the Constitution, and it affirmed the judgment for the board. **Absolute immunity extended to all arms or agencies of the state, including county education boards.** *Ex parte Hale County Board of Educ.*, 14 So.3d 844 (Ala. 2009).

◆   An Alabama five-year-old fell from bleachers at a quarterfinal football playoff game held at a high school by the Alabama High School Athletic Association (AHSAA). The child fell through an opening in the seats and broke both her wrists. Her parents sued the school board for breach of an implied contract and breach of implied warranty of safe premises. The case reached the Supreme Court of Alabama, which stated that **Alabama county education boards are considered state agencies, and are immune from tort actions.** The court agreed with the school board that the AHSAA sponsored and controlled the game, defeating any contract claim. The parents' claim was barred by an absolute immunity provision of the state constitution. *Ex Parte Jackson County Board of Educ.*, 4 So.3d 1099 (Ala. 2008).

◆   A Louisiana child fell on bleachers at a football game at a high school stadium. Her family claimed the fall was caused by a lack of adequate traction tape or guards on the bleachers. A school custodial supervisor submitted a statement that he witnessed the fall. He stated that the child was being chased by another child and that the family did nothing to stop her. The family sued the school board for negligence. A state court found insufficient evidence for a trial. The family appealed to the Court of Appeal of Louisiana, which affirmed the judgment. School employees indicated that there was no defect in the bleachers, steps or guard rails, or in the design or construction of the stadium. **To impose liability on a public entity, the entity must know of "a particular vice or defect" that caused the damage, yet fail to fix the defect after having a reasonable opportunity to do so.** Not every imperfection or irregularity is a "defect" resulting in liability for a school board. There was no evidence that the board knew of any defect. There was also no evidence that the bleachers were slippery or that similar incidents had occurred there. The absence of traction tape was not a defect that created an unreasonable risk of harm. *Mason v. Monroe City School Board*, 996 So.2d 377 (La. Ct. App. 2008).

◆   A West Virginia spectator slipped and fell on ice and snow on school grounds while trying to reach a high school basketball game. She sued the board in a state court, arguing it was negligent to hold a basketball game on a day when the entire school system was closed due to weather. The board claimed immunity under the state Governmental Tort Claims and Insurance Reform Act. The case reached the Supreme Court of Appeals of West Virginia, which rejected the spectator's argument that the decision to hold the basketball game was an affirmative act that was not immunized. **While the act of holding the game may have encouraged her to venture out into the snow, it did not cause the conditions at the school.** The Tort Act provided immunity for losses or claims resulting from snow or ice on public ways resulting from the weather. *Porter v. Grant County Board of Educ.*, 633 S.E.2d 38 (W.Va. 2006).

## III.  OTHER SCHOOL ACTIVITIES

*Courts have held schools liable for injuries during school events which resulted from the failure to provide a reasonably safe environment, failure to warn participants of known hazards (or to remove known dangers), failure to properly instruct participants in the activity, and failure to provide supervision adequate for the type of activity and the ages of the participants involved. Schools and their staff members are not liable for unforeseeable harms, as schools are not the insurers of student safety. The fact that each student is not personally supervised at all times does not itself constitute grounds for liability.*

### A. Physical Education Classes

#### 1. Duty of Care

◆   A California school district was not liable for injuries to a student who was hit by a golf club swung by a classmate in their physical education class. According to the student, the teacher did not give a whistle command for the classmate to hit the ball, as was her usual practice. The student sued the school district for negligence. A state court found that the district did not breach its limited duty of care and held for the district. The student appealed to the Court of Appeal of California, which held that the lower court applied the wrong legal standard. **The Supreme Court of California has applied the "prudent person" standard of care to cases involving students injured during school hours.** This simply requires persons to avoid injuring others by using due care. As the lower court should have applied the prudent person standard, the court reversed the judgment and remanded the case. *Hemady v. Long Beach Unified School Dist.*, 143 Cal.App.4th 566, 49 Cal. Rptr.3d 464 (Cal. Ct. App. 2006). The Supreme Court of California denied review of this case in 2007.

◆   During a gym class, an Ohio eighth grader with a history of mild asthma obtained his teacher's permission to retrieve his prescription inhaler from his locker. Minutes later, another teacher found the student unconscious and not breathing on the locker room floor. Despite the administration of medical treatment, he died. The student's estate sued the school board for wrongful death. A jury found for the school board, and the Court of Appeals of Ohio affirmed. The trial court had allowed a physician to testify that the death of a student previously recognized as having "mild asthma" was "one in a million." **According to the physician, not even medical professionals could have foreseen the death.** The court rejected the estate's additional arguments and affirmed the judgment. *Spencer v. Lakeview School Dist.*, No. 2005-T-0083, 2006 WL 1816452 (Ohio Ct. App. 2006).

◆   A New York student was playing football in a physical education class when a classmate threw a football tee that hit her in the eye. Her parents brought a negligence action against the school district in a state court. A state appellate division court held the district had a duty to adequately supervise and instruct students, and was liable for foreseeable injuries caused by their negligence. But **school districts are not insurers of student safety and will not be held liable for every spontaneous, thoughtless or careless act by which one student injures another**. The degree of care required is what a reasonably prudent parent would exercise under similar circumstances. Here, the teacher had not instructed students on how to properly handle the tee and never told them not to throw it. The evidence differed as to whether students had previously thrown the tee or seen the teacher throw it. In affirming a judgment for the student, the court held that the trial court would have to determine if the injury causing conduct was reasonably foreseeable and preventable. *Oakes v. Massena Cent. School Dist.*, 19 A.D.3d 981, 797 N.Y.S.2d 640 (N.Y. App. Div. 2005).

◆   A 16-year-old Louisiana student who weighed 327 pounds collapsed and began having seizures during a PE class. The class was conducted by a substitute art teacher in a gym that was not air-conditioned, and the temperature inside was at least 90 degrees. After the student collapsed, he was taken to a hospital, where he later died. His teacher had played in the game instead of monitoring students. The student's parent sued the school board and its insurer in a state court for wrongful death, and the court awarded her $500,000. The Court of Appeal of Louisiana found no error in trial court findings that the board had breached its duty to exercise reasonable care and supervision. The lower court was also entitled to hear the testimony of a physical education professor and to consider reliable medical testimony. **Teachers have a duty to exercise reasonable care and supervision over students in their custody, and to avoid exposing them to an unreasonable risk of injury.** As physical education classes may involve dangerous activities, due care must be used in them to minimize the risk of student injury. *James v. Jackson*, 898 So.2d 596 (La. Ct. App. 2005). The state supreme court denied the board's appeal. *James v. Jackson*, 902 So.2d 1005 (La. 2005).

### 2.   Governmental Immunity

*Although state laws grant varying degrees of immunity to school districts in negligence cases, the general rule is that government agencies and employees have immunity from civil liability based on "discretionary actions." An Illinois court held immunity is allowed for "policy decisions," which require the balancing of competing interests so that there must be a "judgment call."*

◆   After a Wisconsin student expressed fear about performing a beginning parallel bar exercise, her physical education teacher moved the bars to their lowest setting. Another student demonstrated the exercise, and the teacher positioned herself to spot the student. However, the teacher's attention was diverted by another student who asked a question. The student caught her leg on the bar and seriously injured her knee. She was the first student injured during the teacher's 32-year career. In the student's negligence action against the teacher and the school district, a state trial court held that the teacher deserved governmental immunity. On appeal, the Court of Appeals of Wisconsin held that **Wisconsin law immunizes government agencies and employees from liability for "discretionary actions."** There was no statute, rule or regulation specifying how the teacher should teach gymnastics. Since any directives she received did not eliminate her discretion, immunity protected her. *Krus v. Community Insurance Corp.*, 324 Wis.2d 306 (Wis. Ct. App. 2010).

◆   Two Minnesota students were injured in a darkened school gym while playing "flashlight tag." Their parents sued the district for negligence, and it asserted immunity under a state law requiring each school district in the state to purchase liability insurance if it was available at a cost of $1.50 or less per student per year. The statutory dollar amount was never changed after 1970, and no school district could now obtain liability insurance for $1.50 per student. The case reached the Supreme Court of Minnesota, which explained that the law had expired in 1974. **Had the legislature intended to completely immunize school districts for tort immunity, it would have drafted a statute announcing such immunity.** The district had been self-insured for tort claims since 1990, and had paid out claims it deemed meritorious. So the court held the district was not entitled to immunity. *Granville v. Minneapolis Public Schools, Special School Dist. No. 1*, 732 N.W.2d 201 (Minn. 2007).

## B. Shop Class Injuries

### 1. Duty of Care

*Schools are required to provide their students with a safe environment. Known shop class dangers must be minimized, and safety devices are to be in place and working. Failure to supervise, warn students of known dangers, or maintain safety devices can result in school liability.*

◆   A Minnesota student amputated a finger in a wood shop class accident. He had experience using the saw, which was equipped with a blade guard. Before students could use the saw, they had to pass a test on a protocol for its use. The protocol stated that the best practice for cutting small strips of wood was to disengage the blade guard and use a push stick to guide the strips through the saw. On the day of the accident, the teacher instructed the student to cut small wood strips using a push stick with the blade guard disengaged. After watching the student cut some strips, he moved to another part of the room. The student then reached over the blade to remove a piece of scrap wood and lost a finger.

The student sued the teacher and school district for negligence. A state court denied the teacher's claim to official immunity, and the school district's motion for statutory immunity. The Supreme Court of Minnesota explained that teachers did not forfeit official immunity because their conduct was "ministerial," if that conduct was established by a policy or protocol that was created though the exercise of discretionary judgment. Both the decision to establish a protocol and the protocol itself involved the exercise of professional judgment. **The teacher was entitled to common law official immunity because his liability was based on compliance with the protocol.** The court reversed the judgment against the teacher and held that the school district was entitled to vicarious immunity. *Anderson v. Anoka Hennepin Independent School Dist. 11*, 678 N.W.2d 651 (Minn. 2004).

### 2. Governmental Immunity

◆   An Ohio student lost fingers on his dominant hand when he tried to operate a jointer machine in his high school shop class. Prior to the accident, the teacher had demonstrated its use and instructed the students on safety issues. Neither the student nor the teacher could later say for sure what had happened. After the accident, the machine was taken out of operation and stored. The student sued the school board in a state court for negligence. An inspection of the machine about a year after the incident revealed that its guard was locked open. The court considered testimony from the teacher that it "would probably take five years" for the guard to remain in the open position. The teacher believed the machine was purchased in 1964 and had been broken and repaired since that time. He believed the guard was functioning properly, and he adjusted it weekly. The court denied the board's motion for state political subdivision immunity. On appeal, the Court of Appeals of Ohio held **employees of political subdivisions are immune from liability unless their actions or omissions are manifestly outside the scope of employment or their official duties**. A jury would have to decide whether the teacher's conduct was reckless, and consider inconsistencies in his statements. *Bolling v. North Olmsted City Schools Board of Educ.*, No. 90669, 2008 WL 4599670 (Ohio Ct. App. 10/16/08).

## C.  Field Trips

*California Education Code Section 35330 creates "field trip immunity" for school districts. All persons making a field trip or excursion shall be deemed to have waived all claims against a school district, a charter school, or the state for injury, accident, illness, or death occurring during or by reason of the field trip or excursion. Under state law, adults and the parents or guardians of pupils taking out-of-state field trips must sign waivers of all claims.*

◆   A California student with asthma went on a field trip to a science camp operated by her school district. When she suffered an asthma attack, camp counselors gave her an asthma inhaler and performed CPR until paramedics arrived. She died as she was being airlifted to a hospital. Her parents sued the school district for negligent failure to provide adequate medical staff and misrepresenting the level of medical staffing that would be available at the camp. A state court held for the district, as did the Court of Appeal of California. **It held the district was entitled to immunity because any person on a school field trip was deemed to have waived all claims against a school district,** charter school or the state for injury, accident, illness or death occurring "during or by reason of the field trip or excursion." The court held this broad grant of immunity was designed to encourage the use of field trips. *Sanchez v. San Diego County Office of Educ.*, 182 Cal.App.4th 1580, 106 Cal.Rptr.3d 750 (Cal. Ct. App. 2010).

◆   A California school held a year-end field trip for seventh-graders to a waterpark. It notified families that the event would be "a closed party" supervised by teaching staff. The notice also advised families that waterpark lifeguards would be present. A student drowned during the event, and his family sued the waterpark for wrongful death. The waterpark in turn sought to apportion part of the liability to the school district and indemnify it for any loss. According to the waterpark, the district failed to comply with its own policy requiring a minimum ratio of one adult chaperone for every 13 students.

According to the waterpark, district chaperones caused the death because they failed to determine the student's swimming ability, warn him of risks or watch him while he attempted to swim. The superior court dismissed the district from the case, and the waterpark appealed. The California Court of Appeal held that the district was shielded from liability by the California Education Code, which created "field trip immunity" for California school districts. All persons making a field trip or excursion in connection with a school-related activity were deemed to have waived all claims against a school district for injury, accident, illness or death. **Under the law, the student was deemed to have waived all claims against the district arising from the excursion to the waterpark.** It was irrelevant that the student's parent or guardian had not signed a school permission slip. The court affirmed the judgment for the school district. *Windsor R/V Waterworks Park Co. v. Santa Rosa City Schools*, No. A118090, 2008 WL 4601138 (Cal. Ct. App. 10/16/08).

◆　An autistic Ohio eighth-grader weighed 150 pounds and had a history of behavior problems. A teacher's aide agreed to supervise her on school buses, even though she knew the child had previously hurt others. The child hit and bit the aide on one occasion while they were on a bus. Despite this, the aide agreed to supervise her on a field trip to a bowling alley. The aide received additional pay for this assignment. While at the bowling alley, the child wandered onto a lane and tried to hit a student from another school. When the aide intervened, the child hit and choked her. As a result, the aide suffered two herniated disks in her neck. She sued the school board, its superintendent, and the child's parents. The parents settled the case and the aide appealed a judgment for the board and superintendent to the U.S. Court of Appeals, Sixth Circuit.

The court held the board was charged by the federal Individuals with Disabilities Education Act (IDEA) with providing autistic children a free appropriate public education in the least restrictive environment. Here, the board was attempting to discharge its duties under the IDEA. A more restrictive setting might have violated the IDEA. According to the court, **it would not create "a Catch 22 situation by imposing substantive due process liability for failure to do an act that might itself have exposed the actor to liability on another theory."** The district could not simply decline to educate the child on the basis of behavior that was a manifestation of her disability. In any event, the aide was entirely aware of the child's history and accepted additional pay for extra assignments that required her to control her actions. The board did not act arbitrarily, and the judgment in its favor was upheld. *Hunt v. Sycamore Community School Dist. Board of Educ.*, 542 F.3d 529 (6th Cir. 2008).

◆　A profoundly mentally disabled Kentucky student broke his ankle during a school field trip to a roller rink. An adult supervisor was on the floor taking pictures of students at the time of the accident. The student fell when he leaned over to kiss one of his peer tutors for a picture. His parents sued the school board and teacher for personal injury. A state trial court held that the board was entitled to governmental immunity, and the teacher had qualified immunity. On appeal, the state court of appeals held **qualified official immunity applies when public employees perform acts involving the exercise of discretion and judgment, if they are made in good faith and within the scope of their employment authority**. According to the court, there is no "bright line" rule of demarcation between discretionary and ministerial acts. There was no clear error by the trial court, as the teacher had to exercise her personal judgment and deliberation numerous times during the day of the field trip. This included how best to implement the student's individualized education program and how to supervise him. As the teacher's actions required deliberation and judgment, and she acted in good faith and within the course and scope of her employment, the court affirmed the judgment. *Pennington v. Greenup County Board of Educ.*, No. 2006-CA-001942-MR, 2008 WL 1757209 (Ky. Ct. App. 4/18/08).

## D.  Other Supervised Activities

### 1.  Duty of Care

*School districts have a duty to use reasonable care to supervise and protect students against hazards on school property that create an unreasonable risk of harm. Liability may also exist if supervision is negligently performed.*

◆  A 16-year-old Iowa student collapsed while listening to guest speeches as she stood at attention following a band performance at an outdoor bandshell. Two and a half years later, she sued the school district in a state court, claiming that the band director negligently failed to supply water and failed to recognize the signs of heat stroke, heat exhaustion and/or dehydration. She also asserted claims against the school district. A state trial court held the action was untimely under the state's two-year statute of limitations. The Supreme Court of Iowa rejected the student's claim that she had up to a year after her eighteenth birthday to initiate a lawsuit. Instead, Iowa Code Chapter 670 is the exclusive remedy for tort actions against municipalities and their employees. That law provided that every action against a municipality must be filed within six months, or within two years if the person seeking damages files a notice of a claim of loss with the government. In this case, **the student had not filed a notice with the school district**. The court commented that the legislature had now simplified the law by removing the notice requirement. It also changed the statute so that minors will now have one year from the attainment of majority within which to file a complaint, but that did not help the student here. *Rucker v. Humboldt Community School Dist.*, 737 N.W.2d 292 (Iowa 2007).

◆  A Montana high school freshman rode home from an out-of-town school basketball game on a pep band bus. The driver teased students by pumping the brakes and jarring the bus. The student asked for a restroom break, but the band instructor denied the request. Many students threw food and candy during the trip. As the bus neared the school, the band instructor announced that no one could leave the bus until it was cleaned up. The student told the instructor twice "you let me off this fucking bus." The driver pumped the brakes while stopping the bus, and the student wet himself. The school suspended the student for using profanity and placed him on detention. Eight days later, the student was hospitalized with ketoacidosis. After remaining in a life-threatening condition for several days, he recovered but was diagnosed with Type I diabetes and post-traumatic stress disorder (PTSD). The student and his parents sued the district, band instructor and driver for causing or accelerating his diabetes and PTSD.

A state trial court held for the school district. On appeal, the Supreme Court of Montana explained that **to impose liability on a school district in a**

**negligence case, it must first be shown the district had a duty of care.** In this case, the trial court had erroneously found that the district owed no duty to the student. But the trial court had been unable to determine if the student's diabetes was caused or accelerated by the events resulting from the bus trip. Even his doctor could not establish that diabetes was a likely result of the bus trip or its aftermath. Since the family could not prove the injuries were caused by the district's conduct, the court affirmed the judgment. *Hinkle v. Shepherd School Dist. #37*, 322 Mont. 80, 93 P.3d 1239 (Mont. 2004).

◆ A North Dakota school district operated a middle school in a building owned by the U.S. Bureau of Indian Affairs (BIA). The district and BIA had an agreement to jointly operate the school, which was primarily attended by American Indian students. The principal was a BIA employee who supervised both BIA and district staff. BIA teachers supervised the lunchroom under a plan created through a collective bargaining agreement. A BIA teacher tried to break up a fight between two students during her lunchroom supervision period and suffered a disabling, traumatic brain injury. The teacher sued the district for personal injury, alleging negligent failure to maintain a safe environment. A state court held for the district, finding that it did not own, supervise or control the building at the time of the injury, and thus owed the teacher no duty of care.

The teacher appealed to the Supreme Court of North Dakota. On appeal, the court found no evidence to show district control over the lunchroom, lunchroom supervision plan or teacher. This was true even assuming the district maintained some control over the school through state funding, accreditation and the arrangement with the BIA. The teacher was a BIA employee performing her lunchroom duties under the collective bargaining agreement. **As she did not show a relationship between herself and the district that imposed a legal duty to provide her with a safe working environment, the trial court had correctly held for the school district.** *Azure v. Belcourt Public School Dist.*, 681 N.W.2d 816 (N.D. 2004).

## 2. Governmental Immunity

*As discussed in the immunity sections of other areas in this chapter, state laws typically grant immunity to school districts and their employees based on the exercise of discretion. A Wisconsin court has held the decision to provide students with safety instructions was a discretionary act and thus did not subject the district to liability.*

◆ A North Dakota teacher held a "60s Day" as part of a unit of study for her history class curriculum each year. She showed a video of another student who had ridden a bicycle off the school auditorium stage and onto the floor during a 60s Day event two years earlier. A student believed that the video meant he was allowed to perform the stunt. After school, he and another student went to the auditorium to practice the stunt. They ran into the teacher, who told them she thought it was not a good idea. However, they snuck in a side door anyway. The student was injured when he crashed and struck his head on the auditorium floor. His father sued the school district and teacher in the state court system for negligence. A state trial court ruled for the district, but the Supreme Court of North Dakota allowed the lawsuit to proceed. Although the incident occurred after classes had ended, administrators and teachers were still present and the "school day had not come to an end." **The state's recreational use immunity statutes did not bar the lawsuit.** As for the claims against the teacher, the student's viewing of the video of the previous bicycle stunt could be seen as implying that the stunt would be permissible. *M.M. v. Fargo Public School Dist. No. 1*, 783 N.W.2d 806 (N.D. 2010).

◆   An Idaho school district held a carnival to celebrate the last day of the school year. A contractor provided the activities. Participants in a "bungee run" wore harnesses tethered to a fixed object by a bungee cord. They raced over an inflated rubberized surface until the cord snapped them backward. A student was injured on the bungee run. She sued the district and contractor in a state court for negligence. The court found the school's conduct was not reckless and held it was therefore immune from liability under the Idaho Tort Claims Act.

On appeal, the state supreme court held the Tort Claims Act generally made governmental entities liable for monetary damages to the same extent that a private person would be under the circumstances. Schools generally have a duty to supervise student activities, including extracurricular and school-sponsored events, and a duty to protect students from reasonably foreseeable risks. The court found the student had stated valid claims based on allowing her to participate in an unreasonably hazardous activity, failing to supervise her during the activity, and failing to supervise the contractor to ensure it provided adequate instruction and supervision. **The district court had correctly found the district was immune from liability for negligent supervision and failing to inspect the bungee equipment.** But the student should have been allowed to pursue a theory of direct liability for planning and sponsoring an unreasonably dangerous activity, and the court returned the case to the trial court. *Sherer v. Pocatello School Dist. #25*, 143 Idaho 486, 148 P.3d 1232 (Idaho 2006).

## IV.  UNSUPERVISED ACCIDENTS

*Schools are required to exercise reasonable care in maintaining safe buildings, grounds and facilities. They can be found liable for negligently maintaining buildings or tolerating hazardous structures, fixtures or grounds.*

### A.  On School Grounds

#### 1.  Duty of Care

◆   A New York child fractured her clavicle and femur after falling off a slide on a playground maintained by a city and school district. According to the child's family, the playground used no protective ground cover and was grass and dirt. Other playgrounds operated by the city and district had protective ground cover such as pea stone to lessen injuries, as recommended by the U.S. Consumer Product Safety Commission (CPSC). The family sued the school district and city. After the trial court denied pretrial dismissal, a state appellate division court held that the school's expert witness established that lack of adequate ground cover was not the legal cause of the injuries. On appeal, the New York Court of Appeals held the expert had calculated the force of the child when she landed on the ground, relying on prior tests in which he had used rubber mats. By contrast, CPSC and similar guidelines were based on use of various ground covers. **The expert witness did not provide a scientific or mathematical foundation to substantiate his opinion that the type of ground cover did not cause injury.** So the court reinstated the claims. *Butler v. City of Gloversville*, 12 N.Y.3d 902, 885 N.Y.S.2d 245 (N.Y. 2009).

◆ A California student joined other children on school property who were picking oranges from a tree on the other side of the fence. He placed a bike next to the fence and poked the handlebar through the fence for stability. However, the bike slipped, and he fell and cut his arm on the fence. The student's parents sued the school district for negligence. A state superior court awarded pretrial judgment to the district, and the family appealed. The Court of Appeal of California noted that for at least 16 years prior to the accident, there had been no complaints about the fence. The state Government Code makes a public entity liable for injuries caused by dangerous conditions on public property. A "dangerous condition" is one that creates a substantial risk of injury when the property is used with due care, and in the manner intended. **The student could not show that he was using "due care" while using the fence in a way that was reasonably foreseeable to the school district.** The danger was obvious since "fences are not meant to be climbed, they are meant to keep people out." Common sense would demonstrate that even a nine-year old child could see the danger of injury created by attempting to use a bike as a ladder to reach over a chain link fence. The lower court had properly found the metal tines on the top of the fence were not a "dangerous condition of public property." The court affirmed the judgment. *Biscotti v. Yuba City Unified School Dist.*, 158 Cal.App.4th, 69 Cal.Rptr.3d 825 (Cal. Ct. App. 2007).

## 2. Governmental Immunity

◆ At recess, a Massachusetts student chased a first-grader around an enclosed area and pushed him. The first-grader fell against the corner of a bench wall, suffering a severe injury. The principal had directed that first-graders have recess in the enclosed area, despite its sharp-cornered concrete bench-walls. In a state court action against the school system for negligence, school officials claimed immunity under the Massachusetts Tort Claims Act (MTCA). The Appeals Court of Massachusetts explained that the MTCA prevents liability for claims asserting an act (or failure to act) to prevent or diminish harmful acts by a third person "not originally caused by the public employer." In this case, the principal had ordered that first-grade recess be held in the concrete courtyard. According to the court, the causal link between the decision to hold recess in the enclosure and the injury was "not so remote" as to hold that the principal's decision was not an "original cause" of the injury. **The principal's decision to hold recess in the courtyard was not a "policymaking decision," and it was**

**not entitled to discretionary immunity.** *Gennari v. Reading Public Schools,* 933 N.E.2d 1027 (Mass. App. Ct. 2010).

◆   The Court of Appeals of Wisconsin affirmed a trial court order granting immunity to a school district in a preschool student's negligence action. The parents sued the district after their child fell from play equipment in her classroom. The court held that the district was not required to transfer her to a new room based on a special education evaluation indicating that she required speech/language services. **The classroom teacher had exercised her discretion and judgment in creating classroom safety rules.** State law conferred immunity on political subdivisions and school officials for their discretionary acts. *Nagel v. Green Bay Area Public School Dist.,* 293 Wis.2d 362, 715 N.W.2d 240 (Table) (Wis. Ct. App. 2006).

◆   A 10-year-old Georgia student's teacher instructed her to get paper from heavy, eight-foot-high rolls standing upright in a storage garage. The student was killed when the roll fell on her as she tried to get paper from it. Her parents sued the district, its board and the teacher for wrongful death and intentional misconduct. A state trial court awarded pretrial judgment against the parents, finding the teacher and board were entitled to immunity. On appeal, the Georgia Court of Appeals stated that **the Georgia Supreme Court has previously held that supervising and disciplining students involves discretionary acts.** The teacher was found to be exercising her discretionary authority to monitor, control and supervise students when she sent fourth-graders to the garage. Because she was entitled to immunity, she could be liable only if her actions were motivated by actual malice or intent to cause injury. As there was no evidence of malice or intentional conduct, the court affirmed the judgment. *Aliffi v. Liberty County School Dist.,* 578 S.E.2d 146 (Ga. Ct. App. 2003).

## B.  Off School Grounds

### 1.  Duty of Care

*Courts have disagreed about the duty of a school to supervise students after they are dismissed from school. The age of the student plays a role in whether school liability exists. In a case involving an elementary student, New Jersey's Supreme Court held that "dismissal is part of the school day," creating a legal duty for schools to supervise dismissal. On the other hand, a Florida court recently found no duty to supervise high school students from unforeseen off-campus hazards. Courts in Louisiana and California have imposed a duty to supervise student safety at dismissal. And New York's highest court held that if a student is injured off school grounds, a school district could not be held liable because the district's duty of care only extended to its own boundaries.*

◆   The New York Court of Appeals held that a school district was not liable for injuries suffered by a tenth-grader who was struck by a vehicle while crossing a street off school property. The district was not responsible for any hazardous condition off school grounds where the student was injured. A school's duty to its students "is co-extensive with the school's physical custody and control over them ..., and **when a student is injured off school premises the school district cannot be held liable for the breach of a duty that generally extends only to the boundaries of the school property.**" The accident in this case occurred after school and off school property, and the municipality that owned the road was responsible for warning of any hazards on it. *Hess v. West Seneca Cent. School Dist.*, 15 N.Y.3d 813 (N.Y. 2010).

◆   Two female students in Idaho reported that two males were planning a Columbine-style attack at school. The principal confronted one of the male students, who said he was "going to have a school shooting" on a specified date. The two male students were warned about their threatening conduct, and they agreed not to make further statements. But one month later, the students were accused of threatening to shoot guns at a school dance. Two years after these incidents, one of the male students wrote threatening notes that were viewed by his locker partner. Although the threats were brought to the attention of the school resource officer and a vice principal, they were "dismissed." The same month as the notes were found, the student and a male accomplice murdered a female student at the house of her friend. When her parents sued the school district in a state trial court, it was found that the district owed no duty to protect the student off school grounds and after school hours. On appeal, the Supreme Court of Idaho affirmed the judgment. Nothing in the record convinced the court that the district knew that one of the male students would commit a murder based on information received about him some 30 months earlier. **As the murder was not foreseeable, the district had no duty to prevent it.** *Stoddart v. Pocatello School Dist. #25*, 239 P.3d 784 (Idaho 2010).

◆   A six-year-old California student took the bus irregularly, due to his parents' schedules. About a month after starting school, he got on his bus, but soon told the driver that he saw his father's car. The driver grabbed him by the arm and asked if he was sure, and he said he was. When the student left the bus, he could not find his father and began walking with other students. He was later struck by a car as he tried to cross a busy street. The family sued the school district, bus driver and car driver for personal injuries. A state superior court held for the district under the California Education Code, which provided immunity for accidents occurring off campus and after school hours.

The case reached the Court of Appeal of California, which recited the general rule in the state that **"a school district owes a duty of care to its students because a special relationship exists between the students and the district."** Once a district agreed to provide transportation for its students, it had a legal duty to exercise reasonable care. It rejected the district's claim that "transportation" occurred only while a bus was in motion. In this case, the district had undertaken a duty of care to its students for some time after dismissal. During the loading process, students were still on school premises, and under school supervision. As a result, the fact that the injury took place later and off-campus did not decide the case. The lower court should have considered whether there had been a duty of supervision, and whether the duty was breached. Once the child was on the bus, the district had a duty to exercise ordinary care over him. The case was returned to the superior court to consider questions such as the foreseeability of harm and whether the bus driver should have done more to help the student. *Eric M. v. Cajon Valley Union School Dist.*, 174 Cal.App.4th 285, 95 Cal.Rptr.3d 428 (Cal. Ct. App. 2009).

◆ Washington high school seniors bought six kegs of beer for an off-campus party at a remote location without adult supervision. At the party, three seniors confronted the only junior class member who attended. One of the seniors hit him on the forehead with a beer mug. Although the wound appeared minor, the junior collapsed and fell into a coma four months later. After surviving four years in a persistent vegetative state, the junior died. His estate sued the seniors who had bought the beer, the students who confronted him at the party, and the beer distributor that made the beer kegs available. The Court of Appeals of Washington held that **the non-assailant seniors could not be held liable for the attack on the junior without evidence that they knew the assailants had violent tendencies**. A state law forbidding the purchase of alcohol by minors did not give rise to a duty of care because the law was not intended to protect against assaults. *Cameron v. Murray*, 214 P.3d 150 (Wash. Ct. App. 2009).

◆ A nine-year-old New Jersey student was left quadriplegic after being struck by a car several blocks from school and about two hours after school dismissal. His family sued the car driver, the school principal and the board of education. They asserted that the district and principal breached their duty of reasonable supervision during dismissal. The complaint claimed the parents did not have advance notice on the day of the accident that it was an early-dismissal day. The family settled its claims against the car driver. But a state trial court then held that the board's duty did not apply to an accident that occurred two hours after dismissal and several blocks from school. A state appellate division court reversed the judgment, holding that school boards have a duty of reasonable care to supervise children at dismissal. The case was returned to the trial court.

The school district appealed to the Supreme Court of New Jersey, which explained that dangers to students continued at dismissal time because they were susceptible to numerous risks. It was foreseeable that young students leaving school grounds without parental supervision were vulnerable. A school's duty to exercise reasonable care for students was integral to the state's public education system. **"Dismissal is part of the school day." The school's duty of supervision did not disappear when the school bell rang.** The duty required school districts to create a reasonable dismissal supervision policy, provide notice to parents, and to comply with the policy and with parental requests concerning the dismissal of students from school. The court affirmed the decision of the appellate division court, and returned the case to the trial court for further proceedings. *Jerkins v. Anderson*, 191 N.J. 285, 922 A.2d 1279 (N.J. 2007).

◆ A New York kindergartner with asthma attended an early childhood center. His mother gave the school nurse asthma medication, an inhaler, and an authorization and directive from his pediatrician. A teacher and an aide noticed he was coughing and decided he should see the nurse. The aide walked him to the office, where the nurse gave him his medication. The student was reported as "breathing, alert and in no distress." He returned to class, and his mother was notified. When the mother arrived at school one hour later, the student was still able to breathe, walk and talk. She planned to take him to his pediatrician, but he became hot and ill in the car and she went home instead. The mother called 911, and emergency personnel treated the student without success. He was pronounced dead at a hospital emergency room. The mother sued the school district. A New York appellate division court noted that the student had been released to his mother's custody prior to his death. **Since she had removed him from the geographic boundaries of the district and the control of district staff, no legal duty existed that would create district liability.** *Williams v. Hempstead School Dist.*, 46 A.D.3d 550 (N.Y. App. Div. 2007).

◆   A Florida student died in an automobile crash after skipping class with several other eleventh-graders who simply walked to their cars and left school grounds. The car in which she was riding was driven at over 70 miles per hour. This occurred on wet roads in a residential area with a 35-mile-an-hour speed limit. The car crashed into a tree, killing the student. The student's estate sued the driver of the vehicle and the school board for negligence. A state trial court rejected the estate's argument that the board had a duty to prevent students from leaving campus, and that there was no duty to lessen the risk of injury off campus by preventing students from leaving campus. The estate appealed, claiming that lax enforcement of truancy rules made the death foreseeable.

A Florida District Court of Appeal found that none of the students had accumulated 15 unexcused absences, so they were not "habitually truant." **The court held that even if they were deemed habitually truant, there was no duty of the school board to protect them from unforeseen off-campus hazards.** The primary purpose of Florida truancy laws was to promote academic success, not to enhance student safety. School attendance rules did not impose a legal duty of care on the district to protect students from off-campus traffic injuries. The court found that "the decision whether to have an open campus, a 'fortress,' or something in-between, is a policy decision that should be left to school professionals and not second-guessed by civil juries." The court affirmed the judgment for the school board. *Kazanjian v. School Board of Palm Beach County,* 967 So.2d 259 (Fla. Dist. Ct. App. 2007).

◆   Two emotionally disturbed North Carolina students rode a public school bus to a program for violent students. A bus attendant overheard them speak about committing robbery and murder with a gun one of them had at home. The attendant reported their conversation to the bus driver, but neither employee informed school officials, the school board or the police department. A week later, the students and two other youths stopped cars at an intersection between 7:00 p.m. and 8:15 p.m. A student shot a driver in the head and severely injured her. The victim sued city and county education officials for personal injuries. A state trial court held for the board, and the victim appealed. The Supreme Court of North Carolina said school personnel who overheard students planning criminal conduct had a moral and civic obligation to report it. But this did not create a legal duty which afforded the victim relief. **No legal duty exists unless** an injury **"was foreseeable and avoidable through due care."** The board could not be held liable for actions by students without a "special relationship" with them. The victim was attempting to hold the board liable for the actions of students who were outside its control at 8:15 p.m. and not on school property. *Stein v. Asheville City Board of Educ.*, 626 S.E.2d 263 (N.C. 2005).

## 2.  Governmental Immunity

*In the next case, the Supreme Court of Alabama restated a general rule that an agent of the state is immune from civil liability for conduct based on the formulation of plans, policies or designs.*

◆   An Alabama sixth-grade student told her teacher she was sick and wanted to go home. The teacher instructed her to telephone her mother and she went to the office to do so. Later, an 18-year-old former student arrived at the office and identified himself as the student's brother. An instructional assistant who had been assigned to check students in and out from school allowed the student to leave with the former student. Staff members realized she had left school under false pretenses, and left school to search for her. After the former student sexually assaulted the student in a car, the student's family sued the school board, principal, instructional assistant, and secretary for negligence. A state trial court held the school board and the secretary were entitled to immunity.

But the court denied state-agent immunity to the teaching assistant and the principal. On appeal, **the Supreme Court of Alabama stated the general rule that an agent of the state is immune from civil liability for conduct based on the formulation of plans, policies or designs**. State agents are immune for claims based on the exercise of judgment in the discharge of duties imposed by statute, rule or regulation when educating students. The school's standard checkout procedure allowed students to leave with an older sibling, and the incident occurred while the principal and assistant were "discharging their official duties." The student did not show they acted "willfully, maliciously, fraudulently, in bad faith, or beyond their authority." The trial court should not have denied pretrial judgment to the principal and the teaching assistant. *In re T.W. v. Russell County Board of Educ.*, 965 So.2d 780 (Ala. 2007).

◆   The Court of Appeal of Florida held that a school board had sovereign immunity in a negligence lawsuit filed by a parent whose 13-year-old son was killed while walking home from school. The death occurred at an intersection with no crossing guard. The student was the fourth child to die in transit to or from the school in a seven-year period. The mother asserted that the decision to operate the school from 9:00 a.m. to 4:00 p.m. negligently exposed students to rush-hour traffic. **The court found the scheduling of school hours was a planning-level decision that deserved immunity.** The board did not create a hidden or dangerous condition for which there was no proper warning. Traffic hazards at the site were readily apparent, and court held the school board had no authority over the regulation of traffic. *Orlando v. Broward County, Florida*, 920 So.2d 54 (Fla. Dist. Ct. App. 2005).

## V.  LIABILITY FOR INTENTIONAL CONDUCT

*"Willful or wanton misconduct" refers to intentional conduct. A finding of intentional. willful or wanton misconduct typically defeats immunity. Courts have found school districts liable for intentional acts of third parties on or near school grounds. In such cases, a court must find the district should have foreseen the potential misconduct. For intentional misconduct cases involving coaches, please see Chapter Thirteen, Section III.D. For corporal punishment cases, see Chapter One, Section VI. Additional cases involving sexual harassment and abuse appear in Section III.D. of Chapter Eight, and in Chapter One, Section I.*

### A.  Employee Misconduct

#### 1.  Types of Misconduct

◆   A Georgia teacher was accused of shoving a disabled student's head into a trash can and then pulling him out by his legs. The principal investigated and, after finding that the teacher and student had often engaged in horseplay prior to the trash can incident, determined it was only horseplay. He found no evidence that the teacher acted maliciously. Although the teacher was counseled to end this type of conduct with students, the parents decided to sue. A federal court awarded pretrial judgment to the school district and officials, finding they were all entitled to qualified immunity. The Eleventh Circuit affirmed the judgment, finding the trash can incident did not violate the student's substantive due process rights. **Only intentional actions by officials that shock the conscience may be found to violate the Constitution.** As the lower court had found, the student did not suffer physical injury and there was no evidence that the teacher acted with malice or intent to harm him. Not all injuries to a student by a teacher amounted to corporal punishment. *Mahone v. Ben Hill County School System*, 377 Fed.Appx. 913 (11th Cir. 2010).

◆   A Louisiana high school teacher twice assaulted a student who had volunteered to work with special education students. Others complained about him and criminal charges were filed. He pleaded guilty to simple battery, was fined small amounts and served 30 days in jail. After settling claims against the teacher in a state court civil action, the student pursued the school board for further damages. A jury found the board should pay her $45,000, and the board appealed to the Court of Appeal of Louisiana. There, the board claimed it could not be held liable because the teacher was "merely dealing with a student-at-large who was not one of his students" at the time. The court held **the teacher was engaged in business so closely related to his teaching duties that the board was liable for his conduct**. The state supreme court has held employers should be held liable for employee misconduct if a wrongful act was rooted in employment, reasonably incidental to employment duties, occurred on the employer's premises and occurred during work hours. As the teacher's conduct met this test, and the damages were not excessive, the judgment was affirmed. *T.S. v. Rapides Parish School Board*, 11 So.3d 628 (La. Ct. App. 2009).

◆   A Michigan elementary school student claimed that classmates assaulted him at school twice within a few days. He said that he reported both incidents to the principal's secretary, who failed to notify the principal. The student's parent sued the school district and principal for negligence and gross negligence in a state trial court, which held for the school district. The parent appealed to the Court of Appeals of Michigan. The court explained that the operation of a school or a school system constitutes a governmental function. For this reason, the district had immunity from tort liability for any negligence or gross negligence. Accordingly, the lower court had correctly dismissed the tort action.

Government employees also enjoy immunity from tort liability if the injury is caused while they act in the course of their employment, or in the reasonable belief they are acting within the scope of their employment. On the other hand, a governmental employee is not immune from tort liability if an injury is caused by the employee's gross negligence. **"Gross negligence" is conduct so reckless that it demonstrates a substantial lack of concern for whether an injury results. It is an almost willful disregard for safety or precautions.** The student could not show gross negligence by the district or employees. He did not report either incident to his teacher. While the student claimed he reported the first incident to the principal's secretary, this did not show that she relayed the message to the principal. As the student failed to present evidence that the principal knew or should have known of the first fight, the court found no reasonable person could find her negligent, much less grossly negligent, for failure to investigate. The judgment was affirmed. *Reynolds v. Detroit Public Schools*, No. 276369, 2008 WL 2389492 (Mich. Ct. App. 6/12/08).

◆   The U.S. Court of Appeals, Fifth Circuit, affirmed a damage award for two Mississippi students who claimed a school bus driver arbitrarily excluded them from their bus based on their odor. A federal magistrate judge found the driver drove off while one student had his hand trapped in the bus door. On another occasion, the driver directly sprayed a student with deodorizer. The magistrate judge found the driver had arbitrarily suspended the children from their bus privileges. The Fifth Circuit agreed, finding that **"the bus driver acted preemptively and offensively rather than to control or discipline the children." This satisfied state Tort Claims Act standards.** As there was evidence of damages, the court affirmed the judgment for the students. *Turner v. North Panola School Dist.*, 299 Fed.Appx. 330 (5th Cir. 2008).

◆   In 2001, a California parent's 15-year-old daughter attended the same high school that the parent had attended about 25 years earlier. The daughter began to encounter an English teacher who had taught at the high school when her parent attended. The parent became upset, claiming that when she was 15 years old, the English teacher engaged her in sexual conduct both on and off school grounds for over two years. The parent did not notify the school district of the contact until 2003. A licensed mental health practitioner interviewed the parent and concluded that she still suffered from psychological injury from the sexual abuse. She sued the school district and the English teacher. The Court of Appeal of California found that a party is required to present a timely written claim for damages before suing a public entity. **The deadline for filing a lawsuit against**

**a public entity is the statute of limitations for presenting claims against an entity such as a school district.** The parent was required to make a claim against the district by May 1980, six months after the last molestation. As the parent did not make a timely claim, the case was barred. *Shirk v. Vista Unified School Dist.*, 42 Cal.4th 201, 54 Cal.Rptr.3d 210, 164 P.3d 630 (Cal. 2007).

◆   A Missouri school district assigned a substitute to an elementary school classroom. He grabbed a student by the neck and lifted him off the ground. The teacher later pleaded guilty in state criminal court proceedings to third degree criminal assault and endangering the welfare of a child. The family accepted $20,000 in settlement of negligence claims against the district and board members, and agreed to settle claims against the teacher for $100,000. The agreement provided that any judgment would be sought from the district's insurer. The district had liability coverage through the Missouri United School Insurance Council (MUSIC), a pool of self-insuring school districts. After MUSIC declined to pay the judgment, the family sued for coverage. A state trial court awarded pretrial judgment to MUSIC. The case reached the Supreme Court of Missouri, which affirmed the judgment. It held that **the assault was an intentional act, and not a covered "occurrence" under the policy.** *Todd v. Missouri United School Insurance Council*, No. 223 S.W.3d 156 (Mo. 2007).

◆   An Arkansas student attended a band competition in Atlanta with his school band. He became ill and missed the entire competition while remaining in his hotel room. Shortly after the student returned home, his mother took him to a medical center. He suffered a cardiac arrest and died of a diabetic condition the next day. His mother sued the school district and officials for negligence and deliberate indifference to her son's medical needs. A federal court dismissed her constitutional claims, and the case went before the U.S. Court of Appeals, Eighth Circuit. It held the Due Process Clause does not confer affirmative rights to government aid. States assume a constitutional duty to protect safety only when they have restrained an individual's liberty through incarceration, institutionalization or a restraint that renders the individual incapable of self care. That did not happen here. **School officials have no duty to care for students who participate in voluntary school-related activities such as school band trips.** *Lee v. Pine Bluff School Dist.*, 472 F.3d 1026 (8th Cir. 2007).

## 2.  Governmental Immunity

◆   An Alabama fifth-grader repeatedly disrupted his class. An education board policy required the presence of a witness whenever corporal punishment was administered. When the student avoided his teacher's attempts to hit his palms with two taped-together rulers, she retrieved a paddle and hit him with it. She claimed this was the end of the incident. But the student claimed she kept hitting him, causing injury. He enrolled in another school and then sued the school board and teacher for negligence. A state court denied claims by both the education board and the teacher for judgment based on absolute immunity. On appeal, the Supreme Court of Alabama held the board had been wrongly denied immunity. It reversed that part of the judgment. But the board's policy required the presence of a witness whenever corporal punishment was administered. **The teacher's rationale for deviating from the policy was that she could not leave her other students alone to find a witness.** While this was supported by her statement and those of her supervisors, further inquiry by the trial court was necessary. *Ex Parte Monroe County Board of Educ.*, 48 So.3d 621 (Ala. 2010).

◆  A disabled Ohio student rode a bus with three middle school boys with special needs. An aide on the afternoon route saw a male student with his hand up the student's dress. They were immediately separated. When questioned, the female student said the male student had sexually molested her each day on the afternoon route. The parents claimed that the assaulting student had serious behavior problems and exhibited physical and verbal aggression. They sued the school board and officials in the state court system, asserting negligence and related claims. A trial court denied the board's motion for state law immunity.

The case reached the Supreme Court of Ohio, which noted that state law barred immunity for injuries arising from the "operation of any motor vehicle," but did not define the term "operation." According to the family, the term meant all the essential functions that a driver is trained or required to do by law, not just driving. A dictionary definition of "operate" is to "control or direct the functioning of." This suggested to the court that the term is limited to driving the vehicle itself. **The court held the exception to immunity for negligent operation of a motor vehicle applied only to negligence in driving the vehicle.** It held for the school board. *Doe v. Marlington Local School Dist. Board of Educ.*, 122 Ohio St.3d 124, 907 N.E.2d 706 (Ohio 2009).

◆  A Tennessee alternative school student repeated grade nine at another school in the same system. His disciplinary record was not forwarded from the alternative school. At his new school, the student began harassing a female student, and his name-calling and "unpleasant noises quickly escalated." An assistant principal received repeated reports from the female, her parents and others about the male student, and told the male student to avoid contact with the female. But he later knocked her unconscious in a school hallway and broke her jaw. She was hospitalized and underwent surgery. Her father sued the male student, his mother, the assistant principal and the school board in a Tennessee court. The assistant principal was dismissed from the case, but the court found the assault foreseeable and the school board negligent for failing to protect the female student. She received $75,000 for emotional distress, pain and suffering, and her parents won over $10,000 for medical costs. The state court of appeals rejected the board's claim to immunity under the doctrine of public duty. **School systems, teachers and administrators have a duty of reasonable care to supervise and protect students.** The board had a duty to protect students from foreseeable intentional acts of third parties such as the male student. As a result, the judgment was affirmed. *Dean v. Weakley County Board of Educ.*, No. W2007-00159-COA-R3-CV, 2008 WL 948882 (Tenn. Ct. App. 4/9/08).

◆  An Indiana high school student was shot to death before school started, in an area where students congregated prior to classes. The shooter was a former student with aggressive behavior and homicidal ideation. He was convicted of murder. At the time of the shooting, the school's security officers were inside the building, attending to other duties. The student's parents sued the school corporation for negligence. A state court held a jury trial and allowed evidence of several prior acts of violence involving district schools, including a drive-by shooting. After the trial, a jury awarded a verdict to the parents. On appeal, the Court of Appeals of Indiana agreed with the school corporation's argument that the prior incidents were not similar enough to the shooting to be admitted as evidence of school negligence. **Evidence of a dangerous condition and notice about the condition must be similar to the one at issue in order to be admissible.** But the court rejected the school corporation's claim to immunity under the state tort claims act. Officials did not show they made any policy decision regarding the placement of security staff. A new trial would be held. *Gary Community School Corp. v. Boyd*, 890 N.E.2d 794 (Ind. Ct. App. 2008).

◆  The parents of a 14-year-old South Carolina student learned a substitute had sexual relations with their child. The substitute was convicted of criminal sexual conduct with a minor. The parents sued the school district in a separate action, and a state court held for the district. On appeal, the Supreme Court of South Carolina affirmed the judgment on a claim for infliction of emotional distress. But it agreed with the parents that their claim for negligent supervision had been wrongly dismissed. The state Tort Claims Act precluded government liability for losses resulting from any responsibility or duty such as the supervision, protection, control, confinement, or custody of a student, except where the responsibility or duty was exercised in a "grossly negligent manner." Here, **the parents had alleged gross negligence by the district**. As a result, that claim had been improperly dismissed. The case had to be reconsidered. *Doe v. Greenville County School Dist.*, 375 S.C. 63, 651 S.E.2d 305 (S.C. 2007).

## B.  Student Misconduct

### 1.  Types of Misconduct

*In* Dailey v. Los Angeles Unified School Dist., *2 Cal.3d 741, 87 Cal.Rptr. 376 (1970), the Supreme Court of California held school authorities are to "supervise at all times the conduct of the children on school grounds and to enforce those rules and regulations necessary to their protection." The standard of care for supervising students is that which a "person of ordinary prudence" would exercise when performing comparable duties.*

◆  A California student sued his school district for injuries caused by another student who beat him with a baseball bat off school grounds after school hours. According to the student, the district allowed his assailant to carry a bat around school during school hours, in view of teachers and administrators. He claimed the assailant threatened others with violence and had a history of violence and discipline at school. The district claimed discretionary immunity and argued it could not be held liable for an injury taking place off school grounds after school hours. The Court of Appeal of California agreed, finding **neither school districts nor their employees are liable for the conduct or safety of any**

**student when not on school property, unless there is a specific undertaking by a school district** or a sponsored activity, which was not the case here. *Cortinez v. South Pasadena Unified School Dist.*, No. 2352046, 2010 WL 2352046 (Cal. Ct. App. 6/14/10).

◆    A 185-pound Louisiana student with autism began to hit himself on the head. His teacher was pushed into a wall while trying to keep a mat under him to prevent injury. During the 45-50 minute struggle, the teacher was "twisting and sliding the entire time" but was not hit, knocked down or bitten by the student. She reported injuries to her hand, knee and buttocks. Claiming entitlement to "assault pay" under a state law provision, the teacher sued the school board. A state trial court granted pretrial judgment to the board, but the Court of Appeal of Louisiana held that a trial was required. **"Assault pay" is available to teachers injured or disabled while acting in an official capacity as a result of an assault or battery.** Under the assault pay provision, injured or disabled teachers receive sick pay with no reduction in pay or accrued sick leave days while disabled as the result of the assault or battery. A separate provision covers teachers who are injured as a result of "physical contact" while assisting students. Here, the facts would determine if the teacher's injuries resulted from an "assault" by the student. *Miller v. St. Tammany Parish School Board*, Nos. 2008 CA 2582-2583, 2009 WL 3135208 (La. Ct. App. 9/11/09).

◆    A California school district operated a free after-school program on a school playground. Between 200 and 300 children participated, with two adults typically present to supervise them. One day, only one supervisor was present to watch over 113 participants. A second-grade girl was led by an older girl to an unlocked shed on campus that was off-limits to program participants. The older girl forced a boy to have sexual contact with the second-grader. Both the boy and the second-grader later said the girl held them against their wills and threatened to hit them. The second-grader's mother sued the school district for negligent supervision, claiming the district and employees knew for some time that some of the children had been kissing and engaging in other inappropriate activity. The case reached the state court of appeal, which noted that the after-school program was voluntary. A question remained regarding whether the absence of a supervisor from her post contributed to the injury. As a result, the case required further fact-finding. **If the supervisor allowed dangerous conduct to go on, liability could be imposed.** *J.H. v. Los Angeles Unified School Dist.*, 183 Cal.App.4th 123, 107 Cal.Rptr.3d 182 (Cal. Ct. App. 2010).

◆    A 14-year-old California student with multiple disabilities functioned in her public school on a "borderline basis." During a lunch period, a male special needs student led her from the cafeteria to a hidden alcove under a stairway and sexually assaulted her. A parent observed the students from a sidewalk and reported them to the school office. In the resulting negligence action against the district, a state court noted that the alcove was hidden from anyone on campus but visible from the sidewalk. The alcove was marked as off-limits by a yellow chain. While there had been no reported sexual assaults or other illicit activity in the alcove during school hours, it was considered a "problem area." A "tardy sweep" of the campus should have been conducted six minutes after every lunch period. But the students were found about 14 minutes after the final check of the alcove. The court held for the school district, and the student appealed.

The Court of Appeal of California held that **school officials had a special relationship to special needs students and had to adequately supervise them due to the foreseeability of harm**. School officials were on notice that the alcove was a problem area. As the district had an affirmative duty to protect the student based on a "special relationship" with her, it could be held liable. It also had potential liability for maintaining a dangerous condition of public property, since a yellow chain would not keep out a child who could not appreciate danger. *Jennifer C. v. Los Angeles Unified School Dist.*, 168 Cal.App.4th 1320, 86 Cal.Rptr.3d 274 (Cal. Ct. App. 2008).

◆   A Washington school district declared a school safe for a student who had been named on a "2 kill list" written by two others. The student's parents wanted one of the list writers suspended for the rest of the school year, and they sued the school district for negligence. A trial court held for the school district, and the parents appealed to the Court of Appeals of Washington. The court explained that school districts must protect students from reasonably anticipated dangers. **A duty to use reasonable care only extends to risks of harm that are foreseeable.** The court rejected the parents' claim that the list writer had to be expelled for the rest of the school year. The district had to consider his educational needs. The district acted within its authority by first expelling the writer on an emergency basis, then suspending him, and ultimately reducing the suspension on the basis of a psychiatrist's report. **The district was not obligated to impose discipline to accommodate the student's family.** It acted reasonably and according to the law and its own policies by relying on the psychiatrist's judgment. The judgment was affirmed. *Jachetta v. Warden Joint Consolidated School Dist.*, 142 Wash.App. 918, 176 P.3d 545 (Wash. Ct. App. 2008).

◆   Montana high school boys worked as towel boys and secretly watched and videotaped female students undressing in the school locker room over a period of almost two years. They showed the tapes to classmates during school hours. A teacher and the superintendent heard reports of possible videotaping, but took limited action. After a janitor discovered the boys' activity, several criminal and civil actions were filed. In one case, the female students sued the school district for privacy rights violations and interference with family relationships. A federal court held against the female students. To impose municipal liability, there must be a policy of inaction that is more than just negligence. The hiring of towel boys to serve in locker rooms for females was not a "state-created danger." **The failure to be more attentive or to supervise the boys may have been negligent, but it did not create any constitutional liability.** On appeal, the U.S. Court of Appeals, Ninth Circuit, cited a long-standing rule of federal law: a state's failure to protect persons from private violence does not create a constitutional injury. The district and officials were not deliberately indifferent to student rights and were not the "moving force" behind any violation of rights. *Harry A. v. Duncan*, 234 Fed.Appx. 463 (9th Cir. 2007).

◆   A Michigan teacher lined up most of her students in a hallway and led them to a computer class. She left five students in the classroom because they had not completed their work. One of the students who remained took a pistol out of his desk, put bullets into it, then shot and killed a classmate. The teacher was in the hallway at the time. The classmate's parent claimed the student was involved in several behavior incidents in the months before the shooting, including beating up other students and stabbing another student with a pencil. The parent sued the teacher, principal and school district in a federal district court for a variety of civil rights violations. The court held for the district and school employees, and the parent appealed. The U.S. Court of Appeals, Sixth Circuit, held **the teacher's act of leaving five students unsupervised in the classroom was not an "affirmative act" creating a specific risk to the classmate**. She would have been in about the same degree of danger had the teacher remained. The danger was the student's possession of the gun, not the teacher's positioning. The district was not liable for a civil rights violation because there was no evidence of a district policy or custom of depriving persons of constitutional rights. *McQueen v. Beecher Community Schools*, 433 F.3d 460 (6th Cir. 2006).

◆   A Tennessee student had a history of aggressive behavior and fighting in classes, but was not identified as having a disability. Soon after an assessment team evaluated him, he struck his teacher. The principal suspended him for 10 days and prepared to expel him. She then arranged an individualized education program (IEP) team meeting. The IEP team found the student ineligible for special education. But it found he had a "suspected disability" and that his case should be reopened. The principal decided to return the student to his classroom with a teacher's aide. On his first day back, he assaulted his teacher and the aide.

The teacher sued the school board in a state court. It granted the board immunity, and appeal went to the state court of appeals. According to the court, a school official's decision deserved immunity if it was based on a discretionary function. In this case, the principal was not bound by state and local zero-tolerance policies. She had to balance these mandates against conflicting IDEA requirements. While the student had not yet been declared eligible for special education, the IEP team indicated that further evaluation was warranted. **A federal "stay-put" rule did not allow the principal to expel the student.** Her testimony showed she exercised discretion in balancing competing policies. The judgment was affirmed. *Babb v. Hamilton County Board of Educ.*, No. E2004-00782-COA-R3-CV, 2004 WL 2094538 (Tenn. Ct. App. 2004).

### 2.  Bullying

*In* Mirand v. City of New York, *84 N.Y. 44, 637 N.E.2d 263 (1994), New York's highest court held **a school is liable for student-on-student violence only if it had "specific, prior knowledge of the danger that caused the injury." A student's acts must have been foreseeable by the district to impose liability.***

◆   An Arizona parent called school administrators to report that a classmate was threatening her seventh-grade daughter. But the bullying and threats by the classmate escalated. A teacher called the mother to report rumors that the classmate was planning to attack the daughter. That afternoon, the classmate assaulted the daughter at school. Her family sued the school district and school and law enforcement officers in a federal court for civil rights violations. One of the claims alleged a deprivation of federal due process rights, while others asserted state law negligence and failure to train employees under Arizona's Anti-Bullying law. The court noted that under *DeShaney v. Winnebago County Dep't of Social Services*, 489 U.S. 189 (1989), the Fourteenth Amendment does not generally require the government to prevent private citizens from harming each other. **No special relationship existed in this case that imposed an affirmative duty on school officials to protect the daughter from the classmate.** As Arizona courts had yet to interpret the anti-bullying statute, that claim was sent to a state court. *O'Dell v. Casa Grande Elementary School Dist. No. 4*, No. CV-08-0240-PHX-GMS, 2008 WL 5215329 (D. Ariz. 12/12/08).

◆   An Ohio student said that he was assaulted by a classmate he described as a "known bully." The classmate had been suspended before for fighting, but the district superintendent overturned the discipline after determining he did not instigate the fight. He was evaluated for a disability, but that was interrupted by a brief transfer to another school district. When he returned, he had disciplinary problems based on minor misconduct such as improper language and horseplay. The classmate attacked the student after gym class without provocation. The student was seriously injured, and his parents sued the school district in a state court for negligent supervision. The court granted the district immunity, and the parents appealed. The state court of appeals found earlier incidents involving the classmate were not unprovoked attacks. Staff members testified that he was not viewed as a bully or a disciplinary problem. While the classmate was disruptive at times, earlier incidents only showed he might be involved in horseplay or a provoked fight. **The classmate's prior disciplinary incidents did not make it foreseeable that he would commit an unprovoked criminal assault on the student.** The fact that he had been incarcerated was not enough to put the school on notice that he might attack the student. The court affirmed the judgment for the district. *Aratari v. Leetonia Exempt Village School Dist.*, No. 06 CO 11, 2007 -Ohio- 1567, 2007 WL 969402 (Ohio Ct. App. 3/26/07).

◆   Connecticut students persistently harassed and bullied a ninth-grade student with attention deficit hyperactivity disorder (ADHD) who was under five feet tall and weighed only 75 pounds. He claimed school employees knew of the harassment and bullying, but did nothing about it. He withdrew from school, and his family sued the school board in a federal court. They asserted claims under the IDEA, conspiracy to deprive the student of his due process and equal protection rights, and negligence. The court dismissed the case, and the family appealed. The Second Circuit held that the Due Process Clause of the Fourteenth Amendment creates no affirmative right to government protection. **Failure of school employees to respond to harassment and bullying conduct, while "highly unfortunate," did not create constitutional liability.** The lower court also properly dismissed the student's equal protection claim. He did not allege that school employees treated him differently because of his size or his ADHD. But the Second Circuit has recognized monetary claims based on IDEA violations under 42 U.S.C. § 1983, and the lower court would have to reconsider that claim. State law negligence claims were also reinstated. *Smith v. Guilford Board of Educ.*, 226 Fed.Appx. 58 (2d Cir. 2007).

◆   An Illinois student was reluctant to go to school after being bullied, shoved and kicked. His mother complained to the principal but did not identify the bullies. She later called a school social worker to obtain counseling for her son. She told the social worker the names of the bullies and said that her son did not wish them to be revealed. The social worker agreed not to disclose their names but soon provided them to the principal. The principal then met with the bullies and revealed the student's name before assigning them to detention. The student claimed to suffer emotional distress from the disclosure of his name to the bullies. He transferred schools and filed a state court privacy rights violation action against the principal, social worker, school board and the rural special education cooperative that employed the social worker. The Appellate Court of Illinois held the social worker was protected by state law, which **permits a good-faith disclosure to protect a person against a clear, imminent risk of serious injury**. He had discretion to decide whether disclosing confidential information was necessary to protect the student and relayed this information to the principal in the belief there was a risk of further harm. And the principal's handling of bullying fell within the definition of "discretionary" action. *Albers v. Breen*, 346 Ill.App.3d 799, 806 N.E.2d 667 (Ill. App. Ct. 2004).

## 3.  Governmental Immunity

◆   Parents of an Ohio student with Down syndrome claimed he was sexually assaulted at school by a school district employee. Their state court complaint said the assault occurred under circumstances that showed recklessness and "an extreme lack of teacher oversight" in a classroom. The parents claimed the school knew one of the attackers had a history of psychological problems and that dangerous students were recklessly placed in the classroom. Also, regular and substitute teachers were reckless in monitoring class activities. The Court of Appeals of Ohio noted that school employees were accused of failing to monitor student behavior. This activity was within the scope of their official job duties. **An assault under circumstances of recklessness and "an extreme lack of teacher oversight" was sufficient to establish potential liability.** *E.F. v. Oberlin City School Dist.*, No. 09CA009640, 2010 WL 1227703 (Ohio Ct. App. 3/31/10).

◆   A Nebraska student claimed that she was sexually assaulted by a classmate at their high school during school hours. She claimed he had a history of physical and/or sexual misconduct toward other students, but that school officials took no steps to restrain him. The family sued the school district for negligence. A court held that the district was immunized from liability by the Nebraska Political Subdivisions Tort Claims Act (PSTCA). The family appealed to the Supreme Court of Nebraska, which explained that the PSTCA eliminated in part the traditional immunity of school districts for the negligent acts of their employees. **Districts are now generally liable for wrongful acts to the same extent as a private individual in a similar case.** The complaint alleged that the district had prior knowledge of specific behavior by the classmate that made violent conduct reasonably foreseeable. The court therefore rejected the district's sovereign immunity defense. *Doe v. Omaha Public School Dist.*, 273 Neb. 79, 724 N.W.2d 447 (Neb. 2007).

◆  A Mississippi cheerleader claimed male students surreptitiously videotaped her changing into a swimsuit at an off-campus pool party. Her mother sued the parents of the male students and obtained a restraining order against the boys. Juvenile court proceedings were also instituted. But the principal found no evidence of harassment. The school was unable to place one of the boys in a separate accelerated biology class, as it was the only such class offered at the time. The mother claimed that the boys and their parents harassed the cheerleader at sporting events. She sued the school system for negligence.

A state trial court found much of her testimony about harassment concerned off-campus conduct. It found the school system took reasonable steps to prevent the harassment and was immune from suit under the Mississippi Tort Claims Act (MTCA). The mother appealed to the Court of Appeals of Mississippi. It held the evidence did not support a finding that the school system breached a duty to the student. Instead, there was "substantial proof that the district met and exceeded any duty owed" the student. **The school system was not responsible for any harassment the student suffered outside of school that was linked to the videotaping.** The school system took reasonable steps to investigate the cafeteria incident, and the teacher monitored the students in class. The school system was immune from any liability under the MTCA. *Beacham v. City of Starkville School System*, 984 So.2d 1073 (Miss. Ct. App. 2008).

## C.  Parent Misconduct

### 1.  Sign-Out Policies

◆  After a Kentucky child was picked up from school by an unauthorized individual, the parent sued the education board and superintendent for negligence. The case reached the Court of Appeals of Kentucky, which stated that immunity applied to the board if it was performing a "governmental function." Here, the board's after-school pick-up and drop-off policy directly furthered the education of students, which was a governmental function. So the board was entitled to immunity. According to the parent, the superintendent did not investigate, take disciplinary action or enact policies to prevent future incidents. But the court held these alleged failures did not strip the superintendent of immunity. **Nothing in the complaint alleged any failure by the superintendent to exercise personal discretion, in good faith and within the scope of his authority.** Both the school board and superintendent were entitled to immunity. *Breathitt County Board of Educ. v. Combs*, No. 2009-CA-000607-MR, 2010 WL 3515747 (Ky. Ct. App. 9/10/10).

◆  A Louisiana father gave his children's middle school documentation that he had their sole "provisional custody." He claimed that they could only be released to him. School policy allowed only the persons listed on a check out form to sign a student out of school. When the children's mother appeared at their school prior to a holiday break, the principal telephoned the father. He stated that under no circumstances could they be released to her, and that he would come to the school. But when the father arrived at school 20 minutes later, the principal had already released the children to the mother. The father sued the school board, principal and insurer. After the case was dismissed, the Court of Appeal of Louisiana held that the father's claims for out-of-pocket expenses could proceed if the school officials owed him a duty to refrain from allowing the mother to check the children out of school. **Schools have a "duty to make the appropriate supervisory decisions concerning a student's departure from campus during regular school hours."** As the father asserted violation of the policy on checking-out students, and claimed the sole authority to do so, the principal had violated the policy and her duty to the children and father. *Peters v. Allen Parish School Board*, 996 So.2d 1230 (La. Ct. App. 2008).

◆   A Tennessee couple began divorce proceedings. The wife obtained a temporary restraining order splitting custody of the children. She told school staff not to release the children to their father, but a staff member told her that would require a court order. The husband signed the children out of school early the next day, giving as a reason: "keeping promise by mother" for the daughter and "pay back" for the son. A staff member read the reasons for early dismissal on the sign-out sheet after the father left, and she told the principal. Police were called. They arrived at the father's house to find it ablaze. The father brandished a knife, and the police shot him to death. The children's bodies were found inside the house. Later, the mother sued the school board for negligence in the state court system. A trial court held for the board, and the mother appealed.

The state court of appeals held that the board was not liable for negligently violating its own sign-out policy. There was no evidence that staff knew of a dispute until the mother called the day before the murders. The trial court had correctly held that a **school has no legal duty to follow the instruction of one parent not to release a child to the other parent without a court order to this effect**. But failure to read the father's reasons for signing out the children was evidence of breach of the duty to exercise ordinary care for safety. The court rejected a claim that the board had no duty to examine the reason for signing out a child. The trial court was to further consider this claim. *Haney v. Bradley County Board of Educ.*, 160 S.W.3d 886 (Tenn. Ct. App. 2004).

◆   An Alaska father had legal custody of his son, and the child's mother had visitation during the Christmas and summer vacations. The father warned the principal that the mother would attempt an abduction. A state court stayed enforcement of the parties' custody order pending investigations in Alaska and Washington. Just before Christmas vacation, the mother arrived at school to pick up the student, accompanied by a police officer. The principal noted that the custody order provided by the father did not specify visitation terms. The mother produced her copy of a previous order granting her visitation rights. The principal called the father, who objected to releasing the student. However, the principal released the student to the mother after a discussion with the police officer. The mother refused to return the student to the father after the Christmas break and he was unable to regain custody for over five months. The father sued the district and principal for interference with his custodial rights.

A state trial court held the principal and district were entitled to qualified immunity. On appeal, the Supreme Court of Alaska held state law established official immunity for "discretionary actions," which require personal deliberation, decision and judgment. The court found **the principal's actions were discretionary, since he acted with deliberation and made a considered judgment** after speaking with the father, verifying the mother's identification, reviewing legal documents and consulting with the police. His actions were not malicious, corrupt or in bad faith and were not subject to any exception to immunity. *Pauley v. Anchorage School Dist.,* 31 P.3d 1284 (Alaska 2001).

## 2. Parental Liability

*Section 316 of the Restatement of Torts (a legal encyclopedia) states there is no legal duty for parents to prevent harm by their children unless "they are in a position to exercise immediate control over their children to prevent some foreseeable harm." Parents have no duty "to take precautionary disciplinary measures or to regulate their children's behavior on an ongoing basis."*

◆   A Minnesota teacher had several confrontations with a parent. Eventually, the teacher obtained a restraining order against the parent and sent a copy of the order to her principal. The school district's counsel determined the order did not prohibit the parent from entering the school. It only prevented her from coming near the teacher's classroom. Within three months, the teacher saw the parent in the school and called 911 to report a violation of the order. She then left school for the rest of the day. The district maintained that the parent had not violated the harassment order and suspended the teacher without pay for three days.

Near the end of the school year, the teacher saw the parent while she was escorting her class to a school bus. She left school for the day and later sued the district and the parent for negligence. A state court held that the district was entitled to official immunity. The teacher won a judgment against the parent for $32,205 for assault, then appealed the decision for the school district to the state court of appeals. The court found the teacher's whistleblowing was not a "report" within the meaning of Minnesota law. Also, a state law requirement for schools to adopt anti-harassment policies did not concern parents; it applied only to students, teachers, school employees and administrators. **The parent's harassment did not violate any contractual obligation of the district.** The judgment for the district was affirmed. *Ellison-Harpole v. Special School Dist. No. 1,* No. A07-1070, 2008 WL 933537 (Minn. Ct. App. 4/8/08).

◆   An Illinois teacher claimed that a student charged at her with scissors and threatened to stab her while screaming obscenities. She was able to disarm the student, who ran out of the room, kicked the door, and slammed it shut on her finger. The teacher sued the school district and the student's mother. She claimed that the parent had prior knowledge of the student's arrest record, mental illness, conduct disorder, character, and history of outbursts in class. A federal court held the parent could not be held liable simply because she was the student's mother. Liability required proof that the parent did not adequately control or supervise her son. To state a claim for negligent supervision, the teacher had to show the parent was aware of specific prior conduct that put her on notice that the assault was likely to occur, and had the opportunity to control the student. **Parents have a duty to exercise "reasonable care" to control their minor children and prevent them from intentionally harming others.** The court found no duty of parents to "take precautionary disciplinary measures or to regulate their children's behavior on an ongoing basis." Since parental liability may result only if parents are in position to exercise immediate control over their children to prevent some foreseeable harm, the court granted the parent's motion to dismiss the teacher's claim against her. *Bland v. Candioto*, No. 3:05-CV-716RM, 2006 WL 2735501 (N.D. Ill. 2006).

◆    Under Louisiana law, parents are legally accountable for the acts of their children. An 11-year-old student with impulsivity and aggression problems pointed a toy gun at a teaching assistant (TA). The TA did not know the gun was a toy and claimed to be emotionally and mentally traumatized. The TA received workers' compensation benefits for psychological injuries. The school board sued the student's mother, claiming that the student was negligent and that the mother was personally liable for his actions. A trial court held for the mother. On appeal, the state court of appeal held **Louisiana parents of minor children can be liable for harm caused by a child's conduct even where a parent is not personally negligent**. But the student could be deemed negligent only if a court found that he violated the applicable standard of care. Here, given the student's maturity level, lack of awareness of risks and his inclination to be impulsive and aggressive, he did not breach the standard. As the student was not negligent, his mother could not be held liable for his actions. *Lafayette Parish School Board v. Cormier*, 901 So. 2d 1197 (La. Ct. App. 2005).

### D.  Suicide

◆    A New Hampshire student with learning disabilities was having problems at his middle school. During his seventh-grade year, a teacher's aide overheard him say he "wanted to blow his brains out." A guidance counselor called the student's mother, and had the student sign a contract for safety, but she took no other action. Several weeks later, the mother claimed that a special education teacher made a false and knowing attempt to impose discipline on her son. The next day, the student was reported to the vice principal and suspended. After the suspension, the student returned home, went to his room and hanged himself.

The mother sued the school administrative unit, a teacher and the guidance counselor for negligence, intentional infliction of emotional distress and wrongful death. A court dismissed the case, and the Supreme Court of New Hampshire affirmed. **It rejected the mother's claim that the counselor and administrative unit had a special duty to prevent the suicide** and that the counselor voluntarily assumed a duty to prevent it. There was no intentional or malicious conduct in this case that might create a duty to prevent the suicide. The administrative unit did not have actual physical custody over the student in such a manner that liability could be imposed. A false statement by the teacher leading to the student's discipline did not satisfy the high standard of "extreme and outrageous conduct" for infliction of emotional distress claims. *Mikell v. School Administrative Unit #33*, 972 A.2d 1050 (N.H. 2009).

◆   A Minnesota student killed himself after returning home from school. The student used a gun and ammunition he found in the house. A suicide note and his mid-term grades were found next to his body. The family sued the school district, claiming the suicide was a foreseeable consequence of bullying and school negligence that the district had a duty to prevent. A court held for the district, as did the state court of appeals. While Minnesota schools have a duty to protect students, they are not liable for sudden, unanticipated misconduct. Here, the suicide was not foreseeable. School staff had no reason to know of the student's continuing problems with bullying, because he did not report them. As there was no foreseeable harm, there was no duty to protect him. The court rejected claims by the estate that the principal should have proactively intervened with the bullies. **There was no evidence that a school bullying policy would have prevented the tragedy.** *Jasperson v. Anoka-Hennepin Independent School Dist. No. 11*, No. A06-1904, 2007 WL 3153456 (Minn. Ct. App. 10/30/07).

◆   A student who formerly attended an Idaho high school committed suicide. His estate tried to hold the Idaho district liable because an essay he wrote for a class showed that he had contemplated suicide in the past. He also wrote that he had "turned his life around" and was currently happy. The state legislature had enacted a law providing that **neither a school district nor a teacher had a duty to warn of a student's suicidal tendencies "absent the teacher's knowledge of direct evidence of such suicidal tendencies."** The law stated that "direct evidence" included "unequivocal and unambiguous oral or written statements by a student" that would not cause doubts in a reasonable teacher. The legislature adopted the new provision specifically to narrow the duty of a teacher to warn of a student's suicidal tendencies. The student's words provided an opposite conclusion to the one urged by his parents. *Carrier v. Lake Pend Oreille School Dist. No. 84*, 142 Idaho 804, 134 P.3d 655 (Idaho 2006).

## E.  Defamation

*As teachers are deemed "public officials," they must show a false statement has been published to a third party, with "actual malice" and damages in order to recover in a defamation case. The actual malice standard is difficult to meet. A person seeking recovery in a defamation suit must prove the publication has caused damage to his or her reputation. Privilege is a defense to certain defamation claims. Persons with a common interest in the subject matter of speech (such as a teacher's performance) may enjoy a privilege to discuss their common interest in protecting students. For defamation cases involving coaches, please see Chapter Thirteen, Section III.B. of this volume.*

◆   Most of the students attending a Minnesota charter school were Somali Muslims. The American Civil Liberties Union of Minnesota (ACLU) sued the charter school, its directors and state education officials in a federal court to halt the school's allegedly religious practices – such as the posting of prayers, school prayer sessions, the enforcement of a school dress code, dietary practices and the bus schedule. In responding to the lawsuit, the school filed five counterclaims against the ACLU, including defamation and interference with its business relationships with the parents of students. These claims were based on comments made by the ACLU outside of the litigation. However, the court refused to allow the claims to move forward. The Charter School Law made charter schools a part of the state system of public education. And **established law prohibited government bodies from suing for libel, defeating the defamation claim**. Since the claim for interference with business relationships only duplicated the defamation claim, the ACLU was entitled to dismissal of both claims. *ACLU of Minnesota v. Tarek Ibn Ziyad Academy*, No. 09-138, 2009 WL 4823378 (D. Minn. 12/9/09).

◆   A South Carolina special education teacher formed a close bond with a student and let him use her car, unaware that he did not have a license. She also gave him school computer passwords and wrote him excuses from his classes. The principal fired her after learning of this. She was also arrested and charged with contributing to the delinquency of a minor. Later, the principal told a staff member that the teacher had "cleaned [them] out," referring to the fact that when she left, she took a great deal of equipment that she had purchased. She sued the principal for defamation and raised other claims. The state court of appeals held that she could pursue the defamation claim against the principal because **she was accused of a crime involving moral turpitude**. *McBride v. School Dist. of Greenville County*, 698 S.E.2d 845 (S.C. Ct. App. 2010).

◆   An Indiana principal notified a parent that his access to the school where his three children attended would be restricted because he was a convicted sex offender. After the parent supplied proof that he was not the sex offender, the principal wrote him a formal apology. But the parent stated that school officials continued to treat him as a sex offender and spread this belief throughout the community. He and his wife sued the school board, school officials and the city, alleging slander, civil rights violations and other claims. The defendants sought to have the case dismissed. But a federal court refused to do so. The parents alleged intentional treatment different from other parents regarding the pick-up and drop-off of their children, without a rational basis. **The parents also raised an issue of false allegations by the principal "accusing them of being on the run from Florida law enforcement."** *Luera v. City of Ft. Wayne*, 2010 No. 1:09-CV-136 JVB, 2010 WL 3021514 (N.D. Ind. 7/29/10).

◆   A Maine student left a ham sandwich on a cafeteria table where Somali Muslim students were sitting. The school suspended the student for 10 days and classified the incident as a hate crime/bias offense. A reporter contacted the superintendent and quoted him as saying that work had to be done to bring the community together. A user of a website platform called "Associated Content" posted an Internet article that mischaracterized facts and described the response to the incident by a Somali community center as an "anti-ham response plan." Fox Network staff members retrieved the user's contrived article, read the reporter's original article, and based a three-hour cablecast on the incident. Two Fox co-hosts repeatedly ridiculed the superintendent and attributed a contrived anti-Somali statement to him. Fox later issued a retraction and apology, but the superintendent sued one of the cohosts and others for defamation.

A federal court held the statements were protected, and appeal went to the U.S. Court of Appeals, First Circuit. It held discussions of public officials such as the superintendent deserved "breathing space" under the Constitution. **A conditional privilege of free speech may only be overcome by clear and convincing evidence that a speaker made a defamatory statement with actual knowledge of its falsity.** Courts describe this as the "actual malice" standard. While some statements were defamatory, they did not meet the actual malice standard. The "anti-ham response plan" statement was not defamatory, as the court found it "imaginative expression" or "rhetorical hyperbole." It was not suggested that the co-hosts knew the Associated Content posting was false. While the cohosts carelessly relied on the Associated Content posting, this was negligence, not actual malice. *Levesque v. Doocy*, 560 F.3d 82 (1st Cir. 2009).

◆   A West Virginia school employee learned he would be transferred due to declining enrollment. He requested a hearing, posted the location and date of the hearing and wrote "This is the night to expose the cockroaches." He accused the board treasurer and superintendent of being "thieves," and implied that another board member lived with "his mistress." He claimed that funds for the school golf team were "stolen" for team travel, although this claim had been investigated and no impropriety found. At his hearing, the employee reasserted his accusations against board members and the superintendent, never reaching the substance of his own transfer. The superintendent advised the employee he would be recommending employment termination based on insubordination. In response, the employee called the superintendent more epithets. The board then voted to fire the employee for insubordination. After a grievance board upheld the action, a state court ordered him reinstated, finding his speech protected.

On appeal, the Supreme Court of Appeals of West Virginia noted the grievance board had found the employee's conduct was insubordinate. A school board's need to conduct its affairs far outweighed any right to make personal and potentially unfounded and damaging remarks against school officials. **Statements that are knowingly false, or made with reckless disregard of whether they are true, are unprotected** by the First Amendment. The employee's speech was not protected. *Alderman v. Pocahontas County Board of Educ.*, 223 W.Va. 431, 675 S.E.2d 907 (W.Va. 2009).

◆   A Nevada school administrator obtained an evaluation of courses offered by a distance learning software seller and found that they did not comply with salary enhancement provisions of the relevant collective bargaining agreement. The seller demanded recognition of its classes and threatened legal action. The administrator wrote to the seller that its courses were not "credit bearing toward any degree" offered by three universities. She noted that some courses could be completed in three to five hours and that tests could be passed without reading the material. According to the letter, no safeguards assured a candidate actually took the test. The administrator then emailed three different teachers to explain that the seller's courses were not credit-bearing toward a degree. She said some courses were not eligible for elective credit at the universities offering them.

The seller sued the district for defamation and related claims in a state court. A jury found some of the administrator's comments were defamatory and awarded the seller over $340,000. On appeal, the Supreme Court of Nevada explained that **an absolute privilege protected the administrator's letter because the seller had already demanded that the district recognize its courses and threatened legal action if it did not**. This privilege extended to non-lawyers as well as lawyers. At the trial court level, the seller attempted only to show that its business was down, and did not link this claim to the letter or emails. The administrator's writings did not impugn the seller's fitness for trade. The communications concerned the fitness of the seller's products, and the administrator had no intent to harm the seller's business interests. As she did not show reckless disregard for the truth, the judgment was reversed. *Clark County School Dist. v. Virtual Educ. Software*, 213 P.3d 496 (Nev. 2009).

◆   A former temporary teacher lost his defamation action against a Louisiana school board. A high school principal sent the board's human resources office a brief letter stating the teacher's dates of employment and noting only that "it is recommended that Mr. Tatum not be returned to Cohen School." The Court of Appeal of Louisiana affirmed a trial court's dismissal of the case. It held that **a communication is defamatory if it tends to harm one's reputation in the community**, deters association with others, or exposes the person to contempt or ridicule. The principal's recommendation against rehiring the teacher was not defamatory. Expression of opinion is actionable only if it implies false factual assertions, is defamatory, and is made with actual malice. *Tatum v. Orleans Parish School Board*, 982 So.2d 923 (La. Ct. App. 2008).

◆   A California high school principal served with distinction at several inner city schools before being assigned to Jefferson High School in Los Angeles. Jefferson significantly improved its traditionally low-achievement standing, but a series of violent disturbances occurred that resulted in several student injuries and arrests. The superintendent of schools was quoted in the media as saying "stronger leadership was needed at Jefferson," and that the principal had "retirement plans that did not fit with the district's needs." The principal was removed from the school and reassigned to a "desk job." He retired six months later and sued the school district and two superintendents in a state court for defamation and invasion of privacy. The case reached the state court of appeal. It held **the superintendent "had an official duty to communicate with the press about matters of public concern."** His duty was to inform the public about how the district would respond to the violence, and these statements were privileged. The principal's leadership was a subject of legitimate public concern, and none of the statements divulged private information. The superintendent's statements were privileged in his capacity as chief executive officer for the district. The court upheld the judgment and held the school officials were entitled to their attorneys' fees. *Morrow v. Los Angeles Unified School Dist.*, 149 Cal.App.4th 1424, 57 Cal.Rptr.3d 885 (Cal. Ct. App. 2007).

◆   A 74-year-old Massachusetts foreign language teacher filed a defamation and discrimination lawsuit against her principal. The principal had criticized the teacher's handling of a class trip to Germany, alleging that she left a sick child unattended while she visited another town. A state trial court dismissed the case, but the court of appeals held that the teacher raised valid concerns about the principal's statements to a group of parents concerning her performance. **His statements and his "ongoing antagonistic relationship" with her were enough to allow the defamation claim to proceed.** While the principal was entitled to discuss the teacher's performance with parents, this privilege would be lost if the teacher showed that he spoke with malice. *Dragonis v. School Committee of Melrose*, 64 Mass. App. Ct. 429, 833 N.E.2d 679 (Mass. App. Ct. 2005). The Supreme Judicial Court of Massachusetts denied further review.

## VI.  SCHOOL BUS ACCIDENTS

*Courts have found school bus drivers and districts liable for injuries to students resulting from the failure to exercise reasonable care in the operation of a vehicle or the design of a bus route. Districts are not liable for injuries caused by sudden and unforeseeable attacks of students on school buses.*

### A.  Duty of Care

*Florida's Supreme Court has held that school boards are not insurers of school safety. A school board's duty of care to students regarding transportation extends from when a bus picked up the student at a bus stop, to when they reached the school door. This stemmed from the board's custody of the student.*

◆   A Florida middle school student was killed while crossing a street to get to her bus stop. She was using the stop because of problems she had with other students at the stop on her side of the road. Her school counselor told her to use the stop across the street. Her family sued the board in a state court. Appeal reached the state court of appeal. It found that if a student was harmed before reaching a designated bus stop (or after leaving one), the student was outside the board's duty of care. Florida regulations placed the burden on parents to ensure the safe travel of students to and from home, when they were not in school custody. **Since the student was under the exclusive control of her parents while she walked to the bus stop, the school district had no duty to ensure her safe arrival.** The court affirmed the judgment for the board. *Francis v. School Board of Palm Beach County*, 29 So.3d 441 (Fla. Dist. Ct. App. 2010).

◆   A nine-year-old North Carolina student was seated on a school bus next to another student who was poking holes in paper with a pencil. The driver told the other student to put the pencil away and told the student to turn around in the seat and stay out of the aisle. When the bus went over a dip in the road, the driver heard a scream. The student's left eye was punctured by the other student's pencil, causing a serious injury. In a State Tort Claims Act proceeding before the North Carolina Industrial Commission, the student's parents claimed the bus driver's failure to supervise the other student was the cause of the eye injury. The commission found the student's injuries resulted from the driver's negligence and awarded the student $150,000 in damages. The state court of appeals upheld the award. **Evidence supported the commission's finding that the driver had a duty of care to enforce school safety policies but failed to do so.** And this failure was the legal cause of the student's eye injury. *Lucas v. Rockingham County Schools,* 692 S.E.2d 890 (N.C. Ct. App. 2010).

◆   A 15-year-old Louisiana student asked her school bus driver if she could exit a bus a few blocks from home. She had no written permission slip as required by school board policy, but the driver allowed her to leave as she was not a behavior problem. The student spent the day with her 18-year-old boyfriend and had sex with him. The principal called the family home during the school day to report her absence. The student did not return home, fearing consequences from her parents. Law officers found her a few days later in an abandoned building where she had been hiding. The student's family sued the school board for negligence. A trial court found that the board breached a duty owed to the student, but that this did not cause the harm she alleged.

The Court of Appeal of Louisiana reviewed evidence that the two students had been observed displaying affection at school, and that the principal had warned the student of the possible legal consequences of attempting a relationship with an 18-year-old. He had also issued her a three-day suspension for her conduct at school. There was evidence that the student's parents knew of the relationship. While they claimed that the truancy incident would not have occurred if the driver had not let her off the bus, the court disagreed. The driver's conduct was not the cause-in-fact of any harm. **The injury was not within the scope of any school board duty because of the lack of its foreseeability.** Accordingly, the court affirmed the judgment for the school board. *J.M. v. Acadia Parish School Board,* 7 So.3d 150 (La. Ct. App. 2009).

◆   A four-year-old Florida child with disabilities endured a four-hour bus ride on his first day of school because the driver lost his way. The child's father took him to a pediatrician, who found no signs of abuse or injury. But the child began having nightmares and wetting his bed. His parents sued the school board for negligence and false imprisonment. Appeal reached the state court of appeal. It held **the "impact rule" requires a personal injury plaintiff to show that any emotional distress must "flow from the physical injuries" suffered from an impact.** Neither the pediatrician nor the psychologist who examined the child found any physical or emotional injury. As the impact rule barred recovery for emotional injury, the court reversed the judgment on the negligence claim. It affirmed the appeal on the false imprisonment claim. There was no evidence of any intent to confine the child or keep him on the bus. *School Board of Miami-Dade County, Florida v. Trujillo,* 906 So.2d 1109 (Fla. Dist. Ct. App. 2005).

◆   A Washington school bus driver dropped a student off past her usual stop, but closer to her home and on the same side of the street as her house. After the bus pulled away, the student started walking across the street to get her mail and was severely injured when struck by another vehicle. She sued the school district and bus driver for negligence. A court held for the district and driver, and the state court of appeals affirmed. The accident was not caused by the drop-off location. The only proof offered to show that the drop-off point was dangerous was the accident itself. The bus driver did not violate a legal duty towards the student. **State rules governing school bus drivers required drivers to take reasonable action to assure a student crosses a road safely, but only if the student must cross the road.** The student did not need to cross the street to get home, and the driver was unaware that she intended to cross it. *Claar v. Auburn School Dist. No. 408*, 125 Wash. App. 1048 (Wash. Ct. App. 2005).

## B. Governmental Immunity

◆   A seven-year-old Alabama student with disabilities attended an intensive therapeutic placement center for students with behavioral and emotional problems. Each day, he rode a five-seat special education bus about 30 miles to the center. According to the student, a classmate sexually assaulted him on a day when a substitute driver drove the bus. The classmate claimed that the two boys had only exposed themselves to each other. The student's parents sued the board and school officials for negligence and civil rights violations. A court held that the assault did not result from a school board policy. The substitute driver was entitled to immunity, as driving the bus was a discretionary duty.

The parents appealed to the Eleventh Circuit, which held public schools do not generally have any constitutional duty to protect students from violent acts by third parties. The student's special education status did not form a "special relationship" creating a duty to protect him. The parents failed to show any board policy was the "moving force" behind the incident. There was no evidence that the classmate had previously committed sexual assault or was a known threat to do so. The Alabama Supreme Court has repeatedly held that **the supervision of students involves discretion and judgment**. Persons who supervise students are entitled to immunity in negligence cases. *Worthington v. Elmore County Board of Educ.*, 160 Fed.Appx. 877 (11th Cir. 2005).

◆   A Texas pre-kindergartner fell asleep on her school bus and was locked inside it for a full afternoon. After arriving at school, the driver and bus monitor failed to check the bus before locking it. The child's parents sued the school district for negligence. The district claimed sovereign immunity, and the case reached the Court of Appeals of Texas. It explained that the Texas Code waives immunity for property damage, personal injury and death that "arises from the operation or use of a motor-driven vehicle." The court noted that in an earlier case, **the Supreme Court of Texas had found that the unloading of a school bus was part of the transportation process**. Here, the family's claim was based on the "use of the bus." Since the locking of bus doors was distinguished from negligent supervision, sovereign immunity was waived. *Elgin Independent School Dist. v. R.N.*, 191 S.W.3d 263 (Tex. Ct. App. 2006).

◆   After an accident between a school bus and a car, the car driver sued the school board and bus driver in a Virginia trial court. The bus driver and the board asserted the defense of sovereign immunity, and the court granted their request, ruling the bus driver was entitled to sovereign immunity for simple negligence and that the board's liability was entirely dependent upon and derived from his negligence. Because the car driver did not allege gross negligence against the bus driver and the board, the court held that the board was entitled to judgment. The car driver appealed to the state supreme court, which observed that **state law abrogated school board immunity for acts of simple negligence up to the amount of a board's insurance coverage**. The statute imposed liability on school boards for simple negligence, even where their employees were liable only for gross negligence. The court reversed the judgment, as transportation of students on school buses was a governmental function over which the district exercised significant control. Transportation of students involved discretion and judgment by bus drivers. *Linhart v. Lawson*, 540 S.E.2d 875 (Va. 2001).

## VII. SCHOOL SECURITY

*State legislatures have enacted laws regarding school safety, but to this date, most of the lawsuits arising from breaches of school security remain rooted in negligence principles. School districts owe their students a duty of reasonable care, and the duty of teachers and administrators to supervise and protect their students is well-established. In A.W. v. Lancaster County School District 0001, 784 N.W.2d 907 (Neb. 2010), below, the Supreme Court of Nebraska held that foreseeability questions in negligence cases are generally for juries to determine. It found that questions of foreseeability are not "legal" questions, but involve common sense, common experience, and the application of community standards and behavioral norms. So juries, rather than judges are typically entitled to review questions of foreseeability in negligence cases.*

### A.  Duty of Care

◆   A Nebraska school policy required visitors to check in at the main office of the school. However, an intruder entered the school without being observed by school secretaries. Teachers asked the intruder if they could help him, but he ignored them. One teacher directed him to a restroom and told him to report to the office after he was finished. Another teacher reported him to the office, but she did not continue observing him. After the teachers lost sight of the intruder, he went to another restroom and sexually assaulted a five-year-old student. The student's mother sued the school district for negligence. A state court awarded pretrial judgment to the district, but on appeal, the Supreme Court of Nebraska stated that a trial was required. In this case, the district owed the student a duty of reasonable care. But the question of whether the assault was reasonably foreseeable involved a fact-specific inquiry for a jury. **As the teachers had permitted the intruder to evade them, reasonable minds could differ as to whether the assault was foreseeable.** It had been improper for the lower court to award judgment to the district, and the case was returned to it for further proceedings. *A.W. v. Lancaster County School District 0001*, 784 N.W.2d 907 (Neb. 2010).

◆  Four Michigan teachers and their union brought a lawsuit against their school board, asserting it improperly failed to expel students who had assaulted them. They maintained that state law required the expulsion of students who assaulted others, and argued that school administrators who failed to follow the law should have their contracts cancelled. The Court of Appeals of Michigan ruled against them, holding that they did not have standing to pursue the case. On further appeal, the Michigan Supreme Court held that the teachers had standing to pursue their action. They were likely to suffer an injury that other members of the public wouldn't face. Thus, **the teachers had a substantial and distinct interest in enforcing the law that a student be expelled for assaulting a teacher**. *Lansing Schools Educ. Ass'n MEA/NEA v. Lansing Board of Educ.*, 487 Mich. 387, 792 N.W.2d 686 (Mich. 2010).

◆  An Iowa student used a BB gun to shoot a classmate on a sidewalk outside their high school at dismissal time. Law officers arrested the student and two other boys later in the day when they used the same BB gun during a theft. Although the student claimed the shooting was accidental, he was placed in juvenile detention and expelled. Dissatisfied with the school's handling of the matter, the classmate's mother sued the school district and officials for negligence. A jury returned a verdict for the school district and officials.

The mother appealed to the Court of Appeals of Iowa, which noted that **schools must exercise the same care as a parent of ordinary prudence would in comparable circumstances**. In the month before the shooting, the student had been involved in three fights at school. The school had responded with a student responsibility plan and placed him on "full escort" by a staff member at all times. In addition, the student was suspended and recommended for alternative placement the next year. The court found evidence from which the jury could find the school had responded appropriately to the prior incidents. School administrators followed district disciplinary policies in dealing with the student. Moreover, the fights may have been provoked and were "mutual" in nature. The judgment for the district and officials was affirmed. *Herrig v. Dubuque Community School Dist.*, 772 N.W.2d 15 (Iowa Ct. App. 2009).

◆  In 2005, an Oregon school district adopted a policy that any employee having a firearm in school or at a school event would face discipline up to and including termination. A teacher had an ex-husband whom she feared might turn violent. She sought to bring a handgun to school, asserting that she was licensed to carry a concealed weapon and that she needed it for self-defense. The district's human resources department warned her that she could be fired for bringing the gun to school, and she sued. She claimed that the policy was illegal because Oregon law states that only the legislature can "regulate" firearms or pass ordinances concerning them. A court dismissed her claim, holding that the law didn't apply to workplace policies, and the Oregon Court of Appeals affirmed. The state law was only intended to prevent cities and counties from creating a patchwork of conflicting laws concerning firearms. It was not intended to reach as far as internal employment policies. *Doe v. Medford School Dist. 549C*, 221 P.3d 787 (Or. Ct. App. 2009).

## B.  Governmental Immunity

*As in other tort liability areas, public officers and employees enjoy qualified official immunity if they are performing discretionary acts involving the exercise of judgment or personal deliberation. It is further required that the government official or employee be acting in good faith and within the scope of their authority.*

◆   A Minnesota kindergartner said that he did not want to go outside with his class for recess. He stayed in a supervised detention room in the school office, but an aide instructed him to use a lavatory down the hallway instead of the one in the detention area. While in the lavatory, the kindergartner was sexually assaulted by a recent high school graduate who had been inside the school several times in the days before the assault to do janitorial work. On the day of the assault, he entered the school through a side door without signing in and obtaining a visitor badge. The kindergartner's mother sued the school district for negligent supervision and failure to have and enforce a specific policy on school security. A court denied pretrial judgment on the negligent supervision claim, and the Court of Appeals of Minnesota agreed that a trial was required on that issue. The aide had let the kindergartner go unaccompanied to a restroom outside a detention room equipped with its own lavatory, and the graduate somehow got in the school building without signing in and wearing a badge. But **the school district was entitled to immunity for not having a specific policy to protect elementary children from intruders**. These decisions took place at the planning level and involved the evaluation of financial, political, economic and social factors. *Doe v. Independent School Dist. No. 2154*, No. A09-2235, 2010 WL 3545585 (Minn. Ct. App. 9/14/10).

◆   A Georgia student was severely beaten by a classmate after they left their classroom. The principal and vice principal found the student unconscious and bleeding profusely in the hallway. According to the student's parents, the school's only effort to assist him was taking him to the school clinic, where a nurse cleaned his wounds. They claimed he was placed in an intensive care unit for traumatic brain injury due to the lack of immediate treatment. The parents filed a negligence action against the district, asserting that the school knew of the classmate's extensive history of violence and that a teacher ignored his threats against the student. The court awarded judgment to the district, and the parents appealed. The Supreme Court of Georgia found a state constitutional provision requires schools to prepare safety plans to address violence in schools, and to provide a safe environment. But qualified immunity protects officials for their discretionary actions taken within the scope of their official authority. **Public officials and employees may be held personally liable only for ministerial acts that are negligently performed, and for those acts performed with malice or intent to injure.** School officials had exercised discretion in how they created a school safety plan. Their alleged malice in not providing the student immediate medical care did not deprive them of immunity. *Murphy v. Bajjani*, 282 Ga. 197, 647 S.E.2d 54 (Ga. 2007).

◆   A student at Philadelphia's Olney High School was punched by an unknown attacker who was trying to hit someone else. The attack occurred on the stairwell, where there were no surveillance cameras or security staff. The intended victim ducked, and the attacker hit the student in the eye, severely injuring him. Neither the attacker nor the intended victim was ever identified. The student's mother sued the school district and school officials in a federal court, asserting due process violations and willful misconduct. The court rejected the claims, including one alleging that school officials had created the danger leading to the injury. On appeal, the U.S. Court of Appeals, Third Circuit, affirmed. Although the school was short four security officers that day, and had been short of a full security staff on 83 of the previous 85 school days, **the injury to the student was not foreseeable**. The atmosphere of violence at the school did not make it foreseeable that he would be attacked. Additional surveillance or security might have helped apprehend the attacker, but it was speculation to say this would have prevented the attack. *Mohammed v. School Dist. of Philadelphia*, 196 Fed.Appx. 79 (3d Cir. 2006).

## C.  Building and Grounds

### 1.  Visitors and Intruders

◆   Washington school employees identified a former student as the person who broke into a junior high school and damaged it, based on their review of surveillance camera video. After police arrested him and charged him with criminal conduct, fingerprint analysis showed he was not the offender. By the time the fingerprint analysis exonerated him, the former student had spent 19 days in jail. He sued the school district in the state court system for malicious prosecution. The state court of appeals held the former student did not satisfy the legal requirements for a malicious prosecution claim. **He had to show more than just a mistake by proving "evil intent," but he failed to do so.** *Hubbard v. Eastmont School Dist. No. 206*, 152 Wash.App. 1040 (Wash. Ct. App. 2009).

◆   A Kansas jogger was approached by a municipal police officer because her dog was running loose on school grounds. She had an unloaded handgun with her. A state court acquitted the jogger of a criminal charge of possessing a firearm on school property, since there were no classes in session and no school-sponsored activities at the time. The Court of Appeals of Kansas noted **state law declared that possession of a firearm by any person (other than a law enforcement officer) in or on any school property or grounds was a criminal offense**. None of the exceptions to the law applied here. Whether school was in session was irrelevant, and the court reversed the judgment. *State of Kansas v. Toler*, 41 Kan.App.2d 986, 206 P.3d 548 (Kan. Ct. App. 2009).

◆   A Louisiana high school student was stabbed in a hallway by an intruder who was leaving the school office, where he had been denied a visitor's pass. Staff members watched him exit the building but did not escort him out as he walked to a school parking lot. He re-entered the building unobserved through an unlocked side door. The intruder apparently recognized the student as a person who had laughed at him some years earlier about a personal slight. The student and her parents sued the school board for negligence. A state trial court dismissed the case, and appeal went to the state court of appeal. It held school boards have a duty of reasonable supervision over their students. Supervision must be reasonable and competent, according to the circumstances of the case. But school board were not insurers of children's safety. **"Constant supervision of all students is not possible nor required for educators to discharge their duty to provide adequate supervision."** Before liability may be imposed, there must be proof of negligent supervision and a causal connection between the lack of supervision and the accident. *Boudreaux v. St. Tammany Parish School Board*, No. 2007 CA 0089, 2007 WL 4480703 (La. Ct. App. 12/21/07).

## 2. Building Entry Policies

◆   After a sex offender entered a Texas school and exposed himself to a child, the district implemented a regulation requiring every visitor to produce a state-issued photo identification as a condition of entering secure areas where students were present. Under the regulation, pictures were taken of visitor identification cards but no other information was taken. The system enabled schools to check visitor names and birth dates to determine if they were listed on national registered sex-offender databases. A parent refused to allow her child's school to either scan her driver's license or permit manual entry of her information. As a result, she was denied access to areas of the school. She and her husband sued, challenging the policy as a violation of their constitutional rights. A federal court held for the district, and the Fifth Circuit affirmed. **The regulation addressed a compelling state interest and was not overly intrusive.** The system took only the minimal information needed to determine sex offender status. *Meadows v. Lake Travis Independent School Dist.*, 397 Fed.Appx. 1 (5th Cir. 2010).

◆   A Chicago third-grader had conflicts with another girl at school. The other girl's mother and a companion threatened the student's mother at her home. The school principal set up a meeting between the families. Near the end of a school day, the other girl's parent and an adult cousin fought the student's mother and grandmother in a school office. The principal called police and swore out criminal complaints for disorderly conduct against all four adults. Criminal charges were dismissed, and the principal later said he had made a mistake and should have only had two of the women arrested. The parent and grandparent sued. The U.S. Court of Appeals, Seventh Circuit, noted the issue was not whether a parent or grandparent had actually committed disorderly conduct. **It was only necessary to show a reasonable person in the principal's position had probable cause to believe there was disorderly conduct.** The principal entered a chaotic situation and could easily have viewed the mother to be an equal participant in the fight. Each of the family's civil rights claims failed. *Stokes v. Board of Educ. of City of Chicago*, 599 F.3d 617 (7th Cir. 2010).

# CHAPTER THIRTEEN

## Interscholastic Athletics

## I. HIGH SCHOOL ATHLETICS

### A. Eligibility Rules and Restrictions

*State athletic association eligibility rules requiring a sit-out period for athletes transferring into a district from a neighboring school district, private school or from out of state may be enforced if they are reasonably related to the prevention of recruiting student-athletes. Many courts, including the Louisiana Court of Appeal, have held there is no constitutional right to play varsity sports. Challenges by students with disabilities are considered in Section II C., below.*

### 1. Transfer Students

◆ A Louisiana student transferred to a different public high school. He asked the Louisiana High School Athletic Association (LHSAA) to rule on his eligibility. The LHSAA determined there had not been a bona fide change of residence under its "transfer rule" and that he was ineligible to play football during his first year at the new school. His parents sued the LHSAA in a state court for an order allowing him to compete in varsity athletics at his new school. The case was dismissed on a legal technicality, and by the time an appeal reached the state court of appeal the student had graduated from high school.

For this reason, the court held the claim for an order against the LHSAA requiring the association to allow his participation in sports was moot.

As for the student's challenge to the transfer rule and the LHSAA's eligibility ruling, the court found **LHSAA actions were "internal affairs of a voluntary association."** According to the court, an amateur organization conducting sports competitions maintained exclusive authority over a specific class of amateur athletes. While the lower court had incorrectly declined to consider claims for damages for alleged deprivation of constitutional rights, the court of appeal rejected the constitutional issues. LHSAA investigations and the enforcement of its rules were not "state action." Even if the LHSAA was deemed a "state actor," the court held "[a] student's interest in participating in a single year of interscholastic athletics amounts to an expectation, not a constitutionally protected claim of entitlement." The possibility of obtaining a college athletic scholarship was speculative and was not a protected property interest. As the student had no due process right to interscholastic athletic participation and did not advance a valid equal protection claim, the court affirmed the judgment on those claims. *Menard v. Louisiana High School Athletic Ass'n*, 30 So.3d 790 (La. Ct. App. 2009).

◆ An Oklahoma student athlete's parent made a negative comment about the basketball coach after a game and later refused to discuss the incident with the district superintendent. The parents were then barred from school property. The student quit the team and two months later transferred to a different school. The Oklahoma Secondary School Activities Association (OSSAA) denied the student's request for a waiver from its transfer rule, which bars transfer students from playing varsity sports for one year unless the OSSAA grants a waiver. A state court granted the family's petition for relief from the OSSAA ruling.

On appeal, the Supreme Court of Oklahoma noted that OSSAA rules explicitly bar hardship waivers when circumstances indicate discontent with the school in which eligibility has been established. **Participation in interscholastic athletics is not a right but a privilege subject to OSSAA eligibility rules.** Courts do not generally interfere in a voluntary association's internal affairs unless a member's financial or property rights are involved or there is evidence of a serious mistake or wrongdoing. No such mistake had occurred here, and the lower court committed error in ruling otherwise. *Morgan v. Oklahoma Secondary School Activities Ass'n*, 207 P.3d 362 (Okla. 2009).

◆ A student athlete at Barren County High School violated the school's alcohol policy and was declared ineligible for interscholastic athletic competition for the next school year. His family moved, and he enrolled at Glasgow High School. He asked the Kentucky High School Athletic Association (KHSAA) to declare him eligible for interscholastic athletics there based on a bona fide change in address exception to KHSAA's transfer rule. The KHSAA denied the request. While the student had established a new address, he was still ineligible under the penalty imposed at Barren High School. A Kentucky court granted the student's request for a restraining order barring the KHSAA's enforcement of the decision. The order was made in an *ex parte* proceeding, in which the KHSAA did not receive notice or an opportunity to appear. The Court of Appeals of Kentucky refused to disturb the order, and the KHSAA appealed. On appeal to the Supreme Court of Kentucky, the court noted that when the party being restrained is brought to court, the order has served its purpose and should be extinguished. **The correct way to challenge the restraining order was to ask the court issuing it to dissolve the order.** The court vacated the court of appeals' order. *Kentucky High School Athletic Ass'n v. Edwards*, 256 S.W.3d 1 (Ky. 2008).

◆   The U.S. Court of Appeals, Eleventh Circuit, affirmed a court ruling against a Georgia high school football coach and former players who alleged harm when the state high school association forfeited their games for a season. The association found that **the school improperly included a nonresident player on the team.** The lower court rejected student claims based on lost opportunities to receive college scholarships. Students have no constitutional right to participate in athletics. As the coach was not discharged or demoted, his constitutional rights were also not violated. *Stewart v. Bibb County Board of Educ.*, 195 Fed.Appx. 927 (11th Cir. 2006).

◆   The Louisiana High School Athletic Association (LHSAA) received a complaint about a student residency issue. The student's parents claimed that two LHSAA officers demanded to search their house and threatened to immediately declare the student ineligible from athletic participation if they refused. They let the officers search the house. The LHSAA commissioner held that the student's school violated its transfer and change of residence rules by letting the student play basketball. The student sued the district in a state court, which dismissed the case. On appeal, the Court of Appeal of Louisiana found **the student's claim to "an opportunity for an athletic scholarship to college" was a speculative and uncertain expectation, not a protected property interest.** The student had no due process rights to participate in interscholastic sports. The court found her equal protection claim did not specifically allege how she was treated differently from others. The state high school athletic association was not a state actor that could be held liable for an unlawful search of a private home. However, the complaint stated sufficient facts to support a claim for invasion of privacy under state law. The court reversed that part of the judgment. *Johansen v. Louisiana High School Athletic Ass'n*, 916 So.2d 1081 (La. Ct. App. 2005).

◆   A Kansas parent claimed that a public high school athletic director recruited his son extensively. The student attended the school for two half-days and then decided to transfer. He sent the athletic director a "limited eligibility transfer form" that would allow him to remain eligible for non-varsity sports after a transfer. The director refused to sign the eligibility form, asserting that the transfer was athletically motivated. The state athletic association approved the denial, relying on statements by school officials, who declared that the parent considered his son's athletic opportunities when making the transfer decision. The parent claimed the transfer was not motivated by athletics, and he sued. The court considered the parent's request for a preliminary injunction and noted that the student would not suffer any irreparable harm if it failed to intervene. He would miss only 18 weeks of basketball eligibility and could still practice with the football team. The board had a legitimate basis for denying the eligibility request. **As there is no recognized property interest in playing non-varsity sports, the court found no equal protection violation.** *Love v. Kansas State High School Activities Ass'n,* 2004 WL 2357879 (D. Kan. 2004).

## 2. Other Rules

*State laws typically vest state athletic associations with broad powers to interpret their own rules. Constitutional claims generally fail, as many court decisions have held there is no constitutionally protected interest to participate in interscholastic athletics or other extracurricular activities.*

◆ West Virginia state athletic association rules imposed a two-game suspension on any student-athlete who was ejected from a basketball game. After being ejected from a game, a student-athlete had physical contact with a referee, triggering another rules violation. He sued the West Virginia Secondary Schools Activities Commission (SSAC), seeking an order to prevent enforcement of the two-game suspension. Meanwhile, his school suspended him for four games. By the time the court held a hearing, the parties had reached an agreement by which he would miss three games. Despite the agreement, the court proceeded to consider an SSAC rule regarding the forfeiture of games involving suspended players. The court struck down the rule and another SSAC rule based on its lack of provisions for administrative review. The SSAC appealed to the Supreme Court of Appeals of West Virginia, which reversed. **The lower court's attempt to declare an SSAC rule on multi-game suspensions unconstitutional was improper.** The SSAC was not a state actor, and no due process right was implicated. *Mayo v. West Virginia Secondary Schools Activities Comm'n,* 223 W.Va. 88, 672 S.E.2d 224 (W.Va. 2008).

◆ A Delaware student played varsity basketball and remained in the school district when his mother moved to Georgia. She executed a power of attorney authorizing the basketball coach and a lawyer to make decisions regarding her son. After the lawyer came to the school for a copy of the student's transcript, the school investigated his relationship with the student. The principal concluded that the power of attorney was insufficient and that the student was not a resident. The principal informed the Delaware Interscholastic Athletic Association (DIAA) that the school had used an ineligible player, and stated that the school planned to forfeit all the games in which the student participated. He asked the DIAA to waive the applicable forfeiture penalties. The DIAA denied the waiver request, and the state education board (SBE) upheld that decision. A court then issued a letter opinion which explained that **Delaware law vested the DIAA with the power to decide all controversies involving its rules, regulations and waivers.** State law provided for appeals of DIAA decisions to the SBE, but declared that "the decision of the SBE shall be final and not subject to further appeal." *Cape Henlopen School Dist. v. Delaware Interscholastic Athletic Ass'n.,* No. 08A-01-003 ESB, 2009 WL 388944 (Del. Super. 1/28/09).

◆ The Oklahoma Secondary School Activities Association required private schools to obtain a majority vote of members for admission. However, any public school that applied for membership was automatically admitted. The Christian Heritage Academy twice sought to join the association. Both its applications were rejected, even after it reduced its boundaries to reduce its competitive advantage. The academy sued the association for equal protection violations. The case reached the U.S. Court of Appeals, Tenth Circuit, which held that the association violated the Equal Protection Clause. **There was no legitimate purpose for the different admission rules.** The association was a state actor because 98% of its members were public schools. Its directors were public school employees and its authority to determine eligibility and hold playoffs was granted by the state. The association treated the academy differently from public schools with comparable student populations and locations. *Christian Heritage Academy v. Oklahoma Secondary School Activities Ass'n*, 483 F.3d 1025 (10th Cir. 2007).

◆ A West Virginia student who had been home-schooled sought to participate on a middle school wrestling team. The West Virginia Secondary School Activities Commission (WVSSAC) denied the request, and the case reached the state supreme court of appeals. The court noted that WVSSAC rules required students to maintain a 2.0 grade average to remain eligible for interscholastic sports. Students also had to do passing work in four subjects per week in which they could earn credit toward graduation. Home-schooled students were evaluated only once per year. The court held school boards should not be required to spend funds to support home-schooled student participation in interscholastic sports. Participation in extracurricular activities did not rise to the level of a fundamental or constitutional right under the West Virginia Constitution. **Excluding home-schooled students from interscholastic sports did not violate equal protection.** Like the parents of private school students, the parents of home-schooled children voluntarily chose not to participate in the state's public school system. In making this choice, these parents agreed to forgo the privileges of a public school education, one of which was the opportunity to qualify for interscholastic sports. The court held that the WVSSAC did not exceed its authority in issuing the eligibility rules. *Jones v. West Virginia State Board of Educ.*, 218 W.Va. 52, 622 S.E.2d 289 (W.Va. 2005).

◆ A Pennsylvania student was home-schooled for her seventh- and eighth-grade years. A school district allowed her to play interscholastic basketball both years. The student ended her home school program in grade nine and enrolled in a state-chartered and certified "cyber charter school." The school district let the student play on an interscholastic basketball team, but it later excluded her for failing to meet district requirements. Her family sued. The case reached the U.S. Court of Appeals, Third Circuit, which noted that the district's interscholastic sports participation requirements included verifiable attendance documentation. All of the student's attendance and class time was self-verified, under a curriculum provided by the University of Missouri. As her attendance was not verified by certified instructors and her curriculum was not approved by the state board of education, the school district could find her ineligible for interscholastic sports. **The decision denying the student's participation in interscholastic sports did not violate her constitutional rights.** *Angstadt v. Midd-West School Dist.*, 377 F.3d 338 (3d Cir. 2004).

## B. Athletic and Extracurricular Suspensions

*In addition to refusing to recognize any constitutional right to participate in interscholastic athletics or other extracurricular activities, the courts have rejected the argument that the possibility of obtaining a college athletic scholarship is an interest protected by any constitutional provision.*

◆ Upset that his son was not playing a particular position, a parent approached a coach during a high school baseball game. A harsh exchange of words followed, and school officials banned the parent from all athletic events for one year. The parent sued the school board in a federal court for constitutional rights violations. After the court denied him temporary relief, he filed a notice of dismissal. The school district opposed dismissal because it appeared that the parent had filed a complaint with the Ohio Civil Rights Commission. Under federal rules, this meant he lost the right to voluntary dismissal. **The court exercised its discretion to dismiss the case, even though he would simply be pursuing his claims with the state.** *Pennington v. Lake Local Schools Board of Educ.*, 257 F.R.D. 629 (N.D. Ohio 2009).

◆ A Kentucky high school student admitted to the school principal that he had been drinking alcohol before coming to a school dance. The school board excluded him from playing basketball and all other extracurricular activities. He sued the board and principal, asserting that the discipline was arbitrary and capricious. He further alleged discrimination and due process violations. A court dismissed the complaint, and the student appealed. The Court of Appeals of Kentucky noted that students have no fundamental or vested property right to participate in interscholastic athletics. For that reason, the student's constitutional claims had been properly dismissed. **A school board may suspend or expel a student for violating lawful school regulations.** However, the student claimed that the board acted arbitrarily and capriciously in denying his opportunity to participate in interscholastic athletics. The court held that he stated a viable claim for arbitrary and capricious action by the board and principal. Thus, the case required a trial. *Critchelow v. Breckinridge County Board of Educ.*, 2006 WL 3456658 (Ky. Ct. App. 2006).

◆ Parents told school officials that a Washington student-athlete and several other football players were drinking alcohol at a school dance. A staff member saw a beer container in the student's car, and a search of the car yielded an empty beer carton, cigars and tobacco. The school suspended the student for 10 days for violating a school policy against drinking alcohol as a member of the football team. He appealed the discipline, and the athletic board suspended him from a football game and five wrestling matches. He had to forfeit his football letter and individual honors and was recommended for alcohol evaluation and treatment. The principal upheld both the academic and athletic sanctions pursuant to an informal conference, as did a district hearing officer and the school board. When the student sued, a state court held for the district. The state court of appeals held that **interscholastic sports participation is a privilege, not a constitutionally protected property or liberty interest**. The district provided the student with more process than required under the circumstances by applying the state law procedures for short-term academic suspensions. It was not required to provide him with the kind of protections he would receive for an expulsion proceeding. The judgment for the district was affirmed. *Taylor v. Enumclaw School Dist. No. 216*, 133 P.3d 492 (Wash. Ct. App. 2006).

◆ A Pennsylvania coach suspected that a student was taking drugs and required him to take a drug test. A drug treatment facility determined that the student had no drug abuse problem, but he claimed that the principal did not reinstate him to swim and water polo teams despite the evaluation results. He claimed the coach cut a lock off his locker, performed a search, and seized his property. His family sued. A court held that the privacy expectations of student/athletes are even lower than those of the general student population. The coach suspected the student was using drugs because his behavior was unusual. There was an immediate concern for safety. The student did not assert a valid Fourth Amendment claim based on the locker search. His First Amendment claim failed, as he was not prevented from associating with team members. The removal of a student from school athletic teams did not implicate any due process rights. **Students do not have a due process property interest in any particular component of a public education**, such as extracurricular activities participation. There was also no due process violation based on the disclosure of medical information. The results of the drug testing were only revealed to the student's parents and his medical condition was not indicated. The court held for the district and school officials on all the claims. *Dominic J. v. Wyoming Valley West High School*, 362 F.Supp.2d 560 (M.D. Pa. 2005).

## C. Drug Testing

*Drug testing by urinalysis has been deemed a "search" under the Fourth Amendment to the U.S. Constitution. Testing limited to potential interscholastic sports participants has met with widespread court approval. For drug search cases involving a broader student population, see Chapter Two, Section II.B.*

*Courts have held student-athletes to a higher standard of conduct than the general student population in drug-testing cases, due to the representative role they play and their reduced expectations of privacy. In the next case, a California school district could not justify expanding a mandatory random drug-testing program for student athletes to include a broader range of participants in competitive recreational activities under the state constitution.*

◆ A California school board expanded a random drug-testing program that had been previously limited to student-athletes. Anecdotal evidence indicated that students, including those taking music, were using drugs and alcohol. Although the superintendent later said he had little reason to suspect students involved in competitive recreational activities (CRAs) used substances at a higher rate than others, he wanted to test as many students as possible. When the policy was approved, it applied to CRAs such as choir, band, science bowl, "tri-mathalon," mock trial and the Future Farmers of America. Some CRA activities were used for student class grades and some satisfied state university admissions requirements. The expanded testing program covered 56.8% of high school students in the district. No procedure was in the testing program for challenging a positive test result. Consequences for a false positive were limited to CRA eligibility, and results were not shared with law enforcement agencies.

Parents of two honor roll students sued the school district in a state superior court for violation of their privacy rights under the state constitution. The court granted the students' request for a preliminary order halting the testing. Appeal went to the state court of appeal. It found the district offered "vague and shifting justifications" for testing CRA participants, and held the policy intruded upon privacy interests protected by the state constitution. Privacy rights were implicated by testing urine samples and requiring parents to disclose medications a child might be taking. **"Unlike the federal Constitution, the California Constitution contains an explicit guarantee of the right to privacy."** A state supreme court decision had held the California Constitution creates "a legal and enforceable right of privacy for every Californian." CRA participants were not shown to have reduced expectations of privacy in comparison to others. Some CRAs were curricular and some fulfilled college admissions requirements. The court held the superior court did not abuse its discretion in finding the students were entitled to injunctive relief. They were likely to prevail in further court activity by showing a sufficient expectation of privacy to pursue state constitutional claims. *Brown v. Shasta Union High School Dist.*, No. C061972, 2010 WL 3442147 (Cal. Ct. App. 9/2/10).

◆  After a 2000 survey indicated that 50% of student-athletes in a Washington school district self-identified as drug and/or alcohol users, the district began a random testing program. Participants had to agree to be tested for drug use as a condition of playing extracurricular sports. Drug test results under the program were not sent to law enforcement agencies. Students who tested positive were suspended from sports, but not from school. Parents of several students who played high school sports sued the school district, asserting the policy violated the state constitution. A state court upheld the policy, and the parents appealed.

The Supreme Court of Washington found "stark differences" between the Fourth Amendment and the Washington Constitution, which prohibits a search of a person "without authority of law." Under *New Jersey v. T.L.O.*, 469 U.S. 325 (1985), school officials may search students based on reasonable grounds for suspecting the search will turn up evidence of a violation of school rules. In *Vernonia School Dist. 47J v. Acton*, below, the Supreme Court upheld a random, suspicionless drug-testing program for student-athletes. The Washington court found the Supreme Court "never adequately explained why individual suspicion was needed in *T.L.O.* but not in *Acton*." **The state constitution provided greater protection than the Fourth Amendment**, and as students had a fundamental privacy interest in their bodily functions, the judgment was reversed. *York v. Wahkiakum School Dist. No. 200*, 178 P.3d 995 (Wash. 2008).

◆   An Oregon school district responded to increased student drug use by instituting a random drug-testing policy for all students wishing to participate in varsity athletics. Each student-athlete was to submit a consent form authorizing a test at the beginning of the season and weekly random testing thereafter. Students who refused testing were suspended from sports for the rest of the season. A seventh-grader who wanted to play football refused to sign the drug-testing consent form and was suspended from sports for the season. His parents sued the district, arguing that the policy violated the Fourth Amendment and the Oregon Constitution. A court upheld the policy, but the Ninth Circuit held that it violated both the U.S. and Oregon Constitutions.

On appeal, the U.S. Supreme Court stated that the reasonableness of a student search under the Fourth Amendment is determined by balancing the interests between the government and individual. **Students have a lesser expectation of privacy than the general populace, and student-athletes have an even lower expectation of privacy in the locker room.** The invasion of privacy in this case was no worse than what was typically encountered in public restrooms. Positive test results were disclosed to only a few school employees. The insignificant invasion of student privacy was outweighed by the district's important interest in addressing drug use by students who risked physical harm while playing sports. The Court vacated and remanded the decision of the court of appeals. *Vernonia School Dist. 47J v. Acton*, 515 U.S. 646 (1995).

◆   In 2002, the Supreme Court expanded the reach of its *Vernonia* decision in *Board of Educ. of Independent School Dist. 92 of Pottawatomie County v. Earls*. The Court held that an Oklahoma school district with no discernible drug problem could implement a program of testing for all students seeking to participate in extracurricular activities. **The Court found no reason to limit random drug testing to student-athletes**, extending *Vernonia* to cover all extracurricular activities participants. For a full summary of the case, please see Chapter Two, Section II.B. *Board of Educ. of Independent School Dist. 92 of Pottawatomie County v. Earls*, 536 U.S. 822 (2002).

## II.  DISCRIMINATION AND EQUITY

*Federal civil rights laws forbid discrimination based on sex, race or disability in federally funded school athletic programs. All public school entities must also comply with the Equal Protection Clause.*

### A.  Gender Equity

*Title IX of the Education Amendments of 1972, 20 U.S.C. § 1681(a), prohibits sex discrimination and exclusion from participation in any educational program on the basis of sex by any program or activity receiving federal funding. Federal regulations at 34 C.F.R. Part 106.41 provide guidance on equal athletic opportunities for members of both sexes. In determining whether equal opportunities exist, the U.S. Department of Education's Office for Civil Rights (OCR) considers several factors including: (1) whether selection of sports and levels of competition accommodate both sexes; (2) the provision of equipment or supplies; (3) the scheduling of games and practices; (4) travel and per diem allowances; (5) coaching and tutoring opportunities; (6) coaching and tutoring assignments and compensation; (7) provision of locker rooms, practice and competitive facilities; (8) provision of medical and training facilities and services; and publicity. See 34 C.F.R. Part 106.41(c).*

◆   As the only female on her school's freshman football team, a Wisconsin student claimed discrimination by her head coach. She said he denied her access to the girls' locker room and kept snacks and practice schedules in the boys' locker room, where she was not allowed to go. According to the student, the coach told her to get her haircut "like a boy." After her mother complained to school officials that the coach was not letting her child obtain her equipment, the student practiced without pads and injured a shoulder and clavicle. She sued the school district and coach in a federal district court for civil rights violations.

**The court held that to impose Title IX liability on a federal funding recipient, the institution must have actual notice of discrimination by employees and yet have "deliberate indifference" to it.** There was evidence that when other players came to practice without equipment, the usual response was to find appropriate gear. The district did not contest the coach's departure from this general rule or his hostility to the mother's complaints. The student made out a valid equal protection claim against the coach. A state law claim against the coach for disregarding a known danger also deserved further consideration. But the student did not show the district had notice of any discriminatory acts, particularly the denial of her access to the girls' locker room. As the district had no actual notice of the coach's allegedly discriminatory actions, the Title IX claim against it was dismissed. The student did not show the district created a dangerous situation, but claimed only that no official stopped her from harming herself by practicing without pads. This did not support her due process claim against the school district. *Elborough v. Evansville Community School Dist.*, 636 F.2d 812 (W.D. Wis. 2009).

◆   California high school girls sued their school district in a federal court, asserting Title IX violations. They produced evidence that the difference between their enrollment numbers and the percentage of girls participating in sports was from 6.7 to 10.3 % in the three most recent school years. The court found a 6.7 % difference represented 47 girls or at least one competitive team. Thus, the district failed the substantial proportionality inquiry of Title IX's regulations. The court also found that female athletic participation rates at the high school were not expanding. As a result, the district failed the second part of the regulatory test. Finally, the district failed the third part of the regulatory test because it discontinued a viable field hockey program twice due to its inability to retain a coach. **Student interest and ability, not the ability to retain a coach, determined whether the test was met.** As the district failed each part of the Title IX regulatory compliance test, the court found the district was not in compliance with Title IX. *Ollier v. Sweetwater Union High School Dist.*, 604 F.Supp.2d 1264 (S.D. Cal. 2009).

◆   Two female Tennessee students enrolled in a weightlifting/conditioning class along with 35 boys. The principal removed the girls from the class out of concern for inappropriate behavior by males, and a staff member told them to report to the guidance office to work as helpers. One student objected. A state official contacted the district's director of schools, and within a few days the principal permitted the student to return to the class. She missed only three days of class, earned an A grade, and graduated. However, she claimed the stress of being removed from the class made her unable to eat and that she contracted mononucleosis as a result. The family sued the school board and officials in a federal court for violating the Equal Protection Clause and Title IX, claiming $1 million in damages. After the court granted the board's dismissal motion, the U.S. Court of Appeals, Sixth Circuit, affirmed. **The principal was not executing an official policy of the board at the time he ordered her removal, and did not act as a board policy maker.** Here, the board took immediate corrective action on her behalf as soon as the director of schools learned about the incident. As the board had no prior notice of the student's claim, it could not be found deliberately indifferent to known acts of discrimination. *Phillips v. Anderson County Board of Educ.*, 259 Fed.Appx. 842 (6th Cir. 2008).

◆   The Michigan High School Athletic Association (MHSAA) scheduled girls' basketball, volleyball and soccer seasons during non-traditional seasons throughout the state. Female student-athletes sued the MHSAA for violating the Equal Protection Clause, Title IX and the state Civil Rights Act. A federal court noted that psychological harm was done to female athletes in the form of a message that they were subordinate to males. The scheduling created many disadvantages for girls, including lost scholarships and the inability to participate in "March Madness" events and tournaments. The court prohibited the MHSAA from continuing to schedule girls' sports in disadvantageous seasons. The Sixth Circuit then held that **competition in non-traditional seasons harmed girls, particularly by sending them a message that they were "second class" or were less valued than boys.** The MHSAA's evidence did not establish that separate seasons for boys and girls maximized opportunities for their participation. Female athletes were always required to play in disadvantageous seasons. The scheduling differences were properly found to be discriminatory, as boys' and girls' schedules were separate and treated unequally. *Communities for Equity v. Michigan High School Athletic Ass'n*, 459 F.3d 676 (6th Cir. 2006).

◆   A Wisconsin boy wanted to participate on the girls' gymnastics team at his high school. He filed a state court action against the Wisconsin Interscholastic Athletic Association (WIAA), alleging constitutional and Title IX claims. The student challenged a WIAA rule prohibiting all interscholastic activity involving boys and girls competing against each other, except as permitted by law and board of control interpretations. He added Wisconsin statutory and constitutional claims for injunctive relief. The court denied any relief, noting that the WIAA is a private, voluntary association. As the WIAA was not a public entity, no equal protection suit could be brought against it. The WIAA received no federal funds and could not be sued under Title IX. The student appealed to the Court of Appeals of Wisconsin, which found that **he failed to offer any evidence that the WIAA was engaged in action traditionally reserved to the state**. His equal protection and Title IX claims could not succeed. The court affirmed the judgment for the WIAA. *Bukowski v. Wisconsin Interscholastic Ass'n*, 726 N.W.2d 356 (Table) (Wis. Ct. App. 2006).

◆   New York state and regional championships for girls' soccer were held in the fall, and 649 of 714 schools offering soccer scheduled it accordingly. Some districts scheduled girls' soccer in spring to avoid jeopardizing field hockey programs. Two districts scheduled boys' soccer in fall, and the boys' teams remained eligible for state and regional competition. Girls' soccer was the only sport held outside the state championship season in either district. The families of two students who sought to play girls' soccer for district schools sued the districts for Title IX violations. A federal court held that the scheduling of girls' soccer seasons in spring violated Title IX. The districts appealed to the Second Circuit, which noted that a Title IX policy interpretation required equivalent treatment, benefits and opportunities, and the accommodation of interests and abilities of both sexes.

The court held that the scheduling of girls' soccer in spring created a disparity that had a negative impact on girls. It sent girls the message that they were not expected to succeed and that the school did not value their athletic ability as much as it valued the ability of boys. There was no reason why soccer and field hockey could not be played in the same season. The court affirmed the judgment and ordered the district court to consider whether boys and girls received equal opportunities for post-season competition. *McCormick v. School Dist. of Mamaroneck*, 370 F.3d 275 (2d Cir. 2004).

◆   The Minnesota State High School League recognized girls hockey as a varsity sport in 1994, many years after it began sponsoring boys hockey. Boys hockey tournaments took place in professional sports arenas, including the Target and Xcel Energy Centers. The league selected Ridder Arena, home of the University of Minnesota women's hockey team, to be the site of the 2004 girls tournament. A group representing girls hockey team members and their parents sued the league for Title IX and state Human Rights Act violations. The court denied a motion for a preliminary order to venue the girls tournament at the Xcel Energy Center, as **neither Title IX nor state law required the identical treatment of boys and girls athletics**. Instead, the laws required "equivalent treatment and equal accommodation."

In later court proceedings, the court found there were differences in the way the league handled tournaments. Other girls sports events were held at Xcel, and a boys tournament there drew smaller or comparable crowds than girls' events. The girls raised the issue of what message the choice of venue sent to female hockey players and fans. The evidence could lead a jury to find the league's scheduling policy violated Title IX, so the court ordered a trial. Less than a month after the decision, the parties announced a settlement under which the 2006 girls tournament would be held at Xcel. *Mason v. Minnesota State High School League*, No. 03-6462(JRT/FLN), 2004 WL 1630968 (D. Minn. 2004).

◆ A male Rhode Island high school student desired to compete as a member of his school's girls' field hockey team. However, the regulations of the Rhode Island Interscholastic League forbade boys from participating on girls' athletic teams. A federal court denied his request for an injunction based on the Fourteenth Amendment's Equal Protection Clause. He then sued the league, seeking an injunction based on the state constitution's equal protection provisions. The trial court granted the injunction, but the Rhode Island Supreme Court vacated the injunction. Gender classifications under the state constitution need only serve important governmental objectives and be substantially related to the achievement of those objectives. **Safety concerns and physical differences between the sexes justified the rule.** *Kleczek v. Rhode Island Interscholastic League,* 612 A.2d 734 (R.I. 1992).

## B. Race Discrimination

*Title VI of the Civil Rights Act of 1964 prohibits intentional race discrimination in any program that receives federal funds. Title VI is based on the Equal Protection Clause, and many discrimination complaints allege violations of Title VI, the Equal Protection Clause, and analogous state laws.*

◆ As a freshman, an Illinois student played for the varsity football team. He received a disciplinary referral for wearing his pants too low, in violation of the school dress code. The school referred him for discipline for failing to follow instructions to leave an area where some other students were fighting. His father learned that the student was at risk of being placed on disciplinary probation. The student finished his sophomore year at the high school but then moved with his father outside the district's boundaries. The father presented administrators with false documents showing that the family still lived in the district. The district allowed the student to work out with the football team during his junior year, but it barred him from Illinois High School Association games. The family moved back into the district, and the student was allowed to play football his senior year. But the family sued for constitutional rights violations. **A federal court found no evidence that other students were disciplined for wearing their pants too low.** But there was evidence that Caucasian students involved in the fighting incident were also disciplined, and 12 Caucasian students were placed on disciplinary probation in the student's sophomore year. The student apparently received the same treatment as others. The court held for the school district. *Bryant v. Board of Educ., Dist. 228,* No. 06 C 5697, 2008 WL 1702162 (N.D. Ill. 2008).

◆ The U.S. Court of Appeals, Eleventh Circuit, held that a lower court properly ruled against an Alabama student who filed an equal protection lawsuit based on his expulsion for striking two football coaches who removed him from a football game. **The claims failed because the student was unable to show that he was treated any differently than others.** He was not "similarly situated" to two other students who were not expelled, as their conduct involved horseplay and lesser misconduct. *Davis v. Houston County, Alabama Board of Educ.,* 291 Fed.Appx. 251 (11th Cir. 2008).

◆   Thirteen suburban Chicago school districts withdrew from the South Inter-Conference Association after over 30 years of membership. They formed two new athletic conferences, excluding two school districts in Thornton, Illinois that served mostly African-American students. The Thornton districts alleged a racially motivated conspiracy among the 13 districts, resulting in three racially segregated conferences. They joined several Thornton parents and students in a federal court action against the 13 districts. The Thornton parties **included a racially charged statement by a board member of one of the 13 districts accusing African-Americans of ruining neighborhoods in Chicago's south suburbs.** They also referenced apartheid, white flight and a racial Mason-Dixon line. Rejecting a claim by the Thornton parties that a reference to *Brown v. Board of Education* stated the grounds of their lawsuit, the court found there was no basis for any of the statements. As a result, the court struck them from the complaint. The lengthy statement by the board member was redundant and served no purpose but to scandalize the conduct of the 13 districts. His remarks might be inadmissible hearsay and had to be stricken. *Board of Educ. of Thornton Township High School Dist. 205 v. Board of Educ. of Argo Community High School Dist. 217,* No. 06 C 2005, 2006 WL 1896068 (N.D. Ill. 2006).


◆   A Mississippi student's parent claimed that the school's head football coach called her son "nigger" and "fat black ass" during team practices. A teammate allegedly repeated these epithets, and along with another player, hit her son's helmet with rocks during practice. The coach allegedly did nothing and the principal took no action when she reported this. In a later practice, the teammate allegedly lunged at the student and gouged his eye, causing permanent injury. When the principal investigated the incident, no one admitted seeing an assault.

The parent sued the school district, coaching staff and school officials in a federal district court, alleging deprivation of her son's civil rights. The court dismissed the claims, and the parent appealed to the U.S. Court of Appeals, Fifth Circuit. It found the teammate was not a "state actor" and thus could not be liable for civil rights violations filed under 42 U.S.C. § 1983. The Due Process Clause did not require coaches to protect the student from the teammate because there was no "special relationship" between the coaches and student. While the conduct of school officials in this case was "morally reprehensible," the teammate's actions could not be attributed to them. **Use of racial epithets, without evidence of harassment or other deprivation of established rights, does not constitute an equal protection violation.** The school investigated the incident, and while its response may have been inadequate, it did not show inaction creating an equal protection violation. Apart from the racial epithets, the parent produced no evidence of bias by school officials. The judgment was affirmed. *Priester v. Lowndes County,* 354 F.3d 414 (5th Cir. 2004).

The case returned to the district court, which found that the student had alleged sufficient facts to avoid pretrial judgment on his discrimination claims against the district. Disputed fact issues surrounded his expulsion, including whether he had shoved the coach and threatened to kill the teammates while disobeying instructions to avoid a confrontation. This required a trial. *Priester v. Starkville School Dist.,* No. 1: 03CV90, 2005 WL 2347285 (N.D. Miss. 2005).

## C. Students with Disabilities

*In* PGA Tour v. Martin, *532 S.Ct. 661 (U.S. 2001), the Supreme Court held the Americans with Disabilities Act (ADA) requires an individualized inquiry to determine whether a requested modification is reasonable and necessary for the disabled individual, and whether the modification would fundamentally alter the nature of the competition.*

◆   A 19-year-old Mississippi senior with learning disabilities transferred to another school and sought a temporary restraining order that would allow him to play basketball. He sued the state athletic association under the ADA, the IDEA and the Constitution. A federal court refused to grant him relief, finding no justification for disrupting the status quo. **The state high school athletic association had found that the transfer was made for athletic reasons**, and he failed to show a substantial likelihood of success on the merits of his claims. The student essentially argued that if he was not allowed to play varsity basketball, he would be less likely to get a professional contract. This could be remedied by an award of money damages, undercutting the claim that he would be irreparably injured in the absence of a court order. On appeal, the U.S. Court of Appeals, Fifth Circuit, rejected the student's arguments. His primary argument was financial and the court rejected claims under federal disability laws and provisions of the U.S. Constitution. *Newsome v. Mississippi High School Activities Ass'n*, 326 Fed.Appx. 878 (5th Cir. 2009).

◆   A New Jersey student with learning disabilities was recruited for football by several NCAA Division I schools. The NCAA ruled that a number of his high school special education classes did not satisfy its core course requirement and declared him ineligible during his freshman season. He sued the NCAA, the universities and the ACT/Clearinghouse, which administers college entrance examinations. After he died, his estate continued the litigation. His mother later revealed to the NCAA and the universities that he had been in and out of drug treatment and mental health programs and that his death resulted from an apparent drug overdose. The court sanctioned the mother and her attorneys, finding that the failure to disclose the information was willful and in bad faith.

The U.S. Court of Appeals, Third Circuit, held that the alleged discrimination took place during the 1995-96 school year, when the student was deemed ineligible for football under NCAA rules. The evidence of any substance abuse by the student in 1995-96 was minimal. **His substance abuse was irrelevant for purposes of establishing liability.** The district court's contrary ruling was reversed. The case was returned to the district court for a determination of whether the NCAA and the universities violated the ADA and Rehabilitation Act. *Bowers v. NCAA*, 475 F.3d 524 (3d Cir. 2007).

◆   A Colorado student was diagnosed with attention deficit disorder (ADD) at age eight. He received medication and attended a speech class for grade four. By middle school, his special education program ended, and he stopped taking medication for ADD. In high school, his academic modifications were limited to additional time for tests and homework, and the provision of class notes. He missed several weeks of school in ninth grade due to a sinus infection, and he repeated grade nine. His parents divorced near this time. When the student reached grade 12, state athletic association rules barred him from playing football as he was in his ninth consecutive semester of high school attendance. The association denied his request for a hardship waiver, and he sought a state court order to declare its eight-semester rule violated a state anti-discrimination act. The court denied his request for preliminary relief. On appeal, the Court of Appeals of Colorado found evidence that he repeated grade nine because of his parents' divorce, problems adjusting to a new school, and his sinus infection. **A single failed year of school was a temporary and short-term event that did not render the student "disabled" under state law or the ADA.** The trial court had properly denied his request for temporary relief. *Tesmer v. Colorado High School Activities Ass'n*, 140 P.3d 249 (Colo. Ct. App. 2006).

◆ Under either Section 504 or the ADA, **a person with disabilities may be excluded from a program if participation presents a direct threat to the health and safety of others.** In a Kentucky case, a school district properly excluded a student with hemophilia and hepatitis B from participation on the junior varsity basketball team while trying to determine if he presented a serious health risk to others. The U.S. Court of Appeals, Sixth Circuit, reasoned that Congress created a narrow exception to the broad prohibition against discrimination contained in the ADA, where an individual with disabilities presents a direct threat to the health and safety of others. School officials had never removed the student from the team but had placed him on hold status while awaiting medical advice. The action was appropriate in view of the potential liability faced by the school if a competitor became infected as a result of his participation. The student had also voluntarily chosen not to participate. *Doe v. Woodford County Board of Educ.*, 213 F.3d 921 (6th Cir. 2000).

## III. ISSUES IN COACHING

### A. Employment

*Coaches typically receive a salary supplement for their coaching duties under separate contracts. In these cases, their property interests in their coaching assignments are limited to the term of the supplemental contract and severable from teaching contracts. Under these circumstances, coaching duties do not have the same statutory protections as regular teaching assignments.*

*A Texas school athletic administrator was unable to convince the state court of appeals that the Texas Whistleblower Act protected him from being demoted after he reported a violation of state interscholastic rules.*

◆ A Texas high school administrator served as athletic director and director of extracurricular activities. He learned that a high school football player might be in violation of a state University Interscholastic League (UIL) residency rule. The administrator discussed the problem with other school officials. With district approval, he submitted a written report to the UIL, and the football team was barred from playoff games. About five weeks later, the district reassigned the administrator to an athletic trainer position. After a hearing, the district reinstated him to the extracurricular activities job. But he was not reinstated as an athletic director and he sued the district under the Texas Whistleblower's Act. On appeal, the Supreme Court of Texas held **the elements of the state Whistleblower Act could be considered in order to determine both a court's jurisdiction and any liability issues**. It returned the case to the lower court for a determination of whether the administrator had stated a Whistleblower violation. *Galveston Independent School Dist. v. Jaco*, 303 S.W.3d 699 (Tex. 2010).

Upon its third review of the case, the court of appeals explained that the Whistleblower Act pertained to the good faith reporting by a public employee of a "violation of law" by the employing governmental entity. According to the school district, the trial court should not have denied pretrial judgment, since UIL rules were not laws. **Agreeing with the district, the court found no state law requiring the UIL to have a residency rule.** UIL rules were not "adopted" by the legislature, but were submitted by the UIL to the state commissioner of education for approval. As UIL rules were not "laws" under the Whistleblower Act and to do so would lead to absurd results, the court held for the district. *Galveston Independent School Dist. v. Jaco*, 331 S.W.3d 182 (Tex. Ct. App. 2011).

◆ Alabama's Supreme Court held that **teachers under contract for supplemental non-teaching duties like coaching do not require notice of non-renewal for such contracts under the state Teacher Tenure Act**. A full summary of the case appears in Chapter Ten, Section I.B.2. *Boone v. Birmingham Board of Educ.*, 45 So.3d 764 (Ala. 2009).

◆ Many complaints were made about an Iowa high school basketball coach's threatening and intimidating treatment of players and his use of profanity. Five players quit the varsity team during his first year. The district renewed the coach's contract, but it also extended his probationary status and notified him of "major concerns" with the boys' basketball program. In the coach's fourth season, he was again the subject of numerous student and parent complaints. Fifteen families wrote letters, complaining that he told injured players not to see their doctors, ignored athletic association rules, set a poor example for ethical behavior and created a negative environment that damaged student self-esteem and confidence.

The district superintendent specifically forbade the coach from correcting players outside the presence of an assistant coach, counselor or parent. In a basketball game held the next year, a player failed to follow coaching instructions. After the game, the coach and player met briefly in a hallway with no other adult present. Administrators ruled that the coach had violated the directive. The school fired the coach, and the Supreme Court of Iowa noted that **the school board had appropriately considered the coach's entire history, as well as the final incident, when voting to terminate his coaching contract**. The coach had been informed throughout his career about the need to respect his players, and the superintendent had specifically notified him that failure to do so could lead to termination. Just cause existed for contract termination. *Board of Directors of Ames Community School Dist. v. Cullinan*, 745 N.W.2d 487 (Iowa 2008).

◆   Tennessee's highest court held school directors have the authority to transfer tenured teachers, including those with coaching responsibilities. For this reason, a tenured teacher who head-coached a high school girls' basketball team for 17 years could be transferred – as to his coaching responsibilities – without regard to a collective bargaining agreement. **The statutory term "teacher" did not extend to contracts for coaching duties, as there was no certification of coaches in the state.** An arbitrator had incorrectly held that a master contract governed the renewal of the coaching contract in this case. Year-to-year appointments were not entitled to the benefits of the collective bargaining process. *Lawrence County Educ. Ass'n v. Lawrence County Board of Educ.*, 244 S.W.3d 302 (Tenn. 2007). For a full summary of this case, see Chapter Seven, Section IV of this volume.

◆   An inner-city Alabama high school basketball coach was a tenured science teacher with 20 years of teaching experience. Before the start of the 2004-05 basketball season, he agreed with players to use a "one-minute drill" or "circle" as a form of discipline in practices. The "drill" consisted of the team encircling the rules violator, then hitting or kicking him for up to one minute. The coach looked on and timed the hitting with a stopwatch. The punishment was used 11 times in a six-week period. After the media reported a player's injuries, the school district placed the coach on administrative leave. A hearing officer found the coach engaged in serious misconduct but did not recommend canceling his contract. Instead, the coach was barred from coaching for four years, suspended without pay for 30 days, and ordered to apologize to all players and parents.

The case reached the Supreme Court of Alabama, which noted that at his hearing, the coach acknowledged his mistake and promised it would never happen again. Players uniformly stated that he was a positive influence in their lives. **The Alabama Teacher Tenure Act permitted consideration of a teacher's employment history, including matters occurring in previous years.** The coach had no prior disciplinary record, and parents and students expressed a strong and almost unanimous desire for him to remain. The coach had been able to improve grades and make college a realistic goal for his players. The hearing officer had attempted to balance a number of vital concerns. That decision was upheld. *Ex parte Dunn*, 962 So.2d 814 (Ala. 2007).

◆   An untenured Alabama teacher was the faculty sponsor for a junior varsity cheerleading squad. Parents complained about unfairness in cheerleading tryouts. The principal investigated and gave the teacher a questionnaire. She responded to the questionnaire and raised her own questions about the tryouts. The principal decided not to renew the teacher's contract, and she sued the school board for speech and due process violations. A federal court held for the board, and the Eleventh Circuit affirmed. A public employee who does not speak as a citizen on a matter of public concern has no First Amendment claim based on his or her employer's reaction to the speech. Public employees are not speaking as "citizens" when they speak about their official duties. **The teacher's responses to the questionnaire were unprotected.** *Gilder-Lucas v. Elmore County Board of Educ.*, 186 Fed.Appx. 885 (11th Cir. 2006).

◆  During a job interview with an Indiana school board, a coach disclosed his criminal convictions, including one for conspiracy to distribute marijuana. He assured the board he had "turned his life around," and the board hired him. The coach was then offered additional positions teaching special education and coaching the girls' basketball team. He obtained a limited one-year teaching license to teach special education. Near the end of the coach's term, an interim district superintendent recommended not renewing his teaching contract due to the expiration of his limited teaching license. The non-renewal of the coach's contract was reported in the media. The board voted to immediately remove him as the girls' basketball coach. He resigned as football coach and sued the board for denial of his equal protection and due process rights.

The Seventh Circuit ruled against him. His sole argument was that the board had singled him out by requiring him to take drug tests. He stated that the district athletic director had been caught stealing from the school but was not required to submit to drug testing. The court held that **the coach and athletic director were not "similarly situated" and could not be compared for purposes of an Equal Protection claim**. The athletic director was never prosecuted for any crimes, while the coach had a felony drug conviction. *Ott v. Edinburgh Community School Corp.*, 189 Fed.Appx. 507 (7th Cir. 2006).

◆  A Mississippi teacher's football coaching duties included summer work, but he refused to attend eight of 24 summer workouts. The school board voted not to renew his primary teaching contract for the next year as a result. After a state chancery court upheld the decision, the teacher appealed to the Court of Appeals of Mississippi. He argued that his coaching rider did not permit the non-renewal of his teaching contract, and that the rider was not enforceable because it required him to work for no pay, in violation of state and federal wage laws. The court held **state law did not prohibit school boards from including riders or attachments in school employment contracts**. The teacher's rider was valid, and the trial court did not commit error by finding that he failed to perform his duties by skipping the summer workouts. There was no merit to his argument that the extended time period specified in his coaching rider violated state and federal wage laws. Federal regulations published under the Fair Labor Standards Act exempt teachers and those with coaching duties from coverage. There was no merit to a claim that the rider applied only to cases of resignation or involuntary termination. The employment contract and rider referred to a single teacher/coach position. As the teacher had defiantly chosen not to attend the summer workouts, the court upheld the judgment for the school district. *Smith v. Petal School Dist.*, 956 So.2d 273 (Miss. Ct. App. 2006).

◆  After working for six years for his district, an Alabama teacher transferred to a high school to teach physical education and coach basketball. He discovered that the girls' team did not receive the same funding or access to equipment and facilities as boys' teams. He claimed that his job was made difficult by lack of adequate funding, equipment and facilities, and he began complaining to supervisors. He stated that the district did not respond to his complaints and gave him negative evaluations before removing him as girls' coach. He sued the school board in a federal court, claiming the loss of his supplemental coaching contracts constituted unlawful retaliation in violation of Title IX. The court dismissed the case, and the Eleventh Circuit affirmed this.

The U.S. Supreme Court stated that **Title IX covers retaliation against a person for complaining about sex discrimination**. "Retaliation is, by definition an intentional act," and is a form of discrimination, since the person who complains is treated differently than others. Without finding that actual discrimination had occurred, the Court held that the teacher was entitled to attempt to show that the board was liable. A private right of action for retaliation was within the statute's prohibition of intentional sex discrimination. Title IX did not require the victim of retaliation to also be the victim of discrimination. Teachers and coaches were often in the best position to vindicate the rights of students by identifying discrimination and notifying administrators. A reasonable school board would realize it could not cover up violations of Title IX by retaliating against teachers. The Court reversed the judgment. *Jackson v. Birmingham Board of Educ.*, 544 U.S. 167 (2005).

## B. Defamation

*Coaches, like other public school officials and teachers, are considered "public officials" in defamation cases. This means that to prevail, they must show that defamatory statements were made with "actual malice." And they must prove the other elements of a defamation claim. Since actual malice is difficult to prove, defamation claimants typically face an uphill battle.*

◆ Several parents of players on a Utah high school basketball team accused their coach of giving preferential treatment to the team's star player, criticized his demeanor and questioned his use of team funds. The administration eventually dismissed the coach from his head coaching duties, citing "his refusal to promise that he would not deny team membership and playing time to the women in retaliation against the Parents." The coach sued the parents for defamation, and a trial court agreed with the parents that the coach was a "public official." This meant he was required to show they made their statements with "actual malice" to prevail on his defamation claims.

The Supreme Court of Utah explained that **persons who are deemed to be public officials or public figures "surrender a sizeable measure of their right to recover damages from those who defame them."** Statements directed at public officials or public figures require proof that the speaker had actual malice. However, the coach did not occupy a position with such "apparent importance" that he had "public official" status. Despite the increasing popularity of athletics, the court rejected the parents' claim that coaches should be treated as public officials. Unlike those in "policy-making positions," Utah teachers and coaches did not surrender their ability to protect their reputations by accepting their jobs. However, the court agreed with the parents that they could be entitled to a conditional privilege based on family relationships. The case was returned to the district court, which was to decide whether the parents' statements were defamatory under the new standard explained by the supreme court. *O'Connor v. Burningham*, 165 P.3d 1214 (Utah 2007).

◆   Michigan High School Athletic Association rules required transfer students to sit out of interscholastic athletic competition for two semesters if a transfer was "athletically motivated." A star student-athlete told his football coach and others he was considering a transfer because "the program was in disarray." The student's mother told the principal the transfer was academically motivated, but the principal filed a complaint with the state athletic association, asserting the transfer was athletically motivated. Two newspapers interviewed school officials, then published articles speculating that the transfer was athletically motivated. The student sued the school district, principal, coach and the district athletic director for defamation and other claims. The case reached the Court of Appeals of Michigan, which held **the principal, coach and athletic director were entitled to speak to reporters who were already aware of the story**. The trial court had properly dismissed defamation and invasion of privacy claims based on governmental immunity. Statements to the association were limited to furthering the district's interest and were made in a proper manner. And the statements to the reporters were not defamation, as there was no evidence that they caused any special harm. The student himself openly spoke about his transfer at school. *Cassise v. Walled Lake Consolidated Schools*, No. 257299, 2006 WL 445960 (Mich. Ct. App. 2006).

◆   A Louisiana student and her mother were spectators at a game. She claimed a coach physically and verbally threatened them and called the police to have them removed from the gym. The student sued the school board and coach in a federal court, claiming "threatening and abusive language is actionable" in actions for federal civil rights violations under 42 U.S.C. § 1983. The coach moved for dismissal, asserting there was no viable Section 1983 claim, and that she was also entitled to qualified immunity. The court agreed with the coach, stating that **the Due Process Clause "does not transform every tort committed by a state actor into a constitutional violation."** Even in a state custodial situation, "the use of words, no matter how violent, does not comprise a Section 1983 violation." The court rejected the student's claim alleging harm to her reputation. The conduct she alleged did not raise a valid constitutional claim. Any harm to reputation was not a deprivation of a constitutional liberty or property interest recognized by state or federal law. *Paige v. Tangipahoa Parish School Board*, No. 04-354, 2005 WL 943636 (E.D. La. 2005).

◆   A Minnesota school district decided not to rehire a varsity football coach. A newspaper published articles quoting sources who said the coach was "known for his temper, inappropriate comments and foul language, which people claim he uses to intimidate players." While news accounts did not identify the source of these comments, one statement was attributed to a former assistant coach. The head coach sued the school district for defamation, breach of contract and other claims. A court twice denied motions by the coach to identify staff members who allegedly defamed him, then held for the district and employees.
    The case eventually reached the state supreme court, which recited the elements for a defamation claim, which are: (1) a false and defamatory statement (2) in an unprivileged publication to a third party that (3) harmed the plaintiff's reputation in the community. **Public officials must also**

demonstrate that the statement was made with "actual malice." In Minnesota, public school teachers and coaches are deemed public officials. Since the speaker was anonymous, the court held that his or her identity would necessarily lead to relevant evidence on the issue of actual malice. The district court had found that the statements, if false, were defamatory. The court reversed, finding that if any school employee was the source of the statements, there was probable cause to believe the speaker had relevant information. *Weinberger v. Maplewood Review*, 668 N.W.2d 667 (Minn. 2003).

## C.  Liability

*Coaches typically avoid liability for student injuries, unless there is a showing of willful or wanton misconduct. For additional cases involving liability in the context of school athletics, see Chapter Twelve, Section II.*

◆   A Tennessee cheerleading sponsor worked in a school cafeteria and was not a certified teacher. She supervised the cheerleading squad for over two years without incident. A cheerleader then broke her arm during a practice when she landed on the floor while attempting a "basket toss" maneuver. At the time of the injury, the sponsor had left the practice for other duties. The cheerleader sued the school board and sponsor for negligence. After a court awarded pretrial judgment to the board and sponsor, the cheerleader appealed. The Court of Appeals of Tennessee held that **the cheerleader failed to show that the sponsor's experience was inadequate or fell below an established standard of care**. Thus, the negligent hiring claim failed. But there was a dispute concerning the sponsor's level of supervision over the squad. While she said she told the squad not to perform stunts in her absence, the cheerleader said there was no such warning. A trial was required on that issue. *Britt v. Maury County Board of Educ.*, 2008 WL 4427190 (Tenn. Ct. App. 9/29/08).

◆   A Pennsylvania junior high school wrestling coach directed a 152-pound wrestler to "live wrestle" a 240-pound teammate during a practice. "Live wrestling" simulated actual competitive conditions, with both wrestlers giving their best efforts. Pennsylvania Interscholastic Athletic Association (PIAA) rules limited wrestling to competitors in their own weight class or one class above. The teammate was three PIAA weight classes above the wrestler, and he injured the wrestler's leg when he collapsed on him. The wrestler sued the school district and employees in a federal court, which held for the district.

The wrestler appealed to the U.S. Court of Appeals, Third Circuit, which explained that **to hold the coach liable for a constitutional violation, it had to be shown that he deprived the wrestler of a federal right in a way that was foreseeable and fairly direct**. In this case, the coach had paired mismatched wrestlers simply because there was no partner for the teammate. The coach apparently had done this previously. As there was at least circumstantial evidence of deliberate indifference to the wrestler's federally protected rights, the court returned the case to the lower court. However, the claims against the school district failed. State agencies are not liable for constitutional violations of their employees, except for policymakers, or where the agency itself has an official policy or custom of violating federally protected rights. *Patrick v. Great Valley School Dist.*, 296 Fed.Appx, 258 (3d Cir. 2008).

◆   Four Tennessee student-athletes claimed their varsity football head coach humiliated and degraded them, used inappropriate language and required them to participate in a year-round conditioning program that violated school rules. They claimed he hit a player in the helmet and threw away college recruiting letters that were sent to "disfavored players." One of them typed a petition that said "I hate Coach Euverard and I don't want to play for him." Eighteen players signed the petition. When the coach learned of this, he summoned players into his office one by one to interview them. Players who signed the petition were allowed to stay on the team if they apologized and said they wanted to play for the head coach. Four players who did not apologize and accept the coach were taken off the team. They sued the coach, school board and other officials for First Amendment violations. A federal district court denied the officials' motion for qualified immunity, and they appealed. The U.S. Court of Appeals, Sixth Circuit, noted that the petition was a direct challenge to the coach's authority, and it would harm team unity and divide teammates into groups. **The petition was reasonably likely to cause substantial disruption to the team and therefore was not protected.** There was no First Amendment violation as the players had implicitly agreed to accept their coach's authority by turning out for the team. *Lowery v. Euverard*, 497 F.3d 584 (6th Cir. 2007).

◆   An Ohio student was injured when a batted ball ricocheted off an L-screen that had been placed in front of him for protection. He was hospitalized and doctors implanted four titanium plates and screws into his head. He sued the school district and coach for negligence, claiming that the coach failed to properly supervise the batting cage and did not provide protective helmets for pitchers. The complaint did not allege malice, bad faith or reckless conduct or claim damages from the coach individually. A court awarded pretrial judgment to the school district and the student appealed. The case reached the state supreme court, which held teachers and coaches have wide discretion to determine what supervision is necessary for student safety. The coach's decisions reflected his discretion. He instructed pitchers regarding the L-screen as well as general guidance on game preparations. **The coach's direction represented the exercise of his judgment and discretion in the use of equipment or facilities in connection with his position.** As the injury resulted from the coach's judgment or discretion, the district could claim immunity. There was no suggestion of reckless conduct, malice or bad faith. *Elston v. Howland Local Schools*, 113 Ohio St.3d 314, 865 N.E.2d 845 (Ohio 2007).

◆   A Texas cross country coach had his team warm up on the paved shoulder of a two-lane state highway. He followed the team in his personal vehicle. The warmup took place about 7:00 a.m., in low-light conditions. After warming up, the team gathered on the shoulder of the eastbound lane of the highway. The coach parked on the westbound shoulder and activated his emergency flashers. An oncoming vehicle drove onto the eastbound shoulder, striking and killing a team member. The team member's parent sued the school board and coach in a state court, alleging that the coach negligently operated his emergency flashers. The court held that the board and coach were entitled to immunity under the Texas Tort Claims Act. The state court of appeals affirmed the judgment. Government units can be liable for property damage, personal injury and death in cases involving the use or operation of a motor vehicle. But the activation of the emergency flashers on the coach's car did not create a waiver of immunity under the Act. Even if it did, there was no evidence that the death arose from this use. The student was killed by the vehicle that struck him. **The coach's actions were supervisory in nature and did not involve the operation or use of a motor vehicle.** *Morales v. Barnette*, 219 S.W.3d 477 (Tex. Ct. App. 2007).

◆    A Michigan middle school wrestling coach injured a student when he performed a maneuver in practice without prior warning. The student sued, and a state court denied pretrial judgment to the coach, finding that he was grossly negligent in performing the maneuver without prior notice. The case reached the Supreme Court of Michigan, which held that even if the coach had grabbed the student from behind and took him to the mat as alleged, this did not produce injury. **The injury occurred when the coach and student were engaged in wrestling activity.** The student testified that after he completed a body roll, he did what he had been coached to do – brace his arm and try to escape. This was what caused the injury. As the lack of adequate notice of the initial maneuver was not a basis for injury, the court reversed the judgment. *Jefferson Middle School v. Nadeau*, 477 Mich. 1109, 729 N.W.2d 840 (Mich. 2007).

◆    A Texas basketball coach and an athletic trainer were blamed for the death of a student who collapsed after completing a two-mile run with her team. The student's parents claimed the coach and trainer failed to perform CPR or give her other necessary medical attention and that their delays caused her death. They sued the district, coach and trainer in a federal district court. **The court held that to show a school employee has violated a constitutional interest in bodily integrity, there must be proof of deliberate indifference toward the victim.** The family had alleged only negligence, not deliberate indifference. The coach attended to the student about five minutes after she finished running, and the trainer saw her about 12 minutes later. As this was not "conscious disregard" for her health and safety, the employees had qualified immunity. The district was entitled to immunity for the constitutional and state law claims. *Livingston v. DeSoto Independent School Dist.*, 391 F.Supp.2d 463 (N.D. Tex. 2005).

◆    A 15-year-old Mississippi student became fatigued at a football practice on a hot August day. He told the coach he felt weak and needed a water break, but the coach thought he was "faking it" and refused the request for a break. After allegedly suffering a heatstroke, the student sued the district and coach in a state court for negligence. The court held a trial and found the student suffered damages of $350,000, including $68,000 in medical bills. However, the court found the coach and district were entitled to immunity under the Mississippi Torts Claims Act (MTCA) because their conduct was discretionary. The student appealed to the Supreme Court of Mississippi. The court explained that government entities and their employees are entitled to MTCA immunity against all claims based on the exercise of discretionary duties. Here, the coach was in the best position to know his team and had to motivate and discipline players. **Imposing liability on the coach and district would result in their loss of control over high school football programs due to the risk of lawsuits.** Since the coach's actions were discretionary within the meaning of the MTCA, the supreme court affirmed the judgment for the district and coach. *Harris v. McCray*, 867 So.2d 188 (Miss. 2003).

◆ A 14-year-old California student told two coaches of her great fear of diving into shallow water. They allowed her to swim the first leg of team relay races during the first meets of the season, which allowed her to start in the water. Minutes before the start of a meet, a coach told her that she could not start the relay and would have to dive into the pool. She panicked and begged him to change the rotation to allow her to start from the water. He refused and allegedly threatened to exclude her from the meet. She broke her neck on a practice dive, and later sued the school district and coach. She presented evidence from a certified water safety instructor that the dive she tried was ultra-hazardous if done by an inadequately trained swimmer. A state court held for the district and coach, but the state supreme court ruled that the case required a trial. **The court held a school district generally has no duty to protect a student from the inherent risks in a sport.** But sports instructors and coaches have a duty not to increase the risks of sports participation beyond what is inherent in the sport. The trial court had to credit the student's expert and her statements concerning the lack of instruction, her fear of diving into shallow water, and her claim that the coach threatened her if she did not dive. *Kahn v. East Side Union High School Dist.*, 31 Cal.4th 990, 4 Cal.Rptr.3d 103, 75 P.3d 30 (Cal. 2003).

◆ A Nebraska high school football player was struck on his head during a game. He felt dizzy and disoriented, but stayed in the game a few plays before taking himself out. Coaches observed he was short of breath but attributed this to hyperventilation. As the student made normal eye contact and had normal speech and movement, no medical attention was sought. The student later asked to return to the game, and coaches allowed him to do so. He suffered a headache the entire weekend, but coaches denied he said anything about it the next week. They allowed him to practice with the team, and he suffered a closed-head traumatic brain injury. The student sued the school district in a state court for personal injuries. After the court dismissed the case, the Nebraska Supreme Court held it should not have discredited testimony by expert witnesses.

Certified athletic trainers who taught state-required courses for coaching endorsements had testified for the student that Nebraska **high school coaches should know that headache, dizziness and disorientation are symptomatic of a concussion.** The case then returned to the trial court. It heard testimony that little training or literature was available to coaches about head injury at the time of the injury. The court dismissed the case, as the coaching staff complied with the duty of care required of a reasonably prudent person with a state coaching endorsement. The supreme court later affirmed this decision. *Cerny v. Cedar Bluffs Junior/Senior Public School*, 268 Neb. 958, 679 N.W.2d 198 (Neb. 2004).

### D. Misconduct

◆ A California freshman made her varsity softball team. This achievement and her relationship with the team's head coach "stirred up some resentment among the other softball team members." Rumors began that she was having a lesbian relationship with the coach. The principal warned the coach to avoid favoritism, "maintain a proper professional distance" and avoid being alone with the student. After the coach disobeyed the warning, the district did not renew her probationary contract. The student claimed that students continued calling her "homo" and that teachers who witnessed the harassment did nothing to stop it. However, she reported only one incident to the school, and when she did, a vice principal met with the student and a harasser. The new coach then dismissed her from the team, stating that she had been a "cancer on the team." She sued the district, principal, vice principal and other staff.

A court awarded pretrial judgment to the district and staff, and the Court of Appeal of California affirmed. Here, the student had been rude and disrespectful to the new head coach, an assistant coach and her teammates. Only one potentially harassing remark was ever reported to the school, and the vice principal responded to it. **The student sought damages for "school yard insults and name calling," most of which were never brought to the school's attention.** She did not show harassment so severe, pervasive and objectively offensive that it denied her equal access to education under Title IX. *Ashby v. Hesperia Union School Dist.*, 2004 WL 2699940 (Cal. Ct. App. 2004).

◆ A Pennsylvania coach suspected that a member of the high school swim team was pregnant. He repeatedly asked her if this was true. She consistently denied it but eventually agreed to take a pregnancy test. The result was positive and, after learning that there was no medical reason to prevent the student from swimming competitively, the coach let her remain on the team. However, she alleged that after her baby was born, the coach attempted to alienate her from her peers, refused to speak with her and retaliated against her by removing her from competition. She sued him for civil rights violations. A federal district court held that the coach was entitled to qualified immunity.

On appeal, the Third Circuit found that **requiring a student to submit to a pregnancy test, if proven, would be an unlawful search and seizure**. A reasonable swim coach would not have forced a student to take a pregnancy test. Because the coach did not "justify his failure to respect the boundaries of reasonableness," he was not entitled to qualified immunity on the student's Fourth Amendment claim. This aspect of the district court's judgment was reversed and remanded. The court also reversed and remanded the student's claims based on violations of her constitutional privacy rights and state law. Her pregnancy was entitled to privacy protection under the Due Process Clause. The coach was not entitled to qualified immunity, since current law put him on notice that the compelled disclosure of personal information was not objectively reasonable. *Gruenke v. Seip*, 225 F.3d 290 (3d Cir. 2000).

# CHAPTER FOURTEEN

## School Operations

## I.  BUDGET AND FINANCE

### A.  Educational Finance and Equal Opportunity

*Education is not a fundamental right under the U.S. Constitution. However, state constitutional education clauses require states to provide an "adequate," "sound basic" or "thorough and efficient" system of public schools.*

*The U.S. Supreme Court effectively eliminated educational financing claims based on the Equal Protection Clause of the U.S. Constitution by holding education is not a fundamental right in* San Antonio School Dist. v. Rodriguez,

*411 U.S. 1, 93 S.Ct. 1278, 36 L.Ed.2d 16 (1973). State courts continue to consider financial equity and educational adequacy claims under state constitutions. Typical state court challenges to school financing systems involve differing tax bases that result in disparities among school district revenues.*

◆  Two groups challenged Colorado's public school funding system in the state court system. One group consisted of parents of students attending eight different school districts. The other was made up of 14 school districts. They asserted that the system was underfunded by at least $500 million in 2001-02 and that state officials allocated funds irrationally and arbitrarily in violation of the state constitution. They claimed that the state did not provide an adequate education to students with disabilities, those from lower socio-economic backgrounds, ethnic and racial minorities and non-English speaking students. A state court held that the case posed a political question for the legislature to decide. But the Supreme Court of Colorado returned the case to the trial court so **the parents and districts could try to prove the state's current public school financing system was not rationally related to the constitutional mandate to provide a "thorough and uniform" system of public education**. If the court found the current system of public school finance was irrational and thus unconstitutional, the legislature would be given time to change the system. *Lobato v. State*, 218 P.3d 358 (Colo. 2009).

◆  In the 1980s, a group representing students in New Jersey's poorest urban school districts sued state officials, asserting that the legislature failed to provide an adequate public education. In 1990, the state supreme court ordered state officials to develop a funding formula to provide all children, including students in poorer urban districts, with equal educational opportunities under the New Jersey Constitution. A 1994 state supreme court decision coupled the 1990 funding requirement to educational program standards. *Abbott v. Burke*, 136 N.J. 444, 643 A.2d 575 (N.J. 1994).

Remedial orders created "*Abbott* districts," identified as the state's poor urban districts. In 2008, the New Jersey legislators enacted the School Funding Reform Act (SFRA). State officials sought court review of the SFRA's constitutionality and release from prior court remedial orders.

In 2009, the case returned to the state supreme court, which noted that the SFRA was a "weighted school funding formula" with a base cost for students with increased per-pupil amounts reflecting grade level and at-risk status, limited English proficiency (LEP) status and special education status. Under a sliding scale for educating at-risk pupils, the court found that **the SFRA formula provided more funding to districts with higher concentrations of at-risk students**. An adequacy budget covered two-thirds of special education costs, and extraordinary aid was available to fund special education costs in excess of $40,000 for any student. The court upheld the SFRA, finding that the legislation was designed to exceed constitutional requirements for an adequate education. It granted the state's motion declaring the legislation constitutional, and relieved it from prior remedial orders concerning the *Abbott* districts. *Abbott v. Burke*, 199 N.J. 140, 971 A.2d 989 (N.J. 2009).

◆   A group of Missouri school districts, advocacy groups and taxpayers challenged the state's school funding formula in 2004. The focus of the case shifted to Senate Bill Number 287, enacted in 2005. S.B. 287 revised the state funding formula by attempting to remedy inequities resulting from the system's reliance on a combination of state and local funding. Schools with greater "local effort" contributions received less state assistance. After a trial, a court held that the state did not have to provide public schools over 25 % of the state's revenue. The Supreme Court of Missouri accepted an appeal and noted that **Section 1(a) of the Missouri Constitution concerning the "diffusion of knowledge" did not create a free-standing duty to provide certain schools with funding**.

The challengers were improperly attempting to read the 25 % requirement of Section 3(b) as a separate funding duty in Section 1(a). Section 3(b) provided a minimum level of funding for schools and declared that the legislature "may" provide additional funding to account for deficiencies. Thus, the court found no merit to the claim that S.B. 287 created an unconstitutional funding formula. There was no expressed right to equitable education funding in the constitution's provision for free public schools. S.B. 287 was justified by a clearly legitimate end. School funding was achieved through state and local resources, with state funding going disproportionately to districts with fewer local resources. Since none of the challengers' additional arguments had merit, the court affirmed the judgment for the state. *Committee For Educational Equality v. State of Missouri*, 294 S.W.2d 477 (Mo. 2009).

◆   A group of Indiana students sought a court ruling that the state was not satisfying its duty to provide a quality education for all public school students under the Indiana Constitution's Education Clause. The case reached the Supreme Court of Indiana, which explained that the General Assembly had two duties under the Education Clause. The first was to encourage moral, intellectual, scientific and agricultural improvement, and the second was to "provide for a general and uniform system of open common schools without tuition." But the Education Clause spoke only of a general duty to provide a system of common schools. **There was no requirement to attain any standard of educational quality.** Terms like "general and uniform," and "equally open to all" did not prescribe standards. Since there was no affirmative duty for a particular educational standard, the students' challenge failed. *Bonner v. Daniels*, 907 N.E.2d 516 (Ind. 2009).

◆   Educational adequacy and funding appeals reached the Supreme Court of New Hampshire in 1993, 1998, and 2002, when the court held the state had a duty of accountability in *Claremont School Dist. v. Governor*, 794 A.2d 744 (N.H. 2002). In 2005, the legislature mandated student opportunities to acquire skills in core subjects including reading, writing, science and math. Two school district administrative units and an organization representing 19 others filed an action in response to H.B. 616, which governed state education funding and allocation. A state superior court declared H.B. 616 unconstitutional. The Supreme Court of New Hampshire agreed, ruling that **H.B. 616 did not fulfill the state's duty to define and determine the cost of a constitutionally adequate education, failed to satisfy accountability requirements and**

**created a non-uniform tax rate** in violation of the state constitution. *Londonderry School Dist. SAU #12 v. State*, 907 A.2d 988 (N.H. 2006).

The legislature then enacted Chapter 270, which paved the way for the state to determine the cost of an adequate education by creating a joint legislative oversight committee for further study. The administrative units claimed there were still infirmities in the law, such as failure to meet accountability requirements and an insufficient universal cost of education for each student. State officials argued that Chapter 270 represented sufficient steps toward satisfying the constitutional duty to provide adequate education to each child. The court agreed, finding the education funding plan from H.B. 616 was no longer in effect. Because the legislature had acted in good faith to address the previously identified constitutional infirmities in prior legislation, the court dismissed the case. *Londonderry School Dist. SAU #12 v. State of New Hampshire*, 157 N.H. 734, 958 A.2d 930 (N.H. 2008).

◆   In 2002, the Supreme Court of Arkansas held that the state's school funding effort was insufficient. The General Assembly responded with Act 57 and Act 108. Act 57 described the General Assembly's continuing duty to assess what constitutes an "adequate education." The court then ruled that legislative inaction had violated school funding requirements. However, it refused to order the General Assembly to appropriate a specific increase in funding amounts. Instead, it was up to the General Assembly to determine whether, after correcting for constitutional infirmities, more funds should be appropriated. *Lake View School Dist. No. 25 v. Huckabee*, 364 Ark. 398, 220 S.W.3d 645 (Ark. 2006).

The supreme court later reviewed a special masters' report that found the General Assembly had enacted a comprehensive system for accounting and accountability for state oversight of school expenditures. A 2007 act authorized the state to assure the state's basic, per-student foundation funding was being met. An additional $50 million had been appropriated for school facilities in 2006. Categorical funding and teacher salaries were increased. The court held that **the General Assembly had taken necessary steps to assure that public school students were being provided with an adequate education and substantially equal educational opportunities**. *Lake View School Dist. No. 25 v. Huckabee*, 370 Ark. 139, 257 S.W.3d 879 (Ark. 2007).

◆   The New York Constitution requires the state to offer all children the opportunity of a sound basic education. In 2003, the Court of Appeals held that New York City students were not receiving an opportunity for a sound basic education due to the state's failure to comply with its duty. The court directed the state to determine the actual cost of a sound basic education in the city, reform the system of school funding and management, provide for a sound basic education, and ensure an accountability system for the reforms by July 30, 2004. A trial court adopted the recommendation of a panel of judicial referees for compliance that called for annual expenditures of $5.63 billion, phased in over four years, plus $9.179 billion in capital improvements over five years.

These amounts reflected proposals by the group representing the students who filed a lawsuit. In 2004, the governor proposed spending $1.93 billion to close the gap in operating expenses for city schools with an additional $4.7 billion over five years. The legislature increased funding by only $300 million, and the state failed to meet the July 30, 2004 deadline. The case returned to the court of appeals, which stated that **the job of the courts was not to calculate the cost of a sound basic education in New York City schools, but to review whether the state's proposal for calculating this cost was rational.** The state had found the cost of providing a sound basic education in city schools could be met with $1.93 billion in additional operating funds. The governor's proposal exceeded this constitutional minimum by adding $4.7 billion during the next five years. As the governor's proposal was a reasonable estimate of the cost of a sound basic education in city schools, the court approved it. *Campaign for Fiscal Equity v. State of New York*, 8 N.Y.3d 14, 861 N.E.2d 50, 828 N.Y.S.2d 235 (N.Y. 2006).

◆    An association of Idaho school districts, superintendents and students sued the state, asserting that state funding levels and the funding method violated the Idaho Constitution. The case reached the Supreme Court of Idaho, which reviewed district court findings of myriad structural problems and fire hazards. The court rejected the state's attempts to "refocus this litigation into small, district-by-district battles" instead of addressing the larger issue of the legislature's constitutional duty toward public education in Idaho. The district court had compiled thousands of pages of testimony and exhibits. The overwhelming evidence documented serious facility and funding problems in the state's public education system.

The state itself documented facilities deficiencies in a 1993 assessment concluding that 57% of all Idaho school buildings had serious safety concerns. A 1999 report found the situation had further deteriorated. The "glaring gap" in the funding system was the lack of a mechanism to quickly deal with major, costly and potentially catastrophic conditions in low-population districts with low tax bases in economically depressed areas. The "list of safety concerns and difficulties in getting funds for repairs or replacements is distressingly long." **The funding system was inadequate to meet the state constitutional mandate for a thorough system of education in a safe environment.** While the legislature failed in its constitutional mandate, an appropriate remedy was a task for the legislature, not the court. *Idaho Schools for Equal Educational Opportunity v. State of Idaho*, 129 P.3d 1199 (Idaho 2005).

◆    Forty-seven Texas school districts claimed that state control of the levy, assessment and disbursement of revenue resulted in a statewide property tax. Other districts claimed that funding for school operations and facilities was unconstitutional because children in property-poor districts did not have substantially equal access to revenue. The state supreme court noted that over half the annual cost of public education in the state was funded by ad valorem taxes imposed by independent school districts on local property. The legislature's decision to rely heavily on local property taxes did not in itself violate the Texas Constitution, but the disparity between districts in size and wealth made it difficult to achieve efficient education funding. Some districts had to pay disproportionately high property taxes. School maintenance and operations were funded by a separate tax capped at $1.50 per $100 of valuation. Revenue disparities among districts were reduced by supplementing property-poor district tax revenue with state funds.

The court held that **the school financing system did not violate the efficiency requirement of the constitution. However, state control of local taxation for education amounted to an unconstitutional state property tax.** The number of districts taxing at the maximum "maintenance and operations" rate had risen from 2% of districts to 48%, and 67% of districts were taxing at or above $1.45. The state controlled more than $1 billion in local tax revenues recaptured from 134 districts. Recapture had doubled in less than a decade, and the number of districts and the amount of revenue subject to recapture had almost tripled since 1994. The school districts had lost any meaningful discretion to tax below maximum rates and still provide students with an accredited education. Districts were forced by educational requirements and economic necessities to tax at the valuation cap. This violated the state constitutional prohibition on a state property tax. As removing the cap would only increase the disparity between rich and poor districts, the court held that the cap had to be raised or the system had to be changed by June 1, 2006. *Neeley v. West Orange-Cove Consolidated Independent School Dist.*, 176 S.W.3d 746 (Tex. 2005).

◆   In 1997, the Supreme Court of Vermont held that the state was denying students equal educational opportunities. The legislature responded with Act 60, also known as the Equal Educational Opportunity Act of 1997. A group of students asserted that nondiscretionary expenditures on special education, transportation and facilities resulted in less funding for instruction and curriculum. They claimed that their high school was in poor condition and offered such a limited curriculum that many students had taken all course offerings and had to take gym classes to fill their senior year schedules. Taxpayers claimed that Act 60 required them to pay disproportionately high state and local education taxes when compared to taxpayers in other Vermont towns. The students and taxpayers sued the state for equal protection violations. A trial court dismissed the case, ruling that recent legislation had remedied the claims. The taxpayers and students appealed to the state supreme court, which held that the trial court had improperly dismissed the case. The court found the allegations of the taxpayers and students sufficient to proceed with the case. **As they alleged that recent legislation caused the same fundamental violations as Act 60, the case was remanded for further proceedings.** *Brigham v. State*, 889 A.2d 715 (Vt. 2005).

◆   The Montana Legislature created the state's current educational funding system in 1993. House Bill (H.B.) 667 addressed a 1989 Montana Supreme Court decision concluding that the spending disparities among the state's school districts denied students equal educational opportunity under the state constitution. H.B. 667 addressed inequities by relying on a regression analysis to address the financial disparities among districts. The bill created a general fund with built-in maximum and minimum amounts computed by a statutory formula. A coalition of schools, school districts, parents and educational associations sued, alleging that H.B. 667 violated two provisions of the state constitution. The coalition stated that most districts were at or over their maximum budgets. Some districts said they could not provide a quality education unless they could spend more than their general fund maximum.

A state court found serious problems with the current system's funding and held that the system violated the Public Schools and Indian Education Clauses of the Montana Constitution. The state appealed to the Supreme Court of Montana, which found that **the current system was constitutionally deficient**, based on evidence of budgeting at or near the maximum budget authority, growing accreditation problems, the cutting of programs, teacher flight to other states, deterioration of buildings and increased competition between special and general education programs for general fund dollars. The court upheld the decision on the Public Schools Clause issue. *Columbia Falls Elementary School Dist. No. 6 v. State of Montana*, 326 Mont. 304, 109 P.3d 257 (Mont. 2005).

## B.  Property Taxes and Other Local Funding Issues

*Courts usually refrain from intervening in state and local tax or funding questions. For example, the Supreme Court of North Carolina held that the legislature, not the judiciary, was vested with budgetary responsibilities.*

♦   A Missouri land developer bought a parcel of land. It learned that Central School District owned and taxed it, despite the fact that it was surrounded by property included in the Farmington School District. It sought an order that the land was within the Farmington district, but a state trial court agreed with Central School District that the parcel was within its boundaries even though it was non-contiguous with the rest of the district. On appeal, the Supreme Court of Missouri held that the trial court did not err by relying on an assessor's map rather than on school district records. **State law and a state constitutional provision referring to contiguous boundaries for school districts applied to reorganization plans and boundary changes and did not require contiguity in other cases.** *MC Development Co. v. Cent. R-3 School Dist. of St. Francois County*, 299 S.W.3d 600 (Mo. 2009).

♦   Beaufort County (North Carolina) Commissioners allocated $2.7 million less than the county school board requested for fiscal year 2006-07. After mediation failed, the board sued the commission. A jury found that the board needed an additional $766,000. The court ordered the commissioners to appropriate this amount. Appeal reached the Supreme Court of North Carolina, where the commission argued that allowing the court system to decide public education funding levels impermissibly delegated a legislative duty under the state constitution. But the court disagreed, finding that the separation of powers clause of the North Carolina Constitution did not prevent the General Assembly from seeking assistance, "within proper limits," from other government branches – like determining the annual cost of education in the county. Fact-finding of this kind was within the historic and proper role of the judiciary.

**The legislature, not the judiciary, allocated budgetary responsibility to local entities and required judgments against a county commission if school**

**board costs exceeded the allocation.** The court found the legislature did not assign policymaking to the courts or otherwise make an improper delegation of its authority. But the trial court had improperly instructed the jury regarding the term "needed" in the context of funding under Section 431(c). The case was returned to the lower court for a new trial. The jury was to be instructed that Section 431(c) required the county commission to appropriate the amount legally necessary to support a system of free public schools. In addition, the jury was to be instructed to consider state educational goals and policies, the board's budgetary request, the financial resources of the county, and county fiscal policies. *Beaufort County Board of Educ. v. Beaufort County Board of Commissioners*, 681 S.E.2d 278 (N.C. 2009).

◆   The Supreme Court of South Dakota permitted a group of school districts to proceed with an action asserting underfunding of K-12 public education in the state. In prior challenges involving tax levies, the court had held that school districts lacked standing. But in this case, the districts asserted that the entire state public school system was under-funded. **The court held that the districts were designated by the South Dakota Constitution as the trustees of school trust funds and fines and taxes earmarked for education.** Based on this constitutionally defined status, the districts could pursue the action. *Olson v. Guindon*, 771. N.W.2d 318 (S.D. 2009).

◆   After Iowa legislators authorized a local sales tax option in 1998, school districts in Polk County, including the Des Moines School District, adopted a local sales tax referendum. The school board proposed a 10-year plan to improve school facilities. It noted that the cost of improvements exceeded revenue projections from the sales tax and stated that the plan was subject to modification. By 2004, the Des Moines board found that local option sales tax revenues were short of projections. The district faced higher building costs and lower enrollment. The board modified the 10-year plan by closing four elementary schools and selling a central facility. It spent funds on facilities that were not part of the original plan and hired a firm to create a management plan.

Taxpayers sued the school board, challenging the modification of the original plan. A state trial court agreed with the board that the proper remedy was an appeal to the state department of education. The Supreme Court of Iowa then stated that school boards are authorized by state regulations to determine the number of schools to operate, and they are required to provide public notice and encourage public consideration when closing a school. Here, the board's decision did not jeopardize any student's right to attend a public school – it only meant that some students would be attending different schools. **This was a "legislative decision" that only a school board could make, and it was not subject to review by a court.** As the lower court held, the taxpayers could appeal to the education department. *Wallace v. Des Moines Independent Community School Dist. Board of Directors*, 754 N.W.2d 854 (Iowa 2008).

◆   The Cobb County (Georgia) School Board improperly bought laptop computers for its middle and high school students with proceeds from a special purpose local option sales tax (SPLOST) that had been authorized for certain capital outlay projects such as technology and information systems hardware and software, and technology infrastructure. A taxpayer sued the board, arguing that the laptop purchase was an abuse of discretion. The case reached the Supreme Court of Georgia, which noted that **state law limited the use of SPLOST proceeds for the exclusive purpose or purposes specified in the resolution or ordinance calling for the imposition of the measure**. In this case, the board resolution authorizing the SPLOST stated that the funds would be used on designated capital outlay projects, such as "system-wide technology improvements." The board could not use SPLOST proceeds for an entirely different purpose. The court ruled for the taxpayer. *Johnstone v. Thompson*, 631 S.E.2d 650 (Ga. 2006).

◆ A New York school board's proposed budget eliminated 18 positions and $786,000 in spending, but district voters twice voted it down. Even with the cuts, the proposals would have increased district spending by $1.1 million and increased district property taxes by 12.68%. The district adopted a contingency or "austerity" budget nearly $500,000 less than the one voters had rejected. About $350,000 was saved by eliminating all funding for field trips, interscholastic sports and extracurricular activities. The contingency budget still increased district spending by over $600,000 from the prior year, due to higher costs of employee health insurance premiums and retirement system contributions, special education costs and debt servicing. A taxpayer group sued, claiming that Education Law Section 2023 required the funding of field trips, athletics and other extracurricular activities. The New York Supreme Court, Appellate Division, held that **there was no requirement for a board of education to fund interscholastic athletics, field trips and other extracurricular activities** as part of a district budget submitted to voters. *Polmanteer v. Bobo*, 794 N.Y.S.2d 171 (N.Y. App. Div. 2005).

## C. Federal Funding

*Federal funding in education is within the jurisdiction of the Secretary of the U.S. Department of Education. Like other questions of budget and finance, the courts do not closely scrutinize these decisions.*

◆ The Federal Impact Aid Act provides funding to school districts whose financial conditions are adversely affected by a federal presence, such as a large tract of tax-exempt land. States may not offset Impact Aid by reducing aid to school districts, but may reduce funding to equalize per-pupil expenditures among districts. The Act instructed the U.S. Education Secretary to calculate a disparity in per-pupil expenditures among school districts in a state. When doing so, the Secretary disregarded districts with per-pupil expenditures above the 95th percentile or below the fifth percentile of such expenditures in the state. New Mexico excluded 23 of its 89 districts for determining the equalization formula under the Impact Aid Program. Two school districts challenged the calculation, as they stood to lose state funding due to an offset of Federal Impact Aid. **The case reached the U.S. Supreme Court, which found strong indications that Congress intended to leave the Secretary free to decide**

**whether a state aid program equalized expenditures.** The alternative urged by the districts would permit gross disparities in district expenditures. The Secretary's method complied with the Impact Aid Act by comparing per-pupil expenditures made by the state's highest and lowest spending districts. The Court upheld the calculation by the Secretary. *Zuni Public School Dist. No. 89 v. Dep't of Educ.*, 550 U.S. 81 (2007).

◆    **The U.S. Supreme Court held that the Secretary of Education has the authority to demand a refund of misused funds granted to states under Title I** of the Elementary and Secondary Education Act of 1965. Title I provides funding for local educational agencies to prepare economically underprivileged children for school. Recipient states must provide assurances to the secretary that local educational agencies will spend the funds only on qualifying programs. After federal auditors determined that the states of New Jersey and Pennsylvania had misapplied funds, the secretary ordered them to refund the amount of misapplied funds. Both states appealed to the U.S. Supreme Court, arguing that the secretary exceeded his statutory authority in ordering the refunds. The Supreme Court held that Title I, as originally enacted, gave the federal government a right to demand repayment once liability was established. The 1978 amendments to Title I were designed merely to clarify the secretary's legal authority and responsibility to audit recipient state programs and to specify the procedures to be used in the collection of any debts. *Bell v. New Jersey*, 461 U.S. 773, 103 S.Ct. 2187, 76 L.Ed.2d 312 (1983).

◆    The Supreme Court held that the 1978 Title I amendments' new, relaxed standards concerning local schools' eligibility to receive Title I funds could not be applied retroactively. *Bennett v. New Jersey*, 470 U.S. 632, 105 S.Ct. 1555, 84 L.Ed.2d 572 (1985). In a companion case, the Court held that the state of Kentucky's lack of bad faith was irrelevant in assessing its liability to repay misused Title I funds. *Bennett v. Kentucky Dep't of Educ.*, 470 U.S. 656, 105 S.Ct. 1544, 84 L.Ed.2d 590 (1985).

## D.  School Expenditures and State Appropriations

*Washington's highest court rejected a lawsuit asserting legislative funding formulas which allowed differing salaries among employees in various school districts violated the state constitution. Local variations were permitted, since the legislature was aware of the relevant political and economic issues.* Federal Way School Dist. No. 210 v. State of Washington, *219 P.3d 941 (Wash. 2009).*

◆    The Florida Legislature approved an amendment to the state constitution that modified a 2002 citizen initiative limiting public school class sizes. The proposal revised the class size requirements of the 2002 initiative, setting an average maximum number of students rather than just setting a maximum number of students. The ballot title and summary for the proposed 2010 amendment explained that 2002 limits on the maximum number of students assigned to each teacher in public school classrooms would become limits on the average number of students assigned per class to each teacher. The Florida

Education Association sued state officials, asserting the 2010 proposal violated state constitutional and statutory requirements for accuracy and clarity. It argued that the proposal would substantially reduce the state's constitutional obligation to fund class size restrictions and claimed that the ballot summary was defective because it did not state the amendment's chief purpose. The case reached the Supreme Court of Florida, which found that **the constitutional obligation of the state to provide "sufficient funds" for class sizes remained unchanged under the 2010 measure**. There would be the same right to state provision of sufficient funds for mandated class sizes. The 2010 proposal had a stated purpose of establishing maximum class sizes, and the ballot summary was not misleading. The measure could appear on the November 2010 ballot. *Florida Educ. Ass'n v. Florida Dep't of State*, 48 So.2d 694 (Fla. 2010).

◆   Parents of students attending English language learner (ELL) programs in Nogales (Arizona) Unified School District sued the district for violating the Equal Educational Opportunities Act (EEOA). The EEOA requires states to take appropriate action to overcome language barriers in schools. In 2000, the court held that Arizona's funding to ELL students was arbitrary and unrelated to the actual cost of ELL instruction in Nogales. The order was later extended to the entire state. Over the next eight years, the court issued more orders, found the state in contempt and fined it from $500,000 to $2 million a day. After fines grew to over $20 million in 2006, the legislature passed HB 2064. HB 2064 increased ELL incremental funding and created new funds to cover additional ELL costs, but permitted state funds to be offset by available federal funds.

   The case reached the Supreme Court, which held that **the lower courts should have determined whether enforcement of the 2000 order was supported by ongoing EEOA violations**. The EEOA gave state and local authorities substantial latitude to take appropriate action to overcome language barriers. By focusing on Arizona's incremental funding for ELL students under HB 2064, the Ninth Circuit improperly substituted its judgment for that of state and local officials. The Court reversed and remanded the case to the lower courts to consider the factors that might justify relief. Factors included: 1) Arizona's new "structured English immersion" ELL instruction mandate; 2) evidence of student progress; 3) structural and management reforms in Nogales schools; and 4) an overall increase in Arizona's school funding since 2000. The lower court was to vacate its order extending relief beyond Nogales, unless it found a statewide EEOA violation. *Horne v. Flores*, 129 S.Ct. 2579 (U.S. 2009).

◆   Two education proposals were placed on the ballot for Florida voters in 2008. One would have eliminated restrictions on the use of state funds to aid religion. The other would have required school districts to spend at least 65% of their funding on classroom instruction. It also would have said the state's duty to provide for public education was not limited to free public schools. The proposals were submitted by the state Taxation Budget Reform Commission (TBRC). Opponents sought a state court order to prevent the items from going before voters. A Florida court awarded judgment to the state, and the opponents appealed. The Supreme Court of Florida held **the TBRC's duties were limited to dealing with the state budgetary process**. The proposal titled "Religious

Freedom" clearly did not address taxation or the state budgetary process. Thus, the proposal for public funding of education was a subject for which the TBRC had exceeded its constitutional authority. The court ordered the secretary of state to prevent either of the constitutional amendments from appearing on the November 2008 ballot. *Ford v. Browning*, 992 So.2d 132 (Fla. 2008).

◆   Michigan's Headlee Amendment prohibits the state from reducing funding for necessary costs of existing activities or services mandated by the legislature. It obligates the state to fund the necessary costs of new or increased activities that the legislature mandates. A group of taxpayers and school districts sued the state for violating the amendment. After years of litigation, the state supreme court held that the legislature could not reduce its share of funding for special education in *Durant v. Michigan*, 456 Mich. 175, 566 N.W.2d 272 (Mich. 1997) ("*Durant I*"). The legislature then passed M.C.L. § 388.1611f, which gave relief to districts that were not plaintiffs in *Durant I*. To receive funds, districts had to waive any right or interest similar to that asserted in *Durant I*.

A new group of taxpayers and districts sued in 1998, claiming continuing violations of the Headlee Amendment from 1997 to 2001. The court of appeals largely held in their favor in *Durant II*, but a third case, *Durant III*, resulted in a decision for state officials. A new challenge was brought against state officials, asserting insufficient funding for new or increased levels of activity. The case returned to the supreme court, which noted that the districts stated a claim as a result of an executive order establishing the Center for Educational Performance and Information (CEPI), which required districts to create and maintain student data. If proven, this unfunded "off-loading of state funding responsibilities onto local units of government" would violate the Headlee Amendment. *Adair v. State of Michigan*, 680 N.W.2d 386 (Mich. 2004).

The case returned to the court of appeals, which appointed a special master to consider the remaining claims. The court later affirmed the master's findings, holding that data collection and reporting implemented through the CEPI resulted in the state's offloading of some responsibilities onto school districts. **The state had made a conscious decision to impose new activities and an increased level of activities regarding the design and updating of software to perform data collection to avoid state Headlee Amendment funding obligations.** The state failed to fund the necessary costs associated with data collection and reporting mandates associated with the CEPI. *Adair v. State of Michigan*, 279 Mich.App. 507, 760 N.W.2d 544 (Mich. Ct. App. 2008).

◆   In January 2005, the Supreme Court of Kansas held that the state's public school finance system violated the Kansas Constitution. The legislature enacted 2005 H.B. 2247, which increased school funding by $142 million for the 2005-06 school year and authorized a study to find the cost of delivering a K-12 curriculum and required programs. In June 2005, the supreme court held that H.B. 2247 was unconstitutional because it was not based on actual cost considerations. The court also held that H.B. 2247 exacerbated existing funding inequities. Under-funding by the state forced some districts to use their local option budgets to fund the state's constitutional obligation. A legislative division of post-audit (LPA) cost study was insufficient to determine the actual costs of providing a constitutionally suitable education. The governor called a special legislative session, which resulted in the passage of S.B. 3. This authorized an additional $147 million for the 2005-06 school year.

The court then found that S.B. 3 complied with its order and approved the finance formula for interim purposes. In January 2006, the legislature enacted S.B. 549, containing vast changes to the school finance formula. The case returned to the supreme court, which held that S.B. 549 created additional at-risk weightings for districts with high numbers of at-risk students and students who were not proficient in reading or math. More districts with lower assessed valuation per pupil would now receive supplemental aid on local option budgets, bringing them up to par with other districts. The three-year cumulative total of aid under the laws was $121.7 million greater than in January 2005. S.B. 549 essentially made local option budget state aid a part of the foundation level of funding. The legislature had substantially responded to the court's concerns that the funding formula did not provide adequate funding for students in districts with high minority, at-risk and special education populations. **Equity did not require equal funding for each student or district.** What was required was an equitable and fair distribution of funding to provide opportunities for each student to obtain a suitable education. As the 2005 and 2006 acts substantially complied with the prior court orders, the case was dismissed. *Montoy v. State of Kansas*, 138 P.3d 755 (Kan. 2006).

◆   In 1994, the Arizona Supreme Court held that the state's property-tax-based funding scheme resulted in significant disparities among districts that violated the state constitution. *Hull v. Albrecht*, 950 P.2d 1141 (Ariz. 1997).

The legislature enacted new legislation, which the court struck down. The Students FIRST Act created a capital finance program funded by dedicated revenue from a state transaction privilege tax. The supreme court upheld the Act's minimum adequacy standards for capital facilities, but it disapproved of a provision allowing districts to opt out of state capital funding requirements through local funding. The legislature amended the Act by establishing three mechanisms to fund school facilities, including the Building Renewal Fund (BRF). It disregarded the formula for the 1998-99 school year and simply increased BRF funding by 10% over the prior year. This resulted in $27 million less for the BRF than the formula required. While the formula for the 2001-2002 school year would have resulted in over $122 million to the BRF, the legislature allowed only $672,093 to reach schools. The BRF formula for 2002-2003 called for $128 million, but only $38 million went into the fund.

The legislature suspended the BRF formula for 2003-2004. A state court ordered the legislature to restore $90 million it had subtracted from the BRF. The Arizona Court of Appeals held that **the state's constitutional obligation was to fund an "adequate" public school system**. This included a minimum quality and quantity standard for buildings and sufficient funding for necessary facilities and equipment to enable students to master educational goals. The Students FIRST Act reflected the supreme court's mandate to provide facilities necessary for student academic achievement and prioritized funding for district facilities "directly necessary for scholastic success." Failure to fund the BRF formula was not a constitutional violation. There was no unequivocal evidence that the cuts had an impact on student academic achievement. *Roosevelt Elementary School Dist. No. 66 v. State of Arizona*, 74 P.3d 258 (Ariz. Ct. App. 2003). The Arizona Supreme Court decided not to review this decision in 2004.

◆   The California Constitution requires the state to reimburse local districts for the cost of new programs or higher levels of service mandated by the state. The San Diego Unified School District filed a test claim for reimbursement of the increased costs of hearings to expel students under two statutes. Education Code § 48915 compelled suspension with a recommendation for expulsion of students found in possession of a firearm at school or school activities. It permitted expulsions at the discretion of the principal for damaging or stealing property, receiving stolen property, selling or using illegal drugs, possessing tobacco or drug paraphernalia, and disruption. Section 48918 granted students a hearing and appeal rights if expulsion was recommended.

The case reached the Supreme Court of California. It found **the compelled expulsion provision of Section 48915 was a state mandate for which all hearing costs were fully reimbursable**. But the discretionary expulsion provision of Section 48915 was not a new program or higher level of services required by the state. Hearings for Section 48915 discretionary expulsions only implemented federal due process mandates. Neither Section 48918 nor federal law required an expulsion recommendation. This was true despite a No Child Left Behind Act requirement which, like Section 48915, mandated expulsion for firearms possession. The court found the cost of these hearings was minimal and not reimbursable. *San Diego Unified School Dist. v. Comm'n on State Mandates*, 33 Cal.4th 859, 16 Cal.Rptr.3d 466, 94 P.3d 589 (Cal. 2004).

## E.  Student Fees and Tuition

### 1.  Transportation Fees

*In the next case, the Supreme Court held the Equal Protection Clause does not require free transportation in public schools. Its rationale was rooted in the lack of a fundamental right to education under the U.S. Constitution.*

◆   North Dakota statutes authorized thinly populated school districts to reorganize into larger districts for efficiency. Reorganized districts had to provide for student transportation to and from their homes. School districts choosing not to reorganize were authorized by statute to charge students a portion of their costs for transportation. The parents of a nine-year-old student refused to sign a transportation contract with the school district. The family was near or at the poverty level. Claiming inability to pay the fee, the family made private transportation arrangements that were more costly than the school's fee. The parents sued the school district in a North Dakota trial court for an order to prevent the district from collecting the fee on grounds that it violated the state constitution and the Equal Protection Clause. After losing at the trial court level, the parents appealed to the North Dakota Supreme Court.

The court upheld the lower court decision on state and federal constitutional grounds. On appeal to the U.S. Supreme Court, the parents claimed that the user fee for bus service unconstitutionally deprived poor persons of minimum access to education and placed an unconstitutional obstacle on education for poor students. The Court noted that the student had continued to attend school during the time she claimed she was denied access to the school bus. **The Equal Protection Clause does not require free transportation.** Education is not a fundamental right under the U.S. Constitution. The Court upheld the statute, as it bore a reasonable relationship to the state's legitimate objective of encouraging school districts to provide bus service. The statute did not directly impose a bus fee requirement. It did not discriminate against any class or interfere with any constitutional rights. *Kadrmas v. Dickinson Public Schools*, 487 U.S. 450, 108 S.Ct. 2481, 101 L.Ed.2d 399 (1988).

◆ A Kentucky school board furnished bus transportation and allowed students to attend schools that were outside their attendance area but within the same district. But to limit class sizes, the board instituted a revised transportation policy permitting students to attend schools within the district but outside their attendance areas only if they utilized private transportation. The parent of a student affected by the change sued, claiming that the transportation policy was arbitrary, capricious and unreasonable, and violated his constitutional rights to due process. A court granted pretrial judgment to the school board, and the parent appealed to the Kentucky Court of Appeals. The court upheld the judgment, finding the board's decision was not arbitrary, capricious or unreasonable. The due process rights of students and parents had been protected by numerous public meetings held during the policy revision. Its impact on students already availing themselves of the policy was mitigated by the use of a grandfather clause. **Any change in school policies might have an adverse impact on some students, but some such impacts could not be avoided.** *Swift v. Breckinridge County Board of Educ.*, 878 S.W.2d 810 (Ky. Ct. App. 1994).

## 2. Tuition and Other Fees

*The Supreme Court of Indiana held that a mandatory fee imposed by a school district on all its students, was a "charge for attending a public school and obtaining a public education" in violation of the Indiana Constitution.*

◆ A group of St. Louis parents enrolled their children in schools within the Clayton School District. They signed agreements obligating themselves to pay the tuition. After the parents took this action, the transitional school district of St. Louis lost its state accreditation. The parents asked Clayton to charge the transitional school district for their children's tuition because Missouri law required unaccredited districts to pay tuition for students attending accredited schools in adjoining districts. When Clayton rejected the parents' claim, they sued. A state court held for the school districts, and the parents appealed. The case reached the Supreme Court of Missouri, which noted that the unaccredited district was obligated to pay tuition for students attending accredited schools in other districts. But it rejected the parents' claim to a right to restitution for tuition they already paid. The contracts were valid, and the parents had no right to restitution. **The parents had contractually obligated themselves to pay Clayton for tuition, and there was no requirement for Clayton to seek payment from the transitional school district.** *Turner v. School Dist. of Clayton*, 318 S.W.3d 660 (Mo. 2010).


◆   An Indiana school district charged each of its students a mandatory $20 fee to address a $2.3 million budget deficit for 2002 that was projected to increase to $5.5 million in 2003. The district deposited the fees in its general fund with state funds and local property tax receipts to help pay the salaries of nurses, media specialists, counselors and a student services coordinator. The district also used the fees to pay for alternative education, a police liaison program, and for athletic, drama and music programs. The parents of students who qualified for reduced or free school lunch and textbook programs filed a class action against the school district, asserting that the fee violated the state constitution.

The case reached the Supreme Court of Indiana, which noted that Article 8, Section 1 does not provide for a system of "free schools," as many state constitutions do. Instead, it provides for "a general and uniform system of Common Schools, wherein tuition shall be without charge, and equally open to all." But without a specific statutory authority, fees or charges could not be directly or indirectly assessed against students or parents for public education cost items. Here, the fee was imposed on all students and was deposited into the district's general fund to offset the cost of non-instructional staff salaries, a police liaison program, alternative education program, and music and drama programs. The state board had already deemed these items as "part and parcel of a public school education." **A mandatory fee, imposed generally on all students, was a "charge for attending a public school and obtaining a public education" in violation of Article 8, Section 1.** *Nagy v. Evansville-Vanderburgh School Corp.*, 844 N.E.2d 481 (Ind. 2006).


◆   As a result of increased enrollment, a Pennsylvania school board approved a program providing for a district-financed tuition scholarship for any student legally residing in the district for attendance at any private school or non-district public school. A group of resident taxpayers filed a declaratory judgment action against the district in the state court system challenging the program. The trial court agreed with the taxpayers and granted their motion for judgment on the pleadings, ruling that the district lacked authority to implement the plan. On appeal, the Commonwealth Court of Pennsylvania held school districts have no powers except those authorized by express statutory grant and necessary implication. **State law did not expressly authorize reimbursement of tuition and fees.** If a district found its financing insufficient, its options were to either obtain a court order or follow procedures set by the secretary of education. The legislature did not authorize tuition payments to parents in this case, and there was no implied authority for the district plan. A statewide program resembling the plan was struck down by the U.S. Supreme Court in *Sloan v. Lemon*, 413 U.S. 825 (1973). The district had clearly acted outside the scope of its statutory authority, and the court affirmed the trial court order. *Giacomucci v. Southeast Delco School Dist.*, 742 A.2d 1165 (Pa. Commw. Ct. 1999).

## F.  Private Contractors

*The Arizona Supreme Court found nothing in the state code prohibited a public entity from withdrawing a bid after acceptance, but prior to the award of a contract. And the Supreme Court of South Carolina found a state code provision allows correction or withdrawal of an erroneous bid before or after an award. It held bid awards or contracts may be cancelled if there was a mistake.*

◆    The Los Angeles Unified School District contracted to build an elementary school, but later terminated the contract for material breach and default. It sought proposals from other contractors to complete the school and offered prospective bidders copies of a 108-page correction list that detailed defective, incomplete or missing work by the original contractor. A new contractor then submitted a bid to complete the school and repair deficiencies. It later found additional problems and sought more money. The district rejected its claim for extra compensation for "latent defects" but agreed to pay the contractor $1 million beyond the contract amount with a reservation of rights. It then sued the contractor and its insurer to recover the additional amount paid. After the court held for the school district, the Supreme Court of California held that **contractors cannot avoid obligations or seek additional compensation because of unanticipated difficulties.** But they may recover for extra work or expenses made necessary because conditions were not as represented by the public entity. A contractor does not have to show active misrepresentation or fraudulent concealment to recover expenses from a public entity that fails to disclose material information affecting the cost of performing a contract. The court returned the case to the trial court. *Los Angeles Unified School Dist. v. Great American Insurance Co.*, 49 Cal.4th 739 (Cal. 2010).

◆    A disappointed bidder claimed a Georgia school board had to accept its bid because of an immaterial defect by the low bidder on a construction project. The invitation for bids disallowed changes without board approval, but reserved the board's right to reject bids and waive "technicalities and informalities" in its best interest. The low bidder did not initially provide a subcontractor list, as required by the project specifications. It provided the list within two hours of the opening of bids, and the board accepted it. The contractor that submitted the next-lowest bid sought a court order declaring it the winner. The court denied its request for relief. The supreme court accepted the contractor's appeal and held that state law did not require every statement in an invitation for bids to be met precisely and without deviation. **The district retained statutory powers to waive technicalities.** There was no law, regulation or ordinance requiring all project subcontractors to be listed on public bids. The trial court did not commit error by concluding that the list of subcontractors was immaterial and could be waived. The supreme court affirmed the judgment. *R.D. Brown Contractors v. Board of Educ. of Columbia County*, 626 S.E.2d 471 (Ga. 2006).

◆    A 2007 legislative amendment placed private contractor employees under Florida Statutes Section 1012.467. This provision required criminal background screening for all non-instructional contractors with permission to be on school grounds when students were present. Those convicted of child abuse and certain other charges were denied access to public school grounds when students were present. An employee of a private contractor pleaded no contest to a child abuse charge in 1996. He underwent a criminal background screen as required by the new law and was notified he would no longer have access to school property due to his 1996 no-contest plea. As a result, the contractor fired the employee. A state court enjoined the school board from barring him from school property. On appeal, the employee argued that the 2007 amendment retroactively converted his no-contest plea to a conviction, depriving him of a vested right to enter school property. The Florida District Court of Appeal found that the school board never terminated the relationship or demanded that the contractor fire him. He had no vested right to go onto school grounds. **Since the employee failed to show the board had divested him of any right, the court reversed the judgment.** *School Board of Miami-Dade County, Florida v. Carralero*, 992 So.2d 353 (Fla. Dist. Ct. App. 2008).

◆   An Arizona school district solicited bids for the construction of new classrooms. The low bidder was a contractor that had performed work for the district four years earlier. It had begun that project prematurely, prior to the completion of asbestos removal, and the district was fined for violations. The district required the contractor to acknowledge that it would ensure this would not be repeated. The school board voted to accept the contractor's bid on the new project. The board's executive director signed a notice to proceed, and a meeting was scheduled to execute the contract. The night before the meeting, the contractor began work at the construction site. The district refused to sign the contract and cancelled the contractor's bid. The contractor denied it had been instructed not to begin work before signing the contract, and it claimed the district had no authority to cancel or modify the contract. The district re-bid the project. The contractor sued the district, arguing that the signing of a contract and posting of a performance bond were "mere formalities" and were not a prerequisite to the formation of a contract. A jury returned a verdict for the contractor. The state court of appeals affirmed, and the district appealed.

The Supreme Court of Arizona held that a public agency accepting a bid was not bound until a formal contract existed. **Nothing in state law prohibited a public entity from withdrawing a bid after acceptance of the bid, but prior to the award of a contract.** The court remanded the case to the trial court with instructions to enter judgment for the district. *Ry-Tan Construction v. Washington Elementary School Dist. No. 6*, 111 P.3d 1019 (Ariz. 2005).

◆   A South Carolina contractor bid $16.3 million on a school renovation project and was the low bidder by over $1 million. After bids were opened, the contractor advised the school district that it had failed to include a roofing subcontractor's bid and asked to either add $613,500 to its bid or to withdraw the entire bid. The district allowed the adjustment, and the contractor's bid was still $461,500 less than the second-lowest bidder. The second-lowest bidder sued to prevent the district from accepting the contractor's bid. The court held that the bid adjustment complied with the district's procurement code and regulations. On appeal, the Supreme Court of South Carolina examined a procurement code provision that allowed the correction or withdrawal of an erroneous bid before or after award. The same provision allowed the cancellation of bid awards or contracts based on mistaken bids.

**The procurement provision stated that no change in bid prices could be made if this would be prejudicial to the interest of the school district or fair competition.** The court found no violation of district rules. The mistake was clear, and the amount the contractor had intended to bid for the roof was evident from examining the subcontractor's bid, as this had been submitted to several general contractors. The court held that the correction did not jeopardize the integrity of the sealed bidding process, and was not prejudicial to the interests of the district or fair competition. It would have been prejudicial to the district had it been bound to accept the second-lowest bidder's bid, which was $461,500 higher. The court affirmed the judgment. *Martin Engineering v. Lexington County School Dist. One*, 365 S.C. 1, 615 S.E.2d 110 (S.C. 2005).

◆ A California contractor was the low bidder for a $6 million elementary school improvement project. The project was delayed by heavy rains, and the parties agreed to delay the completion date. The school district terminated the contract after the project remained unfinished for four more months. The district demanded completion of the project from the contractor's surety under its performance bond. The surety hired another party to complete the job. The contractor sued the district and one of its employees for many claims, including breach of contract. The contractor presented evidence that the district's action cut its bonding limit in half, resulting in over $3.1 million in lost profits on "unidentified projects." The jury returned a verdict for the contractor, awarding the lost profits claimed due to reduction or loss of bonding capacity.

The case reached the Supreme Court of California, which explained that **damage awards cannot exceed what an injured party would have been paid had there been no breach**. The contract did not include potential profits on future unidentified projects. Termination of the contract did not directly cause the contractor to lose potential profits or future contracts. Any loss resulted from the limits on the contractor's bonding imposed by the surety. Since the lower courts had erroneously awarded the contractor damages based on the imposition of bonding limits after the contract termination, the court reversed the judgment. *Lewis Jorge Construction Management v. Pomona Unified School Dist.*, 34 Cal.4th 960, 102 P.3d 257, 22 Cal.Rptr.3d 340 (Cal. 2004).

## G.  Insurance Cases

*State education laws require school employers to defend employees who cause harm while acting in the course and scope of their employment" and "without malice." Insurance policies universally exclude injuries that result from intentional conduct.*

◆ A due process hearing officer held that a Virginia school board violated the IDEA and ordered the board to reimburse a family for almost $118,000 in education costs and attorneys' fees. After a federal court approved the award, the Fourth Circuit affirmed. When attorneys' fees for the family were calculated, it was discovered that the board had expended almost $192,000 to fight the case. It sought coverage from the Virginia Commonwealth Division of Risk Management plan. When the plan denied coverage, the board sued. The plan argued that the IDEA due process hearing did not involve a "claim" and that the reimbursement of education costs was not "damages" under plan language. Under this theory, the board was never exposed to a damage award in the family's IDEA action, and there was no duty to provide legal defense to the board. The Supreme Court of Virginia disagreed. It found that **the family had made a "claim" as defined by the plan and that the amount the board was ordered to pay was not excluded from coverage**. As the duty to defend is broader than the duty to provide coverage, the plan was necessarily liable for defending the case. This meant the plan had to pay the school board's legal fees. *School Board of City of Newport News v. Comwlth. of Virginia*, 689 S.E.2d 731 (Va. 2010).

◆   A Michigan school district's insurer sued the district to enforce its rights under state law with respect to the provision of nursing services to a student. It sought reimbursement for services it believed the district was providing and it was paying for. But the court of appeals noted that the student's IEPs did not specify the services in dispute, and the services being provided by the district were not being paid for by the insurer. Further, **the insurer had no right to try to determine, through a lawsuit, whether the district should be providing nursing services to the student**. *Progressive Michigan Insurance Co. v. Calhoun Intermediate School Dist.*, No. 290564, 2010 WL 2680112 (Mich. Ct. App. 7/6/10).

◆   A Maryland high school vice principal was accused of assaulting a student who was in his office discussing a report of harassment by another student. The vice principal claimed he showed the student a small knife he kept in his drawer and asked him how he would feel if someone he had picked on brought a knife to school. He told the student that this was "where harassment could lead." But the student claimed the vice principal shut the door and brandished the knife in front of him. He filed an assault action against the vice principal, who asked the board of education to defend him. The board was a self-insuring member of the Maryland Association of Boards of Education Group Insurance Pool. Asserting that an assault was intentional and malicious conduct that was excluded from coverage, the board refused to defend the vice principal. He obtained defense under his educators employment liability policy.

After a jury found that the vice principal did not commit assault, the educators liability insurer sought reimbursement from the board. A state court held that the board had to provide a defense for the vice principal. The Court of Appeals of Maryland then noted that **state law required a board to defend an employee who was both "acting in the scope of his employment" and "without malice."** Here, the vice principal won his case. The court of appeals found nothing in state law that would relieve a school board of its statutory duty based on the type of insurance coverage it had purchased. As the vice principal's response to the student's complaint asserted he was acting in pursuit of his duties, in the scope of his employment and without malice, the education board had a duty to defend him in the student's action. *Board of Educ. of Worcester County v. Horace Mann Insurance Co.*, 408 Md. 278, 969 A.2d 305 (Md. 2009).

◆   A Pennsylvania school hired a contractor to renovate an elementary school. The contract included a liquidated damages clause for work delays, and a performance bond was acquired from a surety to cover default by the contractor. The terms of the bond made the surety responsible for any remaining work after default, and made it eligible for any contract balance. Near completion of the project, the school district claimed that the contractor's work was untimely and deficient. It declared the contractor in default and withheld its final payment, also refusing to pay the balance to the surety. The contractor sued the school district, and the district counter-claimed against the contractor.

The district agreed to release all claims against the contractor and pay it $430,000. However, the district refused to release its claims against the surety, claiming it reserved all rights under the performance bond. The settlement was placed into the record before a judge, with no mention of the surety's rights or duties. The court held that the release of the contractor also discharged the surety. The case reached the Supreme Court of Pennsylvania, where the surety argued that it stood in the shoes of the contractor, and had no remaining liability after a settlement. The district argued that the release did not fully resolve all issues relating to the contractor's default. The court noted that **the district sought to have it both ways by releasing the contractor, then claiming additional rights against the surety**. However, the district was only entitled to performance by either the contractor or the surety. *Kiski Area School Dist. v. Mid-State Surety Corp.*, 600 Pa. 444, 967 A.2d 368 (Pa. 2008).

◆   The Texas Political Subdivisions Property/Casualty Joint Self-Insurance Fund is a self-insurance risk pool and claim administrator for member districts and political subdivisions. A school district submitted a claim for extensive water and mold damage to some of its facilities. The fund denied the claim. The district sued the fund, which claimed state law immunity. The case reached the Supreme Court of Texas, which found that although the fund was a combination of political subdivisions that enjoyed local government status, it was not entitled to immunity. *Ben Bolt-Palito Blanco Consolidated Independent School Dist. v. Texas Political Subdivisions Property/Casualty Joint Self-Insurance Fund*, 212 S.W.3d 320 (Tex. 2006).

◆   The family of an Illinois student with disabilities sued their school district for violating the Individuals with Disabilities Education Act (IDEA), Section 504 of the Rehabilitation Act, and the Americans with Disabilities Act (ADA). The district tendered defense of the lawsuit to its insurer. The insurer paid the district $50,000 under a supplementary payments provision of its policy that limited coverage for defense costs to $50,000 for non-monetary claims involving disputes in special education. The insurer denied responsibility for further defense costs, relying on a policy exclusion precluding coverage for relief "other than monetary damages." It asserted that the family's suit was limited to the special education placement and did not seek damages. A federal court and the Seventh Circuit Court of Appeals held for the district. The family appealed the

IDEA claims to the U.S. Supreme Court. The Court declined the case, but the appeal cost the district an additional $9,901 in legal costs and fees.

The school district filed a separate action against the insurer in a state court for additional defense costs. The court held that since monetary damages are available under the ADA and Section 504, the insurer had to defend those claims. The Appellate Court of Illinois noted that the ADA, Section 504 and IDEA claims sought reimbursement for the cost of obtaining independent evaluations and services. The family would have been entitled to payment from the district had these claims succeeded. **The claims for reimbursement sought monetary damages as contemplated by the policy, and the insurer was required to defend the district.** The court affirmed the judgment for defense costs arising under the ADA and Section 504, and it reversed the judgment denying defense of the IDEA claims. The district was entitled to the additional costs of defending the Supreme Court appeal, as it involved an IDEA claim. *General Star Indemnity Co. v. Lake Bluff School Dist. No. 65*, 819 N.E.2d 784 (Ill. App. Ct. 2004).

◆   Louisiana school board employees sued the board for injury and illness from exposure to toxic substances, safety hazards and toxic mold. They claimed the board was negligent in the upkeep and repair of a high school. The board sought coverage from its general liability insurer, which claimed coverage was barred by exclusions for employees and for expected or intended injury. A Louisiana court awarded pretrial judgment to the insurer, and the board appealed. The Court of Appeal of Louisiana found that the policy's employers liability exclusion applied to bodily injury to an employee, arising out of and in the course of his or her employment. **The policy's expected or intended bodily injury exclusion applied to any intentional injury.** These provisions unambiguously excluded coverage for employees and for intentional conduct. The court rejected the employees' assertion that the policy did not bar coverage because they made their claims against "administrators" as well as the board. The judgment was affirmed. *Hemstad v. Jefferson Parish School Board*, 916 So.2d 1174 (La. Ct. App. 2005).

◆   The Court of Appeals of Maryland explained that local boards of education may satisfy their state law obligation to carry comprehensive liability insurance through self-insurance programs. Such insurance must conform to terms and conditions of private liability insurance. The state Education Article independently **requires education boards to provide counsel for teachers who are sued for claims "in the performance of their duties, within the scope of employment, and without malice,"** and where a board determines the teacher acted within his or her official capacity. Liability insurers are obligated to defend actions against their insureds "if there was any potentiality of coverage." In this case, a student who claimed sexual abuse by a teacher had asserted contacts that went beyond the proper teacher/mentor role. This indicated potential coverage by the board's self-insurance. *Montgomery County Board of Educ. v. Horace Mann Insurance Co.*, 860 A.2d 909 (Md. 2004).

## II.  DESEGREGATION

*In* Brown v. Board of Education, *347 U.S. 483, 74 S.Ct. 686, 98 L.Ed. 873 (1954), the U.S. Supreme Court declared unconstitutional separate but equal systems of segregation in public schools. Fourteen years after its landmark decision in* Brown, *the Court responded to widespread resistance by school districts to federal court desegregation orders by ruling that segregation must be eliminated "root and branch."* Green v. County School Board of New Kent County, *391 U.S. 430, 88 S.Ct. 1689, 20 L.Ed.2d 716 (1968).*

*By 1992, the Court declared that formerly segregated, dual school districts could be released from federal court supervision upon a demonstration of good-faith compliance with a desegregation decree, where the "vestiges of past discrimination have been eliminated to the extent practicable."* Freeman v. Pitts, *503 U.S. 467, 112 S.Ct. 1430, 118 L.Ed.2d 108 (1992). Courts rely on the factors identified in* Green *to determine if a district should be declared unitary and released from federal court supervision. They also consider more recent cases such as* Freeman, Board of Educ. of Oklahoma City Public Schools v. Dowell, *498 U.S. 237, 111 S.Ct. 630, 112 L.Ed.2d 715 (1991), and* Missouri v. Jenkins, *495 U.S. 33, 110 S.Ct. 1651, 109 L.Ed.2d 31 (1990).*

*The test from* Freeman *and* Dowell *for releasing a school system from federal court supervision is whether there has been compliance with the decree, whether retention of the case by the court is necessary or practicable to achieve compliance with the decree, and whether the school district has demonstrated a good-faith commitment to the desegregation decree to the public and to minority parents and students. The* Freeman *decision is also important for approving the concept of the withdrawal of federal court supervision in stages as partial unitary status is achieved with respect to specific programs and areas including school facilities, faculty and staff assignments, extracurricular activities, transportation and student assignments.*

***In a 1991 Oklahoma case, the Supreme Court held that the supervision of local school districts by the federal courts was meant as a temporary means to remedy past discrimination.*** *It returned the case to a lower court with instructions to determine whether a school district that achieved unitary status in 1977 had complied with constitutional requirements when it later adopted a student reassignment plan.* Board of Educ. of Oklahoma City Public Schools v. Dowell, *498 U.S. 237, 111 S.Ct. 630, 112 L.Ed.2d 715 (1991).*

### A.  Release from Federal Court Supervision

◆   Federal court oversight of Shelby County (Tennessee) public schools began in 1963 with a class action alleging racial segregation. Over the years, the federal district court issued many orders requiring elimination of all vestiges of state-imposed segregation in accordance with *Brown v. Board of Education*. A court-approved desegregation plan was implemented. In 2006, the school board and a class of students sought to end the lawsuit. After two fairness hearings, the court found that the goals of the desegregation plan had not been met. It refused to dismiss court oversight regarding student assignment, faculty integration and extracurricular activities, and it set "racial ratios" for student and faculty members to be met by 2012. A target for the end of court supervision was set for 2015. The school board and the U.S. government appealed to the U.S. Court of Appeals, Sixth Circuit. The court noted that a **"unitary" school system is one having unitary assignment of students, faculty and staff, and unitary school facilities, resources, transportation and extracurricular activities**. If a school district complies in good faith with a desegregation decree, and eliminates the vestiges of past discrimination to the extent practicable, the system is entitled to be released from supervision.

Student assignment remained racially imbalanced in Shelby County schools, but the court found this was due to demographic factors. Political and social decisions beyond the board's control affected the district's racial balance. These influences were unrelated to the prior constitutional violation and were outside a court's power to resolve. As the Supreme Court has observed, "racial balance is not to be achieved for its own sake." The lower court had incorrectly found the board out of compliance with the decree based on variations in teacher ratio in some schools. Race-based hiring as ordered by the district court was unconstitutional. As the district court had denied the request for unitary status for extracurricular activities without explanation, the court rejected this part of the order, and reversed the judgment with instructions to dismiss the case. *Robinson v. Shelby County Board of Educ.*, 566 F.3d 642 (6th Cir. 2009).

◆   Little Rock (Arkansas) School District (LRSD) was in desegregation litigation since 1956. In 1989, a federal court approved an interdistrict settlement plan that allowed court supervision of remedial desegregation by LRSD and two neighboring districts. The parties agreed in 1998 that if LRSD substantially complied with a revised desegregation plan, the district would be declared unitary after the 2000-01 school year. In 2002, the court granted LRSD "partial unitary status" based on compliance with all plan provisions except those governing academic programs for improving African-American student achievement. The court imposed a compliance remedy upon LRSD. In 2004, the U.S. Court of Appeals, Eighth Circuit, affirmed the finding of substantial compliance. When LRSD asked to be declared unitary, a federal court held that it was still not in compliance with the academic assessment provisions. The Eighth Circuit rejected LRSD's claim that this was an error.

The case returned to the lower court, which found that **the LRSD acted in good faith to implement the program assessment process as required** by the 1998 revised plan. After the court declared the LRSD system unitary, a group of intervenors appealed. The Eighth Circuit expressed complete agreement with the lower court that LRSD had substantially complied with its desegregation obligations. No evidence supported the current appeal. *Little Rock School Dist. v. North Little Rock School Dist.*, 561 F.3d 746 (8th Cir. 2009).

◆   In 1969, a federal court held that a Mississippi school district operated a segregated, dual school system. Under later orders, the court divided the school district into three attendance zones and required the transportation of students in non-segregated, nondiscriminatory ways. The district also had to select locations for school construction and consolidate its schools to prevent recurrence of a dual system. In 2004, the district sought a declaration of full unitary status which, if granted, would end federal court oversight. The U.S. Government and private parties agreed that many areas of operation were unitary. But they alleged that the district did not act in good faith with court orders regarding facilities and a magnet high school that was still 98.5% African-American. The court held that the district was unitary and dissolved all its desegregation orders.

The case reached the U.S. Court of Appeals, Fifth Circuit, which held that the magnet program at the high school had been in operation long enough for the court to make informed findings about it. The district's good-faith compliance was seen in the expenditure of considerable resources for renovating the high school and implementing the magnet program. It had implemented minority recruitment, set up a biracial advisory committee, and fulfilled its reporting obligations. Racial imbalance in schools, by itself, does not create a constitutional violation. **While the magnet high school had failed to draw white students, there was evidence that this was primarily due to demographic and cultural factors.** The school district had achieved unitary status in all of its operations, and further judicial oversight was neither required nor desirable. *Anderson v. School Board of Madison County*, 517 F.3d 292 (5th Cir. 2008).

◆  In 1964, a federal court held that Alabama operated a *de jure* segregated system of dual schools and required all school districts to desegregate. In 1970, the court ordered the Roanoke City Board of Education to implement a desegregation plan proposed by the federal government. By 1997, the court ordered the parties to consider whether the Roanoke school system had achieved unitary status in several areas. In 1998, the court approved a consent decree which found the Roanoke schools had achieved unitary status in student assignment, facilities and transportation. These functions were returned to local control. The board agreed to take action in other identified areas to eliminate any remaining vestiges of segregation. These included faculty hiring and assignment, student assignment and instruction, special education, extracurricular activities, student discipline and graduation rates. During the 2006-07 school year, the board sought a declaration of unitary status and termination of the lawsuit.

A federal court found that the board had made considerable efforts to recruit and hire minority applicants for faculty positions, and had encouraged student assignment on a nondiscriminatory basis through special programs and courses. It had taken reasonable steps to ensure equal participation opportunities in extracurricular activities. Student discipline had been addressed through cultural diversity training, activities and workshops. The board hired a consultant to work with repeat offenders, significantly reducing disciplinary problems. The district dropout rate was 4% lower than the statewide average. African-American student participation in a high school math club and local chapter of the National Honor Society was increasing. **The city board and its members had met standards entitling the district to a declaration of unitary status.** *Lee v. Roanoke City Board of Educ.*, Civil Action No. 3:70cv855-MHT, 2007 WL 1196482 (M.D. Ala. 4/23/07).

◆ In 1969, a Georgia school system was ordered to close all legally recognized black schools. The system complied. In 1983, a plaintiff class contended that the school system improperly limited minority transfers to a predominantly white school and that the proposed expansion of a white high school would perpetuate segregation. The court ruled that the school system had achieved unitary status and did not have a discriminatory intent in deciding to expand the high school. The U.S. Court of Appeals, Eleventh Circuit, stated that the system had not discharged its duty in the areas of student assignment, transportation, and extracurricular activities by closing all legally recognized black schools in response to the 1969 order. The system would not achieve unitary status until it maintained at least three years of racial equality in the six categories set out in *Green*: student assignment, faculty, staff, transportation, extracurricular activities, and facilities. The U.S. Supreme Court, however, held on appeal that the *Green* framework did not need to be applied as construed by the court of appeals. **Through relinquishing control in areas deemed to be unitary, a court and school district may more effectively concentrate on the areas in need of further attention.** The Court held that the "incremental" approach was constitutional, and that a court may declare that it will order no further remedy in any area that is found to be unitary. The order of the court of appeals was reversed, and the case was remanded to the district court. *Freeman v. Pitts,* 503 U.S. 467, 112 S.Ct. 1430, 118 L.Ed.2d 108 (1992).

The case returned to the district court, which found the evidence did not demonstrate a pattern of discrimination or absence of good faith by the school district. It therefore granted the district's motion to be released from federal court jurisdiction. *Mills v. Freeman,* 942 F.Supp. 1449 (N.D. Ga. 1996).

## B. Liability Issues

*Courts reviewing the actions of government officials in desegregation cases may find liability for civil rights violations where actions by the officials foreseeably perpetuate racial segregation in schools. Relief for constitutional violations may be apportioned among state and local school agencies.*

### 1. Government Liability

◆ Illinois residents petitioned the state board of education to detach land from Joliet Township High School District and annex it to Lincoln Way Community High School District. Joliet objected to the petition, arguing that the state law under which the petition was filed violated the federal Equal Educational Opportunities Act (EEOA). According to Joliet, the state school code forbade state education department hearing officers from considering EEOA issues when ruling on school district detachment and annexation petitions.

The hearing officer found the conditions of the code were met and recommended granting the petition. Appeal reached the Supreme Court of Illinois, which explained that the Supremacy Clause of the U.S. Constitution declares the laws of the U.S. to be the supreme law of the land. Any state law that conflicts with a federal law is preempted by the Supremacy Clause and is unconstitutional. The court found the parties were in agreement that the EEOA claim should be heard, but were in disagreement over what court or agency should consider it. **The EEOA was a remedial statute designed to specify appropriate remedies for the orderly removal of vestiges of the dual system of racially segregated schools.** It was clear that Congress intended the states and their educational agencies to refrain from discrimination. As the courts of Illinois had an obligation to review and enforce the EEOA, the court held the proper means for redress of an EEOA violation was an original action in a state court. Joliet's EEOA claim could be fully litigated in the state court system, avoiding a court ruling that would invalidate the state law. *Board of Educ., Joliet Township High School Dist. No. 204 v. Board of Educ., Lincoln Way Community High School Dist. No. 210*, 231 Ill.2d 184, 897 N.E.2d 756 (Ill. 2008).

◆ A Georgia school district relied on ability grouping since the end of *de jure* school segregation. Teachers grouped elementary school students based on their perceived abilities and their actual performance. The local NAACP branch and several African-American families sued the district, asserting that the practice violated the Equal Protection Clause of the Fourteenth Amendment and Title VI of the Civil Rights Act of 1964. A federal court held that many areas of school operations had racial imbalances, but attributed them to demographics and other "external factors." Although disproportionate numbers of low-income children, most of them African-American, were put in lower ability groups and stayed there throughout their academic careers, there was no federal law violation. The court attributed this to an "impoverished environment," not discrimination. The case reached the Eleventh Circuit which held that **a school district's obligation is only to eliminate the vestiges of past discrimination "to the extent practicable."** Here, the record supported the finding that the imbalances in the ability grouping program did not result from intentional discrimination, but from poverty. The Eleventh Circuit upheld the lower court decision. *Holton v. City of Thomasville School Dist.*, 490 F.3d 1257 (11th Cir. 2007).

## 2. Inter-District Remedies

◆ The U.S. Supreme Court affirmed an intra-district school desegregation plan that included busing in *Columbus Board of Educ. v. Penick*, 443 U.S. 449, 99 S.Ct. 2941, 61 L.Ed.2d 666 (1979). However, in the landmark Detroit school busing case, the Court rejected a plan that would have required multi-district, inter-district busing. It said there was no evidence that suburban districts outside Detroit which were included in the plan either operated segregated school systems or by their actions affected segregation in other districts. The Court held that **absent some inter-district constitutional violations with inter-district effects, racial segregation existing in one district could not be remedied by inter-district solutions.** *Milliken v. Bradley*, 418 U.S. 717, 94 S.Ct. 311, 41 L.Ed.2d 1069 (1974).

◆ In 1985, the Englewood Cliffs Board of Education petitioned the New Jersey state education commissioner to sever a longstanding agreement with the city of Englewood Board of Education, under which Englewood Cliffs students attended one of Englewood's high schools. Englewood opposed the petition, seeking to prevent further racial imbalance that would result from termination of the agreement. It also joined as a party to the action the Board of Education of Tenafly, a wealthy community that in 1982 began accepting nonresident students to Tenafly High School on a tuition-paying basis. An administrative law judge (ALJ) held that the Tenafly policy enticed white and Asian students from Englewood, exacerbating Englewood's racial imbalance. The ALJ held that state education officials had a constitutional and statutory responsibility to prevent segregation and ordered the Tenafly Board to stop accepting tuition-paying students from both Englewood and Englewood Cliffs.

The case reached the state supreme court, which held that **the state board and commissioner had an affirmative duty to take action to remedy racial imbalances at the high school**. The school had gone from 65.8% black and Hispanic in 1982-83 to 84% in 1987-88. The first step in achieving a racial balance that would effectuate state policy was to enjoin all other districts, including Tenafly, from accepting Englewood and Englewood Cliffs students into their schools. The state board had improperly and perhaps unintentionally allocated the responsibility for addressing racial imbalances to the Englewood Board. The court rejected compulsory regionalization, and the commissioner and state board retained ultimate responsibility for addressing racial imbalance at the school. *Board of Educ. of Borough of Englewood Cliffs v. Board of Educ. of City of Englewood*, 170 N.J. 323, 788 A.2d 729 (N.J. 2002).

◆   In 1979, a federal district court required the inter-district busing of students between primarily black Indianapolis public schools and primarily white public schools in local suburban areas. The court found Indianapolis Public School District (IPSD) boundaries were deliberately maintained to preserve segregated schools and that the city's housing authority refused to build public housing that would encourage desegregation. Years later, the Indianapolis school board moved the court to lift the busing injunction, observing that the lawsuit was 30 years old and claiming that the district had achieved unitary status.

The court denied the motion and ordered all kindergarten students in designated sections of the city to participate in mandatory busing, rescinding an earlier order permitting parents to select busing at their option. IPSD appealed to the U.S. Court of Appeals, Seventh Circuit. **The court held that the school board should have received an opportunity to present evidence at a hearing to consider whether the order should be dissolved.** The district court had erroneously denied the board this opportunity. In addition, the district court had improperly modified the decree to include the compulsory busing of kindergartners. The court vacated and remanded the case, so that the district court could develop a record based upon an evidentiary hearing. *U.S. v. Board of School Commissioners of City of Indianapolis*, 128 F.3d 507 (7th Cir. 1997).

### 3. Budget Issues

◆   An Arkansas taxpayer and 14 school districts sued the governor for diverting equalization funds, (later known as "foundation funds") to satisfy court-ordered desegregation costs in Pulaski County, and to provide additional base funding for districts that did not meet other funding standards. They claimed the diversion violated Amendment 74 to the Arkansas Constitution, which assessed a uniform rate of taxation (URT) of 25 mills for each school district on the value of property "solely for the maintenance and operation of the schools." A claim was added that the state unlawfully retained and diverted Amendment 74 property taxes and funds allocated to the state Educational Excellence Trust Fund. A court held for the state officials, and the challengers appealed to the Supreme Court of Arkansas.

The court found that Amendment 74 set a URT of 25 mills for each district on the assessed value of property "solely for the maintenance and operation of the schools." But URT funds only partially funded the basic foundation for any given year. **The court rejected the argument that the state could not reduce its Amendment 74 funding based on increased tax revenues resulting from increasing property values.** Amendment 74 did not place limits on how the General Assembly appropriated these funds, once it established what was needed to provide all students with substantially equal educational opportunities. Amendment 74 permitted variances in school district revenues above the base rate of 25 mills to enhance curriculums, facilities and equipment. There was no retention of URT funds by the state when the growth in URT revenues resulted in a corresponding reduction in state funding. The 25 mill URT set the amount of state foundation aid. Since none of the challengers' other theories had merit, the court affirmed the judgment for the state. *Ft. Smith School Dist. v. Beebe*, 2009 Ark. 333 (Ark. 2009).

◆    Two sparsely populated school districts in the Texas panhandle served fewer than 130 students each, and they depended on transfer students to be viable. "Virtually all" of the students in one district were transfer students. Texas law permits any eligible child to transfer if the receiving district and the parents agree. A 1970 federal court order required the state and the Texas Education Agency (TEA) to desegregate schools. A 1973 court order forbade the TEA from funding or supporting student transfers when the effect in either a sending or receiving school or district would be to reduce or impede school desegregation. The TEA began to track student transfers under an automated system. Both of the panhandle districts failed to report student transfers into TEA's transfer monitoring system. The TEA later informed the districts it would withhold funds for the following year for failing to report the transfers. After unsuccessfully challenging the actions within the TEA, the districts sought to intervene in the federal desegregation case. The court held that its 1973 order applied statewide because it was meant to eliminate the vestiges of race discrimination from Texas' former dual school system. But, as the panhandle districts received a state "sparsity adjustment," they did not receive any additional funds due to the transfers, and the TEA sanctions were disallowed.

On appeal, the U.S. Court of Appeals, Fifth Circuit, agreed with the districts that the 1973 order exceeded the lower court's authority. **The districts had never been subject to a desegregation order, and it was not shown that any of the transfers in this case were approved based on an intent to discriminate.** No state law provided for the sanctions, and the TEA's power to impose them arose solely from the 1973 court order. As the districts had never been found to have discriminated against students based on their race, the TEA could not sanction them. There must be a constitutional violation to sanction a school system. Accordingly, the judgment was reversed. *Samnorwood Independent School Dist. v. Texas Educ. Agency*, 533 F.3d 258 (5th Cir. 2008).

◆ In 1971, a federal district court entered Order 5281, requiring the desegregation of Texas school districts that had taken no steps to comply with *Brown v. Board of Educ.* Order 5281 prohibited the Texas Education Agency (TEA) from allowing student transfers that reduced or impeded desegregation, or that perpetuated discrimination. Hearne Independent School District (HISD) was not a party to Order 5281, but had been the defendant in another desegregation case. Its total student enrollment dropped from near 1,700 in 1991 to under 1,200 in 2004. Mumford Independent School District (MISD) grew from 57 students to over 400 during the same years, largely by receiving students from HISD of Hispanic or African-American descent. HISD and MISD remained "majority-minority" both before and after the transfers. The U.S. government and HISD claimed the transfers violated Order 5281 and sued the TEA and MISD to halt the transfers.

A court prohibited further transfers of white students to MISD. On appeal, the Fifth Circuit noted that the racial composition of Texas public schools had changed drastically since 1971. **During the past decade, HISD had lost students of all races** via transfers, dropouts and changes of residence. The TEA had a "liberal transfer policy" in which state funding followed students across district lines. The lower court had rejected the TEA's balancing approach and ordered the TEA to cease all funding for the transfer of white students, including those who had attended MISD schools for their entire school careers. Small changes in the racial composition of a district due to student transfers did not justify mandatory inter-district desegregation remedies. The TEA's funding of transfers had no significant net racial impact upon either district. The district court order was vacated. *U.S. v. State of Texas*, 457 F.3d 472 (5th Cir. 2006).

◆ In 1977, the Kansas City, Missouri, School District (KCMSD), its school board and a group of resident students sued the state of Missouri and a number of suburban Kansas City school districts, claiming the state had caused and perpetuated racial segregation in Kansas City schools. A court held that the state and KCMSD were liable for an intra-district constitutional violation. The defendants were ordered to eliminate all vestiges of state-imposed segregation.

Because the district's student population was almost 70% African-American, the court ordered a wide range of quality education plans that converted every high school and middle school, and some elementary schools, into magnet schools to attract white students from adjoining suburbs. This action was based upon the court's finding that KCMSD student achievement levels still lagged behind national averages in some grades. The state contested its court-ordered responsibility to help fund capital improvements for KCMSD schools. It also contested orders requiring it to share in the cost of teacher salary increases and quality education plans. Appeal reached the U.S. Supreme Court, which observed that the lower court's remedial plan had been based on a budget that exceeded KCMSD's authority to tax. There was a lack of evidence in the record to substantiate the theory that continuing lack of academic achievement in the district was the result of past segregation. The lower court had exceeded its authority by ordering the construction of a superior school system to attract white students from suburban and private schools. Its mandate was to remove the racial identity of KCMSD schools, and an inter-district remedy went beyond the intra-district violation. **The magnet district concept of KCMSD schools could not be supported by the existence of white flight.** The lower court orders for state contribution to salary increases, quality education programs and capital improvements were reversed. *Missouri v. Jenkins*, 515 U.S. 70 (1995).

## III.  SCHOOL DISTRICT OPERATIONS

*School district powers are created by state laws, and actions exceeding statutory authority may be set aside by a reviewing court. If state law provides, school district territories may be altered by annexation and detachment where economics or demographics make such action necessary.*

### A.  School Closing and District Dissolution Issues

◆  New Hampshire's highest court denied a taxpayer challenge to a school district plan to build and renovate two elementary schools. A pair of taxpayers noted the lot sizes of the schools did not meet state administrative requirements. A state court allowed the school district to intervene in the lawsuit, and it argued that the taxpayers had no legal interest in enforcing the state administrative rule on lot size. In the meantime, the taxpayers raised a new claim that waiver of the minimum lot size violated a state duty to provide a constitutionally adequate education. After the court dismissed the case, the state supreme court affirmed the decision. It noted recent court cases finding that **taxpayers are required to demonstrate that their rights are impaired in order to obtain relief from a court**. It was not enough for the taxpayers to simply allege that they paid taxes in the district. Since they could not show they had any personal rights that were impaired by the lot size waiver, the judgment was affirmed. *Baer v. New Hampshire Dep't of Educ.*, 160 N.H. 727, 8 A.3d 48 (N.H. 2010).

◆  Act 60 of a 2003 Extraordinary Session of the Arkansas General Assembly required school districts with average daily memberships of fewer than 350 students to consolidate with – or be annexed by – other school districts. After Lake View School District was consolidated with another district, a group of challengers sued state officials in a federal court, which dismissed the case. Appeal went to the Eighth Circuit, which held that **the state had a legitimate interest in consolidating school districts to achieve economies of scale and other efficiencies**. *Friends of Lake View School Dist. v. Beebe*, 578 F.3d 753 (8th Cir. 2009).

◆  An Iowa school district closed five schools and the state board of education affirmed the decision. A group of taxpayers sought review, asserting that the board did not comply with its own regulations. After the court upheld the decision, appeal reached the state supreme court. Among the court's findings was that the school district considered revenue forecasts and discussed a staff report with strategic options for dealing with protected revenue shortfalls and cost increases. It considered other options and held meetings to solicit public input on its plans. According to the taxpayers, the district action had to be set aside because of failure to comply with two state board rules describing procedural steps for districts to follow when closing schools. They claimed public participation was limited because of insufficient notice. The court held that while the legislature had authorized the board to adopt rules for many specific subjects, there was no express legislative authorization of rules prescribing the procedures for closing schools. Instead, **the legislature's failure to grant the board such authority fit within the grant of exclusive jurisdiction to school districts in school matters**. The district's decision to close some of its schools clearly entailed discretion. The court ruled for the district. *Wallace v. Iowa State Board of Educ.*, 770 N.W.2d 344 (Iowa 2009).

◆   The Beaumont Texas board of school trustees announced a $388.6 million bond issue "for the purpose of acquiring, constructing, renovating, improving and equipping new and existing school buildings and school facilities." Voters approved of the bond issue and the district began to define projects at various sites. When it became apparent that a particular school would be demolished, the Beaumont Heritage Society sued the district and school officials, claiming the board lacked the authority to demolish the school. At a hearing, the district superintendent testified that no middle school buildings would be retained.

According to the society, school officials had represented prior to the bond issue that the school would not be demolished. The court enjoined demolition of the school pending a full trial. School officials appealed to the Court of Appeals of Texas, which noted that contractors were apparently prepared to tear down the middle school buildings. If the society's evidence was true, school officials had made public misrepresentations prior to the bond issue. The district did not offer any board minutes reflecting a vote to demolish the school. But the superintendent had testified at the lower court hearing that no buildings at the school would be retained. **While school trustees are vested with the duty to manage school property, state law restricted expenditures of public funds to their authorized purposes.** The trial court did not abuse its discretion in halting the demolition pending a trial to consider whether the district's use of bond funds was authorized. *Thomas v. Beaumont Heritage Society*, 296 S.W.2d 350 (Tex. Ct. App. 2009).

## B.  Redistricting and Zoning

◆   A Kansas city planning commission held a hearing to consider a school district's application for a special use permit for a lighted softball complex and stadium. An adjacent property owner objected, and the planning commission voted to deny the application due to the frequency of stadium use and its impact on surrounding properties. After hearing from interested parties, the city council voted 5-3 to return the application to the planning commission for further review and examination of specific items. The planning commission again voted to deny the special use permit, but the city council voted 5-4 to grant it with modifications, with the mayor casting the tie-breaking vote. The objecting property owner sued, claiming violations of Kansas law. A court held that state law did not permit the city council to override the planning commission by a simple majority vote. It reversed the city's action. The city then appealed to the Supreme Court of Kansas, meanwhile voting 6-2 to ratify its action granting the special use permit.

The supreme court held that state law said nothing about a two-thirds majority by a city after a proposal was returned to a planning commission, then resubmitted. As the trial court had incorrectly interpreted the statute to require a two-thirds majority vote after the city returned the case to the planning commission, the court reversed the judgment. **The final authority in zoning matters rested with the agency with legislative power.** The court rejected the property owner's additional arguments, finding that he had received a fair, open and impartial opportunity to contest the application. *Manly v. City of Shawnee*, 287 Kan. 63, 194 P.3d 1 (Kan. 2008).

◆  A New York school district provided special education services at private, religious schools to students with disabilities who were members of the Satmar Hasidic group. The group's religious beliefs include segregation of school-age boys and girls and separation from mainstream society. A U.S. Supreme Court decision in 1985 prohibited the state from paying public school teachers for teaching on parochial school grounds. The state legislature passed a statute establishing a separate school district entirely within the Hasidic community to provide special education services. The New York Court of Appeals held that the statute endorsed religion in violation of the Establishment Clause.

The U.S. Supreme Court agreed to review the case. It held that a state may not delegate authority to a group chosen by religion. Although the statute did not expressly identify the Hasidim as recipients of governmental authority, it had clearly been passed to benefit them. The result was a purposeful and forbidden fusion of governmental and religious functions. **The creation of a school district for the religious community violated the Establishment Clause.** The Court held that the legislation extended a special franchise to the Hasidim that violated the constitutional requirement of religious neutrality by the government. *Board of Educ. of Kiryas Joel Village School Dist. v. Grumet*, 512 U.S. 687, 114 S.Ct. 2481, 129 L.Ed.2d 546 (1994).

The legislature passed new legislation allowing municipalities to establish their own school districts upon the satisfaction of several criteria. Noting that these criteria would restore a Hasidic school district, the taxpayers renewed their challenge. The case reached the state's highest court, which held that **despite the neutral criteria of the amendments, the Hasidic village was the only municipality that could ever avail itself of the amendments**. As no other municipality could be eligible for redistricting under the law, it impermissibly favored the Satmar sect, and the court of appeals held for the taxpayers. *Grumet v. Cuomo*, 90 N.Y.2d 57, 659 N.Y.S.2d 173, 681 N.E.2d 340 (N.Y. 1997).

The legislature amended the law again in 1997, in an attempt to conform with the court of appeals' decision. The case again reached the New York Court of Appeals. Despite the law's facial neutrality with respect to religion, it only benefited Kiryas Joel residents, and its potential benefit extended to only one other district in the state. **Since other religious groups would be unable to benefit from the law in the manner enjoyed by the Satmar sect of Kiryas Joel, the law was not neutral in effect** and it violated the Establishment Clause. *Grumet v. Pataki,* 93 N.Y.2d 677, 720 N.E.2d 66 (N.Y. 1999).

## IV.  SCHOOL BOARDS

### A.  Membership

#### 1.  Appointments, Elections, Residency and Recall

◆  A Washington school board voted to reschedule a school makeup day in violation of a collective bargaining provision. Many teachers did not report for work and those who did received no pay. The board found some substitutes, but it resorted to hiring jugglers and clowns to keep students occupied for the day. An arbitrator held that the board violated the bargaining agreement by unilaterally changing the makeup day, and that board members had "knowingly and willfully" violated contract rights by withholding pay. The incident cost the district almost $75,000. Three district residents filed recall petitions against two board members. The case reached the Supreme Court of Washington, which ruled that to be legally sufficient, **the recall petitions needed only "state with specificity substantial conduct clearly amounting to misfeasance, malfeasance or violation of the oath of office."** Here, the petition alleged that the board members knowingly and willingly broke a collective bargaining agreement and thereby unnecessarily caused substantial financial harm. As the charges against the board members were legally sufficient, the petitioners could continue seeking a special election to recall the members from office. *In re Recall of Young,* 100 P.3d 307 (Wash. 2004).

◆  Section Two of the federal Voting Rights Act of 1965 bars all states and their political subdivisions from maintaining discriminatory voting practices, standards or procedures. Section Five of the act is limited in scope to "covered jurisdictions." It prohibits the passing of new discriminatory laws as soon as old ones are struck down by freezing election procedures in covered jurisdictions unless the changes are nondiscriminatory. A Louisiana school board that was covered under Section 5 addressed population disparities revealed in the 1990 census by adopting a plan preserving a white majority in each of its 12 single-member districts. The board rejected a proposal by the local NAACP that would have created two districts with a majority of African-American voters. The board complied with Section 5 procedures by obtaining pre-clearance from the U.S. District Court for the District of Columbia. The U.S. Attorney General's office appealed to the U.S. Supreme Court, where it joined with the NAACP in arguing that a change in voting practices that violates Section 2 also constitutes an independent reason to deny pre-clearance under Section 5. The Court held that the sections addressed different voting policy concerns. Nothing in the statute justified presuming that a violation of Section 2 was sufficient for denying pre-clearance under Section 5. However, some of the evidence presented in support of a Section 2 claim might be relevant in a Section 5 proceeding. **As the district court had failed to consider evidence of the dilutive impact of the board's redistricting plan, the Court vacated the judgment and remanded the case.** *Reno v. Bossier Parish School Board,* 520 U.S. 471, 117 S.Ct. 1491, 137 L.Ed.2d 73 (1997).

On remand, the district court again granted pre-clearance to the board, and the Attorney General obtained Supreme Court review. The Supreme Court held that Section Five does not prohibit pre-clearance of a redistricting plan enacted with a discriminatory but non-retrogressive purpose. Accordingly, the Court affirmed the judgment. *Reno v. Bossier Parish School Board,* 528 U.S. 320, 120 S.Ct. 866, 145 L.Ed.2d 845 (2000).

◆   Texas is a covered jurisdiction under Section 5 of the Voting Rights Act of 1965. The Texas legislature enacted a comprehensive statutory scheme for holding local school boards accountable to the state for student achievement. The law contained 10 possible sanctions on districts for failing to meet legislative standards governing the assessment of academic skills, development of academic performance indicators, determination of accreditation status and the imposition of accreditation sanctions. The law's most drastic sanctions – appointment of a master or a management team to oversee district operations – required the exhaustion of the lesser sanctions first. In compliance with Section 5, Texas requested administrative pre-clearance for the amendments. The attorney general approved most of the sanctions as not affecting voting but found the appointment of a master or management team could result in a Section 5 violation.

Texas appealed to the U.S. District Court for the District of Columbia, which held that the claim was not ripe for adjudication. The U.S. Supreme Court agreed to review the case, and it stated the general rule that **a claim is not ripe for adjudication if it rests upon contingent future events that may not actually occur**. Texas had not identified any school district in the state that might become subject to the appointment of a master or management team and was not required to implement the sanctions until one of the remedies already approved by the attorney general had been exhausted. Because the issue presented was speculative and unfit for judicial review, the Court affirmed the judgment. *Texas v. U.S.,* 523 U.S. 296, 118 S.Ct. 1257, 140 L.Ed.2d 406 (1998).

◆   The Tennessee Constitution and the Tennessee Education Improvement Act mandate popularly elected school boards. Shelby County Tennessee, which encompasses the city of Memphis, has two school districts, one of which serves only Memphis residents. The county enacted an electoral plan calling for the election of county board members from seven single-member districts throughout the entire county. As a result, Memphis residents could vote in county education board elections, even though students from Memphis attended school in a different system. The county board of commissioners filed a federal court action against state officials including the attorney general, seeking a declaration that the Education Improvement Act violated the Fourteenth Amendment rights of county voters who did not reside in Memphis. The court agreed with the commissioners, and the state officials appealed.

The U.S. Court of Appeals, Sixth Circuit, stated that courts have established a number of factors to determine whether non-district voters have a substantial interest in school board elections. These included the degree to which one district finances the other, the voting strength of district voters, the potential for crossover students and joint programs between districts. In this case, Memphis voters did not substantially finance the county school district, and they outnumbered county voters by three to one. There was very little crossover of students and a negligible number of joint programs between city and county districts. Applying these factors, **the Education Improvement Act was unconstitutional as applied to county school board voters**. It improperly diluted votes and placed the majority of votes in the hands of out-of-district voters. The court affirmed the lower court's judgment. *Board of County Commissioners of Shelby County, Tennessee v. Burson*, 121 F.3d 244 (6th Cir. 1997).

### 2.  Misconduct, Conflict of Interest and Nepotism

*New Jersey's Supreme Court held that a school board member who pursued a special education due process action against his school district on behalf of his son had an impermissible conflict of interest.*

◆   A New Jersey school board member resigned from office prior to the filing of a due process hearing request regarding his autistic son. He later reached an agreement with the board and again successfully ran for office. The day before his term began, he signed a settlement agreement with the board. The next year, the board member and his wife requested enforcement of the agreement. They claimed that the board breached the settlement by placing his son in an "abusive environment" due to lack of support by staff. The petition sought compensatory education, extended, at-home day services, attorneys' fees, costs and other relief. An administrative law judge found that the board member's conduct was allowed under the state School Ethics Act, N.J.S.A. Section 18A:12-24(j). But the commissioner rejected this finding and ordered his removal.

The case reached the Supreme Court of New Jersey, which found that **board members should not be removed from office simply because they were pursuing a claim against a school district involving an individual or immediate family interest**. Disqualifying conflicts of interest should be identified by type. That said, the claim in this case sought monetary relief, and the IDEA offered less-adversarial options. A demand for substantial monetary relief could not be reconciled with continued service as a board member. The commissioner had engaged in the correct analysis. In the future, a case-by-case analysis was appropriate to consider claims involving a board member who has filed a claim against his or her own board of education. *Board of Educ. of City of Sea Isle City v. Kennedy*, 951 A.2d 987 (N.J. 2008).

◆   After a Kansas teacher won a four-year term as a school board member, the board sought to disqualify her from service while she continued her teaching duties. It alternatively sought to prevent her from receiving her teaching salary while serving as a board member. A court held that although state law prohibited certain persons from school board membership, it did not specifically exclude teachers. Also, the board's policy prohibiting members from receiving compensation for employment by the district was void as an unlawful attempt to determine who was qualified to serve as a board member. The school board appealed.

According to the Kansas Supreme Court, **the offices of teacher and board member are demonstrably incompatible**. Under the dual-service arrangement, the teacher occupied one position that was subordinate to the other. She was both employer and employee, and she sat on a policymaking body that negotiated with the employees' collective bargaining representative. This presented a clear conflict of interest. She was subject to discipline by the board and could be fired by it in certain circumstances. Applying equitable principles, the court found that her employment as a teacher endured and disqualified her from serving on the board. *Unified School Dist. No. 501, Shawnee County, Kansas v. Baker*, 269 Kan. 239, 6 P.3d 848 (Kan. 2000).

◆   A Georgia citizen complained that three elected school board members had participated in decisions affecting the compensation and benefits of their spouses, who were employees of the school system. The individual also asserted that the board members' recent election of a new superintendent was improper because the new superintendent would "be beholden to the [board members] and would reciprocate by granting [their] spouses additional privileges, compensation or benefits." A Georgia court dismissed the complaint, finding no enforceable duty among the board members to refrain from voting on matters that might affect the financial interests of their employee spouses.

The citizen appealed to the Georgia Supreme Court, which affirmed. The constitutional provision at issue stated that "[p]ublic officers are the trustees and servants of the people and at all times amenable to them." This broad language had been construed in other cases as prohibiting a public officer from financially benefiting as the result of performing official duties. In this case, the alleged benefit to the board members' spouses was speculative, and the language of the state constitution did not support the citizen's construction. **There was no precedent for the position that the familial relationship of locally elected school officials disqualified them from participating in school operations decisions.** The trial court had properly dismissed the complaint. *Ianicelli v. McNeely*, 272 Ga. 234, 527 S.E.2d 189 (Ga. 2000).

## B.  School Board Powers and Duties

*In 2009, North Carolina's highest court found that no state law required a rapidly growing school district to obtain parental consent before it assigned over 20,000 students to mandatory year-round schools.*

◆   A Wisconsin school district received eight open-enrollment applications from resident students who wished to enroll in other districts in 2009. At the time, more than 10% of its resident students attended nonresident districts. It denied the applications, citing a state statute that allowed only 10% of a district's resident student population to enroll in other districts if the resident board chose to apply a statutory cap. As an additional reason for denying the applications, the district claimed financial hardship. When the students' parents requested administrative review, the state education superintendent agreed with them that the limit on the percentage of a district's residents transferring to other districts did not apply after the 2005-06 school year. The superintendent also held that any authority to deny applications based on undue financial burden were limited to cases of eligible students with disabilities.

On appeal, the Court of Appeals of Wisconsin noted that the statute in question provided no authority to limit transfers or open enrollment by percentage of students after the 2005-06 school year. As for the financial burden claim, the court agreed with the state superintendent's finding that only the cost of special education or related services required in an individualized education program could serve as a possible basis for denying an open enrollment application due to an undue financial burden. None of the students in this case had a disability requiring an individualized education program. **No state law provisions restricted student transfers based on the overall financial health of the resident district.** The court affirmed the superintendent's order. *School Dist. of Stockbridge v. Evers*, 792 N.W.2d 615 (Wis. Ct. App. 2010).

◆   A Virginia court approved a sex offender's application to go onto school property to observe his stepson's activities, and to pick him up, drop him off and go to conferences. The court granted the offender conditional rights to be present on school property. It also terminated his duty to re-register every 90 days as a sex offender, instead requiring him to annually register with the state police as a convicted sex offender. The Commonwealth of Virginia and school officials objected to the order, and appealed to the Supreme Court of Virginia. According to the court, **the order lifting the ban on the sex offender violated the school district's constitutional authority to supervise students**. Thus, the court reversed the judgment and returned for a determination of whether and under what circumstances, the ban might be lifted in whole or in part. *Comwlth. v. Doe*, 278 Va. 223, 682 S.E.2d 906 (Va. 2009).

◆   Wake County (North Carolina) has one of the fastest-growing school systems in the nation. After student enrollment increased by over 30% from 2000 to 2006-07, the system expected another 65,000 increase in students by 2015. Despite extensive new construction, county schools remained extremely overcrowded, and some schools used cafeterias, libraries, auditoriums, offices, lounges, common areas and even storage rooms for classrooms. The board of education converted some elementary and middle schools to multi-track, year-round calendars. Students in such schools were divided into four tracks, each with its own schedule. Tracks were staggered so that three tracks were in school and one was out at all times. Multi-track schools using all 12 calendar months could accommodate up to one-third more students than traditional calendar schools. After public hearings to discuss converting more schools to year-round calendars, the board involuntarily assigned over 20,000 students to year-round schools. Parents who opposed the assignments sued the board in a state court.

The case reached the Supreme Court of North Carolina, which noted that a state statute authorized local boards to determine school calendars and appropriate class sizes. The statute did not classify school calendars as "traditional," or "year-round," and did not declare a preference for any calendar.

**Boards could devise calendars to achieve their educational goals, and calendar flexibility was encouraged to meet state-mandated performance standards.** Year-round schools were a legitimate calendar option, and the court found no statutory restriction on their use. While the law contemplated consultation between local boards and parents in the development of school calendars, there was no requirement for parental consent. Parents who were dissatisfied with an assignment could apply to the local board and receive a hearing. The court held that year-round schools were part of a mandated "uniform system of public schools." *Wake Cares v. Wake County Board of Educ.*, 675 S.E.2d 345 (N.C. 2009).

◆ In 1967, South Carolina lawmakers consolidated eight school districts in Charleston County into a unified county district. The eight districts remained in existence as "constituent districts" of the unified district, with authority to control their own matters. The unified district set up a countywide magnet school for gifted children. It was located within constituent District 20. One fourth of the school's openings were reserved for District 20 residents, and another quarter for their siblings. A fourth of the openings were reserved for students who would otherwise attend low-performing schools, and a fourth were to be allocated districtwide. In 2006, District 20 adopted a motion to give priority for all magnet school seats to qualified students residing within District 20. The magnet school principal appealed to the unified county district, asserting that District 20 lacked authority to set the school's attendance guidelines. The unified district's board nullified the District 20 decision to limit the magnet school to its own residents. District 20 appealed.

The state court of appeals found District 20 incorrectly interpreted the 1967 Act as permitting it to set attendance guidelines under its authority to decide which schools students could attend. Because the magnet school's attendance zone was countywide, the authority of constituent districts was not implicated. **The Act gave the unified district authority to provide a program for gifted children.** As District 20's position was inconsistent with the authority given to the unified district, the court held that District 20 lacked authority to set the magnet school's attendance guidelines. *Stewart v. Charleston County School Dist.*, 386 S.C. 373, 688 S.E.2d 579 (S.C. Ct. App. 2009).

◆ The Supreme Court of Georgia upheld a decision refusing to allow a would-be speaker to require a school board to place him on a meeting agenda. The speaker twice requested to be placed on a school board meeting agenda. Board policy vested the authority to grant or deny such requests with the superintendent, subject to a majority vote by the board to change the agenda and add persons wanting to address a meeting. The superintended denied the speaker's requests, and the board did not vote to add him to the agenda. A state superior court granted his request for a hearing but then dismissed the complaint. The Supreme Court of Georgia found no error by the lower court. The court explained that such relief is granted when a person has a clear legal right to compel a public officer to perform a required duty, and there is no other adequate legal remedy. However, **courts generally do not compel officials to follow a course of conduct, perform a discretionary act or**

**undo a past act**. As the setting of a board agenda was a discretionary act, such relief was unavailable. *James v. Montgomery County Board of Educ.*, 283 Ga. 517, 661 S.E.2d 535 (Ga. 2008).

♦   Two Indiana home-schooled students sought to attend public schools on a part-time basis. The superintendent denied their request under a district policy prohibiting non-public school students from enrolling in less than six credit-generating courses, unless they had an individualized education program. The students appealed. An administrative law judge held that they should be allowed to attend classes part time in district schools. The district appealed to an Indiana trial court and sought to stay the administrative order. The court granted the request for a stay and scheduled a "preliminary hearing." The state board asked for and received an extension to respond. Meanwhile, the hearing was held. The trial court invited the parties to submit additional briefs, but they declined. It then vacated the order of the administrative law judge as contrary to law.

The board appealed to the Court of Appeals of Indiana, which held that the board had been denied due process. Due process requires notice, an opportunity to be heard, and a chance to confront any witnesses. Notice must be reasonably calculated to afford parties a chance to present their cases. **It was unreasonable for the parties to expect that a "preliminary hearing" would be their last and only chance to present their cases.** The board received notice of the hearing only seven days in advance. This was not reasonable notice. Statements by the parties indicated that the subject of the hearing was a stay of the administrative order, not a final review. The parties believed the purpose of the preliminary hearing was to consider a stay, and they clearly expected additional hearings. *Indiana State Board of Educ. v. Brownsburg Community School Corp.*, 842 N.E.2d 885 (Ind. Ct. App. 2006).

♦   A Montana citizen sued a school district in the state court system, asserting a right to participate in the selection of a new superintendent. She claimed that the school board failed to notify her of votes and decisions leading to the hiring. A state court dismissed the case, and the Supreme Court of Montana affirmed. It noted that the state constitution grants the right to a reasonable opportunity for citizen participation in the operation of government, and the right to examine documents or observe the deliberations of public bodies and agencies. **In order to satisfy the requirement of standing to bring suit, the citizen had to clearly allege a past, present or threatened injury to a property or civil right.** She further had to claim an injury that was distinguishable from injury to the public at large. The court rejected her claim that being an informed and interested citizen conferred standing. She had no personal stake or interest in the hiring of a new superintendent. *Fleenor v. Darby School Dist.*, 331 Mont. 124, 128 P.3d 1048 (Mont. 2006).

♦   The Salt Lake City School Board considered school facilities usage, school boundaries and school closings for a period of over four years. It eventually closed two elementary schools in one part of the city and planned to build new schools in another area that it identified as underserved. Parents who objected to the actions claimed that the board acted arbitrarily and failed to consider its own policy in closing the schools. A state court held a trial, where the opponents claimed that the board violated a 1973 policy requiring it to follow several factors in making school closing decisions. The factors included keeping neighborhood schools as close as possible to students and communities, student safety, minimizing student transportation, the placement of students in efficient and functional buildings, use of newer school buildings and replacement of older ones. The court found that the opponents did not show the board ignored its closure policy, or act arbitrarily and capriciously in closing the schools. Even if the board did not have the policy before it, the factors enumerated in it were fully incorporated into new documents that guided the closing decisions.

The opponents appealed to the Supreme Court of Utah. The court accepted the trial court's determination that the board considered its policy when it acted. Meeting minutes, instructions to subcommittees and other documents were "replete with discussion of the factors" contained in the policy. **The board had thoroughly discussed the policy factors when it made the closure decisions.** The factors themselves indicated the discretionary nature of the board action. The court was reluctant to disturb the board's discretion in the absence of arbitrary action or a due process violation. The remedy for opponents of the closings was "in the voting booths," and the court affirmed the judgment. *Save Our Schools v. Board of Educ. of Salt Lake City*, 122 P.3d 611 (Utah 2005).

◆ The Supreme Court of Montana held that **a citizen's challenge to the continued use of Native American mascots by a school board had to be heard by the state human rights commission**. The superintendent had no jurisdiction over the challenge to the board's decision to retain mascots named "Chief" and "Maiden" by the district, which is located entirely within the Flathead Reservation. The human rights commission was the appropriate agency for determining whether the mascots created a hostile environment under the state human rights act. A "mere disagreement" with the district did not entitle the citizen to a hearing before the superintendent. *Dupuis v. Board of Trustees, Ronan School Dist. No. 30*, 128 P.3d 1010 (Mont. 2006).

◆ The Bedford New Hampshire School District (BSD) contracted with the Manchester School District (MSD) to educate its high school students. In 2001, MSD notified BSD and several other districts that it would terminate their 20-year tuition contracts at the end of the 2002-03 school year. BSD and MSD then negotiated a three-year tuition contract that included a per-pupil tuition payment. The payment had an operating expense component and a capital expense component. At BSD's annual meeting in 2004, BSD voters approved a $1.8 million deficit appropriation to fund the capital component of the tuition contract. Voters approved a general budget to fund the entire tuition payment for the 2004-05 school year. This included a $4.4 million appropriation for the capital component. Two taxpayers sued BSD and MSD in a state court, challenging the validity of the three-year contract and the votes.

The taxpayers sought an order barring payment of the capital component of the tuition payment and restoration of amounts of capital expenses already paid. The state supreme court found nothing in the law at issue required voter approval before a contract could be made. The taxpayers misapprehended the nature of school districts. **The authority to appropriate money rested with the school board and its voters at a district meeting.** The board had authority to make necessary contracts such as the tuition payment contract. BSD voters had been informed of the contract and its financial consequences before approving of the deficit appropriations. The court ruled against the taxpayers. *Foote v. Manchester School Dist.*, 152 N.H. 599, 883 A.2d 283 (N.H. 2005).

◆   A Minnesota school district reassigned all its junior high school grades to a high school building. The building that housed both elementary and junior high school grades was divided into separate "schools." Grades seven and eight made up 53% of the student population for the building, and classes for these grades occupied about half its space. A district committee issued a report recommending that grades seven and eight be moved from the building and into the district's only high school. The board adopted the committee's recommendation at a meeting, and a citizens' group petitioned the Court of Appeals of Minnesota for an order setting aside the action.

The court held that the building in this case was a single "schoolhouse," even though the junior high and elementary grades had been considered separate "schools." **The legislature intended notice and hearing requirements to apply only when a school shut its doors.** The school-closing statute at issue did not apply when a school remained open with a different student body composition. For a "schoolhouse closing" to take place, a district had to totally suspend or cease all the operations of a facility. While the reassignment action had greatly reduced the student population at the building, the district had not totally suspended or ceased all operations there. The reassignment of grades was not a "schoolhouse closing" as defined by state law, and the board was not required to follow the procedures of the school closing statute. *Citizens Concerned for Kids v. Yellow Medicine East Independent School Dist. No. 2109*, 703 N.W.2d 582 (Minn. Ct. App. 2005).

◆   An Ohio trial court held that parents have no constitutional right to attend school activities or be present on school grounds. School authorities may exclude parents from school activities and property without a hearing. Ohio school boards may govern school activities and property without adopting formal rules on all aspects of governance, subject to the "abuse of discretion standard." There was no abuse of discretion in a case involving the parent of a middle school student who was banned from school activities for three months after a "verbal altercation" with her daughter's volleyball coach at a neighboring school. The right to a free public education belongs to students, not their parents. **Although parents have a liberty interest in the education and upbringing of their children, this did not create any constitutional right for them to attend school activities or be present on school property.** As the parent had no constitutional liberty interest in being on school grounds or attending school activities, the board could exclude her from them without a hearing. *Nichols v. Western Local Board of Educ.*, 805 N.E.2d 206 (Ohio Common Pleas 2003).

## C. Open Meeting Laws

◆   In advance of a scheduled Massachusetts school committee meeting, the chair of the committee emailed the four other committee members regarding the superintendent's job performance. Two committee members emailed their responses only to the chair, while another sent his views to all the members. The fourth member did not respond. At the meeting, the board went into executive session to "discuss collective bargaining," though in fact they discussed the superintendent's evaluation. A newspaper reporter complained to the district attorney about the superintendent's evaluation process, and the committee's failure to release the evaluation. The district attorney found that the school committee violated the open meeting law by conducting the evaluation outside of public view. The case reached the Supreme Judicial Court of Massachusetts.

The court explained that the committee's reason for going into executive session was improper under the open meeting law because it was inaccurate. The superintendent was not covered by collective bargaining. Evidence showed the committee discussed the superintendent's professional competence, which should have been discussed in open session. And the emails had the effect of circumventing the open meeting law (even though some of them were not between a quorum of members). **As the emails were a "deliberation" that violated the letter and spirit of the open meeting law, they had to be made available to the public.** *Dist. Attorney for the Northern Dist. v. School Committee of Wayland*, 455 Mass. 561, 918 N.E.2d 796 (Mass. 2009).

◆   A group of Nebraska residents claimed their school board violated the state Open Meetings Act (OMA) by holding secret meetings prior to resolving to issue construction bonds for a new building. They said the construction issues were fully discussed in the secret meetings and then approved in a public meeting. But they did not file any action against the school board. Instead, they waited to see if the bond issue would pass in the election. After electors voted for the bonds, the residents sued, alleging OMA violations. A court held for the board, and the Supreme Court of Nebraska affirmed. Here, the residents' lawsuit was simply an election contest in the guise of an OMA action. They did not file suit within the time period specified by the election contest statutes. **An election contest was the exclusive remedy once an election has been held.** For this reason, the district court had properly dismissed the action. *Pierce v. Drobny*, 279 Neb. 251, 777 N.W.2d 322 (Neb. 2010).

◆   A Wisconsin school board held two closed meetings to discuss an administrator's employment, then voted in open session not to renew her contract. It did not provide her with the four months' notice of non-renewal, which administrators are to receive under state statute. The board maintained that she did not qualify as an "administrator" under this law because not all her duties were administrative. The administrator sued the school district, seeking the protection of the statute, including salary and other benefits. In the pretrial information-gathering process known as discovery, the administrator sought information from the closed board meetings. The district claimed that the requested data was privileged, but the court ordered the district to provide the information. The Supreme Court of Wisconsin held that **under state discovery rules, parties may have access to another party's information unless a privilege applies, so long as it is relevant to the subject matter of the lawsuit**. The fact that the information might not be admissible at a trial was not grounds for objection, so long as the request for information was reasonably calculated to reveal admissible evidence. The mere fact that the information sought by the administrator related to a closed session did not mean it was privileged. *Sands v. Whitnall School Dist.*, 754 N.W.2d 439 (Wis. 2008).

◆   A Pennsylvania student fired a soft pellet gun at his girlfriend from his car. He was suspended with a recommendation for a one-year expulsion. The superintendent agreed to modify an expulsion recommendation with several conditions, including 50 hours of community service, counseling, and compliance with behavior and academic requirements. The school board voted two weeks later in an open session to ratify the reduced sanctions. The student appealed, arguing that a soft pellet gun was not a "weapon" and that the shooting of a toy gun at a student was not a terroristic threat. He also claimed that the board violated the state Sunshine Act by taking official action in private.

The case reached the Commonwealth Court of Pennsylvania. It found the state Public School Code required expulsion for not less than one year of any student who was determined to have brought a "weapon" onto school property. The code defined "weapons" to include knives, guns and "any other tool, instrument or implement capable of inflicting serious bodily injury." Another court had applied the definition of "weapon" from the state Crimes Code to a student using a carbon dioxide-powered paintball. A pellet gun, like a paintball gun, could inflict serious injury to an eye. It was permissible to find it was a "weapon" under the code. **Even if the board had violated the Sunshine Act, its later vote in open session to modify the expulsion cured any violation.** *Picone v. Bangor Area School Dist.*, 936 A.2d 556 (Pa. Commw. Ct. 2007).

◆   A Colorado school board met in an executive session, where no minutes were taken and discussions were not disclosed. The board decided not to rehire a probationary teacher for the 2004-05 school year. The district superintendent sent him a "letter of intent," stating that the board did not intend to offer him a teaching contract for the next year. The board met twice in May 2005 and voted to renew all probationary teacher contracts, except that of the teacher. It failed to provide him with a non-renewal notice by June 1, as required by the Colorado Teacher Employment Compensation, and Dismissal Act (TECDA).

The teacher sued the district. Meanwhile, the board voted in public session that it would not rehire the teacher for 2004-05 or a later year. The board sent notices of the action to the teacher. The case reached the Supreme Court of Colorado, which held that **the vote to non-renew the teacher's contract in an executive session violated the state Open Meetings Law**. It was therefore not binding. No final policy decisions, including the non-renewal of a teacher's contract, may be made by a board in executive session. The superintendent's "letter of intent" had no effect. The TECDA required each school board to provide timely, written notice of a teacher termination. The failure to provide timely written notice to the teacher of a non-renewal vote resulted in his automatic reemployment. Although he was automatically reemployed for the 2004-05 year, he was not entitled to reinstatement because he received timely notice of the open board meeting decision. *Hanover School Dist. No. 28 v. Barbour*, 171 P.3d 223 (Colo. 2007).

◆  A Washington school board held a meeting for the public to evaluate candidates for an open board position. A citizen sought handouts provided by candidates at the meeting, an audiotape of the meeting and letters of interest from the candidates. The district made an audiotape and the letters available, but said it did not have any copies of the candidates' handouts. The citizen claimed the audiotape did not work in his car stereo and refused to listen to it on a district system. He sued the district for alleged violations of the state Public Disclosure Act (PDA). A court held for the district, and the citizen appealed to the Court of Appeals of Washington. The court held **the PDA did not require an agency to explain, conduct research on, or create documents that did not exist and were not in its possession**. The citizen had no evidence to contradict statements by district employees disclaiming possession of the documents. A document that is not possessed by an agency is not, by definition, a public document. While the PDA required an agency to give the fullest assistance to persons seeking to review public records, the law did not specify a format for audiotapes. The district had complied with the PDA by providing the citizen with the candidates' letters of interest and the tape, and by offering its equipment to listen to it. The court affirmed the judgment for the district. *Boss v. Peninsula School Dist.*, 125 Wash. 1024 (Wash. Ct. App. 2005).

◆  Some New York citizens attempted to videotape a school board meeting. When the board instructed them to discontinue the taping, they protested, and they were allowed to record the proceedings. Later, the board adopted a new resolution to reserve the right to allow or disallow videotaping of its meetings. After the board denied further efforts to videotape meetings, the citizens sued for violation of the New York Open Meetings Law. A state court dismissed the case, and appeal reached a New York appellate division court. It found the Open Meetings Law declared it was essential to the maintenance of a democratic society to perform public business in an open and public manner. The court rejected the board's claim that videotaping meetings would make them "less open" by stifling shy citizens. **Although the Open Meetings Law did not explicitly compel the board to allow videotaping of its meetings, a liberal interpretation of the law allowed citizens the right to record them.** Because the board could not ban the tape recording of its meetings, the court reversed the judgment. *Csorny v. Shoreham-Wading River Cent. School Dist.*, 2003 N.Y. Slip. Op. 14079, 2002 WL 32092581 (N.Y. App. Div. 2003).

◆  **An Ohio trial court ordered three school board members removed for retaining uncertified teachers and systematically violating the state Public Records and Open Meetings Acts.** The board members intentionally violated the Open Meetings Act by going into executive session without notice 10 times in 11 months. The board failed to approve minutes for public review and granted a single board member power to assume the board's full authority when it was not in session. The board members retained two unqualified and uncertified teachers. At the same time, they did not address "explosive issues," such as investigating sexual abuse charges against an employee. One member voted for the district to employ her husband and her daughter. The court held that board members "owed a duty to provide their high school students with competent and certified teachers in a zone of safety." *In re Removal of Kuehnle,* No. 2004 CV-08-214 (Ohio Common Pleas 2004).

◆   California parents complained about an elementary school principal, who received a negative performance evaluation. The superintendent placed her on administrative leave for several incidents of unprofessional conduct. He then presented the board with written, verified charges of her unprofessional conduct and persistent violation of laws in a closed session. The board did not take any testimony, but it initiated termination proceedings and served her with notice of its intent to dismiss her unless she requested a hearing. The principal made such a request, but it was delivered to the wrong address. The board eventually received the principal's request but concluded that it was untimely and that she waived her right to a hearing. It voted to fire her and reaffirmed its decision two months later in a closed session. The principal asserted that the board violated the California Open Meetings Act by failing to notify her of the two meetings.

A state court ordered the board to set aside its decision. On appeal, the California Court of Appeal **rejected the principal's assertion that the presentation of charges by the superintendent to the board was a "hearing" under the open meetings act**. The board did not consider evidence on the charges. It considered whether the charges warranted the initiation of a disciplinary proceeding against the principal. The superintendent's recommendation for termination and the grounds for it did not make the board session a "hearing," and the principal was not entitled to receive any advance notice. The court reversed and remanded the case. *Proud v. San Pasqual Union School Dist. No. D037921,* 2002 WL 31174297 (Cal. Ct. App. 2002).

◆   The Washington Court of Appeals held that the state Open Public Meeting Act (OPMA) **applied not only to school board meetings, but to deliberations, discussions, and other communications**. Courts in other states have applied open meetings acts to telephonic communications, emails, individual meetings between superintendents and board members, and serial electronic communications among a quorum of board members. Email exchanges could be "meetings" if certain statutory factors were present. The OPMA would not be violated if less than a majority of board members was involved in the exchange of emails and the participants did not collectively intend to transact official business. Passive receipt of an email did not qualify as a "meeting." There had to be "action," as defined by OPMA. There was evidence in this case that some emails between board members related to board business, that some board members had knowledge that the OPMA might be implicated, and that there was an active exchange of emails. The case required a trial. *Wood v. Battle Ground School Dist.,* 27 P.3d 1208 (Wash. Ct. App. 2001).

# CHAPTER FIFTEEN

## Private Schools

## I. PRIVATE SCHOOL EMPLOYMENT

*The general consensus among courts is that a "ministerial exception" bars any employment claim that would limit a religious institution's right to select an individual to perform religious functions. The ministerial exception may be raised by religious employers in claims arising under Title VII of the Civil Rights Act of 1964 and similar state laws. In the following case, the Supreme Court of Wisconsin held that "courts around the country have universally*

563

*recognized that the First Amendment protects houses of worship from state interference with the decision of who will teach and lead a congregation."*

## A. Employment Discrimination

◆   A Michigan Lutheran school teacher received a certificate of admission into the teaching ministry and became a "called" teacher, meaning she could be fired only for cause. At a church outing in June, she became ill and took disability leave. She was diagnosed with narcolepsy in December. When the school later fired her, she sued the school for violating the Americans with Disabilities Act (ADA). A federal court dismissed her lawsuit, finding the teacher was a ministerial employee, but the Sixth Circuit reversed the judgment, stating she was not. **She spent six hours and 15 minutes of her seven-hour workday teaching secular subjects using secular textbooks.** She did have some religious duties – such as teaching a religion class and leading a chapel service twice a year. But other teachers had the same duties – not only those not designated "commissioned ministers" but those who did not even share the school's faith. Further, a court wouldn't have to interpret church doctrine to adjudicate the ADA claim. *EEOC v. Hosanna-Tabor Evangelical Lutheran Church and School*, 597 F.3d 769 (6th Cir. 2010).

◆   A Wisconsin first-grade teacher claimed a Catholic school dismissed her on the basis of her age. She complained to the state Labor and Industry Review Commission (LIRC), which denied the school's request to dismiss the case on the basis of a "ministerial exception" rooted in the First Amendment. A state circuit court affirmed the LIRC decision, as did the Court of Appeals of Wisconsin. Appeal reached the Supreme Court of Wisconsin, which found the case arose under the state Fair Employment Act (FEA). According to the school, the teacher occupied a "ministerial" position, barring her claim. The court held **the ministerial exception precluded employment discrimination claims "for employees whose positions were important and closely linked to the religious mission of a religious organization."** In this case, the school was committed to the Catholic faith and worldview, and the teacher's position was important and closely linked to that mission. The school was considered a ministry of the Catholic Church. The teacher led prayers with students, helped celebrate religious holidays, served as a catechist and taught Catholic doctrine and practice. Her FEA age discrimination claim unconstitutionally infringed upon the school's right to religious freedom under the Wisconsin Constitution. The court reversed the lower court judgments. *Coulee Catholic Schools v. Industry Review Comm'n*, 320 Wis.2d 275, 768 N.W.2d 868 (Wis. 2009).

◆   A Michigan teacher worked as a church's director of religious education for eight years. After obtaining a master's degree in teaching, she became a teacher of math and religion courses. Her duties included planning Masses for several grades and assisting an elementary teacher with student liturgies. After a series of employment incidents that did not involve religion, the school discharged her. She sued the Catholic Diocese of Lansing under state laws including the Whistleblowers' Protection and Civil Rights Acts. A state court dismissed the whistleblower claim, but not the civil rights claim. The state court of appeals explained that **the ministerial exception barred any claim that would limit a religious institution's right to select an individual to perform spiritual functions**. It returned the case to the trial court to resolve questions about the teacher's job duties. If they were primarily religious, she could not pursue her civil rights action further. But if they were not ministerial in nature, her civil rights claim could proceed. *Weishuhn v. Catholic Diocese of Lansing*, 279 Mich.App. 150, 756 N.W.2d 483 (Mich. Ct. App. 2008).

When the case returned to the trial court, it found that the ministerial exception applied to the teacher, requiring dismissal of the state Civil Rights Act (CRA) and Whistleblower Protection Act (WPA) claims. Appeal again went to the state court of appeals, which found no error with trial court findings that the teacher was primarily engaged in religious duties. Although she taught math, she also taught religion and was actively involved in masses, religious planning and activities. As the teacher was in a primarily religious position, she was a ministerial employee, and the school was entitled to judgment on the CRA claim. The WPA claim was also subject to the ministerial exception. The judgment for the Diocese was affirmed. *Weishuhn v. Catholic Diocese of Lansing*, 287 Mich.App. 211, 787 N.W.2d 513 (Mich. Ct. App. 2010).

◆   **A Florida District Court of Appeal applied the ministerial exception to a state whistleblower claim by a principal of a Catholic school.** She asserted that when she complained to the Archdiocese about a supervisor's assault and battery, the Archdiocese retaliated against her by discharging her. The court held that the ministerial exception had been applied to federal claims under the Americans with Disabilities Act, the Age Discrimination in Employment Act, and common law claims brought against religious employers. As a result, the court found no reason why the ministerial exception should not apply to a state whistleblower claim. *Archdiocese of Miami v. Minagorri*, 954 So.2d 640 (Fla. Dist. Ct. App. 2007). The Supreme Court of Florida denied further review, as did the U.S. Supreme Court.

◆   A non-Jewish business manager worked at a Michigan Jewish school. In his third year there, co-workers reported him for shouting and swearing and kissing a female co-worker. The business manager apologized in writing to the rabbi, but his contract was not renewed based on unprofessional behavior. The school hired a Jewish employee to replace him. The business manager sued the school for religious discrimination. A trial court found that statements by co-workers and the rabbi were not direct evidence of religious discrimination. To qualify as direct evidence, these statements had to lead to the conclusion that religious discrimination was a motivation behind the decision to terminate him. Hiring a Jew to replace the business manager did not suggest the school was lying about having fired him for behaving in an unprofessional way. The state court of appeals affirmed. To merit a trial, **he would have had to provide evidence that suggested religious discrimination – not his unprofessional behavior – was the real reason he was fired**. *Berg v. Jewish Academy of Metropolitan Detroit*, Nos. 271204 and 273398, 2007 WL 1610448 (Mich. Ct. App. 6/5/07).

◆   A guitar instructor taught music part-time at a Florida Episcopal school. When the school learned he had been arrested on a domestic violence charge, it fired him. The school said he reacted by menacing and threatening to create bad publicity. The teacher filed a discrimination charge with the state Commission on Human Relations, alleging he was fired because of his Hindu faith, gender, unmarried status, and because he had a preschool-age child. At the hearing, the administrative law judge (ALJ) dismissed the religion-based charge because Florida does not allow such claims against religious institutions. The ALJ heard evidence on the other charges and found the instructor's arrest was a valid reason to fire him. The U.S. Court of Appeals, Eleventh Circuit, upheld that decision. **The ALJ properly found that the termination was based on the teacher's domestic abuse arrest.** His threatening behavior confirmed the school's judgment. *Cataldo v. St. James Episcopal School*, 213 Fed.Appx. 966 (11th Cir. 2007).

◆   The U.S. Supreme Court held that the Mormon Church could discriminate on the basis of religion in hiring for a nonreligious job. The case involved an employee who worked at a church-operated gymnasium for 16 years. After being discharged for failing to meet several religious requirements for employment, he sued the church in a U.S. district court, alleging religious discrimination in violation of Title VII of the Civil Rights Act of 1964. The case reached the Supreme Court, which noted that Title VII "shall not apply ... to a religious corporation, association [or] educational institution ... with respect to the employment of individuals of a particular religion to perform work connected with the carrying on by such [an organization] of its activities." **The Court upheld the right of nonprofit religious employers to impose religious conditions for employment in nonreligious positions** involving nonprofit activities. *Corp. of the Presiding Bishop of the Church of Jesus Christ of Latter-Day Saints v. Amos*, 483 U.S. 327, 107 S.Ct. 2862, 97 L.Ed.2d 273 (1987).

◆   A teacher chaired the theology department at a Minnesota Lutheran school. His duties included counseling and he was responsible for ensuring students followed the beliefs and doctrines of the synod – an advisory body of Lutheran congregations and ministers. After 22 years at the school, the teacher admitted he was gay, but said that he was not in a homosexual relationship and had never lived a gay lifestyle. The bishop and the school principal told the teacher he should remain "closeted" and celibate. When the school found a replacement, the teacher resigned. He sued the school, alleging discrimination based on sexual orientation in violation of the Minnesota Human Rights Act. The case reached the Court of Appeals of Minnesota. The teacher contended that although part of his job entailed pastoral duties, he was also a secular teacher, and the court could apply neutral principles of law to decide his case. The court ruled against the teacher because **the lawfulness of a discharge based on sexual orientation would have required it to delve into church doctrine** in violation of the Establishment Clause. There was no evidence that the teacher's position could be split into secular and nonsecular parts. *Doe v. Lutheran High School of Greater Minneapolis*, 702 N.W.2d 322 (Minn. Ct. App. 2005).

## B.  Labor Relations

*The courts have ruled that "pervasively religious" schools may be able to avoid any obligation to bargain with employees under the National Labor Relations Act (NLRA). This exception to the NLRA's coverage is based upon First Amendment religious freedom considerations. Managerial employees are not protected by the NLRA.*

◆   A New York religious academy granted tenure to a teacher in 1996. His annual salary during the seven years up to the 2006-2007 school year averaged more than $100,000. In 2007, the academy discharged the teacher. The parties agreed to arbitrate the matter of his employment termination in accordance with Jewish law. An arbitration panel found the academy had granted the teacher tenure and had wrongfully discharged him without just cause. The panel directed the academy to reinstate him to his teaching position at an annual salary of $100,000 with back wages and contributions to his pension plan. The academy petitioned a state court to vacate the arbitration award, arguing that the award would create a new contract. After the court vacated the award, a New York Appellate Division court reversed. **The arbitration award did not violate a strong public policy,** and the academy didn't show that it was irrational or that it exceeded the arbitrator's powers. As the teacher demonstrated that he could only be discharged for cause, he could enforce the award. *Brisman v. Hebrew Academy of Five Towns & Rockaway*, 70 A.D.3d 935, 895 N.Y.2d 482 (N.Y App. Div. 2010).

◆   A private New Hampshire day school had long-running contracts with three school districts. Two of its teachers filed unfair labor practice charges against the school with the state Public Employee Labor Relations Board. The National Education Association asked the state board to decide whether the school was considered a public employer. The board declared that the school was a "quasi-public corporation" and held that it had authority to decide the complaint. The school appealed to the Supreme Court of New Hampshire, which noted that the National Labor Relations Board **(NLRB) has jurisdiction over labor disputes at nonprofit educational institutions and private nonprofit secondary schools** with gross annual revenues high enough to qualify. The contract between the school and the school districts did not exempt the school from NLRB authority as a "political subdivision." Thus, the state board did not have jurisdiction to decide the complaint. *In re Pinkerton Academy*, 155 N.H. 1, 920 A.2d 1168 (N.H. 2007).

◆   The right of employees of a Catholic school system to form a collective bargaining unit was successfully challenged in a case decided by the U.S. Supreme Court. In this case, the unions were certified by the National Labor Relations Board (NLRB) as bargaining units but the diocese refused to bargain with them. The Court said that the religion clauses of the U.S. Constitution, which require religious organizations to finance their educational systems without governmental aid, also free the religious organizations of the inhibiting effect and impact of unionization of their teachers. The Court agreed with the employers' contention that **the threshold act of certification of the union would necessarily alter and infringe upon the religious character of parochial schools**. This would mean that the bishop would no longer be the sole repository of authority as required by church law. Instead, he would have to share some decisionmaking with the union. The Court held this violated the religion clauses of the U.S. Constitution. *NLRB v. Catholic Bishop of Chicago*, 440 U.S. 490, 99 S.Ct. 1313, 59 L.Ed.2d 533 (1979).

◆  A Roman Catholic secondary school in New York City employed lay and religiously affiliated faculty and taught both secular and religious subjects. After a union began representing the lay faculty, the school administration and the union met repeatedly to negotiate the terms of a collective bargaining agreement. When those efforts failed, the union staged a strike. The school discharged the striking workers and ended negotiations. The state Employment Relations Board cited the school for alleged violations of the state Labor Relations Act. It charged the school with refusing to bargain in good faith and with improperly discharging and failing to reinstate striking employees. The case came before the Court of Appeals of New York. The court held the state Labor Relations Act did not implicate religious conduct or beliefs, and it did not restrict or burden religious belief or activities. The Establishment Clause argument failed because the state board's supervision over collective bargaining with respect to secular terms and conditions of employment was neither comprehensive nor continuing and did not entangle the state with religion. Here, **the government was not forcing the parties to agree on specific terms but was ordering the employer to bargain in good faith on secular subjects**. *New York State Employment Relations Board v. Christ the King Regional High School*, 90 N.Y.2d 244, 660 N.Y.S.2d 359, 682 N.E.2d 960 (N.Y. 1997).

◆  Two teachers at a Pennsylvania Catholic elementary and secondary school attempted to organize a teachers union. Through an association of Catholic teachers, they petitioned the Pennsylvania Labor Relations Board (PLRB) to compel an election. The teachers were fired, and the association filed a second petition that was dismissed on the grounds that the school was not a public employer and the teachers were not public employees under the Public Employee Relations Act (PERA). The case reached the state supreme court, which found the NLRA does not apply to lay teachers employed at church-operated schools. However, the NLRA and the PERA do not have the same scope. The PERA defines a public employee as any individual employed by a public employer but excludes employees at church facilities "when utilized primarily for religious purposes." **As the school was operated primarily for religious purposes, the teachers were excluded under the PERA.** *Ass'n of Catholic Teachers v. PLRB*, 692 A.2d 1039 (Pa. 1997).

◆  In *NLRB v. Yeshiva Univ.*, the U.S. Supreme Court held that in certain circumstances, **faculty members at private educational institutions could be considered managerial employees**. The ruling was based on the conclusion that Yeshiva's faculty decided school curriculum, standards, tuition rates and admissions. The Court's decision applied only to schools that were "like

Yeshiva" and not to schools where the faculty exercised less control. Schools where faculty members do not exercise binding managerial discretion do not fall within the scope of the managerial employee exclusion. *NLRB v. Yeshiva Univ.*, 444 U.S. 672, 100 S.Ct. 856, 63 L.Ed.2d 115 (1980).

## C. Termination from Employment

◆　A teacher at the Missouri Military Academy observed bruises on a cadet's arms and insisted that school officials make a report of evidence of physical abuse to the state Division of Family Services. The academy fired him the same day. He sued for wrongful discharge and breach of contract. A court dismissed the wrongful discharge and emotional distress claims, but held a trial on the breach of contract claim and awarded the teacher $13,300 in damages. Appeal reached the Supreme Court of Missouri, which ruled that **a teacher under contract can sue for wrongful discharge just as "at-will" employees can if the termination violates a clear mandate of public policy**. Allowing contract employees to pursue wrongful discharge claims put them on the same footing as "at-will" employees. The teacher was under a clear statutory mandate to report suspected abuse of a child. He could pursue his wrongful discharge claim, and the judgment in his favor for breach of contract was affirmed. *Keveney v. Missouri Military Academy*, 304 S.W.3d 98 (Mo. 2010).

◆　A Louisiana Christian School hired a principal for its elementary/pre-school division under a contract requiring the submission of all employment-related disputes to Bible-based mediation or arbitration by the Institute for Christian Conciliation (ICC). The school discharged the principal before the end of the school year and paid her salary and benefits through the end of the year. She sued for breach of contract, gender discrimination, sexual harassment and retaliation. A court granted the school's motion to compel arbitration. According to ICC rules, arbitration was conducted under the Montana Uniform Arbitration Act. After a hearing, an arbitrator held the school breached its contract with the principal, violating the law and Matthew 18, and awarded the principal over $150,000 in damages. However, the arbitrator found no evidence of gender discrimination, sexual harassment or retaliation.

　　The principal then sued in a Louisiana federal court, seeking confirmation of the award. The court affirmed the award, finding that Montana law applied. The school appealed to the Fifth Circuit, which held that **the Federal Arbitration Act did not bar parties from structuring their contracts, or preempt state laws on arbitration**. However, while Montana law applied to the arbitration, the contract itself was properly interpreted under Louisiana law. The court vacated the judgment and remanded the case for further proceedings. *Prescott v. Northlake Christian School*, 369 F.3d 491 (5th Cir. 2004).

◆　A teacher contracted with a Nebraska Catholic high school for a year. The contract reserved the school's right to terminate the contract immediately in the event of overt conduct in violation of Catholic Church doctrine, or any other conduct which reflected grave discredit upon the school. Three months later, the teacher sought to be released from his contract to obtain a public school teaching position. The school refused his request and informed him that unless he reaffirmed his commitment to the contract, it would withhold $1,000 in pay and cancel his benefits. When the teacher did not reassert his commitment, the school withheld his pay and canceled his benefits. He petitioned a Nebraska trial court for a declaration that the school constructively terminated his contract. The court held that it lacked jurisdiction to review the terms of the contract because it would be an impermissible inquiry into church doctrine in violation of the First Amendment. The Nebraska Court of Appeals affirmed, focusing on the contract clause permitting the school to immediately terminate a teacher for violating a doctrine of the Roman Catholic Church. **An analysis of whether the contract was unconscionable would require it to examine Roman Catholic doctrine.** This is an impermissible inquiry under the First Amendment. *Parizek v. Roncalli Catholic High School of Omaha*, 11 Neb. App. 482, 655 N.W.2d 404 (Neb. App. 2002).

## II.  STATE AND FEDERAL REGULATION

*Private schools must meet individual state standards for accreditation and compulsory attendance. All public and private school teachers are mandatory child abuse reporters. For additional cases on child abuse reporting, see Chapter Seven, Section V of this volume.*

### A.  Accreditation

◆   A University of California (UC) admission policy evaluated in-state applicants' qualifications by reviewing their high school courses – and only approving those it found college preparatory. A Protestant schools' association, a member school and five of the school's students claimed the practice violated the First Amendment's religious and free speech clauses as well as the Fourteenth Amendment's Equal Protection Clause. The case reached the Ninth Circuit, which upheld the policy as constitutional. It noted that **UC's policy did not prohibit high schools from teaching whatever and however they chose**. And UC approved some courses with religious content and viewpoints that used religious textbooks. Further, the court found no evidence that UC treated students from religious private schools worse than other applicants. *Ass'n of Christian Schools Int'l v. Stearns*, 362 Fed.Appx. 640 (9th Cir. 2010).

◆   The Ohio superintendent of public instruction registered Golden Christian Academy in the Ohio Pilot Project Scholarship Program. As a condition of registration, Golden signed an "assurance of compliance" stating that the school would meet all applicable state minimum standards for nonpublic schools and that all employees who worked with voucher students would pass criminal background investigations. The superintendent informed the school that she intended to revoke its registration for failure to meet the assurance of compliance. After the superintendent revoked Golden's registration, Golden appealed, arguing that the superintendent had no authority to revoke the school's registration. It also claimed that it currently complied with the assurance of compliance. The court of appeals noted that the statue was unclear about the superintendent's authority in this situation. However, **it would be illogical for the statute to grant the superintendent the power to register a school for the voucher program but not to revoke its registration**. The court held that the superintendent could revoke Golden's registration. *Golden Christian Academy v. Zelman*, 760 N.E.2d 889 (Ohio Ct. App. 2001).

## B.  Sex Abuse and Mandatory Reporting

*State laws require all educators and caregivers to timely report suspected child abuse or neglect. The laws provide incentives for reporting by offering immunity for good-faith reporters and imposing criminal penalties for failure to make timely reports. New York and Minnesota require mandated reporters who work for a school to report suspected child abuse or maltreatment themselves, and not through another school employee. New York's highest court has stated that teachers and other state-mandated reporters "ought to err on the side of caution and make a report" if they reasonably suspect child abuse or neglect.*

◆  Parents of a District of Columbia preschooler called her private school, claiming four other preschoolers sexually assaulted her in a school bathroom. Her parents had already taken her to the hospital and called the police and the Child and Family Services Agency (CFSA). The principal and vice principal investigated. After interviewing the other children and their parents, they decided the story was not credible. Neither reported the incident to the police or the CFSA – but the principal gave his written report of the school's investigation to the detective assigned to the case. The District of Columbia later charged both principals with violating the mandatory reporting statute. A judge found both administrators guilty of a misdemeanor, but the court of appeals vacated their convictions. **The mandatory reporting statute did not require them to report suspected sexual abuse involving only students.** *Hargrove v. District of Columbia*, 5 A.3d 632 (D.C. 2010).

◆  A Delaware student alleged that a priest who served as a teacher and later a principal sexually molested him from the time he was eight years old until he was 17. The student sued in 2004, alleging that the last incident of molestation occurred in 1985. He claimed that he told his parents only about the last incident and that they reported it to church officials in 1985. The officials allegedly agreed to deny the priest the opportunity to be near minors. The church sought to dismiss the case, claiming that the action was untimely under Delaware's two-year statute of limitations for personal injury claims, and the state's three-year limitation period for breach of contract claims. The student claimed his delay in filing his claims was excused because he suppressed any memory of the abuse until less than two years before he filed his lawsuit.

   The court noted that **Delaware recognizes "the discovery rule exception" in cases involving child abuse**. This exception delays the start of the limitations period based on suppressed memories of sexual abuse. In this case, the student presented expert testimony indicating he had suppressed memories of the abuse. Although he could not rely on the discovery rule exception with respect to the incident he reported to his parents in 1985, he could rely on the exception with respect to 900 other alleged incidents of sexual abuse. Those claims were not barred by the statute of limitations. The court also found enough evidence to create a factual issue as to whether the church breached a contract with the parents by affirmatively concealing alleged molestations. A trial was required. *Eden v. Oblates of St. Francis de Sales*, No. 04C-01-069 CLS, 2006 WL 3512482 (Del. Super. Ct. 2006).

◆   An Ohio high school student received counseling from a psychologist at her private school for about a year. Sometime during the year, the psychologist made a report to the Cuyahoga County Department of Family Services that she believed the student's father had abused her. The report was investigated and the allegation of abuse deemed unsubstantiated. The father sued the psychologist, claiming she was required to act in good faith when filing the report. An Ohio trial court granted pretrial judgment to the psychologist, and the father appealed. He also appealed the court's failure to allow him access to certain material relating to the report and investigation. The court affirmed the judgment, holding that **the psychologist – statutorily obligated to report suspected child abuse – was entitled to immunity**. Under state child abuse reporting law, if an individual is subject to the mandatory reporting statute, that individual is granted immunity from liability when making a report. There was no statutory requirement that a report be made in good faith, despite the father's assertion to the contrary. As for his contention that he was denied investigation materials, the court held that they were confidential and privileged. *Liedtke v. Carrington*, 763 N.E.2d 213 (Ohio Ct. App. 2001).

◆   In 1984, a 13-year-old New Jersey child told her mother that her father had sexually abused her. The mother took her to their parish pastor. The child did not disclose the abuse to the pastor, but when she was taken for counseling, she told her Catholic Social Services (CSS) caseworker. In 1986, the child reported abuse to a teacher at her Catholic school. The teacher sent her to the principal, who allegedly said, "sometimes it's just best to leave things in the past." In 1987, after her father molested her sister, the child described her own experience with abuse to a pastor. He allegedly said she could no longer work her weekend job at the rectory because of her reports of incest to several priests. The abuse was finally reported to police in 1991, and the father was sentenced to 10 years in prison. In 1994, the child sued three priests, the CSS, the case worker, her parish and the diocese. **The court dismissed the case because it was filed over seven years after the child turned 18.**

On appeal, the Superior Court of New Jersey agreed with the trial court's decision to exclude her experts' testimony. Her first expert, a priest, stated she suffered from "religious duress." Her other expert was a psychiatrist who maintained she did not file her complaint until her father's incarceration because she feared he would hurt her. This testimony was opinion without factual basis. Neither the child nor her experts linked her failure to file a timely complaint to the defendants' actions. The court affirmed the judgment. *Smith v. Estate of Reverend P. Kelly*, 778 A.2d 1162 (N.J. Super. Ct. App. Div. 2001).

## C. Taxation

### 1. Federal Income Taxation

◆ Section 501(c)(3) of the Internal Revenue Code provides that "corporations ... organized and operated exclusively for religious, charitable ... or educational purposes" are entitled to tax-exempt status. The Internal Revenue Service (IRS) routinely granted tax exemptions under Section 501(c)(3) to private schools regardless of whether they had racially discriminatory admissions policies. In 1970, however, **the IRS concluded that it could no longer grant tax-exempt status to racially discriminatory private schools** because such schools were not "charitable" within the meaning of Section 501(c)(3). Two private colleges whose racial admissions policies were rooted in their interpretations of the Bible sued to prevent the IRS from interpreting the federal tax laws in this manner. The U.S. Supreme Court rejected the challenge and upheld the IRS's interpretation. The Court's ruling was based on what it perceived as the strong public policy against racial discrimination in education. Because the colleges were operating in violation of that public policy, the colleges could not be considered "charitable" under Section 501(c)(3). Thus, they were ineligible for tax exemptions. The Court held that the denial of an exemption did not impermissibly burden the colleges' alleged religious freedom interest in practicing racial discrimination. *Bob Jones Univ. v. U.S.*, 461 U.S. 574, 103 S.Ct. 2017, 76 L.Ed.2d 157 (1983).

◆ Parents of African-American public schoolchildren sought a federal court order requiring the IRS to adopt more stringent standards for determining whether private schools had racially discriminatory admissions policies. The parents claimed IRS standards were too lax and that certain private schools were practicing racial discrimination and were still obtaining tax exemptions. **The Supreme Court dismissed the parents' claims, ruling they had shown no injury to themselves as a result of the allegedly lax IRS standards.** None of their children had sought enrollment at the private schools involved, and the abstract stigma attached to living in a community with racially discriminatory private schools was also insufficient to show actual injury. Further, the parents' theory that denial of exempt status to such schools would result in greater white student enrollment in area public schools, and hence result in a greater degree of public school integration, was only speculation. *Allen v. Wright*, 468 U.S. 737, 104 S.Ct. 3315, 82 L.Ed.2d 556 (1984).

### 2. State and Local Taxation

◆ A New York school board developed a tax plan that would close one school and spend less so services to private schools could be improved and money could be freed up for religious school tuition. The board had four Orthodox Jews who were members and two other members who shared their aims. Five parents of public school students sued, alleging that the "Orthodox Majority" had tried to convert the school board "into an Orthodox ruling committee." A federal court and the Second Circuit ruled that the tax plan did not violate the

Constitution because **all parents, whether religious or not, received the same tax breaks**. It did not matter that a large number of Orthodox Jewish taxpayers freely chose to spend their tax savings from the plan on religious education for their children. *Incantalupo v. Laurence Union Free School Dist. No. 15*, 380 Fed.Appx. 59 (2d Cir. 2010).

◆   Arizona Rev. Stat. § 43-1089 allows taxpayers to deduct up to $500 from state income taxes each year for voluntary contributions to qualified "school tuition organizations" (STOs) that distribute grants to students attending private schools. Married couples filing joint returns may deduct up to $625 annually for these donations. The law does not prevent STOs from directing money to schools that provide religious instruction or have admissions preferences on the basis of religion or religious affiliation. Section 43-1089 survived a state court challenge in *Kotterman v. Killian*, 193 Ariz. 273, 972 P.2d 606 (Ariz. 1999).

Another group of taxpayers sued Arizona state officials in a federal court, asserting that Section 43-1089 violated the Establishment Clause. State officials opposed the action on grounds including the federal Tax Injunction Act (TIA). The case reached the Supreme Court, which affirmed the judgment. The TIA prevented federal district courts from enjoining, suspending or restraining "the assessment, levy or collection of any tax under State law where a plain, speedy and efficient remedy may be had in the courts of such State." 28 U.S.C. § 1341. Federal cases interpreting the TIA and the Anti-Injunction Act held that the TIA did not immunize all aspects of state tax administration from court review. It only prevented federal courts from interfering with state tax collections. **The "decades-long understanding" of courts was that the TIA did not bar a third-party constitutional challenge to tax benefits such as this action.** *Hibbs v. Winn*, 542 U.S. 88, 124 S.Ct. 2276, 159 L.E.2d 172 (2004).

◆   A Maine nonprofit corporation operated a summer camp for children of the Christian Science faith. Activities included supervised prayer, meditation and church services. Weekly tuition for the camp was roughly $400. A Maine statute exempted charitable institutions from real estate and personal property taxes. However, institutions operated primarily for the benefit of nonresidents were only entitled to a more limited tax benefit, and then only if the weekly charge for services did not exceed $30 per person. Because most of the campers were not Maine residents and weekly tuition was over $30, the corporation was ineligible for the state tax exemption. It petitioned the town for a refund of the taxes it had paid, arguing the exemption violated the Commerce Clause of the U.S. Constitution. The case reached the U.S. Supreme Court, which found the camp was engaged in commerce not only as a purchaser, but as a provider of goods and services. **A real estate tax, like any other tax, could impermissibly burden interstate commerce.** If the exemption applied to for-profit entities, there would be no question of a Commerce Clause violation. The Court found no reason why an entity's nonprofit status should exclude it from Commerce Clause coverage. Nonprofit institutions are subject to other laws regulating commerce, and federal antitrust laws. *Camps Newfound/Owatonna, Inc. v. Town of Harrison, Maine*, 520 U.S. 564, 117 S.Ct. 1590, 137 L.Ed.2d 852 (1997).

◆   Burr and Burton Academy is a Vermont private high school operated by Burr and Burton Seminary, a nonprofit corporation. In 1996, Burr and Burton constructed "Head House" as a residence for the academy's headmaster. Traditionally, housing had been part of the headmaster's compensation package. In April 1997, the town of Manchester appraised Head House at $290,000 and decided it was subject to applicable property taxes. The next year, the town added a Burr and Burton student dormitory to the taxable property list. However, the dormitory property had been placed on the real estate market in 1994 and had been leased to various tenants until being sold in 1999. Burr and Burton challenged the appraisals, asserting that the properties fell within a state property tax exemption for property owned by educational institutions.

The case reached the state supreme court, which held that Head House qualified for the property tax exemption because it served an educational purpose. During the 1998-99 academic year, Head House held 11 school-related events. **Residences for headmasters and faculty serve an educational purpose.** The fact that Head House was part of a compensation package did not prevent it from qualifying for the exemption. However, the dormitory property was ineligible for the exemption. It had not been used for any educational purpose since 1994. As the dormitory property had been used for commercial purposes, the academy was required to pay the assessed property taxes. *Burr and Burton Seminary v. Town of Manchester*, 782 A.2d 1149 (Vt. 2001).

◆   In a companion case to *Burr and Burton Seminary v. Town of Manchester,* the Berkshire School sought a tax exemption for a 212-acre parcel of land. The land had been donated to the school, which intended to use the property for a student mountain program and environmental science classes. The town of Reading appraised the undeveloped land at $250,000 and assessed taxes against Berkshire. Berkshire grieved the appraisal, asserting that under the language of 32 Vt. Stat. Ann. § 3802(4), mere ownership was sufficient for the exemption. A state court agreed, but the Vermont Supreme Court reversed under *Burr and Burton Seminary*. It reiterated the holding that an educational use requirement was implicit in the statutory language. **Even though the land was not being used for any purpose – educational, commercial or otherwise – nonuse would not qualify for exemption** under the statute. If Berkshire used the land for educational purposes in the future, the issue of exemption could be raised again. *Berkshire School v. Town of Reading,* 781 A.2d 282 (Vt. 2001).

◆   Pennsylvania's Institutions of Purely Public Charity Act exempts qualifying entities from real estate taxes. A private school in Pottstown was founded as an all-boys school. In 1996, the Pottstown School District and the local borough petitioned the county board of assessment appeals to remove the school's real estate tax exemption. They claimed that the school's policy of denying female students admission demonstrated it did not benefit a substantial and indefinite class of persons. The board affirmed the school's tax-exempt status, and the school district appealed to a state court. Meanwhile, the school amended its admittance policy to include females. The Pennsylvania Commonwealth Court held that based on state court precedents, the school's exclusion of females did not undermine its status as a purely public charity under the state constitution. **Pennsylvania courts have long held that single-sex schools are considered purely public charities.** If the legislature had intended to exclude this type of school from the statute, it would have done so. The school was exempt from real estate taxation as a purely public charity. *Pottstown School Dist. v. Hill School*, 786 A.2d 312 (Pa. Commw. Ct. 2001).

## D. Zoning and Local Regulation

◆   A Catholic high school in San Diego sought to update and modernize its 84-year-old campus – including its science labs and art studios as well as the school library and computer lab. It also sought to build a 20,500-square foot classroom building and a two-level, 104-space parking garage. It wanted to demolish two buildings on its property, but neighbors considered them an important part of the neighborhood and formed a protest group. After an extensive review process lasting more than a year, the city planning commission decided to grant the permits it needed for its modernization project. But the neighbors appealed to the city council, which then denied the necessary permits. The school sued the city in federal court, asserting a violation of the Religious Land Use and Institutionalized Persons Act of 2000. That law bars the government from imposing or implementing a land use regulation in a way "that imposes a substantial burden on the religious exercise" of people and institutions. The school sought pretrial judgment, but the court held that a trial was required. **A jury could find that the denial of permits did not constitute a "substantial burden" on the students' religious rights.** *Academy of Our Lady of Peace v. City of San Diego*, 2010 WL 1329014 (S.D. Cal. 4/1/10).

◆   A Florida church claimed that attempted inspections of its school violated its religious free exercise and Fourth Amendment rights. Under Florida law, the state department of health (DOH) conducted periodic, unscheduled inspections of school and food service facilities. While a DOH inspector was inspecting a Baptist school located on the same property as the church, he noticed a playground. He stepped out of the kitchen to inspect the playground, but the pastor of the church stopped him, saying it belonged to the church and was outside his authority to inspect. The church later sued the DOH, its inspectors, and sheriff's officers who assisted them in attempting to inspect the property. The court dismissed the case, and the Eleventh Circuit affirmed. The attempted inspections did not violate the church's right to free exercise of religion under the state or federal constitutions or the Florida Religious Freedom Restoration Act. **The church did not show that the DOH's entry on its property was unlawful,** and there was no unreasonable search. *Youngblood v. Florida Dep't of Health*, 224 Fed.Appx. 909 (11th Cir. 2007).

◆   Georgia's highest court held that increased traffic was a sufficient reason to deny an application for a conditional use permit by a private school seeking to build a football stadium near a residential area. The school's application for a 1,500-seat stadium was part of a plan to construct several new buildings. The expansion was opposed by residents in the adjoining neighborhood. The city planning commission approved most of the project, but it rejected the application for a permit to construct the stadium. The Supreme Court of Georgia held that local government decisions must be upheld if there is any support for them. A school study indicated there were two high school stadiums within a mile of the area. There was already congestion from the existing stadiums, so denial of the conditional use permit was not an abuse of discretion. **Traffic congestion was a valid consideration for the regulation of land use.** *City of Roswell v. Fellowship Christian School*, 281 Ga. 767, 642 S.E.2d 824 (Ga. 2007).

◆   The U.S. Court of Appeals, Second Circuit, affirmed a judgment for a New York private school under the Religious Land Use and Institutionalized Persons Act (RLUIPA). The school was so short of space that groups were being taught in halls and even closets. It sought to renovate two buildings and build a new one, but a village zoning board rejected its request for a special permit. The case reached the Second Circuit, which held that **denying the permit substantially burdened the school's religious exercise by confining it to inadequate facilities.** The zoning board had no compelling government interest in denying the permit. It appeared that the board refused to grant the permit because of pressure created by vocal neighbors who opposed the expansion project. *Westchester Day School v. Village of Mamaroneck*, 504 F.3d 338 (2d Cir. 2007).

◆   Under California law, a joint powers authority (JPA) can issue tax-exempt revenue bonds for public benefit construction projects. About 350 California cities planned to issue tax-exempt bonds to benefit three Christian schools, including a prep school that planned to use bond proceeds to build classrooms, sports facilities and administrative offices. The JPA brought a validation lawsuit in state court, inviting any interested party to make objections before it issued the bonds. No party objected, but the court asked for a state attorney general's opinion. His opinion was that the tax exemptions might violate the separation of church and state principle of both the state and federal constitutions. The case reached the Supreme Court of California, which noted that **bond proceeds could not be used for religious projects.** It was unclear whether the program only "incidentally" benefited religion. The case was returned to the trial court with instructions for determining whether the Christian schools provided a broad curriculum of secular subjects taught in a religiously neutral way. *California Statewide Communities Development Authority v. All Persons Interested in Matter of Validity of a Purchase Agreement*, 40 Cal.4th 788, 152 P.3d 1070 (Cal. 2007).

## III. PRIVATE SCHOOL STUDENT RIGHTS

*Private school students do not enjoy the constitutional protections that the courts have recognized for public school students. Generally, courts have demonstrated a reluctance to interfere with private school academic and disciplinary policies. Federal discrimination and civil rights statutes also only provide limited protection. For example, civil rights cases attempting to assert private school liability under a constitutional theory or federal statutory right pursuant to 42 U.S.C. § 1983 require a determination that the school is a state actor. Although a private school may become a state actor based on performance of duties normally associated with government entities or close cooperation with the government, the U.S. Supreme Court in* Rendell-Baker v. Kohn, *457 U.S. 830, 102 S.Ct. 2764, 73 L.Ed.2d 418 (1982), limited the circumstances in which an ostensibly private institution can be found to be acting "under the color of state law."*

## A. Admissions and Other School Policies

*Although the U.S. Supreme Court has applied 42 U.S.C. § 1981 to private schools to prohibit race discrimination, the Court noted that its holding did not extend to religious schools that practiced racial exclusion on religious grounds. Similarly, Title VI of the Civil Rights Act of 1964 (42 U.S.C. § 2000d) prohibits discrimination on the basis of race, color, or national origin but only applies to "programs or activities" receiving federal financial assistance. In the context of sex discrimination, Title IX applies to recipients of federal funding but also provides a specific exclusion which allows private undergraduate institutions to discriminate on the basis of sex in admissions (20 U.S.C. § 1681(a)(1)).*

◆ A small Kentucky Christian high school accepted students through renewable one-year contracts. A student performed well academically in her first year, but was later suspended or expelled for her negative attitude toward the school and her frequent tardiness. Several students reported that she engaged in sexual conduct with another female student, and the school refused to renew her contract for her senior year. The student sued the school and its headmaster for denial of due process, breach of contract, libel, slander and invasion of privacy. A court held for the school and headmaster, and the student appealed to the Kentucky Court of Appeals.

According to the court, the school did not violate the student's constitutional or contractual due process rights. The law pertaining to due process in private schools differs significantly from public school cases. **The relationship between a private school and its students is contractual in nature.** The court rejected the student's claim to the same due process rights afforded public school students. She received all the process she was due when she met with the headmaster and was allowed to respond and defend her actions. The headmaster's investigations into her conduct did not amount to defamation or invasion of privacy. The allegations were reported by students, and he did nothing more than question them. As a result, the lower court had properly held for the school and the headmaster. *Bentley v. Trinity Christian Academy,* 2009 WL 1491351 (Ky. Ct. App. 2009).

◆ Classmates of a Los Angeles college prep school student posted death threats and insults based on his sexual orientation on websites, and admitted making the threatening postings. Some threats had been made from school computers. The student's family moved. Later, the school paper published a story which reported that several of the website posts had called him a "faggot." When the newspaper revealed the family's new address and the name of his new school, the newspaper faculty advisor approved the story. The student and his parents sued the school for violation of state hate crimes laws. The school enrollment contract had an arbitration agreement, so the case was arbitrated.

According to the arbitrator, the school could not be held responsible for the student postings, even though some of them had used school computers. This ruling was based on **a federal law for the Protection for Private Blocking and Screening of Offensive Material**. The law prohibits providers of interactive computer services from being treated as "the publisher or speaker of any information provided by another information content provider." Under the arbitration agreement, the prevailing party could obtain its costs and legal fees from the losing party. Applying these rules, the arbitrator ordered the parents to pay the school over $521,000 for its arbitration costs and attorneys' fees, but the state court of appeal overturned the award of costs and fees. *D.C. v. Harvard-Westlake School*, 176 Cal.App.4th 836, 98 Cal.Rptr. 300 (Cal. Ct. App. 2009).

◆ In *Runyon v. McCrary*, the U.S. Supreme Court relied on 42 U.S.C. § 1981 to declare that black students could not be excluded from all-white elementary schools. In this Virginia case, the parents of black students sought to enter into contractual relationships with private nonreligious schools for educational services advertised and offered to members of the general public. The students were denied admission because of their race. The Supreme Court recognized that **while parents have a First Amendment right to send their children to educational institutions that promote racial segregation, institutions are not protected by the same principle**. The school's argument that Section 1981 does not govern private acts of racial discrimination was rejected. However, the Court observed that its holding did not extend to religious schools that practiced racial exclusion on religious grounds. *Runyon v. McCrary*, 427 U.S. 160, 96 S.Ct. 2586, 49 L.E.2d 415 (1976).

◆ A non-native Hawaiian student unsuccessfully applied to the Kamehameha Schools, a private K-12 educational institution created via a charitable trust and dedicated to the education of native Hawaiians. The school admits non-native Hawaiians only if openings remain after all qualified applicants of Hawaiian ancestry have been accepted. It conceded that he probably would have been admitted if he was of Hawaiian ancestry. The applicant claimed he was denied admission on the basis of his race, in violation of 42 U.S.C. § 1981. A federal court upheld the schools' admissions policy, and the Ninth Circuit affirmed. The school admittedly considered the race of applicants when making admissions decisions. But the court found that **the policy constituted a valid affirmative action plan**. The policy responded to a significant imbalance in the educational achievement levels of native Hawaiians as compared to other ethnic groups. Non-native Hawaiians did not lack adequate educational opportunities. The policy did no more than was necessary to correct the imbalance suffered by native Hawaiians. The preference would be applied only until the effects of past discrimination were remedied. *Doe v. Kamehameha Schools*, 470 F.3d 827 (9th Cir. 2006).

The case returned to the district court, where the student argued that he should be allowed to proceed anonymously with the case in view of "hundreds" of comments criticizing him on websites. The court refused, finding only a handful of comments, none of which showed an objective risk of severe retaliation. The Ninth Circuit again affirmed. *Doe v. Kamehameha Schools/Bernice Pauahi Bishop Estate*, 596 F.3d 1036 (9th Cir. 2010).

## B.  Athletics and Extracurricular Activities

◆    Three days before a state basketball tournament, the New Jersey State Interscholastic Athletic Association banned a private school team because the coach held practices out of season. The school sued, alleging that the association's undercover investigator violated its privacy rights. Its coach admitted that he inadvertently broke the out-of-season rule. The school asked a federal court to issue an injunction allowing its team to compete in the tournament. The court refused, finding that the school was not likely to win the lawsuit. The school argued that its students would lose an "irreplaceable opportunity to gain college scholarships" by competing on a huge stage before an audience that would include many college coaches, scouts and recruiters. But **the judge quoted courts that found this link to scholarships speculative – and not the kind of harm a court order is intended to remedy.** *St. Patrick High School v. New Jersey Interscholastic Athletic Associations*, No. 10-cv-948 (DMC) 2010 WL 715826 (D.N.J. 3/1/10).

◆    The University Interscholastic League (UIL) is an association of public schools and open-enrollment charter schools that organizes Texas interscholastic and academic competition. Private schools may apply for UIL membership, but the association has narrow, specific qualifications, and only two non-public schools were UIL members. A UIL rule excluded any private school whose right to participate in a league similar to the UIL had been suspended or revoked for violating rules or codes. A Christian college prep school applied for UIL membership after being disqualified from the Texas Association of Private and Parochial Schools (TAPPS). Because the school was eligible for organizations similar to the UIL, its application for UIL membership was denied. The school and the parents of a student attending there sued the UIL, asserting constitutional rights violations.

A court dismissed the case, and the Fifth Circuit affirmed. The UIL rule did not burden the religious free exercise rights of the family. **Parental rights in education extend to the choice of a public, private, or home school, but not to a particular component of that education, such as participation in interscholastic athletics.** UIL rules did not violate equal protection principles. Distinctions drawn in the rules between large and small schools, and between public and private schools were rationally related to the state's interest in reducing unfair competition in the UIL. *Cornerstone Christian Schools v. Univ. Interscholastic League*, 563 F.3d 127 (5th Cir. 2009).

◆    A Massachusetts student transferred to a public school from a prep school in order to repeat her freshman year of high school. She joined the public school's swim team. During the next two years, the student proved to be one of the fastest swimmers in Massachusetts. Prior to her senior year, the Massachusetts Interscholastic Athletic Association (MIAA) deemed her ineligible to compete, based on its "fifth year student rule." The student sued, seeking an order that would allow her to compete as a high school senior on the prep school's swim team. The case reached the Massachusetts Supreme Judicial Court, which noted that the lower court had properly awarded judgment to the MIAA on the student's constitutional rights violation claims. Any right to education she possessed did not extend to participation in extracurricular activities. Moreover, the student had chosen not to participate on any school's swim team as a freshman and had received the full benefit of her four years of varsity sports eligibility under MIAA rules. **She was not treated differently from other swimmers based on her participation in a private swim club during her first freshman year.** And she failed to show she was similarly situated to other swimmers who were granted MIAA waivers. *Mancuso v. Massachusetts Interscholastic Athletic Ass'n,* 453 Mass. 116, 900 N.E.2d 518 (Mass. 2009).

◆   The Ohio High School Athletic Association (OHSAA) was denied an appeal regarding the application of a transfer bylaw to a student who had already graduated by the time his case reached a state appeals court. The case involved a private school student who was a member of his school bowling team for three years. He transferred to a public school for one term and then returned to the private school. A court held that the OHSAA could not exclude the student from the private school team. The coach would decide if he would compete. As no harm would result from the student's participation, the OHSAA was not entitled to an order. **On appeal, the Court of Appeals of Ohio held the case was moot because of the student's graduation.** *Dankoff v. Ohio High School Athletic Ass,n,* 2008 WL 4150285 (Ohio Ct. App. 9/10/08).

◆   The Tennessee Secondary Schools Athletic Association (TSSAA) is made up of about 290 public schools and 55 private schools. Its recruitment rule prohibited member schools from using "undue influence" in recruiting middle school students for athletics. Brentwood Academy, a TSSAA member, has had very successful interscholastic athletic programs, especially in football. In 1998, Brentwood's football coach wrote letters to eighth-grade boys who had enrolled at the academy, inviting them to practice with the team. He then made follow-up calls to their families. The coach also supplied two students with free tickets to Brentwood football games. Public high school coaches reported the coach's conduct, and the TSSAA investigated. It then fined Brentwood $3,000 for violating recruiting rules and excluded the school from football and basketball tournaments for one school year. Brentwood sued. A court held that the TSSAA was a state actor which violated Brentwood's First Amendment rights. The Sixth Circuit reversed, and the U.S. Supreme Court held that the TSSAA had a public character and was a state actor. *Brentwood Academy v. Tennessee Secondary School Athletic Ass'n,* 531 U.S. 288 (2001).

The case returned to the district court, which again ruled for Brentwood. On appeal, the Sixth Circuit found that the TSSAA recruiting rule violated the First Amendment. It also found that the TSSAA violated Brentwood's due process rights. The U.S. Supreme Court again agreed to hear the case. It held that **enforcement of the TSSAA recruitment rule did not abridge the academy's free speech or due process rights.** Brentwood was afforded extensive notices and procedures, including an investigation, a hearing and an appeal. There was no free speech violation, as the rule did not forbid true communications about sports. Instead, it forbade the recruitment of middle school students. Brentwood made a voluntary decision to join the TSSAA and follow its recruitment rule. *Tennessee Secondary Schools Athletic Ass'n v. Brentwood Academy*, 551 U.S. 291 (2007).

◆  The mother of a Florida cheerleader signed a school release form that waived her right to sue the school for any injury or claim resulting from her daughter's athletic participation. The student was injured while practicing routines with the squad in the school gym. She sued the school board for negligence. Because her mother had signed a pre-injury release, the court held for the school. The student appealed, arguing that her mother had no legal authority to sign away her right to sue, but the court affirmed, finding that the mother had state law authority to sign away her daughter's rights. Many schools and other organizations condition participation in sports on an agreement not to hold the organization responsible if the participant is injured. The Florida Supreme Court has held that **parents have the authority to waive their children's rights** to sue in exchange for the ability to participate in activities they consider beneficial. Parents are free to make this decision without being second-guessed by courts, because parents are presumed to act in the best interests of their children. As a result, both the mother and daughter were bound by the release. *Krathen v. School Board of Monroe County*, 972 So.2d 887 (Fla. Dist. Ct. App. 2007).

## C.  Breach of Contract

### 1.  Educational Programs

◆  Parents sued a Kansas military school in which their children were enrolled for negligent supervision, intentional failure to supervise, intentional infliction of emotional distress, breach of contract and related claims. They added a claim in their own capacities for breach of fiduciary duty. The school claimed an arbitration clause directed any disagreement of the parties into arbitration under the rules of the American Arbitration Association. The court noted that **the enrollment contracts did not indicate that personal injury claims were included in either of the arbitration clauses**. It denied the school's motion to enforce the arbitration and forum selection clauses with respect to the personal injury claims of the students. On the other hand, the parents had signed the contracts and were bound by the arbitration and forum selection clauses, and the court held for the school on their claims. *Bizilj v. St. John's Military School*, 2008 WL 4394713 (D. Kan. 9/24/08).

◆  The mother of a student who attended a private Kentucky school became dissatisfied with his progress. A teacher recommended another school and more contact between the student and his estranged father. During a phone conversation with a parent volunteer, the mother said that there could be trouble for the school if the student's father became involved. This was taken as a threat that the father could hurt the teacher or the school. The teacher was informed of the conversation and filed a criminal complaint against the mother for making terroristic threats. The complaint was eventually resolved, and the mother agreed to not have any inappropriate or unlawful contact with either the school or the teacher. The mother then sued the school, teacher and parent volunteer, alleging educational malpractice, defamation and malicious prosecution.

The case reached the Kentucky Court of Appeals, which found no evidence to support the mother's claims. **Kentucky law does not recognize claims for educational malpractice.** Turning to the defamation claim, the court concluded that any defamatory statements were privileged because there was no evidence of actual malice. Finally, because the resolution of the criminal charges was not favorable to the mother, she failed to meet one of the essential elements of a malicious prosecution claim. *McGurl v. Friends School Inc.*, 2003 WL 1343248 (Ky. Ct. App. 2003).

### 2. Tuition

◆ A Maryland private school's re-enrollment contract specified that cancellation of a student's re-enrollment had to be in writing and delivered by May 31. Otherwise, the agreement held parents liable for charges for the entire academic year, plus any cost for collecting tuition from them. Parents paid the school a nonrefundable $1,000 deposit and agreed to pay the remaining $13,500 tuition in two installments. But in July – 44 days after the contract deadline – the parents tried to cancel their daughter's enrollment and asked for their deposit back. The school refused and informed the parents that they had to pay the full year's tuition. When they refused, the school sued them for breach of contract. The Court of Appeals of Maryland held that **the school did not have to mitigate its damages by trying to find another student** since the exact damages were already stated in the contract. Courts in Ohio, Arkansas, Kentucky and North Carolina have held that private schools in similar circumstances had no duty to mitigate damages caused by a breach of contract. The amount of damages based on the actual loss to the school was irrelevant, because the time to determine a liquidated damages clause is when the contract is formed. *Barrie School v. Patch*, 401 Md. 497, 933 A.2d 382 (Md. 2007).

◆ A Georgia private school enrollment contract made parents who withdrew their child liable for a full year's tuition. The only exception to this rule was if the parents notified the school they were moving more than 35 miles away. Less than two months after signing a tuition contract, two parents notified the school they were withdrawing their daughter and enrolling her at a different school. When they refused to pay tuition under the contract, the school brought a successful action against them in a state court.

On appeal, the Court of Appeals of Georgia affirmed the judgment for the school. **Liquidated damages provisions are valid if the damage resulting from a breach of contract is hard to accurately estimate and the amount is a reasonable estimate of the loss.** The parents admitted it would be hard to establish the exact amount it would cost the school if it lost one student. The school's final enrollment and budget were unknown at the time, so the school could not accurately estimate the financial impact of one student's withdrawal. The school was not fully enrolled and was running at a loss when the parents signed the contract. As the clause was a valid liquidated damages provision, rather than an illegal penalty, the parents had to honor it. *Turner v. Atlanta Girls School*, 288 Ga.App. 115, 653 S.E.2d 380 (Ga. Ct. App. 2007).

## D.  Discipline, Suspension and Expulsion

*Pennsylvania has a "deference rule" preventing court review of a religious organization's internal decisions about discipline, faith or ecclesiastical rules. Similarly, Louisiana courts can only overrule private school disciplinary decisions that are arbitrary or capricious.*

◆   An African-American senior at a Catholic school in Louisiana created several Facebook accounts and made mocking references about a bishop – as well as profane and mocking comments about her class, the school and certain teachers and administrators. The activity on Facebook violated several of the school's handbook provisions. Other students also joined the sites and commented on the postings. After administrators discovered the Facebook accounts, they disciplined the students involved. As the creator and administrator of the accounts, the student received a nine-day suspension. She sued the school for race discrimination under Section 1981, but the Fifth Circuit ruled that there was no violation of Section 1981. **The student got the longest suspension because she committed the most serious offense.** *Jegart v. Roman Catholic Church of the Diocese of Houma-Thibodaux*, 384 Fed.Appx. 398 (5th Cir. 2010).

◆   A California Lutheran high school teacher learned from a student that two female students had an ongoing homosexual relationship. After the teacher viewed a number of student MySpace pages, she believed the account and reported it to the school's principal. He expelled the female students on the ground that they had a homosexual relationship in violation of the school's Christian conduct rule. The students sued the school and principal for discrimination based on sexual orientation, in violation of the California Unruh Civil Rights Act. The court held for the school, ruling that it was not a "business enterprise" subject to the Unruh Act. The Court of Appeal of California found no error in the judgment. **Lutherans believed that homosexuality was a sin, and the school's policy was to refuse admission to homosexual students.** The Christian conduct rule permitted expulsion for "immoral or scandalous conduct," whether on or off campus. This would include homosexual conduct. *Doe v. California Lutheran High School Ass'n*, 170 Cal.App.4th 828, 88 Cal.Rptr.3d 475 (Cal. Ct. App. 2009).

◆   A Kansas private middle school principal wrote a letter to parents that formalized an English-only policy, citing name-calling, lack of inclusion, put-downs and bullying as grounds for discipline. Her letter required English to be spoken at school at all times. Three sixth-grade students and their parents claimed the English-only rule discriminated against them on the basis of race or national origin. Each of the families spoke English as their primary language. After the diocese that operated the school affirmed the policy, a student refused to sign a policy-related document. He left school, claiming he was expelled. His family and two others sued under Title VI of the Civil Rights Act of 1964. The families had to show that the students were members of a protected class who suffered adverse action and were treated less favorably than similarly situated students. According to the school, there was no "adverse action" here because there is no right to speak a foreign language at a private Catholic school, and each of the students spoke English as their first language. The court found that **English-only rules as applied to bilingual speakers are generally not discriminatory**. The English-only policy in this case resembled a private school rule mandating uniforms. Just as schools could require uniforms, they could dictate the language spoken when based on an appropriate reason. However, a hostile environment claim could proceed, based on the assertion that staff watched the Spanish speakers more closely than other students. *Silva v. St. Anne Catholic School*, 595 F.Supp.2d 1171 (D. Kan. 2009).

◆  Seventh-grade boys at a Pennsylvania Catholic school became fascinated by gangs and knives after their teacher had them read a book describing gang violence. One student admitted bringing a miniature Swiss Army knife to school and was expelled. The school sent a letter to other parents informing them that an unnamed student had been expelled for bringing a penknife to school. The student's parents sued the principal, pastor, school and archdiocese. They claimed their son had brought a small personal manicure set to school – not a knife. The case reached the Pennsylvania Supreme Court, which noted that **the state's "deference rule" prevents court review of a religious organization's internal decisions about discipline, faith or ecclesiastical rules**. However, the deference rule should not apply at the initial stages of a lawsuit for defamation and infliction of emotional distress. Disputes concerning questions of civil law do not require deference to religious doctrine and may be resolved based on neutral principles. The court allowed the defamation and infliction of emotional distress claims to proceed. *Connor v. Archdiocese of Philadelphia*, 601 Pa. 577, 975 A.2d 1084 (Pa. 2009).

◆  A Louisiana Catholic high school senior played on the varsity basketball team. He was placed on probation for plagiarism after his teacher noticed his paper on "Pride and Prejudice" was virtually identical to papers submitted by 13 others in the class. The student handbook stated that plagiarism was a "Class C" offense calling for a one-day suspension or detention plus a nine-week probation. Dishonesty was a "Class D" offense, requiring a full year of probation. While on probation, students could not participate in varsity sports. Twelve students admitted plagiarizing from a website, but the student didn't. The principal placed him on "special disciplinary probation" for the rest of the school year for dishonesty. When the student's father sued the school for an order to allow his son to play on the basketball team, the Court of Appeal of Louisiana found that the school's handbook vested disciplinary decisions with the principal. **Louisiana courts can only overrule private school disciplinary decisions that are arbitrary or capricious.** The decision in this case was neither. A year-long probation was within the principal's discretion. *Lawrence v. St. Augustine High School*, 955 So.2d 183 (La. Ct. App. 2007).

◆  Four 14-year-old Alabama private school girls played strip poker at a party in a private home. After leaving, they communicated electronically with boys who had been at the party. The boys convinced them to photograph themselves in the nude and email them the pictures. The boys promised that they would delete the pictures after viewing them. Instead, they circulated the photos to others. Copies were distributed throughout the school and an explicit photo was set as the wallpaper on a computer in a sixth-grade computer lab, leading to a shutdown of the system. The school's headmaster expelled the girls and the boy who had taken responsibility for distributing the photos.

The girls sued the school, headmaster and the school board chair for breach of contract, negligence, invasion of privacy and related claims. The case reached the Supreme Court of Alabama, which rejected the students' claims that the school breached the enrollment contract by failing to provide them with due process during the investigation. The headmaster met with the parents, informed them of the situation, showed them the photos, and gave them a chance to respond. **Each of the students and their parents had signed a pledge in which they promised to abide by the student handbook,** and the handbook expressly provided that "[o]ff-campus behavior which is illicit, immoral, illegal and/or which reflects adversely on [the school] subjects the student to immediate expulsion." The school did not breach the enrollment contract. *S.B. v. St. James School*, 959 So.2d 72 (Ala. 2006).

## E.  Students with Disabilities

*Private institutions must comply with laws requiring accommodation of students with disabilities, such as the Americans with Disabilities Act (ADA). Students with disabilities must be reasonably accommodated, but only to the extent that it does not impose an undue hardship on the school. But the Individuals with Disabilities Education Act (IDEA) does not apply to private schools that provide services to students with disabilities under individualized education programs. Private schools are not "local educational agencies" and do not fit into any definition for liability purposes under the IDEA.*

◆  A New York court held a private school had no duty to hold a manifestation hearing prior to expelling a disabled student with an individualized education plan. After the private school expelled the student, his parents obtained a state court order holding this action could not be taken prior to a manifestation determination hearing. The school appealed to a state appellate division court, which noted that the parents failed to exhaust their administrative remedies under the state education law. Even if the parents had exhausted administrative remedies, they still would not be entitled to relief. **The education law places the burden on public schools to provide special education services, and not upon non-public schools.** The lower court decision was reversed. *In re Pelose*, 885 N.Y.S.2d 816 (N.Y. App. Div. 2009).

◆ A private school contracted with a Virginia school district to provide educational services for an autistic student. The contract allowed either party to terminate the agreement upon 30 days' notice. The school could also terminate the contract if the student committed a serious incident. When the school sought to discharge the student over safety concerns, his parents objected and requested a due process hearing. A hearing officer ordered the school to comply with the stay-put provision of the Individuals with Disabilities Education Act (IDEA), finding that **its contract with the district required it to comply with the IDEA**. The school sued the school district to challenge the order and then reached a settlement with the district releasing it from the contract. The federal court then refused to intervene in the dispute, leaving the due process hearing over the decision to expel the student to the hearing officer. *Virginia Institute of Autism v. Virginia Dep't of Educ.*, 537 F.Supp.2d 817 (E.D. Va. 2008).

◆ A student with learning and emotional disabilities attended a public elementary school emotional support class that was staffed by a private mental health and retardation service provider under contract with the School District of Philadelphia. His parent claimed the classroom was chaotic and violent and that staff members improperly restrained her son. She asserted that the provider used uncertified staff, who mismanaged the classroom and did not implement his individualized education program. A hearing officer held that the district did not deny the student a free appropriate public education, and a Pennsylvania special education appeals panel affirmed that decision. The parent appealed to a federal court, asserting that the administrative decisions violated the Individuals with Disabilities Education Act (IDEA) and Section 504 of the Rehabilitation Act. She also sought an award of monetary damages.

The court held that the provider was not directly funded or controlled by the state and had no duty to provide for special education students. **The IDEA imposes no liability on private schools that provide services to students with disabilities.** Private schools are not "local educational agencies" and do not fit into any definition for liability purposes under the IDEA. While other states, such as New Jersey, have elected to impose IDEA liability upon private entities, Pennsylvania has not. The parent's Section 504 claim and her claims for monetary damages failed. *Damian J. v. School Dist. of Philadelphia*, No. 06-3866, 2007 WL 1221216 (E.D. Pa. 4/25/07).

◆ The Third Circuit decided that more evidence was needed to establish if a private school with a strong Quaker affiliation fell within the ADA's religious exemption to lawsuits. The parents of a student with Attention Deficit Disorder and other learning disabilities claimed the school's staff did not give him the help he needed and tried to pressure him into leaving school through a campaign of public humiliation and improper physical discipline. They sued the school in a federal court, claiming the school subjected him to a discriminatory environment and failed to accommodate his disabilities. The court held that the school could not be sued under the ADA because it was a religious organization. The Third Circuit reversed and remanded the case to the lower court for further consideration. **The ADA exemption applied if the school was a religious organization or under the control of one.** As the only evidence presented was an affidavit by the school's headmaster, the parents should have the chance to gather more information to determine if the school was a "religious organization." *Doe v. Abington Friends School*, 480 F.3d 252 (3d Cir. 2007).

◆   The mother of a New Hampshire wheelchair-bound student claimed that his school district failed to follow his IEP and erroneously decertified him from eligibility for special education. She filed a complaint with the state department of education. After an administrative ruling against her, she placed her son in a private school outside the district. When she sued the school district under the IDEA and Section 504, a federal court held that **most of her claims failed because the private school was outside the district and she did not intend to return her son to district schools**. Her tuition reimbursement claim under the IDEA remained viable, but her claims against individual employees under Section 504 failed. *J.P.E.H. v. Hooksett School Dist.*, 2008 WL 4681827, 2008 WL 4681925 (D.N.H. 10/22/08).

Subsequently, the court determined that tuition reimbursement was not in order because the student's classroom performance demonstrated that he was no longer qualified as a child with a disability under the IDEA. *J.P.E.H. v. Hooksett School Dist.*, 2009 WL 1883885 (D. N.H. 6/30/09).

◆   A private school student in Michigan had a brain tumor that was in remission. Because of his problems walking, his mother requested a physical therapy needs evaluation from the school district. The district found that he did not need additional physical therapy. The mother then asked for an individual educational evaluation at the district's expense. When the district refused, a lawsuit resulted. The Michigan Court of Appeals held that state law required special education for "every handicapped person." Further, **nothing in state law limited individual educational evaluations to public school students**. The district had to pay for the evaluation. *Michigan Dep't of Educ. v. Grosse Pointe Public Schools*, 701 N.W.2d 195 (Mich. Ct. App. 2005).

## IV.  PUBLIC AND PRIVATE SCHOOL COOPERATION

*Cooperation between public and private schools must avoid the appearance of government approval of religion and must not constitute government aid to, or excessive entanglement with, religious organizations.*

### A.  Dual Enrollment

◆   Many Indiana local educational agencies and private schools employed dual-enrollment agreements under which the agencies provided secular instruction to private school students at public schools. Public funds were also used to provide computer and Internet services to private schools, including those with religious affiliations. A group of taxpayers opposed the dual-enrollment process as a public subsidy of religious schools. They sued for violations of Article 1, Section 6 of the Indiana Constitution. A court held that the dual-enrollment process did not violate the state constitution. The Supreme

Court of Indiana affirmed. **The dual-enrollment programs did not result in the payment of public funds directly to religious institutions,** and any cost saving realized by parochial schools was relatively minor and incidental. The programs did not confer substantial benefits on religious institutions or directly fund religious activity. *Embry v. O'Bannon,* 798 N.E.2d 157 (Ind. 2003).

◆   An Illinois student tested above grade level at a private school. His mother asked the superintendent of their school district for permission to enroll him in an Algebra II or geometry class in district schools as he entered grade eight. The private school principal made a request on behalf of the student to place him in a public school math class the next year. The superintendent contacted the principal and the independent study teacher, seeking the student's grades, homework, quizzes, tests and scores. The superintendent allowed the student to enroll in district schools on a part-time basis, but placed him in an Honors Algebra I class. The student instead enrolled in an Algebra II course at a local community college while remaining in eighth grade in his private school. The family sued the district and superintendent for due process and equal protection violations. The court noted that an Illinois law permitted private school students to attend public school part time. Here, the superintendent conferred with private school staff and reasonably determined that the student's proper placement was in Honors Algebra I. State law did not create a protected property interest to attend a student's class of choice. **As courts may not interfere with the daily operations of a school system unless a conflict sharply implicates constitutional values,** the court held for the district and superintendent. *Hassberger v. Board of Educ., Cent. Community Unit School Dist. 301,* No. 00 C 7873, 2003 WL 22697481 (N.D. Ill. 2003).

### B.  Textbook Loans and Other Materials

*The provision of textbooks by the state to private and parochial school students is permissible under the First Amendment. In* Cochran v. Louisiana State Board of Educ., *281 U.S. 370, 50 S.Ct. 335, 74 L.Ed.2d 1929 (1930), the U.S. Supreme Court upheld a state law that authorized the purchasing and supplying of textbooks to all schoolchildren, including parochial schoolchildren, on the basis of what is now called the "child benefit" doctrine. The Court held that the textbook loan statute was constitutional because the legislature's purpose in enacting the statute was to benefit children and their parents, not religious schools.*

◆   A group of Louisiana citizens sued the Jefferson Parish School Board in 1985 for violating the First Amendment, alleging that the board improperly provided Chapter Two funds to parochial schools to acquire library materials and media equipment. The group asserted that expenditures for books, computers, software and other audiovisual equipment violated the Establishment Clause. A federal court agreed, granting pretrial judgment to the group because the funding failed the test from *Lemon v. Kurtzman,* 403 U.S. 602 (1971). The court held that the loan of materials to sectarian schools constituted direct government aid under *Meek v. Pittenger,* 421 U.S. 349 (1975) and

*Wolman v. Walter*, 433 U.S. 229 (1977). Two years later, the court reversed itself, citing the intervening *Zobrest v. Catalina Foothills School Dist.*, 509 U.S. 1 (1993), decision. The citizens appealed to the Fifth Circuit, which held that the Chapter Two grants were unconstitutional under *Meek* and *Wolman*.

The U.S. Supreme Court then stated that there was no basis for finding the board's use of Chapter Two funds advanced religion. Use of Chapter Two funds by private schools did not result in government indoctrination because eligibility was determined on a neutral basis and through private choices by parents. **Chapter Two had no impermissible content and did not define its recipients by reference to religion.** A broad array of schools was eligible for assistance without regard to religious affiliation. Students who attended schools receiving Chapter Two funds were the ultimate beneficiaries of the assistance. The Court upheld the board's use of Chapter Two funding and held that the parish did not need to exclude sectarian schools from its program. *Mitchell v. Helms*, 530 U.S. 793, 120 S.Ct. 2530, 147 L.Ed.2d 660 (2000).

◆ A 1997 Wisconsin law created the Technology for Education Achievement (TEACH) Board, which administered the Education Telecommunications Access program. The TEACH board approved access for data lines and video links under a heavily subsidized program in which both public and private schools participated. A taxpayer group objected to the program on constitutional grounds because $58,873 of the program's annual total budget of over $1.9 million was awarded to nine religiously affiliated Wisconsin schools and private colleges. The taxpayer challenge reached the U.S. Court of Appeals, Seventh Circuit, which held that **in the absence of any restriction on the expenditure of public funds by the schools, the expenditures had a primary effect that advanced religion.** The subsidies could easily be used for maintenance, chapels, religious instruction, or connection time to view religious websites. The law did not bar schools from using the grants for these and other constitutionally impermissible purposes. Because direct aid from the government to a sectarian institution in any form is invalid, the provision of direct subsidies to religious schools was unconstitutional. *Freedom From Religion Foundation, Inc. v. Bugher*, 249 F.3d 606 (7th Cir. 2001).

◆ The U.S. Supreme Court reaffirmed the validity of the child benefit doctrine in a case involving a New York textbook loan statute. This statute required local school districts to lend textbooks free of charge to all children in grades seven through twelve. Parochial school students were included. The Court observed that the textbooks loaned to parochial schoolchildren were the same nonreligious textbooks used in the public schools. **The loaning of textbooks was permissible because the parochial school students used them for secular study.** There was no state involvement in religious training. The state of New York was merely providing a secular benefit to all schoolchildren. *Board of Educ. v. Allen*, 392 U.S. 236, 88 S.Ct. 1923, 20 L.Ed.2d 1060 (1968).

◆ The Supreme Court held that **private schools with racially discriminatory admissions policies may not benefit from textbook loan programs**. This ruling was based on the principle that the state may not give assistance to acts of racial discrimination. Textbooks were "a basic educational tool," said the Court, and to permit racially discriminatory private schools to benefit from state textbook loans would be to allow the state to accomplish indirectly what it could not accomplish directly: a state-funded racially segregated school system. *Norwood v. Harrison*, 413 U.S. 455, 93 S.Ct. 2804, 37 L.Ed.2d 723 (1973).

## C.  Transportation

*The use of state funds to reimburse private schools for transportation for field trips was declared unconstitutional by the U.S. Supreme Court in* Wolman v. Walter, *433 U.S. 229 (1977). There was no way public officials could monitor the field trips to assure that they had a secular purpose. Even if monitoring by the state was feasible, the monitoring would be so extensive that the state would become entangled in religion to an impermissible degree.*

◆  South Dakota school district buses picked up Lutheran elementary school students who lived along its bus routes until the state attorney general suggested that transporting private school students might violate the South Dakota Constitution. The state legislature then enacted a new law expressly allowing school districts to provide transportation for private school students, if this did not cost additional public funds. Prior to the reinstatement of busing, parents of students who attended the private school sued the school district for constitutional violations. The case reached the U.S. Court of Appeals, Eighth Circuit, which explained that the parents lacked standing to sue because they "failed to take even the simple step of requesting that the School District resume busing." In fact, the district had advocated for the legislation to allow busing. *Pucket v. Hot Springs School Dist. No. 23-2*, 526 F.3d 1151 (8th Cir. 2008).

◆  Transportation may be provided to parochial school students without violating the First Amendment under a 1947 U.S. Supreme Court case. The case involved a New Jersey law that allowed reimbursement to parents of children attending nonprofit religious schools for costs incurred by the children in using public transportation to travel to and from school. The law's purpose was to provide transportation expenses for all schoolchildren regardless of where they attended school, as long as the school was nonprofit. The Court analogized free transportation to other state benefits such as police and fire protection, connections for sewage disposal, and public roads and sidewalks, which also benefited parochial schoolchildren. **It was not the purpose of the First Amendment to cut off religious institutions from all government benefits.** Rather, the state was only required to be neutral toward religion. *Everson v. Board of Educ.*, 330 U.S. 1, 67 S.Ct. 504, 91 L.Ed.2d 711 (1947).

◆  Before the start of the 2000-01 school year, the Pittsburgh School District notified the Roman Catholic Diocese of Pittsburgh that it would no longer provide busing for half-day kindergarten programs for either public or private school students. The diocese challenged this decision, arguing that the Pennsylvania Public School Code obligated the district to provide midday bus service for kindergartners. Eventually, several students and their parents sued, seeking injunctive relief. A court granted a preliminary injunction ordering the district to provide busing. The district appealed.

The Commonwealth Court of Pennsylvania rejected the diocese's assertion that the School Code required the district to provide busing for all kindergarten students who attended diocesan schools, regardless of which program they attended. **The district was only required to offer the same transportation services to private school students it offered to public school students.** Under the circumstances, the private school students were eligible for a different, upgraded version of the transportation provided to district students. The court held that the preliminary injunction issued by the trial court was too broad. It vacated the injunction and remanded the case. *Crowe v. School Dist. of Pittsburgh*, 805 A.2d 691 (Pa. Commw. Ct. 2002).

◆   Wisconsin law requires high school districts to provide private school students with transportation to and from their schools. Elementary districts may elect to provide the services instead of the high schools and may contract directly with parents to do so. The parents of students who attended Providence Catholic School contracted with elementary school districts to provide transportation. When the amount paid to the parents became less than the cost of transportation, Providence requested additional funding. The districts denied the request, and parents sought a court order requiring the districts to provide transportation to the parochial school. The state court of appeals held that **the school districts were statutorily allowed to contract with the parents of private school students regarding transportation**. The parents' assertion that state law barred these contracts and required the provision of transportation services was rejected, as state law gave the districts assorted options for providing transportation to private school students. One of these options was contracting directly with the parents. *Providence Catholic School v. Bristol School Dist. No. 1,* 605 N.W.2d 238 (Wis. Ct. App. 1999).

## D.  Personnel Sharing and Outsourcing

◆   After the 2002-03 school year, a Tennessee school board voted to eliminate an alternative school and other programs due to budget constraints. Officials asserted that the vote was financially motivated and would save $171,423. Two teachers and the alternative school principal lost their jobs due to the closing. Alternative school services were to be outsourced under a contract. The board chose a private day program for students with behavioral and/or emotional problems for the contract. Employees who lost their jobs after the closing sued the board in a federal court, arguing that the contract with the religious school violated the Establishment Clause of the First Amendment and analogous state constitutional provisions. A court awarded pretrial judgment to the board, and the employees appealed. The Sixth Circuit held that a genuine issue of fact existed regarding whether the board had violated the Establishment Clause.

**If the private school day program had the same focus on Christianity as its residential school, as the teachers alleged, a reasonable person could find that the board acted to endorse religion.** The Establishment Clause claim was returned to the district court to consider the argument that there was no separation between the private school's day and residential programs. On the other hand, the court held that the teachers' due process claims had been properly dismissed. The board was acting in a legislative capacity when it voted to close the alternative school. There was no requirement that the teachers receive notice and an opportunity to be heard prior to the board's decision. Since the board members were entitled to legislative immunity, they could not be sued in their individual capacities. *Smith v. Jefferson County School Board of Comm'rs*, 549 F.3d 641 (6th Cir. 2008).

In 2009, a majority of the active judges of the Sixth Circuit voted to vacate the decision and to rehear the case before the full court.

◆   Title I of the Elementary and Secondary Education Act of 1965 provides federal funding through the states to local educational agencies for remedial education, guidance and job counseling to at-risk students and students residing in low-income areas. Title I requires that funding be made available for all eligible students, including those attending private schools. Local agencies retain control over Title I funds and materials. The New York City Board of Education attempted to implement Title I programs at parochial schools by allowing public employees to instruct students on private school grounds during school hours. The case reached the U.S. Supreme Court, which held that this violated the Establishment Clause in *Aguilar v. Felton*, 473 U.S. 402, 105 S.Ct. 3232, 87 L.Ed.2d 290 (1985).

On remand, a federal court ordered the city board to refrain from using Title I funds for any plan or program under which public school teachers and counselors appeared on sectarian school grounds. In response to *Aguilar*, local education boards modified their Title I programs by moving classes to remote sites including mobile instructional units parked near sectarian schools. However, a new group of parents and parochial school students filed motions seeking relief from the permanent order.

The case again reached the U.S. Supreme Court, which held that it would no longer presume that the presence of a public school teacher on parochial school grounds creates an unconstitutional symbolic union between church and state. The provision of Title I services at parochial schools resembled the provision of the sign language interpreter in *Zobrest* under the Individuals with Disabilities Education Act. **New York City's Title I program was constitutionally permissible** because it did not result in government indoctrination, define funding recipients by reference to religion or create excessive entanglement between education officials and religious schools. *Agostini v. Felton*, 521 U.S. 203, 117 S.Ct. 1997, 138 L.Ed.2d 391 (1997).

◆   In *Lemon v. Kurtzman*, the U.S. Supreme Court invalidated Rhode Island and Pennsylvania statutes that provided state money to finance the operation of parochial schools. It applied a three-part test, which remains in use by the courts today. "First, the statute must have a secular legislative purpose; second, its principal or primary effect must be one that neither advances nor inhibits religion, ... finally, the statute must not foster an excessive government entanglement with religion." **The programs excessively entangled the state**

**with religion** because of the highly religious nature of the Roman Catholic parochial schools that were its primary beneficiaries. Consequently, the programs violated the First Amendment. *Lemon v. Kurtzman*, 403 U.S. 602, 91 S.Ct. 2105, 29 L.Ed.2d 745 (1971).

## E.  School Facilities and Property

◆  A Georgia school board authorized the lease of classroom space at the Buckhead Baptist Church to create a kindergarten annex. The lease required the school system to rent space from the church for over five years and pay for renovations and improvements on church property that would be credited against rent due. A citizen claimed the lease agreement violated the Establishment Clause of the Georgia Constitution and sued the school system to halt payments to the church. A court ruled for the school system.

The Georgia Supreme Court explained that the state constitution's Establishment Clause prevented the state and its political subdivisions from owning, controlling or giving monetary aid to a church or religious institution. However, this did not mean that a state political subdivision could not "enter into an arms-length commercial agreement with a sectarian institution to accomplish a non-sectarian purpose." Here, the school system had simply leased space from the church to run a public kindergarten in a non-sectarian environment. **Lease payments did not foster the education of students in a sectarian school and was not state monetary aid to the church.** As the lease agreement did not violate the Georgia Constitution, the court affirmed the judgment for the school system. *Taetle v. Atlanta Independent School System*, 280 Ga. 137, 625 S.E.2d 770 (Ga. 2006).

◆  The Milwaukee Parental Choice Program was created to subsidize private education for underprivileged students in Milwaukee. A Catholic High School located primarily in St. Francis, but with 20% of its school grounds, including green space, a parking lot, driveway and track area located in Milwaukee, petitioned the state superintendent of public instruction for an order declaring it eligible to participate in the choice program. This request was denied. In the lawsuit that followed, the Court of Appeals of Wisconsin noted that **the statute plainly indicated that the school was not eligible to participate in the program**. The title of the statute was "Milwaukee parental choice program." Had the legislature intended for schools with buildings not located in the city to participate in the program, it would not have required them to submit copies of their certificates of occupancy "issued by the city." Under the school's argument, "any school, anywhere can become a Choice school by buying a small plot in the City of Milwaukee." Without the required certificate of occupancy from the city of Milwaukee, the school was ineligible for the program. *Thomas More High School v. Burmaster*, 704 N.W.2d 349 (Wis. Ct. App. 2005). The Supreme Court of Wisconsin denied further review.

◆  An Iowa parochial school held a fundraiser for its baseball and softball teams. Individuals and businesses purchased 37 boosters signs that were hung from the outfield fences of school athletic fields. The Iowa Department of

Transportation (IDOT) determined that the signs violated a state law prohibiting billboard advertising within 660 feet of a state highway. The school challenged an IDOT directive to remove the signs, claiming they were not visible from the highway and that IDOT was infringing on commercial speech in violation of the First Amendment. The Iowa Supreme Court held that the signs clearly violated the statute, as they were visible from the highway. **The statute regulated signs based on their location, not their content.** Here, the statute did not impermissibly restrict the school's speech rights. IDOT had a compelling state interest in traffic safety and ensuring an aesthetic environment. The statute only prohibited the booster signs from being placed where they were visible from the highway. The school could still place them elsewhere on its property. *Immaculate Conception Corp. and Don Bosco High School v. Iowa Dep't of Transportation*, 656 N.W.2d 513 (Iowa 2003).

◆   The U.S. Court of Appeals, Sixth Circuit, held that the issuance of tax-exempt industrial development bonds to a Tennessee Christian university to fund a renovation project did not violate the Establishment Clause of the U.S. Constitution. **The bonds did not violate the Establishment Clause because public funds were not used to issue them**, and the method for obtaining them did not implicate any public funds. The bonds were issued in a neutral manner and the issue had a secular objective. The court found that the effect of issuing the bonds neither advanced nor inhibited religion because the bonds were available to a variety of entities. There was no perception of impermissible government endorsement of religion. *Steele v. Industrial Development Board of Metropolitan Government of Nashville*, 301 F.3d 401 (6th Cir. 2002).

◆   Under a Montgomery County, Maryland, zoning ordinance, all businesses and organizations must obtain a special exception in order to build a non-residential structure on land designated for residential use. The county appeals board grants petitions for special exceptions only after determining, through a public hearing, that the new building will not disrupt the surrounding community. The ordinance exempts lots owned or leased by religious organizations from having to obtain a special exception. A federal court examined the constitutionality of the exemption after residential neighbors of the Connelly School of the Holy Child, a parochial school, objected to the school's construction of a new building. The court found the exemption unconstitutional. The Connelly School appealed to the Fourth Circuit.

The court of appeals reversed, holding that **the exemption had the secular purpose of allowing the county to prevent government interference with the religious mission of various organizations** and avoided creating a forum during special exception hearings in which anti-religious views might be expressed. The exemption neither advanced nor inhibited religion. The county merely relieved religious schools from the burden of applying for a special exception. Any advancement of religion that followed would be the result of the religious schools' own acts in light of the exemption. Finally, the exemption did not foster an excessive entanglement with religion. *Renzi v. Connelly School of the Holy Child Inc.*, 224 F.3d 283 (4th Cir. 2000).

## F.   Release Time Programs

◆   **An Illinois program allowed public school students to receive religious instruction in their public schools.** Although religious groups supplied the religious education teachers at no cost to school districts, the superintendent of schools exercised supervisory powers over them. A taxpayer sued a local school board, claiming the release time program violated the Establishment Clause. The U.S. Supreme Court agreed. "This is beyond all question a utilization of the tax-established and tax-supported public school system to aid religious groups," said the Court. "[T]he First Amendment has erected a wall between Church and State which must be kept high and impregnable." *McCollum v. Board of Educ.*, 333 U.S. 203, 68 S.Ct. 461, 92 L.Ed.2d 649 (1948).

◆   Four years later, the Supreme Court upheld a different kind of release time program. In this New York program, students could be released from public school classes during the school day for a few hours to attend religious education classes. Unlike the program in the *McCollum* case, students in the New York release time program received their religious instruction off the public school grounds. Church officials made out weekly attendance reports and sent the reports to public school officials, who then checked to assure that the released students had actually reported for their off-school-grounds religious instruction. The Court approved the New York program largely because the religious instruction took place off school grounds. **There was no religious indoctrination taking place in the public school buildings nor was there any expenditure of public funds on behalf of religious training.** Also, there was no evidence of any subtle or overt coercion exerted by any public school officials to induce students to attend the religious classes. The public schools were merely accommodating religion, not aiding it. The Supreme Court declined to invalidate the New York release time program, saying, "We cannot read into the Bill of Rights such a philosophy of hostility to religion." *Zorach v. Clauson*, 343 U.S. 306, 72 S.Ct. 679, 96 L.Ed.2d 954 (1952).

◆   Two former students claimed that a New York district implemented a "released time" program in an unconstitutional way. They asserted that the district released Catholic and Protestant students so they could attend nearby programs at designated times during the school day. Others remained in classrooms with nothing to do until the released students returned. They sued the district in a federal court, asserting that the administration of the released time program violated the Establishment Clause. A court held for the district, ruling that it did not implement the released time provision in a way that advanced Christianity over other religions and non-religion.

The Second Circuit noted that the Supreme Court had upheld the program authorized in *Zorach v. Clauson*, above. It disagreed that the district's implementation of the program violated the Establishment Clause by favoring Christianity over other religions and non-religion. The program used no public funds and involved no on-site religious instruction. As the Supreme Court held in *Zorach*, **the program called for schools to simply adjust their schedules to accommodate student religious needs**. Nothing suggested that the released time program was administered in a coercive manner. As the district implemented the law consistently with *Zorach*, the judgment was affirmed. *Pierce v. Sullivan West Cent. School Dist.*, 379 F.3d 56 (2d Cir. 2004).

## V. STUDENT FINANCIAL ASSISTANCE

*To be constitutional, government financial assistance for religious school students must primarily benefit the students, not their schools. Federal funding of programs and activities requires compliance with federal statutes such as Title VI, Title IX, the Rehabilitation Act, the Americans with Disabilities Act and the Age Discrimination in Employment Act. Students receiving federal grants will be deemed to be receiving assistance for federal law purposes. For more cases involving school voucher programs, please see Chapter Four, Section IV.*

◆   Arizona lawmakers enacted a law that would give students with disabilities who attended public schools up to $5,000 for tuition and fees at private schools. The program included both sectarian and nonsectarian private schools in its scope. Objectors to the program sued state officials, asserting constitutional violations. The case reached the Arizona Court of Appeals, which held that although the program did not violate the Religion Clause of the state constitution, it did violate the Aid Clause, which prohibits the appropriation of public money made in aid of private or sectarian schools. **Even though the payments would be made to the students, who would then give the money to the schools, the program would still transfer state funds to private schools.** *Cain v. Horne*, 183 P.3d 1269 (Ariz. Ct. App. 2008).

◆   A 67-year-old disabled Washington man failed to repay federally reinsured student loans he incurred between 1984 and 1989 under the Guaranteed Student Loan Program. The loans were reassigned to the Department of Education, which certified the debt to the U.S. Department of Treasury through the Treasury Offset Program. The U.S. government began withholding part of the man's Social Security benefits to offset his debt, part of which was more than 10 years overdue. He sued, alleging that the offset was barred by a 10-year statute of limitations of the 1982 Debt Collection Act. The court dismissed the case, and appeal reached the U.S. Supreme Court.

The Court explained that **the Higher Education Technical Amendments of 1991 "sweepingly eliminated time limitations as to certain loans."** This included the student loans in this case. The Debt Collection Improvement Act of 1996 clarified that, notwithstanding any other law, all payments due under the Social Security Act were subject to offset. Moreover, the Amendments removed the 10-year limit that would otherwise bar an offset of Social Security benefits. The Court affirmed the judgment for the U.S. government. *Lockhart v. U.S.*, 546 U.S. 142 (2005).

◆   Washington law created the Promise Scholarship Program, which made state funds available to qualified students for education-related costs. A student who received a Promise Scholarship enrolled as a double major in pastoral ministries and business at a private Christian college. The college director of financial aid advised him that he could not use the scholarship to pursue a devotional theology degree. When the student sued, appeal reached the U.S. Supreme Court, which held that the Constitution permitted states to deny funding to students pursuing devotional theology degrees. Here, **the training of ministers was essentially a religious endeavor that could be treated differently than training for other callings**. There was no evidence of any state hostility toward religion. Only students seeking a theology degree were denied scholarships. Nothing in the history or text of the Washington Constitution or the program suggested anti-religious bias. *Locke v. Davey*, 540 U.S. 712 (2004).

◆  The parents of three Georgia students enrolled in nonsectarian private schools sued the state, the Board of Education and others for the enforcement of the state Tuition Grant Act. The act provided for direct grants of money, under specified conditions, to the parents of students attending grades K-12 in nonsectarian private schools. The parents alleged that they were denied these grants which, in turn, denied them the equal protection of the law since students in pre-kindergarten and post-twelfth grade programs at private schools had state funds available to them. The case reached the Supreme Court of Georgia, which noted that although the two groups in this case were treated differently with regard to educational funding, they were not similarly situated. Children in K-12 had a constitutional right to an education at state expense and were required to attend school. However, the group of children in pre-kindergarten and post-twelfth grade had no constitutional right to education and were not required to be enrolled in educational programs. Public education for the K-12 students was supported by taxation, but the funding for the other students resulted not only from taxation but also from lottery proceeds. **The disparate entitlements and obligations of the two groups meant that the parents were not entitled to relief.** *Lowe v. State of Georgia*, 482 S.E.2d 344 (Ga. 1997).

◆  A private, not-for-profit technical school in Indiana participated in the Guaranteed Student Loan (GSL) program authorized by Title IV of the Higher Education Act. The program required the school to make refunds to the lender if a student withdrew from school during a term. If the school failed to refund loans to the lender, the student would be liable for the full amount of the loan. The treasurer of the school conferred with the school's owners and initiated a practice of not making GSL refunds. As a result, the school owed $139,649 in refunds. After the school lost its accreditation, a federal grand jury indicted the treasurer for "knowingly and willfully misapplying" federally insured student loan funds in violation of 20 U.S.C. § 1097(a). A federal court dismissed the indictment because it lacked an allegation that the treasurer intended to injure or defraud the United States. The U.S. Supreme Court then held that Section 1097(a) did not require the specific intent to injure or defraud. **If the government can prove that the defendant misapplied Title IV funds knowingly and willfully, that is sufficient to show a violation of Section 1097(a).** The treasurer could be prosecuted. *Bates v. U.S.*, 522 U.S. 23 (1997).

◆   The U.S. Supreme Court held that the First Amendment did not prevent the state of Washington from providing financial assistance directly to a disabled individual attending a Christian college. The plaintiff, a blind person, sought vocational rehabilitative services from the Washington Commission for the Blind pursuant to state law. The law provided that visually impaired persons were eligible for educational assistance. However, because the student attended a Christian college intending to pursue a career of service in the church, the Commission for the Blind denied him assistance. The Washington Supreme Court upheld this decision on the ground that the First Amendment prohibited state funding of a student's education at a religious college. The U.S. Supreme Court took a less restrictive view of the First Amendment and reversed. The operation of Washington's program was such that the Commission for the Blind paid money directly to students, who could then attend the schools of their choice. **The fact that the student here chose to attend a religious college did not constitute state support of religion** because "the decision to support religious education is made by the individual, not the state." The First Amendment was therefore not offended. *Witters v. Washington Dep't of Services for the Blind*, 474 U.S. 481 (1986).

On remand, the Washington Supreme Court reconsidered the matter under the state constitution, which is far stricter in its prohibition on the expenditure of public funds for religious instruction than the U.S. Constitution. **Vocational assistance funds for the student's religious education violated the state constitution** because public money would be used for religious instruction. The court reaffirmed its denial of state funding for the student's tuition. *Witters v. State Comm'n for the Blind*, 771 P.2d 1119 (Wash. 1989).

◆   In 1973, the U.S. Supreme Court invalidated a New York program that provided $50-$100 in direct money grants to low income parents with children in private schools, and authorized income tax credits of up to $1,000 for parents with children in private schools. **The program had the primary effect of advancing religion** and thus was constitutionally invalid. The Court characterized the tax credits as akin to tuition grants and observed that they were really cash giveaways by the state for religious schools. *Committee for Public Educ. & Religious Liberty v. Nyquist*, 413 U.S. 756 (1973).

◆   The U.S. Supreme Court upheld a Minnesota program that involved tax deductions (as opposed to tax credits) that were available to parents of public and private schoolchildren alike. The program allowed state income tax deductions for tuition, nonreligious textbooks and transportation. In upholding the program, the Court held that the state had a legitimate interest in assuring that all its citizens were well educated. Also, the tax deductions in question were only a few among many other deductions such as those for medical expenses or charitable contributions. Unlike the program in the *Nyquist* case, **the Minnesota program was part of a bona fide income tax deduction system available to parents of all schoolchildren**. The Court held that the First Amendment was not offended by the Minnesota tax deduction program. *Mueller v. Allen*, 463 U.S. 388 (1983).

# APPENDIX A

## United States Constitution

[Provisions of Interest to Educators]

## ARTICLE I

Section 1. All legislative Powers herein granted shall be vested in a Congress of the United States, which shall consist of a Senate and House of Representatives.

\* \* \*

Section 8. The Congress shall have Power To lay and collect Taxes, Duties, Imposts and Excises, to pay the Debts and provide for the common Defence and general Welfare of the United States; but all Duties, Imposts and Excises shall be uniform throughout the United States:

To borrow money on the credit of the United States;

To regulate Commerce with foreign Nations, and among the several States, and with the Indian Tribes;

To establish an uniform Rule of Naturalization, and uniform Laws on the subject of Bankruptcies throughout the United States;

\* \* \*

To promote the Progress of Science and useful Arts, by securing for limited Times to Authors and Inventors the exclusive Right to their respective Writings and Discoveries;

\* \* \*

To make all Laws which shall be necessary and proper for carrying into Execution for the foregoing Powers, and all other Powers vested by this Constitution in the Government of the United States, or in any Department or Office thereof.

\* \* \*

Section 9. \* \* \* No Bill of Attainder or ex post facto Law shall be passed.

Section 10. No State shall * * * pass any Bill of Attainder, ex post facto Law, or Law impairing the Obligation of Contracts, or grant any Title of Nobility.

* * *

## ARTICLE II

Section 1. The executive Power shall be vested in a President of the United States of America.

* * *

## ARTICLE III

Section 1. The judicial Power of the United States, shall be vested in one Supreme Court, and in such inferior Courts as the Congress may from time to time ordain and establish. The Judges, both of the supreme and inferior courts, shall hold their Offices during good Behaviour, and shall, at stated Times, receive for their Services a Compensation, which shall not be diminished during their Continuance in Office.

Section 2. The judicial Power shall extend to all Cases, in Law and Equity, arising under this Constitution, the Laws of the United States, and Treaties made, or which shall be made; under their Authority; to all Cases affecting Ambassadors, other public Ministers and Consuls; to all Cases of admiralty and maritime Jurisdiction, to Controversies to which the United States shall be a party  to Controversies between two or more States; between a State and Citizens of another State; between Citizens of different States; between Citizens of the same State claiming Lands under the Grants of different States, and between a State, or the Citizens thereof, and foreign States, Citizens or Subjects.

* * *

## ARTICLE IV

Section 1. Full Faith and Credit shall be given in each State to the public Acts, Records and judicial Proceedings of every other State.* * *

Section 2. The Citizens of each State shall be entitled to all Privileges and Immunities of Citizens in the several States.

* * *

Section 4. The United States shall guarantee to every State in this Union a Republican Form of Government, and shall protect each of them against Invasion; and on Application of the Legislature, or of the Executive (when the Legislature cannot be convened) against domestic Violence.

## ARTICLE V

The Congress, whenever two thirds of both Houses shall deem it necessary, shall propose Amendments to this Constitution, or, on the Application of the Legislatures of two thirds of the several States, shall call a Convention for proposing Amendments, which, in either Case, shall be valid to all Intents and Purposes, as part of this Constitution, when ratified by the Legislatures of three fourths of the several States, or by Conventions in three fourths thereof, as the one or the other Mode of Ratification may be proposed by the Congress; Provided that no Amendment which may be made prior to the Year One thousand eight hundred and eight shall in any Manner affect the first and fourth Clauses in the Ninth Section of the first Article; and that no State, without its Consent, shall be deprived of its equal Suffrage in the Senate.

## ARTICLE VI

\* \* \*

This Constitution, and the Laws of the United States which shall be made in Pursuance thereof; and all Treaties made, or which shall be made, under the Authority of the United States, shall be the Supreme Law of the Land; and the Judges in every State shall be bound thereby, any Thing in the Constitution or Laws of any State to the Contrary notwithstanding.

The Senators and Representatives before mentioned, and the Members of the several State Legislatures, and all executive and judicial Officers, both of the United States and of the several States, shall be bound by Oath or Affirmation, to support this Constitution; but no religious Test shall ever be required as a Qualification to any Office or public Trust under the United States.

\* \* \*

## AMENDMENT I

Congress shall make no law respecting an establishment of religion, or prohibiting the free exercise thereof; or abridging the freedom of speech, or of the press; or the right of the people peaceably to assemble, and to petition the Government for a redress of grievances.

\* \* \*

## AMENDMENT IV

The right of the people to be secure in their persons, houses, papers, and effects, against unreasonable searches and seizures, shall not be violated, and no Warrants shall issue, but upon probable cause, supported by Oath or affirmation, and particularly describing the place to be searched, and the persons or things to be seized.

## AMENDMENT V

No person shall be held to answer for a capital, or otherwise infamous crime, unless on a presentment or indictment of a Grand Jury, except in cases arising in the land or naval forces, or in the Militia, when in actual service in time of War or public danger; nor shall any person be subject for the same offence to be twice put in jeopardy of life or limb; nor shall be compelled in any criminal case to be a witness against himself, nor be deprived of life, liberty, or property, without due process of law; nor shall private property be taken for public use, without just compensation.

## AMENDMENT VI

In all criminal prosecutions, the accused shall enjoy the right to a speedy and public trial, by an impartial jury of the State and district wherein the crime shall have been committed, which district shall have been previously ascertained by law, and to be informed of the nature and cause of the accusation; to be confronted with the witnesses against him; to have compulsory process for obtaining witnesses in his favor, and to have the Assistance of Counsel for his defense.

## AMENDMENT VII

In Suits at common law, where the value in controversy shall exceed twenty dollars, the right of trial by jury shall be preserved, and no fact tried by jury, shall be otherwise re-examined in any Court of the United States, than according to the rules of the common law.

## AMENDMENT VIII

Excessive bail shall not be required, nor excessive fines imposed, nor cruel and unusual punishments inflicted.

## AMENDMENT IX

The enumeration in the Constitution, of certain rights, shall not be construed to deny or disparage others retained by the people.

## AMENDMENT X

The powers not delegated to the United States by the Constitution, nor prohibited by it to the States, are reserved to the States respectively, or to the people.

## AMENDMENT XI

The Judicial power of the United States shall not be construed to extend to any suit in law or equity, commenced or prosecuted against one of the United States by Citizens of another State, or by Citizens or Subjects of any Foreign State.

\* \* \*

## AMENDMENT XIII

Section 1. Neither slavery nor involuntary servitude, except as a punishment for crime whereof the party shall have been duly convicted, shall exist within the United States, or any place subject to their jurisdiction.

Section 2. Congress shall have power to enforce this article by appropriate legislation.

## AMENDMENT XIV

Section 1. All persons born or naturalized in the United States, and subject to the jurisdiction thereof, are citizens of the United States and of the State wherein they reside. No State shall make or enforce any law which shall abridge the privileges or immunities of citizens of the United States; nor shall any State deprive any person of life, liberty, or property, without due process of law; nor deny to any person within its jurisdiction the equal protection of the laws.

\* \* \*

Section 5. The Congress shall have power to enforce, by appropriate legislation, the provisions of this article.

# APPENDIX B

## Subject Matter Table of
## Education Cases Decided by the
## United States Supreme Court

Note: Please see the Table of Cases (located at the front of this volume) for Supreme Court cases reported in this Volume.

**Academic Freedom**

U.S. v. American Library Ass'n, Inc., 539 U.S. 194, 123 S.Ct. 2297, 156 L.Ed.2d 221 (2003).

Univ. of Pennsylvania v. EEOC, 493 U.S. 182, 110 S.Ct. 577, 107 L.Ed.2d 571 (1990).

Epperson v. Arkansas, 393 U.S. 97, 89 S.Ct. 266, 21 L.Ed.2d 228 (1968).

Meyer v. Nebraska, 262 U.S. 390, 43 S.Ct. 625, 67 L.Ed.2d 1042 (1923).

**Aliens**

Toll v. Moreno, 458 U.S. 1, 102 S.Ct. 2977, 73 L.Ed.2d 563 (1982).

Plyler v. Doe, 457 U.S. 202, 102 S.Ct. 2382, 72 L.Ed.2d 786 (1982).

Ambach v. Norwick, 441 U.S. 68, 99 S.Ct. 1589, 60 L.Ed.2d 49 (1979).

Vlandis v. Kline, 412 U.S. 441, 93 S.Ct. 2230, 37 L.Ed.2d 63 (1973).

**Collective Bargaining**

Chicago Teachers Union v. Hudson, 475 U.S. 292, 106 S.Ct. 1066, 89 L.Ed.2d 232 (1986).

Minnesota State Board for Community Colleges v. Knight, 465 U.S. 271, 104 S.Ct. 1058, 79 L.Ed.2d 299 (1984).

Perry Educ. Ass'n v. Perry Local Educators' Ass'n, 460 U.S. 37, 103 S.Ct. 948, 74 L.Ed.2d 794 (1983).

City of Madison Joint School Dist. v. WERC, 429 U.S. 167, 97 S.Ct. 421, 50 L.Ed.2d 376 (1976).

**Compulsory Attendance**

Wisconsin v. Yoder, 406 U.S. 205, 92 S.Ct. 526, 32 L.Ed.2d 15 (1972).

Pierce v. Society of Sisters, 268 U.S. 510, 45 S.Ct. 571, 69 L.Ed. 1070 (1925).

**Continuing Education**

Austin ISD v. U.S., 443 U.S. 915, 99 S.Ct. 3106, 61 L.Ed.2d 879 (1979).

Harrah ISD v. Martin, 440 U.S. 194, 99 S.Ct. 1062, 59 L.Ed.2d 248 (1979).

**Corporal Punishment**

Ingraham v. Wright, 430 U.S. 651, 97 S.Ct. 1401, 51 L.Ed.2d 711 (1977).

**Desegregation**

Missouri v. Jenkins, 515 U.S. 70, 115 S. Ct. 2038, 132 L.Ed.2d 63 (1995).

U.S. v. Fordice, 505 U.S. 717, 112 S.Ct. 2727, 120 L.Ed.2d 575 (1992).

Freeman v. Pitts, 503 U.S. 467, 112 S.Ct. 1430, 118 L.Ed.2d 108 (1992).

Board of Educ. of Oklahoma City Public Schools v. Dowell, 498 U.S. 237, 111 S.Ct. 630, 112 L.Ed.2d 715 (1991).

Missouri v. Jenkins, 495 U.S. 33, 110 S.Ct. 1651, 109 L.Ed.2d 31 (1990).

Crawford v. Board of Educ., 458 U.S. 527, 102 S.Ct. 3211, 73 L.Ed.2d 948 (1982).

Washington v. Seattle School Dist. No. 1, 458 U.S. 457, 102 S.Ct. 3187, 73 L.Ed.2d 896 (1982).

Board of Educ. v. Superior Court, 448 U.S. 1343, 101 S.Ct. 21, 65 L.Ed.2d 1166 (1980).

Columbus Board of Educ. v. Penick, 443 U.S. 449, 99 S.Ct. 2941, 61 L.Ed.2d 666 (1979).

Bustop v. Board of Educ., 439 U.S. 1380, 99 S.Ct. 40, 58 L.Ed.2d 88 (1978).

Vetterli v. U.S. Dist. Court, 435 U.S. 1304, 98 S.Ct. 1219, 55 L.Ed.2d 751 (1978).

Dayton Board of Educ. v. Brinkman, 433 U.S. 406, 97 S.Ct. 2766, 53 L.Ed.2d 851 (1977).

Milliken v. Bradley, 433 U.S. 267, 97 S.Ct. 2749, 53 L.Ed.2d 745 (1977).

Pasadena City Board of Educ. v. Spangler, 427 U.S. 424, 96 S.Ct. 2697, 49 L.Ed.2d 599 (1976).

Milliken v. Bradley, 418 U.S. 717, 94 S.Ct. 311, 41 L.Ed.2d 1069 (1974).

Bradley v. School Board of City of Richmond, 416 U.S. 696, 94 S.Ct. 2006, 40 L.Ed.2d 476 (1974).

Keyes v. School Dist. No. 1, 413 U.S. 189, 93 S.Ct. 2686, 37 L.Ed.2d 548 (1973).

Drummond v. Acree, 409 U.S. 1228, 93 S.Ct. 18, 34 L.Ed.2d 33 (1972).

U.S. v. Scotland Neck City Board of Educ., 407 U.S. 484, 92 S.Ct. 2214, 33 L.Ed.2d 75 (1972).

Wright v. Council of City of Emporia, 407 U.S. 451, 92 S.Ct. 2196, 33 L.Ed.2d 51 (1972).

Winston-Salem/Forsyth County Board of Educ. v. Scott, 404 U.S. 1221, 92 S.Ct. 1236, 31 L.Ed.2d 441 (1971).

Dandridge v. Jefferson Parish School Board, 404 U.S. 1219, 92 S.Ct. 18, 30 L.Ed.2d 23 (1971).

Guey Heung Lee v. Johnson, 404 U.S. 1215, 92 S.Ct. 14, 30 L.Ed.2d 19 (1971).

North Carolina State Board of Educ. v. Swann, 402 U.S. 43, 91 S.Ct. 1284, 28 L.Ed.2d 586 (1971).

McDaniel v. Barresi, 402 U.S. 39, 91 S.Ct. 1287, 28 L.Ed.2d 582 (1971).

Davis v. Board of School Commissioners, 402 U.S. 33, 91 S.Ct. 1289, 28 L.Ed.2d 577 (1971).

Swann v. Charlotte-Mecklenburg Board of Educ., 402 U.S. 1, 91 S.Ct. 1267, 28 L.Ed.2d 554 (1971).

Northcross v. Board of Educ., 397 U.S. 232, 90 S.Ct. 891, 25 L.Ed.2d 246 (1970).

Carter v. West Feliciena Parish School Board, 396 U.S. 290, 90 S.Ct. 608, 24 L.Ed.2d 477 (1970).

Dowell v. Board of Educ., 396 U.S. 269, 90 S.Ct. 415, 24 L.Ed.2d 414 (1969).

Alexander v. Holmes County Board of Educ., 396 U.S. 19, 90 S.Ct. 29, 24 L.Ed.2d 19 (1969).

U.S. v. Montgomery County Board of Educ., 395 U.S. 225, 89 S.Ct. 1670, 23 L.Ed.2d 263 (1969).

Monroe v. Board of Commissioners, 391 U.S. 450, 88 S.Ct. 1700, 20 L.Ed.2d 733 (1968).

Raney v. Board of Educ., 391 U.S. 443, 88 S.Ct. 1697, 20 L.Ed.2d 727 (1968).

Green v. New Kent County School Board, 391 U.S. 430, 88 S.Ct. 1689, 20 L.Ed.2d 716 (1968).

Rogers v. Paul, 382 U.S. 198, 86 S.Ct. 358, 15 L.Ed.2d 265 (1965).

Bradley v. School Board, 382 U.S. 103, 86 S.Ct. 224, 15 L.Ed.2d 187 (1965).

Griffin v. County School Board, 377 U.S. 218, 84 S.Ct. 1226, 12 L.Ed.2d 256 (1964).

Goss v. Board of Educ., 373 U.S. 683, 83 S.Ct. 1405, 10 L.Ed.2d 632 (1963).

U.S. v. State of Louisiana, 364 U.S. 500, 81 S.Ct. 260, 5 L.Ed.2d 245 (1960).

Cooper v. Aaron, 358 U.S. 1, 78 S.Ct. 1401, 3 L.Ed.2d 5 (1958).

Brown v. Board of Educ. (II), 349 U.S. 294, 75 S.Ct. 753, 99 L.Ed. 1083 (1955).

Bolling v. Sharpe, 347 U.S. 497, 74 S.Ct. 693, 98 L.Ed. 884 (1954).

Brown v. Board of Educ. (I), 347 U.S. 483, 74 S.Ct. 686, 98 L.Ed. 873 (1954).

## Disabled Students

Forest Grove School Dist. v. T.A., 129 S.Ct. 2484 (U.S. 2009).

Winkleman v. Parma City School Dist., 127 S.Ct. 1994 (U.S. 2007).

Arlington Cent. School Dist. Board of Educ. v. Murphy, 548 U.S. 291, 126 S.Ct. 2455, 165 L.Ed.2d 526 (2006).

Schaffer v. Weast, 546 U.S. 49, 126 S.Ct. 528, 163 L.Ed.2d 387 (2005).

Cedar Rapids Community School Dist. v. Garret F. by Charlene F., 526 U.S. 66, 119 S.Ct. 992, 143 L.Ed.2d 154 (1999).

Lane v. Pena, 518 U.S. 187, 116 S.Ct. 2092, 135 L.Ed.2d 486 (1996).

Florence County School Dist. v. Carter, 510 U.S. 7, 114 S.Ct. 361, 126 L.Ed.2d 284 (1993).

Zobrest v. Catalina Foothills School Dist., 509 U.S. 1, 113 S.Ct. 2462, 125 L.Ed.2d 1 (1993).

Dellmuth v. Muth, 491 U.S. 223, 109 S.Ct. 2397, 105 L.Ed.2d 181 (1989).

Honig v. Doe, 484 U.S. 305, 108 S.Ct. 592, 98 L.Ed.2d 686 (1988).

Honig v. Students of California School for the Blind, 471 U.S. 148, 105 S.Ct. 1820, 85 L.Ed.2d 114 (1985).

Burlington School Committee v. Dep't of Educ., 471 U.S. 359, 105 S.Ct. 1996, 85 L.Ed.2d 385 (1985).

Smith v. Robinson, 468 U.S. 992, 104 S.Ct. 3457, 82 L.Ed.2d 746 (1984).

Irving Independent School Dist. v. Tatro, 468 U.S. 883, 104 S.Ct. 3371, 82 L.Ed.2d 664 (1984).

Board of Educ. v. Rowley, 458 U.S. 176, 102 S.Ct. 3034, 73 L.Ed.2d 690 (1982).

Univ. of Texas v. Camenisch, 451 U.S. 390, 101 S.Ct. 1830, 68 L.Ed.2d 175 (1981).

Southeastern Community College v. Davis, 442 U.S. 397, 99 S.Ct. 2361, 60 L.Ed.2d 980 (1979).

**Discrimination Generally**

Crawford v. Metropolitan Government of Nashville and Davidson County, Tennessee, 129 S.Ct. 846 (U.S. 2009).

Engquist v. Oregon Dep't of Agriculture, 128 S.Ct. 2146 (U.S. 2008).

Kentucky Retirement Systems v. Equal Employment Opportunity Comm'n, 128 S.Ct. 2361 (U.S. 2008).

Smith v. City of Jackson, 544 U.S. 228, 125 S.Ct. 1536, 161 L.Ed.2d 410 (2005).

Lapides v. Board of Regents of Univ. System of Georgia, 535 U.S. 613, 122 S.Ct. 1640, 152 L.Ed.2d 806 (2002).

Toyota Motor Manufacturing, Ky., Inc. v. Williams, 534 U.S. 184, 122 S.Ct. 681, 151 L.Ed.2d 615 (2002).

Reeves v. Sanderson Plumbing Products, 530 U.S. 133, 120 S.Ct. 2097, 147 L.Ed.2d 15 (2000).

Kimel v. Florida Board of Regents, 528 U.S. 62, 120 S.Ct. 631, 145 L.Ed.2d 522 (2000).

Murphy v. United Parcel Service, Inc., 527 U.S. 516, 119 S.Ct. 2133, 144 L.Ed.2d 484 (1999).

Sutton v. United Airlines, Inc., 527 U.S. 471, 119 S.Ct. 2139, 144 L.Ed.2d 450 (1999).

Bragdon v. Abbott, 524 U.S. 624, 118 S.Ct. 2196, 141 L.Ed.2d 540 (1998).

U.S. v. Virginia, 518 U.S. 515, 116 S.Ct. 2264, 135 L.Ed.2d 735 (1996).

Jett v. Dallas Independent School Dist., 491 U.S. 701, 109 S.Ct. 2702, 105 L.Ed.2d 598 (1989).

Carnegie-Mellon Univ. v. Cohill, 484 U.S. 343, 108 S.Ct. 614, 98 L.Ed.2d 720 (1988).

School Board of Nassau County v. Arline, 480 U.S. 273, 107 S.Ct. 1123, 94 L.Ed.2d 307 (1987).

Monell v. Dep't of Social Services, 436 U.S. 658, 98 S.Ct. 2018, 56 L.Ed.2d 611 (1978).

Hazelwood School Dist. v. U.S., 433 U.S. 299, 97 S.Ct. 2736, 53 L.Ed.2d 768 (1977).

DeFunis v. Odegaard, 416 U.S. 312, 94 S.Ct. 1704, 40 L.Ed.2d 164 (1974).

**Due Process**

Gilbert v. Homar, 520 U.S. 924, 117 S.Ct. 1807, 138 L.Ed.2d 120 (1997).

Univ. of Tennessee v. Elliot, 478 U.S. 788, 106 S.Ct. 3220, 92 L.Ed.2d 635 (1986).

Memphis Community School Dist. v. Stachura, 477 U.S. 299, 106 S.Ct. 2537, 91 L.Ed.2d 249 (1986).

Cleveland Board of Educ. v. Loudermill, 470 U.S. 532, 105 S.Ct. 1487, 84 L.Ed.2d 494 (1985).

Perry v. Sindermann, 408 U.S. 593, 92 S.Ct. 2694, 33 L.Ed.2d 570 (1972).

Board of Regents v. Roth, 408 U.S. 564, 92 S.Ct. 2701, 33 L.Ed.2d 548 (1972).

**Elections**

Reno v. Bossier Parish School Board, 528 U.S. 320, 120 S.Ct. 866, 145 L.Ed.2d 845 (2000).

Texas v. U.S., 523 U.S. 296, 118 S.Ct. 1257, 140 L.Ed.2d 406 (1998).

Reno v. Bossier Parish School Board, 520 U.S. 471, 117 S.Ct. 1491, 137 L.Ed.2d 730 (1997).

Dougherty County Board of Educ. v. White, 439 U.S. 32, 99 S.Ct. 368, 58 L.Ed.2d 269 (1978).

Mayor of Philadelphia v. Educ. Equality League, 415 U.S. 605, 94 S.Ct. 1323, 39 L.Ed.2d 630 (1974).

Kramer v. Union Free School Dist. No. 15, 395 U.S. 621, 89 S.Ct. 1886, 23 L.Ed.2d 583 (1969).

Sailors v. Board of Educ., 387 U.S. 105, 87 S.Ct. 1549, 18 L.Ed.2d 650 (1967).

**Federal Aid**

Lockhart v. U.S., 546 U.S. 142, 126 S.Ct. 699, 163 L.Ed.2d 557 (2005).

Traynor v. Turnage, 485 U.S. 535, 108 S.Ct. 1372, 99 L.Ed.2d 618 (1988).

Selective Service System v. MPIRG, 468 U.S. 841, 104 S.Ct. 3348, 82 L.Ed.2d 632 (1984).

Bell v. New Jersey and Pennsylvania, 461 U.S. 773, 103 S.Ct. 2187, 76 L.Ed.2d 312 (1984).

Valley Forge Christian College v. Americans United for Separation of Church and State, 454 U.S. 464, 102 S.Ct. 752, 70 L.Ed.2d 700 (1982).

Board of Educ. v. Harris, 444 U.S. 130, 100 S.Ct. 363, 62 L.Ed.2d 275 (1979).

Wheeler v. Barrera, 417 U.S. 402, 94 S.Ct. 2274, 41 L.Ed.2d 159 (1974).

Tilton v. Richardson, 403 U.S. 672, 91 S.Ct. 2091, 29 L.Ed.2d 790 (1971).

**Financing**

Hibbs v. Winn, 542 U.S. 88, 124 S.Ct. 2276, 159 L.Ed.2d 172 (2004).

Locke v. Davey, 540 U.S. 807, 124 S.Ct. 1307, 158 L.Ed.2d 1 (2004).

Camps Newfound/Owatonna, Inc. v. Town of Harrison, Me., 520 U.S. 564, 117 S.Ct. 1590, 137 L.Ed.2d 852 (1997).

Papasan v. Allain, 478 U.S. 265, 106 S.Ct. 2932, 92 L.Ed.2d 209 (1986).

Bennett v. New Jersey, 470 U.S. 632, 105 S.Ct. 1555, 84 L.Ed.2d 572 (1985).

Bennett v. Kentucky Dep't of Educ., 470 U.S. 656, 105 S.Ct. 1544, 84 L.Ed.2d 590 (1985).

Lawrence County v. Lead-Deadwood School Dist. No. 40-1, 469 U.S. 256, 105 S.Ct. 695, 83 L.Ed.2d 635 (1985).

Grove City College v. Bell, 465 U.S. 555, 104 S.Ct. 1211, 79 L.Ed.2d 516 (1984).

San Antonio v. Rodriguez, 411 U.S. 1, 93 S.Ct. 1278, 36 L.Ed.2d 16 (1973).

**Freedom of Religion (see also Religious Activities)**

Edwards v. Aguillard, 482 U.S. 578, 107 S.Ct. 2573, 96 L.Ed.2d 510 (1987).

Ansonia Board of Educ. v. Philbrook, 499 U.S. 60, 107 S.Ct. 367, 93 L.Ed.2d 305 (1986).

**Freedom of Speech**

Pleasant Grove City, Utah v. Summum, 129 S.Ct. 1125 (U.S. 2009).

Morse v. Frederick, 127 S.Ct. 2618 (U.S. 2007).

Garcetti v. Ceballos, 547 U.S. 410, 126 S.Ct. 1951, 164 L.Ed.2d 689 (2006).

Rumsfeld v. Forum for Academic and Institutional Rights, 547 U.S. 47 (2006).

Board of Regents of Univ. of Wisconsin System v. Southworth, 529 U.S. 217, 120 S.Ct. 1346, 146 L.Ed.2d 193 (2000).

Rosenberger v. Univ. of Virginia, 515 U.S. 819, 115 S.Ct. 2510, 132 L.Ed.2d 700 (1995).

Board of Educ. of Westside Community School v. Mergens, 496 U.S. 226, 110 S.Ct. 2356, 110 L.Ed.2d 191 (1990).

Board of Trustees of the State Univ. of New York v. Fox, 492 U.S. 469, 109 S.Ct. 3028, 106 L.Ed.2d 388 (1989).

Hazelwood School Dist. v. Kuhlmeier, 484 U.S. 261, 108 S.Ct. 562, 98 L.Ed.2d 592 (1988).

Bethel School Dist. v. Fraser, 478 U.S. 675, 106 S.Ct. 3159, 92 L.Ed.2d 549 (1986).

Board of Educ. v. Pico, 457 U.S. 853, 102 S.Ct. 2799, 73 L.Ed.2d 435 (1982).

Givhan v. Western Line Consolidated School Dist., 439 U.S. 410, 99 S.Ct. 693, 58 L.Ed.2d 619 (1979).

Mt. Healthy City School v. Doyle, 429 U.S. 274, 97 S.Ct. 568, 50 L.Ed.2d 471 (1977).

Papish v. Board of Curators, 410 U.S. 667, 93 S.Ct. 1197, 35 L.Ed.2d 618 (1973).

Grayned v. City of Rockford, 408 U.S. 104, 92 S.Ct. 2294, 33 L.Ed.2d 222 (1972).

Police Dep't v. Mosley, 408 U.S. 92, 92 S.Ct. 2286, 33 L.Ed.2d 212 (1972).

Tinker v. Des Moines, 393 U.S. 503, 89 S.Ct. 733, 21 L.Ed.2d 733 (1969).

Pickering v. Board of Educ., 391 U.S. 563, 88 S.Ct. 1731, 20 L.Ed.2d 811 (1968).

Keyishian v. Board of Regents, 385 U.S. 589, 87 S.Ct. 675, 17 L.Ed.2d 629 (1967).

Adler v. Board of Educ., 342 U.S. 485, 72 S.Ct. 380, 96 L.Ed. 517 (1952).

## Labor Relations

Ysursa v. Pocatello Educ. Ass'n, 129 S.Ct. 1093 (U.S. 2009).

Davenport v. Washington Educ. Ass'n, 127 S.Ct. 2372 (U.S. 2007).

Christensen v. Harris County, 529 U.S. 576, 120 S.Ct. 1655, 146 L.Ed.2d 621 (2000).

Central State Univ. v. American Ass'n of Univ. Professors, Cent. State Univ. Chapter, 526 U.S. 124, 119 S.Ct. 1162, 143 L.Ed.2d 227 (1999).

Lehnert v. Ferris Faculty Ass'n, 500 U.S. 507, 111 S.Ct. 1950, 114 L.Ed.2d 572 (1991).

Fort Stewart Schools v. Federal Labor Relations Authority, 495 U.S. 641, 110 S.Ct. 2043, 109 L.Ed.2d 659 (1990).

Minnesota State Board for Community Colleges v. Knight, 465 U.S. 271, 104 S.Ct. 1058, 79 L.Ed.2d 299 (1984).

NLRB v. Yeshiva Univ., 444 U.S. 672, 100 S.Ct. 856, 63 L.Ed.2d 115 (1980).

NLRB v. Catholic Bishop of Chicago, 440 U.S. 490, 99 S.Ct. 1313, 59 L.Ed.2d 533 (1979).

Abood v. Detroit Board of Educ., 431 U.S. 209, 97 S.Ct. 1782, 52 L.Ed.2d 261 (1977).

## Loyalty Oaths

Connell v. Higgenbotham, 403 U.S. 207, 91 S.Ct. 1772, 29 L.Ed.2d 418 (1971).

Whitehill v. Elkins, 389 U.S. 54, 88 S.Ct. 184, 19 L.Ed.2d 228 (1967).

Elfbrandt v. Russell, 384 U.S. 11, 86 S.Ct. 1238, 16 L.Ed.2d 321 (1966).

Baggett v. Bullitt, 377 U.S. 360, 84 S.Ct. 1316, 12 L.Ed.2d 377 (1964).

Cramp v. Board of Educ., 368 U.S. 278, 82 S.Ct. 275, 7 L.Ed.2d 285 (1961).

Slochower v. Board of Higher Educ., 350 U.S. 551, 76 S.Ct. 637, 100 L.Ed. 692 (1956).

**Maternity Leave**

Richmond Unified School Dist. v. Berg, 434 U.S. 158, 98 S.Ct. 623, 54 L.Ed.2d 375 (1977).

Cleveland Board of Educ. v. La Fleur, 414 U.S. 632, 94 S.Ct. 791, 39 L.Ed.2d 52 (1974).

Cohen v. Chesterfield, 414 U.S. 632, 94 S.Ct. 791, 39 L.Ed.2d 52 (1974).

**Private Schools**

Zelman v. Simmons-Harris, 536 U.S. 639, 122 S.Ct. 2460, 153 L.Ed.2d 604 (2002).

Brentwood Academy v. Tennessee Secondary School Athletic Ass'n, 531 U.S. 288, 121 S.Ct. 924, 148 L.Ed.2d 807 (2001).

Mitchell v. Helms, 530 U.S. 793, 120  S.Ct. 2530, 147 L.Ed.2d 660 (2000).

Bates v. U.S., 522 U.S. 23, 118 S.Ct. 285, 139 L.Ed.2d 215 (1997).

Agostini v. Felton, 521 U.S. 203, 117 S.Ct. 1997, 138 L.Ed.2d 391 (1997).

Farrar v. Hobby, 506 U.S. 103, 113 S.Ct. 566, 121 L.Ed.2d 494 (1992).

Corporation of the Presiding Bishop of the Church of Jesus Christ of Latter-Day Saints v. Amos, 483 U.S. 327, 107 S.Ct. 2862, 97 L.Ed.2d 273 (1987).

St. Francis College v. Al-Khazraji, 481 U.S. 604, 107 S.Ct. 2022, 97 L.Ed.2d 749 (1987).

Witters v. Washington Dep't of Services for the Blind, 474 U.S. 481, 106 S.Ct. 748, 88 L.Ed.2d 846 (1986).

Aguilar v. Felton, 473 U.S. 402, 105 S.Ct. 3232, 87 L.Ed.2d 290 (1985).

Grand Rapids School Dist. v. Ball, 473 U.S. 373, 105 S.Ct. 3216, 87 L.Ed.2d 267 (1985).

Grove City College v. Bell, 465 U.S. 555, 104 S.Ct. 1211, 79 L.Ed.2d 516 (1984).

Mueller v. Allen, 463 U.S. 388, 103 S.Ct. 3062, 77 L.Ed.2d 721 (1983).

Bob Jones Univ. v. United States, 461 U.S. 574, 103 S. Ct. 2017, 76 L.Ed.2d 157 (1983).

Valley Forge Christian College v. Americans United for Separation of Church and State, 454 U.S. 464, 102 S.Ct. 752, 70 L.Ed.2d 700 (1982).

St. Martin Evangelical Lutheran Church v. South Dakota, 451 U.S. 772, 101 S.Ct. 2142, 68 L.Ed.2d 612 (1981).

Committee v. Regan, 444 U.S. 646, 100 S.Ct. 840, 63 L.Ed.2d 94 (1980).

NLRB v. Catholic Bishop of Chicago, 440 U.S. 490, 99 S.Ct. 1313, 59 L.Ed.2d 533 (1979).

New York v. Cathedral Academy, 434 U.S. 125, 98 S.Ct. 340, 54 L.Ed.2d 346 (1977).

Wolman v. Walter, 433 U.S. 229, 97 S.Ct. 2593, 53 L.Ed.2d 714 (1977).

Runyon v. McCrary, 427 U.S. 160, 96 S.Ct. 2586, 49 L.Ed.2d 415 (1976).

Roemer v. Board of Public Works, 426 U.S. 736, 96 S.Ct. 2337, 49 L.Ed.2d 179 (1976).

Meek v. Pittenger, 421 U.S. 349, 95 S.Ct. 1753, 44 L.Ed.2d 217 (1975).

Wheeler v. Barrera, 417 U.S. 402, 94 S.Ct. 2274, 41 L.Ed.2d 159 (1974).

Sloan v. Lemon, 413 U.S. 825, 93 S.Ct. 2982, 37 L.Ed.2d 939 (1973).

Committee for Public Educ. and Religious Liberty v. Nyquist, 413 U.S. 756, 93 S.Ct. 2955, 37 L.Ed.2d 948 (1973).

Hunt v. McNair, 413 U.S. 734, 93 S.Ct. 2868, 37 L.Ed.2d 923 (1973).

Levitt v. Committee for Public Educ. and Religious Liberty, 413 U.S. 472, 93 S.Ct. 2814, 37 L.Ed.2d 736 (1973).

Early v. Di Censo, 403 U.S. 602, 91 S.Ct. 2105, 29 L.Ed.2d 745 (1971).

Lemon v. Kurtzman, 403 U.S. 602, 91 S.Ct. 2105, 29 L.Ed.2d 745 (1971).

Board of Educ. v. Allen, 392 U.S. 236, 88 S.Ct. 1923, 20 L.Ed.2d 1060 (1968).

Flast v. Cohen, 392 U.S. 83, 88 S.Ct. 1942, 20 L.Ed.2d 947 (1968).

Zorach v. Clauson, 343 U.S. 306, 72 S.Ct. 679, 96 L.Ed. 954 (1952).

McCollum v. Board of Educ., 333 U.S. 203, 68 S.Ct. 461, 92 L.Ed. 649 (1948).

Everson v. Board of Educ., 330 U.S. 1, 67 S.Ct. 504, 91 L.Ed. 711 (1947).

Farrington v. Tokushige, 273 U.S. 284, 47 S.Ct. 406, 71 L.Ed. 646 (1927).

## Racial Discrimination

Parents Involved in Community Schools v. Seattle School Dist. No. 1, 127 S.Ct. 2738 (U.S. 2007).

Gratz v. Bollinger, 539 U.S. 244, 123 S.Ct. 2411, 156 L.Ed.2d 257 (2003).

Grutter v. Bollinger, 539 U.S. 306, 123 S.Ct. 2325, 156 L.Ed.2d 304 (2003).

Texas v. Lesage, 528 U.S. 18, 120 S.Ct.467, 145 L.Ed.2d (1999).

St. Francis College v. Al-Khazraji, 481 U.S. 604, 107 S.Ct. 2022, 97 L.Ed.2d 749 (1987).

Wygant v. Jackson Board of Educ., 476 U.S. 267, 106 S.Ct. 1842, 90 L.Ed.2d 260 (1986).

Runyon v. McCrary, 427 U.S. 160, 96 S.Ct. 2586, 49 L.Ed.2d 415 (1976).

Lau v. Nichols, 414 U.S. 563, 94 S.Ct. 786, 39 L.Ed.2d 1 (1974).

Norwood v. Harrison, 413 U.S. 455, 93 S.Ct. 2804, 37 L.Ed.2d 723 (1973).

## Religious Activities in Public Schools

Christian Legal Society Chapter of the Univ. of California, Hastings College of Law v. Martinez, 130 S.Ct. 2971 (U.S. 2010)

Elk Grove Unified School Dist. v. Newdow, 542 U.S. 961, 124 S.Ct. 2301, 159 L.Ed.2d 851 (2004).

Santa Fe Independent School Dist. v. Doe, 530 U.S. 290, 120 S.Ct. 2266, 147 L.Ed.2d 295 (2000).

Board of Educ. of Kiryas Joel Village v. Grumet, 512 U.S. 687, 114 S.Ct. 2481, 129 L.Ed.2d 546 (1994).

Lamb's Chapel v. Center Moriches Union Free School Dist., 508 U.S. 384, 113 S.Ct. 2141, 124 L.Ed.2d 352 (1993).

Lee v. Weisman, 505 U.S. 577, 112 S.Ct. 2649, 120 L.Ed.2d 467 (1992).

Karcher v. May, 484 U.S. 72, 108 S.Ct. 388, 98 L.Ed.2d 327 (1987).

Bender v. Williamsport Area School Dist., 475 U.S. 534, 106 S.Ct. 1326, 89 L.Ed.2d 501 (1986).

Wallace v. Jaffree, 472 U.S. 38, 105 S.Ct. 2479, 96 L.Ed.2d 29 (1985).

Widmar v. Vincent, 454 U.S. 263, 102 S.Ct. 269, 70 L.Ed.2d 400 (1981).

Stone v. Graham, 449 U.S. 39, 101 S.Ct. 192, 66 L.Ed.2d 199 (1980).

Epperson v. Arkansas, 393 U.S. 97, 89 S.Ct. 266, 21 L.Ed.2d 228 (1968).

Chamberlin v. Dade County Board of Public Instruction, 377 U.S. 402, 84 S.Ct. 1272, 12 L.Ed.2d 407 (1964).

Abington School Dist. v. Schempp, 374 U.S. 203, 83 S.Ct. 1560, 10 L.Ed.2d 844 (1963).

Engel v. Vitale, 370 U.S. 421, 82 S.Ct. 1261, 8 L.Ed.2d 601 (1962).

McCollum v. Board of Educ., 333 U.S. 203, 68 S.Ct. 461, 92 L.Ed. 649 (1948).

West Virginia Board of Educ. v. Barnette, 319 U.S. 624, 63 S.Ct. 1178, 87 L.Ed. 1628 (1943).

## Residency

Martinez v. Bynum, 461 U.S. 321, 103 S.Ct. 1838, 75 L.Ed.2d 879 (1983).

Elgins v. Moreno, 435 U.S. 647, 98 S.Ct. 1338, 55 L.Ed.2d 614 (1978).

## School Liability

Chavez v. Martinez, 538 U.S. 760, 123 S.Ct. 1994, 155 L.Ed.2d 984 (2003).

Owasso Independent School Dist. No. I-011 v. Falvo, 534 U.S. 426, 122 S.Ct. 934, 151 L.Ed.2d 896 (2002).

Clark County School Dist. v. Breeden, 532 U.S. 268, 121 S.Ct. 1508, 149 L.Ed.2d 509 (2001).

Gebser v. Lago Vista Independent School Dist., 524 U.S. 274, 118 S.Ct. 1989, 141 L.Ed.2d 277 (1998).

Regents of Univ. of California v. Doe, 519 U.S. 337, 117 S.Ct. 900, 137 L.Ed.2d 55 (1997).

Bradford Area School Dist. v. Stoneking, 489 U.S. 1062, 109 S.Ct. 1333, 103 L.Ed.2d 804 (1989).

Smith v. Sowers, 490 U.S. 1002, 109 S.Ct. 1634, 104 L.Ed.2d 150 (1989).

Deshaney v. Winnebago County DSS, 489 U.S. 189, 109 S.Ct. 998, 103 L.Ed.2d 249 (1989).

## Sex Discrimination

Burlington Northern & Santa Fe Railway Co. v. White, 548 U.S. 53, 126 S.Ct. 2405, 165 L.Ed.2d 345 (2006).

Michigan High School Athletic Ass'n v. Communities for Equity, 544 U.S. 1012, 161 L.Ed.2d 845 (2005).

Davis v. Monroe County Board of Educ., 526 U.S. 629, 119 S.Ct. 1661, 143 L.Ed.2d 839 (1999).

National Collegiate Athletic Ass'n v. Smith, 525 U.S. 84, 119 S.Ct. 924, 142 L.Ed.2d 929 (1999).

Burlington Industries, Inc. v. Ellerth, 524 U.S. 742, 118 S.Ct. 2257, 141 L.Ed.2d 633 (1998).

Faragher v. City of Boca Raton, 524 U.S. 775, 118 S.Ct. 2275, 141 L.Ed.2d 662 (1998).

Oncale v. Sundowner Offshore Offshore Services, Inc., 523 U.S. 75, 118 S.Ct. 998, 140 L.Ed.2d 201 (1998).

Franklin v. Gwinnett County Public Schools, 503 U.S. 60, 112 S.Ct. 1028, 117 L.Ed.2d 208 (1992).

Ohio Civil Rights Comm'n v. Dayton Christian Schools, 477 U.S. 619, 106 S.Ct. 2718, 91 L.Ed.2d 512 (1986).

Mississippi Univ. for Women v. Hogan, 458 U.S. 718, 102 S.Ct. 3331, 73 L.Ed.2d 1090 (1982).

Rendell-Baker v. Kohn, 457 U.S. 830, 102 S.Ct. 2764, 73 L.Ed.2d 418 (1982).

Cannon v. Univ. of Chicago, 441 U.S. 677, 99 S.Ct. 1946, 60 L.Ed.2d 560 (1979).

Board of Trustees v. Sweeney, 439 U.S. 24, 99 S.Ct. 295, 58 L.Ed.2d 216 (1978).

## Striking Teachers

Hortonville Joint School Dist. v. Hortonville Educ. Ass'n, 426 U.S. 482, 96 S.Ct. 2308, 49 L.Ed.2d 1 (1976).

## Student Searches

Board of Educ. of Independent School Dist. 92 of Pottawatomie County v. Earls, 536 U.S. 822, 122 S.Ct. 2559, 153 L.Ed.2d 735 (2002).

Vernonia School Dist. 47J v. Acton, 515 U.S. 646, 115 S. Ct. 2386, 132 L.Ed.2d 564 (1995).

New Jersey v. T.L.O., 469 U.S. 325, 105 S.Ct. 733, 83 L.Ed.2d 720 (1985).

## Student Suspensions

Regents v. Ewing, 474 U.S. 214, 106 S.Ct. 507, 88 L.Ed.2d 523 (1985).

Board of Educ. v. McCluskey, 458 U.S. 966, 103 S.Ct. 3469, 73 L.Ed.2d 1273 (1982).

Carey v. Piphus, 435 U.S. 247, 98 S.Ct. 1042, 55 L.Ed.2d 252 (1978).

Board of Curators v. Horowitz, 435 U.S. 78, 98 S.Ct. 948, 55 L.Ed.2d 124 (1978).

Wood v. Strickland, 420 U.S. 308, 95 S.Ct. 992, 43 L.Ed.2d 214 (1975).

Goss v. Lopez, 419 U.S. 565, 95 S.Ct. 729, 42 L.Ed.2d 725 (1975).

## Teacher Termination

Patsy v. Board of Regents, 457 U.S. 496, 102 S.Ct. 2557, 73 L.Ed.2d 172 (1982).

Chardon v. Fernandez, 454 U.S. 6, 102 S.Ct. 28, 70 L.Ed.2d 6 (1981).

Delaware State College v. Ricks, 449 U.S. 250, 101 S.Ct. 498, 66 L.Ed.2d 431 (1980).

Beilan v. Board of Public Educ., 357 U.S. 399, 78 S.Ct. 1317, 2 L.Ed.2d 1414 (1958).

## Textbooks

Norwood v. Harrison, 413 U.S. 455, 93 S.Ct. 2804, 37 L.Ed.2d 723 (1973).

Board of Educ. v. Allen, 392 U.S. 236, 88 S.Ct. 1923, 20 L.Ed.2d 1060 (1968).

Cochran v. Louisiana State Board of Educ., 281 U.S. 370, 50 S.Ct. 335, 74 L.Ed.2d 1929 (1930).

## Transportation Fees

Kadrmas v. Dickinson Public Schools, 487 U.S. 450, 108 S.Ct. 2481, 101 L.Ed.2d 399 (1988).

## Use of School Facilities

Good News Club v. Milford Cent. School, 533 U.S. 98, 121 S.Ct. 2093, 150 L.Ed.2d 151 (2000).

Ellis v. Dixon, 349 U.S. 458, 75 S.Ct. 859, 99 L.Ed. 1231 (1955).

## Weapons Control

U.S. v. Lopez, 514 U.S. 549, 115 S. Ct. 1624, 131 L.Ed.2d 626 (1995).

# THE JUDICIAL SYSTEM

In order to allow you to determine the relative importance of a judicial decision, the cases included in *2012 Deskbook Encyclopedia of American School Law* identify the particular court from which a decision has been issued. For example, a case decided by a state supreme court generally will be of greater significance than a state circuit court case. Hence a basic knowledge of the structure of our judicial system is important to an understanding of school law.

Almost all the reports in this volume are taken from appellate court decisions. Although most education law decisions occur at trial court and administrative levels, appellate court decisions have the effect of binding lower courts and administrators so that appellate court decisions have the effect of law within their court systems.

State and federal court systems generally function independently of each other. Each court system applies its own law according to statutes and the determinations of its highest court. However, judges at all levels often consider opinions from other court systems to settle issues which are new or arise under unique fact situations. Similarly, lawyers look at the opinions of many courts to locate authority which supports their clients' cases.

Once a lawsuit is filed in a particular court system, that system retains the matter until its conclusion. Unsuccessful parties at the administrative or trial court level generally have the right to appeal unfavorable determinations of law to appellate courts within the system. When federal law issues or constitutional grounds are present, lawsuits may be appropriately filed in the federal court system. In those cases, the lawsuit is filed initially in the federal district court for that area.

On rare occasions, the U.S. Supreme Court considers appeals from the highest courts of the states if a distinct federal question exists and at least four justices agree on the question's importance. The federal courts occasionally send cases to state courts for application of state law. These situations are infrequent and, in general, the state and federal court systems should be considered separate from each other.

The most common system, used by nearly all states and also the federal judiciary, is as follows: a legal action is commenced in district court (sometimes called trial court, county court, common pleas court or superior court) where a decision is initially reached. The case may then be appealed to the court of appeals (or appellate court), and in turn this decision may be appealed to the supreme court.

Several states, however, do not have a court of appeals; lower court decisions are appealed directly to the state's supreme court. Additionally, some states have labeled their courts in a nonstandard fashion.

In Maryland, the highest state court is called the Court of Appeals. In the state of New York, the trial court is called the Supreme Court. Decisions of this court may be appealed to the Supreme Court, Appellate Division. The highest court in New York is the Court of Appeals. Pennsylvania has perhaps the most complex court system. The lowest state court is the Court of Common Pleas. Depending on the circumstances of the case, appeals may be taken to either the Commonwealth Court or the Superior Court. In certain instances the Commonwealth Court functions as a trial court as well as an appellate court. The Superior Court, however, is strictly an intermediate appellate court. The highest court in Pennsylvania is the Supreme Court.

While supreme court decisions are generally regarded as the last word in legal matters, it is important to remember that trial and appeals court decisions also create important legal precedents. For the hierarchy of typical state and federal court systems, please see the diagram below.

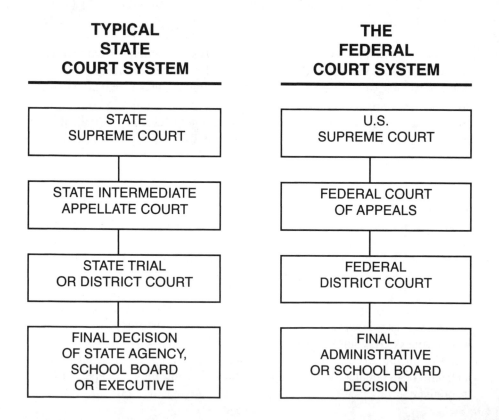

| TYPICAL STATE COURT SYSTEM | THE FEDERAL COURT SYSTEM |
|---|---|
| STATE SUPREME COURT | U.S. SUPREME COURT |
| STATE INTERMEDIATE APPELLATE COURT | FEDERAL COURT OF APPEALS |
| STATE TRIAL OR DISTRICT COURT | FEDERAL DISTRICT COURT |
| FINAL DECISION OF STATE AGENCY, SCHOOL BOARD OR EXECUTIVE | FINAL ADMINISTRATIVE OR SCHOOL BOARD DECISION |

Federal courts of appeals hear appeals from the district courts which are located in their circuits. Below is a list of states matched to the federal circuits in which they are located.

First Circuit — Maine, Massachusetts, New Hampshire, Puerto Rico, Rhode Island

Second Circuit — Connecticut, New York, Vermont

Third Circuit — Delaware, New Jersey, Pennsylvania, Virgin Islands

Fourth Circuit — Maryland, North Carolina, South Carolina, Virginia, West Virginia

Fifth Circuit — Louisiana, Mississippi, Texas

Sixth Circuit — Ohio, Kentucky, Michigan, Tennessee

Seventh Circuit — Illinois, Indiana, Wisconsin

Eighth Circuit — Arkansas, Iowa, Minnesota, Missouri, Nebraska, North Dakota, South Dakota

Ninth Circuit — Alaska, Arizona, California, Guam, Hawaii, Idaho, Montana, Nevada, Northern Mariana Islands, Oregon, Washington

Tenth Circuit — Colorado, Kansas, Oklahoma, New Mexico, Utah, Wyoming

Eleventh Circuit — Alabama, Florida, Georgia

District of Columbia Circuit — Hears cases from the U.S. District Court for the District of Columbia

Federal Circuit Appeals — Sitting in Washington, D.C., the U.S. Court of Federal Circuit, hears patent and trade appeals and certain appeals on claims brought against the federal government and its agencies

# HOW TO READ A CASE CITATION

Generally, court decisions can be located in case reporters at law school or governmental law libraries. Some cases can also be located on the Internet through legal websites or official court websites.

Each case summary contains the citation, or legal reference, to the full text of the case. The diagram below illustrates how to read a case citation.

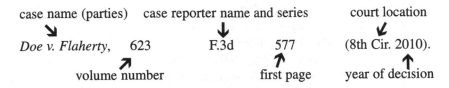

Some cases may have two or three reporter names such as U.S. Supreme Court cases and cases reported in regional case reporters as well as state case reporters. For example, a U.S. Supreme Court case usually contains three case reporter citations.

first reporter          third reporter

*Gratz v. Bollinger*, 539 U.S. 244, 123 S.Ct. 2411, 156 L.Ed.2d 257 (2003).

second reporter

The citations are still read in the same manner as if only one citation has been listed.

Occasionally, a case may contain a citation which does not reference a case reporter. For example, a citation may contain a reference such as:

case name          year of decision    first page      year of decision

*Saxon v. Chapman*,  No. 266077,  2006 WL 1237036  (Mich. Ct. App. 2006).

court file number          WESTLAW[1]          court location

The court file number indicates the specific number assigned to a case by the particular court system deciding the case. In our example, the Michigan Court of Appeals has assigned the case of *Saxon v. Chapman* the case number of

[1]WESTLAW® is a computerized database of court cases available for a fee.

"No. 266077" which will serve as the reference number for the case and any matter relating to the case. Locating a case on the Internet generally requires either the case name and date of the decision, and/or the court file number.

Below, we have listed the full names of the regional reporters. As mentioned previously, many states have individual state reporters. The names of those reporters may be obtained from a reference law librarian.

| | |
|---|---|
| **P.** | **Pacific Reporter** |
| | Alaska, Arizona, California, Colorado, Hawaii, Idaho, Kansas, Montana, Nevada, New Mexico, Oklahoma, Oregon, Utah, Washington, Wyoming |
| **A.** | **Atlantic Reporter** |
| | Connecticut, Delaware, District of Columbia, Maine, Maryland, New Hampshire, New Jersey, Pennsylvania, Rhode Island, Vermont |
| **N.E.** | **Northeastern Reporter** |
| | Illinois, Indiana, Massachusetts, New York, Ohio |
| **N.W.** | **Northwestern Reporter** |
| | Iowa, Michigan, Minnesota, Nebraska, North Dakota, South Dakota, Wisconsin |
| **So.** | **Southern Reporter** |
| | Alabama, Florida, Louisiana, Mississippi |
| **S.E.** | **Southeastern Reporter** |
| | Georgia, North Carolina, South Carolina, Virginia, West Virginia |
| **S.W.** | **Southwestern Reporter** |
| | Arkansas, Kentucky, Missouri, Tennessee, Texas |
| | |
| **F.** | **Federal Reporter** |
| | The thirteen federal judicial circuits courts of appeals decisions. |
| **F.Supp.** | **Federal Supplement** |
| | The thirteen federal judicial circuits district court decisions. *See, The Judicial System, p. 619* for specific state circuits. |
| **Fed.Appx.** | **Federal Appendix** |
| | Contains unpublished decisions of the U.S. Circuit Courts of Appeal. |
| | |
| **U.S.** | **United States Reports** |
| **S.Ct.** | **Supreme Court Reporter** > U.S. Supreme Court Decisions |
| **L.Ed.** | **Lawyers' Edition** |

# GLOSSARY

**Age Discrimination in Employment Act (ADEA)** - The ADEA, 29 U.S.C. § 621 *et seq.*, is part of the Fair Labor Standards Act. It prohibits discrimination against persons who are at least 40 years old, and applies to employers that have 20 or more employees and that affect interstate commerce.

**Americans with Disabilities Act (ADA)** - The ADA, 42 U.S.C. § 12101 *et seq.*, went into effect on July 26, 1992. Among other things, it prohibits discrimination against a qualified individual with a disability because of that person's disability with respect to job application procedures, the hiring, advancement or discharge of employees, employee compensation, job training, and other terms, conditions and privileges of employment.

**Bona fide** - Latin term meaning "good faith." Generally used to note a party's lack of bad intent or fraudulent purpose.

**Class Action Suit** - Federal Rule of Civil Procedure 23 allows members of a class to sue as representatives on behalf of the whole class provided that the class is so large that joinder of all parties is impractical, there are questions of law or fact common to the class, the claims or defenses of the representatives are typical of the claims or defenses of the class, and the representative parties will adequately protect the interests of the class. In addition, there must be some danger of inconsistent verdicts or adjudications if the class action were prosecuted as separate actions. Most states also allow class actions under the same or similar circumstances.

**Collateral Estoppel** - Also known as issue preclusion. The idea that once an issue has been litigated, it may not be re-tried. Similar to the doctrine of *Res Judicata* (see below).

**Due Process Clause** - The clauses of the Fifth and Fourteenth Amendments to the Constitution which guarantee the citizens of the United States "due process of law" (see below). The Fifth Amendment's Due Process Clause applies to the federal government, and the Fourteenth Amendment's Due Process Clause applies to the states.

**Due Process of Law** - The idea of "fair play" in the government's application of law to its citizens, guaranteed by the Fifth and Fourteenth Amendments. Substantive due process is just plain *fairness*, and procedural due process is accorded when the government utilizes adequate procedural safeguards for the protection of an individual's liberty or property interests.

**Education for All Handicapped Children Act (EAHCA)** - [see Individuals with Disabilities Education Act (IDEA).]

**Education of the Handicapped Act (EHA)** - [see Individuals with Disabilities Education Act (IDEA).]

**Employee Retirement Income Security Act (ERISA)** - Federal legislation which sets uniform standards for employee pension benefit plans and employee welfare benefit plans. It is codified at 29 U.S.C. § 1001 *et seq.*

**Enjoin** - (see Injunction).

**Equal Pay Act** - Federal legislation which is part of the Fair Labor Standards Act. It applies to wage discrimination which is based on gender. For race discrimination, employees paid unequally must utilize Title VII or 42 U.S.C. § 1981. Unlike many labor statutes, there is no minimum number of employees necessary to invoke the act's protection.

**Equal Protection Clause** - The clause of the Fourteenth Amendment which prohibits a state from denying any person within its jurisdiction equal protection of its laws. Also, the Due Process Clause of the Fifth Amendment which pertains to the federal government. This has been interpreted by the Supreme Court to grant equal protection even though there is no explicit grant in the Constitution.

**Establishment Clause** - The clause of the First Amendment which prohibits Congress from making "any law respecting an establishment of religion." This clause has been interpreted as creating a "wall of separation" between church and state. The test frequently used to determine whether government action violates the Establishment Clause, referred to as the *Lemon* test, asks whether the action has a secular purpose, whether its primary effect promotes or inhibits religion, and whether it requires excessive entanglement between church and state.

**Fair Labor Standards Act (FLSA)** - Federal legislation which mandates the payment of minimum wages and overtime compensation to covered employees. The overtime provisions require employers to pay at least time-and-one-half to employees who work more than 40 hours per week.

**Federal Tort Claims Act** - Federal legislation which determines the circumstances under which the United States waives its sovereign immunity (see below) and agrees to be sued in court for money damages. The government retains its immunity in cases of intentional torts committed by its employees or agents, and where the tort is the result of a "discretionary function" of a federal employee or agency. Many states have similar acts.

**42 U.S.C. §§ 1981, 1983** - Section 1983 of the federal Civil Rights Act prohibits any person acting under color of state law from depriving any other person of rights protected by the Constitution or by federal laws. A vast majority of lawsuits claiming constitutional violations are brought under Section 1983. Section 1981 provides that all persons enjoy the same right to make and enforce contracts as "white citizens." Section 1981 applies to employment contracts. Further, unlike Section 1983, Section 1981 applies even to private actors. It is not limited to those acting under color of state law. These sections do not apply to the federal government, though the government may be sued directly under the Constitution for any violations.

**Free Exercise Clause** - The clause of the First Amendment which prohibits Congress from interfering with citizens' rights to the free exercise of their religion. Through the Fourteenth Amendment, it has also been made applicable to the states and their sub-entities. The Supreme Court has held that laws of general applicability which have an incidental effect on persons' free exercise rights are not violative of the Free Exercise Clause.

**Handicapped Children's Protection Act (HPCA)** - (see also Individuals with Disabilities Education Act (IDEA).) The HPCA, enacted as an amendment to the EHA, provides for the payment of attorneys' fees to a prevailing parent or guardian in a lawsuit brought under the EHA (and the IDEA).

**Hearing Officer** - Also known as an administrative law judge. The hearing officer decides disputes that arise *at the administrative level*, and has the power to administer oaths, take testimony, rule on evidentiary questions, and make determinations of fact.

**Incorporation Doctrine** - By its own terms, the Bill of Rights applies only to the federal government. The Incorporation Doctrine states that the Fourteenth Amendment makes the Bill of Rights applicable to the states.

**Individualized Educational Program (IEP)** - The IEP is designed to give children with disabilities a free, appropriate education. It is updated annually, with the participation of the child's parents or guardian.

**Individuals with Disabilities Education Act (IDEA)** - Also known as the Education of the Handicapped Act (EHA), the Education for All Handicapped Children Act (EAHCA), and the Handicapped Children's Protection Act (HPCA). Originally enacted as the EHA, the IDEA is the federal legislation which provides for the free, appropriate education of all children with disabilities.

**Injunction** - An equitable remedy (see Remedies) wherein a court orders a party to do or refrain from doing some particular action.

**Jurisdiction** - The power of a court to determine cases and controversies. The Supreme Court's jurisdiction extends to cases arising under the Constitution and under federal law. Federal courts have the power to hear cases where there is diversity of citizenship or where a federal question is involved.

**Mainstreaming** - Part of what is required for a free appropriate education is that each child with a disability be educated in the "least restrictive environment." To the extent that disabled children are educated with nondisabled children in regular education classes, those children are being mainstreamed.

**National Labor Relations Act (NLRA)** - Federal legislation which guarantees to employees the right to form and participate in labor organizations. It prohibits employers from interfering with employees in the exercise of their rights under the NLRA.

**Negligence per se** - Negligence on its face. Usually, the violation of an ordinance or statute will be treated as negligence per se because no careful person would have been guilty of it.

**Occupational Safety and Health Act** - Federal legislation which requires employers to provide a safe workplace. Employers have both general and specific duties under the act. The general duty is to provide a workplace which is free from recognized hazards that are likely to result in serious physical harm. The specific duty is to conform to the health and safety standards promulgated by the Secretary of Labor.

**Overbroad** - A government action is overbroad if, in an attempt to alleviate a specific evil, it impermissibly prohibits or chills a protected action. For example, attempting to deal with street litter by prohibiting the distribution of leaflets or handbills.

**Placement** - A special education student's placement must be appropriate (as well as responsive to the particular child's needs). Under the IDEA's "stay-put" provision, school officials may not remove a special education child from his or her "then current placement" over the parents' objections until the completion of administrative or judicial review proceedings.

**Preemption Doctrine** - Doctrine which states that when federal and state law attempt to regulate the same subject matter, federal law prevents the state law from operating. Based on the Supremacy Clause of Article VI, Clause 2, of the Constitution.

**Prior Restraint** - Restraining a publication before it is distributed. In general, constitutional law doctrine prohibits government from exercising prior restraint.

**Rehabilitation Act** - Section 504 of the Rehabilitation Act prohibits employers who receive federal financial assistance from discriminating against otherwise qualified individuals with handicaps solely becuase of their handicaps. An otherwise qualified individual is one who can perform the "essential functions" of the job with "reasonable accomodation."

**Related Services** - As part of the free, appropriate education due to children with disabilities, school districts may have to provide related services such as transportation, physical and occupational therapy, and medical services which are for diagnostic or evaluative purposes relating to education.

**Remand** - The act of an appellate court in returning a case to the court from which it came for further action.

**Remedies** - There are two general categories of remedies, or relief: legal remedies, which consist of money damages, and equitable remedies, which consist of a court mandate that a specific action be prohibited or required. For example, a claim for compensatory and punitive damages seeks a legal remedy; a claim for an injunction seeks an equitable remedy. Equitable remedies are generally unavailable unless legal remedies are inadequate to address the harm.

**Res Judicata** - The judicial notion that a claim or action may not be tried twice or re-litigated, or that all causes of action arising out of the same set of operative facts should be tried at one time. Also known as claim preclusion.

**Section 1981 & Section 1983** - (see 42 U.S.C. §§ 1981, 1983).

**Sovereign Immunity** - The idea that the government cannot be sued without its consent. It stems from the English notion that the "King could do no wrong." This immunity from suit has been abrogated in most states and by the federal government through legislative acts known as "tort claims acts."

**Standing** - The judicial doctrine which states that in order to maintain a lawsuit a party must have some real interest at stake in the outcome of the trial.

**Statute of Limitations** - A statute of limitation provides the time period in which a specific cause of action may be brought.

**Summary Judgment** - Also referred to as pretrial judgment. Similar to a dismissal. Where there is no genuine issue as to any material fact and all that remains is a question of law, a judge can rule in favor of one party or the other. In general, summary judgment is used to dispose of claims which do not support a legally recognized claim.

**Supremacy Clause** - Clause in Article VI of the Constitution which states that federal legislation is the supreme law of the land. This clause is used to support the Preemption Doctrine (see above).

**Title IX, Education Admendments of 1972** - A federal law that prohibits sex discrimination and exclusion from participation in any educational program on the basis of sex by any program or activity receiving federal funding.

**Title VII, Civil Rights Act of 1964 (Title VII)** - Title VII prohibits discrimination in employment based upon race, color, sex, national origin, or religion. It applies to any employer having fifteen or more employees. Under Title VII, where an employer intentionally discriminates, employees may obtain money damages unless the claim is for race discrimination. For those claims, monetary relief is available under 42 U.S.C. § 1981.

**U.S. Equal Employment Opportunity Commission (EEOC)** - The EEOC is the government entity which is empowered to enforce Title VII (see above) through investigation and/or lawsuits. Private individuals alleging discrimination must pursue administrative remedies within the EEOC before they are allowed to file suit under Title VII.

**Vacate** - The act of annulling the judgment of a court either by an appellate court or by the court itself. The Supreme Court will generally vacate a lower court's judgment without deciding the case itself, and remand the case to the lower court for further consideration in light of some recent controlling decision.

**Void-for-Vagueness Doctrine** - A judicial doctrine based on the Fourteenth Amendment's Due Process Clause. In order for a law which regulates speech, or any criminal statute, to pass muster under the doctrine, the law must make clear what actions are prohibited or made criminal. Under the principles of the Due Process Clause, people of average intelligence should not have to guess at the meaning of a law.

**Writ of Certiorari** - The device used by the Supreme Court to transfer cases from the appellate court's docket to its own. Since the Supreme Court's appellate jurisdiction is largely discretionary, it need only issue such a writ when it desires to rule in the case.

# INDEX